Harmonisation of Securities Law

Custody and Transfer of Securities in European Private Law

Private Law in European Context Series

VOLUME 11

For the
Society of European Contract Law (SECOLA)

Contract law is probably the most dynamic area of European Private Law and also the fundamental private law discipline in all national legal systems. SECOLA was founded to assist the study of European contract law and to enhance its quality. SECOLA organizes an open, truly international and interdisciplinary discussion platform. The focus of the Society is upon newly enacted European Community legal measures, on core concepts in the field of European contract law, and on proposals for further legislation. The Society organizes one or two international conferences each year, arranges for the publication of scholarly discussions in the field including books to be published in this series, and assists with other network activities. In addition, SECOLA has created a journal dedicated to the same aims (see <www.secola.org> and <www.degruyter.de/rs/280_7944_DEU_h.htm>).

A list of previous titles in the series may be found at the end of this volume.

Harmonisation of Securities Law

Custody and Transfer of Securities in European Private Law

Matthias Haentjens

KLUWER LAW
INTERNATIONAL

A C.I.P. Catalogue record for this book is available from the Library of Congress

ISBN 978-90-411-2639-9

Published by:
Kluwer Law International,
P.O. Box 316, 2400 AH Alphen aan den Rijn,
The Netherlands
sales@kluwerlaw.com
<http://www.kluwerlaw.com>

sold and distributed in North, Central and South America
by Aspen Publishers, Inc.,
7201 McKinney Circle,
Frederick, MD 21704, USA

Sold and distributed in all countries by
Turpin Distribution Services Ltd.,
Stratton Business Park,
Pegasus Drive, Biggleswade,
Bedfordshire SG1 8 8TQ,
United Kingdom

Contents-Summary

Contents

Preface

While I was a student of Classics, I managed to have the results of a research project I did on certain technical terms in Greek contracts published as an article in a prestigious papyrology journal.[1] In that article, I presented my findings, which included my discovery that some of the said technical terms could be linked to certain designated areas of Roman Egypt, as well as a precise definition of these terms on the basis of several dozen newly discovered papyri. The terms concerned highly specific references to special gifts that tenants of farmland presented to their landlords at regular intervals, which could be regarded as an important element of the agricultural economy of the time.

Several years later, I had the opportunity to become involved in research on the (legal) infrastructure of economic processes once again. This time, the inquiry concerned the legal aspects of the custody and transfer of securities, generally considered to be important elements in the functioning of the capitalist economies of our time. Securities transfer and custody law becomes especially relevant when securities are transferred after trading, which typically takes place at a stock exchange, and when securities custodians become insolvent. In the findings that presently lie before you, I approach these issues mainly from the perspective of the on-going Europeanisation of private law, and the principal aim of this book is therefore to examine in what way a modernisation and harmonisation of securities custody and transfer laws within the EU can best be achieved.

To that end, the current legal infrastructure of some typical European jurisdictions will be investigated and thus, the laws of Belgium, France and the Netherlands are analysed. The findings of those analyses will subsequently be compared and evaluated against generally accepted standards of modern securities custody and transfer practice, so as to ascertain to what extent the said jurisdictions should

1. *Die Sonderabgaben in den Pachturkunden aus dem römischen Ägypten,* TYCHE, BEITRÄGE ZUR ALTEN GESCHICHTE PAPYROLOGIE UND EPIGRAPHIK 27–45 (2002).

be modernised. In addition, these findings will be compared to the harmonisation brought about in the US through its Uniform Commercial Code. Thereafter, it is questioned whether the proposed measures could be realised by a European instrument of harmonisation.

Once again preoccupied with terminology, I have tried to answer that question through an assessment of whether the proposed modernisation would unacceptably undermine the current systemisation of the European jurisdictions investigated. In many instances, this coherence analysis boils down to a conceptual inquiry, as it is hypothesised that when the relation between securities laws and more general areas of the law is already incoherent, harmonisation will not unacceptably distort that relation. In other words, when certain legal concepts have a meaning in securities law that differs from their meaning in more general areas of law, the relation between securities law and the more general areas of law in which it is embedded is incoherent. In such instance, it must be concluded that a modification of the current conceptual framework cannot be considered undesirable on coherence grounds.

Thus, I will draw conclusions regarding the desirability and form of a future European harmonisation instrument concerning securities custody and transfer law, and because, as yet, no in-depth academic publication has contributed to the decision-making process of the European legislature, I believe this dissertation might be useful, especially because it also assesses the possible impact of harmonisation measures by means of a coherence account. But I am aware that this dissertation does not fall neatly into a traditional legal category. It concerns both private and commercial law, European and national law, securities law and insolvency law, contract law and property law, and even private international law and some legal theory. Although I fully acknowledge ROGERS' statement that '(n)either the generalist practicing lawyer nor the commercial law expert is likely to feel comfortable with this subject',[2] I hope that the present study will at least be of some interest to both.

I am indebted to many persons and institutions who enabled me to conduct my PhD research, to write down its findings, and to get it published. First of all, to my *promotores,* Professors Edgar du Perron and Arthur Salomons, both of the University of Amsterdam. Edgar was the first to say that I should carry out PhD research in law and not something else, and granted me the freedom of choosing my own subject. I am truly grateful to both Arthur and Edgar for their coaching, both professionally and personally. Further, I am grateful to Professor Martijn Hesselink, also of the University of Amsterdam, for directing my attention and ambition towards the Europeanisation of private law and its theoretical ramifications, as well as for his support with regard to the publication of this book by Kluwer Law International; *aux MM. les Professeurs* Michel Grimaldi *et* Alain Gozhi *de l'Université de Paris II, pour la cordialité avec laquelle ils m'ont acceuilli au Panthéon-Assas et aux bibliothèques universitaires juridiques, et pour*

2. ROGERS (1996), 1432.

le temps que M. le professeur Ghozi a consacré pour lire le chapitre sur le droit français; to Wouter Bossu of the International Monetary Fund, for the generosity with which he spared his time to scrutinise the Belgian chapter; to Professor Steven Schuit and Tim Stevens, both partners at Allen & Overy LLP, for their support regarding my private international law research; and to Professor James Rogers of Boston College, for his kindness in discussing his views on the core issues of this book; to Professor Reinier Kraakman of Harvard Law School, for his hospitality and sponsoring my stay at Harvard; and to Professor Harm-Jan de Kluiver of the University of Amsterdam and a partner at De Brauw Blackstone Westbroek, for making possible my stay at Harvard; to Professor Arthur Hartkamp of Radboud University Nijmegen, for enabling me to work with UNIDROIT in Rome at the Convention on Substantive Rules Regarding Intermediated Securities; and to Professor Pim Rank of Radboud University Nijmegen and a partner at NautaDutilh, for his generous help at various stages of the project; to Professor Marjoleine Zieck of the Amsterdam Law School, for facilitating my stay at New York University; to Professor Andreas Lowenfeld of New York University, for challenging all the views I previously had on conflict of laws; to Jacobien Rutgers of the University of Amsterdam, for her support and help, and, not least, to my other colleagues at the Dept. of Private Law, in particular Rolef and Selma, for making writing a dissertation not a dull and lonely activity.

In addition, I am grateful to Professors James Rogers, Pim Rank, Wouter Snijders, Martijn Hesselink, Harm-Jan de Kluiver and Lilian Steffens, members of the doctorate committee, for their time and efforts to review this book. Finally, I am indebted to Peter Morris, for his expert correction of my English, and to Hetty van der Linde, for her translation of the summary into French. But my greatest debts are to Karin, who has supported me more than anyone.

I owe a great deal to the following institutions, all of which generously enabled me to conduct my research abroad: the Royal Dutch Institute in Rome, NWO (the Dutch Research Organisation), Allen & Overy LLP, the Amsterdam Institute of Private Law (I am particularly indebted to Marieke Oderkerk and the Directors Martijn Hesselink and Marco Loos), and the *Stichting Fonds voor de Geld- en Effectenhandel* (Fund for Research on Monetary and Securities Transactions).

A special word of gratitude is due to Professor Bob Brouwer for scrutinizing my first steps in the world of legal theory. He left us far too early and I dedicate this work to him.

Developments have been taken into account up to 1 January 2007.

Abbreviations

ABV	Algemene BankVoorwaarden (General Banking Terms and Conditions)(NL)
ADR	American Depository Receipt (USA)
ALI	American Law Institute (USA)
Amex	American Stock Exchange (USA)
AMF	Autorité des Marchés Financiers (Financial markets authority)(FR)
BIS	Bank of International Settlements
BW	Burgerlijk Wetboek (Civil Code)(B, NL)
Cass. 1re civ.	Première chambre civile de la Cour de cassation (First Private Law Chamber of the Supreme Court)(B, FR)
Cass. com.	Chambre Commercial de la Cour de Cassation (Commercial Law Chamber of the Supreme Court)(FR)
C. civ.	Code civil (Civil Code)(FR)
C. com.	Code de commerce (Commercial Code)(FR)
C. mon. fin.	Code monétaire et financier (Monetary and financial Code)(FR)
CCDVT	Caisse Centrale de Dépôts et Virements de Titres (Central Bank for the Deposit and Transfer of Securities)(FR)
CCP	Central Counter Party
CBFA	Commission Bancaire, Financière et des Assurances/Commissie voor het Bank- en Financiewezen (Commission for Banking and Financial Markets)(B)
CESAME	Clearing and Settlement Advisory and Monitoring Expert Group (EU)
CESR	Committee of European Securities Regulators
CFR	Code of Federal Regulations (US)
CIK	Caisse Interprofessionnelle de Dépôts et de Virement de Titres/Interprofessionele effectendeposito- en girokas (Interprofessional Bank for the Deposit and Transfer of Securities)(B)
CMF	Conseil des Marchés Financiers (Financial Markets Council)(FR)

CNCT	Conseil National du Crédit et du Titre (National Credit and Securities Council)(FR)
CF	Centrum voor Fondsenadministratie (Centre for the administration of interests and dividends)(NL)
CFR	Code of Federal Regulations (USA)
COB	Commissions des Opérations de Bourse (Commission to stock exchange operations)(FR)
CPSS	Committee on Payments and Settlement Systems (BIS)
CSD	Central Securities Depository
DNB	De Nederlandsche Bank (the Netherlands Central Bank)
DTC	Depository Trust Company (USA)
DTCC	The Depository Trust and Clearing Corporation (USA)
DVP	Delivery versus Payment
EC Treaty	Treaty Establishing the European Community (EU)
ECB	European Central Bank
ECJ	European Court of Justice
EFMLG	European Financial Markets Lawyers Group
ESCB	European System of Central Banks
EU	European Union
FCD	Financial Collateral Directive (EU)
FICC	Fixed Income Clearing Corporation (USA)
FR	France
FSAP	Financial Services Action Plan (EU)
Fw	Faillissementswet (Bankruptcy Act)(NL)
HR	Hoge Raad (Supreme Court)(NL)
HSC	Convention on the Law Applicable to Certain Rights in Respect of Securities Held With an Intermediary
ICSD	International Central Securities Depository
IOSCO	International Organisation of Securities Commissions
ISD	Investment Services Directive (EU)
ISD	International Securities Depository
ISSA	International Securities Services Association
KB	Arrêt Royal/Koninklijk Besluit (B)
LCH	London Clearing House
MAF	(Loi sur la) Modernisation des Marchés Financiers (Modernisation of Financial Markets Act)(FR)
MiFID	Directive on Markets in Financial Instruments (EU)
NASDAQ	National Association of Securities Dealers Automatic Quotation (USA)
NBB	Banque Nationale de Belgique/Nationale Bank van België (Central Bank of Belgium)(B)
NCCUSL	National Conference of Commissioners on Uniform State Laws (USA)
NIEC	Nederlands Interprofessioneel EffectenCentrum (Dutch Interprofessional Clearinghouse for Securities)(NL)

NJ	Nederlandse Jurisprudentie (the Netherlands Law Review)
NL	the Netherlands
NSCC	National Securities Clearing Corporation (USA)
NYSE	New York Stock Exchange
OJ	Official Journal (of the European Communities)
OTC	Over The Counter
PRACA	Place of the Relevant securities Account Approach
PRIMA	Place of Relevant Intermediary Approach
RTD com.	Revue Trimestrielle de Droit commercial (Commercial Law Review)(FR)
SBF	Société des Bourses Françaises (French Stock Exchanges Company)
SEC	Securities and Exchange Commission (USA)
SFD	Settlement Finality Directive (EU)
SICOVAM	Société Interprofessionnelle de Compensation des Valeurs Moblières (Interprofessional Company for the netting of securities)(FR)
SIPA	Securities Investor Protection Act (USA)
SIPC	Securities Investor Protection Corporation (USA)
Stb.	Staatsblad (Bulletin of Acts, Orders and Decrees)(NL)
Stc.	Staatscourant (Government Gazette)(NL)
STP	Straight Through Processing
TK	Tweede Kamer (Parliament)(NL)
TRADES	Treasury/Reserve Automated Debt Entry System (USA)
UCC	Uniform Commercial Code (USA)
UNIDROIT	International Institute for the Unification of Private Law
USC	United States Code
USA	United States of America
VABEF	Vereenvoudigde Administratie en Bewaring van Effecten (Simplified Administration and Custody of Securities)(NL)
VOC	Vereenigde Nederlandsche Geoctroyeerde Oost-Indische Compagnie (United Netherlands Chartered East India Company) (NL)
W. Venn.	Code des Sociétés/Wetboek van Vennootschappen (Code of Corporate Law)(B)
Wft	Wet op het financieel toezich (Financial Supervision Act)(NL)
Wge	Wet giraal effectenverkeer (Securities Giro Transfer and Administration Act)(NL)
Wte 1995	Wet Toezicht Effectenverkeer 1995 (1995 Securities Markets Supervision Act)(NL)

Part One
Introductory Chapters

because a man's entire life requires the graces of rhythm and harmony

PLATO[1]

1. PLATO, *Protagoras,* 326b.

Chapter 1
Introduction

1.1 GLOBAL CONVERGENCE, LEGAL RESPONSES

As securities markets gradually merge and expand both in the European Union and world-wide, the volume of securities transactions increases enormously every year.[1] Yet the settlement of these transactions, i.e. the payment of funds and the delivery of the securities, proves to be significantly costlier in the case of cross-border settlements than in the case of domestic transactions being settled.[2] It is generally believed that this discrepancy has its cause for a large part in the legal diversity that currently exists, both with regard to the conflict of laws rules and the substantive laws that concern securities transfer and custody.

In addition to the said diversity of laws, the mismatch between a reality in which dramatic innovations have revolutionised the techniques of securities custody and transfer, and the relevant, yet inflexible legal underpinnings on the other hand, contributes to an extremely undesirable situation of legal uncertainty. Fortunately, various institutions have acknowledged that as a vital element in the functioning of modern economies of scale, the securities settlements infrastructure does not allow for such legal uncertainty, and initiatives have accordingly been undertaken, so as to harmonise and modernise current securities custody and transfer laws.

---

1. *See,* e.g. G30 2003 Plan of Action, 1.
2. Although the exact figures differ, all economic research concludes that cross-border settlement is substantially more expensive than domestic settlement. *See* G30 2003 Plan of Action, 4-5; Scott (2006), Ch. 10, 26; EC Economic Impact Study (2006), 18. The additional costs incurred when securities transactions are settled cross-border consist of direct costs due to higher fees, indirect costs due to extra back-office facilities and opportunity costs due to inefficient use of collateral, a higher incidence of failed trades and a higher incidence of foregone trades; Giovannini Group 2001 Report, ii.

On the global level, the Hague Conference on International Private Law facilitated the recent adoption of a conflict of laws treaty, which aims at a harmonisation of the different conflict of laws rules regarding securities that are held and transferred through a securities account ('book-entry securities').[3] As an important global initiative that targets the current diversity and inadequacy of substantive securities laws, the UNIDROIT harmonisation project must be mentioned.[4] Also on the level of the European Union ('EU'), it has been acknowledged that the current market-led consolidation requires a harmonised legal framework, as it was recognised that a truly cost-effective, integrated clearing and settlement environment within the EU cannot be accomplished without a seamless set of legal rules. But in order to attain a fully integrated internal market, legal harmonisation will probably have to go further than global principles or treaties drafted by non-governmental organisations.

Accordingly, the so-called Giovannini Group explicitly advised the elimination of the most prominent legal barrier to smooth cross-border settlement through a harmonisation of the substantive rules concerning custody, transfer and ownership of securities.[5] The Group's Report in 2003 states: 'The absence of an EU-wide framework for the treatment of interests in securities (including procedures for the creation, perfection and enforcement of security) has been identified as the most important source of legal risk in cross-border transactions'.[6] Consequently, the European Commission established a research group to further investigate the desirability of such a harmonisation instrument and this group essentially confirmed the Giovannini Group's findings.[7]

However, practically all studies on the subject of harmonisation of securities custody and transfer law stress that the law that governs property, contract and commercial law, traditionally the prerogatives of national laws, must be taken into account as 'rooted legal traditions' when drafting a harmonisation instrument.[8]

---

3. The 'Convention on the Law Applicable to Certain Rights in Respect of Securities Held With an Intermediary' was adopted on 13 December 2002 and is available at <www.hcch.net.>
4. UNIDROIT (International Institute for the Harmonisation of Private Law), *Study 78 Harmonised Substantive Rules Regarding Securities Held with an Intermediary,* available at <www.UNIDROIT.org.>
5. The Giovannini Group, set up by the European Commission, issued two reports on the subject of securities custody and transfer law. In its first report of 2001, the Group discerned legal barriers, barriers due to the variation in technical requirements and barriers due to the variation in tax procedures. The Group further concluded that the legal barriers are formed by the absence of a harmonised framework for the substantive rules that concern custody, transfer and ownership of securities (barrier 13), national differences in the legal treatment of bilateral netting (barrier 14) and uneven application of national conflict of laws rules (barrier 15). *See* Ch. 9.3.4.
6. Giovannini Group 2003 Report, 13 and 56.
7. The Legal Certainty Group's advice to the European Commission was published in 2006 and is available at <http://ec.europa.eu/internal_market/>. *See* Ch. 9.3.4. *See also,* e.g. Press Release, European Securities Forum, *Integration of Clearing & Settlement, ESF's Call for Action* (7 May 2003), available at <www.eurosf.com> *and* the EFMLG 2003 Report, all advocating a rapid modernisation and harmonisation of securities law at the EU level.
8. *Cf.* LÖBER (2005), 156 *and* Giovannini Group 2001 Report, 54. *Cf.* letter by G. Morton, Ph. Dupont and A. Maffei to the Legal Certainty Group of February 7 2005, 2 on the UNIDROIT project *and* THAN *in* GUYNN ET AL. (1996), 75. *Cf. also* DE VAUPLANE & BORNET (2001),

More particularly, they argue that the creation of a harmonisation instrument in the field of securities custody and transfer law is highly complicated because of its intimate relationship with the other areas of law just mentioned.[9]

These considerations are in accordance with the analysis recently made by MICHELER, who argued that whereas practices may converge on the functional level, doctrinal path dependence prevents, or at least shapes a corresponding convergence at the formal, i.e. legal level.[10] Indeed, as shall be shown in the following chapters, it was the – albeit not always successful – adaptation of national private and commercial laws to modern, uniform practices of securities custody that has predominantly determined the current form of the infrastructure for securities custody and settlement. It is submitted therefore that other, socio-cultural considerations have not played, nor will they play a directly discernable role in that regard, but that future formal convergence will be mainly determined by doctrinal considerations.[11]

The present book starts from that premise, but principally questions in what way the modernisation and harmonisation of securities custody and transfer laws within the EU can best be achieved.[12] For that purpose, the current legal infrastructure concerning book-entry securities will be analysed regarding some typical European jurisdictions, viz. Belgium, France and the Netherlands. The findings of that analysis will subsequently be tested against generally accepted standards of modern securities custody and transfer practice, and compared with the harmonisation brought about in the US through the Uniform Commercial Code ('UCC'). Then, it will be ascertained whether the modifications proposed would unacceptably undermine the current systemisation of the European jurisdictions investigated. Thus, on both normative and coherence grounds, conclusions will be drawn regarding the desirability and form of a future European harmonisation instrument.

---

no. 1245: 'L'approche factuelle du droit des marchés financiers est simplement le reflet de la complexité des pratiques qu'il est indispensable d'appréhender, de comprendre, et d'encadrer au sein d'un système juridique'.

9. E.g. Giovannini Group 2001 Report, 54 and 60; EFMLG 2003 Report, 22; BNP Paribas Report, 2 *and* LÖBER (2006), 62. *Cf. also* CPSS/IOSCO Recommendations 2001, 5.
10. MICHELER (2006). *Cf. also* CANIVET (2003), 50–51. The functional/formal distinction has been taken from GILSON (2001).
11. *Cf.* WATSON (2000), VI. *But see,* e.g., LEGRAND (1997) *and* TEUBNER (1998), both arguing that social considerations, or 'world-views' are, and should be the prime determinants for the shaping of converging laws. They principally point at supposedly insurmountable differences between common law and civil law systems. In the case of securities laws, that position is falsified by US legislation and the recent Canadian proposal, both jurisdictions that comprise both common and civil law systems. Moreover, civil law Switzerland has recently published a draft Federal Act on the Custody and Transfer of Securities Held with an Intermediary, based on common law concepts; THÉVENOZ (2005).
12. 'Harmonisation' is used here and throughout the present book so as to refer to the approximation of laws. *Cf.* EC Treaty Art. 95 *and see* VAN GERVEN (2004), 502. As opposed to 'unification', which refers to the absolute minimisation of legal diversity, harmonisation usually leaves room for (national) legal differences. Convergence, on the other hand, is used here and elsewhere as a synonym for approximation in a general, i.e. not necessarily legal sense.

1.2 METHODOLOGY

1.2.1 Theoretical Framework

The analysis of the said jurisdictions will thus be conducted in view of the relevance of coherence or, more generally, of the systemisation of law to harmonisation processes. The research presented in this dissertation therefore concerns two different levels, both requiring a different approach. The comparative investigation into the securities laws of the selected jurisdictions demands specific legal questions, which will be discussed in the next section, while the examination of the interaction between different areas of law, on the other hand, demands a more general and theoretical method.

In that respect, the intrastate relationship between securities law and general private or commercial law must be distinguished from the relationship between state law and suprastate law. It is submitted that the relationship between securities law and the more general body of law in which it is embedded determines in what way changes in the former body of law affect the latter.[13] If, for example, a harmonisation instrument would require that national securities laws introduce a new concept that denotes the package of an accountholder's rights in his securities, the relationship between a particular state's securities law and its general private law would determine whether the introduction of that new concept would encroach on the general private law of that state.[14]

As it is assumed that the possibilities of proposals leading to (possibly far-reaching) changes in general bodies of law are slimmer than those for proposals that have less ramifications, it follows that the level of coherence between a functional or specific body of law and the more general body of law in which it is embedded determines the feasibility of a harmonisation initiative directed at a functional body of law.[15] Moreover, it might also determine its success, as it has been argued that the success of a European harmonisation measure must be determined

13. De Vauplane & Bornet (2001), no. 1244 have even argued that on coherence grounds, a harmonisation of securities laws would – and should – also result in a harmonisation of general private law principles: *'C'est pourquoi après l'étape de l' harmonisation des droits des marchés financiers, l'on se dirige, á notre avis rapidement, vers l'unification des composantes essentielles de ces droits, seule réponse* cohérente [emphasis MH] *et satisfaisante aux divers processus d'intégration développés. À défaut, des zones d'incertitudes juridiques génératrices d'insécurité financière naîtraient ce qui ne peut pas être accepté'.*
14. *Cf.* Paech (2002), 1160: 'If the work [of Unidroit, MH] aims at enhancing economic efficiency in cross-border trading and at eliminating legal risk at the same time, it will require the development of a completely new concept which might touch fundamental principles of national legal systems.' *And see* Mooney (1990), 413, arguing from the converse perspective, but the same premise: 'A new model, divorced from common law and U.C.C. property law constructs, also could form a more plausible base for unification of law on the international level. An approach not rooted in longstanding domestic doctrine might provide a more likely basis for harmonizing widely varying doctrine in other nations'.
15. *See* Micheler (2006), 53 *and cf.* Goode (2003-1), 14–16.

by an assessment of whether its policy objective has been accomplished, but also whether the coherence in national jurisdictions is afflicted.[16]

Thus, it is on the basis of an analysis of the coherence of securities law with the more general body of law in which it is embedded, that it will be assessed what type of instrument would be most appropriate for the harmonisation of European securities custody and transfer law.[17] That analysis will be made on the basis of a generally accepted view of coherence as a principle of systemisation of law. The jurisprudential notions of system and coherence will be discussed at greater length in the following chapter, where those concepts will also be made operational for the use of the coherence analysis carried out in the chapters that follow.

However, it should already be noted here that legal theorists differ greatly in their use of the concepts system, integrity, coherence and unity (mostly because these concepts are more or less pivotal elements of their theories of law),[18] and that this study will apply a conception of system and coherence which is believed to be the most suitable for the said analysis. The conception of coherence applied here is therefore non-foundationalist, i.e. it is assumed that not only coherence considerations determine what the law is, and allows for value-pluralism, i.e. it is assumed that not only coherence considerations determine what the law should be.

1.2.2 Comparative Law

The coherence analysis regarding the relationship of securities law with the general body of law in which it is embedded, will be made for some selected jurisdictions that represent typical systems of securities law and are commercially important, viz. Belgium, France, the Netherlands and the US.[19]

Furthermore, harmonisation instruments of the EU, the Hague Conference and Unidroit, will be involved in the analysis.

Belgium's securities custody law has been famous since 1967, when the *Arrêt Royal/Koninklijk Besluit* (Royal Decree, 'KB') no. 62 was enacted. That Decree has modernised legal thinking about securities custody law, was one of the first

16. Smits (2006), 71.
17. *Cf.* the proposal of the European Financial Markets Lawyers Group ('EFMLG'), which identified a specific area of commercial activity, viz. the collateralisation of securities, and proposed uniform legislation for this specific area, thus ring-fencing it from the rest of the law. On the other side of the spectrum, the European Commission proposed a 'European Uniform Securities Code'. *See* EFMLG 2000 Proposal; EFMLG 2003 report, 5–6 and 22; Giovannini Group 2001 Report, 59, *and* the Communication from the Commission to the Council and the European Parliament, *Clearing and settlement in the European Union* (28 May 2002), COM(2002)257, 13. *Cf. also* the Unidroit project, which was originally only concerned with collateralised securities in book-entry accounts; Paech (2002), 1142. *See also* Ch. 12.3.
18. Whether the conception of *integrity* as used by Dworkin amounts to the usual conception *of coherence,* for example, is a matter of debate. *See* Raz (1994), 303–309, Dickson (2001) § 3 and the further references provided there.
19. Here, as in the remainder of this dissertation, countries are listed and discussed in alphabetical order.

statutes to accommodate the transfer of certificates by book-entry[20] and has been a central element of Belgian securities custody law, which is generally considered to be one of the most modern in the world. Moreover, because the Brussels-based Euroclear Bank is the world's largest international central securities depository, Belgian law applies to an enormous number of interests in securities and is therefore commercially extremely relevant.[21]

French securities law has been selected as a typical system, because it abolished, already in 1981, all physical certificates, which is still a distinct feature of most legal regimes. Moreover, the abolition or dematerialisation involved a technical improvement, but also sparked an enormous flow of important legal publications on almost all central notions of securities law. German securities law, on the other hand, represents a system that is still based on the traditional concept of securities as tangible movables, and its rules on the custody and transfer of securities reflect that. But because Dutch law is quite similar to German law in this respect and because of the natural preference to investigate the law of the home country, Dutch law rather than German law has been selected as a typical system of securities law to be analysed. Moreover, although Dutch general private law was originally based on the *Code Napoléon,* it has some characteristics that are quite distinct from Belgian and French private or commercial law.[22]

US securities law has been selected because of its common law heritage, which contrasts with the civil law tradition of the European jurisdictions selected. Furthermore, the Uniform Commercial Code ('UCC') has established a modern, harmonised legal infrastructure for the custody and transfer of book-entry securities within the US,[23] which may be considered exemplary to some extent for a prospective European modernisation and harmonisation. For that reason, US law rather than English law will be investigated.[24]

Thus, the examination of the jurisdictions selected is principally directed at the legal framework for the custody and transfer of securities and its relationship with the more general body or bodies of law in which it is embedded. For that purpose, various specific questions have been phrased, which will be answered for each of the jurisdictions investigated.[25] Those questions principally take a functional approach, i.e. they investigate which legal rules are employed by the

---

20. The German *Depotgesetz* was already enacted in 1937 and had a similar effect; *see,* e.g., MICHELER (2006), 47 and the references provided there.
21. This position assumes the application of a conflict of laws rule that refers to Belgian law. Both under the traditional *lex rei sitae,* and under the more modern PRIMA rule, this is the case; *see infra,* Ch. 3.2.
22. *Cf.* WATSON (2000), II: 'the value of comparative law lies fundamentally in its capacity to explain legal developments, the relationship of law to society [...] the simplest way to exploit comparative law is by examining, and accounting for, similarities and differences in systems that have a historical relationship'.
23. All states, as well as the District of Columbia, have adopted Revised UCC Art. 8 (1994).
24. Moreover, several recent and comprehensive publications are already available on English securities custody and transfer law; *see,* e.g., AUSTEN-PETERS (2000) *and* BENJAMIN (2000).
25. The investigation will therefore involve both macro- and microcomparison; ZWEIGERT & KÖTZ (1998), 4–5 *and* ODERKERK (1999), 33–39.

jurisdictions selected to deal with certain specific issues, while refraining from using the concepts of one specific jurisdiction.[26]

First, it will have to be established which categories of securities are eligible for being credited to a securities account. Second, as one of the main issues of the comparative analysis, it is asked what is the nature of the interests that an accountholder enjoys with regard to the securities he is entitled to? That issue encompasses the following questions: how are an accountholder's interests characterised? How are they evidenced? For example, is a credit entry in a securities account (merely) a proof of ownership or is it a constitutive element for the existence of securities?[27] Are informal dispositions over securities, i.e. dispositions that are not registered by a book-entry in a securities account, at all possible?[28] Are provisional credit entries in securities accounts possible?[29]

Third, as another important question related to the nature of accountholder interests, it is questioned how an accountholder's interests in his securities are protected against the account provider and third parties.[30] This question becomes particularly acute when the account provider becomes insolvent, and the most pertinent questions then become: how are shortfalls availed that occur as to the securities held by the account provider?[31] How are an accountholder's interests in securities separated from the account provider's property, and, more generally, how are accountholder interests protected against the claims of the account provider's general creditors?[32]

Regarding the transfer of securities by book-entry, the specific questions to which an answer is sought are: what are the requirements for a transfer of securities by book-entry?[33] When is a transfer of securities by book-entry effective, i.e. when can the transferee assert his interests in the transferred securities against third parties? Under what circumstances can *bona fide* transferees rely on the crediting of their securities account, especially when having acquired *a non domino*,[34] and, more generally, under what circumstances may credit entries in a securities account be reversed?[35]

Besides the risk which an accountholder runs in its account provider's insolvency, the nature of the security interest(s) which a collateral taker can vest in securities appears to be the most relevant issues for market participants.[36] Consequently, the creation, perfection and enforcement of security rights that can be

26. ZWEIGERT & KÖTZ (1998), 36. The questions take both a functional-institutional, and a problem-solving approach; *cf.* ODERKERK (1999), 67–88 and 236–239.
27. *Cf.* Giovannini Group 2003 Report, 13.
28. *Cf.* UNIDROIT 2003 Position Paper, 20.
29. *Cf. id.*, 24–26.
30. *Cf.* EFMLG 2003 Report, 23–24.
31. *Cf. id*, 26–27.
32. *See* BENJAMIN (2003), 225.
33. *Cf. id.*, 19–20 and EFMLG 2003 Report, 24–25.
34. *Cf.* Giovannini Group 2003 Report, 15; UNIDROIT 2003 Position Paper, 21–22 *and* EFMLG 2003 Report, 26–27.
35. *Cf.* UNIDROIT 2003 Position Paper, 22–24.
36. *Cf.* BENJAMIN & YATES (2002), 62.

vested in securities will be examined in the comparative research presented in this dissertation. More specifically, it will be questioned what the requirements are for the creation of a security right in book-entry securities and how such a security interest may be enforced.[37] Moreover, it is asked whether upper-tier attachment is possible, i.e. whether it is possible for an accountholder's creditor to exercise his rights against higher-tier account providers.[38]

Finally, the conflict of laws rules of the selected jurisdictions will be analysed and compared, insofar as they concern the custody and transfer of securities, both as title transfer and by way of security. No attention is therefore paid to other issues of private international law, such as issues of jurisdiction and execution of judgments.[39]

The findings of the analyses as described, are subsequently compared and evaluated. More in particular, the securities laws of the European jurisdictions investigated will be compared with each other, with US law, with the UNIDROIT draft convention and with the advice of the EU Legal Certainty Group. For the evaluation, the national securities laws investigated will be tested to the standards of modern securities custody practice, which are expressed in various (international) recommendations and reports, and have proven to be generally accepted by lawyers and practitioners alike. Moreover, it will be evaluated whether the national laws investigated achieve financial stability and investor protection to the maximum degree possible.

On the basis of this comparison and evaluation, it will be ascertained to what extent current securities laws of Belgium, France and the Netherlands should be modified. Tested to the overarching policy goals of financial stability and investor protection, proposals for modernisation and harmonisation will thus be made, and it will be consequently assessed whether these proposals would unacceptably undermine the current systemisation of the European jurisdictions investigated. Conclusions regarding a future harmonisation of the jurisdictions investigated are therefore drawn on both normative and coherence grounds. These conclusions could be generalised so as to regard the desirability and form of a future European harmonisation instrument, especially because they are drawn on the basis of a comparison of some typical EU jurisdictions and a general theory of coherence and systemisation of law. But verification of such a generalisation would, of course, require further research into the other jurisdictions of the EU.

1.2.3 ADDITIONAL METHOD ISSUES

From the discussion of the methodological approach taken, it can be inferred that the present study focuses primarily on issues that traditionally classify as issues

37. *Cf.* EFMLG 2003 Report, 25–26.
38. *Cf.* Giovannini Group 2003 Report, 14; UNIDROIT 2003 Position Paper, 18–19 *and* EFMLG 2003 Report, 25.
39. For a summary of these issues, *see* BENJAMIN & YATES (2002), 63 *et seq.*

of commercial or property law, and it is therefore not concerned with the specifics of custody agreements or transfer agreements.[40] Neither will substantive or conflict of laws rules that concern typical issues of corporate or insolvency law be addressed in detail. Operational or technical issues of clearing and settlement systems, prudential requirements for participants in clearing and settlement systems, and, more generally, regulatory law is also considered to lie outside the scope of the present work.

The qualitative research described above has been conducted mainly by following the traditional legal method, i.e. by an analysis of available literature and case law. In addition, courses and seminars on the subject of study have been followed, notably at Université de Paris II (Panthéon-Assas), Harvard Law School and New York University School of Law. Furthermore, conversations with eminent experts in the field have significantly contributed to the research presented in this dissertation.[41]

The results of research on the conflict of laws rules that concern securities custody and transfer has been previously published as part of the Allen & Overy Research Series.[42] Preliminary findings have also been presented in the context of the Ius Commune Research School, in which the law faculties of the Universities of Amsterdam, Edinburgh, Leuven, Maastricht and Utrecht participate, as well as to individual experts.[43]

The present dissertation forms part of a larger research project of the Amsterdam Institute of Private Law and its successor, the Centre for the Study of European Contract Law ('CSECL'), on 'System and Coherence'. That research project is directed at the consequences of Europeanisation on the systemisation of private law and is characterised by a comparative approach. In general, the CSECL's research is directed at the Europeanisation of private law, and it focuses on the consequences of Europeanisation for private law from political and doctrinal perspectives.[44]

This study applies the terminology that is common to international publications in this field.[45]

---

40. For instance, specific problems that occur when book-entry securities are donated are not addressed, since those are generally considered to be of a non-commercial nature; *see, e.g. In re Ferguson,* 18 UCC Rep. Serv. 1284 (NY Sur. 1967).
41. *See* Preface.
42. HAENTJENS (2006).
43. *See* Preface.
44. *See* the Centre for the Study of European Contract Law's *Research Programme 2006–2009,* 3, available at <www.jur.uva.nl/csecl/>.
45. *See* BERNASCONI (2000), 6 *et seq.* and the BIS Glossary. The BIS Glossary consists of a list of definitions used in the 16 reports regarding payment and processing in the international capital markets and is published by the Bank of International Settlements ('BIS'). For a list of commonly used concepts in EU law, *see* the Legal Certainty Group's *Compendium of definitions in Community law,* MARKT/G2/MNCT D(2005), available at <http://ec.europa.eu/internal_market/>. The Legal Certainty Group also released a memorandum that specifically addresses the use of 'intermediary', 'account provider' and 'custodian'; *see* MARKT/G2/MNCT D(2005), available at <http://ec.europa.eu/internal_market/>.

1.3 OUTLINE

In the remainder of Part I (introductory chapters), the jurisprudential notions of system and coherence, as well as their relevance to European harmonisation processes are discussed (chapter 2). In the chapter that follows, the interplay between the reality of securities custody and transfer on the one hand, and the relevant substantive and conflict of laws rules, on the other hand, are examined from a historical perspective (chapter 3). In chapter 4, some general remarks are made on the risks and current practice of clearance and settlement in global securities markets.

In Part II (securities laws of selected jurisdictions), the substantive and private international securities custody and transfer laws of Belgium (chapter 5), France (chapter 6), the Netherlands (chapter 7) and the United States (chapter 8) are analysed on the basis of the questions listed above and against the background of the coherence concept developed in chapter 2.

Part III (harmonisation and modernisation) starts with an overview of current global and regional harmonisation and modernisation initiatives (chapter 9). In the chapter that follows, it is discussed to what extent the European jurisdictions investigated should be modernised so as to meet the generally accepted standards of modern securities custody and transfer practice that are distilled from the various recommendations and reports discussed in the previous chapter. In chapter 11, it is examined whether the advocated modernisation measures would unacceptably infringe on the systemisation of the European jurisdictions investigated. The final chapter of this part discusses the institutional context, the preferred scope and the most appropriate form of a EU harmonisation instrument in the field of securities custody and transfer law (chapter 12).

Subsequently, the conclusions reached are summarised and it is determined whether a European harmonisation instrument that would foster financial stability and investor protection would be prohibitively complicated by the current relationship between securities custody and transfer law with property, contract and commercial law under Belgian, French and Dutch law.

In sum, the present study aims to satisfy HOMMELHOF's admonition, which concerned only the implementation of European harmonisation instruments in German law, but which, it is submitted, applies to any harmonisation instrument and any jurisdiction's legal system:

> *Bei jedem Angleichungsprojekt in Brüssel muß von Anbeginn sorgfältig überlegt werden, wie seine Elemente in das in Deutschland vorhandene Recht eingebaut und mit seinen Prinzipien in Übereinstimmung gebracht werden können. Systemstimmigkeit sollte bereits vor und während der Verhandlungen in Brüssel vorgedacht werden und nicht erst* nach *Erlaß der EG-Richtlinie.*[46]

46. HOMMELHOF (1992), 106.

Chapter 2
System and Coherence

2.1 INTRODUCTION

It has been hypothesised above that the coherence of national systems plays an important role in harmonisation processes, as it has been argued that (the current systemisation of) national legal systems are likely to affect the future form of a harmonisation measure to which it will subject, and vice versa. In the chapters of Part II, some selected jurisdictions will therefore be analysed to determine the current coherence of securities law with the more general body of law in which it is embedded in view of a future harmonisation instrument of securities custody and transfer law.

In order to do so, as well as to assess to what extent (national) systems of law should influence future supra-national legislation, i.e. what the role of coherence should be in such a legislation project, the jurisprudential notions of system and coherence must be made operational. The following sections will therefore make some introductory remarks on those notions and it will be shown how a generally accepted view of coherence as a principle of systemisation of law will be applied.[1]

However, unlike some legal theorists who have developed coherence accounts, a non-foundationalist notion of coherence will be applied here, for it is assumed that not only coherence considerations determine what the law is.[2] Moreover, it is believed that such a notion would not be the most appropriate one

---

1. Thus, a systematic approach to law is chosen here, rather than an approach that is based on the constitutional creation of law by authority and its pre-emptive character; *cf.* e.g. JOERGES (1997), 379, RAZ (1994), 309 *and see* KRESS (1996), 547–548. It is submitted, however, that for the present purposes of assessing the coherence of law, a systematic approach to law is more appropriate.
2. *Cf.* SORIANO (2003), 298 and 300 *and* BERTEA (2005), 157.

in view of the analysis to be made in the current book, which involves a coherence test of positive law, rather than the development of a general theory of law. Furthermore, it will be shown that the most appropriate notion of coherence for the purposes of the present dissertation involves a notion of coherence that allows for value-pluralism, as it is assumed that coherence is only one of the sometimes conflicting principles of the systemisation of law. In other words, it is assumed that not only coherence considerations determine what the law should be.

In the following sections, the systemisation of law and its principles will therefore be discussed first, after which the concept of coherence will be further made operational. Subsequently, some general remarks will be made about the interplay of coherence and supra-national legislation, in particular of the European legislature.

2.2 SYSTEMISATION OF LAW

2.2.1 Relevance and Principles of Systemisation

Most jurists agree that organised bodies of law can be looked upon as systems (of law), and that very few bodies of law are imaginable that are so badly organised that they do not qualify as a system at all.[3] A system of law, as it is understood here, arranges legal material, i.e. court decisions and legislation. Legal material so understood, in its turn, is based on, and formulates rules and norms, as a consequence of which those rules and norms, as well as the individual legal decisions (adjudication and legislation), together form the elements of a system of law. In addition, the principles underlying the said rules and norms are elements of a legal system.[4] In sum, a system of law consists of individual legal decisions, rules, norms, and their underlying principles.

A neatly systemised system is arguably preferable over a body of law that is not or is badly organised, since fairness in general, and equality and legal certainty in particular are enhanced by a well organised set of rules, norms and principles.[5] Systemisation enhances equality, because it requires the formulation (implicitly or explicitly) of rules, norms and principles as well as of the relationships between them. It is therefore clear in a well organised system, which values apply to which

3. *See,* e.g., Wilhelmsson (2002), 80: 'All phenomena of life can be systemised' and 'Legal science creates the system of the legal order'. *See also* e.g. Bloembergen (1992-1), at 564. On the role of codification for systematisation, *see,* e.g., Hesselink (2001), 9–11 *and* Thomas (2005), 41 *et seq.*, from a historical perspective.
4. Because systemisation thus implies the formulation of principles, systems of law also represent expressions of an interpretation of law; *see* e.g. Brouwer (1999), 223 *and* Bloembergen (1992-2), 310 and the further references provided there. On the intricate relation between 'principles' and 'values' in this context, *see* MacCormick (1984b), 40–41.
5. *Cf.* Hesselink (2001), 76–78, Loos (2006), 8 *and* Bloembergen (1992-1), 559, listing simplicity as another advantage of the unity of law, a concept which amounts to *system* as employed here; *cf.* Bloembergen (1992-1), 564 *and* Bloembergen (1992-2), 309.

situations and what the relevant elements of a particular situation are. Thus, systemisation will probably lead to the treatment of like cases alike – provided that the relevant elements are identical.[6] In badly organised systems on the other hand, it is unclear which values (should) apply in which situations, and similar cases are therefore more likely to be treated differently. As another result of the clarity established by systemisation, legal certainty is enhanced, for a well organised system arguably provides its subjects with certainty as to when rules and norms are applied to specific situations.

More generally, systemisation provides for the rationality that is needed for legal decisions to be cogent,[7] as systemisation presents a basis for rational explanations for legal decisions. In other words, through systemisation, reference can be made to a certain set of norms, rules and principles, which is generally necessary for decisions to be acceptable.[8] Thus, the relevance of systemisation is shown, and it must now be discussed when a system of law can be considered to be well organised. BROUWER[9] listed the following principles that systems of law must adhere to: clarity and precision, thrift, comprehensiveness, the optimal realisation of legal values and coherence.

The view that a system of law is well organised when it arranges norms, rules and principles in a clear and precise way (the first principles of systemisation) will probably meet few objections. Related to these principles of clarity and precision is the principle of thrift, which refers to the requirement that a system should not be needlessly complex due to redundant and overly complicated constructions. The principle of comprehensiveness refers to the requirement that a system of law covers all case law and legislation. In other words, in a perfect legal system, all individual legal decisions (in both legislation and adjudication) are covered by the arrangement of norms, rules and principles. But perhaps the most important principle of good systemisation is the optimal realisation of (legal) values, for only a system of law that leads to the reasonable weighing of values can be considered to be well organised.[10] Although the following section will deal with coherence in greater detail, it is notable here that coherence refers to the systemisation requirement that the relations between the elements of a system should be (at least) logically consistent.[11]

However, the principles of systemisation are not always fulfilled. For instance, the more complex and the larger a certain body of law is, the more difficult the realisation of the said principles will be. Moreover, optimal realisation of these principles is under continuous pressure, and as areas of law develop independently

6. Thus, a formal conception of equality is used here; *cf.* BROUWER (1992), 187.
7. BROUWER (1999), 219. *Cf.* CANARIS (1969), 42–43.
8. *Cf. infra,* s. 2.3.2.
9. 1999, at 232. *Cf.* KRESS (1996), 533–534.
10. Consequently, this view considers so-called *Begriffsjurisprudenz,* which refers to a strictly dogmatic organisation and is incapable of adaptation to developments in legal values, not to be good systemisation. *Cf.* CANARIS (1969), 43.
11. Coherence has even been viewed as an intrinsic necessity for a legal system; DESMET (1987), 116. *Cf.* LEVENBOOK (1984), 356 and the references provided there.

of each other and legislators tend to take a functional rather than systematic approach, optimal systematisation is not always reached.[12]

2.2.2 A Mixed-Value Good

As noted above, all principles of systemisation cannot always be realised to the same extent. Moreover, although they reinforce each other in some situations, they conflict in others, and a well-organised system of law must therefore be viewed as a mixed-value good.[13] Consequently, the principles of organisation must be considered as optimisation principles and although their realisation should be aimed at the highest degree possible, it must be realised that full realisation of all principles cannot always be reached.[14]

In a classic example of a situation in which principles of systemisation conflict, a court reaches a decision that is considered fair and just, but which does not fit (easily) into the existing system of law. Assuming that this decision has been preferred over a decision which would be coherent with the system, but would provide an unfair result, a morally better justifiable legal decision has been preferred over a decision which is (logically) more consistent with the system.[15] In that same vein, legislation which deals fairly and satisfactorily with certain problems is sometimes preferred to legislation which is more coherent with other, older legislation and court decisions and thus the optimal realisation of legal values is sometimes preferred to coherence.[16]

Yet it does not prove to be an easy matter to determine in general terms how the principles of systemisation should be weighed when they conflict. Raz, for instance, has stated that whether coherence must be preferred over a morally more correct line, cannot be determined in general, but depends on the circumstances of the case.[17] It is submitted, however, that the weighing of systemisation principles against each other shows significant similarities with the weighing of conflicting legal principles, and the meta-principles that have been shown to determine the latter conflicts can therefore similarly be applied to the weighing of conflicting systemisation principles. More particularly, the meta-principles that have been discerned to enhance the rationality of such a weighing are: the optimisation of all conflicting principles (the result of weighing should be that all conflicting principles are observed as much as possible), consistency in this process (the weighing of principles should be carried out in the same way in similar

12. *Cf.* Bloembergen (1992-1), 327-330, mentioning more practical impediments to the realisation of the 'unity of law', the functional practice of lawyers being one. *Cf. also* Hesselink (2001), 64.
13. *See* Kress (1996), 541. *Cf.* MacCormick (1984a), 244: 'coherence is a desirable ideal feature of a system of law. As such, however, it may compete with other ideal features of law, like substantive justice'. The term 'mixed-value good' is taken from Brouwer (1999), 232.
14. *Cf.* Besson (2004), 266 *and* Curtin & Dekker (1999), 90.
15. Raz (1994), 287–290. *Ibid.,* 288 (with respect to coherence): 'I will take it merely to indicate one desideratum in good judicial decisions'.
16. Raz (1994), 301.
17. Raz (1994), 301. *Accord* Soriano (2003), 316.

situations) and proportionality (one principle should not disproportionately trump other principles).[18]

However, in adjudication, the weighing of coherence against other systemisation principles is made differently than in legislation. For instance, a heavy burden generally lies on judges who are about to give priority to the optimal realisation of values in favour of coherence with existing law, as in many jurisdictions judges do not have much discretion in producing decisions showing little consistency with the rest of the legal system. A legislator on the other hand, is generally in a position to reform an area of law more or less radically, thus introducing a part of a system which may be coherent in itself, but which may or may not display coherence with the rest of the system.[19] It is this weighing of coherence against other systemisation principles by the legislature that will be further elaborated upon in the following sections.

2.3 COHERENCE

2.3.1 Coherence in Systemisation

Whereas many jurists consider coherence to be a special virtue of interpretation in legal reasoning,[20] in these sections, emphasis will lie on coherence as a principle of systemisation of law. But in both approaches, coherence relates to a principle in the analysis of positive law, or to a principle in the process of legal decision making (in adjudication as well as in legislation), and in both approaches, the basic assumption is that the more coherent decisions are the better ones.[21] When considering coherence as a systemisation principle, it is submitted that coherence, more in particular, sees to the relations between all the elements of a system of law as described above, i.e. to the relations between rules, norms, principles and the individual decisions in which these are expressed.[22] Subsequently, it must be questioned whether the relations between the elements of a system are such that this system can be said to be coherent, especially in view of the coherence test to be carried out in the following chapters.

Although general consensus exists that the elements should be systematically interdependent in some way,[23] the precise conditions for coherence and the order

18. Burg (2000), 175.
19. Cf. Raz (1994),300.
20. Dickson (2001) § 3. Such a conception of coherence may relate to an epistemic as well as to a legal theory. *See* Raz (1994), 263–270 and 271. Also, in some coherence accounts diachronic coherence is distinguished from synchronic coherence. Diachronic coherence refers to consistency *over* time, whilst synchronic coherence refers to the consistency *at* a time; *see* Besson (2004), 258 *and* Kress (1996), 540–541.
21. Dickson (2001) §1.
22. *See* Kress (1996), 537–539 providing for an overview of problems (and solutions) in determining the elements of coherence theories. *But cf.* Raz (1994), 273, stating that a valuable coherence test applies to legal principles only (instead of to all legal propositions).
23. Raz (1994), 304. *Cf.* Alexy & Peczenik (1990), 131. *Cf. also* Kress (1996), 533.

between those conditions is subject to debate. Yet most legal theorists agree that the relations between the elements of a legal system should at least be logically consistent. Thus, consistency is a necessary condition for coherence, but it seems to be generally agreed that consistency alone is not sufficient for establishing it.[24] Consequently, when no consistency can be found, the legal system under scrutiny must be considered to be not coherent, i.e. incoherent.

Furthermore, general consensus seems to be that, apart from logical consistency, a coherent system must display some degree of monism or unity,[25] implying that coherence can only be established when the rules and norms of which a system consists are supported by at least *some* common principles.[26] When all rules and norms of a given system are supported by a limited number of principles, this system displays near monistic coherence,[27] whereas when a great many principles support all norms, this system is said to display weak coherence, provided no inconsistencies can be found.

More specifically, the relations between the elements of a legal system are inconsistent if they are not logically valid or inconsistent in other ways.[28] Logical validity in this regard refers to the internal architecture of a system.[29] For instance, when all norms of a specific area of law fit logically into a more general part of law, the relationship between this specific area and the more general body of law in which it is embedded can be said to be logically valid.[30] For example, Article 3:84 of the Dutch *Burgerlijk Wetboek* (Civil Code, 'BW') requires for the perfection of a transfer of ownership the delivery of the property transferred, and the transferor's right of disposal. In its turn, Article 17 of the Securities Giro Transfer and Administration Act which governs the transfer and custody of book-entry securities, prescribes a specific form of delivery as referred to in Article 3:84 BW, viz. a credit entry in the transferee's securities account.[31]

Other inconsistencies result from intrinsic contradictions and from *Wertungswiderspruch*.[32] Intrinsic contradictions are found when the implications of two or

---

24. *See,* e.g. ALEXY & PECZENIK (1990), 130, KRESS (1996), 540 and 546, DICKSON (2001) § 3.1 *and* BERTEA (2005), 156. *Contra* MACCORMICK (1984b), 38. *Cf.* the conditions for a minimally coherent system posed by LEVENBOOK (1984), 361. *Cf. also* DWORKIN (1986), 219 *et seq.*
25. KRESS (1996), 542-543 *and* BERTEA (2005), 156. On the relationship between monism and unity, however, no consensus exists; RAZ (1994), 274–275 for instance, categorises valid internal relations (the ranking of principles) and logical connections as conditions for unity. KRESS (1996), 534, 543–545, on the other hand, names this concept of unity 'monism' and categorises only valid internal relations as conditions for unity. Because the concept of 'unity' is so contested, the focus will lie here on 'monism'.
26. MACCORMICK (1984a), 238 *and* BROUWER (1992), 185.
27. KRESS (1996), 534, 542.
28. *See* CURTIN & DEKKER (1999), 89.
29. KRESS (1996), 542. *See* ALEXY & PECZENIK (1990), 132–139, listing the properties of a supportive structure. *Cf.* DESMET (1987), 133 and 137–139 *and* BERTEA (2005), 159.
30. *Cf.* ALEXY & PECZENIK (1990), 140–141.
31. *See* the Explanatory Notes to the Wge Proposal TK 1975–1976, 13 780, no. 3, 36. On the relationship between Art. 3:84 Civil Code and the Giro Transfer and Administration Act, *see* Ch. 7.4.
32. *See* BROUWER (1999), 232–233.

more (legal) propositions are mutually exclusive. For example, a Dutch working conditions rule requiring that all employees work in a room which has a view of the outside, is (intrinsically) contradictory to the rule of the Dutch Inspectorate for Consumer Goods demanding that rooms where food is processed are shielded from all natural light.[33] Employees who process food are thus obviously subject to two mutually exclusive, and therefore intrinsically inconsistent rules.

Inconsistency in valuation or *Wertungswiderspruch* is established, when norms display contradictory values.[34] Under Dutch law for example, involuntary manslaughter is considered to be a criminal offence and is punishable by a maximum of 9 months imprisonment or detention.[35] All kinds of environmental offences that result from negligence are considered to be summary offences and are therefore valuated as being less serious than criminal offences. However, the said environmental offences are punishable by a maximum of 1 year detention,[36] which thus implies an evaluation that contradicts the evaluation that is implied by their characterisation as summary offences.

Because of the variable character of the conditions for coherence just discussed (monism/unity, logical validity and the absence of inconsistencies), coherence must be a matter of degree.[37] It has already been noted, for instance, that a system displaying almost no monism because a great many principles support all of its norms, can be considered weakly coherent, provided this system displays no inconsistencies (because in such a case the system would be incoherent). Such a system could be absent of inconsistencies because all areas of law with deviating norms are clearly isolated from the rest of the law.[38] In sum, under the coherence account developed here, (value) pluralism does not necessarily lead to incoherence.[39]

Moreover, a given area of the law may be coherent in itself, but may not fit into the rest of the system because no valid logical connections exist between that specific area and the rest of the law.[40] Should this lead to a conflict of norms, the question arises whether the coherence of the specific area of law (local coherence or area-specific coherence) should be upheld against the coherence of the system as a whole (global coherence), and it is generally argued that local coherence should be prioritised.[41]

---

33. *See Strijdige Regels in de Praktijk* (Conflicting Rules in Practice), a report by the Dutch Ministry of Economic Affairs (November 2003), 10.
34. *Cf.* CANARIS (1969), 112 *et seq.*
35. Art. 307 *Wetboekvan Strafrecht* (Criminal Code).
36. Art. 1a(1) in conjunction with Art. 6 (1)(3) *Wet Economische Delicten* (Economic Offences Act).
37. ALEXY & PECZENIK (1990), 145.
38. The isolation of areas of law so that no incoherence arises has been called the coherentist method of scope; KRESS (1996), 541.
39. RAZ (1994), 299. *Cf.* BERTEA (2005), 158.
40. *Cf.* DESMET (1987), 133–139. The same distinction is made with regard to adjudicative coherence; BERTEA (2005), 158.
41. *See* LEVENBOOK (1984), 368, 371; RAZ (1994), 298; KRESS (1996), 540–541 *and* DICKSON(2001) § 3.5 and the further references provided there.

2.3.2 Relevance of Coherence

Thus, the coherence account developed in the preceding sections has only relative normative power on several grounds. First, it has been assumed that not only coherence considerations determine what the law is, which can be described as a non-foundationalist notion of coherence. Second, coherence is viewed here as a principle of the systemisation of law, and it has been shown that, as such, coherence must sometimes recede in favour of the optimal realisation of values. Third, it has been shown that in some instances, coherence allows for value pluralism and, finally, that global coherence may be trumped by local coherence.[42]

However, it is submitted that coherence should play an important role in legal decision making, since as a principle of systemisation, coherence contributes to good systematisation and therefore to the establishment of equality,[43] legal certainty and rationality. Of these, legal certainty and especially rationality are particularly relevant in the coherence context. More particularly, coherence results in legal certainty, because coherence, understood as consistency with earlier decisions, makes new decisions more or less predictable.[44] Moreover, coherence so understood provides a reasonable explanatory basis for individual legal decisions and thus enhances their rationality[45] and intelligibility.[46]

Furthermore, coherence arguably makes a legal system as a whole more efficient, transparent and rational.[47] The efficiency of a legal system is enhanced by coherence, since in systems of strong monism and consistency, few principles, rules and norms govern most factual situations. Monism and consistency also contribute to the transparency of any given legal system, as they render the applicable legal rules easily ascertainable. Finally, as coherence provides a reasonable explanatory basis for individual legal decisions, it also enhances the rationality of the relevant legal system as a whole.

In its turn, that rationality justifies both the system as a whole and individual decisions,[48] because of what is called the argument of authority.[49] Under the argument of authority, legal rules are only likely to be adhered to by the subjects of a given

---

42. As such, the coherence account to be developed here accords with the ECJ's conception of adjudicative coherence; Soriano (2003), 298–299 *and* Bertea (2005), 167.
43. *Cf.* Roth (2002), 770.
44. *Cf.* Raz (1994), 302. Raz also lists social co-ordination as an independent value of coherence. However, social co-ordination could also be considered to be a (side-)effect of legal certainty.
45. *Cf.* Canivet (2003), 58 *and* Bertea (2005), 160.
46. Raz (1994), 264. *But see* Kress (1996), 534. *Cf. supra,* s. 2.2.1.
47. *See* Dworkin (1986), 188-189, Van Gerven (1997), 465 *and* Raz (1994), 273, respectively.
48. Alexy & Peczenik (1990), 144. *See also* Raz (1992), 293, Levenbook (1984), 359, Soriano (2003), 307 *and* Bertea (2005), 170. However, this justification is purely formalistic; MacCormick (1984a), 243. *See also* MacCormick (1984b), 46–47. For a different view, *see* Kennedy (2006), 18, arguing that coherence, even when viewed as having only relative normative power, is obsolete, and at best, a 'counsel of despair'.
49. Besson (2004), 261 and the further references provided there. *See also* Kress (1996), 546–548 *and cf.* Dworkin (1986), 188 *et seq. and* Bertea (2005), 170, specifically applying this argument to EU law.

system if these subjects are able to identify themselves with the authors of these rules. Because such identification is only possible if rules are rational and not inconsistent with other rules issued by the same authority,[50] rationality and thus coherence is of pivotal importance for the justification of any legal system and decisions.

2.4 COHERENCE, SECURITIES LAWS AND EUROPEAN LAW

2.4.1 The EU and Systemisation

The European Union consists of several systems of law. European Community law in its strict sense of the primary and secondary law of the European institutions forms a system of its own, and the laws of all Member States add to that as separate systems of law, while European law must be also be considered an integrated part of the Member States' laws.[51] Consequently, the principles of systemisation require that EU Community law and Member States national legal systems be coherent (national or horizontal coherence),[52] but also that Member States' systems of national law are in coherence with EU law (international or supranational coherence).[53]

Vertical coherence and diagonal coherence can be distinguished as subtypes of supranational coherence, which sees to the relation between EU law and national jurisdictions in their entirety. Vertical coherence concerns the relation between (a certain area of) EU law and the part of national law on which it has its direct effect. Diagonal coherence on the other hand, concerns the relation between (a certain area of) EU law and the more general area of national law in which the directly effected part is embedded, or that national law in its entirety, with the exception of the directly effected part.[54] As will be seen in the following sections, this type of coherence is especially relevant, because the (functional) scope of EU legislative instruments seldom coincides with the scope of national areas of law.

International harmonisation and unification, which aim at coherence between (specific areas of) several national jurisdictions, can be looked upon as transna-

50. *Cf.* Raz (1994), 281: 'It makes no sense to accept an assemblage of norms as one's own norms unless one regards them as valid and justified, and one cannot regard them as justified unless they form a coherent body'.
51. Case 26/62, Van Gend en Loos v. Nederlandse Administratie der Belastingen, 1962 ECR 3. European law in its wide sense as comprising both the law of the EU institutions and the law of national jurisdictions has also been considered as one body of law; Besson (2004), 266–269. Although all Member States have a general obligation (rather than a legal obligation with a statutory basis; Besson (2004), 262–265) to make their jurisdictions mutually coherent, this proposition is not widely accepted.
52. *See,* e.g., Roth (2002), 766, Smits (2002), 66 *and* Müller-Graff (2004), 87, arguing that EU legislation is inconsistent.
53. *See* Besson (2004) *and* Bertea (2005), 155.
54. Van Gerven (1997), 465 calls this form of coherence homogeneity. He contends that there is 'no requirement for Community law to bring about such harmony'.

tional coherence. However, since neither globally, nor within the EU, the collection of states subject to harmonisation or unification form a system as a whole, transnational coherence is not a principle of systemisation[55] and will therefore not be addressed here. But the other types of coherence just mentioned, i.e. horizontal coherence, vertical coherence and diagonal coherence, will be successively discussed in the following sections, especially in view of possible future EU legislation on securities custody and transfer law.

2.4.2 Horizontal and Vertical Coherence

As has been shown above, (horizontal) coherence requires a certain degree of monism or unity of principle, valid logical connections between all elements of the system and the absence of inconsistencies between them. Thus, if a given system contains a body of general private or general commercial law, a body of specific commercial law should be properly embedded therein and should adhere to some extent to the same principles. Furthermore, the rules and norms of specific law should not logically contradict the rules and norms of general law. More specifically, when in the next chapters the relationship between securities law and general private or commercial law within the jurisdictions of Belgium, France, the Netherlands and, to a lesser extent, the US, will be tested, the use of legal concepts will serve as a handle for the coherence test applied to norms, and it will be examined whether certain legal concepts have a meaning in securities law that is different from their meaning in more general areas of law.[56]

If all the conditions for coherence prove to have been satisfied, strong coherence will be found. But if little unity of principle will be found, for example because the securities law proves to be an isolated area of law with typical norms, while the logical connections are correct and there exist no inconsistencies, then it will be concluded that the system concerned is weakly coherent.[57] If logical contradictions are found, for example because of a mismatch between the use of concepts and compartmentalisation, the system will be found to be incoherent.[58]

Although the European legislature has the power to create a whole new area of law, which may or may not be coherent with the rest of the law, its legislative measures should be coherent, at least to some extent with both the directly affected areas of national law (vertical coherence) and the national laws in general (diagonal coherence).[59] However, coherence with the directly affected areas of national law is evaluated differently from coherence with the national laws in general. EU

55. *But see* Besson (2004), 259. But the national (re)codification of law may contribute to international unification (provided the codification is influenced by a comparative analysis of the law) and vice-versa; Hartkamp (1989), 102.
56. *Cf.* Alexy & Peczenik (1990), 140.
57. *Cf.* Ch. 7.7.2 on Dutch law. *See also* Thévenoz (2005), 307, on the recent Swiss reform of securities law.
58. Cf. Ch. 8.7.2 on US law.
59. *Cf.* Besson (2004), 279 and 281. *Cf. also* Ch. 12, where these restraints are based on the (constitutional) principles of subsidiarity and proportionality.

regulations become, by nature, part of the national laws of the Member States, while EU directives require that (parts of) existing national laws be amended. Thus, vertical coherence is simply the result of the primacy of EU legislation, which dictates that the Member States concerned must comply.[60] Furthermore, should any developments on the European level occur, for example because of new case law of the European Court of Justice ('ECJ'), national laws must comply with those developments. Consequently, no vertical incoherence should arise, and EU law has its mechanisms to ensure this.[61]

2.4.3 Diagonal Coherence

As the (functional) scope of EU legislative instruments seldom coincides with the scope of national areas of law, diagonal coherence can become problematical when new EU legislation is drafted, which is exacerbated by the quantity and complexity of the Member States' systems of law with which new EU legislation should be coherent.[62] Furthermore, after the enactment of new EU law, any disrupting decisions by the ECJ and, more generally, the autonomous character of the harmonised part of the law present a continuous threat to diagonal coherence.[63] But here, the focus lies on diagonal coherence and EU legislation in the making.

Once a new EU harmonisation instrument, such as a securities law directive, has been implemented in a given Member State's law, the relation between that Member State's version of the new EU securities legislation and its general private or commercial law is a matter of horizontal coherence. It is therefore submitted, that it can be inferred from a state's horizontal coherence whether new EU securities legislation will be coherent with the general private or commercial law of that state (diagonal coherence).[64] This position will be substantiated *below*, where the consequences of a (radical) EU securities law harmonisation on a weakly coherent, strongly coherent and incoherent national system of law will be successively discussed.

60. Nevertheless, the extent to which existing law has to be amended is an indication of the feasibility of legislative measures.
61. This manner of resolving (possible) conflicts of norms is called the coherentist method of preemption. It refers to the situation in which some areas of law have pre-emptive authority over other areas of law, so that no incoherence arises; Kress (1996), 542.
62. *Cf.* Hommelhof (1992), 106. *But see* Van Gerven (1997), 465. Besson (2004), 265 n.48 has even argued that EU legislative measures should be coherent with all past laws and decisions of all national authorities. *Cf. also* Joerges (1997), 381 and 399 *and* Desmet (1987), 119–121.
63. *See* Van Gerven (1996), 97–98 on the disruptive effect of ECJ decisions on national laws in general. On the disruptive or disintegrative effect of EU Directives on national private laws, *see* Joerges (1997), 392, Hesselink (2001), 37–49, Loos (2006), 8 *et seq. and* Smits (2006), 96–98. *See* Teubner (1998) for a socio-legal perspective. Consequently, it has been argued that full coherence between European and national (private) laws will never be achieved; Van Gerven (1997), 466. *Cf. also,* in the same sense, Hesselink (2006), 295–305.
64. *Cf.* Hesselink (2001), 41 and 47. *See also* Joerges (1997), 396. *But see* Joerges (1997), 394 stating that the impact of European harmonisation on national coherence cannot be predicted.

In this discussion, it is assumed that in the national systems concerned, all harmonised rules are considered part of securities law, and that the implementation measures are confined to (national) securities laws.

Especially in the context of the EU harmonisation of consumer law, it has been noted that EU harmonisation may lead to so-called supererogatory implementation, i.e. broader implementation than the harmonisation instrument required, as EU harmonisation instruments in that field have sometimes been incorporated in a national civil code to avoid the disruption of national coherence.[65]

However, it is submitted that in the context of securities custody and transfer law, the risk of supererogatory implementation is negligible, considering the fact that in all jurisdictions investigated, securities custody and transfer law has been codified in separate statutes, outside a civil code (when present), and that it is unlikely that these jurisdictions will incorporate a harmonised securities law within their civil codes. Consequently, the implementation of a possible future EU harmonisation instrument in the field of securities custody and transfer law is not likely to result in supererogatory implementation, which may also prevent a lack of clarity with regard to the (supranational) origin of the harmonised rules and facilitate easy future amendments on the supranational level.[66]

If, in a given national system of law, the rules of securities law form a distinct area of law which contains rules and norms that are different from general private or commercial law, that national system must be considered to be weakly coherent, as it displays little unity but no inconsistency. Consequently, new EU legislation in the field of securities law would probably not lead to inconsistencies within this national system and thus not to incoherence, as the affected body of securities law has no normative and conceptual connections with general law.[67] Moreover, if an area of law is thus separated from the rest of the law, it will not be under a continuous threat of disrupting decisions by the ECJ nor the autonomous character of this part of the law. As a result, the said system would continue to be weakly coherent, notwithstanding a radical EU harmonisation of securities law.

It is merely theoretical, it is submitted, that a EU harmonisation instrument would turn a system of weak coherence into a strongly coherent one, since that would imply that the EU harmonisation instrument, when implemented, would fit more perfectly into the national system than its former rules of securities law did. In that scenario, the harmonisation measures would have to adhere to all, or most of the same principles as the general principles of this national system, and would have to give rise to no inconsistencies at all.

---

65. *Cf.* SMITS (2006), 99–104, *and* ROTH (2002), 767–769 and 770. WILHELMSSON (2002), 79 has named supererogatory implementation a 'Jack-in-the-Box effect' of EU harmonisation. HESSELINK (2006), 302–304, has expressively called it 'surrender', as one of three strategies for implementing directives.
66. *Cf.* SMITS (2006), 99–104, ROTH (2002), 770 and 773 *and* HESSELINK (2006), 296. *But see* Ch. 12.4.
67. *Cf.* HESSELINK (2006), 299–302, defining this implementation strategy as 'segregation'.

As this is highly unlikely,[68] it is not further considered here, nor in the discussion of the two other possible situations.

If a given national system is strongly coherent, new European harmonisation legislation would probably make that system weakly coherent or incoherent.[69] It is unlikely that that system would remain strongly coherent, as radical harmonisation measures probably adhere to some principles that are different from those of the given national system's general law, which would therefore result in less unity of principle than existed previously. But if the implementation legislation would clarify to which situations the harmonised body of securities law applies and make explicit that these rules of securities law are governed by different principles, the relationship between securities law and the general body of law would be logically valid and would have no inconsistencies. Consequently, weak coherence would be the result.

If, however, the implementation legislation of the given national system would not compartmentalise the harmonised body of securities law in the way just described, the European harmonisation would result in inconsistency, for example because the securities law uses concepts which it has in common with its general law, but which have changed in meaning due to the harmonisation. Inconsistency and thus incoherence would therefore arise between that system's securities law and its general law. In sum, the (technical) form of the implementation legislation – as to which the national legislator has more or less discretion – determines in a national system of strong coherence whether radical harmonisation measures would lead to weak coherence or incoherence.[70]

If a national system is incoherent, for example because of inconsistencies between the rules of securities law and the general rules of private law, that system would, after implementation of a radical EU harmonisation instrument in the field of securities law, probably remain to be incoherent, or become weakly coherent. Again, strong coherence would be a highly unlikely result. Should the implementation legislation not clarify that securities law is governed by different principles, rules and norms than general law, the existing incoherence will be retained, but if the implementation would involve a clear compartmentalisation, the relationship between securities law and the general body of law would become logically valid and absent of inconsistencies. Consequently, the previous incoherence will be turned into weak coherence, and the coherence of the national system concerned would not be diminished, but even improved.

Should the EU legislature foresee that the coherence of the Member States' national systems would decrease because of one of its harmonisation measures, it

68. *Cf.* Joerges (1997), 396.

69. Joerges (1997), 396 seems to assume that this is the case in all parts of European private law *(lato sensu)*. Therefore, and because he argues that EU private law *(stricto sensu)* is contingent in nature, he contends that 'lawyers should *not* at the outset attempt to develop or promote comprehensive and systematic responses to the integration challenge'; and 'the design of new ready-made systems does not seem feasible'.

70. *Cf.* Hesselink (2006), 295–305 on possible implementation strategies for jurisdictions with systematic codifications, with specific attention to the coherence consequences.

should weigh that decrease in coherence against the optimal realisation of values, i.e. the values expressed by the harmonisation measure in question. As noted above, the weighing of coherence against another principle of systemisation must be carried out according to the meta-principles of optimisation, consistency and proportionality.[71] Since compliance with the principle of consistency would be unfeasible, as it would require an investigation into (all) former EU legislation that conflicted with national coherence, only optimisation and proportionality are relevant here.[72] Thus, if the optimal realisation of EU values could be achieved, while coherence could be preserved to some extent and would not be diminished disproportionately, the optimal realisation of EU values should be preferred over retaining coherence.[73]

If, however, the said decrease in coherence would imply that certain general principles would not be effective and that these principles are considered to be essential to a given legal system, for example because they express general considerations of fairness, the coherence of that system would be diminished disproportionately. Moreover, if it is felt that these general principles should be preponderant over the principles expressed by the intended EU measures, the preservation of coherence should be preferred to the optimal realisation of EU values.[74] Consequently, the intended EU legislation should be adjusted to that effect by the European legislature. The optimal realisation of national values is thus weighed via coherence against the optimal realisation of EU values.

2.5 CONCLUSION

In the preceding sections, a non-foundationalist notion of coherence has been developed, which involved that coherence must sometimes recede in favour of the optimal realisation of values, especially when coherence can be preserved to some extent and is not diminished disproportionately. Thus, it has only relative normative power, but it has also been shown that as an important principle of systemisation, coherence should always be realised to the maximum extent possible, as it furthers equality, legal certainty and rationality in a given legal system.

More in particular, it has been shown that a system of law is considered coherent when its elements, i.e. its norms, values and principles, are logically consistent and show some monism or unity of principle. Logical consistency is established when a given system of law demonstrates a sound internal architecture, i.e. if all norms of a specific area of law fit logically into the more general parts of the law, when it has no intrinsic contradictions and instances of *Wertungswiderspruch.* If

71. *See supra,* s. 2.3.
72. *Cf.* HOMMELHOFF (1992), 81 and 102 with regard to the codification of EU law in German (private) law.
73. *See* HESSELINK (2001), 48–49 and 78. *Cf.* Bloembergen (1992-1), 567 *and* HELLNER (1987), 113–114.
74. *See* JOERGES (1997), 382, 393–394.

these conditions are not met, the legal system under scrutiny must be considered not to be coherent, or incoherent. If no inconsistencies can be found, but the rules and norms of the given system are supported by many different principles, that system is weakly coherent.

In the following chapters, the relationship between securities law and general private or commercial law within the jurisdictions of Belgium, France, the Netherlands and, to a lesser extent, the US, will be tested as to coherence, especially with regard to the use of legal concepts. The coherence of (a specific part of) the European jurisdictions mentioned will thus be assessed on a conceptual level.[75] In addition, it will be ascertained to what extent the securities laws of these jurisdictions share the same principles with the more general areas of law in which those securities laws are embedded. Subsequently, it will be tested how a possible future harmonisation instrument in the field of securities law would affect the coherence of the said jurisdictions.

Then, the relevance of so-called diagonal coherence becomes particularly clear, which refers to the relation between certain rules of supra-national law and the body of national law that these supranational rules do not affect directly.[76] For a hypothetical EU proposal that would radically harmonise national securities laws, it has been shown that considerations of coherence should only lead to adjustments to such a proposal if it would lead to a system with strong coherence becoming incoherent or weakly coherent, while coherence could not be preserved to some extent and this coherence would be (felt to be) unjustifiably and disproportionately diminished. Thus, an optimal legislative decision, i.e. one which is both coherent and morally sound would be made.[77]

75. It is reiterated that this conceptual coherence analysis serves as a handle for a coherence test of norms; *see supra*, s. 2.4.1.
76. Cf. Bertea (2005), 170.
77. *Cf.* Soriano (2003), 306.

Chapter 3

Immobilisation, Dematerialisation and the Law

3.1 INTRODUCTION

As in so many instances, a historical perspective may shed some light on the problems of coherence in the modernisation and harmonisation of current securities custody and transfer laws. In other words, the interplay, or tension between the day-to-day practice of the custody and transfer of securities on the one hand, and the relevant substantive and conflict of laws rules, on the other hand, is not a new phenomenon, but has surprisingly old precedents.

In the following sections, a brief overview of the said interplay will be provided, specifically with regard to the custody and transfer of securities, i.e. of the tradable financial instruments that represent either shares in private companies or debt instruments. Although the present study relates to all financial instruments being credited to accounts with the exception of monetary assets, it is mainly concerned with securities, for it is with regard to these instruments that the main differences in national laws exist and thus the principal difficulties for a possible future harmonisation instruments arise.

It will be shown that the legal framework for the custody and transfer of securities, and also the nature of its problems, is determined, to a large extent, by the conception of securities as intangibles or tangibles. Furthermore, the changes in custody or holding structures that have occurred in the last century will be briefly discussed, while the penultimate section will elaborate on the difficulties that these changes pose to private international law concepts.

3.2 REIFICATION, INTERMEDIATION AND DEMATERIALISATION

3.2.1 REIFICATION

Conventional wisdom has it that the earliest issue of shares, in 1602, by the United Netherlands Chartered East India Company *(Vereenigde Nederlandsche Geoctroyeerde Oost-Indische Compagnie,* 'VOC') marks the beginning of the securities trade.[1] As these shares represented intangible rights of ownership in the VOC, they were not physically expressed, except for the entry of the shareholders' names in the books of the company, which therefore also reflected any change of ownership.[2] Soon, however, that practice of registration proved to encourage unregistered and unofficial speculation, and it became a constraint on fast and efficient trade.[3] As a result, the use of bearer certificates began in the Netherlands, but these documents operated merely as certificates evidencing a listing in the issuer's register.

Yet trading in securities *lato sensu* had already begun much earlier, as in the Italian city-states of the 12th and 13th century a lively trade existed in public debt instruments (bonds) that were also generally evidenced by certificates.[4] Interestingly, it was even possible to transfer money during that period by oral instruction to the transferor's bank, regardless of whether the transferee was a client of the same bank, and cross-border transfers occurred via the first international clearing centres.[5]

However, the said trade in securities took place in documents that merely evidenced an intangible right, and although it facilitated easier transfer, it did not provide the transferee with an indisputable right that could be enforced against third parties before the issuer recognised and perfected the change of entitlement. As a solution, late 19th century German jurists, notably von Savigny, developed the idea that the intangible right that a certificate refers to is incorporated in the certificate itself (reification or *Verkörperung).* Thus, the law of tangible movables could be applied to securities, and intangible rights such as shares and bonds could therefore be traded and transferred by a mere agreement between the parties to the transfer or by agreement plus the delivery of the certificate. Moreover, a transferee could immediately assert his entitlement against the issuer of the right and other

1. *See,* e.g., GRUNDMANN-VAN DE KROL (2002), 3 and the further references provided therein. However, the French city of Toulouse could also make that claim on the basis of an issue of 96 shares by the *Société des Moulins du Bazacle* in 1250; *see* <www.euronext.com.> It has even been argued that a lively trade in corporate shares existed in ancient Rome; MALMENDIER (2005).
2. BLOM (1998), 183.
3. *See* DE IONGH (1926), 29 with respect to the shares in the *Vereenigde Oost-Indische Compagnie.*
4. *See,* e.g., PEZZOLO (2005).
5. DE ROOVER (1974), 202–204, discussing the 12th century Genoese banks that created accounts, allowed overdrafts and used the fairs of Champagne as an early international clearing centre.

third parties, including a possibly dispossessed *verus dominus,* on the basis of the possession of the certificate.[6]

However, the protection of possessors of a securities certificate against competing claims found its precedent in the protection of possessors of monetary paper and other 'commercial paper' that was transferred by the endorsement of the traded certificate. This method of transfer was probably introduced on the European continent in the early 16th century and is known in the Anglo-Saxon tradition as the negotiability principle.[7]

English law, however, did not accept the reification theory for securities, which otherwise quickly spread, so that by the mid 20th century, it had been adopted in most Western legal systems.[8] In the US, for instance, the application of the negotiability principle to traded stock was codified in the 1909 Uniform Stock Transfer Act.[9] Thus, the legal fiction of reification significantly enhanced the tradability of securities, but also served the certainty needed in the securities trade.[10]

3.2.2 Intermediation

However, the system just described was based on a reality in which investors were either recorded in the issuer's register or were in physical possession of their certificates, and with quantities of traded (bearer) securities increasing and the services provided by banking institutions improving, more and more investors placed their securities in the custody of banks. Especially because the law now attributed ownership to whoever physically held the certificates, the need to reduce of the risk of loss and theft arose, and again, securities custody followed the practice of money.[11]

Prompted by the post-WWI crisis, the banks of Berlin used the *Kassenverein,* originally established in 1850 for money transfers, as a central securities depository for the processing of securities transfers and their monetary proceeds.[12] As a

6. Micheler (2006), 19 and 25 *et seq. See also* Drobnig (1988), 13: *'Die Erfindung der Effekten als Wertpapiere ist eine juristische Großtat. Sie sind aber auch eine der entscheidene* **rechtstechnischen** *Grundlagen des Hochkapitalismus; denn sie haben die breitgestreute Finanzierung des modernen Wirtschaft und damit das Privateigentum an den Produktionsmitteln wesentlich erleichtert, wenn nicht ermöglicht'.*
7. *Cf. also* De Roover (1974), 220–221 *and see* Rogers (1996), 1452–1453, *and,* extensively, Rogers (2004).
8. But the French lawyer Thaller opposed this theory as early as 1904; De Vauplane & Bornet (2001), no. 47-1 and 47-2.
9. Guttman (1990), 443, Sommer (1998), 1186 *and* Rocks & Bjerre (2004), 1.
10. *Cf.* Drobnig (1988), 13.
11. Guynn (1996), 16. Immobilisation of gold and forms of physical money into the vaults of financial intermediaries and the replacement of physical money with paper certificates took place as early as the fourteenth and fifteenth centuries. But the deposit of money in banks itself is, of course, much older; *cf.,* e.g., De Roover (1974), 201–204.
12. Drobnig (1988), 17 and Micheler (2006), 44–46.

consequence, the investor no longer had a direct relationship with the issuer, but maintained a securities account with his bank which, possibly via further intermediaries, either held the investor's securities in custody (with respect to bearer securities) or was registered as the owner in the issuer's register.[13]

The intermediated holding of securities, or indirect holding system, was followed throughout the world, not in the least because the Group of Thirty recommended in 1989 that the custody of securities be centralised in Central Securities Depositories ('CSDs') or International Central Securities Depositories ('ICSDs').[14] At present, the overwhelming majority of certificated securities are held in the vaults of a CSD or its sub-custodian. Alternatively, they are registered in the issuer's books in the name of the CSD or its nominee in the case of registered securities. In the case of multinational issues, securities are most often held by an ICSD.[15]

3.2.3 Fungibility and Dematerialisation

Thus, in most jurisdictions, a multi-tiered, pyramid-shaped structure of custody was established. In that structure, the first-tier relationship is formed between the CSD and its participants, usually institutional investors or credit institutions, while between these participants and the ultimate investors, several other intermediaries may be interposed.[16] Most often, intermediaries pool their clients' entitlements to securities of the same issue in a fungible or *omnibus* account with the higher-tier intermediary. In some systems, however, an investor's interests are separately recorded, not only on the books of the immediate intermediary, but also on the books of the CSD (non-fungible or traceable accounts).[17] Yet in all of these multi-tiered structures, the account, rather than the certificates, is the root of the investor's entitlement.[18]

Importantly, the systems of fungible custody are based on the interchangeability of securities of the same issue, so that they can be held in pools and transferred without the need for individual administration. Consequently, such fungible custody enables in-house netting for securities transfers between the clients of the same custodian, and, more generally, the transfer of ownership and

13. Consequently, a custodian of securities or an account provider will hereinafter be referred to as an 'intermediary', but no distinction is intended between the concepts of account provider, intermediary, or custodian, unless so indicated. *See* MARKT/G2/MNCT D(2005), available at <http://ec.europa.eu/internal_market/>, for a memorandum that specifically addresses the use of 'intermediary', 'account provider' and 'custodian' in the context of the Legal Certainty Group's advice.
14. G30 1989 Report, recommendation 3, 7. *See* Bernasconi (2000), 12 n.45 for an overview of the history of the world's CSDs and ICSDs.
15. The European ICSDs (Euroclear Bank and Clearstream International) were originally established for the use of the Eurobond market; *see* Giovannini Group 2001 Report, 9 and 20.
16. For some securities, an ICSD forms a top layer above the (national) CSDs.
17. *See* Bernasconi (2000), 10.
18. Bernasconi (2000), 14.

the creation of security interests in securities without physical movement in the case of bearer securities, or without changing the issuer's register in the case of registered securities.[19]

Just as the economic crisis after World War I forced the Berlin banks to centralise the custody of certificated securities, the so-called Wall Street 'paperwork crisis' of 1968 forced New York custodians to change to a system of centralised, fungible custody. In both crises, the labour-intensive, time-consuming and expensive methods of physical delivery and administration on an individualised basis could no longer be managed and in both crises, the same solution was chosen.[20] In the 1968 paperwork crunch, trading had to be delayed, while securities transactions could take months to be settled, so that centralised custody on a fungible basis proved to reduce the risks of loss and theft, illiquidity costs, and, more generally, systemic risk.[21] Furthermore, it reduced the cost of capital to public and private issuers, as well as accountholders by a reduction of the operating costs.[22]

Due to the movement towards the centralisation of custody, or, more accurately, due to the fact that in the last few decades, custodians are only occasionally required to have physical securities in stock, (bearer) securities are increasingly more often kept in a single vault maintained by the CSD or its sub-custodian. The next step – which was given impetus on the European continent by its monetary unification in 1999 – was the replacement of all the physical securities kept in one place by a single paper, the so-called global share or global bond.[23] The process of (gradually) reducing the movements and existence of physical certificates is called immobilisation, which is almost naturally followed by dematerialisation, the process by which all physical certificates are replaced by securities accounts.[24] Thus, all physical certificates are replaced by (securities) accounts, and the risk of loss and theft is excluded completely.[25]

3.2.4 Contemporary Legal Characterisations

Legally, the custody of securities was first regarded as *depositum,* as was the case with the earliest custody of money.[26] This Roman law term characterises the

---

19. *See* Guynn (1996), 16 *and* Peters (2003), 15.
20. Drobnig (1988), 15 and 17 and Micheler (2006), 44 *et seq.*
21. *See* Guynn (1996), 21 and 24 *and* Bernasconi (2000), 2 and 12. *See infra,* Ch. 4.4 for a more detailed discussion of these risks.
22. Guynn (1996), 24.
23. *See* Drobnig (1988), 20–22, discussing different types of globals. *Cf.* Goode (1996), 168. *See* Goode, *ibid.,* for the description of different sub-qualifications of immobilisation, such as compulsory and permanent immobilisation as opposed to optional and revocable immobilisation.
24. In France, for example, the issue of physical certificates has been forbidden by law since the 1980s; Act no. 81-1160 of 30 December 1981, now codified as Art. L. 211-4 C. mon. fin. *See* Ch. 6.1.3. *See also* Goode (1996), 168 *and* Peters (2003), 21.
25. Ripert & Roblot II (1996), 2. *See also* Bernasconi (2000), 9.
26. Guynn (1996), 20.

situation in which the depositor has traceable property rights in individual deposited assets[27] and meant in practice that the custodian had to register the securities numbers held for each individual investor. It has been noted, however, that this practice involved increasingly burdensome administrative costs as the volume of securities in smaller denominations increased enormously.[28]

Many legal systems therefore replaced *depositum* by so-called *depositum irregulare,* which refers to a mixture of the Roman law concept of *mutuum* (loan)[29] and the concept *depositum* just mentioned. *Depositum irregulare* means that through depositing securities, investors acquire a right against their custodian of the delivery of the same amount of securities of the same kind, since the individuality of the deposited assets is lost as they are held in one single pool (fungible custody).[30] Thus, the custody of securities on a fungible basis is a direct result of the fact that custodians no longer administer individual securities for individual clients, but maintain pools in which all securities to which the custodian's clients are entitled may be found.

In most legal systems however, such a commingling of securities implies the loss of ownership, which could leave the investor with a mere contractual claim against his custodian, and provide little or no protection in the case of the custodian's insolvency.[31] Different, sometimes statutory solutions have therefore been developed to deal with this problem.[32] The principal distinction between the solutions contemporarily chosen is between jurisdictions that confer investors with some kind of co-property interest in their securities and still regard securities as tangible movables, and jurisdictions that have developed other views. Co-property interests are known in civil law jurisdictions such as Germany, Spain and the Netherlands, where it is based on the *Depotgesetz,* the *Ley del Mercado de Valores* and the *Wet giraal effectenverkeer,* respectively. In common law jurisdictions such as England and Wales, co-ownership follows from the common law concept of trust.

Co-property rights may be distinguished between co-ownership in actual pools of securities and co-ownership in notional pools of securities. Fungible custody in

---

27. J. Inst. 1.3.14.3. *See also* Guynn (1996), 20 and 50, n.22 *and* Rutgers (1998), 5 and the further reference provided therein. This is still a rule of law in both civil and common law jurisdictions as regards *res mobilia;* Bernasconi 2000, 19.
28. *Cf.* e.g. the Explanatory Notes to the Dutch *Wet Giraal Effectenverkeer* 1976 (Securities Giro Transfer and Administration Act, 'Wge'): TK 1975–1976, 13 780, no. 3, 12.
29. *See* G. Inst. 3.90 *and* J. Inst. 3.14 on *mutuum. Cf. also* Art. 1932 of the French *Code Civil* (Civil Code).
30. *Cf.* the BIS-Glossary definition of fungibility: 'a concept that characterises the method of holding securities by a CSD [Central Securities Depository, MH] or other financial intermediary in which each of a number of issues of physical or dematerialised securities are held in separate fungible pools. No owner has the right to any particular physical or dematerialised security in a particular pool, but has a right to such an amount of physical or dematerialised securities as shown in its account with a CSD or other financial intermediary'. On the precise legal meaning of fungibility in the case of securities however, there is little consensus; *see,* e.g., Annexe VIII.11 (A. Ghozi) to the CNCT 1997 Report, 188 *and* Goode (2003), 211.
31. Although in some jurisdictions this can be prevented contractually; Goode (1996), 170.
32. The following categorisation is largely based on Bernasconi (2000), 20 *et seq.*

Belgium and Luxembourg is based on *Koninklijk Besluit* (Royal Decree) *no. 62* and several *Règlements grand-ducal* (Grand-ducal Decrees) respectively, which establish co-ownership in notional pools of securities.[33] Whereas the former system confers upon investors a direct, traceable property right in the physical certificates themselves, the Belgian/Luxembourgian system grants investors a co-property right, regardless of where the actual securities are located, i.e. irrespective of how many intermediaries are interposed between the investor and the actual custodian of securities.[34]

Although the precise classification of investors' interests in securities is unclear under French law, it is undisputed that investors do not have a co-ownership right in pools of securities.[35] Under US law on the other hand, investors enjoy a package of rights *in rem* as well as *in personam* against their intermediary, as the US Uniform Commercial Code ('UCC') Article 8 provides investors with proprietary and contractual rights in respect of the securities to which they are entitled. Italian and Brazilian law present yet a different solution, by a legal fiction that regards custody on a fungible basis as *depositum,* i.e. the administration of individual assets per individual client.

3.2.5 CONCLUSION

In sum, the practice of securities custody has dramatically changed in the second half of the 20th century, as securities ceased to be physically held on an individualised basis and became registered in pooled securities accounts with multiple layers of intermediaries, while the certificates themselves were immobilised in the vaults of CSDs or abolished altogether.[36] In addition, the settlement of securities transactions is becoming fully international, as issuers, CSDs, ICSDs, intermediaries and investors are increasingly often located in different jurisdictions.

However, most European jurisdictions still regard securities as movable tangibles and apply traditional property law concepts to securities transfers and custody. For example, some systems have retained the direct relationship between investors and their securities (tracing), which seems to be contrary to the fungible and intangible nature of current securities and is most often utterly impractical due to the multiple layers of intermediaries.[37] Furthermore, the application of possession, and in fact all *in rem* actions, to book-entry securities proves to be problematical, not only because of the intangible nature of interests in securities that

33. Of 17 February 1971, of 8 June 1994, of 7 June 1996, of 16 August 2000 and a statute of 3 September 1996. *See* Ch. 5.3.6.
34. In the Netherlands for example, third (or lower)-tier investors are not granted co-ownership rights in the actual pool of securities. *See* Ch. 7.3.5. *See also* GOODE (1996), 171.
35. *See* Ch. 6.3.5.
36. *Cf.* MOONEY (1990), n.340: 'A fungible bulk of securities is the antithesis of a discrete certificate'.
37. *Cf.* SOMMER (1998), 1204 *et seq. and* THEVENOZ (2005), 303. The impracticality of the tracing approach especially comes to light in cross-border situations; *see infra,* s. 3.3.

are expressed through accounts, but also because of the pooling or commingling of securities. For Belgium, France and the Netherlands, these problems will be discussed at greater length in the following chapters.

Consequently, various jurisdictions have modernised their securities laws or are about to do so. In 1994, for instance, the US introduced a new body of law creating a new type of interest for securities account holders.[38] Both Canada and Switzerland have recently published draft acts on the custody and transfer of securities held with an intermediary, that are both based on concepts similar to the US UCC and will thus introduce a new type of accountholder interest.[39] The English Financial Markets Law Committee, on the other hand, has recently recommended that the Law Commission should prepare a statute to modernise securities custody and transfer law, but was of the opinion that no radical changes were necessary.[40] Similarly, it has been argued that German law should abandon the co-ownership construct in favour of the trust concept.[41] Finally, it remains to be seen what the effects of a possible future global and/or EU harmonisation instrument will be on these developments.

3.3 CONFLICT OF LAWS

3.3.1 INTRODUCTION

When a suit in which a conflict of laws has arisen is brought before a court, the court will first have to ascertain its jurisdiction, after which it will have to classify the issue in dispute. An important classification that has to be made in that regard is whether the issue is contractual or proprietary in nature, a distinction known to all jurisdictions investigated.[42] Contrary to the conflict of laws rule applied to proprietary aspects, the private international law rule governing contractual aspects seems fairly settled; parties to an agreement may determine the law which is applicable thereto *(lex contractus),* a rule which is made explicit in the European Rome Convention 1980.[43] The international private law concerning proprietary aspects of custody and transfer law, however, had to face the same challenges as

---

38. UCC Art. 8, Part 5 and corresponding provisions in UCC Art. 9 (1994). *See* Ch. 8.3.4 *and,* e.g., REITZ (2005), 361 and 367.
39. The Canadian proposal for a Uniform Securities Transfer Act was published on 1 August 2003; *see* SPINK & PARÉ (2004). The Swiss draft Federal Act on the Custody and Transfer of Securities Held with an Intermediary was published in December 2004; *see* THÉVENOZ (2005), 307.
40. FMLC 2004 Report, Issue 3, available at <www.fmlc.org>.
41. *See,* e.g., EINSELE (2005), 261.
42. Even if the subject-matter concerned is classified as contractual in nature, e.g. the delivery thereof is considered to have proprietary aspects; *cf.* BENJAMIN (2000), 155.
43. Convention on the Law Applicable to Contractual Obligations, Rome 19 June 1980 (80/934/EEC), OJ L 266/1.

substantive law, and the following sections will show that its solutions have not always been satisfactory.

3.3.2 *Lex Situs, Lex Societatis* and Their Problems

Traditionally, the *lex rei sitae, lex situs cartae* or *lex situs,* all names for the same rule, has been applied as the appropriate conflict of laws rule for proprietary issues concerning bearer securities, referring to the law of the jurisdiction in which the assets concerned are located at the time a conflict of laws occurs. It derives from the mediaeval theory of Statutes and is still applied in most jurisdictions throughout the world, often also to conflicts concerning securities.[44]

Because proprietary claims are enforceable not only *inter partes,* but *erga omnes,* they require clear and easy choice of law rules to provide third parties with legal certainty. As a consequence, the applicability of the law of the jurisdiction where the tangibles concerned are located seems appropriate. This may undoubtedly be true with respect to immovable property, but problems arise from the outset when the rule is applied to movables, because of their ability to move across borders. To demonstrate this inherent difficulty, one only has to consider cases in which the movable object is stolen, cases in which security interests are vested in movable objects and cases of movables in transit.[45]

In the case of securities held through multiple tiers of custodians, these problems become even more urgent. Applying the *lex rei sitae* rule would compel one to 'look through' the whole chain of custody to the place where the securities in question are located,[46] and a number of objections to such an approach have been put forward.[47] First, the *lex rei sitae* itself is not unequivocal, or is at least applied differently in different jurisdictions and sometimes even interpreted differently within a single jurisdiction; it can refer to the law of the certificates' location, to the law of the issuer's location (which is sometimes called the *lex societatis, see below*), to the law of the securities register's location and to the law of the highest tier's location.[48] It will be obvious that these connecting factors do not necessarily refer to the same jurisdiction.

Secondly, in the case of fungible securities, bearer certificates of the same kind are not always kept in one single vault. Therefore, the location of the securities which give rise to the dispute cannot possibly be determined, since it is impossible to establish whether the securities concerned are the ones which are kept in the vault of one intermediary or held on a different level in the chain

44. Kropholler (2004), 541 and on the theory of Statutes *id.,* 11–13. *Cf.* Potok (2002), 8 n.7.
45. *Cf.,* e.g., Strikwerda (2002), nos. 159–162, Siegel (1994), 221, Clarkson & Hill (2002), 487 *and* Verhagen (2000), 114.
46. *See* Bernasconi (2000), 3 and 28–29 *and* Guynn et al. (1996) 27. *Cf.* Potok (2002), 28, stating that in direct holding systems, a look-through approach would still be feasible.
47. *Cf.* Potok (2004), 208–209.
48. Explanatory Report on the Hague Securities Convention, 18.

of custodians, possibly in another jurisdiction.[49] Furthermore, as a result of the multi-layered structure of custody, it is unlikely that the parties to the dispute have access to information known by upper-tier intermediaries concerning the location of the securities in their custody.[50] Especially in a cross-border situation, this inaccessibility of information is not uncommon due to the sometimes highly complicated structures of custody.

Thirdly, if an investor wishes to transfer his international securities portfolio comprising securities of issuers of different nationalities as a whole, multiple jurisdictions would be applicable to the same transfer and its proprietary aspects, which implies large-scale costs and a greater legal risk.[51] Further, some securities transactions permit so-called substitution, i.e. the replacement of securities provided as collateral by other securities, and these are possibly located in a different jurisdiction. In such a situation, it would be impossible to determine the law which is applicable to the proprietary aspects of the transaction.[52]

In the case of registered securities, the *lex societatis* is traditionally applied where conflicts of laws occur as to proprietary matters, referring to the law of the issuer's location. The *lex societatis* rule, however, is also neither easy to use, nor unequivocal. First, the *lex societatis* could refer to either the location of the issuer or the location of the issuer's register, which are not necessarily in the same jurisdiction. Furthermore, a great deal of debate exists in legal literature on an issuer's location; it could refer to either the place of incorporation *(lex incorporationis)* or the place where the issuer performs its main activities or has its headquarters *(siège réel)*. In France, Belgium and Germany, for instance, the *siège réel* theory is employed, whereas in the Netherlands the *lex incorporationis* is implemented.[53]

It should be noted that under the rules just discussed, the preliminary question is whether the securities concerned classify as registered, bearer, certificated or uncertificated securities and even this cannot always be determined with certainty.[54]

3.3.3 PRIMA

To meet these difficulties,[55] a new conflict of laws rule had to be formulated. Taking the practical reality of the indirect holding system as a starting point, the 1998 Oxford Colloquium on Collateral and Conflict of Laws developed the

49. *See also* Austen-Peters (2000), 198 *and* Rogers (2005), 18: 'There is no answer to the question whether the Australian's Investor's position is part of one mass or the other. The question is not factually difficult, it is metaphysically absurd'.
50. Rogers (1996), 1459 *and* Benjamin (2000), 162.
51. *See* Potok (2001), 58–59 *and* Austen-Peters (2000), 204.
52. Benjamin (2000), 162.
53. Strikwerda(2002), no. 199.
54. *See* Rogers (1996), 1457 as to the qualification of global certificates.
55. Described by James Rogers, Reporter to the Drafting Committee to Revise UCC Art. 8 (1994) as being of 'horrendous complexity;' Rogers (1996), 1457.

so-called Place of Relevant Intermediary Approach ('PRIMA'), referring to the rule that proprietary issues concerning indirectly held securities are governed by the law of the place of the most relevant intermediary.[56] The relevant intermediary means the intermediary/custodian with which the relevant party to the dispute maintains his securities account and the law of the first intermediary's jurisdiction (from the point of view of the accountholder concerned) in the chain of custody thus applies to the proprietary issue in question.

At present, several variations of PRIMA may be distinguished. First, under Belgium's private international law, proprietary issues of cross-border securities transactions are governed by the law of the location of the assets transferred,[57] a rule which resembles the traditional *rei sitae* rule. The assets, however, are considered to consist of the accountholder's claims against his intermediary, rather than the underlying securities and, as a result, this rule generally refers to the intermediary's location.

The conflict of laws rule of the EU Settlement Finality Directive ('SFD')[58] also seems to be a variation on the *lex sitae,* as it designates the location where the relevant party's securities are registered as the appropriate connecting factor. The EU Financial Collateral Directive ('FCD')[59] on the other hand, designates the place where the relevant securities account is maintained as the appropriate connecting factor.[60] This variation of PRIMA has therefore also been called 'PRACA', standing for the Place of the Relevant Account Approach.[61]

Moving still further away from the *lex rei sitae* is the variation of PRIMA under which the accountholder and custodian are allowed to designate the law applicable to all aspects of their respective rights and duties. Here, no relation whatsoever exists between the location of the assets concerned and the law which is applicable. This rule is applied in the US UCC and the Hague Securities Convention, but under the HSC, party autonomy to designate the applicable law in the account agreement is restricted and must have some connection with the actual place of the intermediary or one of its branches.

It has been argued that PRIMA – in all its variations – is a modification of the traditional *lex rei sitae* rule, since it considers the place of a securities accountholder's entitlement as an appropriate connecting factor.[62] It is submitted,

---

56. The contributions to the said Oxford Colloquium have been published in Butterworths' Journal of International Banking and Financial Law – Special Supplement/September 1998. The term 'Place of the Relevant Intermediary Approach' and its acronym have been introduced by Richard Potok, *see* Benjamin & Yates (2002), 77, n. 1.
57. *Koninklijk Besluit* (Royal Decree) no. 62 of 1967; *see* Potok (2004), 210.
58. Directive 98/26/EC of the European Parliament and of the Council of 19 May 1998 on settlement finality in payment and securities settlement systems (OJ L 166/45), *see* Ch. 9.3.3.
59. Directive 2002/47/EC of the European Parliament and of the Council of 6 June 2002 on financial collateral arrangements (OJ L 168/43). *See* Ch. 9.3.3.
60. On the discrepancy between the rules of the SFD and the FCD, *see* Haentjens (2006), 37. *But see* Potok (2004), 212.
61. De Vauplane & Daigre (2003), 34.
62. The EU Collateral Directive Recital, no. 8 expressly states so. *See also* Benjamin (2000), 151 *et seq.*

however, that to consider the intermediary's location as a 'place' in the sense of the traditional *situs* rule would be confusing or at least highly artificial. It would suggest the possibility of locating the physical location of the object of the dispute, whilst it is controversial if intangibles have a *situs* at all. Moreover, not all jurisdictions classify the place of the relevant intermediary as the place where the accountholder's entitlement is situated. Thirdly, if PRIMA is understood to allow party autonomy to designate the governing law,[63] as is the case in the HSC and the UCC, even less connection with the traditional *lex situs* rule exists.[64]

In conclusion, PRIMA is being accepted worldwide, both on the national level[65] and on the regional level. On a global level, the Hague Securities Convention has also adopted the PRIMA rule. However, telling differences may be discerned regarding the precise form of PRIMA adopted, even among different EU directives. These differences, together with more traditional conflict of laws rules and relevant substantive securities law, will be investigated further in the next chapters.

3.4 CONCLUSION

In the previous sections, it has been shown that during the last centuries, the law has constantly been adapted to changes in practice of securities custody, in some instances after crises had painfully demonstrated the inadequacy of the contemporary framework. It has also been shown that although the practice of securities custody has dramatically changed in the second half of the 20th century, neither substantive, nor private international law has kept pace with that development, while the modernisation of conflict of laws rules seems a little more advanced.

The main underlying problem seems to be that most European jurisdictions still base their securities custody and transfer laws on traditional property law concepts, and remain to characterise securities as tangible movables. While the change in the conception of securities as tangibles in lieu of intangibles had revolutionised legal thinking in the 19th century, it may be time to introduce a new concept of assets, or to return to the concept of intangibles, thus following the developments that have taken place in the custody of monetary assets.[66]

---

63. It is debatable, however, if such a rule could still be classified as a PRIMA rule; Rank (2005), 250.
64. *Cf.* Tenenbaum (2004), 842.
65. For an overview of the implementation of the PRIMA rule, *see* Bernasconi (2000), 50 *et seq.*
66. *Cf.* Drobnig (1988), 41. *See also* Mouy & De Vauplane (1995), 58: *'Depuis la dématérialisation, les auteurs sont partagés sur la nature juridique des droits du titulaire d'untitre au porteur. Un courant majoritaire considère qu'il s'agit toujours d'un droit de propriété, qui de corporel est alors devenu incorporel. D'autres auteurs pensent au contraire que le titulaire du titre ne dispose, à l'encontre de son teneur de compte, que d'un droit de créance. Dans cette dernière analyse, la relation titulaire du titre/teneur de compte présente des similitudes manifestes avec celle ayant pour objet un compte espèces, puisqu'il est admis que le titulaire du compte espèces ne détient qu'une créance en restitution des sommes y figurant, sans toutefois que ce rapprochement apparaisse convainquant en raison des différences de natures entre les titres et les espèces'.*

Accordingly, various authors have noted the similarities between the current practice of securities custody and modern monetary accounts.[67] But others have stressed the differences, most notably that money accounts generally express purely contractual interests, so that entitlement holders are merely unsecured claimants in their account provider's insolvency, whereas securities account holders are generally protected from the claims of the insolvent intermediary's general creditors.[68] Secondly, a credit institution is typically not under an obligation to keep all monetary funds to which its clients are entitled readily available to be retrieved by these clients, whereas securities account holders usually have the right to retrieve the assets corresponding with their security entitlements at any time.[69] Thirdly, the exercise of voting rights traditionally attached to the ownership of securities warrant a different approach to the custody of securities than to monetary funds.[70]

However, notwithstanding the extent to which the modern practice of securities custody resembles money accounts, it is clear that 'traditional legal garments fit poorly on the frame of current practice'.[71] Yet it will have to be seen in the following chapters whether modernisation in the context of harmonisation would be feasible from a doctrinal perspective.[72] In other words, it will have to be seen whether a transition in the conception of securities from tangibles to intangibles or something else would be as difficult for us as it would have been for the ancient Greeks, who strictly divided their (legal) world into 'visible' and 'invisible' property *(phanera ousia* and *aphanēs ousia).*[73]

---

67. E.g., Mooney (1990), 403–405 *and* Sommer (1998), 1182 and 1201. *Cf. also* Reitz (2005), 367, n.21.
68. *See,* e.g., De Vauplane & Bornet (2001), no. 52.
69. *See* Rocks & Bjerre (2004) 37. *Cf.* Schrans & Steennot (2003), 110 *and* UCC § 8-504 official cmt. 3
70. Guynn (1996), 29.
71. Mooney (1990), 307.
72. *But cf.* Mooney (1990), 413: 'A new model, divorced from common law and U.C.C. property law constructs, also could form a more plausible base for unification of law on the international level. An approach not rooted in longstanding domestic doctrine might provide a more likely basis for harmonizing widely varying doctrine in other nations'.
73. *See,* e.g., Cohen (2005), 290. But the current distinction in civil law jurisdictions has its roots in Roman law; e.g. Van Erp (2004), 536.

Chapter 4

Practice and Risks of the Post-Trade Process

4.1 TRADE, CONFIRMATION, CLEARING, SETTLEMENT

The preceding chapter aimed to provide some insight into today's practice of securities custody, its historic background and legal framework. That overview showed that apart from the safekeeping of investors' assets, the framework of securities custody mainly serves the facilitation of transfers of securities. A closer investigation of current practices of securities transfers reveals that securities transfers are effectuated in an overwhelming variety of fact patterns, but the main distinction is between transfers following from trades concluded on an institutionalised market or exchange, and from other, i.e. over the counter ('OTC') transactions.

Whereas the modern, institutionalised market practice requires four steps to be taken in order to come to a complete or perfected transfer of (rights in) securities, viz. trade, confirmation, clearing and settlement, trade and settlement usually suffice in the instance of OTC transactions.

'Trade' refers to the expressed intention of parties to deliver securities against the payment of funds,[1] and while different exchanges have different rules for the matching of buyers and sellers and the establishment of the conditions for delivery and payment, in OTC situations, the trade stage is often completely left to party autonomy. 'Confirmation' is simply the report of the trade to the parties and, again, different exchanges have different rules for the effectuation and legal significance

---

1. Some deliveries, however, are 'free', i.e. made without corresponding payment; BENJAMIN (2003), 127.

of that confirmation.[2] Clearing is used in a narrow sense as 'the calculation of the mutual post-trade obligations of market participants'[3] or, in a wider sense, as the management of the credit exposures between trade and settlement. The actual transfer of securities against payment is usually classified as settlement, although settlement is sometimes used in a wider sense to mean the post-trade process as a whole.[4] Throughout the present dissertation, 'clearing' and 'settlement' will both be used in their precise, narrower sense.

As noted, the four steps just listed may be taken in various ways, but they may also occur at various times in relation to each other. First, the moment of agreement between parties may be separated from the moment of settlement in various ways. In so-called fixed-settlement systems, settlement takes place after a fixed period of time has elapsed since the conclusion of the contract, while in other systems the moment of settlement is agreed upon. The moment of payment may also be separated from the moment of securities transfer in various ways. However, since the risk of non-performance increases as time elapses, it is preferable to make the moment of transfer and the moment of payment coincide.[5] True coincidence is called Delivery versus Payment ('DVP') or real-time settlement, which means in practice that securities are transferred only upon payment being received.[6]

In the following sections, some general remarks will be successively made on the most common fact patterns of clearing and settlement in both national and international situations. Thereafter, more generally, the risks that have been discerned in the context of securities settlement will be discussed, where it will be argued that harmonisation would be the solution to the legal risk that is currently experienced.

4.2 CLEARING

As noted above, in most situations where securities transactions are concluded on an institutionalised market, the transactions of market participants are cleared, i.e. calculated together. That calculation is made in various ways.[7] In so-called 'gross settlement', or 'trade-for-trade settlement' systems, payment for and the delivery of every single transaction is calculated individually and no netting or set-off takes

2. Confirmation, however, may become complicated when parties to a trade act on behalf of others who are located in different jurisdictions, which is not uncommon; CPSS/IOSCO Recommendations 2001, 37.
3. Benjamin (2003), 128 *and* BIS-Glossary.
4. *See* Giovannini Group 2001 Report 2001, 6 *and* Rank (1999), 76.
5. *See infra,* s. 4.4.2.
6. Furthermore, real-time systems may be distinguished from quasi-DVP systems, in which the moments of delivery and payment are separated, but settlement is guaranteed by a third party, often a central counter party or clearinghouse.
7. *See* Dalhuisen & Van Setten (2003), 130 n.245 *and* Rank (1999), 76.

place.[8] In other systems, the obligations to deliver securities are expressed per transaction (on a gross basis), whilst obligations as to the money side of transactions are offset at an agreed point in time (netted).

However, whereas trade-for-trade settlement systems might provide a high level of transparency, they are increasingly costly and technically difficult to realise, as the volume of securities transactions has grown dramatically over the last decades. Moreover, netting or set-off of securities and payment transfers reduces the risks associated with individual transfers[9] and thus result in a cost reduction. In most systems, both delivery and payment obligations are therefore netted, which is performed by either a CSD, ICSD, or a separate entity that specialises in clearing and netting (clearinghouse).[10]

To complicate matters further, centralised netting is generally organised in either a clearinghouse or central counterparty system.[11] In a clearinghouse system, the clearing house calculates the net positions of all its participants' obligations or all their transfer orders.[12] At the end of the trading cycle, the clearing house submits the netted orders to the settlement agent (typically a CSD or ICSD and a central bank), to which it is usually duly authorised, and the settlement agent credits and debits the participants' accounts accordingly. Although the functions of the clearing house and settlement agent can be combined in one institution, the participants hold securities and/or cash accounts only with the settlement agent and the clearing house does not become a (central) counterparty to its participants.

In a central counterparty system on the other hand, the central counterparty ('CCP') is interposed between all participants' transactions and in that capacity takes over their obligations by novation.[13] Thus, for all transactions, a seller has to deliver securities to the CCP instead of to the buyer, whilst the buyer has to make his payments to the CCP instead of to the seller. The CCP consequently also takes over all the risks attached to non-performance by a defaulting party,[14] and the use

---

8. *Cf.* BIS Glossary 2003.
9. *See infra,* s. 4.4.
10. *Cf.* BIS Glossary 2003 on netting: 'an agreed offsetting of mutual obligations by trading partners or participants. The netting reduces a large number of individual positions or obligations to a smaller number of obligations or positions'. If positions are netted, individual transactions can hardly be reversed, since a single reversal would require the unwinding of the entire set-off process, with serious and systemic consequences for other participants. The legal framework would therefore have to ensure the finality, i.e. non-reversibility, of securities transactions in settlement systems based on netting. For the EU, the Settlement Finality Directive aims at the elimination of that risk; *see* VEREECKEN & NIJENHUIS (2003), *and infra,* Ch. 9.3.3 and 10.2.8.
11. VAN SETTEN *in* VEREECKEN & NIJENHUIS ET AL. (2003), 264-272.
12. *Cf.* Art. 2(e) SFD *and see* VAN SETTEN *in* VEREECKEN & NIJENHUIS ET AL. (2003), 267.
13. *Cf.* Art. 2(c) SFD. But a CCP can also merely guarantee its participants' obligations; SCOTT (2006), Ch. 10,11.
14. *See* BENJAMIN (2003), 173–174, for a discussion of a CCP's possible reactions in the case of a party's default.

of a CCP therefore results in a considerable reduction of settlement risk.[15] Then, i.e. after a trading day, the CCP usually nets all the obligations, thereby reducing 'all outstanding residuals to a single debit/credit between itself and each member (rather than a multiplicity of bilateral exposures between members)'.[16] But the netting may also take place *ex ante,* i.e. prior to the novation.

Although similar, the netting by a CCP and a clearing house must be distinguished, as in a CCP system, the net balance has to be paid/delivered to or by the CCP, whereas in a clearinghouse system, the net balance is paid/delivered between the participants themselves through accounts with the settlement agent. For that purpose, the CCP's participants maintain so-called clearing member accounts with the CCP, and consequently hold both a clearing member account with the CCP and a securities and cash account with the settlement agent.

4.3 SETTLEMENT

4.3.1 Typical Sales and Security Arrangements

Notwithstanding the reality that most securities transactions are concluded at an institutionalised market and are consequently cleared and settled via a CCP, and mindful of the fact that parties to a sale are normally unaware of each other's identity and merely order their intermediaries to buy or sell securities of a certain type,[17] a typical example of a purely domestic settlement (securities side) would be as follows.

Assume seller (A) and buyer (B) are clients of the same intermediary, a participant of the national CSD. Upon A's transfer order, this intermediary debits A's account and credits B's account. The intermediary's account with the CSD remains unchanged, as the transfer can be perfected solely on the books of the intermediary. But if seller (A) and buyer (C) are not clients of the same financial intermediary, seller A orders his intermediary (X), a participant of the CSD, to debit his securities account. Intermediary X then debits A's account and the CSD consequently debits X's account. The CSD then credits Y's account, Y being investor C's intermediary. Finally, Y credits C's account, by which the transfer is completed.[18] In practice, however, Y often credits C's securities account before Y's account with the CSD is correspondingly credited.[19]

15. Especially in the reduction of replacement cost risk and principal risk; *see infra,* s. 4.4.2. The present author is grateful to Professor W.A.K. Rank for pointing out that novation is preferred over assignment or assumption precisely for this reason, i.e. because the CCP thus assumes risk without assuming the defenses that the defaulting party might have.
16. Van Setten *in* Vereecken & Nijenhuis et al. (2003), 269. *See also* Giovannini Group Report, 5 *and* Benjamin (2003), 128.
17. Rogers (2005), 53 *et seq.*
18. *See* Giovannini Group 2001 Report, 11 for a schematic overview of settlement in a domestic context.
19. *See also* Ch. 10.2.5.

Again, it has to be borne in mind that these are highly simplified fact patterns, and provide typical examples of securities transfers only. Other than for sales, securities are increasingly used as collateral to secure loans,[20] and the settlement of these loan agreements does not always involve the transfer of collateralised securities. Collateral may be provided by means of a transfer of title, e.g. as part of a repurchase agreement, but also by the creation of a security interest, e.g. a pledge.

Repurchase agreements have become a common method to secure loans, especially between large financial institutions. Under such an agreement, the borrower typically sells a certain volume of securities that corresponds to the amount of the loan, and at the same time agrees to repurchase the same volume of equivalent securities at a later point in time for the price of the loan plus interest. In a similar agreement, but one that is prompted by a need for securities rather than for money, a certain volume of securities is borrowed under the condition that the same volume will be returned at a later point in time plus interest to the initial lender (securities lending).[21] In both types of transactions, the collateralised securities are transferred as described above.

In general, security interests can be created either with or without the transfer of the collateralised securities to the collateral taker or a third party, but, especially in jurisdictions with a civil law tradition, some form of dispossession is required to render the security interest effective against third parties. In the case of a possessory pledge, the same procedure is followed as described above with regard to an outright transfer between investors A and B or A and C, the sole difference being that the transferred securities are operationally marked as pledged securities in B's or C's account. But it would also be commonly characterised as a possessory pledge when the collateralised securities remain registered in the collateral giver's name, but are (operationally) marked or flagged as pledged securities.[22]

Other ways to create a security interest include the following:[23]

- The collateral provider, his intermediary and the collateral taker enter into a (tripartite) control agreement. In this situation, the securities are not transferred to another account.
- The collateral taker is the same entity as the collateral provider's intermediary, and the collateralised securities are recorded in a special pledged account in either the collateral provider's or the collateral taker's name.

---

20. *See*, e.g., POTOK (2001), 55 *and* GOODE (2002), 3.
21. *See*, e.g., KEIJSER (2006), 11–13. For repurchase agreements, the International Securities Markets Association and the Bond Market Association (currently: the International Capital Market Association and the Securities Industry and Financial Markets Association, respectively) have drafted a standard Global Master Repurchase Agreement, while securities lenders may use the Global Master Securities Lending Agreement drafted by the International Securities Lenders Association.
22. *See* Ch. 10.2.9.
23. OOI (2003), 230 *et seq.*

- The collateral taker is the same entity as the collateral provider's intermediary, and the intermediary and the collateral provider enter into a control agreement. The securities are not transferred to another account.
- The collateral taker is the same entity as the collateral provider's intermediary, and the collateral provider and his intermediary enter into a repurchase agreement. The collateralised securities are transferred from the collateral provider's to the intermediary's account.

4.3.2 Cross-Border Dimensions

As noted in the previous chapters, securities are transferred less and less within a purely domestic context and securities markets are international to an ever greater extent, i.e. parties to the same transaction are increasingly likely to be members of different markets, while the securities, the object of their transaction, may be located in yet another jurisdiction. In this cross-border context, the distinctive feature of settlement is 'that it involves gaining access to a settlement system in another country and/or the interaction of different settlement systems'.[24]

Currently, foreign settlement systems can be accessed in multiple ways, including:[25]

- Direct access, as a participant of the foreign CSD where the securities have been issued and deposited. Because membership of a foreign CSD usually involves stringent (capital) requirements, this option is not widely used.[26]
- Access to the foreign CSD via a local agent, usually a participant of that CSD. This is the most commonly used option.[27]
- Access to an ICSD, either directly as a participant, or indirectly via a local agent. ICSDs have established direct links with multiple CSDs and through their agents. This option used to be particularly popular for the trade in fixed-income instruments, but it has expanded to all kinds of securities trades. Consequently, its participants can often settle their transactions solely on the books of the ICSD.[28]
- Access to a global custodian. These custodians have direct access to national CSDs through a network of sub-custodians, which may be either subsidiaries of the global custodian or local agents.

24. Giovannini Group 2001 Report, 7.
25. Giovannini Group 2001 Report, 8. *See id.,* at 8 for a schematic overview of the possible links in cross-border settlement and *id.,* at 13 for a schematic overview of cross-border clearing and settlement of equities, bonds and derivatives. *See also* CPSS/IOSCO Recommendations 2001, 42–43.
26. Giovannini Group 2001 Report, 8, with reference to surveys conducted by the BIS.
27. *Ibid.*
28. CPSS/IOSCO Recommendations 2001, 42.

- Access to the foreign CSD via the domestic CSD. An increasing number of links between national CSDs have been established, but these links often do not offer payment facilities.

These multiple permutations and the myriad of links among custodians result in a far from transparent network. Moreover, even within the EU, different states have different policies with regard to the accessibility of links to nonresident traders and settlement institutions. In addition to the harmonisation and modernisation of the legal framework for securities custody and transfer, the European Commission has therefore expressed its intention to liberalise and integrate existing securities clearing and settlement systems.[29] The European Parliament, however, recently adopted a motion in which it stated that it saw no need for a framework directive on the regulation of clearing and settlement providers.[30]

On the global level, legal literature has developed several solutions to the present fragmentation, including the 'worldclear model', the 'global hub model', and the 'spokes model'.[31] In the worldclear model, a global CSD would assume all the functions of current CSDs and act as a true global custodian for all securities, which would be extremely efficient, but might not be warranted for reasons of competition and systemic risk. In the global hub model, an ICSD would function as a hub for all CSDs, so that bilateral links between CSDs would not be needed. In the spokes model on the other hand, the bilateral links between CSDs would be intensified so as to improve the present situation in which not all links are reciprocal and far from all CSDs maintain sufficient links with other CSDs.[32] The general consensus, however, seems to be that the integration of clearing and settlement systems should be left to the market, but although the market has seen substantial integration over the last decade,[33] none of the solutions has yet materialised.

4.4 DISCERNED RISKS

4.4.1 Systemic Risk

Before 1968, the risks imminent in financial markets and particularly those connected with securities transfers received very little attention from practitioners and academia alike, but the materialisation of those risks during the paperwork crisis

29. Communication from the Commission to the Council and the European Parliament, Clearing and Settlement in the European Union – The way forward, COM(2004) 312 final, at 8.
30. Motion of the European Parliament of 6 June 2005, A6-0180/2005 final, 14.
31. *See*, e.g., Benjamin (2003), 224 *and* Scott (2006), Ch. 10, essentially based on the Morgan Guaranty Trust Company Report *Cross-border Clearance, Settlement and Custody: Beyond the G30 Recommendations* (1993).
32. *Cf.* CPSS/IOSCO Recommendations 2001, 43.
33. Testify, for instance, the (intended) transatlantic merger of the stock exchanges Euronext and NYSE. *See* Ch. 9.3.2 on the integration that has taken place in the European clearing and settlement industry.

of 1968 and the late 1980s have made the subject more popular ever since.[34] More particularly, several risks have been distinguished since then which may jeopardise the stability of the financial market.

The main distinction is made between specific and systemic risks.[35] Systemic risk refers to the danger that the failure of one market participant may undermine the stability of the market as a whole, as the interdependent relationships of current financial markets may involve that one party's failure initiates a spill-over effect or a chain reaction that affects other market participants.[36] Systemic risk is enhanced by the consolidation of financial markets,[37] for fewer participants now represent larger parts of the market(s), and is further increased by the integration of global financial markets, for almost all financial market participants now form part of a larger interdependent network.[38]

Thus, because of their central role, CSDs and ICSDs are more susceptible to generate systemic risk than other market participants. More generally, payment systems and the financial markets as a whole depend to a large extent on the functioning of securities settlement systems, and confidence in the safety and reliability of those systems is therefore of critical importance.[39] But an outdated legal infrastructure, in combination with dramatic changes in market practice, may undermine that confidence and exacerbate the possibilities of systemic risk materialising.[40]

4.4.2 Specific Risks

Apart from systemic risk, all market participants have to manage specific risks connected with the functioning of the securities settlement system,[41] which include settlement risk and pipeline liquidity risk, referring to the risk of a loss of capital due to 'holes' in the chain of settlement.[42] Here, most attention will be devoted

34. Especially since 1987, when a major US firm in the securities industry became bankrupt and trading on the NYSE could consequently not be resumed until the United States Government intervened; *see*, e.g., De Marez Oyens & Fraenkel (1990), 166 *and* Reitz (2005), 360.
35. Goode (1996), 167.
36. *Cf.* BIS Glossary 2003.
37. Benjamin (2003), 130.
38. Explanatory Report on the Hague Securities Convention (2005), 4.
39. CPSS/IOSCO Recommendations 2001,41.
40. *See* Rogers (1996), 1436-7, referring to a speech by Alan Greenspan, then Chairman of the Federal Reserve Board: 'the greatest threat to the liquidity of our financial markets is the potential for disturbance to the clearance and settlement process for financial transactions'. *Cf.* Mooney (1990), 315 arguing that a modernisation of securities custody and transfer law reduces systemic risk. *See also* Sommer (1998), 1194–1197.
41. *See* EFMLG 2003 Report, 11.
42. Goode (1996), 167. In some publications, settlement risk is used in a narrower sense to refer to what is here called principal risk; *see* CPSS/IOSCO Recommendations 2001, 36 *and* Moloney (2002), 711.

to settlement risk, which comprises other categories of risks such as custody risk, credit risk, liquidity risk, and legal risk.[43]

While operational risk is generally understood so as to arise from 'deficiencies in systems and controls, human error or management failure',[44] custody risk specifically refers to the risk of loss of securities held by intermediaries because of theft, fraud in general or other causes. As more intermediaries are interposed, which is almost inevitably the case in cross-border settlements, this risk becomes both greater and more difficult to assess.[45] Yet it can be countered by an adequate legal framework and the strict enforcement of regulatory supervision, which might include a requirement that intermediaries separate their own assets from the assets they hold for their clients.[46] Further, links between national CSDs could also contribute to the reduction of custody risk, as that would reduce the need to interpose yet more intermediaries to settle cross-border.

When custody risk materialises, it can result in the materialisation of credit risk, which is further distinguished as pre-settlement or replacement cost risk and principal risk.[47] Replacement cost risk refers to the risk that a party does not perform after the trade has been made, but before any settlement has been realised, i.e. before the securities are delivered and the corresponding money has been transferred. The loss or unrealised gain, if any, is therefore measured by the difference between the market price of the securities at the moment of non-settlement and the contract price agreed upon with the defaulting party.[48] The risk is reduced by risk management by the central counterparty ('CCP') and binding netting regimes that ensure the settlement of trades, and by shorter settlement cycles, i.e. by shorter intervals between trade and settlement.

In most securities markets worldwide, the current interval between trade and settlement is three days, or T+3. Developments are underway, however, to shorten that interval to T+2, T+1, or even T+0.[49] But because all intermediaries that are interposed between seller and buyer must usually re-enter the data necessary for settlement, shorter settlement cycles are difficult to realise. Unfortunately, a recent initiative to achieve Straight Through Processing ('STP') by automation of the

43. *See also* Moloney (2002), 711–712, Kern (2002), 441 *and* Dalhuisen & Van Setten (2003), 127–128.
44. CPSS/IOSCO Recommendations 2001, 40. As an example of operational risk materialising, the mistake by the Japanese brokerage firm Mizuho may be referred to. Mizuho intended to sell 1 share of J-Com for 610,000 Japanese yen (JPY); 5,065 US dollars; but instead offered 610,000 shares for JPY 1 a piece. The value of these shares together was then USD 3.1 billion. Because of very strict finality rules of the Japanese clearing and settlement system as well as exchange rules, the order could not be reversed, as a consequence of which the loss could amount to more than JPY 30 billion (USD 250 million); CNN press report of 9 December 2005. *See also* Ch. 10.2.8.
45. CPSS/IOSCO Recommendations 2001, 43.
46. *See* Ch. 10.2.5.
47. CPSS/IOSCO Recommendations 2001, 39.
48. Guynn (1996), 50 n.8.
49. *See* Benjamin (2003), 172. Clearnet, the European clearing house for the Euronext exchanges (*see* Ch. 9.3.2), already provides for T+2 settlement, while the New York based CSD DTCC discusses its objective to achieve a T+1 settlement cycle in the DTCC 2001 White Paper.

post-trade processing that would thus avoid the re-entry of data, seems not to have been successful.[50]

As another form of credit risk, principal risk materialises when a counterparty does not perform after its own obligation has been perfected, so that a buyer risks the loss of the money he transferred and a seller the securities he delivered, which thus represents the entire value of the transaction.[51] Principal risk therefore substantially contributes to systemic risk, but can be mitigated by mechanisms of delivery versus payment ('DVP') and the use of a central counterparty.[52]

In the instance that credit risk materialises, materialisation of liquidity risk may be the result. Liquidity risk involves the possibility that because of non-performance by a counterparty, a seller or buyer is in sudden need of cash or securities, respectively, in order to meet his own obligations. The liquidity of the market determines the efficiency by which that need may be satisfied, but (risk) management by the CCP,[53] infrastructure consolidation and securities lending facilities may contribute to the reduction of liquidity risk.[54] Moreover, strong DVP mechanisms help to prevent the realisation of liquidity risk and its systemic consequences.[55]

4.4.3 Legal Risk

Legal risk refers to the possibility that the applicable law results in a loss of capital because it does not support the rules of the securities settlement system, the performance of related arrangements, or the property rights and other interests held through a settlement system.[56] In other words, its correct application might lead to consequences that are unforeseen by the parties to a particular transaction and contrary to their initial intentions.[57] Assuming that the applicable law is clear and known, legal risk might arise because of the internal unsoundness of that law, as it might not provide a solution to the problem at hand, contain contradicting rules, or, more generally, might not fit (market) reality or be impedingly burdensome

50. Benjamin (2003), 173.
51. In cross-currency settlement contexts, this risk is commonly referred to as *Herstatt risk; see* CPSS/IOSCO Recommendations 2001, 39 *and* Benjamin (2003), 129.
52. *See* Rank et al. (1997), 51, CPSS/IOSCO Recommendations 2001, 39, Dalhuisen & Van Setten (2003), *and* Scott (2006), Ch. 10,11.
53. Scott (2006), Ch. 10,12.
54. *See* Benjamin (2003), 129.
55. CPSS/IOSCO Recommendations 2001, 40.
56. CPSS/IOSCO Recommendations 2001, 40. Legal risk has also been considered a sub-category of operational risk, which then more generally involves 'the risk of direct or indirect loss resulting from inadequate or failed internal processes, people or systems or from external events'. *See* Consultative Document of the New Basel Capital Accord, 94 as quoted by Benjamin (2003), 129.
57. *Cf.* H. Wagner (2005), 31.

or complicated. Finally, that law might be subject to frequent and unforeseeable changes (legal instability).[58]

Legal risk is particularly exacerbated in a cross-border context where it might be unclear both what the applicable law is and where the proceedings will be brought, and different conflict of laws rules may thus refer to different applicable systems of law (legal uncertainty). Moreover, foreign law and especially complex foreign securities laws are little known and may thus withhold intended legal effects, or decree legal effects other than originally intended by the parties. For instance, the applicable law might impose perfection requirements which have not been met by the parties to a securities transaction because the applicable law was unknown to them. As a second example, a conflict of laws rule might state that the substantive law of the *forum* determines whether a transfer classifies as a transfer of title or as a pledge. Thus, a judge might classify a particular securities transaction as a pledge, although the parties intended it to be a transfer of title due to their unfamiliarity with that particular applicable law (recharacterisation risk).

More generally, legal risk is most likely to materialise in the case of a custodian's insolvency, when the interests of both securities accountholders, and the custodian's creditors are truly tested.[59] One of the most typical risks with regard to book-entry securities therefore results from the fact that in an intermediary's insolvency, priority conflicts between creditors and accountholders might arise, which are ultimately determined in a way that is contrary to the parties' expectations (intermediary risk).[60] That risk becomes particularly acute when the intermediary concerned has either intentionally or unintentionally acted as being fully authorised to dispose of his clients' assets.

Legal risk in the field of capital markets materialises dramatically in times of stress, and intensifies the other risks just discussed, thus substantially contributing to systemic risk[61]. Specifically, legal risk may deter parties from entering into uncertain and costly international transactions, and thus lead to a dramatic devaluation of securities and the unavailability of credit. As noted above, legal risk in the field of securities custody and transfer law has particularly increased during the last decades because of the fundamental change in market practices from physical certificates to an intermediated holding system with immobilised or dematerialised securities, without the legal framework keeping pace. An enormous increase in volume of securities transactions that are settled cross-border and the growing

58. H. Wagner (2005), 30–31. *Cf.* Explanatory Notes to the Preliminary Draft UNIDROIT Securities Convention, 44.
59. As a consequence, these situations appear to present the most relevant issues for market participants; *cf.* Benjamin & Yates (2002), 62.
60. *Cf.* Schwarcz (2001), *and see* Ch. 10.2.5 and 11.2.5.
61. CPSS/IOSCO Recommendations 2001, 41. *Cf.* the CPSS 1995 Report, 55, arguing that the difficulty to obtain full understanding of the rules and law governing the settlement process directly contributes to systemic risk.

reliance on collateral[62] adds to the higher urgency of addressing legal risk in the field of capital markets.[63]

As an obvious solution, legal risk would be reduced by the unification of conflict of laws rules, so that they unanimously determine the applicable law, and by the modernisation and harmonisation of substantive securities laws, so that they can be readily known, are easily accessible and support current market practices and structures. Neither, however, has yet been accomplished.

4.5 CONCLUSION

Operational aspects of the current practice of securities transfers have been the main subject of the preceding sections. It has been shown how, in an overwhelming variety of possibilities, securities may be transferred OTC or via institutionalised markets. Some characteristics of the pre-settlement stage or clearing have been discussed, as well as typical fact patterns in the actual transfer of book-entry securities and the creation of security interests in such securities (settlement). As a consequence of the current multiple access model, however, settlement appeared to be extremely complicated in a cross-border context, although key market participants continue to consolidate and integrate.

From the discussion of the risks inherent to financial markets and, more specifically, to securities settlement systems, it follows that most of the risks can be mitigated by operational measures, which have indeed been implemented in many systems. These measures have also been recommended in reports and recommendations drafted mainly by international organisations, which will be discussed at greater length in a later chapter.[64] However, although it has been shown how legal risk substantially contributes to systemic risk and thus represents a threat to the financial markets as a whole, it is hypothesised that that risk has still not been properly addressed. It will therefore be one of the main objectives of the following chapters to ascertain more precisely to what extent the existing legal frameworks are internally sound, i.e. to what extent they support current market practice and do not result in unintended and unforeseen consequences.

---

62. *See* Potok (2001), 55 *and* Löber (2006), 7.
63. *Cf.* Explanatory Notes to the Preliminary Draft Unidroit Securities Convention, 36 and 44–46.
64. Ch. 9.2.2.

Part Two

Securities Laws of Selected Jurisdictions

LE PLAIDEUR
Par quelle étrange barbarie se peut-il que des compatriotes ne vivent pas sous la même loi?
L'AVOCAT
Il en est ainsi de poste en poste dans le royaume: vous changez de jurisprudence en changeant de chevaux.

THE LITIGANT
What strange kind of barbarism is it that citizens must live under different laws?
THE LAYWER
Thus, when you travel in this kingdom you change legal systems as often as you change horses.

VOLTAIRE[1]

1. VOLTAIRE, *Dialogue Entre un Plaideur et un Avocat,* in ŒUVRES (1751), reprinted in DIALOGUES ET ANECDOTES PHILOSOPHIQUES, 10–11 (R. Naves ed., Éditions Garnier 1955).

Chapter 5
Belgium

5.1 INTRODUCTION

5.1.1 Trading, Clearing and Settlement

Under the rule of Napoleon, the *Bourse de Fonds Publics de Bruxelles* was founded as Belgium's first stock exchange (2 July 1801).[1] Since April 1999, this exchange has comprised not only a stock-market, but also a derivatives market called Belfox. On 22 September 2000, the Dutch, Belgian and French markets merged to form Euronext Amsterdam, Euronext Brussels and Euronext Paris with Euronext NV as the Amsterdam-based holding company. Since 2002, Euronext NV also hosts the stock exchange of Lisbon and the London-based derivatives market LIFFE, which became Euronext Lisbon and Euronext LIFFE respectively. Trading takes place on one single trading platform.[2]

LCH.Clearnet SA ('Clearnet')[3] performs the roles of the central counterparty ('CCP') and the clearing house for all these exchanges.[4] In its capacity as CCP, it replaces all transactions concluded between market participants by transactions with Clearnet itself. That legal process, called novation, as well as

---

1. *See* <www.euronext.com>.
2. As a recent development, Euronext and the New York Stock Exchange announced on 2 June 2006 a merger of the two companies, thus forming the world's largest and first transatlantic exchange. At the time of writing however, the merger had not yet taken full effect; *see* <www.euronext.com> *and infra,* Ch. 9.3.2.
3. In February 2001, the French *Banque Centrale de Compensation* (Central Clearinghouse Bank) Clearnet SA merged with the CCP of the Amsterdam and Brussels markets. On 22 December 2003, London Clearing House merged with Clearnet and the group now technically consists of LCH.Clearnet SA and LCH.Clearnet Limited. It is owned by the Euronext group for 80 per cent and by the Euroclear group for 20 per cent. *See* <www.euroclear.com> *and infra,* Ch. 9.3.2.
4. *See* Ch. 4.2 for a discussion of these concepts.

all rules regulating participation in the Clearnet clearing system, are governed by French law.[5]

On 1 April 1968, the *Caisse Interprofessionnelle de Dépôts et de Virement de Titres/Interprofessionele effectendeposito- en girokas* ('CIK') was established by statute as the central securities depository. Since 1991, CIK has managed a settlement system for the settlement of equity, and since 15 July 1998, also for the settlement of public and private sector debt.[6]

International securities transfers were then settled through the Euroclear system, managed by the Morgan Guarantee Trust Company, Brussels branch, which later became the independent Euroclear Bank. On 1 January 2006, CIK was integrated into the Euroclear system and it is now called Euroclear Belgium.[7] Besides its links with the other members of the Euroclear Group (viz. Euroclear Bank, Euroclear France, Euroclear Nederland and CRESTCo of the UK and Ireland), Euroclear Belgium maintains links with SEGA of Switzerland and Clearstream Bank Frankfurt.

The Belgian CSDs and their settlement systems are supervised by the *Banque Nationale de Belgique/Nationale Bank van België* (Central Bank of Belgium, 'NBB') and the *Commission Bancaire, Financière et des Assurances/Commissie voor het Bank- en Financiewezen* ('Commission for Banking and Financial Markets, 'CBFA').[8] At the time of writing, statutorily designated CSDs are CIK, NBB and Euroclear Bank,[9] and their participants are regulated by the NBB and CBFA.[10]

5.1.2 *Sedes Materiae*

Belgium's law on book-entry securities demonstrates a strong connection with general private law, but also with corporate law. Unless derogatory rules are provided for by specific statutory instruments, general rules of private law apply, notably those laid down in the *Code Civil/Burgerlijk Wetboek* (Civil Code, 'BW'). General rules of corporate law, as well as rules concerning corporate securities, have been codified in the *Code des Sociétés/Wetboek van Vennootschappen* (Code of Corporate Law, 'W. Venn'.).

---

5. Clearnet Rules Art. 1.2.3.1.
6. Before 15 July 1998, bonds were cleared and settled by the *Banque Nationale de Belgique/ Nationale Bank van België* (Central Bank of Belgium, 'NBB'), which now only effectuates the transfer of funds, i.e. the money leg of settlement. Giovannini Group 2001 Report, 22.
7. Joint Media Release by Euroclear and Euronext of 14 November 2005, available at <www.euronext.com>.
8. Act of 22 February 1998 Art. 8 *and* Act of 2 August 2002, Art. 23(3). *See also* Act of 2 January 1991 Art. 22 *and* Art. 468 W. Venn.
9. KB no. 62 of 10 November 1967 Art. 1(1)(1) *and* KB of 28 August 2002 Art. 2.
10. Act of 28 April 1999. *Cf.* Explanatory Memorandum to the draft Act of 14 December 2005, Doc 51 1974, 21.

The famous *Arrêt Royal/Koninklijk Besluit* (Royal Decree, 'KB') no. 62 of 10 November 1967[11] is the oldest Belgian statutory instrument that specifically regulates book-entry securities law. This KB was mainly intended to facilitate the circulation of (bearer) securities by book-entry into securities accounts. It accommodates the centralised custody of bearer certificates, as a result of which immobilisation was strongly stimulated. As a general principle, however, immobilised securities remain governed by rules of general private law, in particular by rules regarding movable tangibles, so far as KB no. 62 does not explicitly derogate from those rules.[12] Since its enactment, KB no. 62 has been modified on several occasions.[13]

The Acts of 2 January 1991 and 22 July 1991 created the possibility of completely dematerialised issuance for certain specific categories of securities; the former Act introduced detailed provisions for the custody of dematerialised government bonds, and the latter Act laid down that these provisions must apply to certain categories of commercial paper.[14] The Code of Corporate Law further expanded the category of securities eligible for this method of issuing to all corporate bonds. Thus, while KB no. 62 initiated or at least statutorily stimulated the immobilisation of securities custody and created the possibility to transfer by book-entry, the just named legislation on the dematerialisation of securities created a new mode of issuing and holding securities.[15] A recent Act however, has initiated the gradual abolition of all bearer certificates and envisages the complete dematerialisation of all Belgian securities.[16] The KB of 18 August 1999 statutorily underpins the operation and regulation of clearing and settlement institutions. The Acts of 28 April 1999 and 15 December 2004 transposed into Belgian law the EU Settlement Finality Directive and the Collateral Directive respectively.

It is likely that the up to date and apt legislation that has just been mentioned, has contributed to the success of the Brussels-based Euroclear Bank in becoming the world's largest international central securities depository.[17] In the following sections, the current Belgian legal infrastructure for the custody and transfer of securities, as well as its relationship with more general areas of law will therefore be analysed in greater detail. First, the main doctrinal distinctions with regard to financial instruments will be discussed. In the section that follows, legal aspects of securities custody will be analysed, with particular emphasis on securities accounts, the accountholder/intermediary relationship and the consequences of

11. Hereinafter: KB no. 62.
12. Schrans & Steennot (2003), 107.
13. The latest, important modification dated 23 December 2005.
14. Act of 22 July 1991 Art. 7(1).
15. Boddaert (2004), 94.
16. Act of 14 December 2005.
17. In 2005, Euroclear Bank held € 7.1 trillion in securities for its clients; *see* Euroclear Annual Report 2005, 13 available at <www.euroclear.com>.

intermediary insolvencies. In Sections 4 and 5 of this chapter, the transfer of securities by book-entry, and the creation and enforcement of security interests in securities will subsequently be discussed. Section 6 will deal with Belgian private international law concerning securities custody and transfer. The chapter will conclude with answers to the questions posed in Chapter 1.2.2 and a coherence analysis.

5.2 CATEGORIES OF SECURITIES

As for their function, Belgian law distinguishes securities from derivatives, but both categories are considered to be 'financial instruments'.[18] With regard to securities, an important legal distinction under Belgian law is made as for their form: a distinction is made between *effecten op naam* (registered securities) and *effecten aan toonder* (bearer securities).[19] In time, however, this distinction will become obsolete as all *toondereffecten* will be converted into dematerialised securities by 2014.[20] Dematerialised securities are also generally considered to form a separate, third category of securities.[21]

With regard to *toondereffecten,* Belgian law considers the certificates to incorporate investors' rights.[22] The classification of bearer securities as movable tangibles enhanced the circulation of securities enormously by simplifying the requirements for their transfer,[23] as pursuant to Article 1583 in conjunction with Article 1138 BW, simple *traditio* (delivery) suffices for movables to be transferred. The classification also advanced legal certainty for subsequent acquirers; pursuant to Article 2279 BW, in principle, all *bona fide* possessors of movable tangibles are deemed to be the owners of the movables concerned.[24] Ownership of registered securities is proven and enforceable against third parties by their registration in the issuer's register; Article 504 W. Venn. Although a certificate is often issued to the owners of registered securities, neither these certificates

---

18. *See,* e.g. Act of 2 August 2002 Art. 2(1). The listing of financial instruments which this provision provides, however, must not be generalised since it must be read in the context of this Act only; Schrans & Steennot (2003), 84 and 86 *et seq.*
19. *See also* Schrans & Steennot (2003), 105–106. Order securities exist, but are rare; *see* Schrans & Steennot (2003), 105, n.121.
20. Act of 14 December 2005. Explanatory Memorandum to the draft Act of 14 December 2005, Doc 51 1974, 8.
21. *See* Act of 2 January 1991 Art. 1(1)(3) and Art. 460(2) W. Venn. *Cf.* Schrans & Steennot (2003), 289–290. The distinction however, is not uncontroversial; *see* Sunt (1996), 50-451.
22. Van Ryn & Heenen (1981), 103. A subtle distinction has been made here: although it incorporates the investor's rights, a certificate is not considered to *be* the investor's rights against the issuer; Schrans & Steennot (2003), 109 and 111.
23. Van Ryn & Heenen (1981), 81.
24. *Cf.* Tison (1996), 230–231.

nor registration in the issuer's register represent conclusive, i.e. unchallengeable, evidence of title, as title may be proven 'by all legal means'.[25]

The category of dematerialised securities was introduced in 1991.[26] Originally, only government bonds and certain categories of corporate debt instruments, i.e. commercial paper, were eligible for this mode of issue.[27] As part of an important modification of securities law and company law, the Act of 7 April 1995 created the possibility to issue dematerialised shares, profit-sharing certificates, (convertible) bonds and warrants issued by *naamloze vennootschappen* (public companies).[28] The modification was intended to 'modernise the custody of securities, to accelerate securities transactions and to reduce printing costs'.[29]

To these considerations, the Belgian Government added that the use of bearer certificates may facilitate financial crime and the funding of terrorism,[30] and therefore issued a draft Act on 1 August 2005 that would convert all *toondereffecten* into dematerialised securities by 2014. The Act was adopted 14 December 2005. It results, first, in a prohibition on issuing bearer certificates as of 1 August 2008.[31] Second, on that same date, rights to bearer certificates expressed by securities accounts will statutorily be converted into rights that relate to dematerialised securities.[32] Third, holders of bearer certificates must demand their conversion into dematerialised securities or *effecten op naam* before 31 December 2013.[33] Ownership of dematerialised securities is proven and can be asserted against third parties by book-entry in a securities account.[34]

5.3 CUSTODY OF BOOK-ENTRY SECURITIES

5.3.1 INTRODUCTION

In Belgium, as in most countries, securities may be held in custody on an individualised as well as on a fungible basis. Only fungible custody enables transfer by book-entry[35] and is not hindered by the requirement that deposited assets must

25. VAN RYN & HEENEN (1981), 127 and PEETERS & VAN DER VORST (2001), 450.
26. Acts of 2 January 1991 and 22 July 1991.
27. *See* TISON (1996), 258.
28. W. Venn. Book VIII, Title 3. This listing is probably not intended to be exhaustive; SUNT (1996), 453. It is a matter of debate whether *commanditaire vennootschappen op aandelen* (partnerships limited by shares) are also allowed to issue dematerialised securities under W. Venn.; TISON (1996), 233–234 *and* SUNT (1996), 446. As the latter author indicates however, this debate is not of much practical importance since such companies are only limited in number.
29. TISON (1996), 230.
30. Explanatory Memorandum to the draft Act of 14 December 2005, Doc 51 1974, 4–7.
31. Act of 14 December 2005 Art. 3(1).
32. Act of 14 December 2005 Art. 5.
33. Act of 14 December 2005 Art. 7.
34. *See* further *infra*, s. 2.3.2.
35. SCHRANS & STEENNOT (2003), 253 *and cf.* Ch. 3.1.3.

be returned *in specie.*[36] However, as in most countries, the major problem of fungible custody is that depositors lose their right of ownership when their securities become commingled with other securities of the same kind held by their custodian.

There has been some debate in Belgian legal literature on the precise nature of this loss of ownership. It has been argued that upon deposit, a custodian acquires full power of disposal over the assets, whereas the depositors lose all ownership rights. It has also been argued, quite to the contrary, that depositors acquire a right of co-ownership, even without any statutory provision declaring this.

Both these positions, however, do not seem to be generally accepted.[37] The most generally accepted view is that once deposited assets become commingled, depositors are then unable to revendicate their assets[38] since the individualisation of assets is required for all proprietary rights to be enforced regarding those assets.[39] Although depositors thus remain owners, their right of ownership is not enforceable and they are left with a mere contractual claim against their custodian, who will be considered to be the owner in the eyes of third parties.[40]

As a matter of principle, fungible custody requires securities to be fungible. However, neither *toondereffecten* nor *effecten op naam* are *ipso facto* fungible under Belgian law, since Belgian law deems fungible only those assets that cannot be designated except by reference to size, weight or number.[41] Because *toondereffecten* and *effecten op naam* are individualised by number or registration respectively, specific contractual arrangements or statutory provisions are therefore required to establish fungible custody.[42] The Belgian legislator has enacted KB no. 62 to that effect, and the statute mainly allows for *toondereffecten* to be held in custody on a fungible basis, provided that the depositor has consented. Such consent however, may have been implicit.

Unlike *toondereffecten,* dematerialised securities are considered fungible by nature, but it will be seen that the (legal) treatment of dematerialised securities is in many ways identical to the treatment of fungible securities under KB no. 62. The only major difference seems to be that, subject to the terms of issuance that may declare otherwise, immobilised securities are eligible for delivery

36. BODDAERT (2004), 83.
37. PEETERS & VAN DER VORST (2001), 453.
38. Hof van Beroep te Antwerpen 20 August 1990, *T.R.V.* 1990, 540. *See also* SAGAERT (2003), 391 *and* E. HUYGHE in his annotation of Hof van Beroep te Antwerpen, 20 August 1990, *T.R.V.* 1990,544–545.
39. *See,* e.g., SAGAERT (2003), 380–381.
40. PEETERS & VAN DER VORST (2001), 453.
41. *Contra* SAGAERT (2003), 386–387, who argues that *genera* (assets that are 'fungible' by nature, such as oil and the like) and fungibles (assets that are considered equal with a view to a certain legal relationship between parties) should be clearly distinguished. Commingling of the first kind is called *confusio,* as a result of which a new asset is created, whereas the commingling of the latter kind is known as *commixtio,* which does not form a new asset; *id.*, 394.
42. Some authors argue that bearer securities are fungible by nature, but are individualised by certain actions, e.g. the custodian's obligation to return the deposited assets *in specie;* e.g. SAGAERT (2003), 399; BODDAERT (2004), 138–139.

out of the system,[43] whereas the delivery of dematerialised securities is impossible by nature.[44] Moreover, as of 1 January 2008, the retrieval of bearer certificates in physical form out of the custody system will be prohibited by statute.[45] Therefore, the decision of the legislature to regulate the custody of immobilised bearer securities and of dematerialised securities separately has been severely criticised.[46]

5.3.2 Securities Accounts

5.3.2.1 Entries in Securities Accounts

Both securities immobilised under KB no. 62 and dematerialised securities may be held in book-entry custody. In such instance, entitlements to these securities are expressed by credit balances on securities accounts. Belgian law characterises a securities account as a *rekening-courant* (current account). A securities account credit balance represents all securities to which an accountholder is entitled[47] and debits to the account are set off against credits.

However, only certain, i.e. fixed and permissible, claims or entitlements regarding fungible assets are eligible for set-off; Article 1291 BW. A securities account balance may therefore represent only certain entitlements to securities.[48] Claims that are uncertain as to their object, as well as provisional or future claims, cannot be credited to a regular securities account, but are registered in the so-called *différé*. In an account-holder's insolvency, the *différé* is available to his creditors.[49] An account provider that has (remaining) claims against an insolvent accountholder is therefore allowed to set these claims off against all uncertain claims to securities which this accountholder might have. Such a set-off after the commencement of insolvency proceedings clearly derogates from Article 1298 BW.[50]

---

43. *Cf.* KB no. 62 Art. 6(2).
44. *See* Schrans & Steennot (2003), 287. For a concise overview of other, minor differences (e.g. regarding issuers, instruments and investors eligible for either category of securities), *see* Tison (1996), 261.
45. Act of 14 December 2005, Art. 4.
46. E.g. Tison (1996), 260, Sunt (1996), 429 *and* Servaes (2000), 519–520.
47. Technically however, all securities of the same kind form separate pools, as a result of which as many pools exist as there are kinds of securities admitted to the system; e.g. Sunt (1996), 429, n.12.
48. Boddaert (2004), 212.
49. KB no. 62 Art. 11(1) for immobilised securities and the Act of 2 January 1991 Art. 10(2) and Art. 472(2) W. Venn. for dematerialised securities. Interestingly, the cited Arts. of the KB no. 62 and the Act of 2 January 1991 restrict the *différé* to the (provisional) obligations resulting from the relationship between the accountholder and its (immediate) custodian, Contrary to the W. Venn. which has a broader scope; KB no. 62 Art. 11(3) and the Act of 2 January 1991 Art. 10(3).
50. Boddaert (2004), 213. On the other hand, insolvent accountholders are still prohibited from engaging in new securities transactions; Art. 16 *Loi sur les Faillites/Faillissementswet* (Insolvency Code).

Belgian law does not permit a securities account to indicate a negative balance, as a negative balance is considered to imply the unauthorised creation of securities. In a recent case tried by the Antwerp Court of Appeal, a participant of the CIK had erroneously transferred the same securities twice on behalf of one of its customers; first by physical delivery, and later by book-entry. As a result of the second transfer, the participant's account with the CIK showed a negative balance. The CIK consequently penalised the participant for not replenishing the negative balance in due time. The court ruled however, that the imposed fine was unlawful since the CIK was not permitted to allow a negative balance under any circumstances.[51]

The Act of 2 August 2002 abolished KB no. 62 Article 2(2) and modified Articles 469(1) W. Venn. and the Act of 2 January 1991 Article 4(1). These provisions required intermediaries to separate their own assets from the assets they hold for their clients on the books of the CSD. The rationale behind the abolition of this rule was that the segregation could not be controlled or certified by the CSD and that any such rule could not be imposed on or enforced against possible foreign intermediaries maintaining securities accounts with a Belgian CSD.[52] The obligation to separate one's own assets from clients' assets has now become a matter of regulatory law and is directed at Belgian intermediaries only.[53]

5.3.2.2 Ownership of Book-Entry Securities

It is a settled view in Belgian legal doctrine that general private law rules on the possession of assets are not applicable to the 'possession' of a securities account or a credit balance on such an account,[54] as only movable tangibles can be 'possessed' in the sense of, e.g., Article 2279 BW.[55] Moreover, the distinction between the rights of an accountholder against his account provider and the rights that his securities account refers to, i.e. the security itself or the rights against the issuer, is generally acknowledged in Belgian legal literature;[56] the rights against the issuer, i.e. the security itself, are classified as an uncorporeal movable right, whereas

51. *Hof van Beroep te Antwerpen* (Antwerp Court of Appeal) 21 November 2002, *Forum Financier/Droit Bancaire et Financier* 2003, 313. As a consequence, 'short' positions should be covered by securities lendings; *see* the comment on this case by R. Steennot and M. Tison: *Forum Financier/Droit Bancaire et Financier* 2003, 316. It has been suggested on the other hand, that for administrative purposes, a negative balance in individual cases would be allowed; Boddaert (2004), 122.
52. Explanatory Memorandum to the draft Act of 2 August 2002, Doc 50 1842 and 1843, 116–117. *Cf.* Schrans & Steennot (2003), 268 *and* Boddaert (2004), 123.
53. *See* the Act of 2 August 2002 Art. 26(16).
54. Schrans & Steennot (2003), 106–107. For the purpose of the protection of a *bona fide* acquirer however, KB no. 62 Art. 19, Art. 475bis W. Venn. and the Act of 2 January 1991 Art. 13 bis (all introduced by the Act of 14 December 2005), apply Arts. 2279 and 2280 to the accountholder of immobilised and dematerialised securities respectively; *see* Explanatory Memorandum to the draft Act of 14 December 2005, Doc 51 1974, 24 *and infra.*
55. *See,* e.g., VanNeste (1990), 454. *But see* the Act of 14 December 2005, discussed *infra.*
56. E.g. Schrans & Steennot (2003), 109–112. *See also* explicitly the Explanatory Memorandum to the draft Act of 2 August 2002, Doc 50 1842 and 1843, 116.

the certificate or the securities account is considered a material or immaterial *instrumentum* (bearer), respectively, of those rights. Thus, although a credit entry in a securities account provides the accountholder with proof of ownership of the underlying securities and renders the accountholder's entitlement to the underlying securities opposable against third parties, an entry in a securities account is not constitutive for the creation of an investor's right against the issuer, i.e. it is not constitutive for the existence of the security itself.

Moreover, a (credit entry in a) securities account does not represent unchallengeable evidence of the accountholder's title to the underlying securities.[57] Regarding securities accounts that refer to immobilised securities under KB no. 62, (the possession of) the bearer certificate(s) provide conclusive evidence of title. Regarding dematerialised securities, title to these securities is determined in the last resort by the issue itself,[58] although only the securities accounts can provide any proof of ownership and only crediting these accounts can render the investors' rights opposable against third parties. Furthermore, dematerialised securities can be transferred through book-entries only[59] and securities accounts are thus a necessary element for all transfers of dematerialised securities to be effected. In other words: although it may be possible for an investor to have certain rights against an issuer without these rights being expressed by a securities account, this investor's power regarding his rights against the issuer is extremely limited.

Yet the possibility of errors and fraud by operators of a settlement system can account for the fact that securities accounts provide (mere) challengeable proof of ownership. It has also been argued[60] that as the KB no. 62 system was merely intended to supplement existing systems of custody and to facilitate securities transactions, its technical consequences, i.e. securities accounts, should not be attributed stronger legal force than the original systems attributed to the possession of certificates and to issuer registration, which also provided mere challengeable proof of ownership.

5.3.2.3 Challenges to the Ownership of Book-Entry Securities

As a matter of private law, a *verus dominus* (rightful owner) may always successfully revendicate his assets from other parties, but in the cases of theft or loss, he enjoys this right only during the three years that follow the event. Moreover, if stolen or lost assets are sold on a market, the acquirer in good faith is protected against proprietary challenges and a revendication claim will fail; Articles 2279(2) and 2280 BW. Although it is doctrinally questionable whether these rules apply to securities accountholders, the Act of 14 December 2005 expressly states so.[61]

57. *See infra and cf.* KB no. 62 Art. 7(2).
58. Schrans & Steennot (2003), 107. *But cf.* Tison (1996), 230.
59. *See* Art. 468(2) W. Venn. *and the* Act of 2 January 1991 Art. 6(1).
60. Boddaert (2004), 107.
61. By introducing KB no. 62 Art. 19, Art. 475bis W. Venn. and the Act of 2 January 1991 Art. 13 bis; Act of 14 December 2005, Arts. 21, 34 and 36 respectively.

However, at first sight, the position of an entitlement holder who has been involuntarily dispossessed of his securities seems promising. In the case of a mistake made by the accountholder's intermediary, the accountholder may (contractually) reclaim his assets under Article 1376 BW, provided the latter still holds the assets.[62] If the assets have been transferred to a third party transferee, however, it is unlikely that a (proprietary) claim of revendication would succeed, even before the enactment of the Act of 14 December 2005 was passed.

First, as a practical matter, a claim of revendication against a third party acquirer suggests that the *verus dominus* has been able to track down the acquirer. In the context of modern anonymised stock-markets, this is highly unlikely. Second, as a general rule of private law, assets must be sufficiently individualised to be susceptible to any proprietary claim.[63] Consequently, a claim of revendication can only succeed if the securities concerned have not (yet) been commingled with other securities in the third party acquirer's account.[64] Third, it has been argued that all proprietary claims should have a tangible object and that the uncorporeal character of an accountholder's entitlement would thus prevent successful revendication. Recent literature indicates otherwise however; the doctrine now generally accepts that proprietary claims have intangibles as an object.[65] Fourth, a revendication challenge would fail if Article 2279(1) BW would be applied. Under this rule, all possessors in good faith are deemed to be owners and good faith acquirers are thus protected against competing property claims. Although the provision originally applied to the possessors of movable tangibles only,[66] the Act of 14 December 2005 extended its scope so that it now also applies to *bona fide* holders of entitlements to immobilised and dematerialised securities.

However, before this Act was passed, accountholders were thus liable to revendication claims by dispossessed *veri domini,* provided these accountholders were traced as third party acquirers and the securities concerned had not been commingled with other securities of the same kind in the acquirer's account.[67] This situation had been criticised on grounds of legal certainty and the prevention of systemic risk.[68] The Belgian legislator had therefore granted the accountholder protection against competing claims in three specific situations. First, stolen or lost certificates must be filed; once filed, these securities cannot be acquired in good faith. Conversely, all acquirers are protected against competing claims that concern stolen or lost, but not filed certificates.[69] Second, if an accountholder as a pledgee has received securities in good faith and these securities have been credited to a pledge account in the pledgee's name, the pledgee is protected against competing

62. Moreover, the intermediary may be liable to a criminal charge; BODDAERT (2004), 109.
63. SAGAERT (2003), 380–381.
64. BODDAERT (2004), 111 *and* SUNT (1996), 457, n.153.
65. BODDAERT (2004), 109, with reference to recent French case law.
66. *See,* e.g., VAN NESTE (1990), 454.
67. TISON (1996), 250–251 and 260.
68. TISON (1996), 250–251 and 260 *and* BODDAERT (2004), 112.
69. Act of 24 July 1921 and KB no. 62 Arts. 9 and 10. *See infra,* s. 2.3.3.

claims.[70] Third, a good faith acquirer of government bonds was protected against competing claims if these bonds had been transferred by participants who were not allowed to engage in transactions with these securities as they belonged to their clients.[71] In the latter two instances however, the protection was not absolute.[72]

5.3.3 KB no. 62 Custody

5.3.3.1 Custody Structure

As stated previously, KB no. 62 of 10 November 1967 originally created a system of custody in which *toondereffecten* (bearer securities) are rendered fungible; Article 6. The system is based on the accountholder's (implicit) consent to that effect and is therefore not a mandatory one.[73] As its most important accomplishments, it has enabled the transfer of securities by book-entry with proprietary effect and has resulted in the immobilisation of bearer certificates.[74]

Although KB no. 62 creates a typical pyramid-shaped structure of custody, it allows for multiple CSDs and for the possibility of certificates to be immobilised only in the vaults of a participant. To these securities, KB no. 62 nonetheless applies; Article 17.[75] KB no. 62 also allows CSD and intermediaries to hold securities in sub-custody, either physically or by book-entry; Article 4. Furthermore, although the KB no. 62 seems to assume a 3-tier holding structure, with a CSD and one level of intermediaries interposed between CSD and (ultimate) investors, it also caters for a longer chain of custody with multiple levels of intermediaries. In such a situation also, the ultimate accountholder enjoys proprietary protection in the case of his immediate intermediary's insolvency.[76]

The anonymity of investors to the CSD is considered to be an important feature of the system.[77] Therefore, accountholders can, as a rule, only enforce their rights against their immediate intermediary; Article 12(1), concerning claims of participants against the CSD, and Article 13(1), concerning claims of investors against a participant. But the same Articles list several exceptions to this rule. First, a claim of revendication may be enforced against upper-tier intermediaries in the case of the insolvency of an accountholder's immediate intermediary,[78]

70. Act of 2 January 1991 Art. 7(3) and Art. 470(2) W. Venn. for dematerialised securities, KB no. 62 Art. 7(1)(2) for immobilised securities.
71. Act of 2 January 1991 Art. 5.
72. *See infra,* ss. 2.5.3 and 2.4.3, respectively.
73. In contrast to the French system; *see* Ch. 6.1.3.
74. *Cf.* Boddaert (2004), 84.
75. Such a situation could arise if the securities (although being eligible for KB no. 62 custody) have been refused for custody by the CSD or if the depositor has not agreed to the securities being held by the CSD. As a result of these securities being held by a participant, book-entry transfers are possible only between the lower-tier accountholders; Boddaert (2004), 242–243.
76. *See infra,* s. 2.6.3.
77. *See* Schrans & Steennot (2003), 263.
78. *See also infra,* s. 2.3.7.

and second, investors may enforce their corporate rights (such as voting rights) directly against the issuer.

5.3.3.2 Securities Eligible[79]

Practically, only Belgian bearer securities were originally eligible for admittance to the KB no. 62 system of custody.[80] KB no. 62 Article 2 refers to the Act of 2 August 2002 Article 2(1) to indicate which categories of securities are eligible, and although that provision refers to almost all categories of financial instruments,[81] Article 2 excludes Belgian dematerialised securities as subject to the Act of 2 January 1991, the Act of 22 July 1991 and the W. Venn. But as many legal authors stressed the similarity between the legal regimes regarding immobilised and dematerialised securities, separate legislation for Belgian dematerialised securities was considered redundant.[82] Since the Act of 14 December 2005, however, KB no. 62 also applies to foreign dematerialised securities and foreign securities generally.[83] Moreover, the said act extends the scope of the KB no. 62 to dematerialised securities that are not subject to the acts mentioned *above*.[84]

Since securities are only eligible for the application of KB no. 62 if they can be treated as fungibles, the KB only applies to financially and economically identical securities, i.e. securities of the same category, term, issuer and conferring the same rights.[85] Consequently, it was questioned whether the KB would apply to *effecten op naam* (registered securities), as those securities must be registered in the ultimate investor's name in the issuer's register (Belgian law does not recognise beneficial ownership[86]) and were therefore considered by some not to be fungible by nature. But the Act of 14 December 2005 resolved the controversy as the KB no. 62 now explicitly applies to registered securities also.

Furthermore, securities must be freely transferable by book-entry in order to be eligible. As a consequence, certain derivatives are not eligible if they represent

79. The Arts. of association of the CSDs may determine which institutions are eligible for participation. For a discussion on the institutions eligible for participation in the CIK system, *see* Cerfontaine (2004), 508.
80. *Cf.* Sunt (1996), 431.
81. For an extensive discussion on all the financial instruments listed in the Act of 2 August 2002, *see* Boddaert (2004), 92.
82. Schrans & Steennot (2003), 260.
83. Originally, foreign registered securities had to be admitted to the KB no. 62 system in the following way. Once transferred to a Belgian CSD or other Belgian nominee, the latter issued corresponding bearer certificates called Continental Depository Receipts or International Depositary Receipts, which were subsequently deposited into the KB no. 62 system; Sunt (1996), 435–436 *and* Boddaert (2004), 96. Belgian registered securities cannot be swapped by the same technique; Arts. 242(1)(7) and 503(1)(6) W. Venn. *Cf.* Sunt (1996), 454.
84. *See* Explanatory Memorandum to the draft Act of 14 December 2005, Doc 51 1974, 23–24.
85. Schrans & Steennot (2003), 269; Boddaert (2004), 95 and 138 *and* Sunt (1996), 430.
86. Sunt (1996), 432. Moreover, it is forbidden for non-owners to enjoy corporate rights attached to securities; Arts. 349, 389 and 651 W. Venn.; Boddaert (2004), 97.

a non-transferable contractual relationship between an investor and an issuer.[87] Securities of which the transfer is restricted by the issuer's articles of association are not eligible for the same reason.

5.3.3.3 Deposit

As stated previously, KB no. 62 only applies if the accountholder/depositor has agreed to his securities being treated as fungibles. Such consent may have been given implicitly. The Antwerp Court of Appeal has even held that if securities are transferred to a CSD within the KB no. 62 system of custody, the KB applies automatically. The Court ruled that in such instance, no investor must be denied the proprietary protection which the KB provides.[88] This decision was based on KB no. 62 Article 4 (now Article 6), which declares that all securities that have been deposited with the CSD are fungible.

The current Article 5 explicitly states that the fungible character of deposited securities does not entail any limitation on the depositor's original rights. Where a deposit of fungibles causes the depositor to lose his original right of ownership,[89] KB no. 62 grants a depositor of fungible securities a right of co-ownership instead.[90] Thus, although the delivery of certificates to a custodian classifies as *traditio*,[91] its consequence is a legal 'conversion' of a right of ownership into a right of co-ownership that concerns the entire pool of fungible securities which his custodian(s) may hold.[92]

In order to enhance legal certainty as to the circulation of bearer certificates, the Act of 24 July 1921 protected possessors of bearer securities against competing claims.[93] Pursuant to this Act, an owner whose bearer certificates have been lost, stolen, or who has otherwise been involuntarily dispossessed, must make the dispossession public by filing the securities in question. After filing (called *verzet*), no subsequent acquirer of these securities can claim to have acquired them in good faith.[94] Conversely, all *bona fide* transferees/possessors of bearer securities that have not been filed are protected against competing claims.[95]

KB no. 62 Articles 9 and 10 apply the *verzet* procedure to the deposit of fungible securities: when accepting bearer certificates for deposit, the CSD and its participants must check the *verzet* register in order to be considered a good faith

87. Derivatives may, however, be credited to securities accounts; Schrans & Steennot (2003), 255.
88. Hof van Beroep te Antwerpen, 20 August 1990, *T.R.V.* 1990, 542.
89. *See supra,* s. 2.3.1.
90. As explicitly stated by the Hof van Beroep te Antwerpen, 20 August 1990, *T.R.V.* 1990, 541.
91. Schrans & Steennot (2003), 260.
92. Boddaert (2004), 103 *and* Schrans & Steennot (2003), 272. On the nature of this co-ownership right, *see infra,* s. 2.3.6.1
93. *See extensively* Van Neste (1990), 483 *et seq.*
94. *Cf.* Boddaert (2004), 195.
95. Since 14 December 2006, accountholders entitled to KB no. 62 securities are similarly protected under Art. 2279; *see supra,* s. 5.3.2.

depositee/acquirer; Article 9(1).[96] Further, all filing after deposit is without legal consequence; Article 9(2). Moreover, if no dispossession has been filed, a custodian is protected against all competing claims; Article 10. This provision clearly derogates from Article 2279 BW.[97] By applying the *verzet* procedure to the deposit of securities, Articles 9 and 10 together show that the deposit of securities into the KB no. 62 system is a hybrid figure that combines elements of transfer of ownership with deposit as commonly understood in general private law.

5.3.4 Dematerialised Securities

It is for an issuer to decide whether he will issue securities in dematerialised or in a traditional registered or bearer form,[98] provided the category of securities in question is eligible for dematerialisation.[99] Once issued in a dematerialised form, government bonds and certain types of corporate debt instruments are held in a pyramid-shaped custody structure, with the *Banque Nationale de Belgique/Nationale Bank van België* (Central Bank of Belgium, 'NBB') serving as the CSD.[100] For all other dematerialised corporate bonds and shares, the Belgian government has designated the CIK, now Euroclear Belgium, as the CSD.[101]

Unlike the participants in the KB no. 62 system, who are admitted to participation according to the rules of the CSD concerned,[102] participants that administrate dematerialised securities accounts have to be designated as such by the government; Act of 2 January 1991 Article 3 and Article 468(3) W. Venn. By KB of 12 January 2006, the government has fairly liberally designated certain categories of institutions that may maintain securities accounts, including Belgian credit institutions, Belgian corporations, Belgian CSDs, Belgian branches of certain foreign credit institutions and the NBB.[103]

Also contrary to the KB no. 62 system, the total number of dematerialised securities of a certain issue must be registered in the issuer's register of *effecten op naam* (registered securities) in the CSD's name; Article 468(4) W. Venn. That registration represents the relationship between the issuer and the chain of intermediaries and guarantees the anonymity of the beneficial owners/ultimate investors. But it has been argued that it does not provide accountholders with any proof of ownership and merely involves an administrative registration.[104] Moreover, some

96. When failing to do so, the custodian concerned is liable to the person who filed the dispossession pursuant to Arts. 1382 *et seq.* BW.
97. *See also* Boddaert (2004), 205.
98. Sunt (1996), 449.
99. *See supra,* s. 2.2.
100. KB of 12 January 2006 Art. 6. Being both CSD and Central Bank, the NBB can provide in-house Delivery Versus Payment ('DVP') settlement on the top-tier level; Sunt (1996), 444.
101. *See* Art. 468(3) W. Venn. *and* KB of 12 January 2006 Art. 6.
102. KB no. 62 Art. 1(2).
103. Art. 1(1).
104. Schrans & Steennot (2003), 291; Tison (1996), 238.

have argued that it may cause unnecessary confusion with the category of *effecten op naam* and create the impression of a trust construction, which is unknown in Belgian law.[105]

5.3.5 ACCOUNTHOLDER/INTERMEDIARY RELATIONSHIP

In Belgian legal literature, the classification of the accountholder/intermediary relationship has been a matter of considerable debate[106] (as has been the intermediary – sub-custodian or CSD relationship[107]). Most authors characterise this relationship principally as a contract of *bewaargeving (depositum regulare),* with an additional contract of *lastgeving* (mandate).[108]

The rules that regulate *bewaargeving* have been codified in Articles 1915–1948 BW. Of these provisions, Articles 1930 and 1944 are especially appropriate in the context of securities custody. The former Article forbids custodians to dispose of the deposited assets without the depositor's explicit or implicit consent, while the latter provision imposes upon the custodian the obligation to return the deposited assets at the depositor's request under all circumstances. The obligation to return the deposited assets in due time is considered to include the obligation of safekeeping as far as the deposited assets are concerned. But these last two obligations differ in one fundamental aspect. The obligation to return the assets must be observed under all circumstances and even *force majeure* is sometimes not accepted as a ground for justification, should the custodian not comply.[109] The obligation of safekeeping on the other hand, is (merely) an obligation that should be performed to the best of the intermediary's abilities.[110]

General rules of private law thus regulate the accountholder/intermediary relationship, but specific legislation does derogate from these rules.[111] One of the most important derogating provisions in this regard is KB no. 62 Article 6(2), which states that a custodian (or sub-custodian or CSD) is allowed to return equivalent, but nonetheless different securities than originally deposited. This provision explicitly derogates from Articles 1915 and 1932(1) BW that require deposited assets to be returned *in specie.* Other Civil Code provisions also clearly do not apply to the custody of book-entry securities. Article 1918 BW for instance,

105. SUNT (1996), 450–451.
106. The service of securities custody offered by financial intermediaries on the other hand, is plainly statutorily qualified as an 'auxiliary service'; Act of 6 April 1995 Art. 46(2)(1).
107. *Cf.* SCHRANS & STEENNOT (2003), 265.
108. *See,* e.g. FREDERICQ (1952), 371, DU LAING (2001), 335 and 355 *and* CERFONTAINE (2004), 478 and 480 *et seq. Contra* SAGAERT (2003), 400 *et seq.*
109. Art. 1929 BW.
110. *See* Art. 1927 BW. *Cf.* CERFONTAINE (2004), 492. But the standard of due care is heightened if the custodian has solicited its clients and demands payment for its services; Art. 1928(1) and (2). Moreover, it is a matter of debate whether it includes an obligation to preserve the securities' value; DU LAING (2001), 341-343.
111. *See,* explicitly the *Hof van Beroep te Antwerpen* (Antwerp Court of Appeal) 20 August 1990, *T.R.V.* 1990, 540.

requires that deposited assets are movable tangibles and that, as a consequence, any deposit should take place by the physical delivery *(traditio)* of the assets to the custodian. Not only does this obviously not accord with the custody and 'deposit' of dematerialised securities, but also in the case of immobilised securities, the accountholder/intermediary relationship is most often initiated by the opening of a securities account instead of a physical delivery. Yet it has been argued that the opening of an account should be deemed a deposit in the sense of Article 1918.[112] Furthermore, Article 1917 BW requires custody to be without payment to the custodian for its service, which is clearly not the case in most of securities custody agreements. Also outside the context of securities custody however, this provision has been overruled by both statutory law and case law.[113]

A classification of the accountholder/intermediary relationship as *depositum irregulare* would respond to most of the objections just discussed. First, provisions such as Articles 1918 and 1919 BW are unknown to *depositum irregulare* as this is not a statutorily-regulated contract. Second, a custodian is not obliged to return the deposited assets *in specie* under a contract of *depositum irregulare,*[114] which accords with the practice of fungible securities custody. Under a contract of *depositum irregulare* however, depositors are unable to revindicate their assets[115] and are left with a mere contractual claim against their custodian.[116] Moreover, it has been argued that under a contract of *depositum irregulare,* a custodian acquirers full power of disposal over the deposited assets.[117] Therefore, *depositum irregulare* does not seem to be appropriate as a characterisation of securities custody since both in the instance of immobilised and of dematerialised securities custody, accountholders enjoy a right of co-ownership which provides them with proprietary protection and denies their custodian power of disposal.[118]

The additional contract of mandate[119] regards the custodian's obligation to perform certain administrative tasks. The performance of some of these tasks requires the accountholder's explicit consent or assignment, while others are performed on the basis of an implicit mandate. The custodian's obligation to receive

---

112. Du Laing (2001), 339 *and* Cerfontaine (2004), 486–487.
113. *Cf.* Art. 1928(2) *and see,* e.g., Cas. 1re civ., 26 September 1940, *Pas.* 1940, III, 228. *See also* Cerfontaine (2004), 481 and 487–488.
114. Peeters & Van derVorst (2001), 453–454 *and* Sagaert (2003), 400 *et seq.*
115. This has led some authors to qualify the accountholder – custodian relationship as *verbruikleen* (loan for consumption). *Contra* Sagaert (2003), 392. *Verbruikleen* is the common characterisation of the deposit of money and also denies the depositor a right of revendication; Du Laing (2001), 263–265.
116. This claim is a strong one, as *depositum irregulare* custodians are also under a strict obligation to return the assets, i.e. these custodians cannot exonerate liability even on the grounds of *force majeure;* Du Laing (2001), 266.
117. *Contra* Peeters & Van der Vorst (2001), 453, Sagaert (2003), 391 *and* E. Huyghe in his annotation of Hof van Beroep te Antwerpen, 20 August 1990, *T.R.V.* 1990, 544–545.
118. On the other hand, the fact that statutory provisions are required to grant such proprietary protection could be used as an argument for the position that in the absence of such provisions, depositors would not be able to revindicate, which indicates a *depositum irregulare.*
119. *Cf.* Du Laing (2001), 337–338 *and* Cerfontaine (2004), 482 and 484.

and pass on the proceeds of the securities in his custody to his clients would be an example of the latter category.

The precise scope of the additional contract of mandate however, is a matter of debate.[120] It is unclear, for instance, whether and to what extent it includes an obligation for the custodian to provide its clients with information and advice on securities management.[121] It is generally acknowledged on the other hand, that it includes an obligation for the custodian to enable its clients to perform both the mandatory and voluntary corporate actions connected with the securities in its custody.[122] Further, it is uncontested that the custodian must cooperate in the settlement of securities transactions concluded by his clients. Some authors have considered the custodian's administrative tasks to be more important than the custody of securities itself and have therefore characterised the accountholder – custodian relationship as a *rekening – courant* agreement[123] or as an asset management agreement.[124] However, these characterisations have not found general support.

In conclusion, a classification of the accountholder – custodian relationship with traditional concepts appears highly problematical, especially with regard to fully dematerialised securities. Core elements of both *depositum regulare, depositum irregulare* and mandate seem to be present in the custody of fungible securities.

5.3.6 Nature of Accountholder Interests

Both in the case of dematerialised and immobilised securities, Belgian accountholders enjoy a right of co-ownership as to a notional pool of securities to protect them against their immediate intermediary's insolvency. KB no. 62 Article 2(3) expresses this co-ownership right as follows: 'a right of co-ownership, which is an uncorporeal right, which is enjoyed by the collective depositors upon fungible deposit with the CSD or its participants as to the pool of similar securities deposited with them'.[125] Thus, this co-ownership right is enjoyed as to the pool of securities maintained by their immediate intermediary, but also to the latter's accounts with the CSD, other intermediaries, to the CSD's accounts with other CSDs and the issuer, and to the securities physically held by the CSD's sub-custodian(s).[126] In other words, Belgian investors enjoy a proprietary right as to the aggregate number of securities of the same kind that are held by or via their immediate intermediary.[127]

120. *See,* e.g., Van Ryn & Heenen (1988), 553 *and* Du Laing (2001), 344 *et seq.*
121. Du Laing (2001), 348–351.
122. Boddaert (2004), 120.
123. Van Ryn & Heenen (1988), 552. *Cf. also* Du Laing (2001), 361.
124. *See* Cerfontaine (2004), 483–484.
125. Translation by the author. For dematerialised securities, *cf.* the almost identical Art. 468(5) W. Venn.
126. *Cf.* Boddaert (2004), 103–104 and 222–223.
127. *Cf.* Tison (1996), 254.

Where general private law requires the individualisation of assets for any proprietary right to be enforced against these assets,[128] the notional pool of securities, i.e. the aggregate number of securities held through intermediaries, is considered to be a sufficiently individualised asset in the context of an accountholder's right of co-ownership.[129] Moreover, since the aggregate number of securities held through the custody chain is considered as one asset for the purpose of an accountholder's property rights, the number of intermediaries interposed between the issuer and ultimate investor does not affect the latter's rights. As a consequence, Belgian investors enjoy their rights against their immediate intermediary regardless of where the actual securities are located.[130]

As accountholders enjoy a right of co-ownership, their securities do not become part of the CSD's or the participants' estate.[131] More specifically, an accountholder's right of co-ownership refers to the following rights:[132] (a) a right of disposal as to the balance of his securities account, a right which includes the right to transfer, either outright or by way of security, the right to pledge and to grant any third party a right of usufruct;[133] (b) a right of revendication of equivalent securities in the case of the account provider's insolvency, i.e. a right of retrieval of securities of the same kind and number as deposited. In the case of bearer securities, revendication is perfected by the (physical) delivery of the securities out of the custody system, and it is perfected by a transfer to another securities account in the case of dematerialised securities; (c) a right to enjoy the corporate rights that are attached to the securities on the accountholder's balance.

Together with the rights that have been discussed in the previous section, an accountholder's co-ownership represents the combination of rights which an accountholder enjoys against his immediate intermediary. As mentioned before, these rights must be sharply distinguished from an accountholder's rights to the underlying securities.[134] This distinction becomes apparent when considering that in principle, the accountholder's rights (including his right of co-ownership) may be enforced only against the accountholder's immediate intermediary. Solely in the situation of the immediate intermediary's insolvency can it be said to work *erga omnes*.[135] Furthermore, the accountholder's rights against his intermediary are not affected by the actual location of the securities even if they are located abroad,[136] since the notional pool of securities to which accountholders may enforce their

128. *See,* e.g., Sagaert (2003), 380-381.
129. Van Ryn & Heenen (1981), 148, Du Laing (2001), 359. *Cf.* Sagaert (2003), 398 and 402.
130. Even if they are located abroad; *see infra,* s. 2.6.
131. Sagaert (2003), 402. As a consequence, securities accounts have been compared to a *kwaliteitsrekening* (an account that does not form part of the accountholder's estate); Dirix (1998), 10–11, Servaes (2000), 521, n.28 *and* Peeters & Van der Vorst (2001), 455.
132. *See* Boddaert (2004), 104–105 and 220–221.
133. For an extensive discussion of usufruct of fungible securities, *see* Boddaert (2004), 113–115.
134. *See,* extensively Servaes (2000), 522–523. *See also* Schrans & Steennot (2003), 272 *and* Boddaert (2004), 84 and 104. *Cf.* Guynn (1996), 43.
135. *See infra,* s. 2.3.7.
136. KB no. 62 Art. 4. *Cf. also infra,* s. 2.6.

right of co-ownership is deemed to be located with the immediate intermediary and not with the 'actual' location of the securities.[137]

Therefore, an accountholder's right of co-ownership is fundamentally different from any proprietary right under general private law, in that it is ordinarily limited to the accountholder/intermediary relationship and that it may have an intangible asset as an object. Thus, an accountholder's proprietary right must be considered to be a *sui generis* right.[138]

5.3.7 Intermediary Insolvency and the Treatment of Shortfalls

As discussed in the previous section, accountholders enjoy a right of co-ownership. This right can be enforced in their immediate intermediary's insolvency.[139] As a consequence, accountholders' assets are not available to the intermediary's creditors. This also applies to the securities' proceeds such as interests and dividends, which are paid by the issuer to the CSD and subsequently passed on to the participants and their clients.[140]

Although as a general rule, accountholders may enforce their rights only against their immediate intermediary,[141] they may claim revendication of their securities also against upper-tier intermediaries and other intermediaries with whom the immediate intermediary maintains securities accounts if the immediate intermediary becomes insolvent.[142] Only then, the accountholder's property right is 'traced' through the chain of custody. KB no. 62 Article 13(5) and Article 471(4) W. Venn. must be interpreted in this light too; these provisions grant accountholders that have used an agent to maintain a securities account with a participant the right to enforce their right of ownership directly against this participant, should the agent become insolvent, even if the account is not registered in the ultimate accountholder's name. In other words, investors holding securities accounts with a non-participant also enjoy proprietary protection in the case of this non-participant's insolvency, provided the non-participant holds an account with a participant. Although these investors are beneficial owners and not co-owners in the sense of, e.g. KB no. 62, they enjoy a similar revendication right.[143] This may be considered remarkable for a civil law country that is unfamiliar with the concept of trust.

137. Servaes (2000), 523.
138. *Cf.* Peeters & Van der Vorst (2001), 454 and 456.
139. *Cf.* Art. 471(5) W. Venn. *and see* Bernasconi, 2000, 22, nt.83; Guynn (1996), 43–44 *and* Tison (1996), 254.
140. KB no. 62 Art. 13(2) and *cf.* Boddaert (2004), 232.
141. KB no. 62 Art. 13(1) for immobilised securities and the Act of 2 January 1991 Art. 11(1) and Art. 471(1) W. Venn. for dematerialised securities. KB no. 62 Art. 12 provides the same rules in the case of the CSD's insolvency; where KB no. 62 Art. 13 is mentioned in the following, corresponding paragraphs of Art. 12 are also meant to be included.
142. KB no. 62 Art. 13(2) for immobilised securities and the Act of 2 January 1991 Art. 9 and Art. 471(2) W. Venn. for dematerialised securities.
143. The sole difference would be that these investors may not revendicate directly against the CSD; Boddaert (2004), 228–229.

Should a deficit occur when all accountholders try to revendicate their assets, the insolvent intermediary's own securities are first used to cover this deficit. In legal literature, some controversy exists as to whether this entitlement of the accountholders to the insolvent intermediary's own assets ranks superior to the intermediary's creditors who hold a proprietary security right in the same assets.[144] But in practice, pledgees invariably rank higher than the insolvent intermediary's clients, because creditors that have *bona fide* obtained a security interest are not only protected as such against competing claims of third parties,[145] but may also assert a right of retention on the collateralised securities against the debtor/intermediary until their claim has been satisfied. In the case of a remaining deficit, this deficit is allocated *pro rata*, i.e. in proportion to the accountholder's entitlements.[146]

5.3.8 Intermediary Preference/Statutory Lien

Under Belgian law, intermediaries may obtain a proprietary preference over their clients' assets and this is created by law. The enforcement of this preference or statutory lien is identical to the enforcement of a pledge over book-entry securities, including the right of the security taker to enforce his rights without judicial intervention and his right of appropriation and subsequent netting.[147]

A distinction is made between the statutory lien of intermediaries over their clients' accounts and such lien of a settlement or clearing institution over their participants' accounts. The latter lien is created over a participant's omnibus account with the CSD to secure all claims the CSD might have against this participant, provided that these claims have originated in the context of clearing and settlement; Act of 2 August 2002 Article 31(2). The CSD's lien concerns the participants' own assets, but may also concern participants' clients' assets. These clients must have agreed to this and an intermediary acting without such consent is liable to charged with a criminal offence. It can be questioned, however, to what extent this rule really protects the client; if the participant acts without consent but the CSD has no attributable knowledge of this fact, i.e. if it acted in good faith, the CSD's actions cannot be challenged by the deprived clients; Act of 2 August 2002 Article 31(5).[148]

144. *See* Tison (1996), 255 *and* Sunt (1996), 457. *Cf. also* Boddaert (2004), 223.
145. Act of 2 January 1991 Art. 7(3) and Art. 470(2) W. Venn. for dematerialised securities, and KB no. 62 Art. 7(1)(2) for immobilised securities.
146. KB no. 62 Arts. 13(3) and 13(4) for immobilised securities and the Act of 2 January 1991 Art. 8 and Arts. 471(3) and 471(4) W. Venn. for dematerialised securities. As an additional measure of investor protection, the Directive 97/9/EC of the European Parliament and of the Council of 3 March 1997 on investment-protection schemes (OJ L 84/22), implemented as Act of 17 December 1998, requires that investors be compensated for their losses to the amount of (at least) 20,000 Euros (EUR) To that purpose, the said implementation Act creates a special guarantee fund.
147. Act of 2 August 2002 Arts. 31(4)(1) and 31(4)(2). On the history of these provisions, *see* Devos (2000), 538.
148. The Explanatory Memorandum to the draft Act of 2 August 2002 likened this protection of an actor in good faith to similar rules of general private law codified in Arts. 2279 and 2280 BW, Doc 50 1842 and 1843, 72.

The preference of intermediaries over their clients' assets is intended to protect the intermediary against their clients' insolvency, but may also 'remind clients of the risks attached to securities transactions'.[149] In contrast to the CSD's preference, the intermediaries' lien is more limited in scope as it applies only to securities that are held by or transferred to the intermediary to secure the settlement of transactions for their clients; Act of 2 August 2002 Article 31(1).

5.4 SECURITIES TRANSFERS

5.4.1 INTRODUCTION

As a matter of principle, general private law rules also apply to the transfer of ownership of securities. Theoretically, ownership of securities is therefore transferred *solo consensu* in the case of a sale, i.e. by mere agreement between the parties; Articles 1583 and 1138 BW. But, as will be shown in the following sections, how a securities transfer is evidenced and when it takes proprietary effect, i.e. when it becomes effective against third parties, is usually determined by more specific rules, which are not always found in, or seem consistent with, the civil code.

Ownership and thus any transfer of directly held *effecten op naam* (registered securities), for instance, is ultimately evidenced by registration in the issuer's register and some other, technical formalities connected therewith; Articles 250, 365 and 504 W. Venn.[150] But the effectiveness against third parties of a transfer of directly held registered securities is governed by the rules that govern the assignment of claims; Article 1690 BW. This Article provides that an assignment becomes effective against all third parties except the debtor by the agreement to transfer *(solo consensu).* It can be asserted against the debtor (in the case of registered securities: the issuer) when the latter has been informed of the assignment (e.g. through registration in the issuer's register) or when he has acknowledged it.[151] A transfer of directly held *effecten aan toonder* (bearer securities), on the other hand, is evidenced and made effective against third parties through physical delivery, as Article 2279 BW deems a possessor of a movable asset to be the owner of that asset; Article 504 W. Venn.

5.4.2 MOMENT OF TRANSFER

Analogous to that provision on directly held bearer securities, it may be inferred from KB no. 62 Article 6(3) that a credit entry in a transferee's securities account evidences and renders effective a transfer of immobilised bearer securities. Similarly, a transfer of dematerialised securities is both evidenced and made effective

149. Explanatory Memorandum to the draft Act of 2 August 2002, Doc 50 1842 and 1843, 69.
150. On these provisions and their loose application, *see* LAGA & LIETAER (2001), 476–477.
151. *Cf.* TISON (1996), 231, n.9.

against third parties by a credit entry in the transferee's account.[152] Moreover, dematerialised securities can only be transferred this way; Article 468(2) W. Venn. and the Act of 2 January 1991 Article 6(1).

However, it has also been supposed that dematerialised securities are transferred according to the rules of Article 1690 BW on the assignment of claims, but this view is not generally accepted. First, an accountholder's entitlement to dematerialised securities classifies as a proprietary (be it incorporeal) right and rules that govern the assignment of claims are therefore not applicable.[153] Moreover, if a transfer of dematerialised securities would be perfected and made effective against third parties by agreement alone plus notification to the issuer, a highly impractical discrepancy between balances of securities accounts and legal ownership would be created.[154]

A credit entry in a transferee's securities account thus evidences and renders effective a transfer of both immobilised and dematerialised securities, but the civil code determines that a sale of fungible assets only takes proprietary effect, i.e. is effective against third parties, when the assets are made sufficiently ascertainable; Article 1585 BW.[155] In other words, certainty of subject-matter determines the moment of transfer, and it has been argued that in the case of a sale of fungibles, such certainty is only obtained the moment when the fungibles have been delivered, i.e. credited to the transferee's securities account.[156] The more generally accepted view however, seems to be that a sufficient degree of certainty is reached once the destination of the securities has been determined. From that moment onwards, the category and number, as well as the source and destination of the securities to be transferred can be known,[157] which is considered to have occurred after clearing by the CCP/CSD.[158]

Thus, a discrepancy can be discerned between specific rules of securities law, prescribing that the evidence and effectiveness of a securities transfer are determined by a credit entry in the transferee's account, and general private law, which is generally interpreted so as to imply that fungible securities are transferred when cleared by the CCP or CSD.

---

152. This rule has been inspired by general rules on money payments by book-entry: SCHRANS & STEENNOT (2003), 296. *Cf. also,* e.g., TISON (1996), 231 and 241 *and* SUNT (1996), 457–458. *But see,* e.g. PEETERS & VAN DERVORST (2001), 451.
153. *See* SCHRANS & STEENNOT (2003), 295, n.422. *Cf. also supra,* s. 2.3.6.
154. TISON (1996), 243.
155. But this provision does not apply when fungible assets are (to be) transferred *en bloc,* i.e. without individualisation. When securities, for example, are made subject to a donation or a bequest, the *solo consensu* rule again applies; Art. 1586 BW. *See,* more extensively on the problems that arise when the general private law rules on donation are applied to book-entry securities, TISON (1996), 243–248 *and* SUNT (1996), 459.
156. That would be analogous to the current law of money payments by book-entry; *see,* e.g. *Hof van Beroep te Antwerpen* (Antwerp Court of Appeal), 17 May 1984, *R.W.* 1984–1985, 264.
157. BODDAERT (2004), 106.
158. *See* TISON (1996), 241–242 *and* SCHRANS & STEENNOT (2003), 116–117.

5.4.3 Annulment and Finality

As concluded previously,[159] a book-entry in a securities account represents only a challengeable evidence of title. Prior to modification by the Act of 14 December 2005, even *bona fide* accountholders could therefore be challenged by *veri domini* that were dispossessed by fraud or administrative mistake. The Act of 2 January 1991 Article 5 compensated for this lack of protection in a specific situation: if participants who are not allowed to engage in transactions with their clients' assets do transfer these assets (either outright or as collateral), the acquirers of these assets in good faith cannot be successfully challenged by the deprived clients. Strangely enough, the Act of 2 January 1991 applied to certain dematerialised government bonds only while no such rule had been codified for all other dematerialised securities in the W. Venn.[160]

All acquirers of KB no. 62 securities on the other hand, were protected against competing claims that concern stolen or lost certificates, provided that no dispossession of these securities had been filed prior to their deposit into the KB no. 62 system.[161] To solve this discrepancy, and to protect all *bona fide* transferees, the Act of 14 December 2005 extended the scope of Articles 2279 and 2280 BW, so that *bona fide* holders of entitlements to immobilised and dematerialised securities are now all protected against competing claims of third parties.[162]

However, the rules of general insolvency law may also require the reversal of securities transactions if executed after a declaration of bankruptcy. The implementation of the EU Settlement Finality Directive, on the other hand, ensured the finality of the netting of securities transfers against possible challenges by insolvency administrators.[163] Netting and settlement of securities transactions, as well as orders thereto, are now final if executed or registered in the system before insolvency or in the absence of knowledge of a participant's insolvency by the settlement system; Act of 28 April 1999 Articles 3 and 4.[164] Furthermore, the Act of 28 April 1999 Article 6 derogates from the general rule of Belgian insolvency law that insolvency proceedings have retroactive effect to the beginning of the day on which the bankruptcy has been declared (the 'zero-hour rule').[165] It provides that all transfer orders prior to a bankruptcy declaration may not be revoked nor may any consequent payment, delivery,

159. S. 5.3.2.
160. Although the liability of the intermediaries remains unaffected; Tison (1996), 250–251 and 260.
161. Act of 24 July 1921 and KB no. 62 Arts. 9 and 10. *See supra,* s. 2.3.3.
162. Through the introduction of Art. 475bis W. Venn. (dematerialised securities generally), KB no. 62 Art. 19 (immobilised securities) and the Act of 2 January 1991 Art. 13bis (certain categories of dematerialised securities).
163. *See* Devos (2000), 546. Prior to the implementation of the SFD however, orders could already be made irrevocable by agreement, by the general terms of the settlement system and by the rules of the intermediaries; Devos (2000), 533.
164. The Act of 28 April 1999 only applies to the participants to a (settlement) system. For non-participants, similar rules are provided by the Act of 22 March 1993 Art. 157; Schrans & Steennot (2003), 394 *and* 406–414. On the latter provision, *see* Devos (2000), 534 *et seq.*
165. Act of 8 August 1997 Arts. 17 *et seq. (Loi sur les Faillites/Faillissementswet).*

netting or any other legal act in the process of settlement be reversed. But prior legislation already exempted transfers by or to credit and clearing institutions before insolvency or in the absence of knowledge of that institution's insolvency from the 'zero-hour' rule; Act of 22 March 1993 Article 157(1).

5.5 CREATION AND ENFORCEMENT OF SECURITY RIGHTS

5.5.1 INTRODUCTION

As a civil law country, Belgium recognises a limited number of security rights, of which only *burgerlijk pand* (civil pledge), *handelspand* (commercial pledge), and, to some extent, the transfer of ownership by way of security are relevant in this context. These security rights will be discussed in the following sections, where it will be seen that the creation of those rights when vested in book-entry securities, i.e. securities immobilised under KB no. 62 and dematerialised securities, is governed by special rules. Moreover, the enforcement of security rights on book-entry securities derogates from general private law rules.

5.5.2 TRANSFER OF TITLE

Some unclarity exists as to whether fiduciary transfers are allowed under Belgian law. From an important decision of the Belgian *Cour de Cassation/Hof van Cassatie* (Supreme Court), it may be inferred that, in principle, fiduciary transfers are forbidden although specific statutory provisions may derogate from this. The scope of the decision however, is a matter of debate.[166] On the other hand, a creditor/pledgee is clearly forbidden from appropriating pledged assets in the case of his debtor's/pledgor's default (known as *pactum commissorium).* Article 2078(2) BW and Article 1 Title VI of Book 1 *Code de Commerce/Wetboek van Koophandel* (Commercial Code) render all such agreements void.

The Act of 2 January 1991 already exempted securities transfers of ownership by way of security, such as intended in repurchase agreements and the like, from the fiduciary ban; Articles 23 and 25bis(1).[167] These provisions have now been transferred to the implementation Act of the EU Financial Collateral Directive. The latter Act explicitly excludes all Civil Code provisions as well as all Commercial Code provisions that concern security interests from applicability to transfers of ownership of financial instruments by way of security; Article 12(1) Act of 15 December 2004. The provisions have been extended so as to include margin calls and substitutions in the context of repurchase agreements.

166. Cass. 1re civ. 17 October 1996, 2 *Revue de la Banque/Bank en Financiewezen* 1997, 114 *and* annotation by PEETERS. *See also* PEETERS & VAN DER VORST (2001), 430.
167. *See* DEVOS (2000), 538–540. *See also* SCHRANS & STEENNOT (2003), 280, n.351.

5.5.3 Pledge and Attachment

5.5.3.1 Creation of a Pledge

Under general rules of private and commercial law, a pledge is made effective both *inter partes* and against third parties by the transfer of possession of the pledged assets to the pledgee; Article 2076 BW and Article 1 Title VI of Book 1 Commercial Code. The former provision, which applies to pledges concluded between non-businessmen, further requires a (written) deed of pledge.

In the case of directly held bearer securities, dispossession is effectuated by physical delivery, and in the case of directly held registered securities, by registration of the pledge in the issuer's register.[168] Regarding book-entry securities, a pledge is made effective by a transfer of the securities to a specially designated (pledge) account.[169] Where Article 2074 BW requires the individualisation of the pledged assets in a written deed, the special pledge account is considered to sufficiently individualise the pledged book-entry securities, thus eliminating the difference between a 'commercial law pledge' and a 'private law pledge'.[170] Moreover, the implementation act of the EU Financial Collateral Directive explicitly exempts the creation of security rights on book-entry securities from the formalities required by Articles 2074 and 1328 BW.[171]

Where under KB no. 62 and the W. Venn., the designated pledge account may be opened with all custodians, the Act of 2 January 1991 refers only to the pledgee's intermediary and the CSD; Article 7(1). The special pledge account may be registered in the name of the pledgee, pledgor, or any third party.[172] As a consequence of the dispossession requirement however, a pledgor must not remain in control of the pledged securities. If the pledged securities are transferred to a pledge account registered in the pledgor's name (which is quite common if the pledgee is also the pledgor's intermediary[173]), the dispossession must therefore be technically effectuated by the blocking of the pledged account and some administrative publicity measure that marks the account as 'pledged'.[174]

The implementation act of the EU Financial Collateral Directive further undermines the dispossession requirement by determining that when a pledge account is opened with an intermediary in the context of a financial collateral

168. *See,* e.g., KB of 23 January 1991 Art. 15 *and cf.* Explanatory Memorandum to the draft Act of 15 December 2004, Doc. 51 1407, 33.
169. KB no. 62 Art. 7(1) for immobilised securities and the Act of 2 January 1991 Art. 7(1) and Art. 470(1) W. Venn. for dematerialised securities. *See also* the Act of 15 December 2004 Art. 4(2).
170. *See* Boddaert (2004), 154, Sunt (1996), 461 *and* Explanatory Memorandum to the draft Act of 15 December 2004, Doc. 51 1407, 37.
171. Act of 15 December 2004 Art. 7(1).
172. Sunt (1996), 434–435 *and see* Art. 4(1)(2) and 4(1)(3) Act of 15 December 2004.
173. Tison (1996), 256–257.
174. Boddaert (2004), 148. For an extensive discussion of possible fact patterns when pledging securities accounts, *id.,* 148 *et seq.*

arrangement, such intermediary may act as either pledgee, pledgor or third party.[175] Should the pledgor be an intermediary, it may therefore open a pledge account in its own books, and an intermediary-pledgee is currently allowed to open a pledged account in its own books in its own name.[176] Finally, the Act of 2 January 1991 Article 4(2) already provided that in the case of an intermediary-pledgor transferring pledged securities to another intermediary, the latter may open the pledged account in its own books in the name of the pledgor.

Under Belgian law, a pledge on securities includes its interests and dividends, as well as all (corporate) rights attached to the pledged securities.[177] It is not entirely clear however, whether changes to the securities pledged require a new pledge agreement. On the one hand, 'automatic' changes as a result of corporate actions (e.g. the splitting of shares) result in what is called *subrogatie* (subrogation), which is considered not to change the initial pledge agreement.[178] On the other hand, general private law rules would require a new pledge agreement if a pledge account would be changed on the initiative of the pledgor and executed with the collaboration of the pledgee; *cf.* Articles 2076 BW and 1 *Wetboek van Koophandel.*

Case law, however, has determined that if pledged securities are substituted for other securities, the initial pledge is considered not to have changed provided the value of the pledged assets has not increased.[179] Also, the pledgee must have remained in continuous control over the pledged assets, i.e. no hiatus regarding the object of the pledge is allowed.[180] If these two conditions are met, the initial pledge has not changed against third parties. But it has been argued that between pledgor and pledgee, a new pledge agreement has then been formed that must comply with the ordinary requirements of dispossession, individualisation of the subject-matter and *intentio pignoris* (the intention to pledge).[181]

Prior to the Act of 14 December 2005, securities accountholders were not granted the protection of Article 2279 BW, which indemnifies only the possessors of movable tangibles against third party claims.[182] Provisions were therefore

175. Act of 15 December 2004 Art. 4(2), *and cf.* Explanatory Memorandum to the draft Act of 15 December 2004, Doc. 51 1407, 33.
176. Before the Act of 15 December 2004, however, this was different; *see* Peeters & Van der Vorst (2001), 458 and 150.
177. *See* Boddaert (2004), 145 and the references provided there.
178. Boddaert (2004), 168.
179. *Cf.* Act of 15 December 2004 Art. 7(2); this provision applies the same rules that this Act provides for pledged securities to securities that serve as substituting securities or top-up collateral. Thus, this Art. is the counterpart of Arts. 12(1)(2) and 13(1)(2), which apply the same rules that this Act provides for securities collateralised in the context of a repurchase agreement to securities that are provided subsequent to margin calls; Explanatory Memorandum to the draft Act of 15 December 2004, Doc. 51 1407, 38.
180. It has been argued that the new, substituting securities should be of the same kind as the ones that are being substituted. However, this does not seem to be generally accepted; Boddaert (2004), 163–164.
181. For an extensive discussion, *see* Boddaert (2004), 165–167.
182. *Cf. supra,* s. 2.3.2.

drafted that purported to enhance legal certainty for the holders of pledged securities accounts,[183] but some of these provisions were never enacted. As a recent development mentioned before, the Act of 14 December 2005 now extends the scope of Articles 2279 and 2280 BW, so that all *bona fide* holders of entitlements to immobilised and dematerialised securities, including pledgees, are now protected against competing third party claims.[184]

Thus, a defect in the pledgor's entitlement to the pledged securities does not affect the validity of the pledge, so that a pledgee is protected against competing third party claims when the pledge is granted by a non-owner.[185] But this protection is not unconditional; if a pledgee has received the pledged securities in bad faith, i.e. if a pledgee knew that the pledgor was not a *verus dominus,* the pledge may be successfully challenged by the *verus dominus.* It is unclear however, whether bad faith can be assumed in instances other than when the pledgor has notified the pledgee in writing of his status as not being *verus dominus.*[186] Furthermore, if the pledgee is aware that the pledgor acts on a third party's behalf, the validity of the pledge depends on the authorisation of the *verus dominus* to the pledgor.

5.5.3.2 Enforcement of a Pledge

With regard to the enforcement of a pledge, KB no. 62 Article 7(2) and the Act of 2 January 1991 Article 7(3) explicitly derogate from general private law. Whereas general private law requires judicial intervention, authorisation by a Belgian court and a notification to the debtor,[187] a secured creditor with a security interest in immobilised and some categories of dematerialised securities may simply enforce this pledge by a private or public sale, provided the pledgor has been notified and the sale occurs at short notice.[188] Such enforcement may be carried out regardless of any insolvency procedure whilst the proceeds may be set-off against the debt.[189] The surplus must be returned to the pledgor/debtor. The implementation Act of the Collateral Directive, which applies to all categories of book-entry securities,

183. Act of 2 January 1991 Art. 7(3) and Art. 470(2) W. Venn. for dematerialised securities, and KB no. 62 Art. 7(1)(2) for immobilised securities. These provisions were introduced by the Act of 15 December 2004 and the Act of 2 August 2002 respectively. The latter Act, however, was never given the force of law.
184. Through the introduction of Art. 475bis W. Venn. (dematerialised securities generally), KB no. 62 Art. 19 (immobilised securities) and the Act of 2 January 1991 Art. 13bis (certain categories of dematerialised securities).
185. The pledgor's liability to the *verus dominus* on the other hand, remains unaffected; Boddaert (2004), 156.
186. KB no. 62 Art. 7(1)(2). *See also* Boddaert (2004), 157–158.
187. Arts. 1139 and 2078 BW and 4 and 10 *Wetboek van Koophandel.*
188. Peeters & Van der Vorst (2001), 438.
189. This derogation is supported on the ground of the special character of securities; their fluctuation in value is argued to call for the immediate enforcement of a pledge; Boddaert (2004), 158.

has extended these rules so as to apply to all categories of securities.[190] Moreover, Article 8 of this Act provides that prior notification to the debtor is no longer required for a pledge on book-entry securities to be validly enforced.

The Article just mentioned, but also the rules that regulate the special preference in favour of custodians and clearing and settlement institutions[191] allow a security taker to appropriate the assets in which a security right is vested upon the security giver's default.[192] This blatantly derogates from Article 2078 BW and Article 10 *Wetboek van Koophandel,* provisions which explicitly prohibit the appropriation of pledged assets by the creditor and renders void all prior stipulations to such an effect. Another derogation from general private law is contained in Article 10 of the implementation Act of the Collateral Directive. This provision allows for the security taker's disposal of pledged securities and their rehypothecation. It derogates from Articles 2074 and 2082 BW, which forbade all acts of disposition by the pledgee and which were sanctioned by criminal law.[193]

5.5.3.3 Freezing of Securities Circulation

Under Belgian law, three types of procedures can 'freeze' the circulation of securities and effectively prevent these securities from being validly transferred. Firstly, the *verzet* procedure prevents securities from being admitted and circulated freely within the KB no. 62 system of custody. Moreover, once bearer certificates have been filed as involuntarily dispossessed, the issuer and custodian(s) are obliged to refrain from cooperating in all transfers regarding these securities.[194]

Secondly, the circulation of book-entry securities may be 'frozen' when investors participate in general meetings of shareholders. In such instances, the issuers are not allowed to demand the presentation of individualised securities, but must accept certificates that are issued by the CSD or participants and which testify to the bearers' ownership. The issuing of such testimonies results in the freezing of the securities concerned until the meeting of shareholders; KB no. 62 Article 15 and Article 474 W. Venn. The same rule applies to other corporate actions which require the participation of accountholders.[195]

Thirdly, garnishment prevents book-entry securities from being validly transferred. But the applicable provisions on garnishment explicitly prohibit so-called

---

190. Act of 15 December 2004 Art. 8. *Cf. also* Act of 28 April 1999 Art. 8 (the implementation legislation of the SFD), which provides that preferences and other security rights may be enforced regardless of a participant's insolvency.
191. *See supra,* s. 2.3.8.
192. Nevertheless, the security taker remains under the obligation to return a possible surplus; to that end, the pledged securities are estimated at market value and the consequent amount is set-off against the original debt. Moreover, such appropriation must be explicitly agreed upon; Act of 15 December 2004 Art. 8(2).
193. Art. 491 *Code Pénal/Strafwetboek* (Criminal Code). This prohibition was not a mandatory rule and neither was it a matter of public order, and parties could therefore agree otherwise; Boddaert (2004), 155.
194. Boddaert (2004), 194 *and see supra,* s. 2.3.3.
195. Boddaert (2004), 237.

upper-tier attachment of securities accounts that are maintained with the CSD or with the CSD's sub-custodians.[196] This prohibition seeks to protect the clients of a participant against the latter's creditors. These creditors may want to attach the participant's securities which are registered in an omnibus account with the CSD. Such an omnibus account however, typically also comprises the securities of the participant's clients. Moreover, the participant's own securities that are registered with the CSD thus remain available to the investors, should a deficit occur in the participant's insolvency.[197] As a general consequence, this prohibition enhances the free circulation of fungible securities.[198] The right of creditors of an individual investor to attach and enforce an attachment (as well as other possible rights they may have as to their debtor's assets) on the other hand, remains unaffected.[199] In such an instance, the attachment includes the debtor's so-called *différé*.[200]

5.6 CONFLICT OF LAWS

Traditionally, Belgian private international law has applied the *lex rei sitae* to proprietary conflicts of laws concerning securities; on conflicts concerning bearer certificates, the law of the actual location of the certificates has been applied, while the law of the location of the issuer's register *(lex societatis)* has been applied to conflicts concerning registered securities.[201]

Regarding book-entry securities, Belgian private international law has been argued to apply the *lex rei sitae* as follows: Belgian law always applies if a securities account that is involved in the dispute is maintained by or for a Belgian CSD.[202] This interpretation is grounded on a (strict) interpretation of KB no. 62 Article 4, that states that if a Belgian CSD places securities in the custody of foreign sub-custodians either by book-entry or physically, KB no. 62 applies. It has also been argued that KB no. 62 Article 4 refers to the law of the place where the relevant account is located,[203] a rule which would similarly apply to dematerialised securities. This seems to be the better view, since the applicability of KB no. 62

196. KB no. 62 Art. 11(1) for immobilised securities and the Act of 2 January 1991 Art. 10(2) and Art. 472(2) W. Venn. for dematerialised securities. Furthermore, the implementation act of the EU Settlement Finality Directive has made all monetary clearing accounts immune from attachment; Act of 28 April 1999 Art. 9.
197. *Cf. supra,* s. 2.3.7.
198. Schrans & Steennot (2003), 282 *and* Boddaert (2004), 209.
199. For the attachment of dematerialised government bonds however, a specific provision has been enacted limiting this right: on the (working) day before the transfer and payment of the *inschrijvingsprijs* (price of issue), attachment is not allowed; Act of 2 January 1991 Art. 12bis.
200. KB no. 62 Art. 11(1) for immobilised securities and the Act of 2 January 1991 Art. 10(1) and Art. 472(1) W. Venn. for dematerialised securities. For a discussion of the *différé, see supra,* s. 2.3.2.
201. Peeters & Van der Vorst (2001), 435.
202. Schrans & Steennot (2003), 266.
203. Guynn (1996), 44 *and* Boddaert (2004), 131 and 183.

as required by its Article 4 only sees to the law that applies to the relationship between investors and their Belgian intermediaries, as well as to the relationship between intermediaries and a Belgian CSD.[204]

This position is also underpinned by Article 8(2) of the Act of 28 April 1999 that implements the EU Settlement Finality Directive. It states that security rights vested in securities are determined by the law of the place where these securities are registered or where their account is maintained.[205] The implementation Act of the Financial Collateral Directive further explains that these rights comprise: 'the legal nature and legal consequences of the security', 'the perfection requirements for rendering the security right opposable against third parties', 'possible priority conflicts and possible concurring rights of acquirers in good faith' and the 'possible conditions for enforcing the security right'.[206]

Furthermore, under the heading 'tradable securities', the recently enacted Belgian Code of Private International Law[207] expands the scope of the EU Directives' conflict of laws rules. Where the EU Directives only deal with collateralised securities, the Code of Private International Law covers all proprietary conflicts concerning book-entry securities. Its provision on book-entry securities centres on a 'register' in which securities may be recorded. It is the law of the location of this register that applies to rights regarding securities. 'Register' should be interpreted in a broad sense in that it also refers to securities accounts, since a 'register' 'is deemed to be located at the principle office of the intermediary that maintains the individual accounts'; Article 91(1)(2).[208] As a consequence, Article 91(1)(2) covers registered securities, immobilised and dematerialised securities. Moreover, it explicitly departs from reference to the location of a physical asset.[209] An exception seems to be made in the instance that certificates are held abroad in sub-custody for the CSD. Here, *lex rei sitae* applies.[210]

---

204. Boddaert (2004), 126. For a practical example, *see* Boddaert (2004), 229.
205. The rationale of the provision has been suggested to have been the protection of a security taker; Devos (2000), 548–551.
206. But the scope of the said directives and thus their implementation legislation differ; *see* Ch. 9.3.3.
207. Act of 16 July 2004.
208. Explanatory Memorandum to the draft Act of 16 July 2004, 3-27/1 SE 2003, 116. Interestingly, this Memorandum explains that the problems in locating a securities account caused this provision to be drafted as a challengeable presumption. It may be challenged, for instance, if the investor and intermediary intended to locate the relevant 'register' elsewhere; 3-27/1 SE 2003, 117.
209. Explanatory Memorandum, 3-27/1 SE 2003, 116.
210. Consequently, the Belgian rule that forbids upper-tier attachment does not apply to these certificates; Boddaert (2004), 210–211.

5.7 CONCLUSION

5.7.1 Questions and Answers

(1) *Which securities are admitted to the national systems of giro transfer and administration?*
Belgian law distinguishes two systems of custody through which securities may be held and transferred by book-entry. To the first system, only freely transferable *toondereffecten* (bearer securities) can be admitted which are subsequently immobilised. The second system is based on total dematerialisation: government bonds, certain categories of corporate debt instruments, shares, profit-sharing certificates, (convertible) bonds and warrants issued by *naamloze vennootschappen* (public companies) may be admitted to this system. But the Act of 14 December 2005 diffuses the sharp distinction between these two systems, as it brings about the gradual dematerialisation of all securities, and makes foreign dematerialised securities and foreign securities generally eligible for admittance into the KB no. 62 system.

(2) *What is the nature of investors' interests in securities?*
Belgian investors enjoy a right of co-ownership in a notional pool of securities, i.e. the aggregate number of securities of the same kind that are held by or via their immediate intermediary. In principle, this right may be enforced only against the accountholder's immediate intermediary, but in the case intermediary's insolvency it may also be enforced against other intermediaries.

(2.1) *Is a credit entry in a securities account merely a proof of ownership or is it a constitutive element of ownership of the securities concerned?*
A credit entry in a securities account provides the accountholder with (mere) challengeable proof of ownership and the credit balance is not constitutive for the existence of the (rights in the) securities it refers to. Accountholders are therefore liable to revendication claims by *veri domini,* but since the Act of 14 December 2005, all *bona fide* holders of entitlements to immobilised and dematerialised securities, including pledgees, are protected against competing third party claims. *See also* question 4.2.

(2.2) *Are informal (i.e. not registered by book-entry) dispositions over securities possible?*
In principle, informal dispositions over securities are possible, but they do not take proprietary effect.

(2.3) *Is provisional credit in book-entry securities possible?*
In principle, only certain, i.e. fixed and permissible, claims or entitlements regarding fungible assets may be represented by a securities account balance. But claims that are uncertain with regard to their object, as well as provisional and future claims, are registered

in the so-called *différé,* which is available to the creditors of the accountholder in the case of its insolvency. On the other hand, Belgian law does not permit a securities account to indicate a negative balance.

(3) *How are investors' rights in respect of securities protected against the account provider and third parties?*
As accountholders enjoy a right of co-ownership of their securities, these securities are not available to the intermediary's creditors. On the other hand, account providers may obtain a statutory preference over their clients' assets to secure their claims against those clients, when claims arise in the execution of securities settlements. That preference extends to a broader range of claims when the account provider is a clearing or settlement institution. The enforcement thereof is identical to the enforcement of a pledge over book-entry securities, including the right of the security taker to enforce his rights without judicial intervention and his right of appropriation and subsequent netting. It is debatable whether such a statutory preference represents a protection of the investor's rights against intermediaries, especially since a settlement or clearing institution's lien over their participants' accounts may also concern the assets of participants' clients. For protection against other third parties, *see* the answer to question 2.1.

(3.1) *Should shortfalls occur in accounts, how are they availed?*
Should a deficit occur when all accountholders revendicate their assets, the insolvent intermediary's own securities are first used to cover this deficit. It seems that good faith pledgees rank prior to the insolvent intermediary's clients in such a situation, provided they can assert a retention right, i.e. provided the pledged securities have been registered in the pledgee's name. In the case of a remaining deficit, such deficit is distributed pro rata, i.e. in proportion to the accountholder's entitlements. This deficit is covered up to € 20.000 per investor by the guarantee fund that has been created for that purpose.

(3.2) *How are an investor's interests in securities separated from the account provider's property or how can investors' interests avail the claims of the provider's general creditors?*
The Act of 2 August 2002 abolished the requirement for intermediaries to separate their own assets from the assets they hold for their clients on the books of the CSD. The obligation to separate one's own assets from clients' assets has now become a matter of regulatory law that only applies to Belgian account providers; Act of 2 August 2002 Article 26(16).

(4) *What are the formal requirements for the transfer of ownership of securities?*
As an implementation of the *solo consensu* rule, Article 1585 BW determines that a transfer of fungible assets is effective, i.e. can be asserted

against third parties, when the assets to be transferred are sufficiently ascertainable. According to the generally accepted interpretation of that provision in the context of securities transfers by book-entry, it implies that a securities transfer is effective once it is cleared by the CCP or CSD. The more specific securities law statutes, however, provide that it is the credit entry in the transferee's securities account that evidences and renders effective a transfer of book-entry securities; KB no. 62 Article 6(3), Article 468(2) W. Venn. and the Act of 2 January 1991 Article 6(1).

(4.1) *Can a* bona fide *acquirer rely on the crediting of his account (especially when acquiring* a non domino)?

Since the adoption of the Act of 14 December 2005, *bona fide* acquirers, including security takers, can assuredly rely on the crediting of their account, and are protected against competing claims of *veri domini.*

(4.2) *Is it possible for a credit in a securities account to be reversed and may transfer orders (or other instructions) be revoked?*

The reversal of entries in securities accounts is almost invariably possible on contractual grounds when the entry results from (operational) mistakes by intermediaries. Other than on those grounds, a reversal may be prompted by the insolvency of the transferor and *mala fides* on the part of the transferee. Especially since the explicit statutory application of Articles 2279 and 2280 BW to securities accountholders, *mala fide* acquisition can be successfully challenged by dispossessed third parties, provided that these transferees can be identified as such, the securities concerned have not been commingled with other securities of the same kind, and bad faith has been proven. It is submitted that, especially when the transfer has taken place through an anonymised market system, the coincidence of these circumstances is highly unlikely.

Moreover, the implementation of the EU Settlement Finality Directive has ensured the finality of the netting and settlement of securities transfers as well as orders thereto if executed or registered in the system before insolvency or in the absence of knowledge of a participant's insolvency. These finality rules however, only apply to the level of the CSD. But prior legislation already exempted transfers by or to credit and clearing institutions before insolvency or in the absence of knowledge of that institution's insolvency from the 'zero-hour' rule; Act of 22 March 1993 Article 157(1).

(5) *What are the formal requirements for the creation and enforcement of collateral?*

Book-entry securities may be pledged by transfer to a special pledge account that may be registered in the name of the pledgee or any third party, including the pledgor. As a consequence of the dispossession requirement, however, a pledgor must not remain in control of the pledged securities. Further, all previously existing formalities for the creation and enforcement of collateral have been abolished where the collateral concerns book-entry securities.

(5.1) *Is upper-tier attachment possible, i.e. is it possible for an account holder's claimant to exercise his rights against higher-tier accounts?*

KB no. 62 Article 11(1), the Act of 2 January 1991 Article 10(2) and Article 472(2) W. Venn. explicitly prohibit so-called upper-tier attachment.

5.7.2 Coherence

In the *above*, it has been shown that Belgium's securities custody and transfer law displays a relatively strong connection with general private and corporate law, as for many rules on book-entry securities, these more general areas of law are taken as a starting point. Moreover, the Belgian conception of securities custody and transfer law as the *lex specialis* of, especially, corporate law has been recently enforced by an important addition of securities law provisions to the Code of Corporate law (W. Venn.). In addition, the process that will eventually lead to the complete dematerialisation of all Belgian securities will even further increase the importance of the securities law provisions in the said code, as these provisions are specifically directed at most categories of dematerialised securities. Furthermore, the same, recent statute that initiated the dematerialisation process expressly applies some pivotal articles of the civil code to securities accountholders, who were formerly doctrinally excluded.

On the other hand, legal literature has consistently analysed securities custody and transfer law from the perspective of the law of monetary accounts, which consists of rules that traditionally derogate from commercial law. Perhaps more importantly, book-entry securities custody and transfer law derogates implicitly or explicitly from general rules of, especially, private law, with regard to some of its core elements.

Mainly as a result of recent legislation on the EU level, rules of securities law explicitly derogate from both general insolvency law and general pledge laws. First, specific, statutory provisions of securities law expressly exclude the general 'zero-hour' rule, so that insolvency proceedings against a securities intermediary do not have retroactive effect, thus ensuring the finality of transfer orders and securities transactions.

Second, although prohibited by general pledge law, the so-called *pactum commissorium* which facilitates the fiduciary transfer of collateral to a security taker is permitted by specific rules of securities law in the context of financial collateral arrangements. Moreover, general pledge law requires that pledged assets be transferred by the pledgor to the pledgee or third party ('dispossession requirement'). But pledges on book-entry securities may be created by a transfer of the collateralised securities to a special pledge account that may be registered in the name of the pledgee or any third party, including the pledgor. In even sharper contrast with the said dispossession requirement, an intermediary may now, on a statutory basis, act as either a pledgee, pledgor or third party when it has opened a pledge account on its books. It may therefore open a pledge account on its own books and be the pledgor at the same time.

However, perhaps the most radical derogation from general pledge law concerns the liberalisation of the enforcement formalities. When securities are pledged in the context of a financial collateral arrangement, no judicial intervention is no longer required, and the pledge may be enforced by a private or public sale, or even by appropriation by the pledgee, which is contrary to explicit and long-standing provisions of general private and commercial law.

Finally, the current conflict of laws rule for proprietary issues regarding book-entry securities explicitly departs from the traditional *lex rei sitae* rule, that referred to the location of the physical asset concerning which the conflict arose. With one exception, Belgian private international law now refers to the law of the place where the principal office of the intermediary is located that maintains the securities account in question.

The derogations discussed show that securities custody and transfer law shares few principles with more general areas of law. From a coherence perspective, this indicates a weakly coherent system of law, rather than incoherence. Yet incoherence can also sometimes be established, especially where the rules of book-entry securities law do not fit logically within the more general areas of law. Such logical inconsistency appears, for instance, when central elements of securities custody and transfer law cannot be unequivocally classified in private or commercial law terms.

First, a classification of the legal act of depositing bearer certificates with an intermediary, so that the depositor can become a securities accountholder, is not unequivocal. As the depositor loses ownership of his certificates, it can be classified as a common delivery to effectuate a transfer of ownership. Its consequence, however, is not a transfer of ownership, but a conversion of the depositor's ownership into a co-ownership right.

Second, the classification of the accountholder/intermediary relationship is unclear, because some elementary civil code provisions on *bewaargeving (depositum regulare)* apply, such as the intermediary's obligation of safekeeping and the eventual return of the assets in its custody, but others evidently do not. A classification as *depositum irregulare* also does not fit the *sui generis* character of the accountholder/intermediary relationship, because that classification implies a full transfer of ownership to the intermediary, which would contravene the accountholders' co-ownership rights. Finally, the precise scope of the mandate contract that complements the custody relationship is unclear and debated.

Third, accountholder interests are statutorily classified as co-ownership rights, which, under the rules of general private law, can be asserted against all third parties and relate to individualised assets. But accountholder interests relate to a notional pool of fungible assets and can only be enforced against persons other than the account provider, but only in the latter's insolvency. Although these rules are of paramount importance to the protection of accountholders' rights, they represent a logical inconsistency within the Belgian legal system as a whole, because the private law classification of co-ownership evidently does not fit the securities custody context.

Fourth, according to long-standing doctrine, general private law rules on the possession of assets, such as Articles 2279 and 2280 BW, are not applicable to entries in securities accounts or credit balances on such accounts, because they only apply to movable tangibles. Yet, as mentioned *above*, the same act that initiated the dematerialisation process expressly applies Articles 2279 and 2280 BW to the holders of entitlements to both immobilised and dematerialised securities, which therefore might be considered a logical inconsistency. But it might be argued that this extension of the scope of application of Articles 2279 and 2280 BW represents an abandonment of the principle that these provisions only apply to movable tangibles.

Moreover, it has been argued previously that specific rules of securities transfer law show a discrepancy with the rules of general private law, as the former prescribe that a securities transfer becomes effective when the transferee's account is credited, while the latter are generally interpreted so as to imply that fungible securities are transferred when cleared by the CCP or CSD. This discrepancy might therefore be considered to constitute an intrinsic contradiction.

Finally, it can be questioned whether the special position of clearing and settlement institutions is justified, where they can obtain a broad statutory preference over their participants' accounts, which includes the assets of participants' clients. Other intermediaries cannot vest such an extensive lien and, as a consequence, the position of accountholders depends on whether their account provider holds its omnibus accounts with a (Belgian) CSD that vested such lien. Especially because accountholders cannot evidently ascertain that they are subject to these derogatory rules of clearing and settlement systems, the special rules might be considered to create an unjust dichotomy or *Wertungswiderspruch* and thus represent an instance of incoherence.

In sum, Belgian law has created a very modern and clearly successful legal infrastructure for the custody and transfer of book-entry securities. Accountholders are, overall, well protected and the (legal) certainty of the settlement system seems ensured. But the relationship of book-entry securities custody and transfer law with more general areas of the law is often weakly coherent and sometimes incoherent, in spite of recent legislative amendments.

Chapter 6
France

6.1 INTRODUCTION

6.1.1 Trading, Clearing and Settlement

On 24 September 1724, the stock exchange of Paris was founded, and to this day, it has continued to be operative, albeit with some interruptions.[1] Until 22 January 1988, the agents that operated on the seven French stock exchanges were organised as a national company, the *Compagnie des Agents de Change.*[2] On that date, the *Loi sur les bourses de valeurs* transformed the company, renamed it *Société des Bourses Françaises* ('SBF'), and replaced its agents by member-firms.[3] On 1 June 1999, SBF merged with the *Société du Nouveau Marché,* which is open to high-growth companies, Matif SA (interest-rate futures and options) and Monep SA (futures and options on equities and equity indexes). In its turn, this new group, now named ParisBourse SA, merged in September 2000 with the Euronext Group to form Euronext Paris.[4] Other than the regulated markets *Bourse de Paris,* Matif, Monep and the *Nouveau Marché,* Euronext Paris manages the unregulated *Marché*

1. The Paris exchange, however, is by far not the oldest exchange in France, as the Lyon Bourse was founded in around 1540. *See* <www.euronext.com>.
2. The other exchanges were located in Lyon, Bordeaux, Marseille, Lille, Nantes and Nancy.
3. Stock Market Reform Act no. 88–70.
4. As a recent development, Euronext and the New York Stock Exchange announced on 2 June 2006 a merger of the two companies, thus forming the world's largest and first transatlantic exchange. At the time of writing however, the merger had not yet taken full effect; *see* <www.euronext.com> *and infra,* Ch. 9.3.2.

Libre. As for the whole Euronext Group, LCH.Clearet SA performs the central clearing functioning as the central counterparty ('CCP').[5]

During the War, on 18 June 1941, the deposit of French securities was centralised, and all securities had to be transferred to the *Caisse centrale de dépôts et virements de titres* ('CCDVT'), a centralisation which created the possibility of securities transfer by book-entry. After the War, the mandatory character of deposit with this central securities depository ('CSD') was undone,[6] but the CCDVT remained in service as a facultative central depository.[7] On 6 February 1950, a new institution called the *Société interprofessionnelle pour la compensation des valeurs mobilières* ('SICOVAM') took over. SICOVAM was taken over in its turn by Euroclear Bank in 2001 and became Euroclear France. At the time of writing, Euroclear France is France's only CSD, and it maintains links with (among others) the foreign CSDs Clearstream Bank Frankfurt, OeKB of Austria, Euroclear Bank Belgium, CADE and SCLV of Spain, APK of Finland, Monte Titoli of Italy and Clearstream Bank Luxembourg.[8]

6.1.2 *Sedes Materiae*

Although, generally, the French legal system, and French private law in particular is not considered as a strictly hierarchical structure consisting of different branches of law, commercial law is regarded as *droit d'exception* (exceptional law) and its adjudication is performed by special courts, known as *tribunaux de commerce.* Rules of commercial law apply to a certain issue, either because of the nature of the issue, or because of the legal status of the actors, i.e. because they are classified as *commerçants* (businessmen). If the issue is not governed by the rules of commercial law, it is governed by the general rules of private law, to be found in the *Code civil* (Civil Code, 'C. civ'.).

Most issues concerning securities are considered to be commercial law issues and are therefore governed by the *Code de Commerce* (Commercial Code, 'C. com'.), even if the matter is an issue between *non-commerçants.*[9] But many securities-related issues are also specifically governed by the *Code monétaire et financier* (Monetary and Financial Code, 'C. mon. fin'.),[10] which has codified a great deal of prior decrees and acts.[11] Among them, most importantly, is the act

5. In February 2001, the *Banque Centrale de Compensation* (Central Clearinghouse Bank) Clearnet SA merged with the CCPs of the Amsterdam and Belgium markets. On 22 December 2003, London Clearing House ('LCH') merged with Clearnet and the group now technically consists of LCH.Clearnet SA and LCH.Clearnet Limited. *See* <www.euroclear.com> *and cf.* Ch. 5.1.1.
6. Art. 26 of Act no. 49-874 of 5 July 1949.
7. Art. 46 of Act no. 49-981 of 22 July 1949 and Decree no. 49-1105 of 4 August 1949.
8. Giovannini Group 2001 Report, 25. *See also* Euroclear France 2003 Disclosure Framework, 16, for a full listing of Euroclear France's direct and indirect links with foreign institutions.
9. *See* Ripert & Roblot II (1996), nos. 1732 and 1734.
10. Enacted by Ordinance 2000-1223 of 14 December 2000.
11. *But cf.* Reigné & Delorme (2001), 214–218.

that resulted in the dematerialisation of all French securities[12] and the *Loi de la modernisation des activités financiers* (Financial Modernisation Act, 'MAF').[13] More recently, the C. mon. fin. has been modified by the *Loi de sécurité financière* (Financial Security Act) of 2003,[14] Ordinance no. 2004-604 of 24 June 2004 and the ordinance that implements the EU Financial Collateral Directive.[15]

Other than by the *Code monétaire et financier,* the *Code de commerce* and the *Code civil,* French securities custody and transfer law is formed by the *Règlement Général* (General Regulations) of the *Autorité des marchés financiers* ('AMF').[16] These regulations, drafted on a statutory basis, were approved by the French Minister of Finance on 12 October 2004.[17] In sum, issues that are not governed by what is known as *droit commun,* i.e. *droit civil* and *droit commercial,* are governed by provisions of the *Code monétaire et financier* and by specific regulations such as the *Règlement Général* AMF.

6.1.3 Complete Dematerialisation

Article 94 II of the dematerialisation act just mentioned[18] resulted in the most striking feature of modern French securities law: the mandatory and statutory dematerialisation of almost all securities issued in France under French law. As a consequence, the volume of physical certificates that investors, financial intermediaries or CSD now hold, is negligible.[19] The act came into force on 3 November 1984,[20] and was enacted mainly to reduce costs and improve banking services, as it was estimated that dematerialisation could reduce the costs of custody by 40 per cent

12. Act no. 81-1160 of 30 December 1981.
13. Act no. 96-597 of 2 July 1996.
14. Act no. 2003-706 of 1 August 2003.
15. Ordinance no. 2005-171 of 24 February 2005. The EU Settlement Finality Directive has been implemented through Act no. 2001-420 of 15 May 2001.
16. On 24 November 2003, the *Conseil des marchés financiers* ('CMF') and the *Commission des opérations de bourse* ('COB') merged to form the AMF, pursuant to the Financial Security Act no. 2003-706 of 1 August 2003. The securities custody law provisions of the *Règlement Général* of the AMF are taken from the *Règlement Général* of the CMF, which, in turn, was part of the *Règlement Général* of SICOVAM.
17. Art. L. 621-6, together with Art. L. 621-7 C. mon. fin. represents that statutory basis. For the AMF's power to regulate securities custody, *see* especially Art. L. 621-7 IV(1) and L. 621-7 VI C. mon. fin.
18. The provision referred to is now codified as Art. L. 211-4 C. mon. fin. *Cf.* Art. L. 228-1 C. com.
19. Only very specific types of securities, issued before 3 November 1984, viz. *obligations amortissable par tirage au sort de numéros de titres* and *rentes perpétuelles sur l'État* are excluded from dematerialisation; Art. L. 211-4 fourth paragraph C. mon. fin. Also not dematerialised are warrants, the majority of euro-bonds and foreign securities. *See* Euroclear France 2002 Disclosure Framework, p. 5.
20. Via Decree no. 83-359 of 2 May 1983.

to 45 per cent.[21] The dematerialisation was radical, because it was mandatory and irreversible, for all investors who possessed physical certificates were obliged to deposit them with a financial intermediary. Moreover, because the delivery of securities in physical form from an intermediary to a client is not allowed under French law, the change of custody from the possession of certificates by the investors themselves into entitlements to a securities account was irreversible.[22]

Although the dematerialisation was originally only envisaged as a technical improvement, it led to the re-evaluation of almost all central notions of French securities law, notably because the dematerialisation caused securities to lose individuality and to become 'rigorously' fungible,[23] as all securities of the same sort became interchangeable.[24] As a dogmatic consequence, the moment of transfer, the classification of the relationship between investor and custodian and even the legal nature of securities themselves became subjects of discussion in the legal literature, while case law did not provide definitive answers either.[25]

Especially because of this dematerialisation and the doctrinal debates it sparked, the following sections will analyse in greater detail the current French legal infrastructure for the custody and transfer of securities, as well as its relationship with more general areas of law. First, the main doctrinal distinctions with regard to financial instruments will be discussed. In the section that follows, legal aspects of securities custody will be analysed, with particular emphasis on securities accounts, the accountholder/intermediary relationship and the consequences of intermediary insolvencies. In Sections 4 and 5 of this chapter, the transfer of securities by book-entry, and the creation and enforcement of security interests in securities will subsequently be discussed. Section 6 will deal with French private international law concerning securities custody and transfer. The chapter will conclude with answers to the questions posed in Chapter 1.2.2 and a coherence analysis.

6.2 CATEGORIES OF SECURITIES

On the precise scope of the term *valeurs mobilières* (securities) and its relation to the term *instruments financiers* (financial instruments), no general doctrinal

21. Ripert & Roblot (1996), no. 1758. Moreover, the act greatly facilitated centralised income taxation; Bonneau & Drummond (2005), no. 86.
22. De Vauplane & Bornet (2001), nos. 42 and 221. But foreign investors may request the delivery of French securities in certificated form (then called *certificats représentatives d' actions)* in their own jurisdiction.
23. *See* Art. 9 Decree no. 49-1105 of 4 August 1949, Act no. 81-1160 of 30 December 1981 *and,* e.g., Cass. 1re civ., 28 May 1991, *Bull. Joly,* August-September 1991, p. 813, no. 290.
24. Ripert & Roblot II (1996), no. 1738 *and* De Vauplane & Bornet (2001), no. 51. But some controversy exists as to what exactly must be considered to constitute securities *of the same sort,* i.e., whether it refers to securities of the same issue or to the same 'category'; *see* De Vauplane & Bornet (2001), no. 51, n.51.
25. *See,* e.g., Annexes VIII.6, VIII.8, VIII.9, VIII.11, VIII.12, VIII.14 and VIII.17 of the CNCT 1997 Report *and cf.* Bonneau & Drummond (2005), no. 232.

consensus exists. Although Article L. 211-2 C. mon. fin. provides a definition of *valeurs mobilières,* the meaning and scope of that definition remain unclear, as it derives from Act no. 88-1201 of 23 December 1988 Article 1, which was drafted for the sole purpose of that specific act, directed at certain collective investment funds. But while the legal nature and common characteristics of *valeurs mobilières* have been fiercely debated,[26] the only characteristic that seems to be generally accepted is tradability on a stock exchange.[27]

It is also generally agreed that *instruments financiers* include *valeurs mobilières.* As Article L. 211-1 I C. mon. fin. points out, *instruments financiers* include *actions* (equities), *titres de créance* (bonds) and *parts ou actions d'organismes de placements collectifs* (equities in collective investment funds).[28] These three categories are considered *valeurs mobilières,*[29] but *instruments financiers* also refer to, e.g., *instruments financiers à terme* (options, floors, caps etc.).[30]

Regarding *valeurs mobilières,* the main distinction to be made is between *titres au porteur* and *titres nominatifs.* As to investors' anonymity towards the issuer, *titres au porteur* resemble bearer securities, whereas *titres nominatifs purs* are directly registered in the investors' names with the issuer or its mandatary. *Titres au porteur,* on the other hand, are registered with a participant of the CSD in the investor's name, and ultimately with the CSD in the participant's name.[31] The distinction between *titres nominatifs* and *titres au porteur* thus lies in the anonymity of the ultimate investor towards the issuer: the investor is anonymous towards the issuer in the case of *titres au porteur,* whilst he is known to the issuer in the case of *titres nominatifs.* The distinction also lies in the entity responsible for maintaining the securities account vis-à-vis the investor: a financial intermediary is responsible for maintaining the securities account in the case of *titres au porteur,* whilst the issuer is responsible for maintaining the securities account in the case *of titres nominatifs.*[32]

Dematerialised *titres au porteur* may thus be classified as bearer securities, although they do not exist in a certificated form. Non-dematerialised *titres au porteur*

---

26. *See* De Vauplane & Bornet (2001), nos. 40 and 43-55 *and* Couret & Le Nabasque (2004), 182–183 and the references provided there.
27. *See* Art. L. 228-1 C. com.
28. Art. L. 211-1 I(1), Art. L. 211-1 I(2) and Art. L. 211-1 I(3) C. mon. fin. respectively.
29. *See* Couret & Le Nabasque (2004), 182 *and cf.* Ripert & Roblot I-2 (2002), no. 1772.
30. Art. L. 211-1 II C. mon. fin.
31. With respect to *valeurs mobilières,* another main distinction could be drawn between *actions* (equities) and *créances généraux* (bonds); Art. L. 211-2 C. mon. fin. But some authors have considered this divide to be artificial, because many mix forms exist which have nonetheless been governed by the same rules of law since 1985. *See,* e.g. De Vauplane & Bornet (2001), no. 41. The distinction, however, will appear to be relevant when considering conflict of laws rules regarding non-dematerialised securities.
32. Also, mix forms exist as some *titres nominatifs* come with coupons payable *au porteur* for interest or dividend; Art. 5 of Decree no. 55-1595 of 7 December 1955. Moreover, securities are interchangeable; *titres nominatifs* may always be changed into *titres au porteur* (if titres nominatifs are not mandatory by articles of association or law) and *titres au porteur* may always be changed to *titres nominatifs;* arts. 34 and 53 of Decree no. 55-1595 of 7 December 1955.

on the other hand, are represented either by a single certificate or global, which may be temporary or permanent, or by multiple physical notes. These notes come with a main leaf on which a *numéro d'ordre* (individual number) is written and with a leaf of coupons. The coupons themselves are also considered *titres au porteur.*[33]

Titres nominatifs purs are registered securities in a strict sense, in that they are registered by the issuer. *Titres nominatifs administrés* are registered securities also, but with a financial intermediary acting on behalf of and as a representative of the issuer.[34] Prior to the transfer *of titres nominatifs purs* on a stock exchange, they must be changed into *titres nominatifs adminstrés,* provided this change is not prohibited by law or the issuer's articles of association.[35]

All securities which are not mandatory *nominatifs* by law or articles of association are necessarily *au porteur.* In some instances, the legislature has required that securities be issued in the form of *titres nominatifs.*[36] Article L. 212-3 C. mon. fin., for instance, provides that securities not admitted to a regulated exchange must be *nominatifs,* but this requirement does not apply to securities admitted by the CSD to the central system of custody.[37] An issuer's articles of association, on the other hand, may allow its investors to choose the form of the securities issued – or part of the issue.[38] This is known as an *émission occasionnellement nominative* (occasionally registered issue). The articles of association may also create the possibility for the issuer to request the CSD to communicate the identity of the owners of the *titres au porteur.*[39] These *titres au porteur* are then called *titres au porteur identifiable.*

6.3 CUSTODY OF BOOK-ENTRY SECURITIES

6.3.1 Introduction

Between the Second World War and the dematerialisation of the 1980s, bearer securities were held at three levels: by the investors themselves, by intermediaries, and by the CSD. With the dematerialisation, the first layer was eliminated and a two-layered structure remained.[40] But the direct holding of *titres nominatifs* was retained and the current French system of securities custody therefore consists of both direct and indirect elements. *Titres nominatifs* are now registered in securities

33. Ripert & Roblot (1996), no. 1775.
34. Art. 332-59 *Règlement Général* AMF. Conversely, intermediaries holding *titres nominatifs administrés* have been considered to act as representatives of their clients vis-à-vis the issuer; Bonneau & Drummond (2005), no. 88.
35. Art. L. 228-1 C. com. *See* Ripert & Roblot II (1996), no. 1796.
36. *See* Ripert & Roblot I-2 (2002), no. 1524 for a complete listing of securities *nominatifs* by law. Mandatory rules on the different types of securities have recently changed; *see* Couret & Le Nabasque (2004), 184.
37. Art. L. 211-4 second paragraph C. mon. fin.
38. Art. L. 228-1 C. com. *See also* Couret & Le Nabasque (2004), 184.
39. Art. L. 228-2 I C. com.
40. The very few sorts of securities which remained un-dematerialised, however, can still be held by investors; Art. L. 211-4 fourth paragraph C. mon. fin.

accounts maintained by the issuer or its mandatary, while dematerialised *titres au porteur* are registered in securities accounts held by financial intermediaries and the CSD. Thus, since all securities are dematerialised, both the direct and the indirect holding of securities involve the registration of accountholders' interests and securities transfers by book-entries in securities accounts.

In addition, both financial intermediaries and issuers may have recourse to third parties to maintain their securities accounts via an agreement of *mandat de conservation* (custody mandate). The third party's/mandatee's obligation to separate the mandator's own assets from the mandator's clients' assets is part of this agreement, while in the CSD's accounting, the mandatee's own assets should be separated from his clients' assets, i.e. the assets of the mandator and his clients.[41] Furthermore, the mandator's liability vis-à-vis his clients remains unaffected by the mandate.[42] As a result, the number of (sub-)custodians and thus the length of the chain of custody has no legal consequences with respect to the investor's securities entitlements.

According to the AMF, *tenue de compte conservation* or intermediated custody of securities involves, for the intermediary concerned, the duty to register financial instruments in the name of their entitlement holder, and to preserve the corresponding assets.[43] As a general rule, any institution may offer that service,[44] but securities accounts may only be maintained by the categories of institutions listed in Article L. 542-1 C. mon. fin.[45]

In the following sections, several aspects of securities custody will be discussed. First, some further introductory remarks on the structure of intermediated securities custody in France will be made, followed by a discussion of the custody of non-dematerialised bearer securities and *titres nominatifs,* mainly in relation to intermediated securities custody. Then, some specific aspects of intermediated securities custody will be addressed, such as (the classification of) the accountholder/intermediary relationship, (the classification of) the nature of accountholder interests and intermediary insolvencies and the treatment of shortfalls.

6.3.2 Structure of Intermediated Custody

In general, the AMF supervises the custody and transfer of securities in France, and a CSD can perform its task only after the AMF's consent.[46] Eligible for

41. Arts. 332-4 and 332-39 *Règlement Général* AMF.
42. Art. 332-40 *Règlement Général* AMF. *Cf.* De Vauplane & Bornet (2001), no. 99-1 and Clément *in* CNCT 1997 Report, 251.
43. Art. 312-6 *Règlement Général* AMF.
44. Art. L. 531-1 C. mon. fin. 'Main services', on the other hand, may only be offered by admitted participants to the CSD; Art. L. 321-1 C. mon. fin. (the service of securities custody is statutorily considered a 'secondary' service; Art. L. 321-2 C. mon. fin.).
45. This article has only recently been enacted by the Financial Security Act no. 2003-706 of 1 August 2003.
46. Art. L. 621-7 VI(2) C. mon. fin. Although the law thus provides for the possibility of multiple CSDs, Euroclear France is France's only CSD at the time of writing.

admission to the CSD's central system of custody are investment firms being subject to the Investment Services Directive,[47] the *Banque de France,* issuers whose securities are admitted to Euroclear France and national and international CSDs.[48] The admission of intermediaries to the CSD's system is supervised by the AMF and all intermediaries have to comply with the *Règlement Général* AMF. These rules regulate both the relationship between the intermediaries and the CSD, and the intermediaries' maintaining of securities accounts for their clients.[49] Other than by the *Règlement Général* AMF, the relationship between intermediaries and the CSD is also regulated by the *Règles de Fonctionnement d' Euroclear France,* which is approved by the AMF.[50]

Eligible for admission by Euroclear France are all French securities as defined under Articles L. 211-1(1), L. 211-1(2) and L. 211-1(3) C. mon. fin.,[51] while foreign securities may be admitted as long as they are compatible with French book-entry securities.[52] Furthermore, securities are admitted *ex officio* if they are listed at a regulated French exchange and are transferable by book-entry only, pursuant to a rule of law or issuing rules. Derivatives cannot be admitted to the central system of custody.[53] Custody of securities which are not admitted to the central system takes place more or less similarly to the custody of securities which are deposited with Euroclear France.[54]

Ripert & Roblot have described the CSD's three main tasks as follows:[55] to assure the circulation of securities, to guarantee the security of the system as a whole and to control the regularity of book-entries in accounts.[56] Euroclear France assures the circulation of securities by facilitating securities transfer by book-entry between clients of different financial intermediaries. For this purpose, all admitted intermediaries maintain omnibus accounts in their own names with the CSD, which accounts represent all securities the intermediaries' clients are entitled to.[57] Euroclear France guarantees the security of the custody system as a whole by monitoring, per category of securities, whether the intermediaries' omnibus

47. Council Directive 93/22/EEC of 10 May 1993 on investment services in the securities field (OJ L 141/1).
48. *Cf.* Art. 2.1 *Règles de Fonctionnement d' Euroclear France and* the listing by De Vauplane & Bornet (2001), no. 224.
49. Especially book V, title IV and book III, title III, chapter II, respectively.
50. Art. L. 621-7 VI(2) C. mon. fin. *See also* Auckenthaler (2004), 287–289.
51. Art. 1.1 *Règles de Fonctionnement d'Euroclear France. See also* Arts. 3.1 and 3.2 *Règles de Fonctionnement d'Euroclear France and* Arts. 540-1 and 312-6 *Règlement Général* AMF.
52. De Vauplane & Bornet (2001), no. 226. Euroclear France is the custodian of foreign non-dematerialised securities which are listed at Euronext Paris; De Vauplane & Bornet (2001), no. 227.
53. De Vauplane & Bornet (2001), no. 99-2.
54. *See* Ripert & Roblot (1996), nos. 1818–1822. Not-admitted *titres nominatifs* of small companies are subject to a special regime.
55. Ripert & Roblot (1996), no. 1813. *Cf.* Bonneau & Drummond (2005), no. 231.
56. For a full listing of the CSD's tasks, *see* Art. 540-1 *Règlement Général* AMF.
57. Separated from these accounts are the accounts representing the intermediaries' own securities; Art. 332-4 *Règlement Général* AMF.

accounts match the total amount of securities issued, and the CSD registers this total in a special account *(compte Émission).*[58] Finally, the CSD controls the regularity of their participants' bookkeeping through monitoring, per intermediary, whether the intermediaries' omnibus accounts match the total of securities to which the intermediaries' clients are entitled.

Thus, Euroclear France is responsible for the proper functioning of the settlement system, which further includes ensuring the irrevocability of transfers, all in accordance with the *Règlement Général* AMF and under the supervision of the AMF.[59] Also, the CSD facilitates the payment of dividends and interests by the issuer to the financial intermediaries concerned, while dividends and interests on *titres nominatifs purs* are theoretically paid directly by the issuer to the investor. But as the maintenance of the issuer's register or securities accounts are usually mandated to one or more financial intermediaries, the payment of interests and dividends is also most often performed by these intermediaries.[60]

6.3.3 NON-DEMATERIALISED *TITRES AU PORTEUR* AND *TITRES NOMINATIFS*

6.3.3.1 Historic Background

Under the influence of German legal thinking, French doctrine in the late 19th century deemed bearer securities to incorporate investors' rights vis-à vis the issuer.[61] In the same vein, the issuer's register came to be considered as incorporating investors' rights, or at least to provide absolute proof of the investors' ownership.[62] As a consequence, both *titres nominatifs* and *titres au porteur* were considered to incorporate, as *res corporales* (movable tangibles), investors' rights against the issuer.

Because the dematerialisation of the 1980s was originally intended to constitute only a technical measure, doctrine remained to considered securities as *res corporales.* A credit entry in a securities account or a credit balance was therefore considered to provide the accountholder with possession of his securities, but because of the highly fictional nature of this approach, it is fiercely contested in the legal literature.[63] To non-dematerialised bearer securities, however, it is still generally thought to be applicable.

---

58. RIPERT & ROBLOT (1996), no. 1816 *and* BONNEAU & DRUMMOND (2005), no. 231.
59. Arts. L. 330-1 and L. 621-7 VI(3) C. mon. fin.
60. *See* arts. 5 and 38 of Decree no. 55-1595 of 7 December 1955. *See also* RIPERT & ROBLOT (1996), no. 1815, RIPERT & ROBLOT (1996), no. 1801 *and cf.* DE VAUPLANE & BORNET (2001), no. 100 *and* BONNEAU & DRUMMOND (2005), no. 231.
61. DE VAUPLANE & BORNET (2001), no. 47-1 *and see supra,* Ch. 3.2.1.
62. DE VAUPLANE & BORNET, no. 47-1.
63. *See* DE VAUPLANE & BORNET (2001), no. 47-2 and the references provided there, *and* BONNEAU & DRUMMOND (2005), no. 90. *But cf.* MARTIN (1996) *and* MAFFEI (2005).

6.3.3.2 Non-Dematerialised *Titres Au Porteur*

The overwhelming majority *of titres au porteur* that remain in existence in a physical form are foreign securities and euro-bonds, immobilised in the vaults of Euroclear France.[64] The rest consist of the very few categories of *titres au porteur* that were excluded from the general dematerialisation, and these securities may still be held by investors themselves.[65]

When bearer certificates are deposited with an intermediary so as to be replaced by a securities account, the individuality of the certificates is lost and so is the entitlement holder's right of ownership.[66] However, because the civil code provisions on *dépôt régulier (depositum regulare)* are applied to the investor – intermediary relationship by law, neither the depositee/intermediary, nor the CSD becomes the owner of the securities deposited.[67] Moreover, the deposit does not affect the depositor's prior rights against the issuer and other parties, and the accountholder retains a right of revendication in the custodian's insolvency.[68] Yet a construct of co-ownership is generally rejected, and the *Code civil* does not recognise a *depositum regulare* of fungibles that involves the loss of a depositor's ownership, as it requires that a custodian should deliver the deposited assets *in specie* upon the depositor's request; Article 1932 C. civ.[69] The approach of the French legislator has therefore not been considered to be very coherent.[70]

Directly held, non-dematerialised bearer securities are transferred by physical delivery, or by endorsement in the case of order certificates; Article L. 511-8 C. com. Indirectly held, non-dematerialised *titres au porteur* that have been deposited with the CSD, are transferred through debit and credit entries in the transferor's and transferee's securities accounts, respectively. Provided that the transferee has acted in a *bona fide* manner, the *Chambre commercial de la Cour de Cassation* (Commercial Chamber of the Supreme Court, 'Cass. com'.) has held that a defect in the *causa* of the transfer does not invalidate the transfer of ownership.[71]

Moreover, transferees, as well as pledgees, of such securities are virtually fully protected against competing claims by third parties asserting a revendication right. In theory, these parties, who may have been dispossessed by loss or fraud, can successfully assert a revendication right, but they must first be able to identify

64. Euroclear France 2002 Disclosure Framework, p. 5.
65. *See supra,* n. 16.
66. Ripert & Roblot II (1976), no. 1764.
67. Art. 11 of Decree no. 49-1105 of 4 August 1949. It reads: '(...) the interprofessional institution's [i.e. the CSD's, MH] obligations and responsibility of restitution vis-à-vis its participants, as well as these participants' [obligations and responsibility of restitution, MH] vis-à-vis the depositors are regulated by the provisions regarding the custodian's obligations as stated by the Civil Code [i.e. the provisions on *dépôt]'*. The services which an intermediary provides, other than safe deposit, are considered in the light of an additional contract of *mandat* (mandate); Ripert & Roblot (1996), no. 1789.
68. *See* Art. 12 of Decree no. 49-1105 of 4 August 1949.
69. *See also infra,* s. 6.3.4.
70. Ripert & Roblot II (1976), nos. 1764.
71. Cass. com., 18 October 1994, *Bull. Joly,* December 1994,1296, no. 362.

the third party transferee (which is highly unlikely in the anonymised context of the present stock markets), and then have to repay the *bona fide* transferee the price which the latter has paid, provided the securities were bought at a stock exchange; Article 2280 C. civ.[72]

A pledge on non-dematerialised *titres au porteur* is created in the same way as a transfer of ownership is effectuated, i.e. by physical delivery if the securities concerned are held by investors themselves, and through credit and debit entries in the securities accounts of, respectively, the pledgee and pledgor, if the securities concerned are held by Euroclear France.

6.3.3.3 *Titres Nominatifs*

Legally, the dematerialisation has not had much effect on the custody of *titres nominatifs,* although they are no longer registered in the issuer's register, but are now credited to securities accounts maintained by the issuer or its mandatary. The most important change, however, is that *titres nominatifs* used to be transferred through the deletion of the transferor's name in the issuer's register, and a subsequent new issue of the same quantity and quality of securities to the transferee.[73]

Although, strictly speaking, *titres nominatifs* were thus de-registered and reissued, such a 'transfer' was considered to constitute a transfer in the general private law sense, which implies that ownership is transferred the moment parties agree on the price and object of the sale; arts. 1591 and 1583 C. civ.[74] However, prior to the change of the entitlement holder's name in the issuer's books (whether or not this is a register of securities accounts), a transfer of ownership is not effective, i.e. it cannot be asserted against the issuer and third parties.

As with non-dematerialised *titres au porteur,* imperfections regarding an agreement to transfer *titres nominatifs* do not invalidate its proprietary consequences, since from a property law perspective, it is the issuer who effectuates the de-registration and re-issue (or debit and credit entries), and the issuer has no material interest in the transferor and transferee's contractual relationship.[75] But in contrast to non-dematerialised *titres au porteur,* it is seriously debated and uncertain whether a transferee of *titres nominatifs* takes free of all third party claims,

72. In such instance, the dispossessed owner thus can challenge an accountholder's right of ownership with either Euroclear France or with the issuer (upper-tier attachment), and the challenge results in the 'freezing' of the securities concerned; Decree no. 56-27 of 11 January 1956. All transactions prior to the challenge, on the other hand, remain unaffected, as arts. 2279 and 2280 C. civ. apply. *See* Ripert & Roblot (1996), no. 1778.
73. Ripert & Roblot (1996), nos. 1761, 1764 and 1765.
74. *Cf.* Cass. com., 23 November 1993, *Dr. sociétés,* February 1994, p. 18, no. 41.
75. Ripert & Roblot (1996), no. 1765.

most notably of a dispossessed *verus dominus.*[76] In addition, between transferor and transferee, the transferee's acquired interest remains subject to challenge.[77]

A pledge on *titres nominatifs* is created through a *transfert de garantie,* registered in the issuer's books; Article L. 521-1 C. com.[78] Although the *Cour de Cassation* has held that a pledge may be performed in any other way,[79] legal authors generally maintain that a *transfert de garantie* can only be effectuated on the issuer's book, i.e. similar to a transfer of ownership.[80]

6.3.4 Accountholder/Intermediary Relationship

As mentioned above, the dematerialisation of almost all French securities led to the re-evaluation of the central notions of French securities law, including the relationship between the accountholder and intermediary.[81] On the obligations of an intermediary vis-à-vis his clients/accountholders, however, general consensus exists. In the following section, these obligations will be discussed first, after which the classification of the accountholder/intermediary relationship will be examined.

The *Code monétaire et financier* clearly defines an intermediary's obligations, and further refers to the *Règlement Général* AMF provisions on the maintenance of securities accounts.[82] These rules combined, an intermediary's main obligations can be listed as follows:[83]

- An intermediary has a general obligation to preserve the securities in its custody.[84] The rule that intermediaries are forbidden to use and transfer the securities to which their clients are entitled *(prohibition de tirage sur la*

76. *See* Ripert & Roblot (1996), no. 1766 *and* Bonneau & Drummond (2005), no. 91. *Affirmative:* Reygrobellet (1999), 314–315, Martin (1996) *and* Maffei (2005). *See also infra,* s. 6.3.5.
77. *See,* e.g., Cass. com., 24 January 1989, *Bull. Joly,* March 1989, p. 266, no. 85; Paris, 25 October 1991, *Dr. sociétés,* 1992, no. 1138, as cited by J.-C. Hallouin in his annotation of Cass. com., 18 October 1994, *Bull. Joly,* December 1994, p. 1296, no. 362 *and* Cass. com., 22 October 2002, *Rev. sociétés,* July-September 2003, p. 511, all cases in which ownership was successfully challenged by counterparties.
78. Technicalities are specified in Art. 35, paragraph 3 of Decree no. 55-1595 of 7 December 1955.
79. Cass. Com. 5 November 1977, *RTD com.,* 1979, p. 259. *Cf.* Art. L. 521-1 C. com., which determines that 'a pledge of securities may *also* be created by registration by the issuer'.
80. *See* Ripert & Roblot (1996), no. 1768 *and infra,* s. 6.5.3.
81. *Cf.* Bonneau & Drummond (2005), no. 232.
82. Arts. L. 533-1 *et seq.* C. mon. fin. Art. L. 533-9 C. mon. fin. refers to the *Règlement Général* AMF, which addresses securities custody law mainly in its book III, title III, Chapter II. That Chapter contains the so-called *cahier des charges du teneur de comptes conservateur* (book of obligations of a securities account provider). Other provisions are to be found in, e.g., arts. 321-69, 321-71, 321-74 and 321-75, which represent technical requirements for the custody agreement between the financial intermediary and accountholder.
83. *Cf.* Maffei (2005), 243 *and see* Gavalda & Stoufflet (2002), no. 751 on the custody of non-dematerialised securities.
84. *Cf.* Art. 312-6 *Règlement Général* AMF.

masse) is generally considered to result from that obligation; Article L. 533-7 C. mon. fin.[85] and Article 332-4(2) *Règlement Général* AMF.[86] A violation of this prohibition is considered an *abus de confiance* (abuse of trust) and sanctioned according to criminal law; Article L. 314-1 *Code pénal* (Criminal Code).[87]

- An intermediary is obliged to prevent the loss of the assets in its custody and maintain stringent book-keeping; Article 332-4(1) *Règlement Général* AMF.
- An intermediary should inform its clients of corporate actions, so that they can enforce the rights attached to their securities, such as voting rights; Article 332-4(1) *Règlement Général* AMF.[88]
- An intermediary must be able to return the securities in its custody at all time. With regard to dematerialised securities, effectuation of this obligation involves a transfer of securities to another intermediary; Article 332-4(3) *Règlement Général* AMF. But an intermediary has a retention right concerning these securities if its client(s) do not fulfil their obligations; *cf.* Article L. 431-4 C. mon fin.
- An intermediary should separate its own assets from its clients' assets, both on its own books, and in its accounts with the CSD (an obligation which also applies to the intermediary that has mandated the maintenance of securities accounts to a sub-custodian); Article 332-4 *Règlement Général* AMF.

Further to the obligations just listed, it has been questioned how the accountholder – intermediary relationship should be classified. In the following, four possible private law classifications are examined, all of which have been suggested as the most appropriate classification in legal literature. First, three *contrats nommés* will be examined, and finally a *contrat innommé,* or *sui generis* contract.[89] But whatever the classification may be, freedom of contract is reduced to an important extent, as the conclusion of a custody contract with an intermediary is mandatory

---

85. Art. L. 533-7 C. mon. fin. reads: 'Investment firms and – in some cases – (legal) persons mentioned in art. L. 421-8 protect the investors' rights of ownership as to the financial instruments of which they maintain the accounts. They may not use these securities for their own account but with the investor's explicit consent'. *Cf.* Art. 10 Investment Services Directive (Council Directive 93/22/EEC of 10 May 1993 on investment services in the securities field (OJ L 141/1)). With the investor's explicit consent, a custodian's use of deposited assets thus remains possible under a contract of *prêt de consommation. Cf.* Ghozi *in* CNCT 1997 Report, 199-200 *and see infra,* s. 6.5.2.
86. De Vauplane & Bornet (2001), no. 979. *Cf. also* Art. 332-6 *Règlement Général* AMF .
87. *See* De Vauplane & Bornet (2001), nos. 1144–1150.
88. *See also* De Vauplane & Bornet (2001), no. 99-4 and nos. 978-983.
89. *See,* e.g., Malaurie, Aynès & Gautier (2001), nos. 5 *et seq. and* Huet (2001), no. 8.C. and the references provided there.

and its content is almost non-negotiable. Such a contract is called a *contrat imposé* (compulsory contract).[90]

Securities custody has traditionally been viewed in the light of the contract of *dépôt,* and thus considered to be regulated by arts. 1915 *et seq.* C. civ. That position has been grounded on statute and case law,[91] but these sources date either from the pre-dematerialisation period, or refer to a single criminal law judgment, which has been argued to have no value in any private law discussion.[92] Other than the safekeeping of securities, the services rendered by an intermediary in its capacity as the investor's representative (e.g. in the context of the intermediary's relationship with the CSD or issuer) are traditionally viewed in the light of the contract of *mandat.*[93]

The general private law contract of *dépôt* has four characteristics that are relevant to the securities custody context:[94] the assets deposited must be *choses mobilières* (movable assets); Article 1918 C. civ., a deposit must occur through *tradition réelle* (physical delivery); Article 1919 C. civ., the custodian has an obligation of safekeeping concerning deposited assets; Article 1915 C. civ. and the custodian has an obligation of restitution concerning the deposited assets *in specie*; Article 1932 C. civ. Many agree that the main characteristic of *dépôt,* i.e. the safekeeping/preservation of assets deposited, evidently applies to securities custody.[95] But it is highly contested whether dematerialised securities could classify as movable assets.[96] A custodian's obligation of restitution, on the other hand, arguably accords with a securities intermediary's obligation of restitution, albeit that dematerialised securities cannot be delivered *in specie.*[97] Finally, Article 1930 C. civ. provides that under the contract of *dépôt,* a custodian may not dispose of the deposited assets without explicit permission by the depositor, which clearly corresponds with the just described prohibition of *tirage sur al masse.*[98]

The fungible and dematerialised character of securities, on the other hand, leads to evident incompatibilities with *dépôt.* First, securities' fungibility (whether dematerialised or not), and their subsequent commingling in a custodian's pool,

90. Ripert & Roblot (1996), no. 1789 *and* Bonneau & Drummond (2005), no. 232. *Cf.* Malaurie, Aynes & Gautier (2001), no. 21. This conclusion led some authors to oppose the qualification of the investor – custodian relationship as a contract altogether. However, the fact that (statutory) law determines some aspects of a contract, does not exclude a contract from being qualified as such; Ghozi *in* CNCT 1997 Report, 209. *Cf.* Bénabent (2004), no. 4.
91. Art. 11 of Decree no. 49-1105 of 4 August 1949 (cited *supra) and* Cass. crim., 30 May 1996, *Bull. Joly Bourse* 1996, p. 628, no. 100. *See also,* e.g., Cass. com., 14 December 1965, *Banque,* 1965, p. 211.
92. De Vauplane & Bornet (2001), no. 975. *Contra* Maffei (2005), 244.
93. The combination of contracts *dépôt* and *mandat* is not uncommon to French private law; *see* Huet (2001), no. 33503 *and* Bénabent (2004), no. 721.
94. De Vauplane & Bornet (2001), no. 969. *Cf.* Benabent (2004), no. 716.
95. *See,* e.g., Maffei (2005), 244.
96. *See* Malaurie, Aynès & Gautier (2001), no. 861. *Accord* Martin (1996), 47 *et seq. and* Huet (2001), no. 33127; *contra* Reygrobellet (1999), 311 *and* Bénabent (2004), no. 764.
97. *Cf.* Ghozi *in* CNCT 1997 Report, 197.
98. *See also* Germain *in* CNCT 1997 Report, 175.

renders them impossible to be delivered *in specie* at the depositor's request.[99] Second, because of their dematerialisation, securities cannot be physically deposited.[100] Article 1919 second paragraph C. civ., however, provides for the possibility of a fictional deposit, but that provision only applies when a custodian already holds the assets to be deposited.[101] In addition, it has been argued that because *dépôt* does not require the individualisation of deposited assets, but rather the segregation of the assets deposited from the assets already in custody, *dépôt* would be applicable to the custody of dematerialised securities.[102] That position assumes that although fungible among each other, dematerialised securities are not commingled when credited to separate securities accounts, which does not seem to be generally accepted.[103]

It has also been argued that the accountholder/intermediary relationship classifies as *dépôt irregulier (depositum irregulare),* because that contract does not require the eventual restitution of the assets deposited *in specie,* but rather restitution of the same quality and quantity, which is more compatible with the custody of fungible securities.[104] However, *dépôt irregulier* also involves a transfer of ownership of the deposited assets to the custodian and the latter's full power of disposal over the securities deposited,[105] which is obviously contrary to the prohibition of *tirage sur la masse* discussed *above*. Furthermore, Article 1921 C. civ. determines that (the contract of) *dépôt,* i.e. both *dépôt régulier* and *irrégulier,* must result from a mutual agreement. The deposit of dematerialised securities, however, does not result from a voluntary act resulting in a mutual agreement, but from a statutory provision, viz. Article L. 211-4 C. mon. fin. Neither form of *dépôt* has therefore been argued to be applicable to the accountholder/intermediary relationship.[106]

The accountholder/intermediary relationship has further been classified as *louage d'ouvrage* (services agreement), also known as *contrat d'entreprise* (business agreement), supplemented with a contract of *mandat.*[107] To classify as a *contrat d'entreprise,* a contractor must be under the obligation to do or make something through factual acts in a relationship of independence,[108] while under *mandat,* a

99. *See,* e.g., BONNEAU (2003), no. 765, BONNEAU & DRUMMOND (2005), no. 232 *and* PELTIER *in* CNCT 1997 Report, 166.
100. BONNEAU & DRUMMOND (2005), no. 232.
101. *See* GHOZI *in* CNCT 1997 Report, 182.
102. GHOZI *in* CNCT 1997 Report, 188, 198 and 201. *Cf. also* BONNEAU & DRUMMOND (2005), no. 232.
103. *But see* BONNEAU & DRUMMOND (2005), nos. 232 and 661. BOUÈRE & DE VAUPLANE *in* CNCT 1997 Report, 260-261 argue that dematerialised securities are neither individualised nor indivualisable, as securities are not individualised in the omnibus accounts with the CSD. In their view, securities only become individualised after transfer (cf. Art. 1585 C. civ.). *Contra* AUCKENTHALER (2004), 19, who considers securities to be utterly non-individualisable.
104. *E.g.* BÉNABENT (2004), no. 764 *and* GAVALDA & STOUFFLET (2002), no. 752.
105. *See* MALAURIE, AYNÈS & GAUTIER (2001), no. 886, HUET (2001), no. 33501 *and* BÉNABENT (2004), no. 761.
106. BOUERE & DE VAUPLANE CNCT 1997 Report, 265.
107. Arts. 1787–1799-1 C. civ. *See* MALAURIE, AYNÈS & GAUTIER (2001), no. 881.
108. BÉNABENT (2004), no. 479.

mandatary is given the authority to perform certain legal acts as a representative of the mandator.[109] Although these general definitions certainly apply to the accountholder/intermediary relationship, they do not address the most important characteristics of securities custody, viz. the preservation of assets, the prohibition of *tirage sur la masse* and the intermediary's obligation of restitution.[110]

Finally, it has been argued that the accountholder/intermediary relationship should be classified as a *sui generis* contract with 'most of the characteristics of *dépôt*'.[111] Under this view, the accountholder/intermediary relationship consists of elements of the contracts *dépôt, contrat d'entreprise* and *mandat* as just discussed, and, it is submitted, this classification is therefore the most appropriate one.[112] Doctrinally, such a *sui generis* contract that consists of, or is similar to different *contrats nommés* would be called a *contrat atypique* (an untypical contract) or a *contrat complexe* (a complex contract).[113]

In sum, the classification of the accountholder/intermediary relationship in general private law terms proves to be highly problematical. It is generally agreed, however, that some elements of the contract of *dépôt* are applicable and that an accessory contract of *mandat* must be construed.[114] But in practice, all classification is avoided by referring to the account provider as *conservateur,* rather than *dépositaire,* and to the securities account agreement as *conservation.*[115]

6.3.5 Nature of Accountholder Interests

Already before the dematerialisation, controversy existed in the legal literature on the nature of an investor's interests in his securities. The dematerialisation, however, did not contribute to the determination of that issue, but rather intensified the debate. As of today, the classification of an accountholder's interests in the securities he is entitled to, is still highly contested. It is generally agreed, on the other hand, that accountholder interests do not classify as co-ownership rights.[116]

Scholarly debate has mainly questioned whether accountholder interests are of a proprietary or contractual nature, and persuasive arguments have been brought forward on both sides. First, proprietary rights are generally considered to be

109. *Cf.* Malaurie, Aynès & Gautier (2001), no. 709 on the differences between *mandat* and *contrat d'entreprise. See also* Bonneau (2003), no. 765 *and* Bonneau & Drummond (2005), no. 232.
110. *Cf.* Ghozi *in* CNCT 1997 Report, 206–208.
111. De Vauplane & Bornet (2001), no. 974. *Contra* Huet (2001), no. 33127. Ghozi *in* CNCT 1997 Report, 212 calls this special type of *dépôt 'dépôt d'actif financier'* (although he does not seem to accept a qualification as a *sui generis* contract).
112. *See* De Vauplane & Bornet (2001), no. 974, n.162 for further references.
113. A *contrat sui generis* on the other hand, is a contract to which no elements of any existing *contrat nommé* (statutory contract) is applicable. A *contrat atypique* is a *contrat innommé,* but which has many similarities to a certain *contrat nommé,* whereas a *contrat complexe* is a contract which resembles or is a mixture of several contracts. *See* Malaurie, Aynes & Gautier (2001), nos. 5, 8 and 19.
114. Bonneau & Drummond (2005), no. 232.
115. De Vauplane & Bornet (2001), nos. 970 and 968.
116. *See* Ripert & Roblot II (1976), nos. 1764 *and* Maffei (2005), 243. *Cf.* Bernasconi (2000), 23.

effective *erga omnes,* i.e. can be asserted against all. Accordingly, Article 12 of Decree no. 49-1105 of 4 August 1949 granted investors a right of revendication in the case of their custodian's insolvency, a right which could not be challenged by any creditor of the insolvent custodian.[117] Similarly, the *Code monétaire et financier* currently provides that an insolvent intermediary's administrator must transfer all accountholders' securities to accounts with other intermediaries, but any reference to a 'right of revendication' has been omitted.[118]

Furthermore, it follows from the case law that accountholders take free of all competing claims by third parties, except for cases of an accountholder's *mala fides* and vices regarding the securities concerned.[119] A credit entry in a securities account thus provides a *bona fide* transferee/accountholder with a virtually non-challengeable interest, even if the initial entitlement holder has been involuntarily 'dispossessed'. This strongly resembles arts. 2279 and 2280 C. civ., which provisions protect *bona fide* transferees in possession of movable tangibles from competing third party claims. Consequently, some authors have argued that a credit entry in a securities account or credit balances classify as movable tangibles, while others have contended that arts. 2279 and 2280 should apply, regardless of the classification.[120]

Third, the *Code monétaire et financier* determines that account providers, i.e. intermediaries in the case of *titres au porteur* and issuers in the case of *titres nominatifs,* should protect accountholders' rights of ownership regarding their financial instruments.[121] Moreover, under general French private law, ownership involves, more particularly, the rights *of usus, fructus* and *abusus;* Article 544 C. civ.[122] All of these rights are directly applicable to accountholder interests, as an accountholder is entitled to the collection of dividends and interests, and the enforcement of his corporate rights *(fructus),* and may also freely use *(usus)* and dispose of *(abusus)* his securities.

Yet legal literature has been reluctant to accept that dematerialised securities should be subject to a *droit réel* (right *in rem)* like ownership, since general private law requires rights *in rem* to have an individualised object.[123] It has, on the other hand, been argued that although the securities to which credit balances on securities accounts refer, are indeed fungible and non-individualisable *in abstracto,* the

---

117. That provision has made some authors qualify the rights of investors as *collective ownership,* thus following the German example. *See* RIPERT & ROBLOT (1996), no. 1803.
118. Art. L. 431-6 C. mon. fin.
119. *E.g.,* Paris, 25 October 1991, *Dr. sociétés,* 1992, no. 1138, as cited by J.-C. HALLOUIN in his annotation of Cass. com., 18 October 1994, *Bull. Joly,* December 1994, p. 1296, no. 362 *and* Cass. com., 22 October 2002, *Rev. sociétés,* July-September 2003, p. 511. *Cf.* REYGROBELLET (1999), 309 *et seq.*
120. *See* BONNEAU & DRUMMOND (2005), no. 91. *See* MARTIN (1996) *and* MAFFEI (2005) for the former position. *But see* Paris, 5 July 1990, *Dr. sociétés,* December 1990, 7, no. Q-20, where it was held that 'art. 2279 C. civ. does not apply to dematerialised securities'. *Cf. also* DROBNIG (2004), 748, REYGROBELLET (1999), 314–315 *and* PELTIER *in* CNCT 1997 Report, 171, on the relationship between Art. L. 431-2 first paragraph C. mon. fin., which provides that a transfer of securities 'results from' the credit entry in the transferee's account, and Art. 2279 C. civ.
121. Art. L. 533-7 C. mon. fin.
122. BERGEL, BRUSCHI & CIMAMONTI (1999), nos. 47 and 80 *et seq.*
123. *See* RIPERT & ROBLOT (1996), no. 1795 *and* AUCKENTHALER (2004), 20 and the references provided there.

securities accounts themselves, as well as securities of the same issue thus separated, are sufficiently individualised to be subject to proprietary rights.[124]

Second, from the dependency of an accountholder on the account provider's fulfilment of its obligations, it must be concluded that the rights of the former cannot always be asserted *erga omnes*. If an accountholder does not separate his own securities from those of his clients, for instance, revendication by the latter in the accountholder's insolvency becomes virtually impossible.[125] Moreover, if not duly informed by the accountholder on corporate actions, its clients cannot exercise their (corporate) rights.

Furthermore, although it has been argued as noted above, that case law indicates that accountholders take free of all competing claims by third parties, except for instances of an accountholder's *mala fides* and vices regarding the securities concerned, the cases cited only concerned (successful) challenges by counterparties to a transfer of ownership of securities.[126] Accountholder rights have therefore not (yet) been tested in court against third party property claims. Finally, accountholders' rights are only enforceable against third parties when these rights are recognised as such by an account provider, i.e. when securities are allocated to specific investors by way of a securities account.[127] Consequently, credit entries and credit balances in a securities account have been considered to be constitutive elements for the existence of dematerialised securities.[128]

That position is not generally accepted, but doctrine seems to agree that a (credit balance on) a securities account is a constitutive element for the assertion of an accountholder's rights vis-à-vis third parties, while it provides challengeable proof vis-à-vis counterparties of a transfer.[129] It is submitted that accountholder interests must therefore be classified as a combination of both rights *in rem* and *in personam*,[130] for they can be asserted against third parties, but also depend on the fulfilment of the account provider's obligations and the latter's maintenance of its clients' securities accounts.

---

124. *See* Ghozi *in* CNCT 1997 Report, 182 and 208 *and* Bouère & De Vauplane *in* CNCT 1997 Report, 260. *Cf.* Reygrobellet (1999), 308. *Contra* Auckenthaler (2004), 19.
125. *Cf.* Cass. com., 18 October 1994, *Bull. Joly,* December 1994, p. 1296, no. 362. But in Cass. com. 5 March 2002, *Dalloz,* 2002, no. 13, 1139, a revendication claim to fungible securities was sustained.
126. *See* Reygrobellet (1999), 315 *and* Bonneau & Drummond (2005), no. 86 *et seq. Cf. infra,* s. 6.4.3.
127. *See,* e.g. Paris, 31 October 1991, *Bull. Joly,* 1992, p. 64, no. 14 *and* Bouère & De Vauplane *in* CNCT 1997 Report, 263.
128. *Accord* Maffei (2005), 242 *et seq. and* Reygrobellet (1999), 314 and the further references provided there. *Contra* Clément *in* CNCT 1997 Report, 246.
129. Auckenthaler (2004), 21.
130. *See* Ripert & Roblot (1996), no. 1795. *Contra* Maffei (2005), 242, arguing that accountholder interests are solely proprietary in nature.

6.3.6 Intermediary Insolvency and the Treatment of Shortfalls

General insolvency rules are provided in book VI of the *Code de commerce,* while specific provisions concerning financial intermediary bankruptcies are have been introduced by, notably, the Act MAF and the *Loi de sécurité financière.*[131] As a general rule of bankruptcy law, all of a debtor's assets are affected by the declaration of his bankruptcy, but that declaration does not impede creditors' enforcement of their revendication rights; Article L. 621-16 and L. 621-18 C. com.

However, because of the dematerialisation of all French securities and the consequent absence of physical certificates, accountholders cannot revendicate the securities they are entitled to through physical delivery, should their intermediary become insolvent. Moreover, as general private law requires rights *in rem,* including the right of revendication, to have an individualised object to be enforceable, fungible assets such as dematerialised securities cannot be subject to revendication.[132] Accountholders would therefore be treated as unsecured creditors, but under Article L. 431-6 C. mon. fin., the intermediary's bankruptcy administrator must transfer all its clients' securities to accounts with other intermediaries.[133] Provided there is separation of the insolvent intermediary's assets from those of its clients, this rule thus safeguards accountholders from claims by the intermediary's creditors to the insolvent estate.[134]

When accountholders prove to be entitled to more securities than the intermediary's omnibus account with the CSD indicates, a shortfall occurs, because in all instances where accountholder entitlements do not match their account provider's omnibus account with the CSD, the latter accounts prevail.[135] To cover the resulting deficit, recourse is had first to the intermediary's own assets, as any deficit is deemed to result from illegal *tirage sur la masse.*[136] Any remaining deficit is distributed pro rata amongst accountholders, i.e. the losses are apportioned between the accountholders in proportion to their entitlements.[137] With regard to this deficit, however, accountholders are treated as mere unsecured creditors.[138]

---

131. Act no. 96-597 of 2 July 1996 and Act no. 2003-706 of 1 August 2003, respectively.
132. Ripert & Roblot (1996), no. 1795 *and* De Vauplane & Bornet (2001), no. 1158. *See* Art. L. 621-122 C. com. for a few exceptions. Moreover, in Cass. com. 5 March 2002, *Dalloz,* 2002, no. 13, 1139, a revendication claim to fungible securities was expressly sustained. *Cf. also supra,* s. 6.3.5.
133. *See also* Art. L. 213-2 C. mon. fin.
134. Art. 332-4 *Règlement Général* AMF. *See,* e.g. Paris, 10 December 1999, *RD banc. fin.,* May-June 2000, p. 184, no. 134, where the court held that accountholders could not revendicate because the account provider's bookkeeping was in disorder.
135. De Vauplane & Bornet (2001), no. 1159.
136. *See supra, s.* 6.3.4.
137. Art. L. 431-6 C. mon. fin. No transfer in the sense of the preceding paragraph can therefore be effectuated before all investors have asserted their claims; *see* De Vauplane & Bornet (2001), nos. 1162–1163 on the technicalities of that procedure.
138. Art. L. 621-43 C. com. *See* Piniot *in* CNCT 1997 Report, 222 *and* Maffei (2005), 246. But as an additional measure of investor protection, a special guarantee fund has been created to compensate investors' losses up to the amount of EUR 70,000; arts L. 322-1 through 322-4 C. mon. fin. *and* Resolution of 29 September 1999, esp. Art. 5.

6.4 SECURITIES TRANSFERS

6.4.1 Introduction

The technical procedures to effectuate a transfer of intermediated securities by book-entry are fairly straight-forward. *Titres au porteur* are transferred pursuant to a written instruction by the transferor to his intermediary. This intermediary then debits the transferor's securities account, and passes the instruction on to Euroclear France, which debits the intermediary's omnibus account and credits the transferee's intermediary's omnibus account. That intermediary, in its turn, credits the transferee's account, which completes the transfer.[139]

The procedure is almost the same for *titres nominatives administrés,* except for the fact that after having debited the transferor's account, the transferor's intermediary issues – via the CSD – a *bordereau de références nominatives* (book-entry references note) to the issuer of the securities transferred, so that the transferor is de-registered in that issuer's books.[140] After having credited the transferee's account, the transferee's intermediary issues a similar note via the CSD to the issuer to have the transferee registered as new owner. After that registration, the issuer confirms the settlement to the intermediaries via the CSD.[141]

The legal aspects of securities transfers by book-entry, on the other hand, are a much debated and complicated matter. In an important decision, the *Chambre commercial de la Cour de Cassation* held that a securities transfer should be analysed as common *cession* (transfer of ownership).[142] Under general private law, such a transfer implies that ownership is transferred when the parties consent to the price and object of the sale *(solo consensu).*[143] Under that approach, the credit entry in a transferee's securities account would make the transfer effective, i.e. enforceable against third parties, but not effectuate the transfer of ownership itself.[144] Between agreement and the credit entry in the transferee's securities account, the transferor would thus not be able to assert his interests against third parties, including the issuer and possibly the transferee's insolvency administrator. Moreover, he would not be able to re-transfer the assets to which he was entitled,

139. But when a securities transfer follows a stock exchange transaction, a clearing house is interposed as CCP between the intermediaries and CSD; *see* Ch. 4.2. Moreover, the transferee's intermediary usually credits the transferee's securities account before its omnibus account with Euroclear France has been credited; Auckenthaler (2004), 376.

140. Art. L. 431-1 C. mon. fin.

141. *See* Euroclear France 2003 Disclosure Framework, p. 22.

142. Cass. com., 22 November 1988, *Bull. Joly* 1989, p. 84, no. 19. *See also* Cass. com., 23 November 1993, *Dr. sociétés,* February 1994, p. 18, no. 41.

143. Art. 1591 C. civ. and Art. 1583 C. civ. Art. 1583 C. civ. reads: 'between parties, [sale] is perfected and ownership is legally acquired by the buyer vis-à-vis the seller the moment agreement has been reached on the property and the price (...)'. *See also* Cass. 1re civ., 16 July 1992, *Banque et Droit,* January-February 1993, p. 22, where a transfer of ownership was nullified because of the absence of a price on the transfer order.

144. *Cf.* Piniot *in* CNCT 1997 Report, 217.

while the transferor's securities account would refer to securities to which he would no longer be entitled.[145]

The *Chambre civil de la Cour de Cassation,* however, has held that dematerialised securities classify as *choses de genre* (fungible movable tangibles), and that Article 1585 C. civ. requires such assets to be individualised in order to be effectively transferred. It therefore concluded that, contrary to the *solo consensu* approach of the *Chambre commercial* of the same court, the ownership of dematerialised securities can only be effectively transferred through individualisation by a credit entry in the transferee's account.[146]

6.4.2 Moment of Transfer

The situation has been simplified somewhat since the introduction of Article L. 431-2 first paragraph C. mon. fin., which states that in the case of a sale of financial instruments concluded on a regulated stock exchange, ownership 'results' from a credit entry in the transferee's securities account. But the Article further provides that the moment of, and the conditions under which that book-entry is effectuated are to be determined by the exchange in question, i.e. by the rules of Euronext. Under the current rules of Euronext, a transferee's securities account is credited throughout the trading day (settlement under the *Relit Grande Vitesse* system), or on T+1, i.e. the morning after the day of transaction (settlement under the *Relit* system), although parties may agree otherwise.[147] The omnibus account of the transferee's intermediary with the CSD, however, is credited on T+3, i.e. three days after the transaction, and the transferee's securities account is therefore credited before the settlement has been fully completed.[148]

However, Article L. 431-2 first paragraph C. mon. fin. is applicable only to securities listed at a regulated stock exchange, and if securities are neither admitted to the CSD's system of custody, nor traded on a regulated stock exchange, the transfer is governed by Article L. 228-1 ninth paragraph C. com., which fortunately also provides that a transferee's ownership 'results' from a credit entry in his account.[149]

---

145. *Cf.* Bonneau & Drummond (2005), no. 662.
146. Cass. 1re civ., 6 March 1996, *RD bancaire et bourse,* November-December 1997, p. 238, no. 1. *See also* De Vauplane & Bornet (2001), no. 48 *and* Germain & Frison-Roche, annotation of Cass. 1re civ., 6 March 1996, *RD bancaire et bourse,* November-December 1997, p. 238, no. 1.
147. De Vauplane & Bornet (2001), no. 73 and 77. Since 19 December 2001, *Relit* and *Relit Grande Vitesse* 'merged' into RGV2. RGV2 now comprises the two different ways of settlement; Minor & Maffei *in* Vereecken & Nijenhuis (2003), 166.
148. Auckenthaler (2004), 26.
149. L. 228-1 ninth paragraph C. com. was enacted by Ordinance no. 2004-604 of 24 June 2004. Prior to this ordinance, general rules of private law applied to these OTC transactions, and ownership was transferred *solo consensu;* Art. 1583 C. civ. However, these transfers could be asserted against third parties, including the issuer, only after a credit entry was made in the transferee's account; Art. 2 of Decree no. 83-359 of 2 May 1983. Ordinance no. 2004-604

A transfer of securities admitted to the CSD's system of custody, which does not result from a regulated stock exchange transaction, is subject to still other rules. Pursuant to Article L. 431-2 fourth paragraph C. mon. fin., a transfer of ownership of dematerialised securities that results from a so-called over the counter ('OTC') transaction, takes place the moment the transfer has become final or irrevocable under the rules of the CSD's settlement system. Whereas most transfers become irrevocable at the end of the trading day when the *Banque de France* has controlled the money leg of the transaction, for some designated transactions, including OTC transactions, finality is ensured during 'real time', i.e. throughout the trading day.[150]

Ownership of securities admitted to the CSD's settlement system is thus transferred during 'real time' when the transfer results from an OTC transaction, but the transferee only acquires ownership the moment when the money leg of the transaction has been settled and the account of the transferee's intermediary with Euroclear France has been credited. Prior to that moment, the intermediary in whose name the securities are then credited is deemed to be the owner thereof.[151]

In sum, as a derogation from the *solo consensu* rule of general private law (Article 1583 C. civ.), the ownership of dematerialised securities is most often transferred when the credit entry in the transferee's account has been made. Thus, the effectiveness or enforceability of the transfer currently usually coincides with the transfer of ownership.[152] But in OTC transactions settled trough the CSD's custody system, ownership is transferred to the transferee when the money leg of the transaction has been settled. The contractual aspects of the securities transaction, however, continue to be governed by general rules of private law, such as the rules that concern the formation of the contract.[153]

6.4.3 Annulment and Finality

Although not entirely certain, it seems unlikely, as has been noted above, that third parties can successfully challenge a transfer of dematerialised securities and a subsequent credit entry in the transferee's securities account, unless the transferee's *mala fides* or vices regarding the securities concerned could be proven.[154] But the parties to a sales agreement may challenge the transfer and the credit entry in the transferee's securities account on other grounds also. On the other hand, a success-

of 24 June 2004 sought to unify the transfer of ownership regime; Couret & Le Nabasque (2004), 188. *Cf. also* Maffei (2005), 240-241.

150. Minor & Maffei *in* Vereecken & Nijenhuis (2003), 166.

151. Art. L. 431-2 fifth paragraph C. mon. fin. *Cf.* De Vauplane & Bornet (2001), nos. 1165 and 611-634, Bonneau & Drummond (2005), no. 669 *and infra,* s. 6.4.3.

152. Bonneau & Drummond (2005), no. 90.

153. Arts. 1582 – 1701 C. civ. *See* De Vauplane & Bornet (2001), no. 53-2 *and* Piniot *in* CNCT 1997 Report, 218.

154. *Cf.* Maffei (2005), 248.

ful challenge assumes that the transferor has been able to identify the transferee, which is not always likely in today's anonymised stock markets.[155]

Other than on the general private law grounds just discussed, securities transfers may be reversed for reasons specified by the *Code monétaire et financier.* More specifically, Article L. 431-2 second paragraph C. mon. fin. provides that a securities transfer is *de iure* annulled 'if the securities concerned are not credited to the account of the transferee's intermediary with the CSD at the moment and under the conditions that credit entry was due under the rules of the stock exchange'.[156] In other words, when a seller, his intermediary, or the CSD defaults in delivering, the transfer is annulled, even if the transferee's intermediary has already (provisionally) credited the transferee's securities account.[157]

However, this provision is problematical for a number of reasons. First, its relationship with Article L. 431-3 C. mon. fin. is unclear, as Article L. 431-3 C. mon. fin. also provides that a securities transfer following a sales transaction is *de iure* annulled when the transaction fails to settle.[158] No general doctrinal consensus exists, but the better view seems to be that Article L. 431-3 C. mon. fin. specifically applies when the sale proves to be defective in a preliminary stage of the transaction, i.e. if no consensus has been reached on the price, whereas Article L. 431-2 C. mon. fin. applies when the seller defaults regarding his delivery obligation.[159]

Second, Article L. 431-2 C. mon. fin. does not specify what the consequences of annulment are for the obligations that follow from the initial transaction, and it is debated whether the annulment of the transfer of ownership also involves the annulment of the initial transaction and all obligations resulting from that transaction.[160] But because it is generally considered that a reversal of all credits and debits throughout the custody chain would be an unacceptable consequence,

---

155. Yet a successful challenge has no consequences for the settlement system; Euroclear France 2003 Disclosure Framework, 22.
156. That is, on T+3 or three days after the transaction was concluded; *see supra,* s. 6.4.2.
157. *Cf.* Art. L. 621-28 paragraph 4 C. com. *See also* BONNEAU & DRUMMOND (2005), no. 666 *et seq.*
158. Art. L. 431-3 C. mon. fin. first paragraph reads: 'When financial instruments are to be delivered (...) against payment, defaulting delivery or defaulting payment (...) or if no agreement has been concluded, (...) all the non-defaulting party's obligations are annulled vis-à-vis the defaulting party (...)'.
159. It has also been argued that Art. L. 231-3 C. mon. fin. provides for a *de iure* annulment of the obligations of the transaction as a sort of *exceptio non adimpleti contractus (cf.* Art. 1612 C. civ.), whereas Art. L. 231-2 C. mon. fin. provides for an annulment of the transfer of ownership only; PELTIER *in* CNCT 1997 Report, 171. Furthermore, Art. L. 231-3 C. mon. fin. could be analysed as facilitating close-out netting procedures of repurchase agreements *(see infra,* s. 6.5.2), when the initial seller is in default regarding his payment of the repurchase price. In the latter view, the initial buyer cannot be made subject to any obligation to resell securities to the defaulting initial seller, while the *exceptio non adimpleti contractus* does not provide for an annulment of a debtor's obligation; AUCKENTHALER (2004), 132-133.
160. *Contra* BONNEAU & DRUMMOND (2005), no. 667.

only the provisional credit entry in the transferee's account is rescinded, while the transferor's account remains unaffected.[161]

Third, whereas Article L. 431-2 first paragraph C. mon. fin. provides that a transferee's ownership of securities 'results' from the credit entry in his account, it must be inferred from Article L. 431-2 second paragraph C. mon. fin. that the finality of a securities transfer is only truly secured after a credit entry in the securities account of the buyer's intermediary with Euroclear France. Thus, should a transferee's intermediary become insolvent after having credited its client's account and having received payment for that credit entry, but before its omnibus account with Euroclear France has been credited, the transfer is annulled pursuant to Article L. 431-2 second paragraph C. mon. fin. Consequently, the credit entry in the transferee's account is rescinded and concerning the payment price, the transferee has a mere unsecured claim against the intermediary's bankrupt estate. That seems unfair, but the legislature might have argued that the intermediary's bankrupt estate would be unjustly reduced when a transferee would be allowed to successfully assert a revendication claim, while the intermediary never received a credit entry in its omnibus account with the CSD.[162]

Similarly, but in a more direct way, Article L. 431-2 fourth paragraph C. mon. fin. connects the transfer of ownership to the finality of the transfer. It must here be reiterated that for OTC transactions settled through the CSD's system, Article L. 431-2 fourth paragraph C. mon. fin. provides that the ownership of securities is transferred the moment when the transfer has become final under the rules of the CSD's settlement system. Under such circumstances, a transferee thus only acquires ownership the moment when the money leg of the transaction has been settled and the securities account of the transferee's intermediary with Euroclear France has been credited.[163]

Article L. 431-2 fourth paragraph C. mon. fin. was enacted as an implementation of the EU Settlement Finality Directive ('SDF'),[164] which also led to the present form of arts. L. 330-1 and L. 330-2 C. mon. fin. Article L. 330-1 II C. mon. fin. secures the finality of instructions given to, and payments and settlements executed in settlement systems on the day of an intermediary's insolvency. Instructions, payments and settlements therefore remain valid when given or executed on the day of the declaration of insolvency, whereas under general rules of insolvency law, instructions and legal acts on the day of the declaration of insolvency are considered void.[165] Moreover, all other provisions of general insolvency

161. The transferee's intermediary, having already paid the purchase price, is refunded by the CCP; De Vauplane & Bornet (2001), no. 75-1.

162. *Cf.* De Vauplane & Bornet (2001), no. 1165.

163. Art. L. 431-2 fifth paragraph C. mon. fin. *and* De Vauplane & Bornet (2001), nos. 1165 and 611–634. *Cf. supra,* s. 6.4.2.

164. Directive 98/26/EC of the European Parliament and of the Council of 19 May 1998 on settlement finality in payment and securities settlement systems (OJ L 166/45).

165. Arts. L. 621-32 and L. 621-24 C. com. For the definition of 'instruction', *see* Art. 4.4.3.6. *Règles de compensation de* Clearnet.

law that may have retroactive effect, such as provisions on fraudulent preferences, are thus excluded from applicability.[166]

Pursuant to Article L. 330-2 C. mon. fin., excluded from applicability are all provisions that would render void the creation and enforcement of security rights on securities, including pledges and transfers of title, when those security rights have been created in order to secure payment obligations required by a securities settlement system.[167] This provision constitutes a clear derogation from several provisions of general insolvency law.[168]

6.5 PERFECTION AND ENFORCEMENT OF SECURITY RIGHTS

6.5.1 INTRODUCTION

Under French law, a creditor who wants to prevent *pari passu* ranking with other creditors, can secure his claim both by the creation of a pledge in his debtor's securities, or have the ownership of those securities transferred. As a rule of general commercial law, a pledge may be enforced by the pledgee's assertion of a retention right on the assets pledged and by the sale of the pledged assets, while the pledgee takes free of all other creditors' claims *(droits de rétention, de préférence et d'attribution);* Article L. 622-23 C. com. Also under general commercial law, a transfer of ownership by way of security may be enforced by the assertion of a revendication right, should the collateralised assets be held by the debtor; Article L. 621-18 C. com.[169] But, as will be shown in the following sections, the specific rules that govern both types of security interests derogate, sometimes quite sharply, from general French commercial and private law.

6.5.2 TRANSFER OF TITLE

In principle, fiduciary transfers *(fiducie)* are not allowed under general rules of French law. More in particular, conditional transfers to secure a claim are forbidden as a *pacte commissoire,* and any agreement that purports to effectuate such a transfer is void under both private and commercial law.[170] Although case law has not applied this prohibition extensively,[171] the French legislator has created

166. MINOR & MAFFEI *in* VEREECKEN & NIJENHUIS (2003), 186 and 189.
167. *See,* e.g., arts. L. 431-7 and L. 330-2I C. mon. fin.
168. Most notably, arts. L. 621-24, L. 621-25, L. 621-80, L. 621-107 and L. 621-108 C. com. *Cf.* MINOR & MAFFEI *in* VEREECKEN & NIJENHUIS (2003), 196.
169. *Cf. supra* section 3.3.3.
170. Arts. 2078 second paragraph C. civ. and L. 521-3 fourth paragraph C. com.
171. CABRILLAC & MOULY (2002), no. 542 *and* AUCKENTHALER (2004), 123. *But see* the case law cited by AUCKENTHALER (2004), 153–154 (with respect to *vente à réméré).*

statutory exceptions for a few specific arrangements in order to assail any legal uncertainty. In addition, the implementation legislation of the EU Financial Collateral Directive ('FCD') more generally exempts all transfers of title by way of security from the application of the *pacte commissoire* prohibition, provided that these arrangements are concluded between certain, specified institutions.[172] In circumstances other than those provided for by the FCD, fiduciary transfers can be employed only under certain agreements that will be examined *below*.[173]

First, assets may be sold and repurchased by the initial seller within five years, while that repurchase annuls the initial sale *(vente à reméré);* arts. 1659 and 1660 C. civ.[174] *Vente à reméré* may be used to secure a claim when the debtor transfers ownership of his securities to the creditor against payment of the loan, with the obligation to repurchase the securities thus collateralised when the claim is due. Should the debtor default in the repayment, the sale becomes irrevocable; Article 1662 C. civ. However, the repurchase is optional and cannot always be enforced by the creditor, especially not in the case of the debtor's insolvency.[175] In addition, if the sole purpose of the *vente à reméré* is to secure a claim, the prohibition of *pacte commissoire* might still be applicable,[176] and the financial markets have therefore regarded other constructions as more appropriate to secure claims.[177]

Under general private law, a loan of fungibles *(prêt de consommation)* involves the transfer of ownership from the lender to the borrower; Article 1893 C. civ.[178] The borrower is therefore fully authorised to dispose of the borrowed securities, but must eventually retransfer the same quality and quantity of the securities lent; Article 1902 C. civ. When this construction is used to secure a claim, the creditor borrows securities from the debtor, and agrees that when the lender defaults, the borrower is freed from his obligation of restitution. But such an arrangement would still be void pursuant to the *pacte commissoire* prohibition, and a specific statutory exception therefore had to be created that expressly exempts arrangements of *prêt* to secure loans from the application of the prohibition.[179]

Similar to *prêt de consommation,* under an agreement of *pension livrée* (repurchase agreement), the debtor transfers ownership of his securities to the creditor against payment of the loan, and agrees to repurchase the same quantity

---

172. Arts. L. 431-7 and 431-7-3 paragraph 1 C. mon. fin.
173. These agreements, which may be considered a distinctive type of financial instruments, are also used for purposes other than securing a claim; AUCKENTHALER (2004), 115 *et seq.*
174. To effect the repurchase, a simple expressed intention to repurchase by the initial seller is sufficient; Cass. 1re civ., 28 May 1991, *Bull. Joly,* August-September 1991, p. 813, no. 290.
175. *Cf.* AUCKENTHALER (2004), 152 and 166.
176. AUCKENTHALER (2004), 153-155.
177. DE VAUPLANE & BORNET (2001), no. 832.
178. *Prêt de consommation (mutuum)* is distinguished from *prêt d'usage* (*commodatum*), under which no transfer of ownership takes place. The former type is only applicable to fungibles and *biens consomptibles* (consumable assets), but securities have been considered by both legal literature and case law to belong to both these categories; DE VAUPLANE & BORNET (2001), nos. 52 and 836. *See also* MALAURIE, AYNÈS & GAUTIER(2001), no. 930.
179. Art. 31 of Act no. 87-416 of 17 June 1987, now codified as Art. L. 432-6(3). *See also* Art. 431-7 C. mon. fin., which sanctions close-out netting.

and quality of securities when the claim is due. The debtor and creditor further agree that if the debtor defaults, the creditor is freed from any obligation of restitution. But while a creditor's need for securities is often the main reason for engaging in a *prêt* arrangement, the debtor's need for money most often triggers the conclusion of a *pension livrée* agreement. The *pacte commissoire* prohibition would therefore be applicable,[180] but for certain designated financial institutions, the legislator created an exception.[181]

Many different arrangements under which securities are transferred to a counterparty that agrees to retransfer these securities in due time to a third party or the initial seller classify as *portage.*[182] The arrangement can be used to effectuate a repurchase agreement or securities lending, but because it is considered a *sui generis* agreement, i.e. not statutorily classified, the statutory exceptions to the *pacte commissoire* prohibition are also not applicable. As a consequence, it is far from unproblematic.[183]

6.5.3 PLEDGE AND ATTACHMENT

6.5.3.1 Creation of a Pledge

Specific, derogatory provisions of both the *Code monétaire et financier* and other statutes create a special regime for the creation and enforcement of a pledge vested in dematerialised securities, which is otherwise governed by the *Code de commerce.*[184] For instance, the registration of a pledge is not required for a pledge on securities to be effective, whereas under general private law, a pledge must be registered.[185] Moreover, under the implementation legislation of the FCD, only a written deed that identifies the securities pledged and their way of creation is currently required for the creation of a pledge (*nantissement*) on dematerialised securities.[186]

In addition, the pledged securities must be transferred to a special pledge account in the pledgor's name with any intermediary, or, in the case of *titres nominatifs purs,* with the issuer. The pledge may also be made effective by electronic identification of the pledged securities by the intermediary concerned, or, since the implementation of the FCD, by a control agreement between creditor and debtor.[187] Although the written deed and securities transfer render the pledge

180. CABRILLAC & MOULY (2002), no. 530 *and* AUCKENTHALER (2004), 124.
181. Arts. L. 432-12 – L. 432-19 C. mon. fin., which are provisions that originate from the former Act no. 93-1444 of 31 December 1993. *See* AUCKENTHALER (2004), 123.
182. DE VAUPLANE & BORNET (2001), no. 868.
183. *See* DE VAUPLANE & BORNET (2001), nos. 873–876 *and* CORNU (2004), p. 681.
184. *See* arts. L. 431-4, L. 431-5 and L. 431-6 C. mon. fin., Decree no. 97-509 of 21 May 1997 *and* arts. L. 521-1 – L. 521-3 C. com., respectively.
185. Art. 2074 C. civ. *Cf.* DE VAUPLANE & BORNET (2001), no. 65.
186. Ordinance no. 2005-171 of 42 February 2005, implemented as Art. L. 431-7-3 paragraph 2 C. mon. fin.
187. Art. L. 431-7-3 paragraph 2 C. mon. fin. *See also* AUCKENTHALER (2004), 33.

effective, i.e. enforceable against the issuer and other third parties, they are not a constitutive element for the pledge itself, which is created by the pledge agreement alone (*solo consensu*).[188]

By virtue of the pledge, the pledgee obtains a retention right on the pledged securities,[189] but the pledgee and pledgor may together define the conditions under which the latter may still dispose of the securities pledged.[190] In addition, they may agree to confer the voting rights attached to the securities pledged to the pledgor, whereas the rights to the payment of dividend and interests may remain with the pledgee.[191]

Although the quantity and quality of the pledged securities must be identified in order for a pledge to be effectively created,[192] case law has classified an accountholder's securities portfolio as *universalité des biens* (a single entity of property), when that is to the accountholder's expressed intent.[193] That classification implies that a securities account and all assets to which it refers can be treated as a single legal entity, and may therefore be pledged in its entirety. Moreover, changes in the securities account do not alter the pledge as such, although it is contested in legal literature whether securities that are transferred to a pledged account must also be considered as being covered by the pledge.[194] In addition, dividends and interests that follow from the securities thus pledged are covered by the pledge, even when they are credited to separate accounts; Article L. 431-4 I C. mon. fin.[195]

Thus, specific monetary assets are made subject to a special pledge regime, that would otherwise be governed by Article 2075 C. civ. More generally, a classification of a securities account as a *universalité des biens* does not accord with general private law, as general private law does not accept that a single entity of property is composed of different – and differing – assets.[196] Furthermore, the possibility of later transfers to a pledged account seems contrary to the general commercial law provisions that prohibit fraudulent preferences.[197]

---

188. *See* Cass. com., 7 March 1995, *RTD com.,* October-December 1995, p. 835, no. 13.
189. Art. L. 431-4 III C. mon. fin. *See also* Cass. 1re civ. 4 January 1992, *Bull. I,* no. 4. The pledgee's retention right also includes dividends and interests flowing from the pledged securities; Art. L. 431-4 IV C. mon. fin. *Cf.* MAFFEI (2005), 245.
190. For instance, pledgor and pledgee may agree that the pledgee receives a *mandat de gestion* (management mandate) under which he has to manage the pledged portfolio; DE VAUPLANE & BORNET (2001), no. 69.
191. *See* AUCKENTHALER (2004), 35.
192. Art. L. 431-4 II C. mon. fin.
193. Cass. 1re civ., 12 November 1998, *Dr. sociétés,* January 1999, p. 21, no. 17.
194. *See* AUCKENTHALER (2004), 30–31.
195. Derivatives, on the other hand, are excluded from this rule, as Art. 5 of Decree no. 97-509 of 21 May 1997 provides that only securities expressed in accounts maintained by a financial intermediary, CSD or issuer are subject to the provisions of the *Code monétaire et financier.*
196. DE VAUPLANE & BORNET (2001), no. 63.
197. Art. L. 621-107 C. com. *But see* AUCKENTHALER (2004), 36.

6.5.3.2 Enforcement of a Pledge

Under general private and commercial law, a pledge vested in securities can be enforced when the following three conditions have been met: the secured claim must be certain, i.e. not challenged, precise and due; proof of default must have been sent to the debtor; and a certain time-limit must have passed.[198] But under the implementation legislation of the FCD, and as a derogation from general law, the enforcement of a pledge on securities is not subject to any formalities. When the claim has become due, a pledgee may therefore immediately either sell the pledged securities or appropriate them by set-off or transfer to his own account(s).[199] Yet the FCD applies only to specified institutions and securities transfers that are settled through the CSD's settlement system, and when these conditions are not met, the written deed is still a statutory requirement *(lettre de mise en demeure).*

As a way of enforcement, appropriation clearly derogates from the prohibition of *pacte commissoire* discussed *above*, and under general commercial law, a pledge can only be enforced by public auction.[200] Moreover, for pledges in all categories of securities, sums in cash that are part of, or are attached to the pledged securities account may be appropriated by the pledgee. Finally, if the value of the pledged assets plus the costs of enforcement exceed the secured claim, the surplus must be paid to the pledgor.[201]

In addition, under the implementation legislation of the FCD, a pledgor has full power of disposal over the pledged securities, and can therefore retransfer or rehypothecate the collateralised securities. Yet he is under an obligation to eventually return equivalent securities.[202] Furthermore, clearing and settlement institutions may now create their own regime for the creation and enforcement of security rights that are vested in the context of the settlement systems they maintain.[203] More generally, the C. mon. fin. expressly excludes the enforcement of all security interests from the application of all rules on insolvency proceedings.[204]

6.5.3.3 Attachment

With respect to attachment *(saisie),* a distinction is made between *mesures d'exécution forcée* (measures to liquidate) and *mesures conservatoires* (measures to freeze). Under the first type, securities are attached under the issuer in the case of *titres nominatifs purs,* or under an intermediary in all other instances.[205] But

198. Auckenthaler (2004), 36.
199. Art. L. 431-7-3 paragraph 2 C. mon. fin. Prior to the implementation of the FCD, appropriation was already allowed under Art. 3 of Decree no. 97-509 of 21 May 1997.
200. Art. L. 521-3 C. com.
201. *See* Auckenthaler (2004), 37.
202. Art. L. 431-7-3 paragraph 3 C. mon. fin.
203. Art. L. 330-2 paragraph 2 C. mon. fin.
204. Arts. L. 330-2 paragraph 3 and L. 431-7-2 C. mon. fin.
205. Arts. 178 and 180 of Decree no. 92-755 of 31 July 1992.

if the creditor has been judicially granted the authority to liquidate, this type of attachment is effected through the transfer of the attached securities to a special account, after which these securities may be sold.[206]

Mesures conservatoires can also be effectuated only by duly authorised creditors, and the attached securities may not subsequently be transferred by the debtor. The judgment creditor may only sell the assets if he has obtained proper authorisation. In addition, this type of *mesures conservatoires* is distinguished from *sûreté judiciaire,* under which the debtor is still free to transfer the attached securities; Article 79 of Act no. 91-650 of 9 July 1991.

6.6 CONFLICT OF LAWS

Because, as noted *above*, many issues of substantive law are the subject of considerable debate, private international law regarding dematerialised securities is also muddled. It is unclear, for example, whether the express choice of law rules on the assignment of claims apply to securities.[207] The conflict of laws rules of the European Directives, discussed *above*, have provided more certainty. Their scope, however, is limited.

Under French private international law, conflict of laws issues regarding non-dematerialised *titres auporteur* are traditionally governed by the *lex rei sitae.* Since the certificates are deemed to incorporate the investors' rights, the law of their location governs proprietary claims, such as revendication of lost or stolen securities.[208] To 'non-dematerialised' *titres nominatifs,* the *lex incorporationis* or the law of the register's location applies.[209] Most often, but not necessarily, these rules will point to the same law.

As to the appropriate conflict of laws rule regarding dematerialised securities, uncertainty exists since the classification of dematerialised securities themselves is a matter of discussion. Such classification is of relevance, because if securities are considered *meubles corporels* (tangibles), the *lex rei sitae* applies.[210] If dematerialised securities are classified as *meubles incorporels* (intangibles), the applicability of the *lex rei sitae* is not that obvious.[211] Yet a French court, having

206. Art. 59 of Act no. 91-650 of 9 July 1991.
207. *Cf.* Pardoel (1997), 23–24 *and* Audit (2000), no. 763.
208. *But see* Cass. 1re civ., 25 January 1966, *Dalloz Sirey* 1966, 390 *and* Cass. 1re civ., 17 October 1972, *Revue critique de Droit International Privé* 1973, 520. In these cases, the *lex societatis* was applied, probably because of the *lois de police* having a predominant influence.
209. De Vauplane & Nizard (2001), 410. On the French version of *lex incorporationis (siège social), see,* e.g., Mayer & Heuzé (2004), 717 *et seq.*
210. Cass. 1re civ., 8 July 1969, *Revue critique de Droit International Privé* 1971, 75.
211. Mayer & Heuze (2004), 469.

made the classification under French law as the *lex fori,*[212] is most likely to classify dematerialised securities as intangibles.[213]

Nonetheless, most legal authors assume the applicability of the *lex rei sitae,* without 'looking-through' the chain of custodians. Thus a variation of PRIMA is advocated. The argument is made mainly on practical grounds, such as the inefficiency of the traditional rules due to the disconnected relationship between the issuer and the ultimate accountholder/investor and due to modern portfolios consisting of different types of securities. Others, more theoretically, locate the investors' rights in the custodian's/intermediary's jurisdiction[214] or at the place of the securities account.[215] Still others advocate a general application of the PRIMA rule as defined in the SFD.[216]

To proprietary aspects of transfers of non-dematerialised securities the traditional conflict rules apply: the *lex rei sitae,* i.e. the law of the certificates' location, determines the perfection requirements and the effects of transfers of title in the case of *titres au porteur,* whereas the law of the issuer governs the proprietary aspects in the case of a transfer of *titres nominatifs.*[217] But in the event that a judge would classify a transfer *of titres nominatifs* as an operation *sui generis,*[218] he would apply the law where the issuer's register is located.[219] Most likely, this will refer to the same law as the *lex societatis.* Should this not be the case, then the law of the register's location prevails, provided no *fraus legis* is intended and both the law of the *siège social* and of the register's location recognise the validity of the register.

To the proprietary aspects of transfers of dematerialised securities, a French court would most likely apply PRIMA as a variation of the *lex rei sitae,* which is considered the appropriate conflict rule regarding proprietary matters. However, if the securities in question are not transferred as collateral, as a consequence of which Articles L. 330-2 or L. 431-7-4 paragraph 4 C. mon. fin. would prescribe PRIMA, this cannot be stated with absolute certainty.

In a private international law case decided on 8 July 1969,[220] the *Cour de cassation* stringently applied the *lex rei sitae.* In this case, the German parties had created a security interest in a car that was located in Germany at the time of the creation of the security interest. In due time, however, the car moved to France, where a French garage owner obtained a retention claim with regard to this property. Called upon to hear this claim, the *Cour de cassation* held that French law applied to the validity of the security interest, since the car now stood on French

212. Juris-Classeur International, Fasc. 550, no. 12, p. 4.
213. Court of Paris, 5 July 1990, *Droit des sociétés,* December 1990, 7, no. Q-20. *Cf. also* De Vauplane & Nizard (2001), 404.
214. Mouy & De Vauplane (1995), 59.
215. De Vauplane & Nizard (2001), 411.
216. Bloch (1999), 80.
217. Audit (2000), no. 763 and 765.
218. Ripert & Roblot II (1996), nos. 1761, 1764 and 1765.
219. Juris-Classeur International, Fasc. 564-30, no. 124 *et seq.*, 13.
220. Cass. 1re civ., 8 July 1969, *Revue critique de Droit International Privé,* January-March 1971, 75.

soil. As can be inferred from this case, the *rei sitae* rule is a well established rule of French private international law on the proprietary aspects of security interests.

Already in 1983, on the other hand, a provision was enacted[221] that explicitly applies a certain rule of French substantive law to the enforcement of a pledge vested in securities expressed by a French securities account, whether the securities concerned are French or not.[222] This could be understood as a form of PRIMA, but this provision has not been supported by other, more general provisions. Moreover, it is unlikely that a French judge would conversely apply foreign law in the case of a pledge vested in dematerialised securities expressed by a foreign securities account.[223] Since the enactment of the SFD and the FCD implementation legislation, however, PRIMA, considered as a variation of the *lex sitae,*[224] is applied to collateralised securities, whether outright or by way of security.[225]

Although EU legislation has introduced new rules of private international law, these are not considered to constitute a break with the traditional principle of *lex rei sitae.* Consequently, it is not entirely certain that PRIMA will be applied by French courts when called upon to judge proprietary conflicts of laws regarding book-entry securities, save for cases on collateralised securities. Moreover, even if PRIMA is applied in cases of collateralisation, it is far from clear whether the French courts would apply the law of the intermediary's location or the law of the location of the securities account. In conclusion, it is submitted that much uncertainty still exists under French private international law, which calls for a clarification or perhaps even a statutory modification.

6.7 CONCLUSIONS

6.7.1 Questions and Answers

(1) *Which securities are admitted to the national systems of giro transfer and administration ?*
Although no uncontested general definition of *valeurs mobilières* (securities) exists under French law, France's CSD may admit all securities (dematerialised or in a physical form) as defined under Article L. 211-1 C. mon. fin. This provision includes shares, bonds, and shares in collective investment funds. Foreign securities may be admitted as long as they are compatible with French book-entry securities. In addition, securities are admitted *ex officio* if they are listed at a regulated French stock exchange and are transferable by book-entry only pursuant to a rule of law or issu-

221. Now codified as Art. L. 431-4 IV C. mon. fin.
222. Provided the pledge has been created prior to 4 July 1996: Art. L. 431-5 C. mon. fin.
223. Potok (2002), 44.
224. Bloch (1999), 78 *et seq.*
225. Arts. L. 330-2 paragraph 4 and L. 431-7-4 C. mon. fin.

ing rules. Derivatives are not eligible for admittance to the central system of custody.

(2) *What is the nature of investors' interests in securities?*
Article L. 533-7 C. mon. fin. explicitly refers to accountholder interests as ownership rights. However, the classification is intensely debated, and, as has been shown, the better view seems to be that accountholder interests ought to be classified as a combination of rights *in rem* and *in personam,* for they can be asserted against third parties, but also depend on the fulfilment of the account provider's obligations and the latter's maintenance of its clients' securities accounts.

(2.1) *Is a credit entry in a securities account merely a proof of ownership or is it a constitutive element of ownership of the securities concerned?*
Although it is not entirely certain, it can be concluded from the case law that a credit entry in a securities account provides the accountholder with an effective, i.e. enforceable interest against third parties, provided that the accountholder is *bona fide* and that there is an absence of vices as far as the securities are concerned. Between the parties to a transfer, however, it provides proof of ownership that is more broadly challengeable.

(2.2) *Are informal (i.e. not registered by book-entry) dispositions over securities possible?*
In principle, both ownership and security rights are created *solo consensu,* i.e. by agreement only, and, as a consequence, no book-entry need be effected to reflect such dispositions. Yet ownership and security rights only become effective, i.e. enforceable against third parties, when expressed by a credit entry in the entitlement holder's securities account. Moreover, as a derogation from the *solo consensu* rule, ownership of the greater majority of dematerialised securities is transferred by a credit in the transferee's account.

(2.3) *Is provisional credit in book-entry securities possible?*
Article L. 431-2 second paragraph C. mon. fin. provides that a transfer, and therewith the credit entry in a buyer's account, is *de iure* annulled when the securities account of the buyer's intermediary with Euroclear France has not been credited accordingly. This suggests that, other than in the situation referred to, no provisional credit entries, i.e. credit entries in a securities account that do not correspond with a credit entry at the CSD level, are possible.

(3) *How are investors' rights in respect of securities protected against the account provider and third parties?*
An account provider's obligations are clearly defined by law and enforced by the *Autorité des Marchés Financiers.* In addition, accountholders' rights in respect of dematerialised securities are protected by rules of statutory law (mainly the *Code monétaire et financier)* and regulatory law

(mainly the *Règlement général* AMF). Under the latter, account providers must separate their own assets from those of their clients, a rule which also applies to accounts with the CSD and accounts maintained by mandatees or subcustodians. Under the former, the use, i.e. transfer and hypothecation, of accountholders' securities by an account provider is strictly forbidden as illegal *tirage sur la masse;* Article L. 533-7 C. mon. fin. Account providers therefore do not enjoy any power of disposal over their clients' assets that has not been expressly conferred. They do have, on the other hand, a right of retention to secure their claims against accountholders.

(3.1) *Should shortfalls occur in accounts, how are they availed?*
First, deficits are covered by recourse to the insolvent intermediary's own assets. Remaining losses are apportioned among accountholders *pro rata,* i.e. in proportion to their entitlements; Article L. 431-6 C. mon. fin. These losses are covered up to € 70.000 per investor by the guarantee fund that has been created for that purpose.

(3.2) *How are an investor's interests in securities separated from the account provider's property or how can investors' interests avail the claims of the provider's general creditors?*
Under regulatory law, account providers must separate their own assets from those of their clients, a rule which also applies to accounts with the CSD and accounts maintained by mandatees or sub-custodians. The number of (sub-)custodians does not therefore involve legal consequences with respect to accountholders' interests. Furthermore, accountholders can enforce a statutory right of retention in their account provider's insolvency, and this right cannot be challenged by third parties; Article L. 431-6 C. mon. fin.

(4) *What are the formal requirements for the transfer of ownership of securities?*
The formal requirements for the transfer of ownership depend on the type of securities transferred. Ownership of dematerialised securities that are listed on a regulated stock exchange and settled through the CSD's settlement system, as well as ownership of non-listed securities that are not settled through the CSD's settlement system, is transferred by a credit entry in the transferee's account. But in OTC transactions, settled trough the CSD's custody system, ownership is transferred to the transferee when the money leg of the transaction has been settled.

(4.1) *Can a* bona fide *acquirer rely on the crediting of his account (especially when acquiring* a non domino)?
Although it is not entirely certain, it can be concluded from the case law that a *bona fide* transferee takes free from competing claims

by third parties, provided there is an absence of vices as to the securities concerned. Between parties to a transfer, however, the credit entry merely provides a challengeable proof of ownership.

(4.2) *Is it possible for a credit in a securities account to be reversed and may transfer orders (or other instructions) be revoked?*

Other than the reversal of a credit entry that follows from a successful challenge by a counterparty or third party, credit entries may be reversed when the omnibus account of the buyer's intermediary with the CSD has not been accordingly credited; Article L. 431-2 second paragraph C. mon. fin. Such reversal, however, leads to a debit of the said buyer's account only and has no consequences for any prior credit or debit entries made in securities accounts throughout the rest of the settlement system. Moreover, the implementation of the EU SFD has ensured that instructions, payments and settlements when given or executed on the day of the declaration of insolvency, cannot be reversed; arts. L. 330-1 and L. 330-2 C. mon. fin.

(5) *What are the formal requirements for the creation and enforcement of collateral?*

Security interests may be created by a pledge and the transfer of ownership. Regarding both types, the interest is created by agreement only, although the transfer of ownership is most often effectuated by a credit entry in the transferee's account (see *supra*, question 4). Although in principle, fiduciary transfers of ownership are forbidden, certain agreements, viz. *vente à reméré, prêt* and *pension livrée* are exempt from that prohibition. Moreover, the implementation legislation of the EU FCD, which applies to certain categories of institutions and securities settled through the CSD's custody system, sanctions all transfers of title by way of security.

A pledge is made effective by a written deed sent to the intermediary concerned and a subsequent transfer of the pledged securities to a special pledge account in the pledgor's name with any intermediary, or, in the case of *titres nominatifs purs,* with the issuer. The pledge may also be made effective by electronic identification of the pledged securities by the intermediary concerned. But under the implementation legislation of the EU FCD, a written deed that identifies the securities pledged and a control agreement between creditor and debtor will suffice.

A pledge on securities can be enforced by the sale or appropriation of the securities pledged, after a written deed to the debtor has been sent. Yet under the implementation legislation of the FCD, a pledgee may immediately either sell the pledged securities or appropriate them by set-off or transfer to his own account(s).

(5.1) *Is upper-tier attachment possible, i.e. is it possible for an account holder's claimant to exercise his rights against higher-tier accounts?* Pursuant to arts. 178 and 180 of Decree no. 92-755 of 31 July 1992, a judgment creditor may only attach securities with the issuer or its mandatee in the case of *titres nominatifs purs,* or with a financial intermediary in the case of *titres au porteur* or *nominatifs administrés.* From these provisions, and from the general absence of the 'look-though' approach, it may be inferred that upper-tier attachment is not allowed.[226]

6.7.2 Coherence

It has been shown that French law considers securities custody and transfer law to be part of *droit commercial,* which, in turn, is part of *droit commun* (general private and commercial law). Most pivotal elements of securities law, however, are governed by specific rules of law, notably the *Code monétaire et financier* and regulatory law, such as the *Règlement Général* of the *Autorité des marchés financiers.* In many instances, these specific provisions expressly derogate from the more general rules of law, and thus indicate a relationship of weak coherence, as securities law and the *droit commun* thus share few common principles.

Perhaps most importantly, securities transfer law currently derogates from general private law by departing from the *solo consensu* rule in favour of a regime under which ownership is transferred upon a credit entry in the transferee's securities account, rather than upon agreement between transferor and transferee alone. However, the departure has not been wholehearted, and for OTC transactions settled through the CSD's custody system, ownership is only transferred when the money side of the transaction has been settled. In addition, for all other securities transactions, it is provided that the moment when the ownership is transferred is ultimately to be determined by the exchange in question, and that refers to the day on which the transfer agreement was concluded.[227]

Moreover, the rules concerning the creation and enforcement of a pledge on securities have created a special regime that would otherwise be governed by the *Code de commerce.* Especially the implementation legislation of the EU Financial Collateral Directive has introduced many provisions that involve sharp departures from general commercial law principles. For example, it has abolished all previously existing formal requirements, such as a written notification of default prior to enforcement and a public auction as a way of enforcement. In addition, the FCD has introduced a control agreement between creditor and debtor in French law, as a way to make a pledge effective.

However, also prior to the FCD, the rules for the creation and enforcement of security interests in dematerialised securities already derogated from general commercial

226. *Cf.* Maffei (2005), 247.
227. *Cf.* Bonneau & Drummond (2005), no. 666.

law rules. First, unlike common commercial pledges, a pledge on securities did not need to be registered, and second, a pledge on securities could be enforced through the appropriation of the collateralised assets by the creditor, which contrasts with the *pacte commissoire* prohibition of the *droit commun.* On the other hand, exceptions to that prohibition also existed in *droit commun,* so as to allow fiduciary transfers of title under certain agreements that are not exclusively used in securities contexts.

Furthermore, strong doctrinal coherence has recently been restored with regard to the revendication of accountholders' assets in their intermediary's insolvency. Although securities custody law for a long time required an intermediary's bankruptcy administrator to acknowledge accountholder interests, so that they could enforce their property rights, the owners of fungible assets could theoretically not revendicate these assets on dogmatic grounds. A recent decision by the *Cour de cassation,* however, has changed that, and revendication of dematerialised securities by accountholders in their intermediary's insolvency is currently not only in a practical, but also in a doctrinal respect in accordance with general private law.[228]

Generally, these examples indicate a weakly coherent relationship between securities law and more general areas of law. When the rules of securities custody and transfer law do not fit logically within the more general areas of law, however, incoherence is established. Such incoherence shows especially where central elements of securities custody and transfer law cannot be unequivocally classified in private or commercial law terms. Already before the dematerialisation, leading scholars therefore called the approach of the legislature incoherent with respect to the problematical classification of both accountholder interests and the relationship between accountholder and intermediary.[229]

Unfortunately, neither the legislature nor the judiciary have solved these classification issues after the dematerialisation. Although it is currently generally agreed that the accountholder/intermediary relationship is more in accordance with the contracts of *dépôt, mandat* and *louage d'ouvrage* than with other contracts, the discrepancies of some of the main elements of *dépôt* with securities custody are not solved. More specifically, the impossibility to delivery dematerialised securities *in specie* on a request for retrieval, and to physically deposit these securities have been argued to render a classification as *dépôt* inappropriate. The contracts of *mandat* and *louage d'ouvrage,* on the other hand, seem accurate, but do not indicate the main characteristics of securities custody, maintenance of securities accounts and preservation of the assets to which those accounts refer. Practice therefore correctly considers the relationship, it is submitted, a *sui generis* contract, but that approach has not been generally accepted.

In addition, even greater controversies exist over the question of whether accountholder interests classify as property or contractual rights. Legislation and case law seem to indicate the former, but the issue remains unclear, especially with regard to the applicability of the negotiability principle. Thus, it is not entirely certain whether Article 2279 and 2280 C. civ. apply to securities accountholders, and,

228. Cass. com. 5 March 2002, *Dalloz,* 2002, no. 13, 1139.
229. Ripert & Roblot II (1976), nos. 1764.

although it is unlikely, a *verus dominus* might therefore be able to successfully challenge a *bona fide* accountholder's interests. It is submitted that this instance of incoherence and the consequent legal uncertainty in which it results, is unacceptable from the perspective of the important role that securities custody and transfer play in the modern capital markets.[230]

Similarly, it has been shown that it is not entirely certain, what rule of private international law will be applied by the French courts to determine proprietary conflicts of laws regarding book-entry securities. More specifically, the current PRIMA rule refers to the law of the 'relevant intermediary', but it is considered to be an applied version of the traditional *lex rei sitae* rule, notwithstanding its different effect and theoretical basis. The confusion thus presents an example of inconsistency and incoherence, which leads to legal uncertainty, as the logical inconsistency of the said approach results in uncertainty, whether the law of the intermediary's location, or the law of the location of the securities account, is applied.

Finally, it is submitted that the rule that a credit entry in a transferee's securities account must be rescinded because of a defaulting delivery by the transferor to the transferee's intermediary, presents an example of *Wertungswiderspruch.* As a result of this rule, accountholders may be left with a mere unsecured claim against their intermediary, should the latter become insolvent after having credited its client's account, but before having received the corresponding assets from the transferor or CSD. That result, it is submitted, makes an inconsistent distinction between accountholders who happen to find themselves in the said circumstances, and other accountholders, shielded by otherwise strongly protective regulatory and statutory law, which thus represents a clearly inconsistent approach.

In conclusion, the dematerialisation of all French securities sparked intense scholarly debate about almost every aspect of securities custody and transfer law, and that debate has shown that a substantial part of general private and commercial law do not fit the current practice of securities custody and transfer. As a consequence, the legislature and judiciary have introduced specific and clearly derogatory rules in some instances, but in other instances, the relationship remains unclear and is even sometimes incoherent. As Peltier wrote, regarding a criminal case in which the intermediary had violated its obligation to preserve its clients' dematerialised securities:[231] [some elements of the case] 'illustrate perfectly the obvious inefficiency of general private law to grasp the legal relationship [between custodian and investor] which has been transformed by the dematerialisation'.[232]

230. *Cf.* Maffei (2005), 249.
231. Peltier *in* CNCT 1997 Report, 168, n.8.
232. Cass. crim., 30 May 1996, *Bull. Joly Bourse* 1996, p. 628, no. 100, *see supra,* section 3.3.3.

Chapter 7

The Netherlands

7.1 INTRODUCTION

7.1.1 Trading, Clearing and Settlement

As noted in a previous chapter, the issue of shares by the *Vereenigde Nederlandsche Geoctroyeerde Oost-Indische Compagnie* (United Netherlands Chartered East India Company, 'VOC') in 1602 reputedly marks the beginning of securities trade, and the Amsterdam exchange where trade in that stock was centralised claims to be the world's oldest exchange.[1] Soon after the establishment of the stock exchange, futures and options were also traded on the Amsterdam exchange[2] and it is in that tradition that Amsterdam opened Europe's first options exchange in 1978. As successor to the *Vereniging voor de Effectenhandel* (Association for Securities Trade), AEX-Exchanges NV managed all Amsterdam markets, viz. the AEX-Stock Market, Options Market and Financial Futures Markets, until 22 September 2000, when it joined the Euronext Group under the name of Euronext Amsterdam. Euronext NV, the holding company for the Euronext Group, which currently comprises the Paris, Brussels, Lisbon and London LIFFE exchanges, has its statutory seat in the Netherlands.[3]

Since 3 September 1963, AEX-Effectenclearing BV performed central clearing for all exchange transactions. As it did not operate in a membership structure, all traders were admitted to central clearing facilities, but as of 29 June 1998,

---

1. *See supra,* Ch. 3.1 and <www.euronext.com>.
2. *See,* e.g., Gelderblom & Jonker (2005), 189 *et seq.*
3. As a recent development, Euronext and the New York Stock Exchange announced on 2 June 2006 a merger of the two companies, thus forming the world's largest and first transatlantic exchange. At the time of writing however, the merger had not yet taken full effect; *see* <www.euronext.com> *and infra,* Ch. 9.3.2.

only financially highly solid participants could make use of AEX-Effectenclearing BV, which thus involved a substantial diminishment of systemic risk.[4] Since February 2001, Clearnet Amsterdam Branch is the central counterparty ('CCP') for the Euronext Amsterdam markets, and the rules of AEX-Effectenclearing were consequently incorporated in the Clearing Rule Book of LCH.Clearnet. Accordingly, all participants currently have to enter into an agreement under French law with LCH.Clearnet SA.[5]

The greater part of Dutch securities is held by Euroclear Netherlands, formerly Necigef. Euroclear Netherlands is the Netherlands' only CSD and has been designated as such by the Dutch Minister of Finance.[6] Participants of Euroclear Netherlands, which may hold securities as well, are credit institutions regulated by *De Nederlandsche Bank* (the Netherlands Central Bank, 'DNB'), or other institutions such as DNB itself, *Centrum voor Fondsenadministratie* (Securities Administration Centre, CF), Clearnet, the Dutch Ministry of Finance[7] and foreign CSDs.[8] The foreign CSDs with which Euroclear Netherlands maintains links include: Euroclear France, Euroclear Belgium, CIK, Clearstream, Österreichsche Kontrollbank AG (OeKB) and Sweizerische Effecten Giro AG (SEGA).[9]

7.1.2 *Sedes Materiae*

Dutch securities custody and transfer law is considered to be part of general private law *(privaatrecht)*, and absent provisions of a more specific statute, it is therefore governed by the *Burgerlijk Wetboek* (Civil Code, 'BW') of 1992.[10] The most important specific statute on securities custody and transfer law is the *Wet giraal effectenverkeer* (Securities Giro Transfer and Administration Act, 'Wge'). But, as can be inferred from the Explanatory Notes to the Wge Draft, its provisions should be interpreted as rules that specify the more general rules of the Civil Code.[11]

---

4. *Cf.* Ch. 4.4.
5. Art. 4601 Book I (Clearing and Settlement) of the Euronext Rule Book, in conjunction with Art. I 1.2.3.1 of the Clearnet Clearing Rule Book. *Cf.* Van Beek (2002), 3 *and* Vink (1998), 273 and 283–284.
6. Art. 1 *Wet giraal effectenverkeer* (Securities Giro Transfer and Administration Act, 'Wge') *and see* Ministerial Order of 11 August 1977, Stcrt. 1977, 157.
7. *See* Peters (2003), 49.
8. When the EU Investment Services Directive prohibited any restrictions on the admission of foreign CSDs as participants, several foreign CSDs established links with Euroclear Netherlands; Investment Services Directive Art. 15, *and see* Uniken Venema (2003), 113.
9. *See* Euroclear Netherlands Disclosure Framework 2003, 17.
10. The 'new' Civil Code comprises both commercial and corporate law, which was formerly codified in the *Wetboek van Koophandel* (Commercial Code), and private law. On the distinction between private and commercial law, and its separate codification, *see* e.g. Visser (1938) *and* Hartkamp (2002), 25–27. Issues concerning equity are mainly governed by Book 2 of the Civil Code, while issues concerning debt are governed by the general private law provisions on contract law in Books 6 and 7A BW.
11. *See,* e.g., Explanatory Notes to the Draft Wge TK 1975–1976, 13 780, no. 3, 37.

Other than by the BW and Wge, the relationship between participants and CSD is governed by the *Reglement Girodepots* (Central Securities Deposit Regulations), which has been approved by the Minister of Finance.[12] As CSD participants are mainly banks, the relationship between accountholders and participants is usually also governed by the *Algemene Bankvoorwaarden* (General Banking Terms and Conditions, 'ABV').[13]

7.1.3 Historic Background

Prior to the enactment of the Wge on 8 June 1977,[14] no custody system facilitated the transfer of rights in securities by book-entry on a statutory basis.[15] Rights in bearer securities could be transferred only though the physical delivery of the certificates, and ownership was registered by a custodian through individual administration of securities numbers. The individualised registration prevented commingling, and therewith the loss of investors' property rights, but came to be considered as burdensome, because of the enormous increase in the volume of securities held and the shortage of an apt working force and a sharp increase in labour costs.[16]

To overcome these obstacles, but prior to the enactment of the Wge, a system of 'simplified administration and custody of securities' ('VABEF') enabled the deposit of securities into a fungible pool as of 1 November 1971. The VABEF system minimised the risks from intermediary insolvencies by a separation of the custody entity from the financial institutions that managed the custody and securities accounts. But VABEF did not preserve investors' property rights, nor did it facilitate a system for securities transfers by book-entry, and the government therefore considered the VABEF system to be a temporary solution. For domestic securities that are not eligible for admittance to the Wge system, however, VABEF

12. *Cf.* Art. 4 Wge.
13. *Cf.* especially Arts. 22, 23, 24 and 26 ABV. *See* on the ABV Filott (2000), 99–106; Rank et al. (1997), 38 *and also* Uniken Venema (2003), at 79 (on the relationship between Wge and ABV).
14. Stb. 1977, 333.
15. A letter by the *Vereniging voor de Effectenhandel* (Association for Securities Trade) to the Dutch Minister of Justice on 25 August 1969 represents the starting point of the legislative process that resulted in the Wge. In that letter, the *Vereniging* requested that a statute be enacted which would provide that (a) the abolition of individualised registration would not result in the loss of investors' property rights, but that those rights would be replaced by a co-property right in a fungible pool of securities and (b) that physical delivery would be replaced by a system of transfer by book-entry; *see* Explanatory Notes to the Draft Wge, TK 1975–1976, 13 780, no. 3, 11.
16. Explanatory Notes to the Draft Wge, TK 1975–1976, 13 780, no. 3, 12. *See also* Frielink (1990), 20.

still functions, while VABEF II has been introduced in 1993 as a modern version of VABEF, especially for the administration of securities that are located abroad.[17]

The Wge was based on existing German and French securities laws (French law was then similar to German securities law) and replaced individualised securities registration by fungible pools, in which accountholders obtained co-property rights. The replacement was voluntary, and individualised registration of securities numbers remained available. Custody of securities became centralised with a securities depository, while investors were now able to dispose of their securities only through securities accounts with participants of the CSD. These participants opened omnibus accounts in their own name with the CSD, but accountholder interests were preserved by a direct co-ownership right in the CSD's pools and a separation of their securities from those of the participants and the CSD's own property.[18] It was thought that such a construction of co-ownership was preferable to a statutory preference of accountholders' interests.

As the overwhelming majority of Dutch securities consist of bearer certificates, the Wge of 1977 provided for the custody of this type of securities only. But in 2000, the Wge was modified, so as to make registered securities eligible for admittance to the Wge's custody system.[19] That modification was mainly driven by the introduction of the EMU and the subsequent issuing of European Central Bank notes in registered form, as well as by the increase in cross-border transactions.[20] The adjustment of 2000 involved mere technical modifications, but in the course of its enactment, the government announced a more fundamental revision of the Wge.[21]

Because Dutch securities law, like the securities laws of many other countries including Germany, thus represents a legal framework that is (still) heavily based on the traditional concept of securities as tangible movables, the following sections will analyse in greater detail current Dutch law regarding the custody and transfer of securities, as well as its relationship with more general areas of law. First, the main distinctions with regard to financial instruments will be discussed. In the section that follows, legal aspects of securities custody will be analysed,

17. Explanatory Notes to the Draft Wge, TK 1975–1976, 13 780, no. 3, 12. *See* Rank (1996), 320, Uniken Venema (2003), 101 and 174, Schim (2006), 19 *and,* extensively, Rank (1997). *Cf.* Art. 50 Wge *and* Haentjens (2007, forthcoming), comm. at Art. 50.
18. *Cf.* Explanatory Notes to the Draft Wge TK 1975–1976, 13 780, no. 3, 17.
19. *See* Blom (1998), 199, Van den Bosch (2000), 136, Van Pappelendam-Hemmen (2000), 376, Van Dijk (2001-1), 146 *and* Van den Hoek (2004), 147 *et seq.*
20. Explanatory Notes to the Draft Regarding Adjustments of the Wge TK 1999–2000, 27 164, no. 3, 1.
21. Memorandum pursuant to the Official Report, TK 1999–2000, 27 164, no. 5, 1. As its most recent activity, the Ministry of Finance has disclosed that it is preparing a modification of the Wge that will have to be adopted by 1 July 2008. The Ministry stated that the modification will address the limited scope of the Wge's proprietary protection of accountholders, the current sub-optimal structure for the custody of derivatives and the little progress that has been made regarding the dematerialisation of all Dutch securities; *see* letter by the Minister of Finance to the chairman of the *Tweede Kamer der Staten-Generaal* (Lower House, House of Representatives) of 1 February 2007, *available at* <www.minfin.nl>.

with particular emphasis on securities accounts and the accountholder/intermediary relationship. In Sections 4 and 5 of this chapter, the transfer of securities by book-entry, and the creation and enforcement of security interests in securities will subsequently be discussed. Section 6 will deal with Dutch private international law concerning securities custody and transfer. The chapter will conclude with answers to the questions posed in Chapter 1.2.2 and a coherence analysis.

7.2 CATEGORIES OF SECURITIES

Other than between derivatives and primary products,[22] Dutch law distinguishes between bearer securities (*effecten aan toonder*) and registered securities (*effecten op naam*).[23] The distinctive factor in the latter distinction is the form of investor interests; investor interests in bearer securities must be expressed in a certificate, as the certificates themselves constitute investor interests.[24] Investor interests in registered securities on the other hand, need not be expressed in a physical certificate, and should such a certificate exist, it merely serves as an evidentiary document. Although the issuer's articles of association determine whether registered shares may be issued in a physical form, the issuance of shares in a private company with limited liability (*Besloten Vennootschap*) in a physical form is prohibited by law.[25]

Bearer securities exist in different forms.[26] First, in its most classical form, as certificates that represent a single bond or share (*K-stukken* or K-certificates, K stands for classic). These certificates, however, have become rare due to immobilisation and dematerialisation. Second, they exist as certificates that are deposited with the *Centrum voor Fondsenadministratie* (Centre for the administration of securities, 'CF'). The CF receives interests and dividends paid by issuing companies, and distributes these amounts to its participants, which further distribute to the investors. Finally, bearer securities exist as globals, which represent an entire issue in one single certificate.[27] Under Dutch law, both global shares and global bonds are issued, and these certificates are almost invariably held by either the European ICSDs Euroclear and Cedel, or Euroclear Netherlands.[28]

With respect to the eligibility of securities for admittance to the Wge custody system, Article 1 Wge refers to the CSD to determine which securities are eligible.

---

22. If the value of a financial instrument does not derive from fluctuations in other financial instruments' value, that instrument is considered a primary product; RANK *in* EISMA et al. (2002), 26.
23. Order securities also exist, but are rare; RANK *in* EISMA ET AL. (2002), 26.
24. VERJANS (2002), 468 *and* VAN PAPPELENDAM-HEMMEN (2000), 376 however, argue that identifying the investors by the issuer determines the distinction. But that position does not seem to be in accordance with current law; *see*, e.g., VAN DEN HOEK's reaction to VERJANS' publication.
25. Arts. 2:175 and 2:194 BW.
26. *See* RANK *in* EISMA ET AL. (2003), at 45.
27. When separate from the global, smaller denominated securities may also be issued, the global is called a jumbo certificate; UNIKEN VENEMA (2003), 25.
28. *See* GRAAF (1991), KLIK & KUIPERS (1992), BOELE (1997), 15 and 18 *and* BLOM (1998), 186.

Theoretically, all categories of securities are thus eligible, but in practice the Wge does not cater for the custody of derivatives, and Euroclear Netherlands admits only securities that are fungible and freely tradable.[29] Since the 2000 modification of the Wge, both registered and bearer securities are eligible for admittance to the Wge system. In addition, the 2000 modification of the Wge made globals eligible for admittance to the Wge system, and, as a measure to encourage immobilisation, it introduced Article 36(4) Wge, which provides that the CSD may replace *K-stukken* with globals.

7.3 CUSTODY OF BOOK-ENTRY SECURITIES

7.3.1 Three Types of Custody

As the Wge did not abolish any of the existing types of securities custody, three basic legal types of intermediated securities custody can currently be discerned.[30] First, when securities are held on an individualised basis, i.e. when custodians attribute individual securities numbers to individual investors, investors preserve their ownership rights, but no transfer by book-entry is possible between clients of different custodians. This type of custody will therefore not be further discussed. Second, when securities are held in pools on a fungible basis, investors lose their ownership rights and are left with a mere contractual claim against their custodian. That claim includes the delivery of the same quality and quantity of securities deposited. Third, when the Wge applies to the securities and intermediary concerned, securities are also held on a fungible basis, but investors' property rights are protected by a combination of both contractual and proprietary rights. In the following sections, most attention will be paid to the last form of custody.

7.3.2 Custody With Loss of Ownership

The fact that commingling makes it impossible to attribute (rights in) specific assets to specific entitlement holders has as a consequence that investors lose their ownership rights in securities when securities are held on a fungible basis, rather than with individualised registration of securities numbers. The *Hoge Raad* (Supreme Court, 'HR') determined that as early as in 1934,[31] and in the Teixeira

29. *See* Zebregs (2005), 199–203. The present author has been advised, however, that the government is currently considering making derivatives and other financial products eligible for admittance; Haentjens (forthcoming, 2007), comm. at Art. 1.

30. Direct holding arrangements, including those of mutual funds, will not be discussed. *Cf.* De Jong (1998), 53.

31. 20 December 1934, NJ 1935, 708. Loss of property rights due to commingling is now codified in Art. 5:15 in conjunction with Art. 5:14 BW. These Arts. provide that either the owner of the larger part of the commingled pool has to be considered as the owner of the whole pool, or all owners have to be considered as co-owners. But these provisions only deal with liquids and

de Mattos Bank case, it was affirmed that investors cannot enforce any proprietary right in their custodian's bankruptcy, when their securities are commingled.[32]

Yet under several custody constructions still employed today, securities are held on a fungible basis, resulting in investors' loss of their ownership rights, especially when these securities are not eligible for custody in the Wge system.[33] First, investors still may chose to have their securities held on a non-individualised basis. But, as the Teixeira de Mattos case showed, those investors are subject to a substantial insolvency risk, and this construction is therefore only very infrequently applied to bearer and registered securities. For derivatives, however, it is the most common form of custody.[34]

Second, securities can be held in the VABEF system mentioned *above*, and ownership of securities is then transferred to a depository, a special purpose vehicle that is separated from the institution with which investors hold their securities accounts. The insolvency risk of that vehicle is minimised, as its articles of association exclude any form of commercial activity, while the account provider is liable for its administration. Moreover, these depositories are wholly owned by the *Administratiekantoor VABEF,* a non-commercial entity the sole purpose of which is holding the shares in the custody vehicles and the supervision of their functioning.[35] As a more recent version of this construction, VABEF II has been introduced in 1993 and 1994, and is currently mainly used for foreign securities held outside the Netherlands.[36]

Third, when registered securities were not yet eligible for admission to the Wge system, the *Nederlands Interprofessioneel EffectenCentrum BV* ('NIEC') acted as CSD for that category of securities. Registered securities were then registered in NIEC's name on the issuer's register, but seem also to have been registered directly in investors' names, which thus involved a direct holding system.[37] Yet in

---

gasses on the one hand, and assets that can be determined only by weight, size or number (e.g. grain, coffee or sand) on the other (all tangible movables). Commingling due to the impossibility of attribution, such as in the instance of money notes or bearer securities, is distinguished from those instances. As to the latter type of commingling, prior owners *de facto* lose their property rights because of the rules of evidence; according to Art. 3:109 BW in conjunction with Art. 3:119, a custodian of a commingled pool is deemed to be entitled to the securities in its custody. *See* ASSER-VAN DAM-MIJNSSEN-VAN VELTEN 3-II (2002), nos. 71 and 72, ASSER-MIJNSSEN-DE HAAN 3-I (2001), no. 128 *and* WICHERS (2002), 150 *et seq.*

32. HR 12 January 1968, NJ 1968, 274. In this case, the *Hoge Raad* held that 2 clients, who tried to enforce their property rights against the bank's bankruptcy administrator concerning 4 (!) securities held by the bank, could not succeed, because they could not sufficiently prove that they had given the securities into the bank's custody or that the bank was a mere detentor of the securities. *Cf.* Rechtbank Amsterdam (Amsterdam District Court), 18 April 1991, NJ 1992, 104.
33. *See* RANK (1997), 18.
34. RANK (1997), at 19.
35. *See,* e.g., RANK (1996), 327–328.
36. *See* MEIJER (1974), *and,* extensively, RANK (1996), RANK ET AL. (1997) *and* RANK (1999), 85–86.
37. Art. 23 NIEC Regulations. See LE RÜTTE (1992) *and* LE RÜTTE *in* RANK ET AL. (1997), 133. *See also* UMBGROVE (1991), 18, BLOM (1998), 195, RANK (1999), 86 *and* UNIKEN VENEMA (2003), 180.

both instances, NIEC maintained the issuer's register and performed the function of registrar.[38] Fourth, it has been argued that when globals that are not eligible for admission to the Wge system are held by a financial intermediary, investors cannot obtain a proprietary interest and have a mere contractual claim against their account provider, but, as will be shown *below*, that position is contested.[39]

7.3.2.1 Issues of Classification

Although these types of custody are used on a relatively large scale, many legal aspects, and especially their private law classifications, are unclear and doctrinally contested. First, the classification of the act of deposit has been subject to debate, as *bewaargeving* (*depositum regulare*), requires a custodian to be able to deliver the assets deposited *in specie* upon the depositor's request, which is obviously impossible when fungible securities are held as pooled accounts.[40] But a deposit of securities with an intermediary is also not classified as a transfer of ownership. Mijnssen, for instance, showed that although a depositor loses his ownership rights the moment his securities commingle with other securities of the same kind, no transfer can be construed, because constitutive elements for the transfer of ownership are absent, most notably the depositor's intent to transfer.[41] As a solution, especially in the case of registered securities that are registered in the intermediary's name, a transfer of beneficial ownership to the intermediary could be construed, but under Dutch general private law, such a transfer is forbidden.[42]

Second, an accountholder's contractual claim against his account provider refers primarily to his right to the delivery of the same quantity and quality of securities as deposited, and to the proper performance by the account provider of his duties as a custodian.[43] But the private law classification of these rights is not unequivocal, since, for the reasons mentioned *above*, the accountholder/intermediary relationship is not governed by the provisions of Article 7:600 *et seq.* BW on *bewaargeving* (*depositum regulare*). In addition, neither the provisions of Article 7:414 *et seq.* on contractual agency (*lastgeving*), nor Article 7A:1791 *et seq.* BW on loan for consumption (*verbruikleen*) seems appropriate.

More specifically, a classification as *verbruikleen* is not appropriate, because under that contract, the depositary is entitled to use the assets lent for its own purpose, which might to some extent be in accordance with an account provider's authority to use the securities deposited, but which does not correspond to his obligation to respect an accountholder's rights and duties attached to the securities, such as voting rights and monetary rights. In addition, under *verbruikleen,* a

38. NIEC also offers the possibility of custody with administration of securities numbers (Art. 16 NIEC Regulations).
39. This debate will be commented upon later on in this section.
40. Art. 7:600 *et seq.* BW.
41. Mijnssen (1975), 200. Although Mijnssen referred to general rules of private law that have been changed in 1992, his argument is still valid in this specific instance.
42. Art. 3:84(3) BW. *But see infra,* s. 7.5.1.
43. *See* the ABV *and* Rank (1997), 29.

depositary does not receive a fee, which is clearly at odds with normal practice of securities custody.

On the other hand, when an account provider performs certain tasks, such as the execution of transfer orders, that performance classifies as *lastgeving* (contractual agency). Yet to the performance of most other duties and to the use of securities for an intermediary's own benefit, the provisions on *lastgeving* do not apply. Especially when an intermediary's activities do not classify as legal acts (*rechtshandelingen*), the more general provisions on services agreements (*opdracht*) are applicable. Application of those provisions, however, implies the inapplicability of the provisions on *bewaargeving* (*depositum regulare*).[44]

In sum, the (contractual) accountholder/intermediary relationship, commonly referred to as custody agreement, cannot easily be classified in general private law terms, and must therefore be considered a *sui generis* agreement. But because of standard conditions and the non-mandatory character of the statutory provisions on deposit, loan for consumption and contracts in general, that *sui generis* character does not give rise to many legal issues in practice.[45]

Similarly, when securities are held on a fungible basis and investors lose their property rights, questions of classification arise with regard to the transfer of those securities by book-entry. Practically, transfers take place by a credit entry and a corresponding debit entry in to transferee's and transferor's securities account, respectively. But, as these securities are not delivered physically, and no statutory rule gives the book-entries proprietary effect, these transfers have only contractual effects.[46]

It is even questionable whether the said book-entries classify as transfers (of ownership). When a debit entry of the transferor's securities account is made, that entry effectuates the cancellation of the transferor's right against his intermediary, and a corresponding credit entry in the transferee's account effectuates the creation of a similar, but new claim against the latter's intermediary. Thus, a transferee does not acquire the same asset a transferor disposed, and strict dogmatically analysed, these debit and credit entries therefore do not classify as transfer of ownership ex Article 3:84(1) BW. The non-transferability of an accountholder's claim against his intermediary is especially apparent when both transferor and transferee hold their respective securities accounts with different intermediaries. By the same token, a transfer of fungible securities by book-entry does not classify as an assignment of a debt.[47]

---

44. Art. 7:400(1) BW. *Accord* Asser-Kortmann-De Leede-Thunnissen 5-III (1994), no. 43 *and* Du Perron (1993), 1045. *See also* Meijer (1999), 8 *and* Du Perron (1993), 1046, on the relationship between the contracts of contractual agency and services agreement.
45. *See* Rank et al. (1997), 40.
46. But when parties to a particular securities transaction are clients of different intermediaries, the transferor's intermediary has to deliver the securities concerned physically to the transferee's intermediary, for no central depository exists for this form of custody. This particular transaction thus involves the transfer of ownership, but only between intermediaries, not between accountholders.
47. *Cf.* Rank (2001), 68.

In conclusion, securities custody on a fungible basis that involves investors' loss of ownership is more similar to the management of money accounts than to the custody of movable tangibles, for as with money accounts, accountholders do not enjoy any property right against their account provider, while transfers take place through debit and credit entries in the accounts of transferor and transferee.

7.3.2.2 Globals

Globals are almost invariably held in a multi-tiered system, as CSDs or ICSDs hold the physical certificates in custody and register their participants' entitlements to (parts of) the globals, and these participants, in their turn, register their clients' entitlements.[48] As noted *above*, it is a matter of debate how the nature of an investor's entitlement in a global classifies.

On the one hand, it has been argued that this entitlement classifies as a co-ownership right in a *gemeenschap* (community of property), whereas others have claimed that it classifies as a mere contractual claim against an intermediary.[49]

BOELE, for instance, has argued that investors enjoy co-ownership rights, and that the transfer of these rights is therefore governed by the rules on the transfer of movable tangibles.[50] In this view, delivery has to be effected under Article 3:115(c) BW, which prescribes the requirements for delivery when a third party holds a movable tangible for the transferor and holds it for the transferee after the transfer. But this position cannot, it is submitted, withstand closer scrutiny.

First, should Article 3:115(c) BW be applied, it cannot be determined which intermediary must be considered as the holder for the transferor and transferee, especially when the transfer is effected for investors who hold their securities accounts with different intermediaries; must the *direct* holder (*onmiddellijk houder*), i.e. the holder of the physical certificate, most likely the CSD, or the *first* holder, i.e. the transferor's intermediary, be considered as the holder as meant in Article 3:115 BW? Second, the application of Article 3:115(c) BW implies that ownership of (part of) the global is transferred when either the CSD or the transferor's intermediary has either acknowledged, or received notice of the transfer. But it cannot be maintained, it is submitted, that the transferor's intermediary holds anything for the transferee at any point in time, as the former is usually not even aware of the latter's identity, which also applies to the CSD. Moreover, it is

48. In the case of an international issue, a global will most often be deposited with an ICSD like Euroclear or Cedel. These ICSDs developed the practice of depositing certificates with a mutual or common depository. This common depository deposits the certificate in its turn with a national bank. *See* BOELE (1997), 17.

49. *Gemeenschap* is governed by Art. 3:166 *et seq*. BW. If DNB acts as a custodian of a global, a mixed legal form of custody can be discerned; the DNB's participants are deemed to enjoy a co-property right, whilst investors can only assert a mere contractual claim against these participants; BLOM (1998), 189, n.18 and the further references provided there.

50. Art 3:96 BW, and Art. 3:93 first sentence in conjunction with 3:90 BW; BOELE (1997), 20.

untenable that the transferee would receive a right of ownership before a credit entry has been made in his securities account.[51]

In addition, the application of the provisions of the civil code on *gemeenschap* (section 3.7 BW) would lead to insurmountable legal complications. Apart from specific problems that arise when the co-ownership construct is applied to a multiple tiered structure of custody, its applicability without a statutory basis is questionable. As can be inferred from the aforementioned Teixeira de Mattos Bank case, co-ownership rights cannot be invoked on the grounds of an agreement between an accountholder and intermediary alone. The better view would therefore be that the nature of accountholder interests in globals that are not admitted to the Wge custody system classifies as a contractual claim.

7.3.3 Wge Custody

The majority of Dutch securities are admitted to the Wge system of securities custody.[52] But the system is restricted in two ways, as only admitted participants may hold omnibus accounts with the CSD, and only admitted securities may be a part thereof. Admittance of both securities and participants is determined by the CSD; Article 1 Wge.[53]

The Wge created a three-tiered pyramid-shaped securities custody structure. The top of that pyramid is formed by the so-called *giro pool* (*girodepot*), which is administered by the CSD.[54] The CSD's participants are co-owners in that pool, in proportion to the securities of the same kind which they administer. Thus, securities of different issues form different pools, and as many (giro) pools exist as there are securities admitted to the system.[55] The securities that are administered by the participants form so-called *participant pools* (*verzameldepots*), the second tier of the pyramid. Pursuant to Article 12(2) Wge, investors are co-owners of these pools, in proportion to the securities to which they are entitled. They form the third and last tier of the Wge pyramid.

This pyramid-shaped structure is complicated by the fact that participants may hold securities accounts with each other, and one participant's pool can therefore contain an entitlement to another participant's pool, when the former participant holds a securities account with the latter. In addition, securities that are owned by

51. *Contra* Blom (1998), 188.
52. E.g. Van den Bosch (2000), 137.
53. Specific regulations regarding the admittance of institutions by the CSD can be found in Stc. 1999, no. 110, 11.
54. Art. 34 Wge. As a derogation from company law (Art. 2:85 BW), Art. 50a Wge provides that investors in registered securities no longer need to be individually registered by an issuing company, as registration of the CSD or other account provider suffices.
55. Likewise, an intermediary administers as many participant pools as there are categories of securities to which its clients are entitled. In the following, all pools administered by CSD or participants are referred to when giro pool and participant pools are mentioned.

the participant itself form part of the pool it administers.[56] Thus, an accountholder's securities account may refer to securities that are physically present in the participant pool administered by their account provider, in another participant pool, or in the giro pool administered by the CSD. Moreover, at present, almost no physical securities are held by participants, as they are all immobilised with the CSD.

The omnibus accounts which intermediaries hold with the CSD are registered in their own names, and investors can dispose of their securities only via their immediate intermediaries, as Article 10(c) Wge provides that 'the participant pool also contains its entitlement to the giro pool'. That article thus also establishes a direct (proprietary) link between investors and securities, not only when these securities are held by an intermediary, but also when they are held by the CSD, for the investors enjoy a co-ownership interest in the participant pool, which contains an entitlement to the participant pool's share in the giro pool. This direct proprietary entitlement of investors to their securities was the expressed intention of the 1976 legislature, as it was felt that investors should retain a direct property right in their securities, even when these are registered by the CSD in the name of a participant and can be disposed of only via the participant concerned.[57]

Consequently, intermediaries do not have full authority to dispose of the participant pools maintained by them, for they enjoy neither any property right, nor a statutory right of full disposal over their clients' securities.[58] Another consequence is that no separation of an intermediary's own assets from its clients' assets is required by statute, and the legislative history of the Wge even explicitly indicates that no such separation should be made.[59]

7.3.4 Accountholder/Intermediary Relationship

Classification of the accountholder/intermediary relationship in general private law terms proves to be impossible, or at least highly complicated, especially when the legal act that initiates that relationship is taken into account. In the following section, the deposit of securities into a Wge pool with an intermediary will therefore be discussed in greater detail, but the retrieval of securities and the liquidation

56. Arts. 10(b) and 10(a) Wge, respectively.
57. Explanatory Notes to the Draft Wge TK 1975–1976, 13 780, no. 3, 19–20. *Cf.* Rank-Berenschot (1998), 157–158 *and* Haentjens (forthcoming, 2007), comm. at Art. 10.
58. This property law mechanism of investor protection is strengthened by regulatory law; *see* Art. 6:14 *Nadere Regeling gedragstoezicht financiële ondernemingen Wft* (Further Regulations of Financial Institutions Supervision Wft). *Cf. also* Art. 11(2) Wge, where it is provided that account providers may act as the entitlement holders of their clients' assets only when that would serve the 'proper management' of these assets.
59. *See* Explanatory Notes to the Draft Wge TK 1975–1976, 13 780, no. 3, 21–22 and 44. *Contrast* Art. 4:87 *Wet op het financieel toezich* (Financial Supervision Act, 'Wft') in conjunction with Art. 6:15(1) *et seq. Nadere Regeling gedragstoezicht financiële ondernemingen Wft. Cf.* Haentjens (forthcoming, 2007), comm. at Art. 10, 35 and 42. *But see* Van der Beek (2003), 246, Schim (2004), 420–422, *and* Schim (2006), 47 *et seq.*, arguing that such separation must be possible.

of a securities pool, as well as additional contracts that define the accountholder – intermediary relationship will also be examined. It may be reminded that this relationship is primarily governed by the Wge and the *Algemene Bankvoorwaarden* (General Banking Terms and Conditions, 'ABV').

7.3.4.1 Wge Deposit

As noted *above*, the Wge created a custody system of which only admitted securities can become part, and CSD-approved securities therefore have to be deposited into a participant or giro pool.[60] While investors may deposit their securities into a participant pool, only participants of the CSD can (re)deposit securities into the giro pool. The deposit of bearer securities into the Wge system is distinguished from the deposit of registered securities, in that the Wge classifies the former as a 'deposit', but the latter as 'delivery'.[61] But the distinction raises serious legal issues. It is unclear, for instance, whether the deposit of securities with a custodian classifies as *bewaargeving* (*depositum*) or as transfer (of ownership).

The legislature intended the Wge to be in accordance with the civil code of the time, but current private law provisions on *bewaargeving* (section 7.9 BW) no longer fit the deposit of securities.[62] Specifically, under the Wge, the deposit of securities is effectuated when the securities are accepted by a custodian, but under current private law, *bewaargeving* is established when the deposit agreement is concluded.[63] In addition, the civil code provisions on *bewaargeving* do not apply to the custody of fungible securities, as *bewaargeving* requires a custodian to be able to deliver the assets deposited *in specie* upon the depositor's request.[64] On the other hand, *bewaargeving* also involves the depositor's obligation to reward a custodian for its services, the custodian's obligation to handle the depositor's assets with due care, the prohibition on the custodian using the assets deposited for its own account, and, finally, the custodian's obligation to preserve the proceeds that might flow from the assets deposited.[65] All these aspects of *bewaargeving* also apply to securities custody.

---

60. Art. 12 and 38 Wge. When CSD-approved securities exist outside the Wge system, but are subsequently transferred to an intermediary *qua* transferee, they become *ipso iure* part of the participant pool which that intermediary administers, and thereby part of the Wge system; Art. 13 Wge; *cf.* Uniken Venema (2003), 213–219. But other than securities held under the Wge regime, an intermediary may hold securities on an individualised basis.
61. Arts. 12 and 13 Wge.
62. *But cf.* the Explanatory Notes to the Draft Wge TK 1975–1976, 13 780, no. 3, 42, which stated that it had been debated in the legal literature to what extent the provisions of the Civil Code on deposit are applicable to the deposit of goods, when these goods are not to be returned *in specie*.
63. Arts. 12 and 38 Wge, *and* Art. 7:400 BW, respectively. *But see* Van Ardenne-Stachiw *in* Rank et al. (1997), 85 and 117–118. Under the previous civil code, a deposit agreement was effectuated when the assets deposited were accepted by a custodian.
64. Art. 7:600 *et seq*. BW. *Cf. supra,* s. 7.3.2.
65. Arts. 7:601, 7:602, 7:603 and 7:604, respectively.

Moreover, on both practical and dogmatic grounds, a deposit of securities cannot classify as a transfer of ownership.[66] Although it was acknowledged that upon deposit/delivery, investors lose their ownership rights, the government did not explicitly intend to give the impression that these securities are transferred to the participant's or the CSD's property.[67] Moreover, the legislature found it unacceptable that all other requirements for a valid transfer of ownership would have to be met when the deposit/delivery of securities would be so classified.[68] A valid transfer of ownership requires, other than delivery (*levering*), a valid title, the transferee's power of disposal (*beschikkingsbevoegdheid*) and a proprietary agreement (*goederenrechtelijke overeenkomst*), and the non-fulfilment of one of these requirements results in a non-valid transfer of ownership. In such instance, a previous owner can revendicate his assets under third party transferees, which would unacceptably impair the legal certainty required in securities transactions, should the same rule apply to the deposit of securities. Article 14 Wge therefore provides that the absence of a depositor's power of disposal has no legal consequences for the deposit of securities.[69]

Although the formal requirements for delivery have to be met when securities are deposited, it must be concluded that such delivery does not result in the transfer of ownership rights from the depositor to the custodian/depositee.[70] Consequently, the deposit of securities into a Wge pool has to be considered a *sui generis* legal act.[71]

Notwithstanding these classification difficulties, a deposit of securities into a Wge pool results in the replacement of the investor's right of ownership with a right of co-ownership in the *gemeenschap* (community of property), formed by the Wge pool.[72] Upon deposit, such *gemeenschap* consists of securities previously deposited, plus the newly deposited ones. Consequently, a deposit of securities changes the previous owners' entitlement, i.e. it changes the percentage of the Wge pool to which the previous co-owners were entitled.[73] Thus, because co-owners are

66. *See*, e.g., MIJNSSEN (1975), 202, VAN DIJK (2001–2), 336 *and* SCHIM (2006), 67 *et seq.*
67. Explanatory Notes to the Draft Wge TK 1999–2000, 27 164, no. 3, 4 *and cf.* Explanatory Notes to the Draft Wge TK 1975–1976, 13 780, no. 3, 12.
68. Explanatory Notes to the Draft Wge TK 1999–2000, 27 164, no. 3, 4.
69. *See* HAENTJENS (forthcoming, 2007), comm. at Art. 14.
70. Arts. 2:86c and 2:86 BW (registered shares), Art. 3:94 BW (registered bonds) and Art. 3:93 in conjunction with Art. 3:90 BW (bearer shares), which must all be read in conjunction with Art. 3:84 BW.
71. A government statement confirms this position. The said statement referred to the delivery of registered securities, but must be assumed to apply to bearer securities also; Advice of the Council of State and Additional Report TK 1999–2000, 27 164 A, 5.
72. The investor/owner of the securities deposited need not be the depositor; Art. 12(1) Wge. In Rechtbank Amsterdam, 27 August 2003, JOR 2003, 262, the court held that when an administrator had deposited securities he held for the owner of the securities, the (successor of the) administrator had illegally pledged these securities, as he had no power of disposal.
73. For instance, the credit balance of two accountholders with the same account provider shows 10 securities of a certain type. Thus, these accountholders are entitled to 50per cent of the Wge pool. When the securities account of a third accountholder becomes credited with 10 securities

entitled to a share in the entire pool of securities, rather than to specific securities, a representation by the intermediary that administers the pool in which securities are deposited must be construed. Under such construct, an intermediary represents the existing co-owners of the pool when accepting securities from the depositor. By the same token, an intermediary represents its clients vis-á-vis the CSD or other intermediaries when transferring securities to the CSD or other participants, respectively.[74]

The deposit procedure just discussed assumes that securities are held by investors and subsequently deposited into a Wge pool, which may have been the situation for which the legislature drafted the Wge in 1976, but which seldom happens today. At present, investors usually do not possess bearer certificates, and an issuer often directly deposits the securities it issued into a participant or giro pool.[75] The legal aspects of a direct deposit of securities into a participant pool are identical to what has been discussed *above*. A direct issue into the giro pool, however, is more problematical. For instance, when a global is directly deposited into the giro pool, a representation of the participants by the CSD has to be construed, only to satisfy the Wge's requirement that a deposit must be effected by a participant. An issue of dematerialised securities, on the other hand, is effected through assignment of the securities to a participant pool (the pool is often administered by the *listing agent*), after which they are transferred to the giro pool, and subsequently distributed among other participants.[76]

7.3.4.2 Retrieval and Distribution

Provided the issuer has not prohibited the delivery of its securities out of the Wge system, an investor may retrieve from his account provider the securities to which

---

of the same kind, all accountholders become entitled to 33per cent of the pool. *See* UNIKEN VENEMA (2003), 44–46.

74. Arts. 38 and 10(b) Wge, respectively. UNIKEN VENEMA (2003), 83–86, has argued that these transfers are legally identical to the acts of deposit. But it is submitted that the fact that the former transfers relate to securities that are already part of the Wge system, whereas the latter do not, distinguishes them. A depositor loses his ownership when depositing his securities, while an intermediary's entitlement to the securities it transfers remains the same when transferring them to the CSD. In that instance, the intermediary performs a mere administrative task regarding the securities in its custody, regardless of the fact that for both transfers and deposit, delivery has to be performed according to the same statutory requirements.
75. VAN ARDENNE-STACHIW *in* RANK ET AL. (1997), 92 *and* SCHIM (2006), 72 *et seq.* In addition, accountholders may want to deposit securities that are held in the VABEF system (*see supra*) into the Wge system. The Wge created a legal construction, so that no physical delivery out of the VABEF system is needed, but a fictional deposit into the Wge system must be effectuated nonetheless; *see* HAENTJENS (2007, forthcoming), comm. at Art. 50.
76. *Cf. supra,* s. 7.3.1. *But see* VAN DIJK (2001–2), 337–338 *and* SCHIM (2006), 77 *et seq.*, who argue that the Wge allows for a direct issue into the giro pool. But it is submitted that the current text and meaning of the Wge clearly prevent such an interpretation, although it arguably better facilitates today's practice; *see,* especially, Art. 37(1) Wge. *Cf.* UNIKEN VENEMA (2003), 66–75.

he is entitled.[77] The procedure for retrieval and subsequent delivery is similar to the deposit of securities into the system as discussed *above*. As a result of the delivery of securities out of a Wge pool, for instance, the remaining co-owners' entitlements change, for after delivery, their entitlement is to another, viz. a larger, percentage of the Wge pool in question. As the Wge system is based on fungibility, the intermediary that delivers securities out of the pool which he administers must deliver securities of the correct quantity and quality; Article 26 Wge.

When a Wge pool is liquidated, for instance because of the administering intermediary's insolvency, the securities present in that pool are distributed amongst entitlement holders. If the amount of securities held by the insolvent intermediary turns out to be less than the total amount of securities to which the accountholders are collectively entitled, the resulting deficit is first covered by the intermediary's own share in the pool.[78] Any remaining deficit is apportioned among the intermediary's clients, in proportion of their share; arts. 27 and 28 Wge (participant pools), and Article 42 Wge (giro pool).[79]

However, these procedures of delivery and liquidation represent a derogation from the general private law rules on the liquidation of a *gemeenschap* (community of property).[80] First, Article 3:178(1) BW provides that all individual co-owners may request the liquidation of their *gemeenschap* at any point, which is obviously and explicitly not applicable to Wge pools.[81] Furthermore, 3:182 BW requires the cooperation of all co-owners when a *gemeenschap* is liquidated,[82] whereas under Article 30(1) and Article 48 Wge, the delivery of securities out of a Wge pool occurs without the cooperation of accountholders or participants, respectively. If a representation of accountholders or participants by the delivering intermediary or CSD is construed, however, they would fictionally co-operate with the delivery or liquidation.[83]

Finally, the delivery of separate securities that are expressed in a global proves to be problematical. As a solution, the securities to be delivered are separated from

77. Art. 26 Wge (introduced by the 2000 revision of the Wge). *See* UNIKEN VENEMA (2003), 220–231, objecting to the possibility that an issuer forbids physical retrieval, mainly on corporate law arguments. *Contra* SCHIM (2006), 101 *et seq.*, arguing that the prohibition of retrieval by an issuer concerns a specific (corporate) authority that must be distinguished from the authority to prohibit retrieval in the terms of issue, and that this prohibition is not necessarily detrimental to the investors' interests.
78. Such a deficit could arise, for instance, when, to effectuate a transfer, an intermediary credits its clients' securities accounts, before having been correspondingly credited with the CSD, and then falls insolvent; *see* HAENTJENS (2007, forthcoming), comm. at Art. 16, 18 and 41, *and* GROENHUJSEN & KRISTEN (1999), 215.
79. *See* HAENTJENS (2007, forthcoming), comm. at arts. 27 and 28, for practical distribution examples. As an additional measure of investor protection, a special guarantee fund has been created to compensate investors' losses up to the amount of EUR 20,000; arts. 3:258 through 3:265 Wft *and* Stb. 2004, 77.
80. These rules on liquidation also refer to delivery; *see* ASSER-MIJNSSEN-DE HAAN 3-I (2001), no. 463.
81. *Cf.* UNIKEN VENEMA (2003), 235.
82. *See* SNIJDERS & RANK-BERENSCHOT (1996), no. 224.
83. *Accord* WINTER (1998), 191.

the global in the form of registered securities, and subsequently assigned.[84] It is agreed with BOELE[85] that this procedure does not classify as novation (*novatie*), but as a third-party agreement between issuer, CSD and participants, under which the CSD's participants may receive these registered securities, yet may not further assign them to their clients.[86]

7.3.4.3 Additional Contracts

From the discussion on the deposit of securities into a Wge pool, it follows that the classification of the accountholder/intermediary relationship in general private law terms is not at all obvious, especially because a classification as *bewaargeving* is controversial. But the additional contracts that complement an intermediary's principal obligation, viz. the safekeeping of its clients' assets, prove to be no more easily defined.

When an intermediary, as the manager of a securities pool, acts with third parties on behalf of its clients, the accountholder/intermediary relationship classifies as a special form of representation.[87] For instance, an intermediary represents its clients when transferring their securities to the CSD or other intermediaries for deposit and custody.[88] However, this representation, as well as the intermediary's authority to represent, does not originate from an agreement, but from statute; Article 38 Wge. The general private law provisions on *volmacht* (procuration) are therefore not applicable, as Article 3:60(1) BW requires that the authority to represent must be granted through a legal act. In addition, representation under the Wge derogates from the general private law rules on representation, as representation by an intermediary excludes any interference from its clients, for accountholders are prohibited from disposing of their securities without the accountprovider's co-operation.[89]

Furthermore, the general private law provisions on contractual agency do seem to be applicable.[90] But whereas under the general private law definition of contractual agency, a representative discharges its obligations by performing one or more legal acts, an intermediary is typically not contractually obliged to perform such acts, for its typical acts of administration involve the transfer of securities from the participant pool to the giro pool. In addition, the general private law rules on mandate do not apply to the accountholder/intermediary relationship, because under these rules, the rights of the mandatary (*lasthebber*) against third

84. *See* BOELE (1997), 23–24, WINTER (1998), 189, BLOM (1998), 191–193 *and* VAN DEN HOEK (2004), 154.
85. BOELE (1997), 24.
86. BLOM (1998), 194.
87. *See* VAN ARDENNE-STACHIW *in* RANK ET AL. (1997), 111 *and* Explanatory Notes to the Draft Wge TK 1975–1976, 13 780, no. 3, 17. *See also infra,* s. 7.3.6.
88. *Cf.* UNIKEN VENEMA, 91–92.
89. UNIKEN VENEMA (2003), 77, speaks therefore of a sole and exclusive form of administration (*bewind*). *Cf. also* HAENTJENS (2004–2), 990.
90. Arts. 7:414 *et seq.* BW.

parties can also be asserted by the mandator (*lastgever*), whereas an accountholder is strictly prohibited from asserting his rights against, e.g., the CSD.[91]

More generally, section 7.7 BW on services agreements does not apply in a securities intermediary – accountholder context, because typical acts of administration such as the transfer of securities from a participant pool to the giro pool, are effectuated pursuant to statutory law, whereas in principle, (the fulfilment of obligations arising from) services agreements and contractual agency follow from a specific agreement.[92] In conclusion, the accountholder/intermediary relationship must be considered a *sui generis* relationship.[93]

7.3.5 Accountholder Interests

When an accountholder's securities account shows a credit balance of securities that are admitted to the Wge system, and that securities account is held with a Wge-admitted intermediary, the accountholder enjoys, as stated before, a direct co-ownership interest in the securities that his account refers to. The strict Dutch doctrine, however, only allows the ownership of tangibles, so that a different concept had to be created to refer to shared property rights in intangibles. Consequently, securities pools managed by intermediaries classify as *gemeenschappen* (communities of property), and rights therein as 'community rights'.[94] With the introduction of the community construct, the legislature intended to provide investors with the necessary proprietary protection against intermediary bankruptcies. The following section, however, will show that the community construct of the Wge is inconsistent with general private law.

First, although an investor's right of ownership is replaced with a right of co-ownership in a participant pool upon the deposit of his securities, it can be questioned what this co-ownership interest really involves, as the investor can only dispose of his securities via a participant or via a participant and the CSD.[95] In addition, it is submitted that the (meaning of the) co-ownership concept in the Wge context is inconsistent with general private law, for accountholders do not share identical rights in Wge pools, but rather enjoy a combination of rights that can only occasionally be asserted against third parties. Third, the application of the co-ownership and *gemeenschap* construct implies the applicability of the general private law provisions on *gemeenschap* (section 3.7 BW). The Wge itself, however, provides for several derogations from those provisions, but their application

91. Art. 7:420 BW. By the same token, Art. 6:253 BW on third party clauses does not apply. *Cf.* Uniken Venema (2003), 77 n.160 *and see* Haentjens (2004–2), 990. *See also infra,* s. 7.3.6.
92. *Cf.* arts. 7:400 and 7:414 BW respectively. *See* Asser-Kortmann-De Leede-Thunnissen 5-III (1994), no. 53 *and* Meijer (1999), 12.
93. *Cf.* Van Ardenne-Stachiw *in* Rank et al. (1997), 102–104 *and* Van Ravenhorst (1995), 21.
94. But because 'community rights' are identical to 'co-ownership rights', these rights will continue to be referred to as 'co-ownership rights' to facilitate comparative analysis.
95. *See* Explanatory Notes to the Draft Wge TK 1975–1976, 13 780, no. 3, 34 *and* Asser-Mijnssen-De Haan 3-I (2001), no. 461.

to the securities custody context also conflicts with the Wge's rationale, viz. accountholder protection.

7.3.5.1 Section 3.7 BW

To start with the last position: the Wge explicitly charges intermediaries with the management of securities pools and the exercise of accountholders' rights vis-á-vis third parties in that capacity; Article 11(2) Wge. Art. 3:170 BW, however, states that, generally, co-owners only have the authority to perform acts that concern common property together.[96] Consequently, a fictitious representation of the investors together by the intermediary must be construed so as to achieve the applicability of Article 3:170 BW, albeit indirectly, to the Wge context. In addition, it may be reminded that for the liquidation of a Wge pool and for the delivery of securities out of such pool, a similar representation of accountholders by the managing intermediary had to be construed to retain the applicability Article 3:182 BW, which requires the cooperation of all co-owners in the liquidation of a *gemeenschap.*[97]

More generally, the application of section 3.7 BW results in a failure to achieve one of the Wge's main objectives, viz. the proprietary protection of investors. In Kas-Associatie/Drying Corp., an investor (Drying Corporation) did not hold a securities account with a Wge participant, but with an intermediary that, in its turn, did hold a securities account with a Wge participant, viz. Kas-Associatie. Upon the intermediary's insolvency, Drying Corp. tried to assert its accountholder interests against Kas-Associatie. The *Hoge Raad,* however, held that the intermediary could not make Drying Corp. a co-owner in the pool, administrated by Kas-Associatie, because of the nature of the Wge *gemeenschap.*[98] Consequently, all lower than third-tier accountholders (the CSD being the first and its participants being the second tier) are withheld from the protection the Wge was intended to provide. It must therefore be concluded that the application of the provisions of section 3.7 BW lead to inconsistencies and other unwarranted consequences, notwithstanding regulatory rules that intend to mitigate this lack of accountholder protection.[99]

7.3.5.2 Community

The general private law classification of accountholder interests as a community right or a right of co-ownership is also inconsistent. First, when only one client of an intermediary or CSD is entitled to a certain security, i.e. when a participant or giro pool has only one entitlement holder, that accountholder obviously does not

96. Especially Art. 3:170(2) and (3) BW. *Cf.* Asser-Mijnssen-De Haan 3-I (2001), no. 455.
97. *Cf.* Art. 30(1) Wge. *See supra,* s. 7.3.4.
98. HR 23 September 1994, NJ 1996, 461. *Cf.* Uniken Venema (2003), 105.
99. *Cf.,* e.g., Art. 6:16(1)(a) *Nadere Regeling gedragstoezicht financiële ondernemingen Wft* (Further Regulations of Financial Institutions Supervision Wft), where it is provided that account providers that are no credit institutions must have a credit institution open a securities account directly in the name of the account providers' clients.

share in the pool concerned, nor is he a co-owner together with others. The Wge, however, considers all accountholders as such.[100]

Second, the application of the co-ownership construct to accountholder interests is inconsistent, because accountholders, it is submitted, enjoy a combination of rights that can only occasionally be asserted against third parties, rather than share certain identical rights in the Wge pools.[101] Under general private law, a co-owner enjoys a property right to a *pars pro indiviso,*[102] i.e. a share in an undividable community of property, but accountholders enjoy a specific interest in a dividable pool of fungible rights, i.e. an *indivisum pro parte.*

Thus, an accountholder enjoys an entitlement that is expressed by a credit balance on a securities account, and that entitlement refers (sometimes indirectly) to certain securities, but is not identical with the securities themselves.[103] The Wge provisions on *gemeenschap* are therefore inconsistent with the general private law principle under which co-ownership rights in property are identified with the property itself.[104] That position is affirmed by the aforementioned Kas-Associatie/Drying Corp. case, where it was held that a share in a securities pool classifies as a claim (*recht op naam*),[105] although the pool consisted of bearer securities. Such *recht op naam* not only relates to physical and registered securities situated in either a participant or giro pool, but may also relate to other rights, as Article 10(d) and (e) Wge provide that a participant pool may consist of claims (*vorderingen*) that substitute securities which were previously situated in that pool.[106]

The said *recht op naam* classifies – at least partly – as an *in personam* (contractual) interest, since an accountholder can enforce his main rights only against his immediate account provider, and *in rem* (proprietary) interests are enforceable *erga omnes.* For instance, the payment of dividends and interests, the exercise of voting rights and the delivery of securities out of the Wge system can only be enforced against an accountholder's immediate intermediary. Moreover, his right of disposal, i.e. his right to alienate, the right to pledge and the right to establish an usufruct, is also only enforceable against the account provider. If securities are situated in a participant pool, the managing intermediary acts as (exclusive) mandatary (*privatief lasthebber*) for its accountholders when observing the said

100. *Contrast* Art. 3:166(1) BW. The Explanatory Notes to the Draft Wge TK 1975–1976, no. 3, 22–23, refer to such an instance, but although the government admitted that no co-ownership then exists, it was not of the opinion that the Draft should be accordingly amended, with reference to (not further specified) foreign law.
101. *Cf.* Van Ardenne-Stachiw *in* Rank et al. (1997), 102–104. *See infra,* s. 7.4, for a discussion on the non-transferable nature of accountholder interests.
102. *Cf.* Snijders & Rank-Berenschot (1997), no. 214 *and* Asser-Mijnssen-De Haan 3-I (2001), no. 451.
103. *See* Mijnssen (1975), 205, Schoordijk (1975), 631 *and* Dalhuisen & Van Setten (2003), 126. *Accord* Frielink (1990), 36 *and* Van den Hoek (2003), 433. *Contra* Van den Bosch (2000), 137.
104. Art. 3:96 BW. *See* Asser-Mijnssen-De Haan 3-I (2001), no. 81.
105. Kas-Associatie/Drying Corp., HR 23 September 1994, NJ 1996, 461, Section 3.5. *See also* Van Ardenne-Stachiw *in* Rank et al. (1997), 81 n.6, Schim (2006), 122–123 *and* in full Rank-Berenschot (1998).
106. *Cf.* Schoordijk (1976), 632 *and* Rank-Berenschot (1998), 161–162.

accountholder rights, and if the securities concerned are situated in the giro pool or the participant pool of another participant, the intermediary's acts are more generally classified as representation.[107]

On the other hand, accountholder interests also classify as rights *in rem,* for they relate to an estate that is separated from the managing intermediary's property, viz. a Wge pool. Consequently, accountholders take free of adverse claims, and can successfully assert their interests against third parties, such as the intermediary's creditors. In addition, an intermediary is under the obligation to preserve accountholder interests, i.e. to maintain the (rights in) the quantity and quality of securities to which its clients are entitled, as it has no full authority to dispose of the securities in its custody, and must be able to meet accountholders' requests for retrieval at any point.[108] In sum, accountholder interests have both *in personam* and *in rem* effects, and must classify accordingly.[109]

7.3.6 Intermediary Administration

The Wge protects accountholders from their account provider's insolvency by the creation of securities pools as *gemeenschappen* (communities of property) that are separated from the account providers' own estates, and accountholders therefore take free of the claims of the account provider's creditors.[110] That separation of property also resulted in the need for a special provision that authorises the intermediary's bankruptcy administrator to liquidate the securities pool managed by the insolvent intermediary and to distribute its assets; Article 33 Wge.[111] Thus, an intermediary merely holds its clients' assets.[112]

However, an intermediary is also charged with the administration of the securities it holds, and is empowered to exercise its clients' rights against third parties in that capacity; Article 11 Wge.[113] Such administration of an estate that is

107. But it is reminded that the general private law provisions of arts. 7:414 *et seq.* BW on mandate do not fully apply; *see supra,* 7.3.4, *and infra,* s. 7.3.6.
108. Art. 26 Wge. *Cf.* Dalhuisen & Van Setten (2003), 96–97. *But see* Haentjens (2007, forthcoming), comm. at Art. 12 and Art. 26.
109. *Cf.* Dalhuisen & Van Setten 2003, 104.
110. *See* Explanatory Notes to the Draft Wge TK 1975–1976, 13 780, no. 3, 4 and 12.
111. *Cf.* Explanatory Notes to the Draft Wge TK 1976–1976, 13 780, no. 3, 42–43.
112. *Cf.* Van Ardenne-Stachiw *in* Rank et al. (1997), 82. Schoordijk (1975), 649, assumed that Wge pools have corporate personality, so as to explain the existence of a pool's general terms and conditions, the provisions on attachment and the distribution of losses amongst co-owners. *Accord* Ebeling (1978), 142.
113. Excluded from an intermediary's power of disposal are the exercise of voting rights attached to the securities it holds for its clients; Art. 15 Wge. Consequently, neither an investor's right to attend and participate in a general meeting, nor the right to commence proceedings that might lead to an inquiry into the policy and conduct of the issuer's business can be exercised by a participant. Moreover, the Wge requires that intermediaries facilitate their clients' exercise of the said corporate rights; Art. 15 and 39 Wge. *Cf. also* Art. 24 ABV. *See* Uniken Venema (2003), 94–97.

separated from the administrator's own property[114] closely resembles the common law concept of a trust, under which, when applied to the securities custody context, the intermediary would be the legal owner and the investors the beneficiary owners.[115] The comparison is all the more apt, because of the exclusive nature of the intermediary's administration; as noted *above*, accountholders can only dispose of their securities via an intermediary. But the concept of trust is not acknowledged in Dutch private law, and in principle, the civil code does not give a *fiducia cum amico* transfer any legal effect; Article 3:84(3) BW.[116]

Thus, intermediary administration cannot be classified with certainty in general private law terms, especially because, as has been shown *above*, the general private law provisions on *gemeenschap* and its administration are not fully applicable.[117] Especially when an intermediary acts with third parties, representation can be convincingly construed.[118] Yet again, the precise classification of that representation proves to be difficult, as the provisions on contractual agency and services agreements do not apply in their entirety, for they are based on agreement, rather than statute. In the following, some instances of representation by an intermediary in its capacity as a Wge pool's administrator will be examined, and it will be discussed, whether that representation classifies as direct or indirect representation (*middellijke* or *onmiddellijke vertegenwoordiging*).

7.3.6.1 Instances of Representation

It has been shown previously that when an intermediary's bankruptcy administrator liquidates the participant pool and distributes the assets, he represents all accountholders on a statutory basis, which indicates that the intermediary's administrative acts also classify as representation.[119] It has also been noted *above* that an intermediary represents all existing co-owners when accepting newly deposited securities into a Wge pool, for those co-owners' entitlements change with every deposit into or delivery out of a pool.[120] It is reminded that although the value of their entitlement does not change, previous or remaining accountholders become entitled to a different portion of a different collection of securities upon each deposit or delivery, respectively.[121]

By the same token, when an intermediary attaches one of its clients' shares in the pool it administers, the intermediary represents the other accountholders

114. *Cf.* Explanatory Notes to the Draft Wge TK 1975–1976, 13 780, no. 3, 42–43.
115. *See* Dalhuisen & Van Setten (2003), at 100 *and* Schoordijk (1975), 654.
116. *But see infra,* s. 7.5.1.
117. Art. 3:170 BW. *See supra,* s. 7.3.4. *Cf.* Uniken Venema (2003), 76.
118. *See,* e.g., Explanatory Notes to the Draft Wge TK 1975–1976, 13 780, no. 3, 17 *and* Uniken Venema (2003), 46–52.
119. *See* Schoordijk (1975), 650. *Contra* Schim (2006), 114–117.
120. Uniken Venema (2003), 46.
121. Should the proprietary position of the existing accountholders remain the same, the intermediary would also act in its function as administrator or *qualitate qua,* but would not represent.

vis-á-vis the judgment debtor,[122] because their entitlements change as the attached securities are 'frozen' and made unavailable to the other accountholders. In addition, when an intermediary transfers securities it holds for its clients to the CSD or to other participants, that intermediary represents its clients *ipso iure* vis-á-vis these third participants or CSD, and when an intermediary receives dividends or interests paid by an issuer, the intermediary represents its clients vis-á-vis this issuer.[123]

7.3.6.2 Direct and Indirect Representation

Although representation can thus be construed in a number of instances to classify an intermediary's administration of Wge pools, the precise classification of representation in the said instances is a matter of debate. UNIKEN VENEMA for example, has claimed that representation by an intermediary classifies as direct representation (*onmiddellijke vertegenwoordiging*), but it is argued here that a classification as indirect representation (*middellijke vertegenwoordiging*) would be more appropriate.[124]

Under the generally accepted definition of direct representation, an agent acts in his principal's name.[125] Although the agent is not required to name his principal explicitly, the agent's counterparties should be able to infer the principal's identity from the circumstances, possibly at a later moment in time.[126] But when an intermediary represents its clients, their identity is never to be revealed to third parties. In the case of delivery of securities into the Wge system for example, the depositing investor's identity is not very likely to become known to the existing co-owners of the participant pool, nor vice versa. With regard to the transfer of securities by an intermediary to the CSD, the government stated that 'The CSD has nothing to do with the identity of an intermediary's clients, nor with the composition of their securities portfolio'.[127]

It has been argued, on the other hand, that from the Kas-Associatie/Drying Corp. case, it follows that an intermediary's representation cannot be indirect, as the *Hoge Raad* held that under Article 3:110 BW, a co-owner of a securities pool

---

122. Arts. 24 and 44 Wge. *See* SCHOORDIJK (1975), 651.
123. Arts. 38 and 10(b) Wge, *and cf.* Art. 24 ABV, respectively. *Cf.* VAN ARDENNE-STACHIW *in* RANK ET AL. (1997), 102. If the securities concerned are CF-securities, the issuer pays to the CF, which then transfers the funds to the intermediaries who represent their clients vis-à-vis the CF; *see supra,* s. 7.2.
124. UNIKEN VENEMA (2003), 52.
125. BLOEMBERGEN ET AL. (2001), no. 82.
126. DU PERRON (1999), 40 and 49. *Cf.* HR 26 May 2000, NJ 2000, 442 (Weld-Equip/Van de Pest) (ann. SCJJK), where the *Hoge Raad* held that a legal act performed for a principal who had yet to be named, must be considered an act performed in the agent's own name, if the principal cannot later be identified with certainty; *see* DE VRIES (2003), 525–526.
127. Explanatory Notes to the Draft Wge TK 1975–1976, 13 780, no. 3, 15. The government's argument is unfamiliar to other countries. Art. 151 of the Securities Law of the People's Republic of China, for example, even requires that the CSD informs third parties, such as issuing institutions, about the identity of investors.

cannot indirectly make a third party co-owner of the same pool.[128] But the case does not have any influence, it is submitted, on the classification of an intermediary's representation, because that case concerned the (alleged) representation by an accountholder of its client, and representation by an intermediary of its accountholders must be distinguished.[129]

7.4 SECURITIES TRANSFERS

7.4.1 INTRODUCTION

One of the Wge's most important objectives was to create a custody system that would facilitate the easy transfer of securities by book-entry. Whilst the VABEF system enabled the transfer of securities by book-entry only between clients of the same financial institution, the Wge's multi-tiered, pyramid-shaped structure made giro transfer between all accountholders possible.[130]

The Wge classifies a transfer of securities as the transfer of (a part of) an accountholder's co-ownership interest in a Wge pool to another accountholder.[131] Such a transfer of ownership is perfected upon the credit entry in the transferee's securities account; Article 17 and 41 Wge.[132] A credit balance on a securities account is thus a constitutive element of an accountholder's entitlement, because Dutch general private law does not recognise the creation of a property right prior to delivery (*traditio* transfer regime). Consequently, the credit entry in a transferee's account both represents the transfer of ownership, and makes that transfer effective against third parties.

However, the classification of a Wge transfer in general private law terms and its consequences are subject to doctrinal debate. Some authors have claimed that a securities transfer classifies as a transfer of ownership as defined in Article 3:84

128. Thus, Kas-Associatie/Drying Corp. implies that the delivery of a Wge entitlement cannot be effected by indirect representation. *Cf.* MEIJER (1999), 180 *and* VAN SETTEN (1998), 326. In Amsterdam District Court, 20 February 1985, NJ 1986, 113 (Hadisantoso/Flesseman et al.), the court held that a Wge entitlement was deliverable without any formal requirements; that decision can now be considered to have been overruled by Kas-Associatie/Drying Corp. *Cf.* RANK-BERENSCHOT (1998), 164–167 *and* VAN DELDEN (1988), 55.

129. *Contra* UNIKEN VENEMA (2003), 52–54. *Accord* W. SNIJDERS and AVEZAAT *in* AVEZAAT (2002), 18–19.

130. *Cf. supra* s. 7.1.3.

131. Of course, an accountholder can transfer individual securities, i.e. parts of his co-ownership interest in a participant pool, provided these parts are in proportion to the number of securities to which the accountholder is entitled. Thus, if an accountholder is entitled to three securities, he cannot dispose of a quarter of his share in a participant pool; Art. 16(1) second sentence Wge. This principle prevents the creation of fractions of securities, but it presumably also leads to the identification of securities with a co-ownership interest in a pool.

132. Art. 17 Wge reads: 'Delivery of a share in a participant pool occurs through a credit entry in the name of the transferee in the part of the intermediary's records that is intended for that purpose'. Art. 41(1) Wge provides similar rule for transfer via the giro pool.

BW.[133] Under that view, arts. 17 and 41 Wge prescribe a specific method of delivery, but the other requirements laid down by Article 3:84 BW for a valid transfer, viz. a valid title and a power of disposal (*beschikkingsbevoegdheid*), as well as the requirement of a proprietary agreement (*goederenrechtelijke overeenkomst*), remain applicable.[134] It is submitted, however, that that position overlooks some important contractual and practical aspects of the transfer of securities by book-entry.[135]

7.4.2 Object and Moment of Transfer

Pursuant to arts. 17 and 41 Wge, a securities transfer is effectuated through the transfer of a co-ownership interest (share) in a Wge pool, rather than through the transfer of the securities themselves. Accordingly, the Kas-Associatie/Drying Corp. case showed that a Wge share and its object must not be identified, and the rules on the transfer of co-ownership interests must therefore be applied, rather than the rules on the transfer of securities. It is submitted, however, that Wge shares represent a combination of rights that cannot be transferred as provided for in Article 3:84 BW.

Close analysis of a securities transfer via the CSD shows that a transferee acquires a different entitlement against his account provider than the transferor alienated. Because the transferor's and transferee's immediate account providers are not the same, and an accountholder's entitlement can primarily be asserted only against his own account provider, the entitlements of transferor and transferee against their account providers necessarily differ accordingly.[136] Blom, on the other hand, has argued that accountholder interests are proprietary in nature and that transfers of Wge shares are therefore governed by Article 3:84 BW.[137] Although he acknowledges the contractual aspects of the Wge entitlement, he emphasises its proprietary character. Yet it is submitted that the inseparability of contractual and proprietary rights results in the non-transferability of Wge shares, and thus in the non-applicability of Article 3:84 BW.[138]

In addition, the moment of transfer of securities by book-entry indicates the non-applicability of Article 3:84 BW. Under Article 3:84 BW, a transferor remains the entitlement holder with full power of disposal until the delivery of

133. E.g. Mijnssen (1975), 207, Vincent (1997), 44 and 46, Blom (1999), 377 *and* Van Dijk *in* Eisma et al. (2002), 121. These authors mostly base their position on the parliamentary proceedings, notably the Explanatory Notes to the Draft Wge.
134. *Accord* Advisory Opinion of the Advocate General of the Supreme Court in Kas-Associatie/Drying Corp., *see supra,* s. 7.3.4.
135. *Accord* Schoordijk (1975), 633. *Cf.* Dalhuisen & Van Setten (2003), 103, Van den Hoek (2003), 436, Haentjens (2004-1), 478 *and* Schim (2006), 129 *et seq.*
136. *See* Schim (2002), at 193 *and* Van der Beek (2003), 245–246. *Cf. also supra,* s. 7.3.1, on the transfer of securities not admitted to the Wge system.
137. Blom (1999), 380.
138. *See* Dalhuisen & Van Setten (2003), 123.

the transferred assets has been completed. If Article 3:84 BW would apply to a securities transfer, a transferor would then remain empowered to dispose of his securities until the credit entry in the transferee's securities account would have been made. In reality, however, a transferor cannot enforce any rights regarding his securities once the debit entry in his securities account has been made, which thus ensures the finality of securities transfers. Especially because that debit entry does not coincide with the credit entry in the transferee's account, Article 3:84 BW does not seem applicable.[139]

Similarly, when book-entry securities are transferred conditionally, and the resolutive condition is subsequently fulfilled, the transferor again becomes fully entitled to the assets he has conditionally transferred, even if the retransfer has not (yet) been effectuated.[140] But in practice, the initial transferor cannot enforce any rights regarding the securities he is thus entitled to, unless his securities account has been (re)credited.[141]

Thus, Article 3:84 BW accords badly with transfers of securities by book-entry under the Wge. It is therefore agreed with VAN SETTEN that the transferor's transfer order and the consequent debit entry in his securities account has to be considered a core element in any securities transfer by book-entry, since in principle, that debit entry results in the cancellation of his rights against his account provider.[142] Accordingly, similar rights against the transferee's account provider are established by the credit entry in the latter's securities account.[143] In sum, a securities transfer under the Wge has to be considered a *sui generis* type of transfer.

7.4.3 ANNULMENT AND FINALITY

As a general principle of property law, a transfer is not granted all proprietary effects if the requirements for the transfer of ownership provided by Article 3:84

139. *See* DALHUISEN & VAN SETTEN (2003), 123.
140. Art. 3:84(4) BW. *See*, e.g., Asser-HARTKAMP 4-I (2004), no. 175. The present author is grateful to Professor W.A.K. Rank for pointing out that in the context of conditional money transfers, (re)transfers after fulfilment of the resolutive condition are also of mere administrative nature; *cf.* HR 3 December 2004, NJ 2005, 200 (Mendel q.q./ABN Amro Bank NV)(ann. PvS).
141. *Cf.* VAN ARDENNE-STACHIW (1998), 169, who argues that the rules on conditional transfers and the administrative retransfer under Art. 3:84(4) BW accord badly with the requirement of credit and debit entries ex arts. 17 and 41 Wge for proprietary effect. She further points out that the general private law provisions on the protection of *bona fide* transferees against competing claims in the case of conditional transfers are not in accordance with the rules on *bona fide* transferee protection under the Wge. As a solution, she proposes that intermediaries administrate conditionally transferred securities separately, possibly in a separate pool. *But cf.* SCHIM (2006), 156–160.
142. *Cf.* DALHUISEN & VAN SETTEN (2003), 124.
143. As a strict dogmatic consequence of this analysis, a pledge vested in a Wge share extinguishes when that share is 'transferred', and the pledge has to be vested again in the transferee's share; *see* SCHIM (2002), 207–209 *and* VAN DER BEEK (2003), 246.

BW have not been met.[144] In addition, when one of these requirements prove not to have been fulfilled, the particular transfer's proprietary effects are *de iure* annulled. Provisions of the *Faillissementswet* (Bankruptcy Act, 'Fw') may also result in the annulment of a transfer of ownership, typically by determining retroactively that one of Article 3:84 BW's requirements has not been satisfied.

If a securities transfer by book-entry would be governed by Article 3:84 BW, a defective title to the agreement between transferor and transferee would result in the annulment of all the transfer's proprietary effects. Consequently, the credit entry in the transferee's account, as well as the account balances of all intermediaries involved would be without proprietary effect and those entries would have to be rescinded. Obviously, this would severely impede the smooth functioning of securities settlement, especially in systems of netted clearing and settlement, and the application of Article 3:84 BW is also for that reason unwarranted.[145]

Moreover, the transferor/transferee relationship should be distinguished from the transferor/account provider and transferee/account provider relationships, and the former relationship should not affect, it is submitted, the two latter ones (abstract transfer regime). Apart from the fact that in today's anonymised securities markets, the transferor and transferee are often unable to discover each other's identity, the accountholder/intermediary relationship should not be determined by possible deficiencies in the agreements which the accountholder concludes with third parties. Snijders, one of the draftsmen of the Wge, has therefore argued that the Wge originally intended to establish such an abstract transfer regime, rather than the causal transfer regime of Article 3:84 BW.[146]

Consequently, the finality of an entry in a securities account depends on the power of disposal in the accountholder/intermediary relationship, rather than the contractual strength of the transferor – transferee relationship.[147] In that respect, a securities transfer is similar to the payment of funds, for the finality of entries in money accounts is also not affected by deficiencies in the contractual relation between the debtor and creditor.[148] It is reiterated therefore that the acquisition of securities by book-entry should not to be considered in light of Article 3:84 BW, but as a *sui generis* acquisition.[149]

Finally, the implementation of the EU Settlement Finality Directive ('SFD') has ensured the finality of credit entries in securities accounts in intermediary

144. *See supra,* s. 7.4.1.

145. *Cf.* Ch. 4.2.

146. Snijders (2005), 95–96 *and* Schim (2006), 143–145. But even if Wge entitlements would be governed by a causal transfer regime, then *bona fide* transferees are protected against competing claims of third parties through general property law rules, as under arts. 3:88 and 3:238 BW, *bona fide* transferees and pledgees, respectively, take free of a dispossessed owner's claim of revendication; arts. 19 and 20 Wge. *See* Haentjens (forthcoming, 2007), comm. at arts. 19 and 20. *But see* Schim (2002), 205 *and* Van der Beek (2003), 246.

147. *Cf.* Schim (2002), 205 *and* Van der Beek (2003), 246. *Accord* Dalhuisen & Van Setten (2003), 125 *and* Van Ardenne-Stachiw *in* Rank et al. (1997), 103.

148. *Accord* Schoordijk (1975), 634. *Cf.* Schim (2002), 201 *and* Schim (2006), 141 *et seq. Contra* Mijnssen (1975), 207. *Cf.* Snijders (1972), 173, on finality in money payments.

149. Van Setten (1998), 326, Van der Beek (2003), 246 *and also* Uniken Venema (2003), 6–7.

insolvency situations.[150] As a general rule of insolvency law, Article 23 Fw determines that insolvency proceedings have retroactive effect to the beginning of the day on which the bankruptcy has been declared, and that all legal acts performed by the bankrupt on that day are therefore reversible; Article 35(1) Fw. But Article 212b(1) Fw currently provides that transfer orders given prior to a bankruptcy declaration may not be revoked, nor may any consequent payment, delivery, netting or any other legal act in the process of settlement be reversed on the grounds of insolvency rules. In addition, transfer orders given after, but still on the same day as the bankruptcy declaration, may not be revoked nor may any consequent payment, delivery, netting or any other legal act in the process of settlement be reversed, provided the CCP, CSD or clearinghouse was unaware of the bankruptcy declaration; Article 212b(2) Fw.[151] After the day of the bankruptcy declaration, the insolvency rules apply as always.

7.5 CREATION AND ENFORCEMENT OF SECURITY RIGHTS

7.5.1 Transfer of Title

In order to prevent *pari passu* ranking with a debtor's general creditors, a creditor may secure his claim by the creation of a pledge or mortgage. These security rights, as well as fiduciary transfers of ownership, can be enforced in the debtor's insolvency 'as if no insolvency proceedings had commenced'; Article 57 Fw.[152]

Current financial markets use book-entry securities as collateral in many arrangements, but prior to the implementation of the EU Financial Collateral Directive ('FCD'), statutory requirements for the creation and enforcement of a pledge were felt to be prohibitively burdensome in that particular context. Transfer of title was therefore most often chosen, especially in standardised arrangements such as repurchase agreements, buy/sell-back agreements and securities lending agreements.[153] Article 3:84(3) BW, however, explicitly prohibits the fiduciary transfer of ownership, and it became a matter of debate whether the provision

150. *See* Van Setten *in* Vereecken & Nijenhuis et al. (2003), Wouters (1998), 103 *and* Peters (2003), 36. The implementation of the EU Financial Collateral Directive has resulted in the enactment of similar provisions regarding the conclusion of collateral arrangements and its consequent transfers, payment, netting and delivery; *see infra,* s. 7.5. *See also* Ch. 9.3.3.

151. It is not likely, however, that such unawareness will be convincingly construed, as DNB immediately informs CCPs, CSDs and the clearinghouses of any involuntary liquidation order; Art. 212c(2) Fw.

152. Euronext Rule Book Art. 6 Instruction I.5-1, for example, requires that its participants provide for security interests by a DNB guarantee, by a fiduciary transfer of ownership or by the creation of a pledge under Art. 42 Wge.

153. *Cf.* Raijmakers & Van Beek (2003), 183, n.4 *and see* Ch. 4.3.1.

was applicable to the said collateral arrangements, and what the consequences of applicability would be.[154]

Subsequent legal uncertainty led to the enactment of Article 2a *Wet Toezicht Effectenverkeer 1995* (Securities Markets Supervision Act 1995, 'Wte 1995'), which excluded repurchase agreements from the application of Article 3:84(3) BW. The implementation legislation of the FCD extended this exclusion to all agreements that use book-entry securities as collateral, provided they are concluded by certain, well-defined entities; Article 7:55 BW.[155] It is argued here, however, that these derogatory provisions were not needed to avert recharacterisation risks or the application of Article 3:84(3) BW, since, as has been shown *above*, Article 3:84 BW in its entirety is not applicable to any transfer of securities by book-entry. In addition, it follows from the Keereweer/Sogelease case that Article 3:84(3) BW does not apply to a typical repurchase agreement.[156]

In that case, the *Hoge Raad* held that the fiducia ban only applies to agreements whose sole purpose is the creation of a security interest, and that transfers that are intended to provide the transferee/creditor with 'more than only an entitlement that protects the creditor's interests' are allowed. The court's holding says, in pertinent part, that a transfer of ownership is only prohibited when the transferee's entitlement to the transferred assets is not restricted as if his entitlement were a pledge or mortgage.[157]

Under a repurchase agreement, the initial transferee obtains full power of disposal over the collateralised securities, and from his perspective, that power of disposal is one of the major reasons for entering into such an agreement. A repurchase agreement does not restrict the transferee's/creditor's entitlement in any way, and must therefore not be considered as being prohibited under the *Hoge Raad's* interpretation of Article 3:84(3) BW.[158] Article 7:55 BW, however, currently explicitly exempts all financial collateral arrangements concluded between certain, primarily financial institutions from the application of the fiducia ban.

---

154. *See* SALOMONS (1994), 1261, for an historical account of the provision.
155. Consequently, Art. 2a Wte 1995 was removed. *See* Draft Parliamentary Act TK 2002–2003, 28 874, no. 2 *and* Explanatory Notes to the Draft TK 2002–2003, 28 874, no. 3. *See also* RAIJMAKERS & VAN BEEK (2003), at 183.
156. HR 19 May 1995, NJ 1996, 119 (Keereweer/Sogelease). *Cf.* HR 18 November 2005, JOR 60,425 (BTL Lease/Van Summeren). *See* SCHIM (2002), 209 *and* VAN DER BEEK (2003), 246. *Cf.* VAN ERP (2004), 542 and 546, arguing that the FCD resulted in a derogation from the fiducia ban, rather than an interpretation of the same, as the government stated; Explanatory Notes to the Implementation Act TK 2002–2003, 28 874, no. 3, 7–8.
157. *See* RONGEN (1996), 278. *Cf.* VERHAGEN (1997), 56 *and* RANK (1998), 403.
158. Even if the Keereweer/Sogelease case were interpreted in the broadest way possible, i.e. if Art. 3:84(3) BW would apply to all transfers of ownership that 'solely or most predominantly purport to serve the transferee's security interests', Art. 3:84(3) would not apply to repurchase agreements or like agreements, for full power of disposal and the consequent transferability of the collateralised assets is one of the major reasons for entering into such an agreement. *Cf.* RONGEN (1996), p. 283 *and* KLIEBISCH (1997). In the Keereweer/Sogelease case, however, the transfer of ownership concerned was found to be primarily intended to provide a security interest, but the *Hoge Raad* held that Art. 3:84(3) BW was not applicable. The doctrinal majority opinion adhered to *above* is therefore, it is submitted, the more correct one.

7.5.2 Pledge and Attachment

As to the requirements for the creation of a pledge (*pand*) on securities, the Wge distinguishes between the creation of a pledge in favour of the debtor's account provider and the creation of a pledge in favour of persons other than the debtor's account provider. In the former instance, a pledge agreement between debtor and his account provider suffices, both to create the security interest and to make that interest effective, i.e. enforceable against third parties; Article 21(1) Wge.[159]

In the latter instance, the securities pledged must be credited to a special pledge account in the pledgee's name, held by the pledgee's intermediary; Article 20(1) Wge.[160] Legislative history indicates, however, that such a pledge may also be created by the marking or flagging of the pledged securities in the pledgor's account.[161] The same requirements apply when a pledge is created on an intermediary's securities held with the CSD; Article 42 Wge. But that provision is problematical, because an intermediary does not have full power of disposal over the pool it administers, and the legislative history of Wge explicitly indicates that no separation between an intermediary's own assets and the assets it holds for its clients must be made.[162] Nonetheless, it has been argued that an intermediary must be able to pledge its own assets held with the CSD, and that therefore a *de facto* separation of assets must be assumed.[163]

The creation of a pledge on Wge securities is analysed as the creation of a security interest in (a part of) the pledgor's share in a Wge pool. Should an accountholder's securities be located in the giro pool (as they usually are), a security interest is thus created in the accountholder's share in the participant pool held by his account provider. But because of the direct proprietary link between accountholder and his securities, a pledge on that accountholder's share in the participant pool involves a pledge on the participant pool's share in the giro pool held by the CSD. This instance of upper-tier attachment, however, does not concern the entire giro pool, nor the entire participant pool's share in the giro pool, but affects only the securities intended to be pledged. Other accountholders' interests are therefore not impeded, and Article 44 Wge also explicitly prohibits upper-tier attachment, i.e. attachment of an entire pool at a higher tier.

The enforcement of a pledge on Wge securities closely resembles the enforcement of an attachment. Provided the issuer has not prohibited retrieval, both pledgee and judgment creditor may request the delivery of the pledged securities in order to sell them in the way prescribed by general private law, viz. by public auction; Articles 22(1)(a) and 24(1)(a) Wge, and Article 3:250(2) BW. In addition,

159. The Wge provisions on usufruct of securities is identical to the provisions on the creation of a pledge (*see* Art. 23 Wge), except for the fact that no specific rules provide for usufruct for the participant administrating the securities concerned.
160. *Contra* Schim (2006), 181, arguing that the pledged securities must be credited to a pledge account in the pledgor's name.
161. Explanatory Notes to the Draft Wge, TK 1975–1976, 13 780, no. 7 (NvW), 2.
162. *See* Explanatory Notes to the Draft Wge TK 1975–1976, 13 780, no. 3, 21–22 and 44. *Cf.* Haentjens (forthcoming, 2007), comm. at Art. 10, 35 and 42.
163. Van der Beek (2003), 246, Schim (2004), 420–422, *and cf.* Schim (2006), 176–178 and 182.

pledged or attached securities need not be delivered out of the Wge system, but may also be sold directly, i.e. by book-entry, at a public auction by the pledgee/judgment creditor in the same way; arts. 22(1)(b) and 24(1)(b) Wge.[164]

The implementation legislation of the EU Financial Collateral Directive, however, explicitly exempts collateral arrangements concluded between certain, well-defined institutions from these rules. In the context of such arrangements, a pledgor need not sell the pledged securities by public auction, nor notify the pledgor; arts. 7:54(2) and 7:54(5) BW. A pledgor is currently allowed to sell the pledged securities privately or to appropriate them upon the debtor's default, which clearly contrasts with the longstanding principle that any appropriation of pledged assets was prohibited; 3:235 BW.[165] Moreover, in the context of the said arrangements, a pledgor is allowed to use, i.e. sell or hypothecate, the pledged securities to third parties, prior to the pledgor's account, which also implies an appropriation by the pledgee; 7:53(1) BW.[166]

7.6 CONFLICT OF LAWS

7.6.1 INTRODUCTION

Unlike most other areas of Dutch law, the greater part of conflict of laws rules concerning securities has not been codified in statutory provisions. As practically no case law is available either, considerable legal uncertainty exists as to these matters. The conflict of laws provisions of the EU Settlement Finality Directive ('SFD') and the Financial Collateral Directive ('FCD'), have been implemented into the insolvency and private law code respectively, but the scope of these provisions is limited.[167] The enactment process for an Act on Conflict of Law Rules Relating to Property Law Issues (hereinafter: 'Draft Act'), on the other hand, has recently accelerated.[168]

---

164. *See* Explanatory Notes to the Draft Wge TK 1999–2000, 27 164, no. 3, 9. *Cf.* RANK-BERENSCHOT (1998), 162–164 *and* HAENTJENS (forthcoming, 2007), comm. at Art. 22.
165. That Art. is the Dutch codification of CODE JUST. 8.34.3 (Constantine 326). Contrast with the current Art. 7:54 BW. For a private sale, however, a court order is still required; Art. 7:54(5) BW.
166. *See* KEIJSER (2003), 432, RAIJMAKERS & VAN BEEK (2003), 187, STEFFENS (2005), 63, VAN VLIET (2005), *and* KEIJSER (2006), esp. 175 *et seq.* and 297 *et seq.* The last author extensively argues against these derogations from general private law principles, especially in the context of agreements between parties that do not have equal bargaining power.
167. The provision of the SFD referred to has been implemented as Art. 212(f) Fw, of the FCD as Art. 7:56 BW. *See* Explanatory Notes to the [second, MH] Draft Implementation Act TK 2004–2005, 30 138, no. 3, 1 *and* TK 2004–2005, 30 138, no. 2, 4. *Cf.* RANK & VAN DER LELY (2002), 398.
168. *See* TK 2006–2007, 30 876, nos. 1 through 3, issued on 20 November 2006. The text of this Draft Act is practically identical to the Preliminary Draft that was issued as long ago as November 1998. The Draft Act is part of a larger project to codify all current rules of Dutch private international law, and will be referred to frequently in the following sections as reflecting the current, albeit customary, law. The entire Preliminary Draft for Consolidated Private International Law, as well as the Report of the State Committee for Private International Law

As noted *above*, the *Hoge Raad* held in the Kas-Associatie/Drying Corp. case that an accountholder's entitlement as a co-owner in a Wge pool classifies as a *recht op naam* (claim).[169] Under general Dutch private international law, this would imply the applicability of *lex contractus* (proper law of the contract) to determine all proprietary issues regarding the 'claim'. As a consequence, all proprietary issues would be determined by the proper law of the contract that created the claim – provided no choice of law has been made.[170] Such a rule would be in accordance with the Bechem Chemie/Hansa Chemie case, in which the *Hoge Raad* held that under article 12(1) of the Rome Convention 1980, the law designated by the parties to an assignment of a debt also covers its proprietary aspects.[171]

However, a number of arguments could be formulated against the position that rule applies to accountholder interests. First, it is unlikely that a transfer of securities by book-entry in a securities account classifies as assignment.[172] Second, the decision has met with little approval.[173] In addition, it is highly unlikely that a Dutch court would apply the *lex contractus* rule if it were called upon to determine the law which is applicable to conflicts of laws situations involving participants in the Dutch system. As must be inferred from the purpose of the Wge and its Explanatory Notes,[174] Dutch law applies to the proprietary aspects of the first and second-tier relationship, notwithstanding any choice of law, the issuer's location,[175] or the certificates' location.[176]

More generally, if called upon to determine a conflict of laws issue regarding book-entry securities, a Dutch court would probably first determine under the *lex fori* whether the issue would be proprietary or contractual in nature. If it classified the issue as proprietary, it would then determine whether the securities concerned would be certificated and would classify their nature: whether the issue concerned bearer securities, registered securities or book-entry securities. At present, the last-mentioned category is certainly relevant in situations of the insolvency of financial institutions that have collateralised securities.[177] Since the implementation of Article 9 FCD, the distinction is supported in conflict of laws situations regarding

on the Preliminary Draft Act, are available at the website of the Ministry of Justice: <www.minjus.nl>.

169. *Cf. supra,* s. 7.3.5.
170. *Cf.* Draft Act Art. 10 and the Rome Convention Art. 12.
171. HR 16 May 1997, NJ 1998, 585 (Bechem Chemie/Hansa Chemie).
172. Rather, it should be classified as novation; Goode (2003-2), 215, n. 40, Benjamin (2000), 155, n.38, Haentjens (2004-1), 478–481. *Cf.* Rank (2001), 68. *Contra* Verhagen (2000), 122. *Cf. supra,* s. 7.3.2 *and* 7.4.2.
173. *See,* e.g. Struycken (1998), 345 *et seq.* and Steffens (1997), 212–219. *Cf.* Verhagen (2000), 122 *and see* Bernasconi (2000), 49, n.154.
174. Explanatory Notes to the Draft Wge TK 1975–1976, 13 780, no. 3, 36. The rationale is that the applicability of another law could lead to an impairment of the investors' proprietary position, a position that the Wge seeks to protect.
175. *See* Van Beek & Van Bruggen (2002), 33.
176. *See* Van Beek & Van Bruggen (2002), 46–47.
177. Art. 212(f) Fw, implementation of SFD Art. 9(2).

certain arrangements, but after the enactment of the Draft Act, it will apply to all conflict of laws that concern securities.[178]

As matter of principle, *renvoi* is excluded under Dutch private international law. As to contractual matters, Article 15 of the 1980 Rome Convention excludes *renvoi,* whilst Draft Act Article 1(4), as well as legal literature also excludes *renvoi* regarding proprietary matters.[179]

7.6.2 PRIMA

Thus, traditional conflict of laws rules such as *lex rei sitae* and *lex incorporationis* do not apply in the instance of the insolvency of a financial institution that has collateralised securities by book-entry and when securities have been collateralised between certain institutions under certain financial collateral arrangements.[180] In all these cases, a variation of PRIMA determines the law which is applicable to proprietary conflicts concerning book-entry securities. Draft Act Article 16 also contains a variation of PRIMA, as it copies the implementation provision of Article 9(2) FCD, but extends its scope.[181]

Although it could be inferred from this provision that PRIMA has found acceptance amongst Dutch lawyers, its application by a Dutch court in all cases concerning book-entry securities is not entirely certain under current law.[182] Moreover, the Report of the State Committee on the Preliminary Draft itself indicates that the rule does not apply if securities are certificated ones and located in another jurisdiction, and are not admitted to a foreign settlement system. In such a situation, to apply Dutch law to rights concerning those securities is considered an infringement of a possible foreign *lex rei sitae* principle.[183] It has been objected, however, that the (unacceptable) consequence of this rule would be that in order to determine their rights, investors would have to establish first whether securities are certificated or not and, second, where they are located, information which would be practically impossible to obtain.[184]

On the other hand, the proposed article applies to all indirectly held securities, i.e. both those admitted to the Wge system and those held on a fungible basis.[185] It has even been argued that it applies to directly held (i.e. individually administrated) registered securities and derivatives, since both these financial instruments

178. *See* HAENTJENS (2006), 62–63, for an examination of the Dutch conflict of laws that are applied to determine whether securities classify as shares, bonds, and bearer or registered securities.
179. *See* RANK & VAN DER LELY (2002), 399.
180. Arts. 212(f) Fw *and* 7:56 BW, respectively.
181. TK 2006–2007, 30 876, no. 3, 13.
182. RANK (2001), 67 *and* RANK & VAN DER LELY (2002), 398 and 405.
183. Report of the State Committee for Private International Law (1998), 79. *See also* UNIKEN VENEMA (2003), 120 *and* VERHAGEN (2000), 118.
184. BLOM (1999), 381.
185. *See* Report of the State Committee for International Private Law (1998), 84.

are transferred by book-entry only.[186] This position, however, does not seem to be consistent with the Drafters' intention, as the Report of the State Committee refers to indirectly held securities, and specifically to the Wge system.[187]

Further, the connecting factor designated by Draft Act Article 16 is ambiguous. It points to the law of the jurisdiction where the relevant securities account is administrated, but any further guidance on how to determine the securities account's location is not given. It has been argued[188] that a Dutch court would initially look to the account agreement.[189] Other circumstances which a Dutch court could possibly take into consideration are the terms of the contract as a whole and the place mentioned in an account statement.[190]

In addition, the restrictive nature of the Wge system prevents the application of PRIMA from being wholly satisfactory in two situations.[191] In the first situation, a Dutch investor holds a securities account with a Dutch intermediary, to which account both Dutch Wge securities and foreign securities are credited. The account provider holds the foreign securities through a securities account with a foreign participant of a foreign settlement system. Under PRIMA, Dutch law would govern the proprietary rights of the investor with regard to all securities. An (uninformed) investor might therefore expect that the Wge provides proprietary protection with regard to all securities he holds with his Dutch account provider, and that no distinction in legal regime is made between the securities that are admitted to the Wge system and other securities. But since neither the foreign securities nor the immediate intermediary are admitted to the Wge system or act as such, the investor will have a mere contractual claim with respect to the foreign securities.[192]

In the second situation, the Dutch CSD holds a securities account with a foreign institution. It has been a highly debated matter as to whether Dutch law would apply[193] or the law of the foreign institution.[194] The text of Article 35(b) Wge seems to support the former position, as it states that the rights resulting from the holding of securities 'kept by or deposited with foreign institutions in the Central Institution's name' are part of the giro pool. It is submitted, however, that the latter view is the better one; Article 35(b) Wge can also be interpreted to mean that the Dutch CSD may have an interest in a securities pool under foreign law, an interest which is nonetheless included in the Dutch giro pool. This view

186. Blom (1999), 379.
187. Report of the State Committee for International Private Law (1998), 77 *et seq.*
188. Rank & Van der Lely (2002), 408.
189. The custodian concerned would have to be regulatory supervised, however; *ibid.*
190. Rank & Van der Lely (2002), 409.
191. *Cf. also* Van den Hoek (2004), 152 *and* Van den Hoek (2003), 432–438.
192. Probably against a VABEF II entity; *see,* extensively, Rank (1996), Rank et al. (1997) *and* Rank (1999), 85–86 *and supra,* s. 7.3.2. For a discussion of possible solutions to this problem, such as the designation of foreign ICSDs as CSD as meant under the Wge and the designation of the securities concerned as admitted to the Wge system, *see* Van Beek & Van Bruggen (2002), 87–90.
193. Blom (1999), 381, Rank (2005), 250.
194. Van Beek & Van Bruggen (2002), 21 *and* Verhagen (2000), 118.

is explicitly supported by the Report of the State Committee.[195] Again, the Dutch CSD (and eventually the Dutch investors) would thus lack the proprietary protection of the Wge. However, Dutch investors' rights would still be sufficiently protected; any link between the Dutch CSD and a foreign institution requires the mandatory approval of the Dutch Minister of Finance.[196] He is most likely to approve only links with foreign institutions where their laws provide proprietary protection which is comparable to the Dutch Wge.

7.6.3 Securities Transfers and Security Rights

Under Dutch conflict of laws rules, the proprietary validity of a transfer of directly held securities is determined as follows. First, the securities transferred are classified. Then, to certificated securities, the *lex rei sitae* applies in order to determine whether the perfection requirements have been met, but to non-certificated registered shares, the law of the issuer (*lex incorporationis*) applies, while the *lex contractus* applies to registered debt securities.

On the basis of Article 212(f) Fw and Article 7:56 BW, a Dutch court would probably determine the validity of a transfer of securities by book-entry as well as its effects by the law of the jurisdiction of the transferee's intermediary. However, under present law, a Dutch court might apply the traditional rules and 'look through' to the underlying securities when the case falls outside the scope of either Article 212(f) Fw or Article 7:56 BW. Only in situations in which securities are collateralised and provided that all other requirements for the applicability of the SFD or FCD have been met, is PRIMA currently applied with certainty.[197] The classification of the agreement underlying the transfer is made under Dutch law as the *lex contractus.*

Article 7:56 BW has implemented Article 9(2) FCD, a provision which applies to the proprietary aspects of securities transfers by book-entry under a collateral agreement that is concluded by at least one financial institution. The Government has stated that a connection was sought with the Hague Securities Convention, but it has made no reference to a choice of law, as is provided for in the Hague Securities Convention.[198] Furthermore, it has been announced that Article 7:56 BW would be repealed when the Draft Act would be enacted.[199] It has been argued that a Dutch court, applying PRIMA, would determine the proprietary effects of a pledge under the law of the place of the pledgor's relevant intermediary.[200] As a general rule of Dutch private international law, however, the enforcement of a security interest is judged under the law of the place where the enforcement is sought.

195. State Committee for International Private Law (1998), 83.
196. Van Beek & Van Bruggen (2002), 50.
197. Rank (2005), 250–251 advocates a wider application of the conflict of laws rules contained in the EU legislation.
198. Explanatory Notes to the Implementation Act TK 2002–2003, 28 874, no. 3, 10–11.
199. Draft Act Art. 19; TK 2006–2007, 30 876, no. 2, 5.
200. *See,* e.g. Rank & Van der Lely (2002), 406.

Thus, although PRIMA has been accepted in Dutch private international law, both as part of European legislation and in its own Draft Act, traditional conflicts rules are still predominant. The Report of the State Committee explicitly stated that the proposed provision leaves primacy to the law of the certificates' location.[201] The same Draft Act, on the other hand, allows a choice of law in the case of registered shares traded on a stock exchange.[202] As a result, current Dutch private international law as to non-collateralised book-entry securities is characterised by uncertainty, which becomes apparent in the legal literature as well. Whereas some authors still defend a look-through approach, others have welcomed PRIMA.

7.7 CONCLUSIONS

7.7.1 Questions and Answers

(1) *Which securities are admitted to the national systems of giro transfer and administration?*
The eligibility of securities for admittance to the statutory custody system is determined by Dutch CSD; Article 1 Wge. Since the 2000 modification of the Wge, all categories of securities are thus eligible, but in practice, the Wge does not cater for the custody of derivatives, and Euroclear Netherlands admits only securities that are fungible and freely tradable. Non-Wge admitted securities can be held outside of that system, but no absolute proprietary protection for securities accountholders is then ensured.

(2) *What is the nature of investors' interests in securities?*
Three types of intermediated securities custody, and thus of accountholder interests are distinguished. First, accountholders enjoy a mere contractual right against their account provider. That construct is applied in almost all instances that accountholders hold foreign securities through a securities account with a Dutch account provider. Second, investors can retain ownership of their securities when these are held on an individualised basis. This construct is more rarely applied, as it does not facilitate the transfer of securities by book-entry. Third, the statutory custody system of the Wge provides accountholders with a *sui generis* co-ownership right in securities pools. That system, of which the majority of Dutch securities form part, does not, however, apply to lower than third-tier accountholders, and these accountholders therefore have a mere contractual claim against their intermediary.

201. Report of the State Committee for International Private Law (1998), 79.
202. Draft Act Art. 13(2).

(2.1) *Is a credit entry in a securities account merely a proof of ownership or is it a constitutive element of ownership of the securities concerned?*

From the Wge's rationale and the *traditio* transfer regime, it follows that a credit balance on a securities account constitutes a constitutive element of an accountholder's entitlement. But such entitlement is not identical with the securities themselves, for a credit entry refers to a right of co-ownership in a securities pool.

(2.2) *Are informal (i.e. not registered by book-entry) dispositions over securities possible?*

Generally, informal dispositions over securities have no proprietary effect, i.e. cannot be enforced against third parties under the Wge, since a credit entry in a securities account is a constitutive element for the creation of both a security interest (pledge) and a co-ownership right. If the pledgor is the pledgee's immediate account provider, however, a pledge agreement between accountholder and account provider suffices to create the security interest, and that interest is therefore not recorded in a securities account. For another instance of entitlements to book-entry securities that are not registered by book-entry, *see* next item.

(2.3) *Is provisional credit in book-entry securities possible?*

In principle, provisional credit entries in a securities account are allowed. When securities are transferred conditionally and the resolutive condition is fulfilled, the transferor again becomes fully entitled to the assets he has conditionally transferred, even if the retransfer has not (yet) been effectuated. Accordingly, the transferee is not entitled to the securities that are (still) credited to his account. Yet can be questioned, whether the initial transferor is in a position to enforce any rights regarding the securities that he is entitled to, but that have not (yet) been (re)credited to his account.

(3) *How are investors' rights in respect of securities protected against the account provider and third parties?*

Accountholder interests are primarily protected through the property law rules of the Wge, as that statute provides accountholders with co-ownership rights in the pools of Wge securities which an intermediary administers. These pools therefore form no part of an account provider's estate, and third parties, such as the account provider's general creditors cannot enforce any rights against the accountholders' assets. Moreover, intermediaries do not have full power of disposal over the securities pools they administer, and must therefore always be able to meet any request of retrieval by its clients who thus exercise their right of revendication.

In addition, investors' rights are relatively well protected against their account provider's insolvency when their securities are held through a VABEF II entity, a custody entity that is separated from the institution with which investors hold their securities accounts. Investors enjoy a mere contractual claim against this custody entity, but as its articles of association exclude any form of commercial activity, the insolvency risk of that vehicle is minimised. This construction is currently mainly used to administer (entitlements to) foreign securities held outside the Netherlands.

(3.1) *Should shortfalls occur in accounts, how are they availed?*

Should a shortfall occur, i.e. should the total of the accountholders' entitlements exceed the omnibus account which the account provider holds with the CSD, the deficit is first solved by recourse to the account provider's own share in the securities pool it administers. The remaining deficit is distributed amongst the accountholders pro rata, i.e. in proportion to their share. These losses are covered up to EUR 20,000 per investor by the guarantee fund that has been created for that purpose.

(3.2) *How are an investor's interests in securities separated from the account provider's property or how can investors' interests avail the claims of the provider's general creditors?*

Although there exist explicit provisions of regulatory law requiring that accountholder interests be separated from an account provider's own assets,[203] the legislative history of the Wge indicates that such a separation in an intermediary's account with the CSD is prohibited. But as a consequence of the co-ownership construct, an account provider has no power of disposal over its clients' assets, other than for the purpose of the execution of its administrative obligations. In addition, an account provider's general creditors cannot enforce any rights on the Wge pools it administers for its clients.

However, the Kas-Associatie/Drying Corp. case showed that the proprietary protection of the Wge ends with the third tier, and lower than third tier accountholders are left with a mere contractual claim against their intermediary. On the other hand, an investor's contractual claims regarding his securities may trump the claims of the account provider's general creditors when his securities are held through a VABEF II entity (see item 3).

(4) *What are the formal requirements for the transfer of ownership of securities?*

Although it is a matter of debate, the better view would be that no formal requirements exist for the transfer of a Wge entitlement (which must be distinguished from the formal requirements for the transfer of the securities themselves), other than a credit entry in the transferee's securities account; arts. 17 and 41 Wge. Thus, it has been argued that Article 3:84 BW is not applicable to the transfer of Wge entitlements, and that, other than delivery, the requirements of that provision, viz. a valid title, a power of disposal (*beschikkingsbevoegdheid*) and a proprietary

203. Art. 4:87 Wft *and* Art. 6:14 *et seq. Nadere Regeling Gedragstoezicht financiële ondernemingen Wft.*

agreement (*goederenrechtelijke overeenkomst*), need not be satisfied to effectuate an effective transfer.

(4.1) *Can a* bona fide *acquirer rely on the crediting of his account (especially when acquiring* a non domino)?

Although it is not uncontested, it follows from the view set forth under the previous question that a transferor's lack of power of disposal has no proprietary consequences for the transfer (abstract transfer regime). But even if Wge entitlements would be governed by a causal transfer regime, then *bona fide* transferees are protected against competing claims of third parties through general property law rules, as under arts. 3:88 and 3:238 BW, *bona fide* transferees and pledgees, respectively, take free of a dispossessed owner's claim of revendication; arts. 19 and 20 Wge.

(4.2) *Is it possible for a credit in a securities account to be reversed and may transfer orders (or other instructions) be revoked?*

From the previous questions answered, it follows that credit entries in securities accounts cannot be reversed on the grounds of contractual deficiencies between transferor and transferee (abstract regime of transfer), nor on the ground that the credit entry does reflect a mere provisional credit. Furthermore, the reversal of credit entries is not allowed prior to an account provider's bankruptcy declaration, and is not likely to be allowed after that moment. Revocation of transfer orders is always allowed, but only when the financial institution receiving the transfer order is still able to reverse its consequences; Article 23 Fw.[204]

(5) *What are the formal requirements for the creation and enforcement of collateral?*

Security interests in book-entry securities can be created either by transfer of title or by pledge. Although explicitly forbidden by general private law, fiduciary transfers are allowed under the implementation legislation of the EU Financial Collateral Directive, i.e. when certain defined parties enter into a financial collateral arrangement. More generally, fiduciary transfers are allowed provided the creditor/transferee is provided with 'more than only an entitlement that protects his interests as a creditor'.[205]

A pledge on Wge securities can be created either by the transfer of the pledged securities into a special pledge account in the pledgee's name, or by marking the pledged securities as such in the pledgor's account. In addition, a pledge account suffices when the pledgee is the pledgor's account provider. A pledge must be enforced by a public sale, for which the pledged securities might have been delivered out of the Wge custody system. Under the implementation legislation of the FCD, however, a

204. *See* HR 31 March 1989, NJ 1990, 1 (Vis q.q./NMB).
205. *See* Keerweer/Sogelease *and supra,* s. 7.5.1.

pledge may also be enforced by appropriation or by private sale, although for the latter means of enforcement, a court order is still required.

(5.1) *Is upper-tier attachment possible, i.e. is it possible for an account holder's claimant to exercise his rights against higher-tier accounts?*

Art. 44 Wge explicitly prohibits upper-tier attachment.

7.7.2 Coherence

As the integration of corporate law into the civil code might indicate, Dutch private law is set up as a strongly coherent structure, in which functional bodies of law form integrated parts of general private law. Especially with regard to its property law, Dutch law historically represents a system of law that is characterised by its strict dogmatic structure, arguably to provide market participants with a high level of legal certainty.[206] Consequently, rules of more specific areas of law must be interpreted as specifications of the more general rules of the civil code, and that position was also expressed by the government when presenting the Draft Wge.[207] Thus, securities custody and transfer law is considered by the legislature, the judiciary and the majority of legal literature as apart of private law.

In the previous sections, however, it has been shown that the relationship between general private law and securities custody and transfer law is in many instances either weak, inconsistent, or unclear.[208] In the instances where securities custody and transfer law explicitly derogates from general private law principles, the securities law – general private law relationship must be considered to be weakly coherent, as the explicit derogations indicate that securities law and private law share few common principles.[209]

For instance, the Wge explicitly provides that issuers may prohibit the delivery of securities out of the Wge, which constitutes a derogation from the general principle that (co-)owners may always revendicate their assets, while the Wge also does not provide an alternative method of revendication. Furthermore, under the implementation legislation of the EU Financial Collateral Directive, the general private law prohibition on fiduciary transfers has been explicitly lifted for certain financial collateral arrangements concluded between certain defined institutions. In addition, the said legislation has also liberalised the requirements for the enforcement of security rights, so that under certain circumstances, pledges on securities may now be enforced by appropriation or private sale, which sharply contrasts with long-standing principles of general private law.

Unfortunately, however, the instances in which the securities law/general private law relationship is unclear or inconsistent outnumber, it is submitted, the

206. Van Erp (2004), 534.
207. *See,* e.g., Explanatory Notes to the Draft Wge TK 1975–1976, 13 780, no. 3, 37.
208. *Cf.* Schim (2006), 201.
209. *See* Ch. 2.3.

instances of weak coherence. Especially where central elements of securities custody and transfer law cannot be unambiguously classified in private or commercial law terms, incoherence is established, as these classification difficulties indicate that rules of securities custody and transfer law do not fit logically within the more general areas of law.

First, the deposit of securities with a custodian, so that the investor's physical possession of certificates is replaced by a credit balance on a securities account, cannot be unambiguously classified in general private law terms. It has been shown *above* that neither the deposit of securities into the statutory custody system of the Wge, nor the deposit of securities into a non-statutory system, can be convincingly classified as either *bewaargeving* (*depositum regulare*) or transfer of property, primarily because the assets deposited cannot be retrieved *in specie,* nor are they intended to form part of the custodian's property. Yet some elements of *bewaargeving* and transfer of ownership are present in these deposits, notably the intermediary's obligation to preserve its clients' assets and the formal requirements for delivery, respectively.

Second, it is doctrinally generally accepted that representation and contractual agency play an important part in the accountholder -intermediary relationship, but, again, classification is not uncontested. Specifically, the contracts of *volmacht* (procuration) and *lastgeving* (mandate) do not fully apply, notably because representation by an intermediary is created by statute and because it is exclusive, as accountholders cannot assert their rights against the intermediary's counterparties, elements that are both not in accordance with the contracts just mentioned. Furthermore, it is a matter of debate whether an intermediary's representation of its clients classifies as direct or indirect representation (*middellijke* or *onmiddellijke vertegenwoordiging*), although it has been argued that the latter classification is the better one.

Third, applying general principles of transfer law to the securities transfers by book-entry poses serious difficulties, and this is where securities law seems to fit worst into the dogmatic structure of private law, especially with regard to the transfer of Wge securities. The classification of securities transfers outside the statutory system of the Wge has been fiercely debated, notably in the instance of globals, but concerning the transfer of Wge securities even more so.

It has been argued that the causal transfer regime of general private law accords badly with securities transfers by credit and debit entries in securities accounts, because these accounts relate more to the accountholder/intermediary, than to the transferor – transferee relationship, especially when a securities transfer has to be effectuated via the CSD. But also on a more practical level, general rules of transfer law are clearly inconsistent with the Wge. Under the rules of general private law, for instance, the fulfilment of a resolutive condition immediately reverses provisional transfers and gives them proprietary effect, whereas under the Wge, property rights are only obtained upon a credit entry in an accountholder's securities account. In addition, under general private law, a transferor remains the owner until the delivery has been completed, whereas under securities transfer law, a transferor cannot assert any rights concerning his securities when these securities have been debited from his account, although the transferee's securities account has not yet been credited.

Fourth, the co-ownership construct that forms the basis of the proprietary protection which the Wge intended to provide for investors, is not only inconsistent with its general private law counterpart, but also fails to fully achieve accountholder protection. General private law contains a codified regime for co-owners that share in a *gemeenschap* (community of property), but it has been shown that many aspects of the rights that accountholders can assert regarding Wge pools explicitly derogate from that general private law regime. For instance, Wge accountholders cannot request the liquidation of Wge pools, and all administrative powers are exclusively performed by the intermediary that manages the Wge pool, whereas under the general private law regime, all co-owners may request the liquidation of the *gemeenschap,* and all acts of administration must be performed by the co-owners themselves.

However, while those explicit derogations indicate weak coherence, incoherence is also found. All lower than third-tier accountholders and accountholders that are not entitled to Wge admitted securities lack Wge protection. Thus, contradictory values are applied to situations that do not materially differ, as accountholders usually cannot assess whether an intermediary is a direct CSD participant or whether their securities have been admitted to the Wge system. Their securities accounts do not express such a difference, yet they are treated fundamentally differently when asserting their interests in the account provider's insolvency, for non-Wge accountholders have a mere contractual claim against the insolvent account provider. It is submitted, therefore, that this distinction presents an example of *Wertungswiderspruch.*

Finally, PRIMA as been adopted as the appropriate conflict of laws rule for international private law issues that concern book-entry securities, but it has been shown that traditional conflict of laws rules are still predominant. The precise application of PRIMA has therefore become unclear, which thus presents another instance of the inconsistent relationship between general law and securities law.

In sum, virtually all cornerstones of Dutch securities custody and transfer law, especially those of the Wge system, appear not to fit into general private law. Precisely because of the strict dogmatic structure of Dutch private law, and the application of general private law principles to specific and functional areas of law, the inconsistencies and derogations are clearly apparent, perhaps more so than in less dogmatic systems.[210] But where these inconsistencies result in unwarranted consequences, they must be resolved, notably in the instances that accountholder protection suffers.

---

210. *Cf.* Loos (2006), 8.

Chapter 8
The United States of America

8.1 INTRODUCTION

8.1.1 Trading, Clearing and Settlement

In the USA, the securities market takes place at several stock exchanges. Of the stock exchanges, the New York Stock Exchange ('NYSE') and the American Stock Exchange ('Amex') are the largest.[1] The NYSE was founded in 1817, and was then called the New York Stock and Exchange Board.[2] Amex was founded in 1921. In addition, the National Association of Securities Dealers Automatic Quotation ('NASDAQ'), created in 1971, functions as an electronic marketplace where an impressive number of shares is traded per day.[3] The rest of securities trading occurs at five regional stock exchanges and several specialised markets for commodities and financial products.[4]

It was not until after the 'paperwork crisis'[5] of 1968 that the NYSE established the Depository Trust Company ('DTC') in 1973, a limited purpose trust company organised under New York law, in which physical certificates could be

---

1. At the end of 2004, the NYSE had an astounding market capitalisation of USD 12.7 trillion, while the Nasdaq had a market capitalisation of USD 3.5 trillion; Scott (2006), Ch. 13, 4.
2. As a recent development, NYSE and Euronext announced on 2 June 2006 a merger of the two companies, thus forming the world's largest and first transatlantic exchange. At the time of writing however, the merger had not yet taken full effect; *see* <www.euronext.com> *and infra*, Ch. 9.3.2.
3. On 30 June 2006 for instance, over 690 million shares were executed trough NASDAQ; <www.nasdaq.com>.
4. The other stock exchanges are: the Boston Stock Exchange, the Philadelphia Stock Exchange, the Cincinatti Stock Exchange, the Chicago Stock Exchange and the Pacific Stock Exchange. For full listing of all markets, as well as for listing/quotation requirements, *see* Bartos (2002), 205.
5. *See infra*, s. 8.1.3.

immobilised. Thus, a system for the book-entry settlement of transactions was created. In 1976, the National Securities Clearing Corporation ('NSCC') was founded as a result of a merger between the clearing corporations of the NYSE, Amex and the National Association of Securities Dealers.[6] The NSCC gradually merged with the clearing corporations of the regional exchanges and now performs the multilateral netting of transactions concluded on all US stock exchanges.

The NSCC also acts as the central counterparty ('CCP') for most stock-market transactions. After the NSCC has assumed all debit and credit positions of its participants, it nets these positions. Subsequently, NSCC instructs DTC to credit or debit the accounts that participants maintain with the NSCC. In 1999, the Depository Trust and Clearing Corporation ('DTCC') became the holding company of both agencies.[7] Since 2003, Fixed Income Clearing Corporation ('FICC'), a new subsidiary of DTCC,[8] clears and settles most government-issued securities. DTC has direct links with the CSDs of Canada, Japan, Singapore, Germany, Argentina and Peru. DTC is now the world's largest CSD and NSCC the largest CCP.[9]

8.1.2 *Sedes Materiae*

The United States' system of government is federal, and regulatory authority is conferred to the federal government only in a limited number of matters. General commercial law, contract and property law, and more specific rules that govern the custody and settlement of securities transactions do not fall into that category.[10] These areas of law are left to the discretion of the different states. Both federal statutory and case law, however, may pre-empt state law.

Regulation of the securities markets, on the other hand, is a matter of federal law, and the Securities Act of 1933 and the Securities Exchange Act of 1934 are the most important federal statutes in this field.[11] Federal securities law is principally enforced by the US Securities and Exchange Commission ('SEC'), which has a broad range of powers for that purpose.[12] The accountholder – financial intermediary relationship is in many respects a matter of federal (regulatory) law, since most

6. *See* <www.dtcc.com>.
7. In the US, both CSDs and clearing houses are called 'clearing corporations' and both have to be registered with the Securities and Exchange Commission under the Securities Exchange Act of 1934 § 17A(b).
8. FICC was formed by the merger of Government Securities Clearing Corporation ('GSCC') and Mortgage-Backed Securities Clearing Corporation ('MBSCC'); *see* <www.dtcc.com>.
9. In 2004, the value of securities settled by DTCC subsidiaries exceeded the almost incomprehensible figure of USD 1.1 quadrillion; <www.dtcc.com>.
10. *See Erie Railroad Co. v. Tomkins*, 304 U.S. 46 (1938), where the notion of a federal common law for commercial transactions that Justice Story had formulated in *Swift v. Tyson*, 41 U.S. (16 Pet.) 1 (1824), was rejected. *See,* e.g., Bane (1983), 9.
11. Other important statutes that concern the distribution of securities are the Public Utility Holding Company Act of 1935, the Trust Indenture Act of 1939, the Investment Company Act of 1940, the Investment Advisers Act of 1940 and the Sarbanes-Oxley Act of 2002.
12. On the tension between the enforcement of regulation on the federal and on the state level, *see* Scott (2006), Ch. 2, 53.

securities firms that maintain accounts for their clients are subject to SEC regulation. Banks in all their activities are mainly regulated by the Federal Reserve.[13]

Insolvency law is also a federal matter. The Bankruptcy Act and the Securities Investor Protection Act of 1970 represent the most important legislative federal instruments that concern financial intermediary insolvencies. It must be noted however, that federal common law probably does not pre-empt state law in insolvency matters if no significant federal policy is implicated, although different courts have taken different views on this matter.[14]

Finally, all matters that concern securities issued by the US government and its agencies are governed by federal law. More specifically, the SEC Rules on the Treasury/Reserve Automated Debt Entry System ('TRADES') play an important role with regard to the custody and transfer of these securities.

8.1.3 Harmonisation of State Law

Since *Erie Railroad Co. v. Tomkins*, 304 U.S. 46 (1938), both general private and commercial law lie within the realm of state law, and therefore differ from state to state. But several initiatives have been undertaken to harmonise certain aspects of state laws through uniform statutes, not all of which have been entirely successful. The enactment in all states of the Uniform Stock Transfer Act (1909), the first uniform statute that concerned property rights in stocks, for instance, took forty-seven years.[15] The failure of some model laws to achieve effective uniformity has been attributed to either the resistance of state legislatures, to the fact that states implemented them differently, or to the federalization of the matters which these models laws addressed.[16]

The most successful and comprehensive harmonisation of private law has been brought about by the Uniform Commercial Code ('UCC'), which is directed at the harmonisation of the law that concerns payments and commercial transactions in general. It is therefore not confined to, e.g. relationships between or with merchants. UCC Article 8 deals with the custody and transfer of, and interests in, securities, while Article 9 deals with security interests in property generally. Both Article 8 and Article 9 provide for the harmonisation of both substantive and private international securities custody and transfer law.

The UCC is a model law that has no statutory power in itself, but must be implemented in state law to take effect. It addresses the legal uncertainty that existed because of the complex mixture of state case law, statutory law, the

13. Specifically, the Office of the Comptroller of the Currency and the Federal Deposit Insurance Corporation are federal agencies that regulate financial institutions.
14. *Accord In re Gaston & Snow*, 243 F 3d 599 (2d Cir., 2001), *In re Merritt Dredging*, 839 F 2d 203 (4th Cir, 1988). *Contra In re Lindsay*, 59 F 3d 942 (9th Cir, 1995). *See* Guynn & Rogers (2002), 605.
15. One of the most important features of this act was the protection of *bona fide* transferees against competing claims by *veri domini*, which is called 'negotiability' and continues to play an important role in current law. *Cf.* Rocks & Bjerre (2004), 1–2 and *see infra*, s. 8.4.2.
16. Litowitz (2001), xvi.

non-uniformity of the laws of the different US states and the out-of-date English law concepts still predominant in common private law.[17] Since its first operation in 1945, the UCC has been sponsored by the National Conference of Commissioners on Uniform State Laws ('NCCUSL') and the American Law Institute ('ALI'), with the close cooperation of the American Bar Association. It is kept up to date by a Permanent Editorial Board.[18]

In 1994 and 1999, UCC Articles 8 and 9, respectively, were revised, and James ROGERS served as the Reporter to the Article 8 revision.[19] That revision was an indirect result of the so-called paperwork crunch of 1967, when, because of a dramatic increase in the volume of trade, securities transactions could no longer be settled. At that time, settlement occurred through physical delivery and registration, which proved to be an obstacle for the market to function properly, as the back offices of New York securities firms and financial institutions became unable to effectuate the physical settlement of securities transactions. In order to alleviate the processing of securities trades and to restore market confidence, the US Treasury's Bureau of the Public Debt immediately issued regulations that provided for the dematerialisation of Treasury bills, notes and bonds, which from that moment onwards could therefore only be registered and transferred by book-entry.[20]

In response to those regulations, the NCCUSL and ALI agreed to modify UCC Article 8 in 1978, so as to modernise the legal infrastructure for the settlement of all categories of securities. But the modification did not represent an effective acknowledgment of the fundamental changes in market practices that resulted from the immobilisation of securities certificates.[21] The 1978 modification of UCC Article 8 catered for the custody of completely dematerialised issues, yet was still framed on a system of direct holding and the traditional property law concepts that applied to physical chattels.[22] In addition, the market break of the 1980s and the subsequent insolvencies of several financial institutions not covered by regulatory supervision, proved the inadequacy of the 1978 revision, and a new modification of UCC Article 8 was evidently required.[23]

Thus, it had become clear that a fundamental revision was needed to recognise the change that the modern practice of indirect holding had brought, as outmoded rules apparently had the potential to destabilise financial markets in times of stress.[24] Moreover, US Congress concluded that 'the lack of harmony amongst

17. LITOWITZ (2001), xv.
18. The Permanent Editorial Board also gives opinions on conflicts and inconsistencies within the UCC.
19. Unless otherwise indicated, all future references to UCC Art. 8 and 9 concern the current, revised versions. References to UCC Art. 1 concern the version as revised in 2001.
20. Another direct result of the paperwork crunch and an effort to restore market confidence is the Securities Investor Protection Act ('SIPA'); GUTTMAN (1990), 438. On SIPA, *see infra*, s. 8.3.5.
21. *Cf.* MOONEY (1990), n.9, GUTTMAN (2005), 1–23 *and* ROGERS (1996), 1447. On the other hand, the 1978 version did recognise the possibility of a chain of multiple intermediaries; ROCKS & BJERRE (2004), 2.
22. *See* ROGERS (1996), 1456.
23. Most notable among them was the collapse of the Drexel Burnham Lambert Group in February 1990; *see* ROGERS (1996), 1446 *and* GAO (1997), 60 *et seq.*
24. ROGERS (1996), 1436–1438.

various state laws detracts from the liquidity of the clearance and settlement system by making it burdensome (an in some cases, impracticable) for investors to finance their payment obligations'.[25] The revision process was further stimulated by pressure from the SEC, which was instructed by Congress to promulgate federal regulations, should it find that the absence of such regulations impeded the operation of the clearing and settlement system.[26]

Only a few years after the NCCUSL and ALI had begun the revision project, a new UCC Article 8 was adopted in 1994 and subsequently implemented in all states of the US. UCC Article 8 now accommodates the direct holding of both certificated and uncertificated securities, but also the indirect holding of immobilised securities, and is generally regarded as providing a highly effective legal infrastructure for the custody and transfer of securities by book-entry.[27] Together with federal regulations and state laws, the UCC has thus resulted in a modernisation and unification of US securities law and should therefore be studied as an example for possible future European legislation.[28]

Mainly for that reason, the following sections will analyse in greater detail current US law regarding the custody and transfer of securities, as well as its relationship with more general areas of law. First, the main distinctions with regard to financial instruments will be discussed. In the section that follows, legal aspects of securities custody will be analysed, with particular emphasis on securities accounts, the accountholder/intermediary relationship and the consequences of intermediary insolvencies. In Sections 4 and 5 of this chapter, the transfer of securities by book-entry, and the creation and enforcement of security interests in securities will subsequently be discussed. Section 6 will deal with US private international law concerning securities custody and transfer. The chapter will conclude with answers to the questions posed in Chapter 1.2.2 and a coherence analysis.

8.2 CATEGORIES OF SECURITIES

The characteristics of equity securities and debt instruments are generally determined by state law, with an exception of debt instruments issued by the US government and its agencies. Throughout the US, both equity, i.e. stock and shares, and debt instruments appear in certificated and uncertificated form. But most stock is issued in certificated form, while government bonds and shares in mutual funds are

---

25. *Cf.* Legislative Intent at UCC § 8-101, by the New York legislature; Laws 1997, Ch. 566, § 5. *Cf. also* Rogers (1996), 1543: 'To provide an adequate commercial law foundation for modern securities transactions, it is essential that uniform law be adopted at the state level. Similarly, the legislative history of the Market Reform Act of 1990 identifies the problem of potential and actual nonuniformity among the states as the major problem with the commercial law foundation of the securities clearance and settlement system'.
26. Pursuant to the Market Reform Act of 1990; Mooney (1990), n.11. In the end it was concluded however, that modernisation on the state level was preferable because of complexities as to federal authority; Rogers (1996), 1446 and n.26. *Cf.* 31 CFR § 357, Appendix B.
27. Spink & Paré (2004), 345–346.
28. The securities custody and transfer law provisions of the UCC have been implemented in all US states with no major differences in implementation; *see* Lawrence (2005), at UCC § 8-113.

usually uncertificated, so that immobilisation of physical certificates at the CSD level is the most common type of securities custody in the US. Yet the process of dematerialisation is ongoing, and DTCC is actively engaged in that process.[29]

Uncertificated securities can only appear in registered form,[30] while certificated securities appear in either registered or bearer form. The owner of registered securities is registered on the issuer's register, which is usually maintained by a so-called registrar. An issue of bearer securities typically takes place in the form of a single certificate that is deposited with a CSD, and such a certificate may either contain a varying number of securities, or the entire issue. In the former instance, the certificate is called a balance certificate or jumbo certificate, and the securities not comprised in the jumbo certificate are distributed as individual certificates. When the certificate represents the entire issue, it is called a global, and the securities comprised therein cannot be split up nor distributed individually.[31]

As foreign issuers cannot distribute their securities directly in the American markets, they must issue so-called American Depository Receipts ('ADRs') through a US commercial bank (depository).[32] Against the depository, the ADR holder has certain rights under the depository agreement, such as the right to receive dividends, to vote and the right to exchange the ADR for the foreign, underlying shares. Where the foreign counterparts are denominated in foreign currencies, ADRs are dollar-denominated.[33] Issues of foreign debt instruments denominated in US dollars are called Yankee Bonds. Transactions in these instruments may be settled through either DTC or a foreign (I)CSD, whereas non-US dollar denominated notes are usually settled through a foreign (I)CSD.[34]

8.3 CUSTODY OF BOOK-ENTRY SECURITIES

8.3.1 Introduction

An important distinction to be made when describing the legal aspects of securities custody in the US is between securities that are directly and indirectly held. A direct holding system traditionally concerns the situation that investors themselves hold their securities in a physical form, and in such a custody system issuers thus maintain a direct link with the ultimate investors.[35] Currently, however, certificated securities are only occasionally directly held, while uncertificated securities, i.e. dematerialised securities, may also be held directly under US law.[36] Uncertificated securities that are directly held are evidenced by book-entry

29. *See* <www.dtcc.com> *and* White & Summers (2000), 100.
30. *Cf.* UCC §§ 8-106 (2001) and 8-102 (2001).
31. *See*, e.g., Guttman (2005), 1-25 *et seq. and* Guttman (1990), 447–449.
32. Bartos (2002), 241. *See also* Scott (2006), Ch. 2, 84–88.
33. Scott (2006), Ch. 2, 84.
34. *See* Bartos (2002), 212–213.
35. *Supra*, Ch. 3.2.2.
36. *Cf.* the French practice of custody of *titres nominatifs;* Ch. 6.3.3.

only, but their registration on the issuer's books does not classify as a securities account.[37] Especially US government securities and securities issued by mutual funds are so held.[38]

The great majority of securities are thus indirectly held. Certificated private company securities issued in registered form are typically registered in the name of Cede & Co., the nominee used by the Depository Trust Company ('DTC'), which effectively administers the securities holding. Usually, the certificates of both registered and bearer securities are held in a global form with DTC. Banks and securities firms (generally referred to as broker/dealers) can be admitted to DTC's custody system as participants, and thus maintain omnibus accounts with DTC that express their entitlements to the global.[39] These participants, in their turn, administer the securities accounts of their customers, who may be either the ultimate investors or still other intermediaries.

Another important distinction must be made between the custody of securities that are issued by the US government, i.e. the Treasury, or US government agencies on the one hand, and the custody of securities that are issued by private companies on the other.[40] US Treasury and government agency-issued securities are fully dematerialised by law, and are usually held in the Treasury/Reserve Automated Debt Entry System ('TRADES').[41] In this system, the Federal Reserve Banks act as the Treasury's fiscal agents. Only admitted entities may act as participants to the Federal Reserve Banks, which recognise only these entities as accountholders. The participants, in their turn, may act as intermediaries for ultimate investors or other intermediaries. But investors may also hold US Government securities directly with the Federal Reserve Banks or the Bureau of Public Debt, a system which is called 'Treasury Direct'.

The rules that apply to the government systems of book-entry custody (including conflict of laws rules) are federal rules that are either similar to UCC Article 8 or refer to state law and thus to the implemented versions of UCC Article 8.[42]

---

37. *Cf.* UCC § 8-501(a).
38. A mutual fund is an investment vehicle that allows 'investors to purchase interests representing pro rata shares of the net assets of a pool of securities and other assets'; Scott (2006), Ch. 16, 1.
39. From a regulatory point of view, however, the distinction between banks and broker/dealers is essential, as banks are regulated by a number of Federal agencies including the Federal Reserve Board, whereas broker/dealers are regulated by the SEC. The regulation of banks principally aims at reducing the systemic risk, while the regulation of securities firms is generally aimed at investor protection; Scott (2006), Ch. 3, 1. For the purpose of this book, the distinction is less important, and banks and securities firms will therefore be jointly referred to as 'intermediaries', 'custodians' or 'account providers', when acting in that capacity.
40. Such as the Government National Mortgage Association (known as Ginnie Mae), the Federal National Mortgage Association (known as Fannie Mae) and the Federal Home Loan Mortgage Corporation (known as Freddie Mac).
41. 31 CFR § 306.116(a) refers to 31 CFR § 357 for the rules on book-entry US securities. These rules became effective on 1 January 1997; 31 CFR § 357.1.
42. Incorporation by reference approved by the Director of the Federal Register; 31 CFR § 357.2. *See also* 31 CFR § 357.10 *and Cf.* Guttman (2005), 1–25. *Cf.* 31 CFR § 357, Appendix B: 'The questions inherent in a tiered system of ownership have been analyzed, and in Treasury's

Federal rules apply exclusively to the obligations of the issuer (the Treasury) and the Federal Reserve Banks against their clients/accountholders, and, vice versa, to the claims of the accountholders against these entities. The relationship between the Federal Reserve Banks and their clients is therefore regulated by federal law, but it is reiterated that these rules correspond with those of UCC Article 8. Yet admitted participants have a direct claim against the US, although the Treasury and the Federal Reserve Banks act as account providers.[43] As another difference from UCC Article 8, a security interest in US government-issued securities can only be created and perfected by the marking of these securities as pledged on the books of a Federal Reserve Bank. In addition, a security interest in favour of the US has priority over all other interests.[44] But because of the limited scope of the federal rules and their overall similarity to UCC Articles 8 and 9, the following sections will primarily focus on the UCC.[45]

8.3.2 Indirect Holding Under the UCC

As noted above, the revised Article 8 takes a neutral position in that it caters for different holding practices. The underlying idea was that the development of these practices should be solely determined by market and regulatory forces, and that the UCC should not influence such development.[46] The most important goal of the 1994 revision therefore, was to provide sound legal underpinnings for the indirect holding system based on securities accounts. To that end, a new conceptual framework was created in which 'security entitlement' is the central notion. A security entitlement must be understood as the package of rights an accountholder can assert against his immediate intermediary.[47] Thus, the security itself and the rights an accountholder enjoys as to this security via an intermediary are sharply distinguished.

Generally, investors can assert direct rights to their securities only in a situation of direct holding, and an issuer has 'primary' obligations towards the beneficial owners only in such a situation.[48] When securities are indirectly held on the other hand, the rights of beneficial owners relate to their intermediary's obligation

view, satisfactorily addressed by Revised Art. 8'. The Treasury therefore concluded that the uniformity required for an efficient market for government securities could be attained without an independent system of Federal commercial law.

43. *See* 31 CFR § 357, Appendix B.
44. 31 CFR § 357.12(b) and (c).
45. For a highly detailed treatise with many references to regulatory law as well as case law, *see* Guttman (2005).
46. Quinn (2001), [Rev] § 8-101[A][2].
47. *See* further *infra*, s. 8.3.3 *and* 8.3.4.
48. In the language of UCC Art. 8: the issue of a security does not constitute the establishment of a security entitlement; UCC § 8-501(e). Consequently, the issue of ADRs also does not result directly in the creation of a securities entitlement; UCC § 8-501 official cmt. 5.

to pass on the issuer's primary obligations.[49] UCC Article 8 considers only the first tier in the indirect holding system, i.e. the relationship between the issuer and legal owner/first intermediary, as a direct holding relationship to which the rules connected therewith apply.[50] In other words, beneficial owners in the indirect holding system are always holders of a security entitlement, but only the first-tier intermediaries hold securities themselves.[51]

Since a security entitlement does not represent a claim to securities themselves, but a package of claims against a specific account provider, the concept excludes tracing, and an accountholder has no direct legal relationship with his securities through the chain of intermediaries.[52] Consequently, a security entitlement is not transferable, as it is created by a credit-entry in a securities account and is extinguished by a debit-entry.[53] This approach corresponds perfectly with the modern practice of securities custody, where every intermediary has a securities account in its own name with the next intermediary, CSD or issuer, and where the underlying assets are not only fungible, but also located at different tiers. Moreover, because the drafters of the Revised UCC Article 8 abandoned the concept of tracing, the number of intermediaries that are interposed between issuer and ultimate investor does not influence the substance of the latter's rights.

8.3.2.1 Securities Eligible

For the purpose of Article 8, UCC § 8-102(a)(15) provides a definition of 'security' which is very broad and covers practically all types of financial instruments.[54] Thus, to all kinds of debt instruments and interests in the issuer or its property, the provisions of Article 8 apply. As to form, the definition distinguishes between bearer, registered and uncertificated securities. 'Bearer securities' relate to physical certificates that represent the security and jumbo and global certificates are therefore also considered to fall within this category.[55] Registered securities are characterised by the fact that it is the issuer's register that ultimately determines the investors' ownership and transfers thereof, even though certificates are often issued as a means of evidence.[56] 'Uncertificated securities' relate to dematerialised securities that exist only because of a credit-entry in the issuer's books.

---

49. UCC § 8-501 official cmt. 5.
50. It is to the security itself, and thus to the relationship between issuer and first intermediary, that the definition of 'security' (*see* the next section) should be tested, and not to other relationships, such as the one between the beneficial owner and its account provider; *In re County of Orange*, 219 B.R. 543, 36 UCC Rep. Serv. 2d 181, 552 (Bankr. C.D. Cal 1997).
51. *Cf. In re County of Orange*, 219 B.R. 543, 36 UCC Rep. Serv. 2d 181 (Bankr. C.D. Cal 1997).
52. E.g. UCC § 8-102 official cmt. 17 *and* UCC § 8-104 official cmt. 2. *Cf.* ROGERS (1996), 1456.
53. UCC § 8-501 official cmt. 5. *See also* ROCKS & BJERRE (2004) 35–36.
54. This definition differs substantially from the definition of 'security' as developed for purposes of federal securities laws; ROCKS & BJERRE (2004) 6–7.
55. UCC § 8-102 official cmt. 15. *But see* GUTTMAN (2005), 1–25 *et seq. and* GUTTMAN (1990), 447–449.
56. UCC § 8-102(a)(13).

Furthermore, § 8-102(a)(15)(ii) requires that a 'security' be one of a class or series, or be divisible into a class or series, so as to distinguish it from negotiable instruments (drafts, checks, certificates of deposit, notes[57]). In addition, 'securities' are required to be tradable on a securities market. But should an instrument not be tradable, issuers can opt in for the application of Article 8, provided the instrument is a medium for investment.[58]

The definition of 'security' as just discussed is particularly important in the context of directly held securities. The rules of UCC Article 8 on securities accounts, however, are applicable to an even broader category of financial instruments, as UCC Article 8, Part 5, applies to all assets that are held in an indirect holding system by means of a securities account.[59] Thus, UCC Article 8 considers a security as a type of financial asset, but the Article also caters for the (indirect) custody of other types of financial assets, such as options; § 8-102(a)(9).[60] But financial assets must be tradable in order to fall within the scope of Article 8, although its application can also be opted for, just as non-tradable securities.[61]

Since a security entitlement, i.e. the means by which ownership of a financial asset is evidenced, is also referred to as 'financial asset', both a security entitlement and the underlying asset are referred to as a 'financial asset', which thus represents an exception to the distinction that is generally made between entitlement and underlying asset.

8.3.2.2 Securities Accounts[62]

A securities account is defined very broadly in UCC § 8-501(a) so as to include different types of relationships that have securities or other financial assets as an object. UCC § 8-501(a) intends to include, for instance, both the relationship between a clearing corporation and its participants, and between a securities firm or bank and its customers. To accommodate these different relationships and changing market practices, a relationship classifies as a 'securities account' under the UCC if the subsequent application of the rules of Article 8 would be 'consistent with the expectations of the parties to the relationship'.[63]

A securities account and a corresponding securities entitlement can be created by a credit-entry in the books of a securities account provider,[64] or by an intermediary's acceptance of a security certificate or other financial asset when that asset is to be credited to a securities account; UCC § 8-501(b). An entitlement may thus be created before a securities account is credited. It must be noted, however, that

57. UCC § 3-104.
58. UCC § 8-102(a)(15)(iii)(B).
59. UCC § 8-102 official cmt. 9.
60. *Cf. also* UCC § 8-103(e).
61. UCC § 8-102(a)(9)(iii).
62. *See* GUTTMAN (2005), 1–31 *et seq.*, extensively on operational aspects of securities accounts.
63. UCC § 8-501 official cmt. 1.
64. *Cf.* 31 CFR § 357.12(a) on the creation of a securities entitlement on the books of a Federal Reserve Bank.

the acceptance of a security certificate by an intermediary alone is not sufficient to result in the creation of a securities entitlement, as the accepting intermediary must also intend to credit an accountholder's account accordingly. But if the intermediary fails to make the appropriate and corresponding entry in a securities account, any obligation under non-UCC law to do so results in a *de iure* creation of a security entitlement.[65] In these particular instances, a security entitlement is therefore created without a credit entry in a securities account.

Conversely, when an account provider has credited one of its customers' securities accounts, a securities entitlement is created, even if the account provider does not hold all corresponding assets; UCC § 8-501(c).[66] Thus, 'maintenance of financial assets is a consequence of, not a cause of, the establishment of a security entitlement'.[67] This rule may be thought of as an encroachment on entitlement holders' rights, as it sanctions uncovered credit entries, i.e. credit entries that do not correspond with identical entries in the account provider's omnibus account with the higher tier, which thus reduces the estate against which accountholders can enforce their claims. But good reasons have been advanced to support the provision.

First, it has been argued that it corresponds with current market practice, in which operational gaps exist between the moment that a credit-entry is made in a transferee's securities account, and the moment that the account provider has received the corresponding assets.[68] Second, UCC § 8-501(c) does not imply that an intermediary is free to create securities entitlements without corresponding assets, since both UCC § 8-504 and regulatory law restrict the 'uncovered' crediting of securities accounts by intermediaries to a minimum.[69]

Third, it gives conditional transfers proprietary effect, so that accountholders/putative transferees are protected should their account provider become insolvent, even if that account provider does not hold all corresponding assets. This is generally regarded as a considerable improvement compared to the traditional property law construct employed in the prior version of UCC Article 8. Under that construct, accountholders obtained the status of co-owners only if they were entitled to specific, identifiable assets, and putative transferees were therefore not proprietarily protected.[70] Fourth, UCC § 8-501(c) generally facilitates the extension of credit in the form of securities. More in particular, it facilitates the extension of securities credited to a so-called margin account, i.e. an account to which securities are credited

---

65. UCC § 8-501(b)(3) *and see* UCC § 8-501 official cmt. 2.
66. When an account provider receives the financial assets that correspond to its customers' entitlements, he is considered a 'purchaser for value', and consequently enjoys the protection connected with that status. Thus, such an account provider takes free of third party claims regarding the financial assets it holds for its clients; UCC §§ 8-303 and 8-502. *See also infra*, s. 8.4.2.
67. Rocks & Bjerre (2004), 40.
68. UCC § 8-501 official cmt. 3. *Cf.* SEC rule 15c3-3, 17 CFR § 240.15c3-3(b)(2).
69. *See infra*, s. 8.3.3.
70. Mooney (1990), 335–337 *and* Guttman (1990), 463.

that have not (yet) been fully paid for by the accountholder.[71] In sum, it is submitted that UCC § 8-501(c) represents an important improvement compared to the older version of Article 8 that was based on the traditional property law construct.

8.3.3 Accountholder/Intermediary Relationship

UCC Article 8 governs the accountholder/intermediary relationship, but by no means exclusively. First, an intermediary may perform many services that do not fall within the scope of Article 8, such as investment advice and the like. These aspects of the accountholder/intermediary relationship are left to other laws, such as the law of contract and agency on the one hand, and state and federal regulation on the other. Second, in their capacity as custodians, intermediaries are subject to state and federal regulatory law, and UCC Article 8 only applies when these regulations do not.[72] Finally, the common law of contract and agency may supplement UCC law.[73]

At an early stage in the revision project of UCC Article 8, it was decided not to describe the accountholder/custodian relationship in 'old' legal concepts of the common law.[74] Instead, UCC Article 8 now describes and regulates in a functional way the intermediary's duties towards its customers/securities accountholders.[75] The UCC defines minimum standards that an account provider should comply with, and provides supplementary rules.

Because of the functional approach, the characterisation of the accountholder/intermediary relationship in common law terms has become unnecessary and, as such, characterisation proved to be impossible, so that the new approach better corresponds with the *sui generis* character of the accountholder/intermediary relationship. Yet the common law may supplement UCC law when the latter does not apply, and the following section therefore discusses the common law concepts by which the accountholder/intermediary relationship was traditionally characterised.

8.3.3.1 Common Law Concepts

Bailment is defined as the 'rightful possession of a chattel by one who is not the holder of the title to it'.[76] While few would object to such a minimal definition, the character of bailment is not uncontroversial. It has been analysed both as a property law relationship and as a contractual one, with different legal consequences.[77] The disagreements with regard to bailment are long-standing, and bailment does

71. *See* Guttman (1990), 464–468, on the segregation of these categories of accounts.
72. Yet it is reminded that banks and broker/dealers are regulated by different regulators with different policy goals.
73. *Cf.* UCC § 8-509 official cmt. *and* Legislative Intent at UCC § 8-101, by the New York legislature; Laws 1997, Ch. 566, § 5.
74. Rogers (1996), 1496. *Cf.* Mooney (1990), 310 *et seq.*
75. *Cf.* UCC § 8-102 official cmt. 17.
76. Burke (2003), 182.
77. Brown (1975), 209.

not seem to be applicable to intangibles. For instance, under both the property and contractual approach, bailment requires the 'possession', i.e. the actual physical control, of a 'chattel', i.e. tangible goods.[78] These concepts clearly do not match the holding of interests in fungible financial assets.[79]

Another element of bailment is the bailor's relinquishment of control over the chattel. The relinquishment of control is a central element of trust also, where the trustee has a high degree of control over the affairs of the beneficiary. But unlike bailment, the trust property can be intangible.[80] Further, the fact that the settlor, i.e. the initiator of the trust, loses legal title to the trust property and retains only equitable rights, whilst the bailor remains the legal owner, represents a major difference between bailment and trust.[81] Moreover, if a settlor wants to assert his rights to the trust property (e.g. in the trustee's insolvency), a settlor must show that he can follow the property into the trustee's estate.[82] Since the tracing of fungible intangibles that are located at different tiers of a custody chain is impossible, the trust generally does not apply to the custody of indirectly held securities.[83]

A bailee who has been given the authority to deal with the bailment goods classifies as an agent.[84] Agency is distinguished from trust because an 'agent is ordinarily not the owner of property for the benefit of his principal, while a trustee always holds title'.[85] The pre-1994 versions of UCC Article 8 incorporated agency law into the accountholder/intermediary relationship, but restricted its applicability to situations in which the ultimate investor was registered as the owner in the issuer's books.[86] Because, as a matter of principle, ultimate investors are not registered as owners in modern indirect holding structures, and because an intermediary is – in its capacity as custodian – not empowered to deal with its customers' assets, an agency can generally not be said to apply to the accountholder/intermediary relationship.[87] In conclusion, none of the pertinent common law concepts proves to be fully applicable to the *sui generis* accountholder/intermediary relationship, and the functional approach of the revised UCC Article 8 therefore correctly takes a functional approach.

---

78. Brown (1975), 223.
79. The custody of a fungible chattel is also considered bailment under the common law, although older case law had characterised the bailment of fungibles as a sale; Brown (1975), 237–238. *Cf.* Burke (2003), 208.
80. Restatement Third, Trusts § 40. *See also* Bogert (1987), 2.
81. Bogert (1987), 28.
82. Scott & Fratcher (1987), § 523.
83. *Cf.* Mooney (1990), 377.
84. *See* Hynes & Loewenstein (2005), 29.
85. Bogert (1987), 35.
86. *Cf.* Mooney (1990), 419, Appendix II.
87. *Cf.* Mooney (1990), ns.220 and 257.

8.3.3.2 Flexible Duties

As stated previously, the current version of UCC Article 8 describes an intermediary's duties towards its customers in a functional way. Interestingly, Article 8 not only defines these statutory duties, but also describes the methods by which they can be satisfied, and it will show that the description of these methods allows for greater flexibility in their satisfaction. Generally, an account provider's duties are satisfied either when their performance is specifically defined in an (account) agreement, when the account provider exercises due care as required by reasonable commercial standards, or when the account provider complies with requirements of other law.[88]

The underlying policy consideration for the reference to party autonomy was to protect accountholders' expectations in the best way possible, and to provide for sufficient flexibility at the same time.[89] Such flexibility, it has been argued, could be needed in extraordinary custody situations or when irregular securities were held by the intermediary. The custody of foreign securities over which the intermediary can exercise little control as to their actual safekeeping, for instance, could require a lenient approach towards the performance of the intermediary's duties.[90] Moreover, a variable standard of care is consistent with the common law concept of bailment, in which freedom of contract is only limited to violations of public policies.[91]

However, party autonomy as referred to in, e.g. UCC § 8-504(c)(1), is not entirely unrestricted, for intermediaries are bound by both a practical incentive to preserve their reputations and by the legal obligations required by general contract law. Thus, an intermediary must refrain from fraud and generally act in good faith.[92] Under the UCC, the performance and enforcement of contracts and duties in good faith is understood as an observation of 'honesty in fact' and the 'reasonable commercial standards of fair dealing'.[93] General principles of private law on the other hand, understand 'good faith' as 'faithfulness to an agreed common purpose and consistency with the justified expectations of the other party'.[94] Applied to the accountholder/intermediary relationship, the justified expectation of an accountholder would be that his account provider would allow the accountholder to enjoy the 'benefits of the economic or other rights that comprise ownership of the security'.[95]

---

88. As a matter of legislative technique, the first two ways in which an intermediary's duty may be complied with are repeated in each of the provisions that list these duties; UCC §§ 8-504 up to 8-508. The third way is codified in a separate provision; UCC § 8-509.
89. Rogers (1996), 1503–1504. *Cf.* Mooney (1990), 409–410 *and* Legislative Intent at UCC § 8-101, by the New York legislature; Laws 1997, Ch. 566, § 5.
90. UCC § 8-504 official cmt. 4.
91. Rogers (1996), 1505–1506.
92. *See,* e.g., UCC § 1-304 (Obligation of Good Faith).
93. UCC § 1-201(b)(20).
94. Restatement Second, Contracts, § 205.
95. Rogers (1996), 1508. *Cf.* UCC § 8-501(a) official cmt. 1.

Absent an agreement, it is the standard of 'due care' that determines how an intermediary's duties should be satisfied, and an intermediary must observe such due care both with regard to its own operations and its selection of other intermediaries through which it operates. The due care standard is meant to incorporate the principles of the common law under which all circumstances are taken into account to determine whether the standard is met.[96] More specifically, professional securities custodians exercise due care if they 'provide, for a fee, a level of expertise in securities processing that avoids or minimizes the risk of accidents'.[97] Although this standard corresponds with the standard of good faith discussed immediately above, these standards are distinguished, and it is therefore possible to contract out of the exercise of due care, provided the intermediary remains within the limits set by the standard of good faith.

The intermediary's duties are mainly aimed at passing through the 'primary' rights that are connected with the financial assets to which a securities account refers.[98] More specifically, UCC §§ 8-504 – 8-508 set out the following duties:

(1) To obtain, and thereafter maintain, the amount of financial assets that corresponds to the aggregate amount of assets to which the intermediary's clients are entitled.[99] As a consequence, an intermediary is forbidden from disposing of the securities to which its clients are entitled, either by transfer of title or by granting a security interest.[100] But this prohibition applies only when provisions of federal law do not. SEC rule 15c3-3, for instance, imposes on broker/dealers a duty to 'promptly obtain' and 'thereafter maintain'[101] the securities carried for their customers, while rules 8c-1 and 15c2 forbid the hypothecation of customer securities.[102] Under federal law, a violation of these rules constitutes a criminal offence.[103] In addition, state law forbids these practices under the law of bailment or other laws of contract.[104]
(2) To obtain and pass through the proceeds of the underlying securities.[105]
(3) To comply with the accountholder's directions regarding corporate actions and other rights connected to the accountholder's assets.[106] Since

96. UCC § 8-504 official cmt. 4.
97. Rogers (1996), 1507.
98. *Cf.* UCC § 8-501(a).
99. UCC § 8-504(a).
100. UCC § 8-504(b).
101. 17 CFR § 240.15c3-3(b). This wording was directly included in UCC § 8-504(a); UCC § 8-504 official cmt. 1.
102. 17 CFR §§ 240.8c-1(a) and 240.15c2(a).
103. Securities Exchange Act of 1934 § 32, 15 USC § 78ff (1994).
104. Rogers (1996), 1519. But if customer securities have been (re)hypothecated by an intermediary without its customers' consent, the security taker may take free of and gain priority over the customers' claims; *see infra*, s. 8.4.2.
105. UCC § 8-505(a). *Cf.* SEC rule 14b1-1 that provides a similar rule concerning the forwarding of communications to the beneficial owners by securities firms; 17 CFR § 240.14b-1.
106. UCC § 8-506(a).

as a principle of the indirect holding system, a CSD, its nominee, or other intermediary is registered in the issuer's books as the (legal) owner, UCC § 8-506(a) requires that an account provider must comply with its customers' directions, thus acting as a representative, and not at its own discretion.[107]

(4) To comply with accountholders' entitlement orders, provided that these orders are given by the appropriate person.[108] For that purpose, an intermediary should check the order's genuineness, and the intermediary should reasonably comply.[109] In the case where an intermediary transfers accountholders' assets pursuant to an ineffective entitlement order and thereby wrongfully transfers the assets, the intermediary can be held liable and must reimburse the deprived accountholder.[110] An intermediary is not under an obligation to comply with a third party's orders unless this is agreed upon with the entitlement holder, even if such a third party has been mandated under agency law to act on the entitlement holder's behalf. However, if an intermediary does comply with a duly authorised agent's orders, he is not liable, even in the absence of an agreement to that effect with the entitlement holder.[111]

(5) To comply with accountholders' orders to change the form of holding. An accountholder may require that his account provider transfers his assets to another intermediary, delivers the assets out of the indirect holding system or otherwise provides the entitlement holder with direct ownership of the assets. But this duty is not unconditional, as the requested form of holding must be available and the entitlement holder must be eligible for the requested form of holding.[112]

107. Yet an accountholder may, of course, confer discretionary authority upon his intermediary; UCC § 8-506 official cmt. 1 and 2. An intermediary may also put its client in a position to exercise its rights directly; UCC § 8-506.

108. *See* UCC § 8-107(a)(3) (definition of 'appropriate person') in conjunction with § 8- 102(a)(7) (definition of 'entitlement holder').

109. UCC §§ 8-507(a) and 8-102(a)(8).

110. UCC § 8-107(b). *See, e.g., Powers* v. *American Express Financial Advisors, Inc.* 82 F. Supp 2d 448, 40 U.C.C. Rep. 2d 597 (D. Md. 2000) [43 UCCLL7 (Sept. 2000)], where the court held that the securities transfer concerned followed an ineffective entitlement order, as the order was made without appropriate authority. In addition, it was decided that 'other law' determined that the intermediary should bear the loss (consistent with UCC § 8-507 official cmt. 4), even though the intermediary had exercised due care in accordance with reasonable commercial standards. *Cf. Watson* v. *Sears,* 766 N.E. 2d 784, 47 UCC Rep. Serv. 2d 722 (Ind. Ct. App. 2002).

111. Rocks & Bjerre (2004), 47. *See* further UCC § 8-107(a)(4) and (a)(5) *and* UCC § 8-507 official cmt. 4.

112. UCC §8-508.

8.3.4 Nature of Accountholder Interests

Prior to the 1994 revision of UCC Article 8, investors holding interests in indirectly held securities were considered to enjoy co-ownership rights in pools of securities on the basis of a trust construction. This 'property law construct' was based on the idea that investors are (co-)owners of discrete property in the possession or control of their intermediaries/account providers.[113] However, upon proper analysis of the modern practice of securities custody, the revisors of UCC Article 8 concluded that the property law construct poorly matched that practice. Considering the fact that securities are by definition fungible and may be held at various tiers in various jurisdictions, scholars and practitioners alike argued that the proper approach would be to focus on the accountholder/intermediary relationship, rather than to trace ownership rights from investor to security.[114]

Consequently, the notion of 'security entitlement' was coined, a notion that refers to a *sui generis* package of rights that Article 8 confers upon securities accountholders.[115] A security entitlement is acquired the moment when a securities account relationship has been created, i.e. when a credit-entry has been made in an accountholder's securities account.[116] A security entitlement consists of an accountholder's rights *in rem* as well as *in personam* against the intermediary that maintains the securities account, i.e. the account provider.[117] The contractual rights of an accountholder mainly consist of the intermediary's obligation to hold the accountholder's financial assets in good faith, a rather general obligation which is substantiated by the more specific duties discussed *above*.[118]

---

113. *Cf.* UCC § 8-503 official cmt. 2.
114. *Cf.* UCC § 8-504 official cmt. 1 *and* UCC § 8-502 official cmt. 2, where reference is made to the impossibility of tracing in a clearing system with net settlement. In such a system, all obligations to deliver to a seller's intermediary are set off against its rights to receive, so that a seller's intermediary may ultimately receive, rather than have to transfer assets. A particular fierce advocate of abandoning the property law construct was Mooney (1990), 310: '(...) a property law construct for resolving priorities among claimants to fungible bulks of securities is a fundamentally flawed approach', *ib.,* 313: 'the property law construct is inadequate and unworkable', *and ib.,* 378: 'As observed in the context of same-tier priorities, its [i.e. the property law construct's, MH] application to different-tier priorities is confusing, awkward, and unprincipled'. Rogers (1995), 694 has likened tracing and its underlying technique, i.e. applying the traditional conceptual structure of property law to book-entry securities, to 'the technique made famous by Procrustes'. *Cf. also* Guttman (1990), 453, with reference to the fact that even federal law cannot require a registered owner to disclose the beneficial owners' identity.
115. Spink & Paré (2004), 358 have noted that the concept was known in Canada prior to its recognition in the US.
116. *Cf.* UCC § 8-102 official cmt. 7 *and UCC* § 8-501(b).
117. *See,* e.g., Mooney (1990), 413, Guynn & Rogers (2002), 607 *and* Rocks & Bjerre (2004), 50. Some have, on the other hand, considered the intermediary-investor relationship to be 'basically contractual', albeit supplemented by 'some measure of protection which normally comes from a property interest'; Ooi (2003), 216. *Cf.* Schim (2006), 22.
118. UCC § 8-504 *et seq. See also* UCC §§ 8-102(a)(17) and 8-505 *and supra,* s. 8.3.3.

An accountholder's rights *in rem* are thus evidenced solely by a credit balance in the books of a financial intermediary, while Article 8 does not impose a statutory obligation on that intermediary to separate its own assets from those of its customers. But although an account provider registers all credit balances in an omnibus account in its own name with a higher-tier intermediary, client assets do not form part of the intermediary's property, and customers' claims have priority over their account provider's claims in the case of the latter's insolvency.[119]

Although, in principle, rights *in rem* or proprietary rights are enforceable against all third parties, under UCC Article 8, an accountholder's rights may only be asserted against third parties, i.e. persons other than their account provider, in very specific situations. First, since the Article 8 system is not based on traceable property rights, accountholders' interests in the financial assets held by their intermediary are calculated pro rata, and the traditional property law maxim *prior tempore, potior iure* therefore does not apply.[120] In other words, all accountholders are treated equally as to the moment in time of the acquisition of their interests and, as a consequence, an accountholder cannot assert his rights against his fellow accountholders.[121]

Second, it is only in insolvency situations, that an accountholder can assert his rights against the intermediary's trustee in bankruptcy, the intermediary's creditors and other third parties. Under certain circumstances however, the account provider's secured creditors take free of the accountholders' claims.[122] Moreover, an accountholder can successfully assert his interests against third parties only in extraordinary circumstances, viz. if the insolvent intermediary's estate appears to show a deficit because the intermediary had violated its obligation to obtain sufficient assets, if the trustee in bankruptcy does not enforce the accountholder's claim, and if the third party concerned is not protected under the rule that protects *bona fide* transferees against competing claims.[123]

As a corollary of this limited enforceability of an accountholder's rights, both other accountholders and other financial intermediaries are almost always protected against competing claims.[124] Thus, while an accountholder's rights are protected against competing claims, these rights can usually only be enforced against his own intermediary, and the UCC regime provides accountholders with solid legal certainty as to their security entitlement.

---

119. UCC § 8-503(a).
120. Codex Iust. VIII, xviii, 3.
121. UCC § 8-503(b) *and cf.* UCC § 8-502 official cmt. 4.
122. *See infra,* s. 8.4.2.
123. UCC § 8-503(d). All these conditions were met in *Nathan W. Drage, P.C. v. First Concord Securities, Ltd.,* 184 Misc. 2d 92, 707 N.Y.S. 2d 782, 41 UCC Rep. 2d 673 (2000) [34 UCCLL 10 (Dec. 2000). On the protection of third parties, *see infra,* s. 8.4.2.
124. *See Cotton* v. *Private Bank and Trust Co.,* 49 UCC Rep. Serv. 2d 1281 (N.D. Ill. 2003), where the court held that pursuant to UCC § 8-115, the intermediary in question could not be held liable, because it did not act in collusion with a wrongdoer. *Cf. infra,* s. 8.4.2.

8.3.5 INTERMEDIARY INSOLVENCY AND THE TREATMENT OF SHORTFALLS

8.3.5.1 Federal Law

Federal insolvency law pre-empts the rules of UCC Article 8, which therefore deal with the property position of accountholders, rather than with the distribution of assets of a bankrupt estate.[125] While the allocation of losses in the insolvencies of banking institutions is made under state law, securities firms' bankruptcies are principally governed by federal law.[126]

Under the Securities Investor Protection Act ('SIPA') of 1970, the Securities Investor Protection Corporation ('SIPC') was founded.[127] Membership of that corporation is mandatory for securities firms that are registered with the SEC, and the SIPC is authorised to initiate liquidation proceedings in the case of a securities firm's insolvency. In such instance, the SIPC distributes all securities present in the insolvent estate pro rata between those clients that have 'customer' status, while it makes no separate distribution per category of securities.[128] Should the estate appear to be insufficient to satisfy all customers' claims, the SIPC makes contributions to all customers up to an amount of USD 500,000 per customer to satisfy the deficit.[129]

Securities firms bankruptcies that are not covered by SIPA, are governed by Subchapter III of chapter 7 of the Bankruptcy Code. Under the provisions of that code, a similar procedure is applied as the one just described, but, as a difference, distributions are made by the trustee in bankruptcy, rather than the SIPC.[130] Furthermore, the trustee does not distribute all securities present in the insolvent estate pro rata amongst the account provider's clients, but first reduces the securities to money and then distributes the proceeds pro rata.[131]

8.3.5.2 UCC

As stated previously, the proprietary rights that UCC Article 8 confers upon a securities accountholder become almost exclusively apparent in the insolvency of that accountholder's intermediary. Accountholders' interests are then calculated

125. UCC § 8-503 official cmt. 1 and 2.
126. *Cf.* MOONEY (1990), 361. Deficits arising in a banking institution's insolvency, however, are initially covered by the Federal Deposit Insurance Act; 12 USC §§ 1811-1832.
127. 15 USC §§ 78aaa *et seq.*
128. As an over-simplification, 'customers' are understood as all entitlement holders who are not broker/dealers; 15 USC § 78fff-2(4). *See* MOONEY (1990), n.74. *Cf. also ib.* at 364.
129. USC § 78fff-3(a). The money is funded by mandatory membership fees; 15 USC § 78ddd(c).
130. Clients of non-SIPA covered account providers are therefore not automatically insured against their losses like the SIPA insures investors; *See,* e.g., <www.fdic.gov/consumers/consumer/information/fdiciorn.html>.
131. *See* MOONEY (1990), 352 *et seq. and* GUTTMAN (1990), 460.

pro rata per category of securities, and these pools of securities are distributed accordingly. A possible deficit in any of these pools is also allocated pro rata per pool.[132]

The pro rata sharing mechanism implies that accountholders are treated equally in the event of a winding up of the securities pools, with no distinction being made as to the moment of their acquisition of interest. As stated before, this forms a departure from the traditional property law maxim *prior tempore, potior iure* and is in accordance with a risk allocation approach.[133] It is, on the other hand, analogous to the common law treatment of the commingling or confusion of chattels.[134]

Accountholders' securities entitlements do not form part of the insolvent intermediary's estate and therefore take free of the intermediary's general creditors' claims as if they were identifiable assets that belong to the intermediary's customers.[135] Yet this rule is subject to two important exceptions. First, secured creditors of the intermediary have priority over entitlement holders rights if they have control of the secured assets.[136] Second, all secured creditors of clearing corporations take free of the claims of the clearing corporation's clients, regardless of whether these creditors have obtained control of the secured assets.[137] These two exceptions will now be briefly discussed, but first, the concept of control will be explained.[138]

Under the UCC, a creditor can acquire control over directly held, uncertificated securities either by becoming registered as the owner in the issuer's books, or by instructing the issuer to comply with entitlement orders from the security taker.[139] A creditor can acquire control over indirectly held securities in a number of ways. First, he can obtain legal ownership of the collateralised securities, and the debtor is then left with a mere equitable right. Alternatively, the creditor, debtor and the debtor's account provider can enter into a control agreement under which the securities remain registered in the debtor's name, but the account provider

132. § 8-503 official cmt. 1. Thus, the distribution is made differently under UCC than under SIPA. However, the present author believes that it must be agreed with Mooney (1990), n.191 *and* Mooney (1998), 91–93, that there is no good reason why customers holding entitlements to a certain category of securities should bear the costs of a deficit in this pool of securities (as would be the case under UCC Art. 8), while other customers of the same insolvent intermediary who hold entitlements to another category of interests do not, when neither customer was in a position to assess the likelihood of a deficit in one or another pool of securities held. Moreover, Mooney (1998), 92, also shows that the allocation model he proposes results in a lower risk of large losses and a higher risk of small losses and is therefore also more economically justifiable.
133. *Cf.* Mooney (1990), 329.
134. *See,* e.g., Burke (2003), 369.
135. UCC § 8-503(a). In the instance of a shortfall, *see* UCC § 8-51 1(a). *Cf.* Mooney (1990), n.200.
136. UCC§8-511(b).
137. UCC§8-511(c).
138. The concept of control will also appear to play a crucial role in the rules that concern the protection of *bona fide* transferees and the perfection of security interests. *See infra,* s. 8.4.2. and 8.5.2.
139. UCC §8-106(c).

agrees that it will comply with entitlement orders from the pledgee without further consent by the pledgor. Such a control agreement may also be concluded between the creditor and the debtor's account provider with the debtor's consent, or so as to confer a third party with the authority to give entitlement orders.[140] Thirdly, a third party may obtain control of the collateralised securities on behalf of the creditor, and finally, the creditor automatically obtains control over the debtor's assets if the creditor is the debtor's account provider.[141]

The rule that an intermediary's secured creditors take free of the claims of that intermediary's clients contrasts with the traditional property law principle of *nemo dat quod non habet,* as those creditors can thus assert rights that were not the intermediary's to convey. Yet the intermediary's creditors are protected and can enjoy their rights as if the intermediary's accountholders do not have better claims. On the other hand, this rule is in accordance with another principle of property law, viz. the negotiability principle, under which *bona fide* transferees are protected against competing claims.[142] However, secured creditors are granted priority over entitlement holders' claims, while these creditors are not subject to all requirements that normally apply for purchasers to be protected; secured creditors are not required to have had no notice of the adverse claim in order to be protected against it.[143]

The priority of secured creditors over accountholders has also been justified by other arguments. First, reference has been made to the benefits that the (securities) market as a whole enjoys, when lenders are willing to extend credit to intermediaries, and it has been argued that the extension of credit is more attractive if lenders can obtain collateral that has a low possibility of being challenged by competing claims.[144]

Second, since creditors who acquire control over secured assets by obtaining ownership of those assets do not differ in appearance from other accountholders, there appear to be no good reasons to prioritise one accountholder over another. Consumer protection would also not require a different approach, as it has been pointed out that the difference between secured creditors and accountholders does not translate 'neatly into any lines of class, wealth, power, or the like'.[145] Moreover, the alternative, viz. a first-in-time rule under which claimants with older rights trump younger claimants, would lead to fortuitous results, for it is impossible to establish a connection between the time a right is created and a particular financial asset, when these assets are by definition fungible and untraceable.[146] Finally, the rule cannot be argued to encourage intermediaries to enter into agreements while

140. UCC § 8-106(d)(2) and (3), respectively.
141. UCC § 8-106(d) *and* UCC § 8-106(e), respectively.
142. *Cf.* Rogers (1996), 1522. On the negotiability principle, *see* infra, s. 8.4.2.
143. *See infra,* s. 8.4.2.
144. *Cf.* Rocks & Bjerre (2004), 58.
145. Accountholders may be institutional investors, while creditors (e.g. pension funds) may represent retail consumers; Rogers (1996), 1529.
146. Rogers (1996), 1513 *et seq.* In priority contests between some classes of security takers however, a first-in-time rule applies; *see infra,* s. 8.5.2.

using investors' assets as collateral, since the UCC as well as state law and federal regulations expressly forbid such conduct.[147]

The rule that all secured creditors of clearing corporations take free of the claims of the clearing corporation's clients, regardless of whether these creditors have obtained control of the secured assets, has been justified by the fact that a clearing corporation's creditors are not in a position to take control of the secured assets.[148] A clearing corporation is the highest tier in the custody chain, and securities transfers by book-entry to another intermediary (other than on the clearing corporation's own books) are therefore impossible. Moreover, because of a clearing corporation's pivotal role in the clearing and settlement process, it has been argued that it should be in a better position to provide collateral and obtain credit than someone else.[149] Second, clearing corporations are highly regulated entities and are therefore arguably even less enticed than other intermediaries to enter into security agreements with creditors while using their clients' assets as collateral.[150] Third, the rule corresponds with the previous version of UCC Article 8 that treated all transferees recorded on the books of a clearing corporation as *bona fide* purchasers, and consequently took free of competing claims.[151]

Both rules just discussed result in the priority of upper-tier claimants over lower-tier claimants. Apart from legal considerations, such a result is justifiable on economic grounds. The analysis made by MOONEY, for instance, shows that the priority of upper-tier claimants is more efficient, since it allocates loss (viz. not honoured claims in intermediary insolvencies) to the class of claimants that could avoid or reduce the losses at the lower cost, viz. by choosing another intermediary.[152] In addition, he argues that this class also places a lower value on their priority. Yet the present version of UCC Article 8 takes the position that normative considerations should sometimes be preferred, as upper-tier creditors with unsecured claims, upper-tier creditors who have not obtained control and upper-tier creditors subject to the exception of UCC § 8-503(d) remain subject to entitlement holders' claims.

8.4 SECURITIES TRANSFERS

8.4.1 INTRODUCTION

Prior to the enactment of the Uniform Commercial Code, securities transfers were governed by the Uniform Stock Transfer Act in the states that had adopted that statute. One of its most important features was the 'negotiability principle', i.e. a protection of transferees against competing third party claims. That principle continues to play an important role in the provisions of UCC Article 8.[153] In

147. UCC § 8-504(b). *See* UCC § 8-511 official cmt. 2, ROGERS (1996), 1519 *and supra*, s. 8.3.3.
148. UCC § 8-511 official cmt. 3 *and* UCC § 9-310 official cmt. 6.
149. REITZ (2005), 364–365.
150. ROCKS & BJERRE (2004), 58–59.
151. *See* MOONEY (1990), 400 *et seq. and cf. infra*, s. 8.4.2.
152. MOONEY (1990), 384 *et seq.*
153. *Cf.* GUTTMAN (1990), 443 *and* ROCKS & BJERRE (2004), 1.

the following section, the negotiability principle and its implementation in UCC Article 8 will be discussed, but first, some general remarks will be made on the transfer of securities.

All categories of securities can be transferred without any formal requirement. For instance, general rules of private law determine that the contract that initiated a securities transfer need not be in writing for the transfer to be effective.[154] But a transfer of securities can only be asserted against third parties if certain requirements have been met, and different categories of securities require the fulfilment of different technicalities.

A transfer of directly held bearer securities can be asserted against third parties (including the issuer) only when the transferee has obtained possession of the certificates. A transfer of directly held registered securities on the other hand, is made effective against third parties through the registration of the transferee's name in the issuer's books, or the endorsement of the certificate in the transferee's name and the transferee's possession of that certificate. Transfers of directly held, uncertificated securities can only have proprietary effect through the registration of the transfer in the issuer's books.[155]

In the case of indirectly held securities, a transfer has proprietary effect, i.e. it can be asserted against third parties, when the transferee acquires a security entitlement, resulting in a credit-entry in his securities account.[156] Thus, a securities transfer is 'implemented' when the securities entitlement of the transferor has been extinguished, and the transferee has acquired a corresponding entitlement through a credit-entry in his securities account.[157] Consequently, transfers can only be initiated by an entitlement order from the entitlement holder to his account provider.[158]

8.4.2 NEGOTIABILITY

As a general principle of Anglo-American property law, a transferee can only acquire the rights which his transferor has to transfer (*nemo dat quod non habet*).[159] UCC Articles 8 and 9 derogate from this principle in most instances, to protect innocent purchasers of securities against the adverse claims of third parties that might have been involuntarily dispossessed of their assets. As a related general principle, a transferee acquires all the rights his transferor has to transfer. For example, if a transferee acquires from a *bona fide* transferor, he will be treated

154. *See* ROCKS & BJERRE (2004), 21 and 22.
155. UCC §8-301.
156. UCC § 8-301 official cmt. 1 *and* UCC § 8- 501(b). The intention of one of the parties not to transfer a part of the securities credited to the transferee's account is therefore not relevant as to the result, viz. the transferee's (full) ownership of these securities; *Ennis v. Phillips,* 890 So.2d 313, 55 UCC Rep. Serv. 2d 407 (Fla. Dist. Ct. App. 4th Dist. 2004). On the concept of 'security entitlement' *see supra,* s. 8.3.4.
157. UCC § 8-501 official cmt. 5. *See also* ROCKS & BJERRE (2004) 35–36.
158. UCC § 8-102 official cmt. 8.
159. *Cf.* ROGERS (1996), 1461.

as a *bona fide* purchaser, even though his transferor acquired his interest from a *mala fide* transferor. The present UCC Article 8 codifies that principle, which is also known as the shelter principle, so as to apply to the transfer of directly and indirectly held securities also.[160]

Indeed, one of the main reasons for the 1994 revision of UCC Article 8 was to establish firmly the application of the negotiability principle to all securities transfers, as transferee protection was considered to enhance the transferability of assets, and a requirement for any economy to function properly.[161] More in particular, it was argued that, should a purchaser have to investigate the proprietary position of his transferor in every instance of a securities transfer so as to assure himself of the absence of competing challenges, 'the system's rapidity, inexpensiveness, certainty and finality' would be severely impaired.[162] Moreover, it was thought that a substantial systemic risk would be created if a defect in the transferor's proprietary position would affect the legal position of the transferee.[163] Thus, while the *nemo dat* principle gives priority to first-in-time claimants, Articles 8 and 9 now generally prioritise last-in-time claimants.[164]

However, originally, only a transferee of movable tangibles could be protected against challenges by third parties, because only possessors of those assets could obtain the status of *bona fide* purchasers. Under the previous version of UCC Article 8, a transferee who received certificated securities was therefore protected against third party challenges when he obtained the status of *bona fide* purchaser, i.e. when he acquired possession of the certificate in good faith, against value, and had no notice of adverse claims. Thus, transferee protection was a direct result of the 'reification' of the rights which a certificate represented in that certificate.[165]

Consequently, investors entitled to indirectly held securities could not achieve the status of *bona fide* purchasers, as accountholders are entitled to intangible assets. In addition, under the old Article 8, accountholder interests classified as co-ownership rights in a bulk of fungible assets, and an accountholder could therefore not be considered to be unaware of possible adverse claims, since he would be certain that he would have to compete with his fellow co-owners when their account provider would hold insufficient assets to satisfy all accountholders' claims.[166] Moreover, much uncertainty existed as to the precise relationship between the concepts of 'good faith', 'without notice' and '*bona fide* purchaser', and, for all these reasons, the revisors of UCC Article 8 took a different approach.[167]

Although in its present form, UCC Article 8 does not use the concepts 'good faith' and '*bona fide* purchaser', it is identical in effect, i.e. it extends the

160. UCC §§ 8-302(a) and (b) *and* 8-510(b) respectively.
161. Rogers (1996), 1462–1464.
162. Rocks & Bjerre (2004), 30. *Cf.* Burke (2003), 238 and 240.
163. Rogers (1996), 1461. *Cf.* Mooney (1990), 315 *and* UCC § 8-503 official cmt. 3.
164. *Cf.* Mooney (1990), 379–380.
165. E.g. Mooney (1990), n.332 and Guttman (1990), 443. On the development of reification and its legal consequences, *see also supra*, s. 3.2.1, *and* extensively Rogers (2004).
166. *See* Mooney (1990), n.92, for a critical account of this line of argument.
167. Rogers (1996), 1470.

protection previously granted to a *bona fide* purchaser to all transferees of securities. UCC §§ 8-303, 8-502, and 8-510(a) now provide that a transferee of directly held certificated or uncertificated securities, an 'acquirer' of indirectly held assets, and a 'purchaser' of indirectly held assets or a taker of a security interest therein are protected against competing third party claims.[168]

However, in order to be fully protected against a competing third party claim, a transferee must have had no notice of the third party's adverse claim, must have control over the assets transferred, and must have given value for the transfer.[169] The first requirement is a codification of well established criteria developed in case law, according to which a transferee is required not to be 'wilfully blind to the existence of an adverse claim'.[170] Yet a transferee is not under the obligation to make inquiries as to these claims.[171] More specifically, the 'wilful blindness' criterion turns on whether the transferee is 'aware of a significant probability that the adverse claim exists' and whether the transferee 'deliberately avoids information' that would establish the existence of the adverse claim.[172]

In the case of typical transfers that follow a securities sale, the requirements just discussed are easily met, but the finality of a transfer of indirectly held securities is even more secured than the finality of a directly held securities transfer. Purchasers of indirectly held securities are protected unless they had notice of the specific claim with which they are challenged, whereas purchasers of directly held securities are (only) protected if they had no notice of any adverse claim.[173] Moreover, UCC § 8-502 explicitly cuts off all possible constructions under which revendication claims could be made regarding indirectly held securities.[174] In addition, for any revendication claim, a previous entitlement holder (*verus dominus*) must be able to identify the transferee that has received the assets he was deprived of, which is difficult to imagine in the instance of indirectly held securities that

168. Similarly, a transferee is protected against an issuer that asserts the invalidity of the transfer; UCC § 8-202(d).
169. The fulfilment of these conditions must coincide; a transferee who obtains notice of an adverse claim, before he has given value or obtained control, cannot be protected; UCC § 8-303 official cmt. 2. UCC § 8-106 defines 'control' (*see supra,* s. 8.3.5), while UCC § 1-204 defines 'value' very broadly.
170. *Goodman* v. *Simonds,* 61 U.S. (20 How.) 343 (1857) and *Graham v. White-Phillips Co.,* 296 U.S. 27, 31-32 (1935). *See also First Nat'l Bank* v. *Lewco Sec. Corp.,* 860 F.2d 1407 (7th Cir. 1988). A recent case in which notice of an adverse claim was established is *SEC v. Credit Bancorp, Ltd.,* 386 F. 3d 438, 55 UCC Rep. Serv. 2d 74 (2d Cir. 2004). In this case, the court held that some securities were subject to a claim of revendication, because notice of the adverse claim was established. Although they were credited to the same account, other securities, however, were not subject to that claim, because they were credited before the entitlement holder had taken notice of the adverse claim.
171. UCC § 8-105(a)(2) *and* official cmt. 2 and 4.
172. UCC §§ 8-102(a)(1) and 8-105 define the concept of 'adverse claim' and make clear that an adverse claim must relate to a violation of property interests, including principles of equitable remedies that give rise to property claims.
173. *Cf.* UCC §§ 8-303 *and* 8-502.
174. UCC § 8-502 official cmt. 2 and 3, refer to, e.g., a constructive trust.

are traded on anonymised markets by intermediaries that sell and buy securities in their own name.[175]

Furthermore, UCC § 8-503(e) determines that a previous entitlement holder can only successfully challenge a transferee's rights if the latter acted 'in collusion' with the entitlement holder's account provider that violated its obligations to honour the entitlement holder's rights.[176] This 'collusion standard' seems to be met in all instances that a transferee has been 'wilfully blind' to the adverse claim, yet these standards should be distinguished.[177] The New York legislature, for instance, considered that 'collusion' only occurs if the wrongdoing purchaser acted 'in concert', 'by conspiratorial arrangement', by 'agreement for the purpose of violating the entitlement holder's rights' or 'with actual knowledge that the securities intermediary is violating those rights'.[178] Such 'knowledge' will be determined on a subjective rather than on an objective basis, but, again, the purchaser is under not under a duty of inquiry.[179]

If, however, a transferee has indeed acted 'in collusion', the main rule of *nemo dat* applies and the previous entitlement holder can successfully claim restitution of his assets. UCC § 8-503(d) provides a specific example of such a situation, and determines that a restitution claim can be successfully made when the previous entitlement holder's account provider is insolvent, when that account provider's assets cannot satisfy all of its customers' claims, and when the challenged transfer of assets constituted a violation of the intermediary's duty as codified in § 8-504(a). Obviously, the satisfaction of all these conditions will rarely occur and even more rarely be proven.[180]

---

175. *Cf.* GUTTMAN (1990), 456 *and* UCC § 8-502 official cmt. 2.
176. On UCC § 8-503, *see supra,* s. 8.3.4.
177. ROGERS (1996), 1536.
178. Legislative Intent at UCC § 8-101 by the New York legislature; Laws 1997, Ch. 566, § 5. The Canadian harmonisation instrument for securities custody and transfer law, which is similar to UCC Art. 8 to a large extent, differs in that it contains a definition of 'collusion'; SPINK & PARÉ (2004), 382.
179. In *Cotton v. Private Bank and Trust Co.*, 49 UCC Rep. Serv. 2d 1281 (N.D. Ill. 2003), for instance, no collusion (as a necessary element for a claim under UCC § 8-115(2) to be honoured) was found, since 'actual knowledge' was not proven.
180. *Cf.* ROCKS & BJERRE (2004), 62. Yet it is the only instance in which dispossessed entitlement holders can successfully assert their rights against secured creditors of the intermediary who have obtained control; UCC § 8-51 1(b). This provision is considered an application of UCC § 8-503; UCC § 8-503 official cmt. 3 and UCC § 8-511 official cmt. 1. *Nathan W. Drage, P.C. v. First Concord Securities, Ltd.*, 184 Misc. 2d 92, 707 N.Y.S. 2d 782, 41 UCC Rep. 2d 673 (2000) [34 UCCLL 10 [Dec. 2000] provides an example of such a case. QUINN (2001), [Rev] § 8-504[A][2]: 'Drage did have a potential remedy. But, its successful exercise involved juggling complex sections of Art. 8, marshalling the necessary factual information, and following required procedural consequences. Fortunately for the plaintiff in this case it was a law firm, "Nathan W. Drage, P.C." The rest of us, alas, are not likely to be so felicitously situated'.

8.5 CREATION AND ENFORCEMENT OF SECURITY RIGHTS

8.5.1 INTRODUCTION

Under the laws of most US states, parties are free to define the form of the security interest they want to create. A wide range of arrangements can therefore be found, under which security interests are vested in securities or other financial instruments. Under some constructions, the debtor remains the legal owner and has control of the collateralised securities, which are only operationally marked as pledged securities. But under other constructions, the secured creditor obtains legal ownership as a purchaser, and the debtor is left with a mere equitable right. The former construction is usually known as an 'agreement to pledge', and the latter as a 'hard pledge'.[181]

From a dogmatic point of view, US law treats an agreement to pledge and a hard pledge equally, i.e. it considers both constructions as different practical appearances of the same, viz. a security interest. It will be shown, however, that under the UCC, the (legal) consequences of non-possessory and possessory security interests are quite different, especially with respect to the creditors' priority position in relation to other claimants. In that regard, the position of a taker of a 'hard pledge' is indistinguishable from the position of a taker of an outright transfer.[182]

UCC Article 9 governs security interests in general, and, more specifically, the creation and enforcement of security interests vested in securities. Its provisions on security rights in securities form part of Article 9's specific rules on 'investment property', which includes securities, securities accounts, commodity contracts and commodity accounts.[183] As a matter of interest, from a coherence point of view Article 9 explicitly distinguishes investment property' from 'goods', 'general intangibles' and 'instruments', and provides specific rules for that distinct category of property.[184]

8.5.2 PLEDGE AND ATTACHMENT

Under UCC Article 9, a security interest is created or, in its own terminology, has 'attached', when the interest has been made enforceable amongst parties.[185] Typically, attachment and enforceability occur at the same time, but parties may agree differently.[186] Once a security interest has attached, it follows the collateral,

181. UCC § 9-310 official cmt. 6. *Cf.* ROCKS & BJERRE (2004), 54 *and* ROGERS (1996), 1525.
182. For instance, both the acquirer of a security interest by control and an outright transferee are termed 'purchaser' under the UCC; §§ 1-201(29), 8-303. In this way, the UCC avoids (re)characterisation issues that arise when considering repurchase agreements; MOONEY (1990), n.122 *and* ROGERS (1996), 1527.
183. UCC § 9-102(49). On the inclusion of commodity contracts and accounts, *see* UCC § 9- 102 official cmt. 6.
184. UCC § 9-102(a)(42), (44) and (47), respectively.
185. UCC § 9-203 (a) and (b).
186. QUINN (2001), [Rev] § 9-203 [A][2].

even after the disposition thereof.[187] A security interest is considered 'perfected' if the interest can be asserted against third parties. Security interests may be vested in a particular amount of securities of a certain issue, or in an entire securities account.[188] In principle, a security taker is not entitled to the monetary proceeds of collateralised securities as additional security, but he may appropriate those proceeds so as to reduce the secured obligation.[189]

8.5.2.1 Creation

Under UCC Article 9, a security interest is created by agreement. Such an agreement becomes effective when the debtor has valid rights in the collateral, the secured party has given value, and the debtor has authenticated a (written) security agreement that contains a description of the collateral.[190] This description need not be specific.[191]

8.5.2.2 Perfection

A security interest that has been created by agreement can be perfected, i.e. made opposable against third parties, either by filing or by conferring control over the collateralised securities to the security taker, which applies both to indirectly held securities and directly held uncertificated securities.[192] The filing of a security interest must be effectuated in the UCC register that has been created for that purpose.[193] When a security interest is to be perfected by control, a creditor must obtain control over the secured assets pursuant to the security agreement, and provide value for his interest.[194]

A creditor can obtain control in several ways. First, he may become the entitlement holder and the collateralised securities then have to be credited to an account in his name. When the debtor is an intermediary, that intermediary can execute this transaction on its own books, which was impossible under UCC law before the 1994 revision.[195] A creditor can also obtain control through a control agreement, or when a third party has or obtains control over the collateralised

187. Quinn (2001) [Rev] § 9-315[A][3], has aptly called this principle, known to the civil law tradition as the principle of *droit de suite*, 'the pitbull principle'.
188. UCC § 9-203 (h).
189. UCC § 9-207 (c).
190. UCC § 9-203 (a) and (b).
191. UCC § 9-108 (d).
192. UCC §§ 9-312(a) and 9-134(a), respectively, and UCC § 8-106(c) and (d). For a discussion of the pros and cons of either way of perfection, *see* Rocks & Bjerre (2004), 71.
193. UCC § 9-312(a).
194. UCC § 9-203 (a) in conjunction with UCC § 9-106. *Cf.* Rogers (1995), 697.
195. *Cf.* Mooney (1990), 342: 'A property law construct that denies the effectiveness and perfection of such a security interest, while giving effect to similar transfers of ownership interests, could only be grounded on an historical anomaly or a failure to appreciate the sui generis characteristics of the intermediary control phenomenon within the securities markets'.

securities on behalf of the creditor. In addition, control can be obtained automatically, viz. when the creditor is also the debtor's account provider.[196]

As noted above, the debtor remains entitled to the secured assets' proceeds, even when the secured party has gained control over the collateral. Furthermore, the debtor retains his power of disposal absent an agreement that declares otherwise, and he thus remains entitled to transfer and vest other security interests in the assets. But if the debtor sells the secured assets without the creditor's authorisation to do so, a security interest is attached to the proceeds of the sale in favour of the creditor.[197]

The concept of control had been introduced by the 1994 revision of UCC Article 8 so as to avoid the 'uncertainty and confusion that results from attempting to apply common law possession concepts to modern securities holding practices'.[198] Although the concept may be new, ROGERS has shown that it is 'fully consistent with basic principles of secured transactions; indeed the control concept can usefully be regarded as merely a generalization from several specific rules that have long been part of the law of securities and secured transactions'.[199]

8.5.2.3 Creation and Perfection for Intermediaries

In addition to the methods of creation and perfection just discussed, a security interest can be created and perfected automatically, i.e. *de iure,* when the creditor is an intermediary. UCC § 9-206(a) and (b) determine that a security interest is *de iure* created in favour of the debtor's account provider, if that account provider has credited its accountholder's securities account but not received payment for those assets. Furtherm ore, UCC § 9-309(10) provides that a security interest is perfected *de iure* also if the creditor/intermediary does not already have control over the secured assets as the debtor's account provider. These provisions are a codification of the common law concept of a 'broker's lien', and its underlying policy is that intermediaries would otherwise be reluctant to credit their customers'accounts on margin.[200]

With their clients' consent, intermediaries may rehypothecate clients' assets, as is common practice for securities firms, to obtain the funds needed to provide their clients with margin, i.e. unpaid, securities.[201] If an intermediary's creditor has perfected his security interest by control, or if the intermediary is a clearing corporation, the intermediary's clients cannot assert their accountholder rights against this creditor, even if they did not authorise the rehypothecation.[202] It has been

196. UCC § 8-106(e). *See infra.*
197. UCC § 9-315(a)(2).
198. UCC § 8-106 official cmt. 7.
199. ROGERS (1996), 1481–1482, with reference to the law of negotiable instruments and documents of title.
200. Restatement, Security §12. *Cf.* ROCKS & BJERRE (2004), 78 *and* ROGERS (1996), 1487. On margin accounts, *see supra*, s. 8.3.2.
201. Accountholders commonly authorise their securities firm to 'commingle securities of all margin customers for rehypothecation to the lender who provides the financing'; UCC § 8-504 official cmt. 2.
202. *See supra*, s. 8.3.5.

argued that without such a rule, the availability of funds to securities intermediaries would be severely restricted. In addition, it has been stated that the rule does not encourage rehypothecation without customer consent, for federal regulations prohibit such illegal rehypothecation.[203]

8.5.2.4 Enforcement, Priorities

A creditor with a security interest can enforce this interest either by suing for the debt, by enforcing the interest through judicial process, or by executing certain so-called self-help measures. These self-help measures, which are the most important methods of enforcement in practice, are the following: collecting proceeds of the secured assets, taking possession of the secured assets, disposing of the secured assets by sale or otherwise, and appropriating the secured assets (strict foreclosure).[204] Execution of the self-help measures is, however, restricted by the standard of commercial reasonableness.[205] That standard is highly fact-specific, and it may depend on the situation, for instance, whether a private or public sale would be appropriate as a means of enforcement.[206]

Theoretically, a security interest that has attached, but has not been perfected, can be enforced. But all creditors with a perfected security interest trump imperfected security interest holders, both in and outside of bankruptcy situations, and most secured creditors therefore perfect their interest.[207] Yet if multiple creditors have perfected their security interests, priority conflicts may arise when it comes to enforcement, and intricate rules have been drafted to determine the priority ranking between holders of perfected security interests.[208]

UCC § 9-328(a) codifies the basic rule: a security interest perfected by control has priority over a security interest that has not been perfected by control, while intermediaries that have obtained control rank even higher.[209] This rule thus contrasts with the general property law principle *prior tempore, potior iure,* under which older in time claims trump claims that have been created later in time. But it could be argued that the rule accords with another general principle of property law, viz. the negotiability principle, under which *bona fide* acquirers take free of

203. 17 CFR §§ 240.8c-1(a) and 240.15c2(a) *and see* Rocks & Bjerre (2004), 59.

204. UCC § 9-601, 9-607, 609, 610 and 620 *and see* Rocks & Bjerre (2004), 85. For a concise overview, *see also* Quinn(2001), [Rev] § 9-601 [A].

205. UCC § 9-610(b).

206. Rocks & Bjerre (2004), 87.

207. UCC § 9-322(a)(2).

208. Whether principles of equity displace these priority rules is a matter of debate. Although case law seems to support the application of principles of equity, UCC § 9-328 official cmt. 8 argues that this would render security interests in securities less certain and that it may thus contribute to systemic risk. *See* Rocks & Bjerre (2004), 85, referring to *General Insurance Co. v. Lowry*, 412 F. Supp. 21 (S.D. Ohio 1976), *aff'd*, 570 F.2d 120 (6th Cir. 1978) *and* Rogers (1996), 1491–1992.

209. UCC § 9-328(c). UCC § 8-510(c) and (d) apply the same rules of priority to outright transfers, rather than to security interests. These sections have been drafted so as to provide for the same rules as Art. 9, but apply when Art. 9 is not applicable, e.g. because a repurchase agreement is classified as an outright transfer, rather than a security interest; UCC § 8-510 official cmt. 4.

competing claims.[210] The rationale for prioritising control, rather than seniority, thus seems to have been that secured parties that have *bona fide* put themselves in a position to liquidate, should be able to rely on that position. The stronger position of intermediaries, on the other hand, has been justified with reference to the safety of the banking and financial system.[211] Whereas that argument might or might not be wholly persuasive, it has also been pointed out that the untraceability of fungible and indirectly held securities prevents an effective first-in-time rule.[212]

Yet in some instances, especially when it is an easy matter to determine the time of perfection, *prior tempore* is used as a default rule. First, secured creditors who have obtained control take free of claims by creditors who have subsequently obtained control over the same collateral.[213] But, as stated previously, higher-tier claimants with control always take free of other security takers with control, even if the latter have perfected their interest earlier in time.[214] Second, the *prior tempore* rule also applies to determine the priority ranking between security takers who have perfected their security interest by filing.[215] Because the exact time that a security interest is automatically created cannot be determined, no priority rule is given to solve a possible conflict between creditors who have obtained such a security interest, i.e. a security interest against an intermediary.[216]

8.5.2.5 Attachment

Under the UCC indirect holding system, no upper-tier attachment is possible, as creditors cannot trace their debtor's assets to securities pools held by higher-tier intermediaries.[217] Thus, attachment can only be effected upon the debtor's account provider, and must be authorised with a court order. Uncertificated, directly held securities on the other hand, must be seized against the issuer.[218]

8.6 CONFLICT OF LAWS

8.6.1 Introduction

The UCC effectively harmonised state securities custody and transfer laws, but its drafters still thought that a uniform conflict of laws rule would be necessary, firstly

210. The author is grateful to Professor J.S. Rogers for his explanation on this point. Professor Rogers further explained that the priority of control is primarily needed because filing would not have been introduced as a perfection method if perfection by control would not be prioritised. On the negotiability principle, *see supra*, s. 8.4.2.
211. Rogers (1996), 1479–1483.
212. Rogers (1996), 1513 *et seq. Cf. supra*, s. 8.3.5.
213. UCC § 9-328(b).
214. *Cf.* UCC § 8-510(c) and (d).
215. UCC § 9-328(g) in conjunction with UCC § 9-322(a)(1).
216. UCC § 9-328(f). *Cf.* Rocks & Bjerre (2004), 83.
217. *Cf. supra,* s. 8.3.2.
218. UCC § 8-112(c) and (d), respectively.

because different states might implement the UCC differently, and secondly, because different state courts might interpret the UCC provisions differently. Moreover, cross-border securities transactions with non-US counterparties would continue to require a uniform conflict of laws rule.[219]

UCC § 8-106, the predecessor of the current private international law provision of UCC Article 8, provided that 'general choice of law rules' determine the law applicable to the transfer of certificated and some uncertificated securities. Regarding uncertificated securities, that 'general choice of law rule' was the *lex incorporationis,* and thus referred to the law of the place where the issuer was incorporated.[220] Current UCC conflict of laws provisions, however, distinguish between directly and indirectly held securities, and more or less radically depart from the *lex incorporationis* rule. For the purpose of a conflict of laws analysis, the UCC determines that securities are directly held only if they are either registered with the issuer or its registrar in the investor's name, or specifically endorsed in favour of the investor.[221]

8.6.2 Accountholder Interests

UCC § 8-110 contains the current, uniform conflict of laws rule that determines which law to apply to proprietary interests in securities. In short, it employs the *lex rei sitae* rule in the case of directly held, certificated securities, the *lex societatis* to determine the law applicable to proprietary interests in directly held, uncertificated securities, and a variation of the law of the place of the 'relevant intermediary' ('PRIMA') in the case of indirectly held securities.[222]

More accurately, *lex rei sitae,* as referred to in UCC § 8-110, governs the proprietary rights of an acquirer of certificated securities, and points to the law of the location of the securities at the time of delivery. UCC § 8-110(d) substantiates the *lex societatis* rule, and explains that it refers to the law of the jurisdiction under which the issuer is incorporated (*lex incorporationis*) or to the law designated by the issuer itself, provided the *lex incorporationis* permits such autonomy. The drafters of that rule considered that an issuer and others – including the investors, the protection of whose interests depends on their registration by the issuer – should be able to easily determine the applicable law. They therefore referred to the law chosen by the issuer as the one single applicable law, rather than a conflict of laws rule that would result in different laws to apply to the interests of different securities holders.[223]

The same policy consideration lies behind the PRIMA rule of UCC Article 8, which gives primacy to party autonomy, and leaves the parties to a securities

219. *See* Rogers (1996), 1460, Rocks & Bjerre (2004), 89 and Siegel (1994), 216–217.
220. *See* Quinn (2001), § 8-106[A][2].
221. Guynn & Rogers (2002), 607.
222. UCC §§ 8-110(b), 8-110(a), and 8-110(c), respectively.
223. UCC § 8-110 official cmt. 2.

account agreement free to choose the law applicable to the property law aspects of the securities entitlement resulting from that account agreement.[224] It was thought that an account provider and others should look at a single law to determine the rights and duties of an accountholder against his account provider and vice versa, rather than having to look to the laws of the locations of the underlying securities or their issuers.[225] The law designated by the parties may either have been chosen to govern the account agreement itself, or to govern specific proprietary issues. But if no choice of law has thus been made, the law of the place where the securities account is maintained applies, a place which may also have been designated by the parties.[226] It is only as a last resort that the location of the account provider is used as the connecting factor. More specifically, either the law of the location of the office that serves the securities account (which may be designated by the parties), or the law of the location of the account provider's chief executive office applies.

Thus, in order to establish *ex ante* certainty, parties are granted a very large degree of autonomy, as the UCC variation of PRIMA not only extends the effects of a choice of law in the account agreement to proprietary issues and thus to third parties, but neither limits this choice of law in any way.[227] Whereas under general US private international law, a 'reasonable relation' is required with the jurisdiction chosen, and the application of the law of the chosen state must not be contrary to a 'fundamental policy of a state which has a materially greater interest than the chosen state in the determination of the particular issue', the more specific rules of UCC Article 8 do not require such conditions to be met.[228]

---

224. UCC § 8-110(e)(1). This variation of PRIMA is the result of an effort to bring into conformity UCC § 8-110(e)(1) with UCC § 9-304(b)(1), a provision which determines that the parties to a deposit account agreement are free to choose the law applicable to the perfection and priority of security interests in the deposit account; UCC § 9-304 official cmt. 2. *Cf. also* UCC § 4A-507(2) (1990); the underlying policy consideration there was also the idea that party autonomy 'provides a greater degree of certainty with respect to rights of various parties'; UCC § 4A-507 official cmt. 3. *Cf.* Scoles et al. (2000), 984.

225. UCC § 8-110 official cmt. 3.

226. This reference to the place where the securities account is maintained has been considered by the Reporter to the Drafting Committee to Revise UCC Art. 8 (1994) to 'specify the jurisdiction that is most appropriately associated with the package of rights'; Rogers (1996), 1460.

227. UCC § 8-110 official cmt. 3 *and cf.* Rome Convention Art. 3. When the current version of UCC Art. 8 was adopted in 1994, its reference to party autonomy went further than the autonomy granted to parties to a common commercial agreement, which was limited to laws that had a 'reasonable relation to the State or country designated'. But in the present version of UCC § 1-301(c) (2001), that requirement has been abolished, and choice of law is currently limited only when one of the parties qualifies as a 'consumer'; UCC § 1-301(c) and (e) (2001).

228. Restatement (Second) of Conflict of Laws s 187(2)(a) and (b) (1971). But note that private international law, even in international cases, is a matter of state law; *Klaxon Company v. Stentor Electric Manufacturing Co.*, 313 U.S. 487 (1941).

8.6.3 Security Interests

The conflict of laws rules just described apply to accountholder interests, but also to securities transfers, and proprietary issues arising from a transfer of securities by book-entry are governed by the law that applies to the securities account (agreement) of the transferee.[229] But a classification of a securities transfer is made under the substantive law of the *forum,* and it is that law that determines, for instance, whether a securities transfer classifies as a transfer of title or as a security interest.[230]

UCC Article 9 provides a specific conflict of laws rule for issues arising out of the creation and enforcement of security interests in investment securities, but this rule is similar to the rules as discussed in the previous section.[231] Thus, the *lex rei sitae* applies to issues concerning security interests in directly held, certificated securities, *lex societatis* to issues concerning directly held, uncertificated securities, and a variation of PRIMA determines the law that governs security interests in indirectly held securities.[232] These rules point to substantive law only and consequently prohibit *renvoi.*[233]

Yet under the general rule of UCC Article 9, the creation, perfection and priority ranking of security interests is governed by the law of the debtor's jurisdiction.[234] Regarding investment property, this general rule only applies if the security interest is perfected by filing or if it is perfected automatically, and then overrides the conflict of laws rules just mentioned.[235] In these instances, the location of a debtor is determined as follows. First, a distinction is made between companies and other debtors. When a company is incorporated, as the great majority of companies is, the state of registration applies.[236] In the rare case of a company that is not incorporated, the main rule refers to its 'place of business', i.e. the place where its affairs are conducted.[237] When a not-incorporated company has more than one place of business, the jurisdiction of the location of the chief executive office applies. To institutions organised under federal law (such as banks), and a branch

229. *Cf.* Guynn & Rogers (2002), 612. On the transfer of funds, *Cf.* UCC § 4A-507(c) (1990). Whether payment has been made 'is governed by the law of the jurisdiction in which the beneficiary's bank is located'. The policy behind this rule is that payment to the beneficiary is made through the beneficiary's bank; UCC § 4A-507 official cmt. 2 (1990). The law applicable to contractual issues is left to the autonomy of the parties to the agreement: UCC § 1-301(c). Public policy rules may, however, override party autonomy; UCC § 1-301(f) *and cf.* White & Summers (2000), 125.
230. UCC § 9-109(a)(1).
231. UCC § 9-305. As is the case with contractual aspects of a transfer of title, the contractual aspects of security interests in securities are governed by the law chosen by the parties: UCC § 1-301(c) and (e) (2001).
232. UCC §§ 9-305(a)(1), 9-305(a)(2) and 9-305(a)(3), respectively.
233. Scoles et al. (2000), 984–985. *Cf.* Restatement (Second) of Conflict of Laws s 4 (1971).
234. UCC § 9-301. *Cf.* Quinn(2001), at § 9-301[A][5] and [Rev] § 9-305[A][3].
235. UCC § 9-305(c). *See supra,* s. 8.5.2.
236. UCC § 9-307(e).
237. UCC § 9-307(b)(2).

or agency of a bank that is not organised under federal law, still other rules apply; these institutions are considered to be located in the state which is designated by federal law, or in the state designated by the bank, provided that federal law allows such a choice of law. If federal law does not designate a state and if the bank has not chosen a location, the District of Columbia is deemed to be the location of this debtor.[238]

In the most common situation, viz. when a security interest in indirectly held securities is perfected by control, the PRIMA variation determines the applicable law. Consequently, the applicable law changes with the way in which control is obtained, as PRIMA refers to the law of the creditor's securities account when the collateralised securities are transferred to his account, but to the law of the debtor's securities account when the securities pledged remain credited in the latter's name.[239] In short, the law of the account agreement with the intermediary that administers the securities account to which the collateralised securities are booked, applies to the security interests vested in those securities.[240]

8.7 CONCLUSIONS

8.7.1 Questions and Answers

(1) *Which securities are admitted to the national systems of giro transfer and administration ?*

The legal infrastructure for the custody and transfer of securities by book-entry in the US is principally formed by the Uniform Commercial Code ('UCC'), which harmonised the state laws in this field, and federal regulations. Custody and transfer of securities that are issued by the US government, i.e. the Treasury, or US government agencies, are held in the Treasury/Reserve Automated Debt Entry System ('TRADES') with its own (federal) rules, while securities issued by private companies are generally subject to the provisions of UCC Article 8. Yet the federal rules that apply to the government systems of book-entry custody are either similar to UCC Article 8 (with some minor differences), or refer to state law and thus to UCC Article 8, which has been implemented in all states.

As a matter of principle, UCC Article 8, in its current version, caters for different holding practices, and it facilitates the direct holding of certificated (both bearer and registered) and dematerialised securities, as well as the indirect holding of securities. The definition of securities that can be subject to the UCC's provisions is very broad and covers practically all

238. For an overview of the different rules which apply to the different categories of debtors, *see* Cooper (2000), 49.

239. UCC § 9-305(c)(2) in conjunction with UCC § 9-309(10). *See also* Guynn & Rogers (2002), 609 and 610.

240. *See* Guynn & Rogers (2002), 608 and 613.

types of financial instruments. But the category of financial instruments to which the provisions of UCC Article 8 on the indirect holding system apply, is even broader. As a consequence of the definition of 'financial asset' in UCC § 8-102(a)(9), virtually all assets that are held in an indirect holding system by means of a securities account are eligible for application of UCC Article 8 Part 5, either *ipso facto* or because application has been opted for by the account provider and its client.

(2) *What is the nature of investors' interests in securities?*
In 1994, some important modifications to UCC Article 8 were made, most notably the introduction of a Part 5 that is solely directed at the custody and transfer of securities by book-entry. Under the provisions of that Part, an accountholder does not enjoy an interest in his securities that can be classified as a traditional common law concept. Instead, an accountholder enjoys a *sui generis* 'security entitlement', which must be understood as a package of rights that an accountholder can assert against his immediate intermediary/account provider. Thus, the security itself and the rights an accountholder enjoys as to this security via an intermediary are sharply distinguished.

Generally, investors can assert direct rights to their securities only in a situation of direct holding, and when securities are indirectly held, the rights of beneficial owners relate to their intermediary's obligation to pass on the issuer's primary obligations. Thus, a security entitlement does not establish a direct legal relationship between an accountholder and the securities themselves to which he is entitled, and the concept therefore excludes tracing. Consequently, the number of intermediaries that are interposed between the issuer and ultimate investor does not influence the substance of the latter's rights.

A security entitlement consists both of rights *in rem* as well as *in personam.* The contractual rights of an accountholder against his account provider mainly concern the account provider's obligation to hold the accountholder's financial assets in good faith. That rather general obligation is substantiated by more specific duties explicitly codified in UCC Article 8, viz. the duty to obtain, and thereafter maintain the amount of financial assets that corresponds to the aggregate amount of assets to which the intermediary's clients are entitled, the duty to obtain and pass on the proceeds of the underlying securities, the duty to comply with the accountholder's directions regarding corporate actions and other rights connected to the accountholder's assets, the duty to comply with accountholder's entitlement orders, and the duty to comply with the accountholder's orders to change the form of holding. But these duties can be contractually avoided, provided the intermediary remains within the limits set by the standard of good faith.

Although an accountholder's security entitlement does not form part of his account provider's estate, his rights *in rem* are enforceable against third parties, i.e. against persons other than his account provider, but only in very specific situations. First, it is only in insolvency situations, that an accountholder can assert his rights against the intermediary's trustee in bankruptcy, the intermediary's creditors and other third parties. But an accountholder can only successfully assert his interests against third parties in extraordinary circumstances, viz. if the insolvent intermediary's estate appears to show a deficit because the intermediary had violated its obligation to obtain sufficient assets, if the trustee in bankruptcy does not enforce the accountholder's claim, and if the third party concerned is not protected under the rule that protects *bona fide* transferees against competing claims. Outside of an account provider's bankruptcy, a dispossessed accountholder can only rarely assert a right of revendication against third parties, as all transferees (including security takers) who had no notice of the dispossessed accountholder's adverse claim, have control over the assets transferred, and have given value for the transfer, cannot be successfully challenged by a dispossessed accountholder.

(2.1) *Is a credit entry in a securities account merely a proof of ownership or is it a constitutive element of ownership of the securities concerned?*

A security entitlement is the constitutive element of an accountholder's ownership rights, and his rights cannot be proven in another way. Such entitlement is created by a credit-entry in a securities account, and extinguished by a debit-entry. Thus, a securities accountholder can assert his ownership rights to the securities which his account refers to, even if his account provider does not hold the corresponding assets with a higher tier. But while a security entitlement is the constitutive element of ownership in indirectly held securities, an investor can also have ownership rights in securities that are held in other ways, viz. directly.

(2.2) *Are informal (i.e. not registered by book-entry) dispositions over securities possible?*

In principle, a security entitlement is the constitutive element of an accountholder's ownership rights, and a security entitlement can only be created and extinguished by credit- and debit-entries in a securities account. Yet an entitlement may be created without a corresponding credit entry in a securities account when an intermediary has accepted a financial asset for credit in a securities account but has not already done so, or when an intermediary has not complied with any obligation under non-UCC law to credit a securities account; UCC § 8-501(b)(2) and (3). It is only in these particular instances, that a security entitlement is created without a credit entry, and only then, 'informal dispositions' over indirectly held securities are possible.

(2.3) *Is provisional credit in book-entry securities possible?*
Against his account provider, a securities accountholder can always assert the rights that follow from his security entitlement. Thus, when an account provider has credited its clients' securities accounts, those clients can assert their security entitlements, even when the account provider does not hold the corresponding assets with a higher tier. Consequently, provisional credits in book-entry securities are possible and have proprietary effect, i.e. can be enforced as if they were final.

Accountholders therefore do not suffer from any illegal activities of their account provider with client assets, or from the unwanted consequences of operational gaps between the moment that a credit-entry is made in their securities account, and the moment their account provider has received the corresponding assets. In addition, the possibility of provisional credit-entries greatly facilitates the extension of securities on margin, i.e. securities that have not (yet) been fully paid for by the accountholder.

(3) *How are investors' rights in respect of securities protected against the account provider and third parties?*
Under UCC Article 8, accountholder interests in securities held through an intermediary do not form part of that intermediary's estate. In addition, both the UCC and federal regulations forbid an account provider from disposing of its clients' securities, either by transfer of title or by granting a security interest, while under federal law, a violation of this prohibition constitutes a criminal offence. An accountholder's rights in respect of the securities he holds through an intermediary are thus protected against that intermediary. But when an account provider violates the prohibition and transfers or vests security rights in assets that belong to its clients, those clients can only very rarely successfully reclaim their assets under the transferees, as these transferees are generally protected under the negotiability principle.

(3.1) *Should shortfalls occur in accounts, how are they availed?*
Under federal law, the Securities Investor Protection Corporation ('SIPC') initiates liquidation proceedings in the case of a securities firm's insolvency. When a securities firm acts as account provider and its insolvent estate appears to be insufficient to satisfy all its customers' claims, SIPC makes contributions to an amount of USD 500,000 per customer to satisfy the deficit. Securities firms bankruptcies that are not covered by SIPA, are governed by Subchapter III of chapter 7 of the Bankruptcy Code. Under the provisions of that code, a similar procedure is applied as just described, but, as a difference, distributions are made by the trustee in bankruptcy, rather than the SIPC.

(3.2) *How are an investor's interests in securities separated from the account provider's property or how can investors' interests avail the claims of the provider's general creditors?*
Article 8 does not impose an express obligation on account providers to separate their own assets from their customers' assets. But although an account provider registers all credit balances in an omnibus account in its own name with a higher-tier intermediary, client assets do not form part of the intermediary's property, and customers' claims have priority over their account provider's claims in the case of the latter's insolvency.

Accordingly, accountholders take free of the claims of their account provider's general creditors. If, however, an account provider's creditors have secured their claims with a security interest in the assets held by that account provider, and that security interest is perfected by control over the secured assets, the secured creditors' claims trump the accountholders' claims. In addition, all secured creditors of clearing corporations take free of the claims of the clearing corporation's clients, regardless of whether these creditors have obtained control of the secured assets.

(4) *What are the formal requirements for the transfer of ownership of securities?*
For the 'transfer' of securities by book-entry, a debit-entry in the transferor's securities account and an identical credit-entry in the transferee's securities account is the only formal requirement to be fulfilled.

(4.1) *Can a* bona fide *acquirer rely on the crediting of his account (especially when acquiring* a non domino*)?*
It is only in extremely rare circumstances, that the UCC allows a third party to successfully challenge an accountholder's interests, and its version of the negotiability principle expressly protects *bona fide* acquirers against claims by a *verus dominus*. Thus, both other accountholders and financial intermediaries are almost always protected against competing claims, and the UCC regime provides accountholders with concrete legal certainty as to their security entitlement.

(4.2) *Is it possible for a credit in a securities account to be reversed and may transfer orders (or other instructions) be revoked?*
Other than for operational reasons, credit entries are seldom reversed, while the UCC does not provide for specific rules on the revocation of a transfer order or other instructions.

(5) *What are the formal requirements for the creation and enforcement of collateral?*
Theoretically, security rights in (indirectly held) securities can be created and enforced without the fulfilment of any formal requirement. Yet a security interest can only be asserted against third parties when it is

perfected. Perfection is effected through 'control', by filing the security interest in the UCC register, or automatically, i.e. *de iure,* when the creditor is the debtor's account provider. The UCC specifically prescribes the ways in which control over book-entry securities can be obtained. A creditor obtains control when the collateralised securities have been credited to an account in his name, or through a control agreement.

A creditor with a security interest can enforce this interest either by suing for the debt, by enforcing the interest through judicial process, or by executing certain so-called self-help measures. These self-help measures, which are the most important methods of enforcement in practice, are the following: collecting proceeds of the secured assets, taking possession of the secured assets, disposing of the secured assets by sale or otherwise, and appropriating the secured assets (strict foreclosure). Execution of the self-help measures is, however, restricted by the standard of commercial reasonableness.

(5.1) *Is upper-tier attachment possible, i.e. is it possible for an account holder's claimant to exercise his rights against higher-tier accounts?*

Under the UCC indirect holding system, no upper-tier attachment is possible, as creditors cannot trace their debtor's assets to securities pools held by higher-tier intermediaries.

8.7.2 Coherence

Any coherence account of US securities custody and transfer law is complicated by the fact that it is, in principle, a state law matter. A comprehensive research would therefore have to investigate the relation between, notably, the implemented version of UCC Articles 8 and 9, and the more general areas of law in each US state. In addition, securities custody and transfer law is also governed by rules of federal law, and a specific state-by-state investigation of the said relation and its interplay with US federal regulations would obviously not fit within the set-up of the present study. Moreover, it has been argued that 'US law is so thoroughly lacking in coherence that no one would think it useful either to criticize it or to reform it with coherence in mind'.[241]

A coherence analysis of the relation between securities law and the more general areas of law in which it is embedded can therefore not be made for US law in the same way as it has been made for Belgian, French and Dutch law. However, the fact that some provisions of UCC Article 8 explicitly refer to 'other law' prove that its drafters were conscious of the coherence implications.[242] Moreover, several publications by scholars who have been closely involved with the drafting of the

241. Kennedy (2006), 10.
242. *See,* e.g., UCC § 8-102, official cmt. 13 *and* § 8-107(b)(2).

1994 revision of UCC Article 8 expressly address those implications.[243] These coherence considerations typically concern the relation of specific UCC provisions on securities custody and transfer law on the one hand, and common private and commercial law on the other. A coherent, comprehensive civil code may be absent in US law, but from the Restatements, the UCC and case law, some general principles can be construed, and a comparison with the relevant provisions of the UCC might indeed be valuable.[244]

From that comparison, however, it is apparent that the present rules of securities custody and transfer law differ to a large extent from those general rules. First, and most obviously, the 1994 revision of UCC Article 8 introduced the 'security entitlement' concept to classify the package of rights an accountholder enjoys against his account provider, which represented a sharp departure from the common law approach of the pre-1994 UCC Article 8. Under the latter approach, accountholder interests were classified as traditional, common law concepts, viz. co-ownership and trust. Yet that approach proved to be ill-suited to the modern practice of indirect securities holding, and thus, the 1994 revision eliminated a discrepancy that formerly existed when common law concepts of contract and property law were thought to be applicable to the *sui generis* accountholder – intermediary relationship and accountholder interests.

Second, as an acknowledgement of the fungible and intangible nature of book-entry securities, the application of the general property law principle *prior tempore potior iure* was consciously abandoned when the new UCC Article 8 was adopted. Prior to the revision of that article in 1994, a property law construct was applied that attempted to (fictionally) link accountholder rights to specific, identifiable assets, so that these rights could be distributed under the *prior tempore* principle. But as it was recognised that such an approach led to fortuitous results when applied to fungible and intangible assets that are typically commingled, the new version of UCC Article 8 correctly ranks accountholders' claims pro rata, i.e. in the order of their value, rather than in the order of their seniority.

Third, UCC Article 8 explicitly excludes the application of general doctrines to securities custody and transfer law in some instances. For example, the application of the so-called statute of frauds, which requires a contract to be in writing in order to be enforceable, is explicitly excluded for securities transfers, which are thus enforceable without the fulfilment of any formal requirement, other than a credit-entry in the transferee's securities account.[245]

In other words, US securities custody and transfer law currently shares few common principles with more general areas of law, which indicates a weakly

243. *See*, e.g. ROGERS (1996). *Cf. also* MOONEY (1990), 413: 'A new model, divorced from common law and U.C.C. property law constructs, also could form a more plausible base for unification of law on the international level. An approach not rooted in longstanding domestic doctrine might provide a more likely basis for harmonizing widely varying doctrine in other nations'.

244. On the other hand, the UCC has been referred to as a 'unified and coherent statute' that covers an entire field of law; LITOWITZ (2001), xiv.

245. *Cf.* QUINN (2005), 570–571.

coherent system of law.[246] But it is submitted that, also from a coherence perspective, the new version of UCC Article 8 is preferable to its former version, because it replaced the incoherence that previously existed with weak coherence, and expressly applies different concepts to distinctly different legal phenomena.[247] In the same vein, the revised UCC Article 9 treats investment property differently from other categories of property in the context of the creation and enforcement of security interests, and it is interesting to note that new rules for security interests in deposit accounts have been modelled on UCC Article 8.[248]

On the other hand, strong coherence has been maintained or restored in those instances where 'other law' is explicitly made applicable to certain issues of securities custody and transfer law. In its provisions on securities transfers, for instance, UCC Article 8 explicitly refers to general agency law to determine the effectiveness of an entitlement order. In addition, the way in which an intermediary must perform its duties as an account provider is determined by explicit reference to the general doctrine of 'good faith' and 'fraud'. Furthermore, the general negotiability principle has been given a specific application in the context of securities transfers, although no reference is made to the concepts of 'good faith' and '*bona fide* purchaser' that are generally used in the context of transfers of assets. More specifically, all transferees of book-entry securities are protected against competing third party claims, provided they had no notice of the third party's adverse claim, obtained control over the assets transferred, and had given value for the transfer.

As has been shown in the previous sections, this rule and its elements derive from general principles of private/commercial law that similarly protect purchasers for value, and the current version of UCC Article 8 thus maintains a strongly coherent, albeit functional, relation with those general principles of commercial law. A similar approach has been taken with regard to the UCC rules on the creation and enforcement of security interests in investment property. The 1994 revision of UCC Article 8 introduced the concept of 'control' as a central element in the legal framework for security interests in investment property, but in effect, that approach restored coherence with the general principles of creation and enforcement of security interests, as they are also applied to negotiable instruments and documents of title.

In sum, by introducing new concepts for *sui generis* phenomena, and (functionally) maintaining coherence with other parts of the law, the 1994 revision of UCC Article 8 has turned incoherence into weak coherence, and also retained its strong coherence with general principles of US private and commercial law. Whereas a later chapter must examine whether all normative choices made by the drafters of the UCC should be implemented in a European harmonisation instrument, it is concluded here that the UCC should be regarded as an example from a coherence point of view.

246. *See* Ch. 2.3.1.
247. *Cf. also* Rogers (1996), 1450–1451 and 1456.
248. Rocks & Bjerre (2004), 76.

Part Three

Harmonisation and Modernisation

nec erit alia lex Rome, alia Athenis, alia munc alia posthac, sed et omnes gentes et omni tempore una lex et sempiterna et inmutabilis continebit

nor will there be one law in Rome, another in Athens, one now and another one later, but one eternal and never-changing law will rule all peoples at all time

CICERO[1]

1. M. TULLIUS CICERO, DE RE PUBLICA, 3.22.

Chapter 9

Harmonisation Initiatives

9.1 INTRODUCTION

9.1.1 The Case for Harmonisation

As has been indicated in Chapter 4.4, legal harmonisation by legislative instruments in the field of capital markets can be justified by an analysis of the risks currently inherent in the settlement of international securities transactions. In such an analysis, harmonisation reduces legal risk, thus increasing the stability and efficiency of the financial markets as a whole. In other words, harmonisation contributes to the reduction of systemic risk and is thereby justified.

On the other hand, this argument would leave out important objections to harmonisation and would therefore not present a balanced view. Such a balanced view must be obtained by weighing the pros and cons, or, in economic terms: the costs and benefits.[1] These costs include, firstly, the expenses of the necessary changes to national laws and (perhaps) its procedures. As a general matter, however, these costs represent static or 'one-off' losses, whereas it is submitted that harmonisation leads to both static and dynamic benefits and growth.[2] Moreover, it will be shown that where harmonisation in the field of capital markets is concerned, both the dynamic and static benefits are considerable.

Secondly, harmonisation has been said to reduce or minimise competition between legal systems. The minimisation of competition should be taken seriously as it is generally agreed that competition between legal systems furthers (legal)

---

1. An impressive amount of publications has been produced on this subject, also from a 'law and economics' perspective, but mainly on the harmonisation of contract law; *see, e.g,* G. Wagner (2002) *and* H. Wagner (2005) and the references provided there. In the context of the present study, it is only possible to summarise the main argumentation.
2. *Cf.* H. Wagner (2005), 33–35.

innovation and satisfies the differing preferences of the subjects of these systems. It may therefore represent a way to identify the most efficient solution to a certain problem.[3] It is the author's view, however, that the harmonisation of securities custody and transfer law does not necessarily exclude all competition between the relevant legal systems.

Competition is only minimised when legal systems are fully harmonised or unified.[4] In European legislation, on the other hand, various types of harmonisation instruments preserve the possibility of competition without foregoing all benefits of harmonisation. But even if the European jurisdictions were to be wholly unified, competition would remain possible on the global level as complete harmonisation on this level is highly unrealistic.[5] In short, competition between legal systems will always be possible on the global level, whereas on the European level, certain instruments of harmonisation such as directives, might allow for some competition to be preserved.[6]

Moreover, while the choice of applicable law by (physically) relocating has been shown not to be a realistic option, especially not for most European corporations and citizens,[7] competition as just referred to must be ensured by a conflict of laws rule that ensures party autonomy. It will be seen that under the Hague Securities Convention, the law applicable to many securities custody and transfer issues is within certain limits determined by the law that is chosen by the parties.[8]

Thirdly, it has been argued that harmonisation involves costs that cannot be quantified in an economic analysis, or but with great difficulty. These 'costs' relate to socio-cultural aspects that would be harmed by harmonisation. However, these costs are indeed virtually impossible to quantify and therefore difficult to take into account in an objective cost-benefit analysis. Although possible harm to socio-cultural aspects cannot be denied all value as an objection against harmonisation in general, it is difficult to imagine its worth when harmonisation concerns a field of law that is mainly financial in nature and where harmonisation is claimed not only to result in substantial economic benefits, but also to contribute significantly to investor/consumer protection.

Harmonisation of securities custody and transfer law will contribute to enhanced investor protection as it will safeguard the investor to a large extent

3. G. Wagner (2002), 1001–1003 *and* Smits (2006), 79–80. *Cf. also* Hesselink (2001), 57.
4. On the distinction between these terms, *see supra,* Ch. 1.1, n.15.
5. Global competition presupposes a global marketplace, and it is submitted that with regard to securities custody and transfer law, the marketplace is indeed increasingly global. That statement is proven by the (intended) transatlantic merger of the stock exchanges Euronext and NYSE, the countries that participate in the drafting of the Unidroit instrument on this subject and the jurisdictions that have been taken into account by the EU Legal Certainty Group in the preparation of a future EU harmonisation instrument; *see infra.*
6. *Cf. infra,* Ch. 12.4.1. Furthermore, such a restricted form of legal competition will prevent the sometimes much feared 'race for the bottom'. *Cf.* G. Wagner (2002), 1003–1006, who argues that a race for the bottom can only occur in a market where participants can choose the applicable law and doubts that – should it in fact occur – it would have negative consequences.
7. *See* G. Wagner (2002), 1007–1008.
8. *See also,* Ch. 3.3.3 and 9.3.4.

against legal uncertainty, i.e. the current uncertainty in the identification of the law applicable to his rights and duties, the current multiplicity of rules and the difficulty in understanding them.[9] In the words of the New York legislature; clarity and certainty as well as uniformity must be attained 'so that the securities market will function in such a way that it will be more stable, and so that investors, both individual and corporate, will be more secure and their rights and interests better protected'.[10] Moreover, it will be shown that harmonisation will directly enhance investor protection through the modernisation of less protective systems, notably in the cases of intermediary insolvencies.[11]

Another 'cost factor' that is difficult to quantify, but might outweigh the benefits of harmonisation, is the encroachment on the coherence of national systems. Indeed, especially in the field of capital markets where harmonisation must necessarily address matters of property law, contract law, company law and insolvency law, encroachment may present a realistic fear.[12] In this vein, it might be argued that the preservation of the coherence of national systems of law does not permit the harmonisation and accompanying modernisation of securities custody and transfer law.[13] It is this objection that will be the main subject of the following chapters, where it will be shown that the harmonisation and modernisation of securities custody and transfer law are not likely to cause the jurisdictions investigated to become incoherent.

On the benefit side, it has already been mentioned that the reduction of legal risk or legal uncertainty through harmonisation results in considerable (economic) benefits while contributing to enhanced investor protection. More in particular, it has been shown that the reduction of legal uncertainty as described in Chapter 4.4.2, i.e. uncertainty as to what the applicable law is and what its consequences are, is likely to imply (economic) growth.[14] In this view, legal uncertainty both statically and dynamically requires additional time and money spent on contractual agreements and operational measures.[15] Moreover, these so-called transaction costs are exacerbated by higher costs of litigation under foreign laws and for foreign forums, and by the costs of instability that is caused by changes in foreign laws.[16]

As a result, legal uncertainty translates into higher prices for services rendered and lower revenues enjoyed, as a consequence of which, respectively, less

9. *See* Lambrecht & Haljan (1999), 259–260: 'The best form of protection is to give investors certainty as to their rights and responsibilities'. *Cf.* Blom (1999), 376.
10. Laws 1997, Ch. 566, § 5 (Legislative Intent formulated at UCC § 8–101).
11. *See,* e.g., Ch. 10.2.6.
12. *Cf.* Fialho de Oliveira (2005), 831: 'we must set the level of harmony that can be achieved among systems against the need for changes in internal rules and decide to what extent the former compensates for the latter'. *Cf. also* Smits (2006), 71.
13. *Cf.* Micheler (2006).
14. H. Wagner (2005) and see the references provided there.
15. Explanatory Notes to the Preliminary Draft Unidroit Securities Convention, 52. *Cf.* Taylor (1978), 104.
16. G. Wagner (2005), 1014.

consumption and less investments are made.[17] The final result is less national income. Furthermore, it is generally believed that harmonisation has a positive influence on the competitiveness of participants in the relevant marketplace and that, as a consequence, the uniform enactment of (efficient) rules is economically beneficial.[18]

With regard to securities custody and transfer law, economic analyses have been carried out both for the regional (US and EU) and the global level that confirm these arguments. Generally, they focus on the operational consolidation of the settlement industry, but this implies a legal interoperability.[19] For the US, it has been concluded that 'The lack of harmony amongst various state laws detracts from the liquidity of the clearance and settlement system by making it burdensome (and in some cases, impracticable) for investors to finance their payment obligations'.[20] For the EU, it has been calculated that the settlement of international, i.e. intrastate, transactions costs 7–10 times more than it would in the US,[21] while a recent study commissioned by the European Commission estimated that the harmonisation of national laws and, more generally, a reduction in post-trading costs would lead to a higher GDP of between 0.2 per cent and 0.6 per cent in the subsequent years.[22]

In other fields of law, a growth in national income may not outweigh the costs that the harmonisation of laws imply.[23] But it is submitted that both economic and other reasons require a different conclusion when it comes to the reduction of legal uncertainty through the harmonisation of securities custody and transfer law. First, legal uncertainty in securities custody and transfer law involves systemic risk. Although systemic risk might not be quantifiable and has to be inferred from

---

17. It has to be noted that the transaction costs will be prohibitively high where it concerns relatively low-value transactions, whereas high-value transactions may absorb these costs. *See* H. Wagner (2005), 32–35.
18. *See* Spink & Paré (2004), 323 (with regard to Canadian harmonisation with US law) *and* Löber (2006), 4 (with regard to possible future EU harmonisation). Spink & Paré (2004), 345–346, further argue that in the light of the integration of the Canadian and the US markets, Canada should harmonise with the US UCC Art. 8 'to take advantage of the proven effectiveness of Rev8 [Revised UCC Art. 8]', while UCC Art. 8 'enjoys the highest level of global system-confidence'.
19. Scott (2006), Ch. 10, 25, for instance, refers to the problems encountered when ICSDs try to enter national markets. He concludes (Ch. 10, 41): 'Harmonization has been demanded because of the economies of scale achievable from using common systems worldwide and because of the high cross-border level of transaction. In this area, home or host country rules do not appear acceptable'. *Cf. also* Lambrecht & Haljan (1999), 275.
20. Rogers (1996), n.25.
21. Scott (2006), Ch. 10, 26. The Center for European Policy Studies however, estimated this to be 2 to 8 times; *see* G30 2003 Plan of Action, 4. The sources Scott cites calculate that one single CCP would reduce costs by USD 950 million per year. Yet, he must conclude that the creation of a single clearing and settlement organisation is prevented by the 'vertical silo' of ownership, where national exchanges are linked to national clearing and settlement systems; Scott (2006), Ch. 10, 28.
22. This estimate is robust in different model specifications; EC Economic Impact Study (2006), 18.
23. *Cf.* Smits (2006), 73 *et seq.*

circumstantial evidence,[24] legal risk in the field of capital markets materialises dramatically in times of stress, unlike in other fields of law.[25] This became painfully clear in 1987, as a major US firm in the securities industry became bankrupt and trading on the NYSE could therefore not be resumed, except after intervention by the United States Government.[26]

Where, under normal circumstances, legal risk may materialise simply as economic inefficiency, legal risk in financial markets is likely to materialise in times of stress as a dramatic devaluation of securities and the unavailability of credit when parties are deterred from entering into uncertain and costly international transactions.[27] Moreover, legal risk in the field of securities custody and transfer law is particularly increased during the last few decades because of the fundamental change in market practices from physical certificates to an intermediated holding system with immobilised or dematerialised securities. An enormous increase in the volume of securities transactions that are settled cross-border and the growing reliance on collateral[28] adds to the higher urgency of addressing legal risk in the field of capital markets.[29]

The argument that legal uncertainty requires the harmonisation of laws, especially in the field of securities custody and transfer law, also follows from the fact that the value of investors' assets is to a large extent determined by the law.[30] A devaluation of investors' assets because of legal diversity can and should therefore only be addressed by legal harmonisation.[31] Furthermore, securities custody and transfer law mainly has a mandatory character, often to ensure investor protection. It is therefore only the harmonisation of laws that can solve legal uncertainty resulting from legal diversity.[32]

In sum, it must be agreed with GUYNN[33] that harmonisation in the field of capital markets finds its justification in the legal uncertainties and friction costs currently inherent in the legal infrastructure, which will eventually lead

---

24. *Report from the Commission, Evaluation report on the Settlement Finality Directive 98/26/EC (EU 25)*, COM(2005), 657 final/2, 10.
25. *Cf.* the CPSS 1995 Report, 55, where it argues that the difficulty in attaining a complete understanding of the rules and law governing the settlement process directly contributes to systemic risk.
26. REITZ (2005), 360.
27. *Cf.* Explanatory Report on the Hague Securities Convention (2005), 4, SOMMER (1998), 1194 *et seq. and* ROGERS (2005), 14. *Cf.* the 1995 comments from Alan Greenspan, then Chairman of the Board of Governors of the US Federal Reserve System, in the aftermath of the fall of Barings Bank, as quoted by ROGERS (1996), 1438: 'my experience with financial crises has convinced me that the greatest threat to the liquidity of our financial markets is the potential for disturbance to the clearance and settlement process for financial transactions'.
28. *See* LÖBER (2006), 7.
29. *Cf.* Explanatory Notes to the Preliminary Draft UNIDROIT Securities Convention, 36 and 44–46.
30. *Cf.* SOMMER (1998), 1183.
31. Contrary to, for instance, the law that relates to chattels; *see* G. WAGNER (2002), 1014.
32. Contrary to areas of law where rules are not binding; in those instances, harmonisation may not be necessary. *See* HARTKAMP (2003), 98–99 and 101.
33. GUYNN (1996), 6.

to the higher cost of credit and the lower value of securities.[34] Moreover, the increase in the volume of the securities markets has contributed to the value of this justification. In the following chapters, it will therefore be assumed that harmonisation by legislative action and the subsequent formation of a pan-EU legal framework is a necessary condition for an efficient EU clearing and settlement environment.[35]

9.1.2 Three Levels of Challenge

In his comment that accompanies Guynn's influential discussion paper,[36] Rogers discerns three 'levels of challenge' in the process of achieving international harmonisation of securities custody and transfer law: first, consensus has to be reached on the fundamental principles that should be implemented; second, these principles must be integrated into the legal regimes of the participating states; and third, common choice of law principles must be agreed upon so that the 'inevitable elements of international non-uniformity in legal analysis or results will not impair the planning of securities transactions'.[37] With regard to the legal infrastructure of securities settlement and custody, the need for global harmonisation and modernisation has been recognised for a long time, but harmonisation has not been achieved on any of the three levels just mentioned.[38]

Yet harmonisation or even unification seems to be most advanced at the third level. Under the auspices of the Hague Conference for Private International Law, a 'Convention on the Law Applicable to Certain Rights in Respect of Securities Held with an Intermediary' ('Hague Securities Convention', or 'HSC') has been drafted. This convention provides uniform conflict of laws rules for proprietary issues concerning international securities transactions.[39] Although on 13 December 2002, all participating states signed the text of the convention, it will only become effective when 3 states have ratified the treaty. But, at the time of writing, it is only Switzerland and the US that have set in motion an internal ratification procedure. The European Commission has recently reiterated its recommendation that the EU

34. For the harmonisation of contract law on the other hand, such economic benefits are not that evident; Smits (2006), 76.
35. *Cf.* the Communication from the Commission to the Council and the European Parliament, Clearing and settlement in the European Union, Main policy issues and future challenges. Communication of 28 May 2002, COM(2002) 257 def., *and* the Giovannini 2003 Report, 25.
36. The discussion paper Modernizing securities ownership, transfer and pledging laws (1996) which Randall Guynn wrote for the International Bar Association sparked international (legal) interest in the harmonisation of securities custody and transfer law.
37. Guynn et al. (1996), 59.
38. This book focuses on European harmonisation, but the author considers global integration and harmonisation to be equally important for the EU.
39. *Available at* <www.hcch.net>.

and its Member States should sign the convention.[40] The HSC will be discussed in greater detail below.

With regard to the first level of challenge, various international organisations such as the G30, BIS and IOSCO have expressed their views on the (fundamental) principles that should underlie a global harmonisation instrument. The latest and, until now, the most far-reaching global initiative has been undertaken by the International Institute for the Unification of Private Law ('UNIDROIT').[41] These and other global initiatives will be discussed in the following section. On the EU level on the other hand, several Directives have harmonised certain aspects of substantive and private international law concerning securities custody and settlement. Moreover, the so-called 'Legal Certainty Group' has investigated the desirability of a legislative instrument that will harmonise the legal infrastructure of securities settlement within the EU. The European Directives currently in force and the work of this group will be elaborated upon in the third section of this Chapter.

The extent to which the jurisdictions examined in the preceding chapters satisfy the standards that can be distilled from the recommendations of the G30, BIS, IOSCO and the UNIDROIT project is the subject of the next chapter. The outcome of this test is extremely relevant for a future European harmonisation instrument. It will indicate to what extent the legal infrastructure currently in place in these selected jurisdictions should be modernised so as to bring it up to speed with what is generally considered best practice. In the terminology used in the context of the UNIDROIT project: it will indicate the internal soundness of the jurisdictions examined. In other words: it will indicate to what extent the present rules can do with modification rather than replacement, a relevant issue also with respect to the second level of challenge.

Whereas relative consensus thus seem to exist on the first and third levels of the challenge, the second level, i.e. how principles or standards of harmonisation should be integrated into the legal regimes of participating states, remains very unclear. However, it is submitted that harmonisation is highly unlikely to be achieved if its consequences for participating jurisdictions are not understood completely. For the European jurisdictions investigated, an impact assessment of harmonisation is therefore made in the second following chapter. The assessment is carried out by an analysis of the relationship or coherence between the securities law of these jurisdictions and the more general areas of the law in which it is embedded. It is this relationship that will determine to what extent the proposed rules of harmonisation will encroach upon the law as a whole and will therefore also be indicative for the extent that modernisation will be feasible.[42] In sum, the

40. Proposal for a Council decision concerning the signing of the Hague Securities Convention, COM(2003) 783 final *and* Legal assessment of certain aspects of the Hague Securities Convention, of 3 July 2006, SEC(2006), 910. *But see* RANK & BIERMAN (2006) for a critical account of that assessment.
41. *Available at* <http://www.UNIDROIT.org/english/workprogramme/study078/item1/main.htm>.
42. *Cf.* SONO *in* GUYNN ET AL. (1996), 66.

feasibility of harmonisation depends on both the extent to which modernisation must be realised and on the coherence of national systems.[43]

9.2 GLOBAL HARMONISATION

9.2.1 Introduction

The following sections will discuss the global initiatives that have been undertaken in the last few decades to achieve a harmonised legal infrastructure for the transfer and custody of securities. First, it will be explained what recommendations have been brought forward in that field by high-level international organisations such as the Group of 30, the Bank for International Settlements, the International Securities Services Association and the International Organisation of Securities Commissions. These recommendations represent the generally accepted standards of securities custody and transfer law, and will therefore be used in the following chapter as the basis for its evaluation of the European jurisdictions previsously analysed. Thereafter, the as yet most far-reaching global initiatives of legal harmonisation will be discussed. These initiatives concern a harmonisation instrument of substantive law set up by Unidroit, and a convention on private international law drafted under the auspices of the Hague Conference. It is against the background of these instruments that the chapters that follow will examine how harmonisation and modernisation should be achieved within the EU.

9.2.2 Recommendations

It has just been stated that various international organisations have expressed their thoughts on the principles that should underlie a global harmonisation of securities custody and settlement law and on the problems that the current legal diversity pose. The first of these was the Group of 30 ('G30'), a non-governmental organisation that consists of senior members of both the public and private sectors and academia. In 1989, the G30 published its report 'Clearance and Settlement in the World's Securities Markets'.

While it concluded that a centralised, single global clearing would not be feasible, this report formulated nine recommendations with which all markets should comply in order to create a safe post-trade process environment. The nine recommendations address operational differences in the practice of clearing and settlement. Most importantly, they recommend a shortening of the time between the trade date and settlement date to three days (T+3), the practice of Delivery versus Payment, the elimination of the movement of physical certificates by dematerialisation or immobilisation at CSDs, and the use of netting systems.

43. *Cf.* Goode (2003-1), 14–16.

While the drafters of the report recognised that the implementation of these minimum standards would imply alterations to each market's 'own history, traditions and practices', they believed that 'the investments involved will be more than offset in time by the local as well as international benefits which will result from a concerted effort to modernise and make compatible each of the markets'.[44] According to the report, implementation would result in enhanced efficiency and reduced risk.

The Bank for International Settlements ('BIS') was created in 1930 and has since then been a forum for central banks. Its Committee on Payments and Settlement Systems ('CPSS') has prepared various reports on clearing and settlement. In 1995, the CPSS issued an important report on cross-border securities settlements which, for the first time, also paid attention to its legal aspects. The report provides an overview of various schemes of book-entry securities custody[45] and provides an introduction to the problems of the finality of securities transactions and intermediary insolvencies. Further, it links the complexity of different applicable rules and law to the existence of systemic risk.

The International Securities Services Association ('ISSA'), a private sector group, collaborated closely with the G30 when it drafted its recommendations in 1989. Thereafter, the ISSA regularly reviewed the G30 recommendations and published a full revision in 2000.[46] This revision contains eight recommendations, the last of which is devoted to the legal infrastructure of securities clearing and settlement. It states:

> Local laws and regulations should ensure that there is segregation of client assets from the principal assets of their custodian; and no possible claim on client assets in the event of custodian bankruptcy or a similar event. Regulators and markets, to further improve investor protection, should work: to ensure clarity on the applicable law on cross border transactions, to seek international agreement on a legally enforceable definition of finality in a securities transaction, to ensure that local law fully protects the rights of beneficial owners, to strengthen securities law both to secure the rights of the pledgee and the protection accorded to client assets held in Securities Systems.[47]

Recommendation 8 further concludes that, in many countries, securities laws are 'inappropriate for the age of modern electronic clearing and settlement processes' and that it is 'often difficult to establish the prevailing law governing a specific cross border transaction or collateral movement'.[48] The recommendation is

---

44. G30 1989 Report, iii-iv.
45. CPSS 1995 Report, 51.
46. A similar project was undertaken by the International Federation of Stock Exchanges; *See* the FIBV Clearing and Settlement Best Practices Report 1996, *available at* <www.world-exchanges.org>.
47. ISSA Recommendations 2000, 9.
48. ISSA Recommendations 2000, 20.

rather detailed but the ISSA project has not found widespread support or official endorsement.[49]

In 2001, the CPSS of BIS issued a set of 19 recommendations in a collaborated effort with the International Organisation of Securities Commissions ('IOSCO').[50] These recommendations identify a set of minimum standards for securities settlement systems. Its first recommendation reads: 'Securities settlement systems should have a well founded, clear and transparent legal basis in the relevant jurisdictions'. The 2001 Report does not go into great detail about the specific elements that such a legal basis should consist of, but states that

> key aspects of the settlement process that the legal framework should support include: enforceability of transactions, protection of customer assets (particularly against loss upon the insolvency of a custodian), immobilisation or dematerialisation of securities, netting arrangements, securities lending (including repurchase agreements and other economically equivalent transactions), finality of settlement, arrangements for achieving delivery versus payment, default rules, and liquidation of assets pledged or transferred as collateral.

Further, recommendation 12 of the 2001 CPSS/IOSCO Report states that 'entities holding securities in custody should employ accounting practices and safekeeping procedures that fully protect customers' securities. It is essential that customers' securities be protected against the claims of a custodian's creditors'. The recommendation thus mainly addresses custody risk and concludes that besides accurate accounting, segregation could contribute to safekeeping and that 'ideally, a customer's securities are immune from claims made by third-party creditors of the custodian'. In addition, 'it should be highly improbable that a customer's securities could be frozen or made unavailable for an extended period of time',[51] e.g. by segregation. Finally, recommendation 12 refers to the importance of assessing the legal framework by global custodians, especially when custody concerns multinational layers.[52]

In 2003, the G30, in its turn, issued 'A Plan of Action'.[53] This document contains twenty recommendations that should improve the safety and efficiency of international capital markets in the light of their rapid growth and structural change, as well as market shocks as occurred on 11 September 2001. It is considered by its drafters to go further than the CPSS/IOSCO recommendations in setting more ambitious goals, more concrete time frames and providing ways of implementation. Whereas the CPSS/IOSCO recommendations provided minimum standards, the 2003 G30 Plan of Action contains rules for 'best practices', while focusing more on the cross-border aspect of today's internationalised markets. It concludes that 'characteristics of performance' should be globally consistent so

49. CPSS/IOSCO Recommendations 2001, 1.
50. CPSS/IOSCO Recommendations 2001.
51. CPSS/IOSCO Recommendations 2001, 19.
52. *Cf. also* Recommendation 19, 24.
53. An executive summary is available through <www.group30.org>.

as to 'create the cross-system linkages ultimately required to produce a seamless global infrastructure'.[54]

Besides recommendations that concern operational aspects and aim at the creation of an 'interoperable global network',[55] the 2003 Plan of Action also contains recommendations that address the current legal diversity so as to mitigate legal risk. Other recommendations concern the improvement of the governance of providers of clearing and settlement services. The report finds that 'the legal and regulatory frameworks on which clearing and settlement systems are founded continue to develop piecemeal and largely on a domestic basis'.[56] The most important legal recommendation for the purpose of this study is recommendation 15, which reads: 'Advance legal certainty over rights to securities, cash, or collateral'.

In May 2006, the G30 published a 'Final Report on Global Clearing and Settlement', in which the implementation of the 2003 Plan of Action was assessed.[57] It concludes that much progress in the area of interoperability has been achieved in the EU. With regard to the legal recommendations on the other hand, it had to conclude that the call for legal certainty 'raised complex legal issues', which are currently being addressed by the HSC and UNIDROIT.

9.2.3 UNIDROIT INSTRUMENT ON SUBSTANTIVE LAW

Since its establishment in 1926, the International Institute for the Unification of Private Law ('UNIDROIT') has facilitated the creation of harmonisation instruments in the field of private and commercial law as an intergovernmental organisation.[58] Traditionally, these instruments take the form of International Conventions, but other, less binding instruments have also been promulgated, such as the 2004 Principles of International Commercial Contracts.

In 2002, UNIDROIT started a project that would have to result in a harmonisation instrument on the substantive law regarding securities held with an intermediary. At the time of writing, several meetings of governmental experts have taken place, but the text of the instrument has yet to be finalised. Final agreement on the form of the instrument has also not been reached. The following section will therefore be based on the text of the preliminary draft convention as the third meeting of governmental experts had adopted in November 2006.[59]

54. G30 2003 Plan of Action, 6.
55. Of this category of recommendations, recommendation 1 is the most relevant in the context of this book: 'eliminate paper and automate communication, data capture, and enrichment'.
56. G30 2003 Plan of Action, 3.
57. An executive summary of the report is available through <www.group30.org>.
58. From 1926 until the demise of the League of Nations in 1940, UNIDROIT was an auxiliary organ of the League.
59. Preliminary Draft Convention on Substantive Rules Regarding Intermediated Securities as adopted by the Committee of Governmental Experts at its third session, 6–15 November 2006, Doc. 57 of Study LXXVIII, hereinafter referred to as 'UNIDROIT draft convention' or

The UNIDROIT secretariat has explained that, as a matter of principle, provisions have only been drafted when thought necessary for the reduction of legal or systemic risk, or for the promotion of market efficiency.[60] In addition, all provisions drafted were considered necessary for achieving international compatibility and internally sound systems of securities custody and transfer law, especially with a view to investor protection and efficiency. The instrument thus addresses both purely domestic and cross-border situations.

Furthermore, UNIDROIT has explicitly stated that it would take a functional approach that seeks to leave the technical, legal implementation to the participating states.[61] This was thought essential because

> the law governing securities holding and transfer is embedded in national legislation and integrated within several different legal areas: commercial law, corporate law, tax law, insolvency law, etc., as well as through measures carried out by regulatory authorities.[62] As a consequence, the UNIDROIT instrument was drafted so that it provides neutral language which avoids legal classifications.[63]

Nonetheless, it became clear in the course of the project that the functional approach could not avoid some participating states being forced to amend 'significant' areas of their laws. It was considered, however, that an even more functional, model law approach would not be able to guarantee the degree of harmonisation required, and was therefore rejected.[64] Consequently, the preliminary draft convention currently proposes to address the soundness of national securities laws in the following ways, mainly so as to accommodate the needs of principal market participants:

- First, it seeks to establish the effectiveness against third parties of a book-entry in a securities account.[65] Article 7(2) of the present preliminary draft convention therefore provides that a credit entry in a securities account is effective without any necessary further step. The draft convention allows for the reversal of debit entries or designations of a securities account (for instance, in the context of the creation of a security interest) if the relevant intermediary was not duly authorised to do so, either by the accountholder, collateral taker or non-convention law.[66] The draft convention allows for the reversal of credit entries if the acquirer had (actual or construed)

'preliminary draft convention'. Provisions are only discussed that are not indicated to be subject to further consideration.

60. Explanatory Notes to the Preliminary Draft UNIDROIT Securities Convention, 68.
61. *See,* e.g., Explanatory Notes to the Preliminary Draft UNIDROIT Securities Convention, 70.
62. Explanatory Notes to the Preliminary Draft UNIDROIT Securities Convention, 70.
63. Initially however, the introduction of a completely new concept was considered that should denote the package of rights enjoyed by an accountholder; PAECH (2002), 1160.
64. Implementation Report, February 2006, Doc. 26 of Study LXXVIII, 9.
65. Art. 5(2).
66. Art. 11(1). The consequences of ineffectiveness or reversal are to be determined by the non-convention law; Art. 11(2)(c).

knowledge of an adverse claim or if his account was gratuitously credited and an adverse claim has subsequently been brought forward.[67]

- Second, it seeks to establish the effectiveness against third parties of a security interest that has been created by a collateral agreement and by either a designating entry to mark the pledged securities as collateralised, by the simple fact that the collateral taker is the collateral giver's intermediary, or by control agreement.[68] But in order for one or more of these methods to be effective, the relevant contracting state must have made a declaration to that effect.[69] The convention further provides rules on the enforcement of a security interest and other rules concerning collateral transactions in its Chapter VI, but an opt-out provision for the entirety of this chapter has been included to avoid conflicts with relevant existing legislation.[70]
- Third, it seeks to harmonise the priority rules for competing security interests. Article 13 states that security takers that have obtained their interest by being the collateral giver's intermediary, by designation of the collateralised securities as such or by control agreement, are ranked equally according to the time of, respectively, the conclusion of the collateral agreement, the designation of the entry, or the conclusion of the control agreement. Yet if the security giver is an intermediary, the priority ranking is not to be determined by the convention, but by non-convention law. In addition, all priority rules are made subject to party agreements that determine otherwise.[71]
- Fourth, it seeks to establish that accountholders may enjoy their rights undisturbed, and these rights include: the right to enjoy the monetary and voting rights attached to an accountholder's securities, and his right to dispose of the securities to which he is entitled.[72] But an accountholder's right to obtain his securities otherwise than through a securities account (for instance, by physical delivery out of the book-entry custody system) is made subject to, *inter alia,* the law under which the securities are constituted, the terms of the securities and the account agreement.[73] Furthermore, the UNIDROIT convention expressly provides that, although effective against all third parties, the latter two of these three rights can only be exercised

67. Art. 12(1), (2) and (3).
68. Art. 8(1) and (2). Art. 1(k) defines 'control agreement'.
69. Art. 8(4).
70. Art. 32. This provision has been drafted especially in view of the European Financial Collateral Directive, *see infra,* s. 9.3.3.
71. Arts. 13(6) and 14, respectively.
72. Art. 5(1)(a) and (b), respectively. The convention further provides that the law of the participating states must permit voting and the exercise of other accountholders' rights by persons other than the accountholders themselves, such as the intermediaries; Art. 24(2). *Cf.* Art. 13 of the proposed EU Shareholders Rights Directive, *see infra,* s. 1.3.3.
73. Art. 5(1)(c).

against the relevant intermediary, while the first right can only be exercised against the relevant intermediary as well as against the issuer.[74]
- Fifth, it seeks to preserve the integrity of the intermediated holding system. Under these rules no attachment of accountholders' securities is allowed at any other tier than that of an accountholder's immediate intermediary.[75] Furthermore, Article 18 states that, in principle, an intermediary is bound, and only entitled to follow its own accountholders' instructions.[76] In the same vein, Article 19 requires an intermediary to hold an amount of assets with other intermediaries or the issuer itself that corresponds to (at least) the aggregate amount of its clients' entitlements. Yet these obligations imposed on intermediaries are made subject to the relevant provisions of non-convention law, as well as account agreements or rules of a securities settlement system.

While the provisions just discussed are likely to contribute to the facilitation of the interconnection between national systems, UNIDROIT also envisaged provisions specifically designed to further cross-border connections. These provisions include a set of basic concepts and address the allocation of losses in the case of a shortfall of available securities in an intermediary insolvency.[77] For instance, the current version of Article 1 provides that securities are 'of the same description' if they are of the same class (in the case of shares or stock), or of the same currency and denomination and form part of the same issue (in the case of other instruments).

Losses that occur as a result of a shortfall in an intermediary insolvency are shared by the accountholders entitled to the type of securities in which the shortfall occurs, in proportion to their entitlements. If an intermediary operates a settlement system, the rules of this system may determine otherwise, while the allocation rule is further subject to domestic non-convention rules on insolvency proceedings and rules on fraudulent preferences.[78]

As the discussion of the preliminary draft convention's provisions shows, the domestic laws of participating states retain a fair amount of discretion. Most provisions of the convention have been made subject to domestic non-convention law, account agreements, as well as the rules of a securities settlement system. In addition, its standards and functional approach do not seem to require (radical) amendments of domestic laws. The latter issue will be examined in greater detail in the following chapter, but it can be preliminarily concluded, and only with regard to the jurisdictions analysed in the previous chapters, that the current draft

74. Art. 5(2).
75. Art. 17.
76. Exceptions are made for instructions by security takers, persons designated by agreement, court decisions, any non-convention law rule and rules of a settlement system (when the intermediary is the operator of a settlement system); Art. 18(2). Moreover, the consequences of a lack of authorisation are determined by domestic non-convention law; Art. 11(2).
77. PAECH (2002), 1160.
78. Arts. 22 and 16.

UNIDROIT convention will enhance the interoperability and internal soundness of these jurisdictions to a limited extent only.

9.2.4 HAGUE CONVENTION ON PRIVATE INTERNATIONAL LAW

Unification of private international law is generally seen as preliminary to the harmonisation of substantive law;[79] once the rules of substantive law have been harmonised, the need for uniform conflict of laws rules will become less urgent. At present, however, differences in domestic rules on securities custody, transfer and ownership are many and conflicts of laws regularly arise. Moreover, it has already been stated that international non-uniformity is inevitable, even after harmonisation measures have become effective. Consequently, many studies on the cross-border settlement of securities transactions have stressed the need for uniform conflict of laws rules, especially in the context of legal certainty.[80] However, current conflict of laws rules not only differ from jurisdiction to jurisdiction, but are also often unclear and outdated.

In May 2000, Australia, the United Kingdom and the United States proposed to the Hague Conference that it should facilitate a convention that addressed the problems and possible systemic risk[81] caused by differences in private international law regarding indirectly held securities. In February 2003, the final text of the Hague Securities Convention ('HSC') was released.[82]

The present Hague Securities Convention caters for all systems of indirect holding as it does not cover 'direct' relationships between investors and the issuer or between investors and the securities themselves.[83] Also, it does not cover the purely contractual aspects of relationships between parties to a securities transfer or between an investor and his intermediary (although a conceptual distinction between 'proprietary issues' and 'contractual issues' has been avoided).[84] Consequently, the HSC applies mainly to 'proprietary' issues, even if these arise in a custody relationship that is purely contractual in nature. Furthermore, the HSC is not confined to specific types of transactions or situations; it applies to all situations with some international aspect.[85] As usual, the convention has been made

79. E.g., CPSS/IOSCO Recommendations 2001, 9.
80. E.g., CPSS 1995 Report, 55, Recommendation 8 of the ISSA Recommendations 2000, CPSS/IOSCO Recommendations 2001, 43, Recommendation 15 of the G30 2003 Plan of Action, 10.
81. *Cf.*, e.g., POTOK (2004), 205.
82. Its text is available at <www.hcch.net>. Recently, an extensive Explanatory Report on the HSC by Roy Goode, Hideki Kanda and Karl Kreuzer has been published (hereinafter referred to as 'Explanatory Report (2005)'), the reading of which is highly recommended, not least because of the numerous examples and fact patterns provided.
83. Explanatory Report (2005), 11.
84. The issues covered are enumerated in Art. 2(1).
85. Art. 3.

subject to public policy rules[86] and core insolvency rules of national law.[87] Rights that have been established before insolvency, however, remain subject to the law designated by the HSC.[88]

At an early stage in the development of the HSC, it was concluded that the conflict rules that traditionally determined the applicable law for property law issues regarding securities were insufficient to match the reality of indirect holding systems.[89] In the course of the convention negotiations, it also became clear that neither the place of the relevant intermediary ('PRIMA'), nor the place of the relevant securities account ('PRACA') provided practical connecting factors in today's world of electronic agility.[90] Primacy was therefore given to the autonomy of the parties to a securities account agreement to determine the applicable law.

The pivotal article of the HSC in this regard is Article 4(1), under which the applicable law is determined by the parties to the relevant securities account agreement. Parties may either have agreed on a certain law to apply to the account agreement as a whole, as a consequence of which this law applies to all of the (property law) issues mentioned in Article 2(1), or parties may have agreed on a law to govern specifically all Article 2(1) issues. In the latter case, purely contractual issues may thus be governed by the law of another jurisdiction.[91]

Party autonomy, however, is not unlimited as it has been made subject to a reality check. This reality check concerns the relevant intermediary's location; the law designated by the parties must be the law of a so-called 'qualifying office' of the intermediary concerned. Article 4(1)(a)(iii) provides the general rule in this respect: an office of an intermediary is classified as a 'qualifying office' if it is 'engaged in a business or other regular activity of maintaining securities accounts'. Since this criterion might be considered too general,[92] paragraphs 4(1)(a)(i), 4(1)(a)(ii) and 4(1)(b) have been added, representing specific 'safe harbours'; in the event that one of the criteria there listed has been met, an office is undoubtedly classified as a 'qualifying office'. Article 4(2) lists elements that must be disregarded in this respect.[93]

If the rule just discussed does not lead to a result, either because the law chosen does not meet the qualifying office requirement, or because no choice of law has been made, or because there has been no account agreement at all, Article 5 provides fall-back rules. These rules also refer to the law of the relevant intermediary, underpinned by the traditional *lex incorporationis* (Article 5(2)) or *siège réel* (Article 5(3)) rules.

---

86. Art. 11.
87. Art. 8.
88. *Cf.* the EU Settlement Finality Directive; *see infra,* s. 9.3.3. *See also* Explanatory Report (2005), 24.
89. Explanatory Report (2005), 4–5 and 18–19.
90. Explanatory Report (2005), 7. On PRIMA, *see also supra,* Ch. 3.3.
91. Rogers (2005), 40.
92. *Cf.* Rogers (2005), 33.
93. On the reality check, *contra* Rank (2005), 258, *pro* Tenenbaum (2004), 847 *and* Haentjens (2006), 83–84.

The HSC does not provide specific provisions on the law that applies to transfers of title or security interests in book-entry securities. Rather, the general rule of Article 4(1) also governs perfection requirements and their effects; as a result, once securities have been credited to the securities account of the transferee, the law governing this account governs the nature of the latter's interest, its creation, the proprietary validity of the transfer and the like.[94] The HSC thus does not require a preliminary characterisation of the other interests in the chain of custody.[95]

This approach, however, does not solve conflicts of laws when a transferee obtains a valid interest under the law of his securities account, while the transferor has remained the owner under the law of his securities account. The same problem occurs when a transferee obtains a valid interest under the law of his securities account, while a second transferee who has acquired the same securities in good faith also obtains a valid interest under the law governing his securities account. In short, the HSC does not solve these problems of priority as it does not refer to a single law. However, it does make clear to which double liability intermediaries may be subject.[96]

The Hague Securities Convention provides a modern conflict of laws rule that is adapted to the needs of modern practice. It is submitted that it makes the applicable law readily identifiable, although it can be questioned how an express choice of law in an account agreement could be known to third parties. Therefore, and because it moves away even further from the *lex rei sitae* than the current EU Directives do,[97] it remains to be seen whether it will find much support in the European jurisdictions that still depend heavily on traditional conflict of laws rules.[98] At the time of writing, no countries have yet formally ratified the Convention, which should take effect once it has been ratified by three or more countries.[99]

---

94. It has been argued that the law of the transferor should apply *(lex creationis)* to these issues; Ooi (2003), 301. However this does not seem to have been the intention of the drafters of the HSC; *see* Explanatory Report, 84–85 *and,* e.g. Potok (2004), 216.
95. Explanatory Report (2005), 52. *But see* Ooi (2003), 305–306.
96. According to the Explanatory Report, the double liability 'was not created by the Convention' but 'has always existed with respect to cross-border transfers of securities through a chain of intermediaries'; Explanatory Report (2005), 86.
97. *Cf.* Tenenbaum (2004), 842 *and see infra.*
98. For a further discussion of the possible objections against the HSC and its merits, *see* Haentjens (2006), 96 *et seq.*
99. Whereas the US and Switzerland have recently set in motion national procedures to ratify the Treaty, the EU Council is currently reluctant to do so. The European Commission, however, had published a proposal and recommendation in which ratification was advocated; Proposal for a Council decision concerning the signing of the Hague Securities Convention, COM(2003) 783 final *and* Legal assessment of certain aspects of the Hague Securities Convention, of 3 July 2006, SEC(2006), 910). Probably a cautioning opinion of the European Central Bank (of 17 March 2005, CON/2005/7, OJ C 81/10) has contributed to this position; *see* Haentjens (2006), 96–98.

9.3 EUROPEAN HARMONISATION

9.3.1 Introduction

Since 1973, the European Community and later on, the European Union ('EU') have undertaken to establish a single market for financial services. Although the introduction of a single currency has accelerated this development[100] and a significant integration of market participants has occurred since then, a true single market has not yet been established because of legal and operational barriers. Various studies show that the legal barriers result from a lack of a harmonised legal framework and stress the need for the creation of such a framework.[101]

The lack of a legal framework is addressed at different levels, mainly by the European Commission. At the most general level, the feasibility of a harmonised contract law is currently investigated,[102] while at a more specific level, directives that purport to harmonise financial services law have been put in place and continue to be drafted. Most specifically, the so-called Legal Certainty Group has examined the desirability of the harmonisation of securities custody and transfer law. In the following sections, both the financial law harmonisation, and the initiatives to bring about a harmonisation of securities custody and transfer law will be discussed. But first, some introductory remarks on the private, sector-driven integration of the European markets will be made, because the legal harmonisation to be discussed is undertaken in order to accommodate and further this (functional) integration.

9.3.2 Sector-Driven Harmonisation

The technical operation of national clearing and settlement systems has been given a strong impetus towards harmonisation by recent mergers of stock exchanges, CSDs and clearing companies.[103] Yet, the European clearing and settlement infrastructure still suffers from fragmentation, especially where it concerns equities settlement. The cross-border settlement of fixed-income securities is less affected, since the settlement of these securities is predominantly carried out by International Central Securities Depositories (ICSDs).[104]

---

100. Löber (2005), 155.
101. On the subject of securities law, *see,* e.g., Giovannini 2001 Report, 55 *and* EFMLG 2003 Report. *See infra,* s. 9.3.4. It must be noted however, that the EU Treaty limits its own legislative authority by the principles of subsidiarity and proportionality; Art. 5 EU Treaty *and see infra,* Ch. 12.2.2.
102. *See* <http://ec.europa.eu/consumers/cons_int/safe_shop/fair_bus_pract/cont_law/index_en.htm> for an overview of the latest developments and the most important documents on this subject. *See also,* e.g., Hartkamp et al. (2004) *and* Smits (2005), both collections of essays.
103. *See* Benjamin (2003), 224.
104. Derivatives are settled by clearing houses and are predominantly contractual in nature, as a consequence of which less problems arise in the settlement of cross-border transactions; Giovannini Group 2001 Report, 20.

Currently, the EU-based ICSDs Clearstream International and Euroclear provide clearance and settlement facilities for domestic as well as cross-border transactions. Already since 1980, the settlement of transactions between these institutions and their participants is facilitated by an electronic 'bridge' between them.[105] Clearstream International is the merged entity of the Luxembourg-based Cedel International and Germany's CSD Deutsche Börse Clearing AG. Clearstream International holds Clearstream Bank Luxembourg (CBL), Clearstream Bank Frankfurt (CBF) and Clearstream Services Luxembourg (CSL). Euroclear was founded in 1968 by the New York-based Morgan Guarantee Trust Company. As a result of various mergers that took place in the last decade, Euroclear SA/NV held as of 1 January 2005: the ICSD, Euroclear Netherlands (the CSD of the Netherlands, formerly known as Necigef), Euroclear France (France's CSD, formerly known as Sicovam SA) and CrestCo of the UK. Soon, it will also incorporate CIK of Belgium.[106]

Prominent European exchanges have also been the subject of recent mergers and takeovers. On 22 September 2000, the Dutch, Belgian and French markets merged to form, respectively, Euronext Amsterdam, Euronext Brussels and Euronext Paris, with Euronext NV as the Amsterdam-based holding company. Since 2002, Euronext NV also holds the stock exchanges of Lisbon and the London-based derivatives market LIFFE. It is the purpose of this pan-European exchange that trading takes place on one single trading platform. As a recent and interesting development, Euronext and the New York Stock Exchange announced on 2 June 2006 a merger of the two companies, thus forming the world's largest and first transatlantic exchange.[107] At the time of writing however, the merger had not yet taken full effect.

For all the exchanges of the Euronext group, LCH.Clearnet performs the roles of the central counterparty ('CCP') and clearing house. LCH.Clearnet developed from its first merger in February 2001 between French Clearnet SA and the CCPs of the Amsterdam and Brussels markets. Shortly thereafter, the merger with the Lisbon exchange was approved by the Portuguese shareholders. On 22 December 2003, Clearnet merged with the London Clearing House ('LCH'), which clears transactions for the London exchanges.[108] In its capacity of CCP, LCH.Clearnet replaces all transactions concluded between market participants with transactions with Clearnet itself.[109] This process as well as all the rules regulating participation in the Clearnet clearing system are governed by French law.[110]

---

105. *See* Euroclear Annual Report 2002, 46 *and* Giovannini Group 2001 Report, 30.
106. Euroclear Annual Report 2004, 60.
107. *See* <www.euronext.com>.
108. Technically, LCH.Clearnet consists of LCH.Clearnet SA and LCH.Clearnet Limited. LCH. Clearnet is owned by the Euronext group for 80 per cent and by the Euroclear group for 20 per cent. *See* <www.euroclear.com and <http://www.lch.com>.
109. *See also supra,* Ch. 4.2.
110. Clearnet Rules Art. 1.2.3.1.

9.3.3 Harmonisation of Financial Law

In order to create a legal infrastructure that supports the integration of market participants as just described, several instruments of EU legislation have already been put in place, while others are currently on the drawing board. In 1999, the European Commission endorsed a 'Financial Services Action Plan' ('FSAP') that aimed at achieving an integrated internal market for financial services generally. The plan led to the adoption of 42 Community instruments, but although the European Commission acknowledged that the number of cross-border transactions had multiplied in the past decade, that collateral had increasingly been used to secure international transactions and that the international competition between clearing and settlement institutions had intensified, clearing and settlement was not separately addressed.[111]

On the other hand, some legislative instruments that have been adopted in the context of the FSAP deal with aspects of clearing and settlement law.[112] The Commission has followed a two-pronged path in that respect. First, it addressed the access of securities services providers to the integrated market and, second, it made an effort to manage the systemic risk inherent in the current infrastructure of clearing and settlement systems.[113] The former policy objective has resulted in mainly regulatory legislation, while the latter also led to the enactment of provisions that are traditionally considered to be matters of private or commercial law.

The European Commission itself considered the FSAP to be a success.[114] However, the influential Lamfalussy Report, called after the chairman of its preparatory committee and published in 2001, found a regulatory deficiency in the European legislation on securities law. In this report, the piece-meal approach of the European legislature to the harmonisation challenge was criticised and a more coherent approach was recommended.[115] Further, the report suggested that consolidation should primarily remain in the hands of the industry, while competition issues and excessive costs should be addressed in the public sphere.[116]

On 5 December 2005, the European Commission issued a White Book in which it announced its policy goals for the period 2005–2010. It stated that during this period it plans to focus on the enforcement and amendment of existing legislation rather than on the enactment of new legislation. On the other hand, it

---

111. *See also* Communication from the Commission to the Council and the European Parliament, Clearing and settlement in the European Union, Main policy issues and future challenges. Communication of 28 May 2002, COM(2002) 257 def., Peters (2003), 34–43, Benjamin (2003), 225–226 *and* Löber (2006), 155.
112. *Cf.* Löber (2005), 155–156.
113. *Cf.* Moloney (2002), 712–713. On systemic risk, *see also supra,* Ch. 4.4.1.
114. *See,* e.g., *White Paper, Financial Services Policy 2005–2010,* 4.
115. *Cf. supra,* Ch. 2.4.1 *and infra,* Ch. 12.4.1.
116. *Cf.* Moloney (2002), 716. The suggestion is in accordance with the case made in the first section of this Chapter, where legislative action in the field of securities custody and settlement law was advocated with reference to analyses that found the cross-border settlement of securities transactions to be excessively costly.

identified the removing of 'remaining economically significant barriers' also as a 'key axe' of its policy.[117] This presumably includes the drafting process for a future instrument on securities custody and transfer law.

In the following section, both effective Community legislation and an instrument that may possibly be enacted in the not too distant future will be discussed in chronological order. Some of the legislation has been drafted in the context of the FSAP, while other instruments were adopted either before that or are currently being considered for enactment. The process that may result in an instrument that will specifically address securities custody and transfer law will be the subject of the next section.

9.3.3.1 Settlement Finality Directive

The Settlement Finality Directive[118] ('SFD') was adopted on 19 May 1998. Its main purpose was to reduce the systemic risk associated with participation in payment and securities settlement systems, and, more specifically, the risk that materialises when a participant in such a system becomes insolvent.[119] The SFD therefore determines that transfer orders and payment netting be final and non-revocable in nature, it determines which insolvency rules are applicable to claims and obligations in a payment/securities settlement system, and it insulates (the enforcement of) collateral from insolvency proceedings. Moreover, the SFD provides for a conflict of laws rule regarding some proprietary issues of securities custody and transfer law. As a general matter, the SFD constitutes a departure from traditional European securities law legislation, where the focus lies on mutual recognition of home-country supervision.[120]

Article 3 is the SFD's pivotal provision of substantive law. It requires national laws to ensure that transfer orders and netting are enforceable once entered into a settlement system. Enforceability is to be ensured regardless of the commencement of insolvency proceedings against a participant of the settlement system after that entry, while Article 3 further states that the moment of entry should be defined by the rules of the system itself. From which moment onwards a transfer order cannot be revoked is also to be defined by the rules of the settlement system; Article 5.

Article 7 determines that the insolvency of a participant in the settlement system have no retroactive effects with regard to this and other participants' rights and obligations towards the system. This provision is complemented by Article 9(1), requiring the EU Member States to implement legislation that insulates (the enforcement of) collateral from the effects of insolvency proceedings commenced against a participant in a settlement system.

117. *White Paper, Financial Services Policy 2005–2010,* 4.
118. Directive 98/26/EC of the European Parliament and of the Council of 19 May 1998 on settlement finality in payment and securities settlement systems (OJ L 166/45).
119. *See* Recitals 2, 4 and 9.
120. *Cf.* Scott (2006), Ch. 10, 41.

Conflict of laws rules are found in Articles 8 and 9. The rationale behind both provisions is that neither the operator of a settlement system, nor its participants should have to take into account all national (insolvency) laws of the participants to determine their rights and obligations against the system. Article 8 provides that the effects of one of the participant's insolvency be determined by the law designated by the operator of the settlement system, thus deviating from the general rule under which the law of the jurisdiction where insolvency proceedings commenced will apply (*lex concursus*).[121]

When a participant has obtained collateral in the form of securities, Article 9(2) refers to the law of the EU jurisdiction where this participant's/collateral taker's rights are registered to determine their nature.[122] Although Article 9(2) may seem a straightforward application of the PRIMA rule,[123] several problems can be discerned, the most important of which appears to be its unclear scope.[124] Second, Article 9(2) may either refer to the law of the jurisdiction where the collateralised securities themselves are recorded (be it in the collateral provider's or in the collateral taker's name) or to the jurisdiction where the collateral taker's account is recorded. Third, this variation of PRIMA is widely criticised for the opacity of the criterion 'where the right is recorded', since a place of record appears to be arbitrary and extremely difficult, if not impossible, to establish in this age of computerisation.[125] Finally, Article 9(2) may refer to a non-Member State jurisdiction, whereas Article 9(2) also requires that a securities account be located in a Member State in order to be applicable, as a consequence of which the scope of the Article is further restricted.

Notwithstanding these difficulties and the diverging interpretations of the definitions used, the SFD has been implemented in all Member States with no significant deviations.[126] Moreover, the SFD has been evaluated by all Member States and the European Commission and it appears that it has contributed to the reduction of systemic risk.[127] On the other hand, it was noted that some clarifications, improvements, better definitions and possibly simplification would be appropriate, while the choice of law provisions were especially considered problematical.[128]

---

121. *See* Ooi (2003), 250. *Cf.* EU Insolvency Regulation Art. 9 (Council Regulation 1346/2000/EC of 29 May 2000 on insolvency proceedings (OJ L 160/1)).
122. *Cf.*, in slightly different wording, the Winding-up Directive Art. 25; *see infra.*
123. *See supra,* Ch. 3.3.3 *and infra,* Ch. 10.2.11.
124. Indeed, it has been considered to raise more questions than that it provides answers; Van Setten (2003), 296. *See also* Potok (2001), 60–61 *and* Haentjens (2006), 30–34.
125. *Cf.* Hague Securities Convention Art. 4(2)(a), Rogers (2005), 26 *and* Ooi (2003), 234. *Contra* Rank (2005), 259.
126. *Report from the Commission, Evaluation report on the Settlement Finality Directive 98/26/EC (EU25),* COM(2005), 657 final/2, 9. *Cf. also* Potok (2001), 62–63.
127. Although this cannot be quantified and has to be inferred from circumstantial evidence; *Report from the Commission, Evaluation report on the Settlement Finality Directive 98/26/EC (EU25),* COM(2005), 657 final/2, 10. *See also* Löber (2006), 19.
128. *Report from the Commission, Evaluation report on the Settlement Finality Directive 98/26/EC (EU 25),* COM(2005), 657 final/2, 9.

Finally, the fact that the SFD creates a special regime for very specific situations might also be a serious problem that should be addressed.[129]

9.3.3.2 Winding-Up Directive

The Winding-Up Directive[130] purports to harmonise rules on the reorganisation and winding-up of credit institutions, and in that context, it provides that the right of set-off of the insolvent credit institution's creditors must be acknowledged; Article 23. This directive also contains a conflict of laws rule. But unlike the rule of the SFD, which is confined to collateralised securities and participants of settlement systems, Winding-up Directive Article 24 applies to the enforcement of all property rights in the event of any credit institution's insolvency. Apart from this extension, the rule is similar to the SFD Article 9(2).[131] Notable is that the heading of this Article reads '*lex rei sitae*'.

9.3.3.3 Financial Collateral Directive

As a follow-up to the SFD, the purpose of the Financial Collateral Directive 2002 ('FCD')[132] was to solve the most important barriers hampering the easy provision of collateral. The FCD therefore applies both in and outside insolvency situations and is thus broader in scope than the SFD, but its applicability is also restricted to certain financial instruments as defined in Article 2(e)[133] and certain categories of counterparties as defined in Article 1(2). It must further be noted that, as does the SFD, the FCD aims at the complete harmonisation of substantive and private international law, rather than at minimum harmonisation and mutual recognition.[134]

It was thought that market liquidity would increase if national rules that impede the transfer of title by way of security and restrain the execution of collateral would be removed.[135] More in particular, the FCD extends the SFD in that it protects certain market participants from national insolvency rules when perfecting or exercising certain collateral arrangements as defined in Article 2(1). Secondly, the FCD harmonises national rules of enforcement and close-out netting. Notably, it requires national laws to allow for the enforcement of security interests by sale or appropriation without court approval or formalities; Article 4. Thirdly, under the directive, collateral agreements may authorise the collateral taker to

129. *See* Ch. 11.2.7, *and cf.* Partsch-Bobricheff (2005), 45, who defined this special regime as a 'parallel world'.
130. Directive 2001/24/EC of the European Parliament and of the Council of 4 April 2001 on the reorganisation and winding-up of credit institutions (OJ L 125/15).
131. Recital 25 explicitly refers to the SFD.
132. Directive 2002/47/EC of the European Parliament and of the Council of 6 June 2002 on financial collateral arrangements (OJ L 168/43).
133. The FCD's definition of financial instruments does not entirely coincide with the definition of financial instruments of the SFD; Van Beek & Van Bruggen (2002), 38.
134. Löber (2006), 21.
135. Recital 13.

dispose of the collateralised assets even before the security right is enforced (the right of use); Article 5.

Furthermore, the FCD provides a conflict of laws rule that addresses a number of problems which were not solved by the SFD. For instance, it explicitly excludes *renvoi* and its scope has been clarified to a certain extent. Most notably, the creation and therewith the validity of a security interest has been included in the list that enumerates the issues governed by the FCDS's conflict of laws rule. The conflict of laws rule itself, however, still seems sub-optimal. This variation of PRIMA, or more accurately PRACA for the Place of the Relevant Account Approach,[136] is both inconsistent with the SFD's rule and impractical.[137]

It is inconsistent with the SFD's rule, as the SFD's rule probably points to the place where the securities themselves are registered, i.e. where the securities are technically or operationally administered. The FCD's rule, on the other hand, points to the intermediary's location since it is the intermediary that must be considered to maintain the account. These two variations of PRIMA do not necessarily lead to different outcomes, however. It has further been argued that the FCD's deviation from the SFD's rule is 'merely a reflection of the fact that a securities account is "maintained" and not "located" in a specific place'.[138] Moreover, the connecting factor which the FCD employs ('the place where the relevant account is maintained') is an opaque one.[139] Does it point to the local branch of the custodian where the account is opened, to its head offices, to its place of incorporation or indeed to the place where the account is technically administrated?[140]

Besides the conflict of laws rule, the introduction of the collateral taker's right of appropriation as an enforcement mechanism and the collateral taker's right of use have led to fierce criticism.[141] Because of these objections and as a result of non-uniform implementation, modifications to the FCD might be considered in the evaluation process that the FCD itself provides for.[142]

9.3.3.4 MiFID

The Directive on Markets in Financial Instruments ('MiFID') was adopted on April 21, 2004.[143] Because of implementation difficulties, however, the European

136. De Vauplane & Daigre (2003), 34.
137. *See further* Haentjens (2006), 37–38.
138. Potok (2004), 212.
139. Regrettably, the definition of 'relevant account' provides no further guidance; FCD Art. 2(1)(h).
140. *Cf.* De Vauplane & Daigre (2003), 39, who argue that the provision should be interpreted in the light of the Hague Securities Convention.
141. *See,* extensively, Keijser (2006). *See also,* e.g., Johansson (2005) *and infra,* Ch. 10.1.
142. Löber (2005), 169.
143. Directive 2004/39/EC of the European Parliament and of the Council of 21 April 2004 on markets in financial instruments (PB L 145/1). *See further* COM(2000) 625 def. (OJ C 71 E/62), published on 19 November 2002, the European Central Bank's advice published on 12 June 2003: COM/2003/9 (OJ C 144/6) *and* the Explanatory Memorandum: COM(2000) 625 def. (OJ C 71 E/62), 87–88.

Commission proposed to extend the implementation deadline for the MiFID and the Council and Parliament agreed. At the time of writing, the deadline for effective application is November 2007.[144] The directive replaces the Investment Services Directive ('ISD')[145] of 1993, which grants authorised investment firms and banks a 'European passport' to employ their activities throughout the EU. Consequently, the passport gives direct or indirect access to clearing and settlement facilities provided for members of regulated EU markets. The MiFID extends this approach, on the basis of home-country authorisation.

From a securities custody law perspective, Article 13 is of particular interest as the MiFID determines that this provision is applicable to both investment firms and credit institutions,[146] whereas in principle, the directive addresses investment firms only and is not directed at credit institutions or custodians in general.[147] More importantly, Article 13(7) requires custodians to safeguard their clients' ownership rights, especially in the event of a custodian's insolvency, and to prevent the use of clients' instruments by custodians, except with the client's express consent.

As the legislative process of the MiFID followed the comitology procedure advocated in the already mentioned Lamfalussy 2001 Report, it has been drafted as a framework directive and leaves the details to the relevant specialist groups. In the case of MiFID Article 13, the Committee of European Securities Regulators ('CESR') has been designated as the relevant specialist group and it has accordingly advised that Article 13 requires a custodian to separate its own assets from those of its clients.[148]

Although Article 13 has been broadly drafted, CESR has thus only picked up its regulatory aspect, rather than interpreting it so as to refer to non-regulatory custody law as well. As will be argued below,[149] this is the better view, since the non-regulatory issues of securities custody law should be addressed elsewhere. Separation of assets by custodians, on the other hand, must indeed be considered a matter of regulatory law and is therefore justifiably addressed by CESR in the context of the implementation of the MiFID.

---

144. *See* COM(2005) 253 final *and* SEC(2006) 17, 6.
145. Council Directive 93/22/EEC of 10 May 1993 on investment services in the securities field (OJ L 141/1). This Directive follows the Second Council Directive 84/646/EEC on the coordination of laws, regulations and administrative provisions relating to the taking up and pursuit of the business of credit institutions and amending Directive 77/780/EEC, OJ L 386/27.
146. As defined in Directive 2000/12/EC; MiFID Art. 1(2).
147. *See also* Motion of the European Parliament of 6 June 2005, A6-0180/2005 final, 6, where the Parliament regrets this omission.
148. *See* Löber (2006), 27. But MiFID Art. 13 is very similar to its predecessor, ISD Art. 10, as Professor W.A.K. Rank has generously explained.
149. *Infra*, Ch. 10.2.5 *and* 12.3.5.

9.3.3.5 Shareholders' Rights Directive

As a recent development, the European Commission has issued a proposal for a directive on shareholders' rights.[150] This directive addresses problems of corporate law that arise when securities are held through an indirect holding system. More specifically, it proposes to abolish any requirement that shares be blocked, i.e. become non-tradable for a certain period of time, as a prerequisite for the exercise of voting rights at a general meeting of shareholders. Secondly, the directive purports to tackle the difficult and late access to corporate information that investors currently experience. Finally, it proposes to remove (national) legal obstacles to electronic participation in general meetings.

However, the proposed directive also directly covers aspects of securities custody law where it states that investors should have the choice between individual or omnibus securities accounts.[151] The directive further determines that where an intermediary manages omnibus accounts, it is not under the obligation to separate certain shares prior to a general meeting of shareholders, when the separation is a prerequisite for investors to exercise the voting rights attached to these shares.[152] Most importantly, Article 13(3) ensures that intermediaries may be authorised to exercise their clients' voting rights following their instruction. In the same vein, the Article expressly provides that an intermediary does not necessarily have to exercise all voting rights attached to the securities in its custody in the same manner.[153] Finally, Article 13(5) provides that an intermediary in whose name securities are registered at a higher tier should have the possibility to issue proxies to all its clients.

The topics that the just discussed provisions address arguably lie more within the scope of a possible future directive on substantive securities custody and transfer law than that they are typical of a company law directive. Especially where it does not specifically concern voting rights or the exercise thereof, it is submitted that legislation should be left to other instruments, either to regulatory instruments on the management of securities accounts or to an instrument that specifically addresses securities custody and transfer law. Such an approach would avoid difficult issues of scope, as the enjoyment of the rights attached to an accountholder's securities concern both corporate securities and non-corporate financial instruments, while the indirect holding system has the potential to hamper that enjoyment for both types of instruments.[154] At the same time, this approach would respond to the need for an internally coherent and comprehensive harmonised securities custody and transfer law within the EU.

150. Proposal for a Directive of the European Parliament and of the Council on the exercise of voting rights by shareholders of companies having their registered office in a Member State and whose shares are admitted to trading on a regulated market and amending Directive 2004/109/EC, COM(2005) 685 final.
151. Art. 13(1).
152. Art. 13(2).
153. Art. 13(4).
154. *See also infra,* Ch. 12.3.4.

9.3.4 Harmonisation of Securities Custody and Transfer Law

As has been shown in the previous section, several directives have been adopted that aim to harmonise securities law within the EU. But few directives provide for rules on book-entry securities custody and transfer law. Most important in this respect are the SFD and the FCD. Yet, these directives address rather specific transactions (collateral agreements) and situations (the insolvency of participants of the settlement systems). Other EU instruments must be classified as being either of regulatory law (MiFID) or corporate law (the proposed Shareholders' Rights Directive).

As a consequence, the European commercial law infrastructure of securities settlement remains as fragmented as the national securities custody and transfer laws of the EU Member States are diverse. It has become clear from the preceding chapters that virtually all existing legal types of custody can be found in the European Union, having been developed in very different systems of law and reflecting the specific socio-economic culture of each Member State.[155] Especially property and contract law regarding the custody and transfer of (book-entry) securities still varies to a large extent. To address the legal uncertainty and defective functioning of the internal market that this diversity causes, the European Commission first set up the Giovannini Group and later the Legal Certainty Group. The work of these groups and others will be discussed next.

9.3.4.1 Giovannini Group 2001 Report

In 1996, the European Commission set up the Giovannini Group (named after its chairman) to investigate the impediments hampering efficient cross-border settlement and the further integration of the European market. After the publication of reports on other issues,[156] it published a report in 2001 on the clearing and settlement infrastructure of the European Union. The report discerned fifteen barriers to the smooth functioning of the internal market, three of which were legal in nature.

The three legal barriers are listed as follows: the absence of a EU-wide framework for the treatment of interests in securities (barrier 13), national differences in the legal treatment of bilateral netting (barrier 14) and the uneven application of national conflict of laws rules (barrier 15). More specifically, the Giovannini Group 2001 Report attributed the absence of a EU-wide framework for the treatment of interests in securities (barrier 13) to national differences with regard to the characteristics of equities, to the diversity in the treatment of ownership and to the differences in the form of securities.[157]

155. Giovannini Group 2001 Report, 54.
156. Such as the impact of the introduction of the Euro and the efficiency of the euro-denominated government bond markets; *see* Löber (2006), 33.
157. Giovannini Group 2001 Report, 55.

It further concluded that the absence of an EU-wide framework for the treatment of interests in securities is most acutely felt when securities serve as collateral in cross-border situations. It found that legal differences as to the transfer of ownership and pledge then most clearly come to the fore, as a consequence of which cross-border collateralisation of securities represents a severe legal risk. Situations of insolvency are equally risk-prone, due to differences regarding the finality of transactions which is also directly related to the legal arrangement of securities transfer and ownership.[158]

Since the publication of the report, some aspects of barriers 13–15 have been addressed, mainly by the SFD and FCD, and the European Commission recognised that a global unification of conflict of laws rules could result from the endorsement of the Hague Securities Convention. It consequently proposed that the European Council should accordingly sign the HSC on behalf of the Member States and to amend the directives currently in force.[159] However, no decision to that effect has yet been taken, to which position a cautionary opinion from the European Central Bank ('ECB') has probably contributed.[160] Moreover, a EU-wide framework for the treatment of interests in securities is far from accomplished and barrier 13 therefore still remains as the greatest challenge to be tackled.

9.3.4.2 Giovannini Group and EFMLG 2003 Reports

As a follow-up to the first report of the Giovannini Group on securities clearing and settlement in 2001, the European Commission issued a consultation document through which it sought to investigate the market's opinion on the removal of the legal and tax barriers identified, as well as on the removal of competitive distortions between clearing and settlement providers.[161] In this document, the European Commission announced its intention to draft a 'Uniform Securities Code', but also acknowledged that such a code would be 'far from easy to design', because of the intricate links it would have with various areas of national law.[162]

In 2003, the Giovannini Group issued a second report on clearing and settlement within the EU. In this report, it did not express support for the Commission's idea of a European Securities Code. It argued that the EU should confine itself to the reform and harmonisation of certain aspects of securities law, most notably

158. Giovannini Group 2001 Report, 56.
159. Proposal for a Council decision concerning the signing of the Hague Securities Convention, COM(2003) 783 final. The proposal has been reiterated in the form of a recommendation after a legal assessment; Legal assessment of certain aspects of the Hague Securities Convention, of 3 July 2006, SEC(2006), 910. On the Hague Securities Convention, *see supra,* s. 9.2.4.
160. Opinion of the European Central Bank ('ECB') of 17 March 2005, CON/2005/7, OJ C 81/10. At the time of writing, a legal assessment was being carried out to help the Council decide whether to accept the Commission's proposal for signature; *White Paper, Financial Services Policy 2005–2010,* 13.
161. Communication from the Commission to the Council and the European Parliament, *Clearing and Settlement in the European Union, Main policy issues and future challenges,* COM(2002) 275. The competition issue has been addressed by the MiFID, *see supra,* s. 9.3.3.
162. COM(2002) 275, 12.

ownership of book-entry securities. The Group further substantiated the issues it addressed in its first report and proposed that a future harmonisation instrument should cover investors' ownership rights, but also investor protection from intermediary insolvency, the tradability of book-entry securities, priority issues and shortfalls in securities accounts.

The European Financial Market Lawyers Group ('EFMLG'), a private organisation set up in 1999 by the ECB, also issued a report in 2003, in which it supported the idea of a future European directive on the custody and transfer of book-entry securities. Moreover, it expressed further thoughts on the issues that such a directive should cover. First, the EFMLG indicated that a future directive should abolish all certificates, thus accomplishing full statutory dematerialisation at a Community level.[163] Second, it should describe the exact nature and extent of an investor's rights. Third, it should provide for the protection of investor's rights in intermediary insolvencies. Moreover, it should ensure the full tradability of book-entry securities, for instance by the protection of acquirers in good faith, and it should safeguard the safety of settlement systems by double-entry bookkeeping[164] and by the separation of an intermediary's own assets from those of its clients. In sum, a future framework directive should focus on the effects of the registration of securities by book-entry and, at the same time, address the organisation of securities infrastructure. On the other hand, the report acknowledged that the legal relationship between investor and intermediary should remain the prerogative of the Member States.[165]

The European Commission took due notice of both reports and released a second consultative document in April 2004.[166] In this document, the Commission acknowledged the findings of the second Giovannini Group report and subsequently set up a 'Clearing and Settlement Advisory and Monitoring Expert Group' ('CESAME') that would have to focus on operational and competitive aspects. The Commission further announced its intention to draft a directive that should provide market participants with access to clearing and settlement systems throughout the EU, a common regulatory framework and governance arrangements.[167]

With regard to the legal barriers discerned by the Giovannini Group, the Commission argued that barrier 14 had been addressed by the SFD and FCD, while barrier 15 had been removed not only by these same directives, but also by the Hague Securities Convention. Yet it recognised that the absence of an EU-wide framework for the treatment of interests in securities still hampers legal clarity and the overall soundness and efficiency of the Community infrastructure for securities

163. EFMLG 2003 Report, 21.
164. 'Double bookkeeping' refers to the direct correspondence of credits and debits of a beneficiary's account with the crediting and debiting of the counterparty's account; *see* ESCB-CESR 2004 Report, 86. *See also* EFMLG 2003 Report, 19.
165. EFMLG 2003 Report, 22.
166. Communication from the Commission to the Council and the European Parliament, *Clearing and Settlement in the European Union, The way forward,* COM(2004) 312 final.
167. COM(2004) 312 final, 13.

custody and settlement (barrier 13).[168] Consequently, it set up two study groups to investigate the issue further and to advise the Commission accordingly. First, the fiscal compliance group or FISCO examines the need for European harmonisation in view of the variations in national tax procedures and second, the Legal Certainty Group focuses on substantive law issues of custody, ownership and transfer of book-entry securities. As a first step, this group issued a detailed questionnaire to investigate the exact nature of the differences in the current national legal systems of all the EU Member States.

Finally, the Commission stated that future EU legislation should also address the diversity of national rules on the consequences of securities transfers for the exercise of corporate rights and that issuers should be able to choose the location of their securities.[169] The recent proposal for a directive on shareholders' rights has taken up the first of these two corporate law issues,[170] while the second one will perhaps be examined by the Legal Certainty Group.[171]

9.3.4.3 ESCB-CESR 2004 Report

In a joint effort by the Committee of European Securities Regulators ('CESR') and the European System of Central Banks ('ESCB'), they issued 'Standards for Securities Clearing and Settlement in the European Union' in September 2004. While the legal status of these standards is still unclear, they could serve as a basis for regulation by national authorities and be used as oversight standards by central banks.[172] In a motion adopted in June 2005, the European Parliament expressed very serious criticism of the timing, the legal basis and the content of these standards.[173]

The ESCB-CESR standards are based on the CPSS/IOSCO Recommendations 2001 and address mainly operational technicalities.[174] As does CPSS/IOSCO standard 1, the ESCB-CESR standards require a well-founded, clear and transparent legal basis for clearing and settlement systems and the links between them.[175] But unlike the CPSS/IOSCO standards, ESCB-CESR standard 1 refers to the SFD and, more importantly, promotes European harmonisation of laws in order to reduce systemic risk by minimising the discrepancies between national rules.[176] Standard 12 is similar to CPSS/IOSCO standard 12 in that it also requires intermediaries to 'fully' protect customers' securities and stresses that it is 'essential'

168. COM(2004) 312 final, 24.
169. COM(2004), 312 final, 26. *See also* LÖBER (2005), 183–184.
170. *See supra,* 9.3.3.
171. *See* Advice of the EU Clearing and Settlement Legal Certainty Group of 11 August 2006 (hereinafter: Legal Certainty Group Advice), 1, *available at* <http://ec.europa.eu/internal_market/>.
172. LÖBER (2005), 187.
173. Motion of the European Parliament of June 6 2005, A6-0180/2005 final, 7–8.
174. *See supra,* s. 9.2.2.
175. ESCB-CESR 2004 Report, 15.
176. ESCB-CESR 2004 Report, 15 and 19.

that 'customers' securities be protected against the claims of the creditors of all entities involved in the custody chain'. Compared to the CPSS/IOSCO Standards, ESCB-CESR standard 12 requires more explicitly a customer's consent before an intermediary may use (or vest a lien in) this customer's securities for its own business. Furthermore, it is more detailed in its support of double bookkeeping and segregation of intermediary's securities from its clients'.[177]

9.3.4.4 Recent Developments

The European Parliament closely followed the work of the Commission and that of the groups which the Commission had established. In June 2005, it adopted a motion in which it stated that it saw no need for a framework directive on the regulation of clearing and settlement providers. Further, it concluded that the higher costs of cross-border settlement of securities transactions are mainly caused by inconsistencies between national laws. Consequently, the motion supported the work of the Legal Certainty Group investigating the desirability of a directive on securities custody and transfer law. It even urged the Commission to make this work a 'priority instrument for promoting convergence at European level', [178] but it also acknowledged that it might take 'many years' to achieve such harmonisation. It further required that economic and impact assessments be made before legislative instruments would be drafted.[179]

As a follow-up, a study group set up by the European Commission found in its 'Draft Working Document on Post-Trading' that the harmonisation of national securities laws and, more generally, a reduction in post-trading costs, would lead to a higher GDP of between 0.2 per cent and 0.6 per cent in the subsequent years.[180] These (preliminary) findings stress the economic benefits of European harmonisation and the Legal Certainty Group therefore continued to prepare its advice to the Commission.

Most recently, the Legal Certainty Group completed a concise report of the responses to the questionnaire mentioned above and published its advice to the European Commission. In short, the Group advised that legislative action be taken to harmonise the legal effects of book-entries, but did not disclose a view on the specific form which harmonisation should take. It further suggested that

177. ESCB-CESR 2004 Report, 60–62. On double bookkeeping, *see* Ch. 10.2.5.
178. Motion of the European Parliament of 6 June 2005, A6-0180/2005 final, 14.
179. This requirement is in accordance with the European Commission's policy for the years 2005–2010 to legislate only when strictly necessary and only when tangible benefits have been *ex ante* determined; *see,* e.g., Commission Staff Working Document, *Single Market in Financial Services Progress Report 2004–2005,* SEC(2006), 17, 3.
180. This estimate is the result of different model specifications. Further, it should be noted that the figure is dependent on the competitive form of the market and changes in the behaviour of economic agents have not been calculated; Draft Working Document on Post-Trading, 48–50.

ratification of a possible future UNIDROIT instrument might be preferable to the enactment of separate EU legislation.[181]

More specifically, the Legal Certainty Group argued that any harmonisation instrument should be based on the following principles: an accountholder should have the right to dispose of his securities, and to retrieve them when requested. These rights should be of a mandatory law nature. Furthermore, an accountholder should have the right to exercise the corporate rights attached to his securities, and to receive the corporate information necessary for such exercise. These rights, however, might be addressed by the proposed Shareholders' Rights Directive. All accountholder's rights should arise at the moment of a credit, and extinguish at the moment of a debit entry in an accountholder's securities account.

The Legal Certainty Group further advised that any intermediary should be under the obligation to: maintain sufficient assets to satisfy its clients' claims, to provide its clients with corporate information, to pass on corporate information and to exercise instructions with regard to corporate actions, to exercise instructions with regard to its clients' securities account, to segregate its own assets from its clients' assets and to replace those assets when required. Only the first of these obligations should be of a mandatory law nature, while the two following obligations might be addressed by the proposed Shareholders' Rights Directive. Other mechanisms that the Legal Certainty Group proposed in order to protect an accountholder's rights include: protection of a *bona fide* purchaser of book-entry securities, a prohibition of upper-tier attachment and an insulation of an accountholder's rights from his intermediary's insolvency.

At the time of writing, the European Commission had not yet responded to the Legal Certainty Group's advice.

9.4 CONCLUSION

The analyses just discussed show that a fully efficient functioning of the European internal market is still hampered by legal barriers. It has further become clear that these barriers are neither sufficiently, exhaustingly nor adequately dealt with by either existing EU legislation or the recommendations discussed above.[182] The global recommendations mentioned could not result in the dramatic legal modernisation and harmonisation that is currently necessary, while the EU instruments discussed have been proven to be limited in scope as they cover rather specific transactions and situations. In addition, they have not addressed national differences that still exist with regard to investors' ownership rights, investor protection from intermediary insolvency, the tradability of book-entry securities, priority

181. Legal Certainty Group Advice, 10.

182. *Cf. Operational Conclusions established at the CESAME meeting of 8 June 2006,* 17 and 18. The current EU legislation on securities accounts has even been referred to as a 'legal patchwork'; PARTSCH-BOBRICHEFF (2005), 40.

issues and shortfalls. Moreover, the conflict of law rules provided for in these instruments are inconsistent and not globally compatible.[183]

As a consequence, the European Commission and other entities are investigating the desirability and substance of a harmonisation instrument that addresses these issues so as to provide a European legal framework on book-entry securities.[184] Such an instrument should principally aim at the limitation of risk and investor protection.[185] Furthermore, it should be consistent with existing Community legislation and be compatible globally, notably with the recommendations discussed above.[186] In the next chapter, it will be discussed in detail to what extent the European jurisdictions that have been analysed in the previous chapters should be modified to meet these policy goals, especially in the light of existing US law, the UNIDROIT initiative and the advice of the Legal Certainty Group. Whether a European harmonisation instrument that fosters financial stability and investor protection will be prohibitively complicated by the relationship between securities custody and transfer law with property, contract and commercial law, will be the subject of Chapter 11.

183. *Cf.* HAENTJENS (2006), 38.

184. The Commission also considers legislative action to eliminate the current barriers that exist in the area of bank accounts (current, savings and as well as securities accounts); *White Paper, Financial Services Policy 2005–2010,* 14.

185. *Cf.* LÖBER (2005), 156 and 188 *and* LÖBER (2006), 61. *See* SMITS (2006), 72 *et seq.* for a (critical) discussion of these policy goals in the area of European private law harmonisation.

186. LÖBER (2005), 185. On 20 December 2005, the European Commission announced that it had been granted authority by the European Council to take part in the UNIDROIT negotiations on behalf of the EU; press release of 20 December 2005, IP/05/1637.

Chapter 10
National Securities Laws Compared and Evaluated

10.1 INTRODUCTION

As has been shown in the preceding chapter, the barriers that impede the smooth functioning of the European internal market with regard to the settlement of securities transactions are neither sufficiently, exhaustively, nor adequately addressed by existing EU legislation. Both for substantive law and conflict of laws rules a common legal framework is lacking, which leads to legal uncertainty and higher costs in the settlement of cross-border transactions. It has been argued that as a consequence, the European Commission and other entities are justifiably investigating the feasibility and substance of a harmonisation instrument to provide such a framework.

It is submitted that the smooth functioning of the European internal market is as much hampered by legal diversity as it is frustrated by outdated doctrines that do not fit current market practices. The process of European harmonisation should therefore not only result in the international compatibility of national laws, but also be considered an opportunity to modernise outdated domestic systems. In other words, a new European regime of securities custody and transfer law should be sought, rather than merely making the laws of all Member States compatible.

The joint objectives of 'compatibility' and 'internal soundness' have accordingly been formulated as explicit policy goals for a future instrument of global harmonisation for the UNIDROIT project.[1] It is the present author's view that with regard to the European harmonisation process, the 'internal soundness' of national securities custody and transfer laws could be achieved through a modernisation that aims at minimising the legal risk (thus contributing to the financial stability of

1. UNIDROIT 2003 Position Paper 5 and 13.

the market) and maximising investor protection.[2] Furthermore, all modernisation initiated at the Community level should be consistent with existing Community legislation or the *acquis communautaire* and be compatible globally, notably with the recommendations that have been examined in the previous chapter and with the proposed UNIDROIT instrument.[3]

It has been argued, however, that the European harmonisation and modernisation should go further than the UNIDROIT project, i.e. a higher degree of uniformity should be the objective of an EU instrument, because European systems would already show a degree of integration that is absent at the global level.[4] However, all Community legislation initiatives are curbed by the principle of subsidiarity, according to which supranational law should restrict itself to matters that cannot be better left to the national sphere. This principle has been codified in the EC Treaty and it will be ascertained in a later chapter whether the modernisation measures that will be proposed in the following sections exceed the boundaries of the Treaty.[5]

While it is generally accepted that national securities custody and transfer laws should have a clear and transparent legal basis,[6] so that parties are able 'to determine in advance with certainty and predictability the substantive law that will govern their rights and obligations',[7] this rather general principle must be substantiated in more detailed standards. In the next sections therefore, principal aspects of the securities laws of Belgium, France and the Netherlands, as analysed in chapters 5 to 7, will be compared and evaluated. For the evaluation, the said aspects will be tested against the recommendations as discussed in the previous chapter, in order to ascertain to what extent the jurisdictions investigated must be modernised in the context of a possible European harmonisation.

10.2 PRINCIPLES OF MODERNISATION AND POLICY PERSPECTIVES

10.2.1 INTRODUCTION

As has just been indicated, a modernisation of European securities custody and transfer laws should aim at achieving financial stability and investor

2. *Cf.* LÖBER (2005), 156 and 188 *and* LÖBER (2006), 61. *See* SMITS (2006), 72 *et seq.* for a (critical) discussion of these policy goals in the area of European private law harmonisation. The most recent economic impact assessment estimates that the result of a reduction in post-trading costs results in an increase of GDP of between 0.2per cent and 0.6per cent in the subsequent years; Draft Working Document on Post-Trading, 48-50. Interestingly, the UNIDROIT 2003 Position Paper, 28 states that the issues that require the 'balancing of considerations such as investor protection, freedom of contract and economic efficiency' should remain the prerogatives of national legislature.
3. LÖBER (2005), 185. On 20 December 2005, the European Commission announced that it had been granted authority by the European Council to take part in the UNIDROIT negotiations on behalf of the EU; press release of 20 December 2005, IP/05/1637.
4. *Cf.* LÖBER (2005), 188. *See* Ch. 12.4.3.
5. Ch. 12.2.
6. CPSS/IOSCO Recommendations 2001, Recommendation 1 *and* ESCB-CESR 2004 Report, 15.
7. GUYNN (1996), 33.

protection.[8] Although these policy goals necessarily intertwine because financial stability contributes to the optimal protection of accountholders and vice versa, the latter one is specifically served with rules that preserve an accountholder's rights in intermediary insolvencies, with rules that ensure the processing of information related to corporate actions and the exercise thereof, and with a prohibition of upper-tier attachment. Intimately connected to these rules, but more general in character, are the rules that clearly state the effects of credit entries in a securities account and define the nature of an entitlement to securities held in a securities account. Financial stability on the other hand, is specifically served with clear rules on the transfer of securities by book-entry, with the protection of an acquirer in good faith, with the ensured finality of securities transfers, with clear rules on the collateralisation of securities, and with harmonised rules on the eligibility of securities and intermediaries.[9]

It has been argued, however, that modern rules on these subjects would alter current security, property and insolvency law mechanisms and structures.[10] In this view, the alteration would unacceptably weaken the position of investors and result in a shift in balance between creditors, merely to the advantage of large financial institutions.[11] Especially liberal regimes for the enforcement of security interests in financial collateral, the protection of an intermediary's creditors in good faith and party autonomy with regard to the choice of law have given cause for such criticism.

The extent to which modern legal regimes for book-entry securities would alter security and property law (and, to a lesser extent, insolvency law), is the subject of the next chapter, where it will be shown that the modernisation of securities custody and transfer laws need not result in any substantial alteration of more general areas of law. The argument that the modernisation of securities custody and transfer laws will necessarily weaken the position of investors will be discussed in greater detail below, but it must already be briefly stated here that that argument cannot withstand closer scrutiny, principally because it assumes an equalisation of investors/accountholders to (retail) consumers, and creditors to financial institutions. But, as Rogers has put it: the divide between (secured) creditors and accountholders does not translate 'neatly into any lines of class, wealth, power, or the like', since accountholders may just as plausibly be 'large

8. *Cf.* Art. 3(1)(c), (h), (m) and (t) of the Treaty Establishing the European Community. Sections (c) and (h) refer to the establishment of a common or internal market and the according 'approximation' of laws, while section (t) refers to consumer protection as a policy goal of which the European Community has the authority to act. Section (m) refers to the strengthening of the competitiveness of the Community as a policy goal.
9. *Cf.* the EFMLG 2003 Report, in which the Group advocates a European harmonisation instrument that is based on two pillars, viz. the organisation of the securities infrastructure on the one hand, and the effects of book-entries on the other.
10. According to Johansson (2005), 1109 and 1114, 'clear examples' of this could be given. Unfortunately, she does not provide such examples, nor does she substantiate her statement.
11. Johansson (2005), 1115.

financial institutions', as creditors may represent retail consumers (e.g. pension funds and the like).[12]

10.2.2 Securities Infrastructure

10.2.2.1 Securities Eligible[13]

Various reports support the full dematerialisation of securities and recommend that all certificates be replaced by book-entries in securities accounts or registers.[14] Market stability is arguably enhanced when no disputes can arise over lost, stolen or otherwise disappeared certificates. Moreover, it has been calculated that the costs of custody and administration are substantially reduced by complete dematerialisation.[15] This recommendation is, of course, mainly directed at jurisdictions where certificated bearer securities form the majority of securities in circulation. Of the jurisdictions investigated in the previous chapters, it therefore concerns the Netherlands and the US, as practically all French securities have been dematerialised since the 1980s, while Belgian securities will be dematerialised over the next decade.

On the other hand, mistakes can also be made when securities are processed by book-entry, with costly litigation as a consequence (operational risk).[16] In addition, (full) dematerialisation may increase the risk that intermediaries create interests in securities by credit entries in their clients' securities accounts without having obtained the corresponding assets at the higher tier.[17] Furthermore, measures to achieve full dematerialisation may also come at substantial costs, since it has serious consequences for both legislation and market practices. The (market-driven!)

12. Rogers (1996), 1529.
13. On the harmonisation of the concepts 'securities' and 'financial instruments', *see infra,* Ch. 12.3.2.
14. Giovannini Group 2001 Report, 59, Giovannini Group 2003 Report, 14, EFMLG 2003 Report, 7 and 20 *and* G30 2003 Plan of Action, Recommendation 1.
15. DTCC estimates that the annual costs of issuing, storing and processing paper certificates in the US is USD 250 million, while the costs of processing a single paper certificate transfer is estimated to be USD 32 more than a non-certificated one; *see* 'USD 250 million – The Annual Cost of Processing Paper Securities', the first in DTCC's 'no-more-paper' series. In France, it was estimated that the costs of custody could be reduced by 40per cent to 45per cent by the dematerialisation of all securities; Ripert & Roblot (1996), no. 1758.
16. *Cf.* Ch. 4.4. As anecdotal evidence, a mistake by the Japanese brokerage firm Mizuho may be referred to. Mizuho intended to sell 1 share of J-Com for JPY 610,000 (USD 5,065), but instead offered 610,000 shares for JPY 1 a piece. The value of these shares together was then USD 3.1 billion. Because of the very strict finality rules of the Japanese clearing and settlement system as well as exchange rules, the order could not be reversed, as a consequence of which the loss could amount to more than JPY 30 billion (USD 250 million); CNN press report of 9 December 2005. *Cf. also infra,* s. 10.2.8.
17. The author is grateful to Professor W.A.K. Rank for his explanation on this point. *See also infra,* s. 10.2.5.

efforts to dematerialise US securities custody,[18] the complex Belgian legislation[19] and the rigorous French legislation of 1981[20] may testify to this statement. Moreover, it could be questioned to what extent market stability will be enhanced when certificates are already immobilised at a CSD.

While perhaps not eliminating all risks of theft and the like, the immobilisation of securities certificates in the vaults of a CSD certainly minimises these risks, since physical movements of certificates are thus reduced to a minimum and virtually all transfers must be settled by book-entries. In some legal systems, however, immobilisation has resulted in the impairment of investors' rights; whereas investors may have enjoyed property rights as to their directly held securities, immobilisation may have resulted in the conversion of these rights into a purely contractual entitlement. In the Netherlands, for example, the practice of immobilisation led to the enactment of the Wge. But this Act only protects certain investors in domestic securities. Investors in foreign securities are ordinarily left with a mere contractual claim, while fourth and lower than fourth-tier investors also remain unprotected.[21]

It must be concluded that where immobilisation of securities results in complex and unclear legal constructions, for instance because rules of direct holding are applied to securities held through accounts, or has the impairment of investor protection as a consequence, full statutory dematerialisation could be considered at the national level. However, it should not be a top priority for a future European harmonisation instrument that provides investor protection while catering for both immobilisation and dematerialisation.[22]

10.2.2.2 Intermediaries Eligible

Which intermediaries may be admitted to a national system of book-entry securities custody to act as account providers is in most jurisdictions left to the discretion of the CSD. Under French and Dutch law, for instance, the CSD determines the admission of intermediaries, under the supervision of the Government or one of its agencies.[23] Under Belgian law, the CSD determines the eligibility of intermediaries to provide securities accounts for immobilised securities, while the Government itself decides on the admission of dematerialised securities account providers.[24]

18. *See,* e.g., <www.dtcc.com/nomorepaper> for the 'no more paper' campaign of DTCC.
19. *See* Ch. 5.2.
20. *See* Ch. 6.1.3.
21. *See supra,* Ch. 7.3.1 and 7.3.5.
22. The Legal Certainty Group has taken a similar position; *see* Legal Certainty Group Advice, 5. *Cf. also* Drobnig (1988), 40-41.
23. Art. L. 621-7 VI(2) C. mon. fin. (the admission of intermediaries to the CSD's central system of custody is supervised by the *Autorité des Marchés Financiers,* France) and Art. 1 Wge (the CSD determines which securities and which institutions are admitted, the Netherlands). *See* Chapters 6.3.1 *and* 7.3.4 respectively.
24. KB no. 62 Art. 1(2) (for immobilised securities) *and* the Act of 2 January 1991 Art. 3 and Art. 468(3) W. Venn. (for dematerialised securities). *See* Ch. 5.3.4.

Although an important matter, it is submitted that it lies more within the realm of regulatory and competition law, so that no modernisation measure on this issue would be advisable in the context of a substantive law instrument on securities custody and transfer law.[25]

10.2.3 Characterisation of Accountholder Interests

At the international level, no consensus exists on what the dogmatic nature, or legal classification of accountholders' rights should be.[26] General consensus does seem to exist, on the other hand, on what the effects of a credit in a securities account should be; from an accountholder's perspective, these effects include the right to dispose of and to vest security interests in his securities, the right to enjoy the 'fruits' (i.e. dividends etc.) and the exercise of corporate actions attached to his securities, as well as the right to revendicate and retrieve his assets.[27]

These rights are all elements of the traditional concept of ownership in continental European jurisdictions and it has therefore been argued that investors' entitlements should be classified as constructions of (co-)ownership.[28] In this view, accountholder entitlements that are contractual and not proprietary in nature provide less investor protection, also because, contrary to contractual interests, a proprietary entitlement may be asserted *erga omnes.* Any harmonisation or modernisation of securities laws should therefore adopt a property law approach.[29]

Yet investor protection may be ensured by other means than a traditional property right. A contractual right with an absolute priority or a statutory obligation of an insolvent intermediary's liquidator such as provided for under French law[30] for instance, guarantee the protection of investors' interests in an intermediary insolvency. A prohibition for intermediaries to dispose of accountholders' assets would further contribute to that protection. With such rules, a contractual regime protects accountholder interests in a way that is similar to any proprietary regime, especially because a proprietary entitlement can normally, i.e. outside of intermediary insolvency situations, only be enforced against the immediate intermediary.

Under Belgian law, for instance, accountholders enjoy a right of co-ownership with respect to the securities that their securities accounts refer to. This co-ownership right, however, may be enforced only against an accountholder's immediate intermediary and is effective *erga omnes* solely in the instance of the

25. *Accord* Legal Certainty Group Advice, 10. *Cf. also* EU Parliament: 'Sees no evidence that the providers of clearing and settlement services are poorly regulated at the national level, albeit in different ways across the EU, or that any systemic risk they pose in inadequately controlled'; Motion of the European Parliament of 6 June 2005, A6-0180/2005 final, 5.
26. *See,* e.g., Legal Certainty Group Advice, 4.
27. *See,* e.g., Unidroit draft convention Art. 5(1).
28. *See infra,* Ch. 11.2.2.
29. Than *in* Guynn et al. (1996), 76. *Cf.* Schwarcz (2001), 295 *et seq.*
30. Art. L. 431-6 C. mon. fin. *See* Ch. 6.3.5.

immediate intermediary's insolvency.[31] In Dutch law, accountholders' co-ownership rights are also not enforceable *erga omnes.* Moreover, they also differ in other aspects from the private law rules on co-ownership.[32] In other countries, the distinction between a contractual and a proprietary interest has become so fuzzy where it concerns accountholder entitlements that authors disagree vehemently as to the correct classification. In France, for instance, accountholders' rights can be asserted against third parties, but the intangible character of dematerialised securities, the object of these rights, does not allow classification as a right *in rem.*[33]

Because of these (and other) difficulties, the drafters of the 1994 US UCC reform decided to refrain from a property or contract law classification and to introduce the concept of 'securities entitlement'. This *sui generis* concept was considered to refer most adequately to the fundamentally hybrid character of accountholder interests. Although it is the author's view that this approach best corresponds with modern practice and has the highest potential to protect account holder's rights, it is questionable whether the dogmatic tradition of continental European jurisdictions will allow the introduction of such a concept.[34]

As a consequence, UNIDROIT, the Hague Conference and the Legal Certainty Group considered a functional approach the best course to take.[35] In such an approach, legislation refrains from prescribing any legal classification. Although characterisation plays an important role in the private international law of many jurisdictions, the HSC avoids all substantive classifications and provides a conflict of laws rule that expressly caters for accountholder interests of both a purely contractual and proprietary nature.[36] The UNIDROIT instrument will probably neither require its participating states to characterise accountholder interests nor to implement a specific legal construct, but focuses on the effects of a credit entry and provides minimum standards with regard to these effects.[37] The Legal Certainty Group ultimately copied this approach, although some members of the group expressed their strong disagreement with the position.[38]

It is indeed questionable whether the functional approach can guarantee a required degree of harmonisation in view of interstate compatibility, even if the substantive elements of accountholder interests are harmonised.[39] In view of the

31. *See supra,* Ch. 5.3.6.
32. Ch. 7.3.5.
33. *See* Ch. 6.3.5. *Cf.,* e.g., SMITS (1996), esp. 50 *et seq.*, arguing that in general, modern legal practice can draw little benefit from a (sharp) dogmatic boundary between property law and contract law as Von Savigny had advocated.
34. *See infra,* Ch. 11.2.2.
35. *Cf.* EFMLG 2003 Report, 14.
36. *See* HAENTJENS (2006), 97–98.
37. In first instance, however, UNIDROIT considered the introduction of a 'securities entitlement' concept; *see* PAECH (2002), 1160. *Cf. also supra,* Ch. 9.2.3.
38. Legal Certainty Group Advice, 3–4 *and* Annex to the advice of the Group (July 2006), 11–12 (Italian contribution). *See also* the earlier draft of the group's advice ('LCG Draft Advice'), 10–11, where the group considered advising the introduction of a new name for the package of accountholder rights.
39. UNIDROIT Implementation Report, February 2006, Doc. 26 of Study LXXVIII, 9.

'internal soundness' of European jurisdictions on the other hand, modernising the characterisation of accountholder interests is not essential, provided the substantive elements of accountholder interests are adequately modernised, i.e. they provide a sufficient degree of investor protection. This question will be investigated *below*.

10.2.4 Effects of a Credit Entry

10.2.4.1 Tracing

In many jurisdictions, securities held through an intermediary are administered in a so-called pool and registered in the intermediary's name at the higher tier. As a consequence, securities that belong to the different clients of the intermediary are commingled. Commingling poses problems of ownership, which are solved differently by different jurisdictions.[40] Some jurisdictions, to a varying extent, hold on to the traditional property law principle of *droit de suite,* so that accountholders remain entitled to a property right on individual assets.[41] Such a direct property right implies the tracing of that right from the investor asserting it through the custody chain, up to the location of the securities and the person holding them.

Mooney and others have convincingly shown that such a traceable property right in individual securities corresponds poorly to the modern practice of indirect holding, in which numerous intermediaries may be interposed between the ultimate investor and the securities themselves, while the securities might be located in different countries.[42] In the same vein, Guynn has advocated that, as the first of his four 'fundamental principles' of the modernisation of securities law, interests in securities held through an intermediary should relate to an untraceable and pro rata portion of the pool of securities or interests in securities held by that intermediary.[43] It is submitted that such an interest indeed corresponds best with the modern practice of indirect holding with multiple intermediaries interposed between issuer and ultimate accountholder and that investors are therefore most likely to be best protected under such an approach.[44]

The view that traceable interests do not serve investor protection is exemplified by the current Netherlands law. Under Dutch law, an investor enjoys proprietary protection in intermediary insolvencies as a result of his direct property right in the (actual) securities to which he is entitled. Under the applicable Act, however, this direct property right can only be conferred upon participants of the CSD and their clients. Thus, lower-tier accountholders are not granted proprietary

40. Bernasconi (2000), 20 *and cf.* Ch. 3.2.4.
41. *See* Ch. 11.2.2.
42. Mooney (1990), 310, 313 and 378. *Cf. also* Rogers (1995), 694 *and* Guttman (1990), 453. *Cf. also* Sommer (1998), 1184 *et seq.*
43. Guynn *in* Guynn et al. (1996), 10 and 33–35.
44. *Cf.* Einsele (1997), 273, advocating the abolition of the co-ownership construct in favour of a UCC-like construct for German law.

protection and are left with a mere contractual claim against their insolvent account provider's liquidator.[45] Under Belgian law on the other hand, accountholders also enjoy a property right, but not one in actual securities. It is the aggregate number of securities of the same kind that are held by or via their immediate intermediary to which Belgian accountholders are entitled under the applicable Act(s).[46] As a consequence, investors enjoy their property rights against their immediate intermediary regardless of where the actual securities are located and regardless of the number of intermediaries interposed. The 'direct' character of these rights only emerges in the account provider's insolvency, when accountholders may enforce their property rights against all upper-tier intermediaries, including the CSD.

In France, accountholders do not unequivocally enjoy a property law interest, but the protection of their interest is ensured by statutory law, which requires that the account provider's bankruptcy administrator transfers all investors' securities to accounts with other intermediaries.[47] Under the US UCC, on the other hand, accountholders also do not enjoy a traditional property law interest, but they take free of the intermediary's general creditors' claims because accountholders' securities entitlements do not form part of the insolvent intermediary's estate.[48]

In sum, a modernisation of securities custody law in this respect would be advisable, especially in systems like the Dutch, but only to the extent that national laws should not be required to withhold accountholders their due protection in intermediary insolvencies. As the Belgian situation shows, the direct property law character of accountholder interests is not necessarily detrimental to the soundness of the custody system nor to accountholder interests, provided that tracing is confined to insolvency situations and not subject to a limited number of intermediaries interposed. French and US law provide examples of non-property law constructs that provide adequate accountholder protection in their intermediary's insolvency. The UNIDROIT draft convention includes a minimum standard of investor protection in intermediary insolvencies,[49] while the Legal Certainty Group ultimately decided to copy this approach and did not advise the abolition of all tracing mechanisms.[50]

---

45. Notwithstanding regulatory rules such as Art. 6:14 *et seq. Nadere Regeling gedragstoezicht financiële ondernemingen Wft* (Further Regulations of Financial Institutions Supervision Wft), that intend to mitigate this lack of accountholder protection. *See* Kas-Associatie/Drying Corp., HR 23 September 1994, NJ 1996, 461. Paradoxically, it was the intangible nature of investor interests that prevented the applicability of Art. 3:110 BW, which would have allowed lower tier accountholders to obtain such a (direct) property right. *See* Ch. 7.3.5.
46. *See* Ch. 6.3.6.
47. Art. L. 431-6 C. mon. fin. *See also* Art. L. 213-2 C. mon. fin. *and* Ch. 6.3.5.
48. UCC § 8-503(a). *See* Ch. 8.3.4.
49. *Cf.* UNIDROIT draft convention Art. 15.
50. Interestingly, the Legal Certainty Group ultimately decided not to advise the prohibition or impediment of 'any market practice for holding securities', including tracing systems; Legal Certainty Group Advice, 5. In the LCG Draft Advice, however, it stressed the 'artificiality' of tracing and showed the inefficiency of systems that are based on a direct property right; LCG Draft Advice, 8–9.

10.2.4.2 Evidence

Guynn has argued that interests in securities held through an intermediary should be evidenced solely by the interest holder's account with that intermediary,[51] while the Giovannini Group stated that securities accounts must provide accountholders with certainty as to their 'ownership'.[52] In these views, a credit entry in a securities account should ensure that an accountholder can enjoy the rights he is entitled to, and also represent the only way to evidence investors' interests.

In this regard, evidence of the existence of securities themselves, which is ultimately provided by the issuer's register in most jurisdictions, must be distinguished from evidence of interests in those securities. In situations of direct holding, i.e. when no intermediaries are interposed between issuer and investor, these two coincide and the issuer's register prevails in the case of conflict over (the existence of) interests in securities. But when securities are indirectly held, discrepancies arise more easily between the existence of securities as evidenced by the issuer's register and interests in securities as evidenced by securities accounts.

As a consequence, securities may exist that are not evidenced by any securities account, while interests in securities may be evidenced by securities accounts that do not relate to existing securities. The latter is also known as 'over-issuance' and happens when the aggregate amount of securities held by an intermediary's clients does not match the number of securities expressed by that intermediary's (omnibus) account with the CSD or (other) higher intermediary. In those situations, the latter accounts prevail.[53]

Over-issuance can result from both unauthorised and authorised actions by an intermediary. If an unauthorised intermediary disposes of its clients' securities, a deficit and over-issuance consequently arises, provided the intermediary cannot make up the deficit with its own assets. Such unauthorised disposals and its consequences will be discussed in greater detail *below*.[54] On the other hand, an intermediary may be instructed to credit a client account without maintaining sufficient assets at the higher tier(s). As will be discussed *infra,* however, such authorised over-issuance or conditional credits are not always allowed in the jurisdictions investigated.[55]

However, under the laws of all jurisdictions investigated, a credit to a securities account evidences the accountholder's interests in securities, even in situations of over-issuance. In principle, however, the deficit that thus occurs will only have to be allocated in intermediary insolvency situations and the different possible

51. Guynn *in* Guynn et al. (1996), 33–35.
52. Giovannini Group 2003 Report, 14.
53. The relationship between the issuer and CSD may be considered one of direct holding and when a conflict arises between the CSD's account and the issuer's register, the issuer's register prevails.
54. Section 10.2.5.
55. Section 10.2.5.

mechanisms of allocation will be examined *below*.[56] Moreover, interests in securities that are not evidenced by a securities account are only honoured in the rare circumstances that the rights of an accountholder who unlawfully holds his account can successfully be challenged. These circumstances will be further discussed in the context of the finality of securities transfers.[57]

As it is acknowledged that it is imperative, both from an investor protection and a market stability perspective, that accountholders can rely on credit entries in their securities accounts, such credits in securities accounts should represent interests in securities that cannot successfully be challenged except in rare instances and whose enforceability is independent from the existence of the securities themselves. As shall be shown in greater detail *below*, all jurisdictions investigated generally adhere to this principle concerning its components as just discussed and, therefore, no general modernisation is needed in this respect.

10.2.5 Accountholder Protection Against the Intermediary

It is a basic characteristic of the indirect holding system that accountholders allow intermediaries to administer their assets. Perhaps the most important principle to be observed when modernising or harmonising securities law from an investor protection perspective therefore refers to the protection of accountholders against any abuse of the accountholders' assets by the intermediaries and their creditors. Protection can be provided in several ways, of which ownership rights and priorities in intermediary insolvencies are the most important.[58] Some characteristics of ownership rights have already been discussed, while priority issues in intermediary insolvencies will be dealt with in a later section.[59] But besides these methods of protecting investors, other, more specific rules are warranted, which will be discussed in the following section.

10.2.5.1 Illegal Disposal by Intermediaries

First, intermediaries should not be allowed to dispose of their clients' assets without the explicit consent of the clients concerned.[60] If the relationship between accountholder and intermediary would be classified as a contract of *depositum* (*regulare*), the prohibition would follow from this classification, as under the laws of all European jurisdictions investigated, *depositum* prohibits intermediaries from using deposited assets.[61] This classification, however, is fiercely debated and is indeed debateable.

56. Section 10.2.6.
57. Section 10.2.8.
58. Guynn *in* Guynn et al. (1996), 33 *and* G30 2003 Plan of Action, 10.
59. Section 10.2.3 *and* 10.2.6, respectively.
60. ESCB-CESR 2004 Report, 60–62 (Recommendation 12). *See also* EFMLG 2003 Report, 23.
61. Arts. 1930 BW (Belgian Civil Code), 1915 C. civ. (French Civil Code), 7:603(1) BW (Dutch Civil Code). *See* Ch. 5.3.5, 6.3.4 *and* 7.3.4, respectively.

In Belgian and Dutch law, the prohibition on intermediaries from disposing of their clients' securities is therefore generally considered to follow from the classification of accountholder interests as co-ownership. From the co-ownership construct, it follows that the securities that accountholders are entitled to, do not become part of their intermediary's estate and that these securities are not available to the intermediary's creditors. Moreover, this right can be enforced in intermediary insolvency 'as if there were no insolvency'.[62]

When the accountholder/intermediary relationship would be classified as *depositum irregulare* (for instance because of the fungible character of the assets) and the intermediary would consequently obtain (full) ownership rights over the securities in its custody,[63] explicit legislation would be necessary to mitigate the effects thereof. Under French law, for instance, the prohibition on intermediaries from disposing of their clients' assets without explicit consent has been explicitly codified as the prohibition of *tirage sur la masse.*[64] The prohibition implies that an intermediary does not have full power of disposal over the securities in his custody and that both the use and the transfer of ownership of investors' securities by the intermediary are forbidden. A violation of this rule is considered a criminal offence.[65] Similarly, under US law, securities entitlements of accountholders do not form part of their intermediary's estate and therefore take free of the intermediary's general creditors' claims, but UCC Article 8 also expressly states that an intermediary is forbidden from disposing of his clients' securities by transfer of title or by granting a security interest. The latter prohibition is strengthened by regulatory provisions, the violation of which is considered a criminal offence.[66]

Also on the EU level, a similar, explicit prohibition of *tirage sur la masse* has been codified in the MiFID.[67] No modernisation therefore seems to be needed in this respect and neither UNIDROIT nor the Legal Certainty Group has proposed any explicit provision to the effect of such a prohibition.

Yet it should be noted that in many jurisdictions the effectiveness of the *tirage sur la masse* prohibition is mitigated by other rules and principles. For example, the protection of transferees and creditors that have *bona fide* acquired interests in securities from an intermediary that was not authorised to dispose of these assets may thwart the prohibition. The common practice of intermediaries vesting a security interest or lien in their customers' assets, either statutorily or as part of the general provisions of the account agreement, could also be considered detrimental to the spirit of the

62. *See* Ch. 5.3.6 and 5.3.7 (Belgium) *and* Ch. 7.3.4 (the Netherlands). The prohibition on intermediaries from disposing of their clients' securities is generally strengthened by regulatory law. *See,* e.g., Art. 6:14 *Nadere Regeling gedragstoezicht financiële ondernemingen Wft* (the Netherlands).
63. *Contra* SONO *in* GUYNN ET AL. (1996), 71. *See also supra,* Ch. 3.2.4.
64. But note that the qualification of the relationship between accountholder and intermediary is far from unequivocal under French law; *see* Ch. 6.3.3.
65. Art. L. 533-7 C. mon. fin. and Art. 332-4(2) *Règlement Général* AMF; *see* Ch. 6.3.4.
66. UCC § 8-503(a) and UCC § 8-504(b) respectively. *See* Ch. 8.3.5 *and* Ch. 8.3.3.
67. Art. 13(7). Although the MiFID is primarily directed at investment institutions, it may be reminded that this Art. also applies to credit institutions; MiFID Art. 1(2).

prohibition. These rules, however, will be discussed in further detail *below*, where it will be seen that they do not unjustifiably infringe on accountholders' rights.[68]

10.2.5.2 Right of Disposal

Accountholders can only dispose of the securities credited to their account by means of an instruction to their account provider, and, as a corollary of the *tirage sur la masse* prohibition, intermediaries should therefore be bound to effect only dispositions over securities accounts on the instructions of the relevant accountholder or a person that has been duly authorised by him.[69] Such a rule would serve investor protection, but also intermediary protection and thus market stability, since it would provide the legal certainty that prevents intermediaries from being liable for violations of the *tirage* prohibition. The US UCC, as well as the UNIDROIT draft convention therefore provide specific rules on this issue.[70] In all European jurisdictions investigated, on the other hand, it is left to general contract or agency law to determine which parties are duly authorised and empowered to instruct the relevant intermediary.

Under Belgian and Dutch law, an accountholder's right to dispose of his securities and thus to instruct his account provider to that effect follows from the nature of his interest as a co-ownership interest.[71] Although under French law the classification of accountholders' interests is not unequivocal, a similar right must be inferred from the *tirage* prohibition and the intermediary's duty to conserve the assets in its custody. Both the UNIDROIT draft convention and the Legal Certainty Group Advice, on the other hand, propose provisions that explicitly affirm accountholders' right of disposal by means of instructions to their account provider.[72] It is submitted that modernisation might indeed be warranted, especially where the nature of accountholder interests are unclear.

10.2.5.3 Double Bookkeeping

Other than by means of the *tirage* prohibition, accountholders should be protected against their intermediary and its creditors by strict bookkeeping rules. More in particular, it has been suggested that these rules should include the requirement that a credit or debit of an investor's account always corresponds with an identical credit or debit of the account that this investor's intermediary maintains with the higher tier.[73] The objective of the 'double bookkeeping' requirement, as this rule is commonly referred to, is to prevent intermediaries from crediting their clients' accounts without having obtained the corresponding assets. As a result of

68. Sections 10.2.8 and 10.2.9, respectively.
69. EFMLG 2003 Report, 23.
70. UCC § 8-107, *see* Ch. 8.3.3 *and* UNIDROIT draft convention Art. 18.
71. Ch. 5.3.6.
72. UNIDROIT draft convention Art. 5(1)(b) *and* Legal Certainty Group Advice, 5.
73. EFMLG 2003 Report, 19.

such a credit, accountholder interests in securities are created that would exceed the aggregate amount of securities as expressed by the intermediary's omnibus account with the higher tier, if the deficit would not be covered by drawing on the intermediary's own assets.[74]

Under Dutch and Belgian law, it follows from the property law nature of accountholder interests as a direct right of co-ownership that no crediting of securities accounts is possible without an identical corresponding debit at a higher tier. As a consequence, accountholders principally have only a contractual claim against their intermediary when the intermediary credits accountholder accounts with 'uncovered' securities. The relevant Dutch statute, however, provides that if an accountholder has no knowledge of the fact that the credit entry in his securities account is uncovered, that accountholder also has a proprietary claim, which involves recourse to the intermediary's own assets to make up the deficit.[75] Although Belgian law has no explicit provision to this effect, the same rule must be inferred from its provisions on deficits in securities pools and the protection of *bona fide* acquirers of interests in securities.[76]

Under French law on the other hand, the finality of a credit entry is only truly secured after a corresponding credit entry in the securities account of the acquiring investor's intermediary with the CSD.[77] French accountholders therefore lack (proprietary) protection when an intermediary becomes insolvent after having made the credit entry in a client's account, but before the corresponding credit has been effected. However, as any deficit is deemed to result from illegal *tirage sur la masse,* it is first covered by recourse to the intermediary's own assets and the effects of the lack of accountholder protection might therefore be minimised to the same extent as under Belgian and Dutch law.[78]

As a matter of US law, the UCC expressly provides that an accountholder obtains a securities entitlement, even if his account provider does not hold all corresponding assets. But the UCC also contains the obligation 'to obtain, and thereafter maintain' the amount of financial assets that corresponds to the aggregate amount of assets to which the intermediary's clients are entitled.[79] This requirement is further strengthened by federal regulations and by the UCC's explicit prohibition of *tirage sur la masse,* so as to prevent abuse of the rule that intermediaries need not always maintain an aggregate amount of assets that corresponds to the aggregate of its clients entitlements.[80] Moreover, all securities entitlements of accountholders are enforceable in intermediary insolvencies.

It is submitted that the UCC regime best facilitates market practice, without disregarding the protection of accountholder interests. First, operational gaps in

---

74. On the subject of over-issuance, *cf. supra,* s. 10.2.5.
75. Art. 18 Wge, *see* Ch. 7.3.4.
76. *See* Ch. 5.3.7 *and* 5.3.2, respectively.
77. Arts. 332-4(1) *Règlement Général* AMF and L. 431-2 second paragraph C. mon. fin. respectively. *See* Ch. 6.4.2 *and* 6.4.3.
78. *See* Ch. 6.3.6.
79. UCC § 8-501(c) and UCC § 8-504(a), respectively; *see* Ch. 8.3.3.
80. The *tirage* prohibition is also supported by federal regulation; *cf. supra.*

time between the crediting of a client's account and the collection of securities from another intermediary are common, especially when the securities in question are held abroad. On the other hand, investors whose accounts are credited with uncovered securities are adequately protected, since any credit entry in their securities account creates a security entitlement that can be enforced in intermediary insolvencies. Moreover, regulatory authorities can effectively monitor and enforce the intermediaries' obligation to replace missing securities, as well as the prohibition of *tirage sur la masse.*[81]

A system with these characteristics is therefore to be preferred over systems that rely on an unrealistic requirement of immediate corresponding debit and credit entries or over any system in which accountholder protection depends on the distribution of assets in intermediary insolvencies, while the insolvent intermediary might turn out not to have sufficient securities to satisfy the deficit.[82] Both under the UNIDROIT draft convention and the Legal Certainty Group's advice, however, states may opt for imposing a requirement of double bookkeeping.[83] Moreover, the Legal Certainty Group's advice is even less compelling where it concerns the obligation of intermediaries to replace missing assets.[84] It is submitted that a European modernisation instrument should be less informal and be committed to serve market practice and accountholder protection instead, through clear rules that permit uncovered credits, but require the replacement of missing assets, supported by regulation.

10.2.5.4 Segregation

A second rule of bookkeeping that has the potential of protecting accountholders' interests concerns the separation of the assets which an intermediary holds for its own account from the assets which this intermediary holds for its clients. At the higher tier, an intermediary should therefore hold an omnibus account for its clients' assets, but also one for its own assets.[85] Such separation facilitates the detection of any *tirage sur la masse,* i.e. the use of clients' assets for the intermediary's own business, as well as the distribution of securities in an intermediary's insolvency.[86]

In Belgium and France, the intermediary's obligation to separate is a matter of regulatory law.[87] Until recently, however, it was Belgian statutory law that required the separation of intermediaries' own assets from their clients' assets at the CSD level. Yet the legislature became convinced that the segregation could not

81. *Cf.* EFMLG 2003 Report, 19.
82. *Accord* SPINK & PARÉ (2004), 374–375, in the context of the Canadian harmonisation of securities custody and transfer law.
83. UNIDROIT draft convention Art. 11(2) and Legal Certainty Group Advice, 7.
84. Art. 19.
85. ISSA Recommendations 2000, 20.
86. *Cf. infra,* s. 10.2.6.
87. Act of 2 August 2002 Art. 26(16), Art. 469(1) W. Venn. and the Act of 2 January 1991 Art. 4(1) (Belgium); Arts. 332-4, 332-39 and 332-40 *Règlement Général* AMF (France).

be controlled or certified by the CSD and that any such rule could not be imposed or enforced on possible foreign intermediaries maintaining securities accounts with a Belgian CSD.[88]

The Dutch situation, on the other hand, is not unequivocal. Although it must be inferred from the text of and the official comments on the relevant statute that intermediaries' omnibus accounts maintained by the CSD are not to be divided, it has been convincingly argued that separation is necessary, both to protect accountholder interests and to facilitate free disposal by intermediaries of their own assets.[89] Moreover, separation is required by the relevant regulatory provisions.[90]

It must be concluded that as an important means of ensuring investor protection, a separation of assets at the higher tier should be effected, which, at the same time, would facilitate the common practice of intermediaries disposing of their own securities. As the Belgian legislature has shown, the rule that requires separation of assets should not have its place in an instrument for (the modernisation of) private law aspects of securities law, but in the regulatory context so as to ensure its effective enforcement. In the context of the recent EU directive on the regulation of financial markets, CESR has advised similarly.[91]

10.2.5.5 Right of Retrieval

Under the traditional concept of *depositum*, a depositor, as a matter of principle, is always entitled to retrieve the deposited assets from his custodian. In France, for instance, the corollary of this rule, which imposes a permanent obligation of restitution on a custodian, can be found in the provisions of the *Code Civil* on the contract of *dépôt*, and in Belgium and the Netherlands in identical provisions on *bewaargeving* (*depositum*).[92] This obligation of general private law is a strict one; under Belgian law for instance, not even *force majeure* is accepted as a ground for justification should the custodian not comply with the depositor's request for retrieval.[93]

Accordingly, it has been argued that accountholders should always be entitled to retrieve the securities to which they are entitled from their intermediary.[94] It is questionable, however, whether modern practice permits such an unconditional right of retrieval. First, *depositum* presupposes that accountholder interests can be classified as a right of (co-)ownership. Under Belgian and Dutch law, this is the case, but under French law the classification is a highly debated matter. In addition, under the contract of *depositum*, only identical assets to those deposited may be delivered. Yet it has been shown in the preceding chapters that it is a basic characteristic of the indirect holding system that securities cannot be retrieved

88. *See* Ch. 5.3.2.
89. *Compare* Art. 35 Wge *with*, e.g., SCHIM (2006), 47 *et seq.*; *see* Ch. 7.3.3 and 7.5.2.
90. Art. 4:87 Wft in conjunction with Art. 6:15(1) *et seq. Nadere Regeling gedragstoezicht financiële ondernemingen Wft.*
91. *See* CESR Advice regarding implementation of MiFID Art. 13(7) *and* LÖBER (2006), 27.
92. Arts. 1932 C. civ., 1944 BW and 7:605 BW respectively. *See* Ch. 6.3.4, 5.3.5 *and* 7.3.4.
93. *See* Ch. 5.3.5.
94. EFLMG 2003 Report, 23.

in specie. Belgian law therefore allows by statute for a derogation from this characteristic of *depositum* in the case of immobilised securities.[95] Thus, as the classification of *depositum* proves to be founded on a far from solid dogmatic basis in all of the European jurisdictions investigated, the unconditionality of the right of retrieval, which follows from such classification, also becomes questionable.

Second, (physical) delivery of dematerialised securities and global certificates involves serious complications, as the physical retrieval of dematerialised securities is by their nature impossible, while the physical retrieval of globals requires intricate legal conjuring.[96] France, the US, and, recently, Belgium have solved the problem by requiring that retrieval should occur through the crediting of equivalent securities to a securities account with another intermediary.[97] Third, the retrieval of securities as certificates may be forbidden by the issuer concerned, as is the case under Dutch law.[98] It is unclear, however, how this rule relates to the strict obligation of an intermediary to deliver the securities held for its customers at their request.[99]

Hence, the right of accountholders to have their securities physically delivered at their request, either as equivalent securities or *in specie,* cannot be considered a principle with which modern jurisdictions should comply. But the right of accountholders to change the form in which their securities are held, either by transfer to another intermediary or by delivery (if possible), seems to be a fundamental right from the perspective of accountholder protection. This right should therefore be expressly stated in relevant legislation. French law provides such a rule, which is enforced under regulatory law,[100] but Belgian and Dutch law should be modified to this effect.

Although the UNIDROIT draft convention contains a similar rule, it is made subject to, *inter alia,* the law under which the securities are issued, to the terms of the issue, to non-convention law and to the account agreement.[101] The Legal Certainty Group on the other hand, seemed to consider the right of retrieval to be of a mandatory character and did not consequently – and correctly, it is submitted – advise party autonomy in this respect, but left the decision to provide for a rule as proposed to the discretion of the states concerned.[102]

10.2.6 INTERMEDIARY INSOLVENCY

As has already been stated, rules that preserve accountholders' assets in their account provider's insolvency are of paramount importance in protecting

95. KB no. 62 Art. 6(2).
96. *See* Ch. 7.3.4.
97. Art. 332-4(3) *Règlement Général* AMF (France) and UCC § 8-508 (US).
98. Art. 26 Wge.
99. Or to other principles of company law; UNIKEN VENEMA (2003), 220–231. *Cf. supra,* s. 7.3.3.
100. Art. 332-4(3) *Règlement Général* AMF.
101. UNIDROIT draft convention Art. 5(1)(c).
102. Legal Certainty Group Advice, 5.

accountholder interests against their intermediary and its creditors.[103] The priorities of competing claimants in an intermediary's insolvency and the way in which shortfalls are addressed therefore require specific consideration in the context of (a modernisation of) securities custody and transfer law, and these two issues will be consecutively discussed next.

10.2.6.1 Preservation of Accountholder Interests

It is generally agreed that accountholder interests should be ranked higher than the insolvent intermediary's and its creditors' interests,[104] as a result of which the intermediary's creditors would have no possible claim on client assets in the event of an intermediary's bankruptcy or any similar event.[105] Under the laws of several systems, accountholder interests indeed enjoy such a top-priority because of its proprietary character, which, by its nature, is enforceable *erga omnes.*[106] For example, if accountholder interests are classified as rights of (co-)ownership, an accountholder may commonly assert a right of revendication, i.e. claim retrieval of his securities by delivery or transfer of his assets as if there were no insolvency.[107] The EFLMG has consequently argued that in intermediary insolvencies, accountholders should obtain a direct right of retrieval against the relevant CSD.[108]

In Belgium, this is current law, as Belgian law confers upon accountholders the right to revendicate the securities to which they are entitled, not only against their account provider('s liquidator) itself, but also against upper-tier intermediaries and other intermediaries with whom the immediate intermediary might maintain securities accounts.[109] It can be questioned, however, whether such a broad right of revendication is warranted, since in insolvency situations the account provider('s liquidator) itself probably has, and indeed should have, claimed all the assets it holds for its clients via other intermediaries.

Perhaps more importantly, Belgian law grants accountholders a right of revendication against their account provider, regardless of whether that account provider maintains its (omnibus) account directly with the CSD. As a consequence, accountholders that maintain their securities accounts with a non-participant also enjoy a revendication right in the case of this non-participant's insolvency.[110] In the Netherlands, on the other hand, accountholders that maintain securities accounts with participants of the CSD are adequately protected because they can assert their co-ownership right, but any lower-tier accountholder is left with a mere

103. G30 2003 Plan of Action, 10 (Recommendation 15). *See also supra,* Ch. 9.2.2.
104. Guynn *in* Guynn et al. (1996), 71, EFMLG 2003 Report, Giovannini Group 2003 Report.
105. ISSA Recommendations 2000, 20. *Cf.* Schwarcz (2001), 290 *et seq.*, basing his arguments on a law and economics analysis.
106. *But see* Ch. 11.2.2.
107. *Cf.* Unidroit draft convention Art. 15.
108. EFMLG 2003 Report, 23.
109. KB no. 62 Art. 13(2) for immobilised securities and the Act of 2 January 1991 Art. 9 and Art. 471(2) W. Venn. for dematerialised securities.
110. Provided the non-participant maintains an account with a participant; *see* Ch. 5.3.7.

contractual claim against his insolvent account provider.[111] It is submitted that this situation constitutes an unjust dichotomy that is unacceptable from an investor protection perspective. Accountholders who cannot, except with difficulty, assess whether an intermediary is a direct CSD participant or not should not experience serious consequences thereof that run contrary to a generally accepted principle of securities custody law, should the intermediary prove to be a non-participant.

In France, accountholders do not enjoy a co-ownership interest, nor can they assert its accompanying right of revendication, since under French law, proprietary rights can only be enforced when they concern an individualised object. No revendication of fungible intangibles is therefore possible and accountholders entitled to dematerialised securities would thus be treated as unsecured creditors in their intermediary's insolvency. But Article L. 431-6 C. mon. fin. guarantees the preservation of accountholder interests by requiring an intermediary's bankruptcy administrator to transfer all client securities to accounts with other intermediaries.[112] Under US legislation, accountholders also do not enjoy a traditional property law interest, but they take free of the claims of the intermediary's general creditors because accountholders' securities entitlements do not form part of the insolvent intermediary's estate.[113]

It is submitted that the precise legal methods through which accountholder interests are preserved, whether by a special revendication provision, priority rules or as a result of the classification of accountholder interests, is unimportant. What is important is that accountholders take free of the intermediary's general creditors' claims under rules of commercial law, regardless of the number of intermediaries interposed between accountholder and CSD or issuer.[114] The UNIDROIT draft convention also contains a provision to that effect.[115] Moreover, should a legislature wish to exert control over the account providers in its jurisdiction, it should do so by means of regulatory law, and not by limiting the rights that a credit-entry in a securities account entails, as these rights should be enjoyed regardless of whether the securities account concerned is maintained either directly or indirectly with a CSD.[116] Unfortunately, not all jurisdictions investigated meet these principles. Especially Dutch law should therefore be modernised in this respect.[117]

10.2.6.2 Exception: Secured Creditors

As an exception to the preservation of accountholder interests, principles of good faith acquisition can entail that the claims of certain creditors of an insolvent intermediary trump the claims of that intermediary's clients, even when these

111. Notwithstanding provisions of regulatory law and constructs such as VABEF II that intend to mitigate this lack of accountholder protection; Ch. 7.1.3 and 7.3.5.
112. *See also* Art. L. 213-2 C. mon. fin. *and* Ch. 6.3.6.
113. UCC § 8-503(a). *See* Ch. 8.3.5.
114. An intermediary's secured creditors' claims, on the other hand, might justifiably trump accountholder interests; *see* the next section.
115. Art. 21(2).
116. *Cf.* Ch. 12.3.5.
117. *Cf.* SCHIM (2006), 203.

creditors have received security interests in securities to which the intermediary's clients are entitled. Under the laws of all jurisdictions investigated, creditors that have in good faith obtained collateral by means of an outright transfer of securities are protected against the claims of the (insolvent) intermediary's clients.[118] With regard to security interests that have been created by means other than an outright transfer (of ownership), the laws of all European jurisdictions investigated require that creditors obtain a possessory security interest in the collateralised securities in order to obtain this priority.[119] Under US law, on the other hand, security takers with a control agreement, intermediary-pledgees and all secured creditors of clearing corporations also fall within this class of privileged creditors, without having obtained any form of possession.[120]

It is submitted that this exception to the preservation of accountholder interests is justified on the ground of market stability. First, it is imperative that accountholders can assuredly rely on credit entries in their securities accounts as evidence of an indisputable (security) interest. It is the author's view that no accountholder should be denied this right, whether it is a secured creditor of an intermediary or its client. As Rogers has convincingly shown, creditors may represent retail consumers, whilst the insolvent intermediary's clients are just as likely to be institutional investors.[121] Second, the extension of credit is only attractive if lenders can obtain collateral that has a low possibility of being challenged by competing claims, and the exception as just discussed therefore clearly serves the policy of market stability, especially in a market where credit plays an important role in ensuring efficiency and stability.

It can be questioned, however, whether an intermediary's secured creditors should also be protected when their security interest is perfected without any form of dispossession, as is the case under US law. It is the author's view that such a rule might produce unfair results, also considering the fact that secured creditors of an intermediary can thus more easily obtain a privileged position than any other secured creditor. The Unidroit instrument, however, caters for preference for all secured creditors, regardless of the way in which the security interest is created.[122] The Legal Certainty Group follows this approach, but allows the applicable law to be more restrictive.[123]

As none of the European jurisdictions investigated prioritises the claims of an intermediary's creditors over the claims of the intermediary's clients when these creditors have not obtained a possessory security interest, the creditors of

118. *See also infra,* s. 10.2.8.
119. Act of 2 January 1991 Art. 7(3) and Art. 470(2) W. Venn. for dematerialised securities, and KB no. 62 Art. 7(1)(2) for immobilised securities (Belgium); Art. 3:238 BW (the Netherlands); UCC § 8-511(b) (US). *See* Ch. 5.3.2 (Belgium), 7.4.4 (the Netherlands), 8.3.5 (US). No express provision has been found in French legislation, but the rule can be inferred from other rules on the protection of good faith acquirers; *see* Ch. 6.4.3.
120. UCC § 8-511(b) in conjunction with UCC § 8-106(d)(2) and (3), UCC § 8-106(e) and UCC § 8-511(c). *See* Ch. 8.3.5. Moreover, security takers are not required to have had no notice of the adverse claim in order to be prioritised; *Cf.* Ch. 8.4.2.
121. Rogers (1996), 1529.
122. Art. 12(2).
123. Legal Certainty Group Advice, 6.

an intermediary are not in a position to obtain a privileged position more easily than others, while they do become prioritised when their security interest can be known, i.e. when they have met some form of publicity requirement. It is submitted, therefore, that the European jurisdictions investigated need not be modernised in this respect.[124]

10.2.6.3 Shortfalls

Besides the preservation of accountholders' securities in an intermediary insolvency, the just allocation of losses that occur in intermediary insolvencies is of obvious importance in the context of protecting accountholder interests. Important mechanisms of recourse to systemic capital and insurance will not be discussed here, but the focus will lie on the rules of commercial or private law that allocate the losses that might occur in an intermediary insolvency.

The majority of international recommendations agree that in the instance of a deficit in securities of a certain type, i.e. when the aggregate amount of a certain type of securities which an intermediary holds for its clients exceeds the amount of those securities as expressed in the intermediary's omnibus account at the higher tier, this deficit should first be covered by drawing on the securities of that type that the insolvent intermediary holds for its own account.[125] The generally accepted view is that the securities that have thus become available to the insolvent intermediary's clients should be distributed amongst the accountholders entitled to this type of security, in proportion to their original entitlement[126] and regardless of the moment in time when they acquired their original interests.[127] If this distribution does not cover the deficit, the remaining claims should not be given further preferential treatment and the losses should be allocated pro rata.[128]

Unfortunately, the UNIDROIT draft convention allows participating states to provide that securities held for the insolvent intermediary's own account should not be drawn upon,[129] while the Legal Certainty Group has left the entire matter of loss allocation to 'policy makers'.[130] However, the rules as just proposed are followed in all the European jurisdictions investigated, although this is not always expressly stated in the legislation.[131] In France, for instance, any deficit is deemed

124. *See also infra,* s. 10.2.9 *and* 11.2.5.
125. E.g., ISSA Recommendations 2000, 20.
126. E.g., EFMLG 2003 Report, 24.
127. Thus deviating from the traditional property law maxim *prior tempore, potior iure. See infra,* Ch. 11.2.2.
128. Additional investor protection measures may, however, been put in place to cover these losses up to a certain amount. *See,* e.g., Directive 97/9/EC of the European Parliament and of the Council of 3 March 1997 on investment-protection schemes (OJ L 84/22) (EU) *and* Ch. 8.3.5 (US).
129. Art. 21(5).
130. Legal Certainty Group Advice, 6.
131. KB no. 62 Art. 13(3) and 13(4) for immobilised securities and the Act of 2 January 1991 Art. 8 and Art. 471(3) and 471(4) W. Venn. for dematerialised securities (Belgium), Arts. 27, 28 and 42 Wge (the Netherlands), UCC § 8-503 official cmt. 1 (US). *See* Ch. 5.3.7 (Belgium), 6.3.6 (France), 7.3.4 (the Netherlands) *and* 8.3.5 (US).

to result from an intermediary's violation of the *tirage sur la masse* prohibition and the intermediary is therefore liable for replacing the missing assets.[132] No modernisation therefore seems to be immediately required.

Mooney has convincingly argued, however, that a deficit in a certain type of securities should not only be shared amongst the accountholders entitled to that type of securities, but should be distributed pro rata amongst all the accountholders of the insolvent intermediary, regardless of the type of security in which the deficit occurs.[133] It must be agreed that accountholders are not in a position to assess the likelihood of a deficit in one or another pool of securities held, which will be arbitrary in most situations. The allocation model which Mooney proposes, on the other hand, treats all accountholders equally, and prioritises them over the intermediary's general creditors. In addition, his model results in a lower risk of large losses and a higher risk of small losses and is therefore also economically more justifiable.[134]

It is therefore submitted that the preference of accountholders entitled to securities in which no deficit occurs over accountholders entitled to securities in which the deficit does occur, while these accountholders are both clients of the same insolvent intermediary, is unjustified, both on normative and economic grounds. Since all of the jurisdictions investigated distribute a deficit in a certain type of securities only among the accountholders entitled to that type of securities, it submitted that this sub-optimal rule should be modified in the course of a future European harmonisation.

10.2.7 Corporate Action Processing

Probably the two most important reasons why investors acquire (interests in) securities are, first, to receive and exercise the rights attached to the securities, i.e. to enjoy its monetary and voting rights and, second, to (eventually) dispose of the securities.[135] It is therefore a well-founded principle that accountholders should enjoy these rights undisturbed and it represents a clear example of one of the basic elements of ownership, viz. the enjoyment of the fruits of the property (*fructus*).[136]

The indirect holding system, however, can cause difficulties with regard to the enjoyment of the 'fruits' of securities, because of the interposition of intermediaries between investor and issuer, a fundamental characteristic of that system. First, information about corporate events is required for an investor so as to be able to exercise his rights relating thereto. But, since an issuer commonly knows only the

132. *See* Ch. 5.3.7 (Belgium), 6.3.6 (France), 7.3.4 (the Netherlands).
133. ISSA Recommendations 2000,20 *and* Mooney (1990), n.191 *and* Mooney (1998), 91–93. Spink & Paré (2004), 375, where they refer to such an allocation mechanism as part of the Canadian harmonisation of securities custody and transfer law.
134. *See* Mooney (1998), 92.
135. *Cf.* Unidroit draft convention Art. 5(1)(a) and (b), respectively.
136. *See infra,* Ch. 11.2.2.

CSD or other intermediary as the holder of its securities, it can only provide these intermediaries with information about its events.[137] It is therefore of great importance that intermediaries pass on relevant information about corporate events to its customers. Second, an intermediary's cooperation is often needed when accountholders wish to exercise their corporate rights, as intermediaries may be required to testify to the ownership of the securities concerned vis-à-vis the issuer or may be requested to act on the accountholder's behalf.

Although the securities custody and transfer laws in none of the jurisdictions investigated restrict the passing on of corporate information and monetary funds, or hamper the exercise of accountholders' corporate rights, in some of the jurisdictions more explicit provisions on this subject are promulgated than in others. The UCC, for instance, contains explicit provisions that require intermediaries to obtain and pass on the proceeds of the securities to the intermediary's customers[138] and to comply with accountholders' directions concerning corporate actions and other rights connected to the accountholders' assets.[139] The Dutch relevant statute on the other hand, only refers to the obligation of an intermediary to enable its accountholders to exercise their voting rights,[140] while Belgian law only refers to securities' proceeds in the context of intermediary insolvency.[141] In French legislation, explicit provisions on this subject can only be found in the context of directly held securities, the pledging of securities and in regulatory law.[142]

The absence of express provisions can perhaps be explained with reference to the structural organisation of the law in the European jurisdictions investigated, where these issues are considered to lie more within the scope of company law than that of securities custody and transfer law.[143] However, the enjoyment of the rights attached to securities is equally important to both corporate securities and non-corporate, other financial instruments, while the indirect holding system has the potential to hamper the enjoyment of both types of instruments.[144] It is therefore advisable that a modernisation of securities custody and transfer law should stimulate jurisdictions to enact explicit provisions that address both the passing on of issuer information by intermediaries and the facilitation by intermediaries of the

---

137. In the Netherlands, for example, an electronic system has therefore been set up to facilitate the transmission of issuer information directly from issuers to investors; *see* <www.communicatiekanaal.nl>, the website of the *communicatiekanaal aandeelhouders* (communication channel shareholders) *and* TIMMERMAN & DOORMAN (2005), 31.
138. *Cf.* SEC rule 14b1-1 that provides a similar rule concerning the passing on of communications to the beneficial owners by securities firms; 17 CFR § 240.14b-1.
139. UCC § 8-505(a) and UCC § 8-506(a) respectively. *See* Ch. 8.3.3.
140. Art. 15 and 39 Wge. *See* Ch. 7.3.4.
141. KB no. 62 Art. 13(2). *See* Ch. 5.3.7.
142. Arts. 5 and 38 of Decree no. 55-1595 of 7 December 1955 *and* Art. 332-4(1) *Règlement Général* AMF. *See* Ch. 3.3.2 and 3.5.3.
143. In the jurisdictions where accountholders enjoy a co-ownership interest, the right to receive and exercise the rights attached to securities can also be considered to follow from that property interest; *see infra,* Ch. 11.2.2.
144. *See also* Ch. 12.3.5.

exercise of rights attached to securities. Fortunately, the UNIDROIT draft convention, as well as the Legal Certainty Group Advice, contain such provisions.[145]

10.2.8 SECURITIES TRANSFER

From a market stability perspective, but, albeit to a lesser extent, also from the perspective of accountholder protection, it is imperative that clear rules exist with regard to the finality of securities transfers and their requirements.[146] First, market stability requires that no uncertainty exists at any time as to who has ownership rights or similar interests in transferred securities, especially in view of possible (intermediary) insolvencies. Second, it must be unequivocal until what point in time and under what circumstances securities transfers may be reversed, for instance in view of the creation of a security interest in those securities or retransferring them. The moment of and the requirements for a securities transfer will be discussed in greater detail *below*, while the following sections will address certain aspects of finality or the possibility of reversing securities transactions.

10.2.8.1 Finality

Other than for reasons of (operational) mistakes by intermediaries,[147] the reversal of entries in securities accounts is mainly prompted by the insolvency of the transferor and *mala fides* on the part of the transferee. The European legislature has addressed the reversal of securities transfers because of transferor insolvencies in the context of clearing and settlement systems at a relatively early stage. It acknowledged that legal uncertainty should be minimised, particularly in the context of such a vital element of modern economies and recognised that in clearing and settlement systems, an enormous amount of transactions between numerous participants is multilaterally netted on a daily basis, while the reversal of settlements in that context is cumbersome and often impossible.

Consequently, the Settlement Finality Directive was adopted in 1998, which focuses on the entry of transfer orders into clearing and settlement systems, or, more accurately, on the enforceability of transfer orders in view of subsequent insolvency proceedings against the transferor.[148] In addition, Article 9(1) SFD provides that the enforcement of security interests in collateral is insulated from the effects of insolvency proceedings commenced against a participant of a settlement

145. UNIDROIT draft convention Arts. 5(1)(a) and 6 *and* Legal Certainty Group Advice, 5 and 7.
146. *See,* e.g., G30 2003 Plan of Action Recommendation 11 *and* ISSA Recommendations 2000, 20. *Cf. also* BENJAMIN (2003), 225.
147. The (operational) mistake by the Japanese brokerage firm Mizuho, however, could not be reversed; *see,* e.g., CNN report of 9 December 2005. But Dutch law, for instance, does allow a reversal for such a reason; *Cf.* Tweede Kamer, 1975–1976, 13780, no. 3 MvT, 38.
148. *Cf. supra,* Ch. 9.3.3.

system. The Financial Collateral Directive extends the insulation of the enforcement of security interests in financial collateral to all collateral takers.[149]

It is submitted that with regard to the specific issue of the effect of transferor insolvency on (the enforcement of) security interests in securities, no further European modernisation is needed. But, as stated *above*, it should more generally be certain when a credit in a securities account takes secure legal effect against the issuer, the immediate intermediary and third parties. The UNIDROIT draft convention therefore dedicates several provisions to the subject of finality in a more general way.

Under the preliminary draft convention, a debit entry and the designation of an account as collateralised can only be reversed if the entry or designation occurred without due authorisation from the accountholder, collateral taker or domestic non-convention law.[150] A credit entry in a securities account on the other hand, is reversible if the (*mala fide*) transferee had actual or construed knowledge of an adverse claim or if his account was gratuitously credited and an adverse claim has subsequently been made.[151] Furthermore, the draft convention leaves it to the participating states to determine whether the effectiveness of credit and debit entries depends on corresponding credits and debits made at other tiers.[152]

French law, for instance, makes the finality of a credit entry in a transferee's securities account subject to a corresponding credit entry in the account of the transferee's intermediary with the CSD.[153] Furthermore, the precise moment of transfer and thereby its effect against third parties and the possibility of a reversal depends in some instances on whether the price of the sale has been effectively delivered.[154] Finally, a credit entry in a transferee's account remains challengeable by the counterparty to the contract that initiated the transfer, while credit entries in a *mala fide* transferee's account can always be challenged by a third party with a more legitimate interest.[155]

Under Belgian and Dutch law on the other hand, the finality of a credit entry in a transferee's securities account is ensured as, in most instances, credits take proprietary effect, even if these credits are uncovered through a corresponding credit entry in the account of the transferee's intermediary with the CSD.[156]

149. Art. 4. But note that the Collateral Directive remains limited to certain categories of financial instruments and counterparties; Ch. 9.3.3.
150. Art. 11(2). The consequences of ineffectiveness or reversal are determined by domestic non-convention law; Art. 11(2).
151. Art. 11(1)(a) and (b).
152. But it also leaves it to non-convention law to determine the validity of a debit, credit or designating entry whether such entries are liable to be reversed and whether such entries are made subject to a condition; Art. 11(2). *See also supra,* s. 10.2.5.
153. Art. L. 431-2 second paragraph C. mon. fin. for the sale of (admitted) financial instruments on a regulated stock exchange and Art. L. 431-2 fourth paragraph C. mon. fin. for OTC transactions in admitted securities. *See* Ch. 6.4.3 *and supra,* s. 10.2.5.
154. Art. L. 431-2 fifth paragraph C. mon. fin., referring to over the counter transfers of securities. *See also infra.*
155. *See* Ch. 6.4.3.
156. *See supra,* s. 10.2.5.

Moreover, the link between the transaction and the subsequent credit entry in a securities account has been released to some extent. As will be shown below in greater detail, neither under Dutch nor under Belgian law is the moment of transfer determined by (the performance of) the contract that initiated the credit, but it is not entirely certain whether a credit can be reversed because of contractual flaws. Furthermore, credit entries in a *mala fide* transferee's account can always be challenged by a third party with a more legitimate interest under Belgian and Dutch law also.

In conclusion, finality is not always ensured in all European jurisdictions investigated when it does not concern situations covered by the relevant European Directives, i.e. transfers of (collateralised) securities and a subsequent transferor's insolvency. Especially under French law, certainty in finality is not achieved because of the requirement of corresponding credits at a higher tier, because the moment of transfer depends on the delivery of the payment price and because of the requirement of the validity of the underlying contract. The last requirement probably also plays a role in determining the finality of securities transfers under the laws of Belgium and the Netherlands. In all jurisdictions examined, a credit entry in a securities account in the name of a *mala fide* transferee can be challenged.

The UNIDROIT draft convention leaves a large amount of discretion to the participating states and currently even allows them to make the finality of credit or debit entries subject to the requirement that a corresponding credit or debit entry is made at another tier, or any other condition.[157] The Legal Certainty Group, on the other hand, has not (yet) formulated a view on the finality or validity of book-entries.[158] But it is submitted that the finality of securities transfers should be subject to the fulfilment of as few conditions as possible, since every condition involves a level of uncertainty, which is unacceptable in this area of the law and economic importance.[159] Other than with respect to the rule under which *mala fide* transferees can be challenged and which is common to all jurisdictions investigated, the laws examined should therefore be modernised to the extent indicated *below*, where the underlying principles of transfer law that have the potential to endanger finality, viz. consensualism and causality, as well as their applicability to book-entry securities law will be further discussed.

10.2.8.2 Negotiability

As stressed before, it is imperative from an investor protection perspective that accountholders can rely on credit entries in their securities accounts as evidence of an indisputable interest in securities. It has also been noted that from a market stability perspective, today's practice of multilateral netting warrants the avoidance or impossibility of a reversal of securities settlements and that the economic

157. Art. 11(2).
158. *See* Legal Certainty Group Advice, 6.
159. *Cf.* Ch. 9.1.1.

importance of securities settlement systems requires the minimisation of legal uncertainty.[160] Besides intermediary and transferor insolvencies and double book-keeping requirements, the major threat to the finality of book-entry securities credits is the applicability of reversal rules that originate from principles of general private law.

These principles include, first, the well-founded property law principle that a transferee can only acquire what his transferor has to transfer (*nemo dat quod non habet*). As a result, transferees that have acquired assets *a non domino,* i.e. from a transferor who was not entitled to dispose of the assets transferred, are subject to challenges by the *verus dominus* or the third party that asserts his prior entitlement. Second, under the laws of several jurisdictions, defects in the contract that initiated a transfer of assets affect the validity of the transferee's interests in those assets, a principle which is commonly referred to as causality. Third, French and Belgian property laws determine that interests in assets are transferred the moment when an agreement to that effect has been reached. This principle is often known as consensualism.

As a general objection of a dogmatic nature to the application of these principles, it has been argued that a 'transfer' of securities by book-entry is not a transfer in the traditional, private law sense. A close analysis of, especially, a securities transfer between clients of different account providers shows that the transferee does not acquire the very same (accountholder) interest which the transferor had, but obtains a new interest against his own account provider. From a strict dogmatic point of view, a securities transfer by book-entry thus involves the cancellation of the transferor's interests and the subsequent creation of corresponding interests in the transferee's name. It is therefore classified as novation, rather than transfer, so that the principles *of nemo dat,* causality and consensualism find no application.[161]

In addition, it is submitted that these principles should not (always) apply to book-entry securities transfers as they diminish the certainty which a credit entry in a securities account must provide. As a result of the *nemo dat quod non habet* rule for instance, accountholders in whose name securities are credited are exposed to the risk of being challenged by *domini veri* or dispossessed owners with (allegedly) better rights. On practical as well as dogmatic grounds, however, this rule is not always applied in the jurisdictions investigated. First, a successful claim by a prior entitlement holder presupposes the possibility of tracing the securities transferred from the prior entitlement holder, via a transferor, to the transferee. But in modern, anonymised stock-market environments, this possibility is virtually non-existent.

---

160. *Cf. supra,* Ch. 9.1.1.
161. *See,* e.g., BENJAMIN (2000), 155, n.38, GOODE (2003-2), 215, n.40, DALHUISEN & VAN SETTEN (2003), 124, HAENTJENS (2004-1), 478- 481, SCHIM (2006), 133 *et seq.* Yet neither this position, nor all of its (dogmatic) consequences are generally accepted, and the following sections will therefore assume the usual 'transfer' analysis. *See also infra,* s. 11.2.3.

Second, the laws of all jurisdictions investigated protect *bona fide* transferees, i.e. transferees that were not or should not have been aware of the adverse claim of a prior entitlement holder, against claims of prior entitlement holders.[162] In the US legal literature, this exception to the *nemo dat quod non habet* principle is commonly referred to as the negotiability principle. It has been codified in UCC Article 8, so that it protects *bona fide* transferees, as well as takers of security interests in book-entry securities.[163] Under Dutch law, *bona fide* transferees, as well as *bona fide* pledgees of book-entry securities are protected under specific provisions of the relevant statute, which are inspired by similar rules of general property law.[164]

Under Belgian and French law, general private law would not protect *bona fide* accountholders as its protection provision arguably applies to the possessors of tangible assets only.[165] But recent Belgian legislation has explicitly extended its application to good faith transferees of book-entry securities.[166] Moreover, as a matter of Belgian and French general private law, assets must be sufficiently individualised to be the object of any proprietary claim and therefore, transferees whose securities have been commingled with other securities (for instance in an intermediary's omnibus account with the higher tier) cannot be challenged by prior entitlement holders. Finally, under both French and Belgian law, a similar protection must be assumed to apply to pledgees that have been credited with collateralised securities in their (pledge) account.[167]

As a corollary to the rule that protects *bona fide* transferees, transferees that were or should have been aware of an adverse claim by a prior entitlement holder are not protected, but remain, as *mala fide* transferees, subject to the claims asserted by the holders of an older right. As to these transferees, the *nemo dat quod non habet* principle thus remains applicable. It is submitted that because of fairness considerations, the improbability of its application and its connection with general principles of private law, this rule represents a justifiable threat to the finality of credit entries in securities accounts.[168]

However, it would be advisable that the circumstances under which credit entries in a *mala fide* transferee's account can be successfully challenged are made

---

162. In fact, it was this need for the protection of *bona fide* acquirers of securities that caused German lawyers (notably Savigny) to consider securities as tangibles in the mid 19th century; *see* MICHELER (2006), 37–42.
163. UCC §§ 8-502, 8-510(a) and 8-510(b). *See* Ch. 8.4.2.
164. *Compare* Arts. 19 and 20 Wge *with* Arts. 3:88 and 3:238 BW. But these provisions protect fewer good faith acquirers than, for instance, UCC Art. 8, as they do not extend to good faith transferees when the prior transfer was invalid because the original transferor lacked the power of disposal; *see* HAENTJENS (forthcoming, 2007), comm. at arts. 19 and 20.
165. *See* Ch. 5.3.2 *and* 6.3.4 respectively.
166. Applicability of Arts. 2279 and 2280 BW through KB no. 62 Art. 19, Art. 475 bis W. Venn. and the Act of 2 January 1991 Art. 13 bis. *See* Ch. 5.3.2.
167. Act of 2 January 1991 Art. 7(3) and Art. 470(2) W. Venn. for dematerialised securities, KB no. 62 Art. 9(1)(2) for immobilised securities. *See* Ch. 5.3.2. In French legislation, on the other hand, no explicit provisions to that effect can be found.
168. *See also infra,* Ch. 11.2.3.

explicit. The UNIDROIT draft convention therefore contains such express provisions, while the Legal Certainty Group's advice also proposes the harmonisation of the rule and its application.[169] Of the European jurisdictions investigated, these proposals will probably affect French law most, where the legal position is least clear.[170]

10.2.8.3 Causality

In the previous sections, it has been argued that transfers of securities by book-entry should not be made subject to the principle of causality. In other words, defects in the contract that initiated a transfer of book-entry securities should not affect the validity of the transferee's interests in those securities. The argument was advanced that such a transfer system unacceptably threatens the finality of credit entries in a securities account, both from an investor protection and market stability perspective. This argument can be supplemented by two others.

First, the application of the causality principle, as does the application of the *nemo plus* principle, presupposes a possibility of tracing the securities transferred from transferor to the transferee. But it may be reiterated that the modern, anonymised stock market environment virtually prevents such tracing, as a consequence of which transferors seldom know their transferees. Second, the application of the causality principle to book-entry transfers of securities is dogmatically questionable. It is submitted that the proprietary position of an accountholder, i.e. the effectiveness of an accountholder's interests against third parties, should not depend on a contract entered into with an unknown party, but solely on a credit entry in a securities account held with an intermediary.

Third parties may rely on a credit entry as an expression of the relationship of a transferee (or transferor, for that matter) with his intermediary, and deficiencies in the contract between a transferor and a transferee should have as little to do with that relationship between a transferee and his intermediary, as events in the chain of settlement with the transferor – transferee relationship. Moreover, as noted above, an analysis of a transfer of securities by book-entry shows that the transferor's interests in the securities concerned are not transferred, but his interests are extinguished by the debit entry in his securities account, while the transferee's interests of the same quantity and quality are created correspondingly by the credit entry.

A so-called abstract system of transfer, i.e. a system in which defects in the contract between transferor and transferee may give rise to contractual claims, but do not affect the validity of credit entries made as a result of that contract, would therefore better serve market stability and accountholder protection, while being dogmatically correct, as well as being more in line with current market practice. It is submitted that these considerations outweigh the interests of the transferor and his (general) creditors, who may still assert contractual claims against the

169. UNIDROIT draft convention Art. 12 and Legal Certainty Group Advice, 6.
170. *Cf.* MAFFEI (2005), 249.

transferee and probably against the transferor's intermediary also. Such a system seems to be effective in the US.[171]

Under French and Belgian law, however, a transfer of property is traditionally linked to the contract that initiated the transfer. The general property laws of these countries provide that the moment when assets are transferred coincides with the moment when the contract is concluded,[172] but also that the validity of the contract determines whether the transfer is (proprietarily) challengeable. In French case law, challenges by transferors/counterparties to a securities transfer have thus been honoured on several occasions, as a consequence of which the transfer in question had to be reversed and the credit entries undone.[173] Under Belgian law, on the other hand, a credit entry in a transferee's account renders a securities transfer unchallengeable by third parties,[174] but the clearing of the transfer by CCP or CSD has also been argued to achieve that effect. In Dutch legal literature also, it is very much debated whether a general provision of property law applies to securities transactions, requiring a flawless contractual relationship between transferor and transferee for the transfer to have proprietary effect, but that seems to be the current law.[175]

The UNIDROIT draft convention does not require its participating states to amend their laws with regard to this issue, whilst the Legal Certainty Group has not formulated a view.[176] Yet it is reiterated that the finality of securities transfers should be subject to the fulfilment of as few conditions as possible, and that a flawless contractual relationship between transferor and transferee should not be one of them.[177] As a consequence, Dutch and French law should be amended so as to introduce an abstract system of transfer in the context of securities transactions by book-entry. Belgium's law might require clarification in this respect.

10.2.8.4 Consensualism

As has been stated *above*, the general property laws of several countries determine that interests in assets are transferred the moment when a contract to that effect has been concluded (*solo consensu*), a transfer regime that is commonly known as consensualism. It has been repeated that both from an investor protection and market stability perspective, the highest level of legal certainty is required with regard to the reversibility of credit entries in securities accounts. It is submitted that factual and legal reality in this context should coincide and that, therefore, a

171. E.g. *Ennis* v. *Phillips,* 890 So.2d 313, 55 UCC Rep. Serv. 2d 407 (Fla. Dist. Ct. App. 4th Dist. 2004). *See* Ch. 8.4.2. It is also a general principle of German law; DROBNIG (2004-1), 737.
172. *See also infra.*
173. *See* Ch. 6.4.3.
174. KB no. 62 Art. 6(3) for immobilised securities and Art. 468(2) W. Venn. and the Act of 2 January 1991 Art. 6(1) for dematerialised securities; *see* Ch. 5.4.2.
175. Art. 3:84 BW; *see* Ch. 7.4.2.
176. UNIDROIT draft convention Art. 9 *and see* Legal Certainty Group Advice, 6.
177. DROBNIG (2004-1), 739.

transfer of securities should take proprietary effect, i.e. be effective against third parties, neither earlier, nor later than the crediting of a transferee's account.[178]

Thus, a regime of transfer law in which interests in securities are transferred the moment when a credit entry is made in a transferee's account, or the so-called traditional regime, is to be preferred over the consensual regime when applied to securities transfers by book-entry. Under Dutch law, transfer of (interests in) property is generally effected by the delivery of that property. In the case of book-entry securities, delivery is considered to occur through credit entries in the transferee's securities account.[179] Under US law also, a transfer of indirectly held securities is effected when the transferee acquires a security entitlement, which results in a credit to a securities account.[180]

Under French and Belgian general sales law, on the other hand, property is transferred the moment when parties agree on the price and object of the sale.[181] But French securities law derogates from this principle, in that sales and the subsequent transfers of book-entry securities are governed by different rules. Transfers of securities that take place via a regulated stock exchange as well as transfers of securities that are neither admitted to the CSD's system of custody nor transferred via a regulated stock exchange are effected by a credit entry in the transferee's securities account.[182] Over the counter transfers of admitted securities on the other hand, take place the moment the transfer has become irrevocable under the rules of the settlement system concerned.[183] It has been argued that under Belgian law property interests in fungible securities are transferred the moment when credit entries are made in the transferee's securities account, but the more generally accepted view seems to be that those interests are already transferred when the transaction is cleared by the CCP/CSD.[184]

Again, the UNIDROIT draft convention does not require its participating states to amend their laws with regard to this issue, but the Legal Certainty Group has explicitly stated that, in its view, no harmonisation would be needed regarding the moment of transfer.[185] However, a diversity of rules that determine the moment of transfer inevitably leads to situations in which neither the transferor nor the transferee or, perhaps even worse, both transferor and transferee are entitled to the same securities at the same time.[186] Moreover, it is reiterated, once again, that from both an investor protection and market stability perspective, legal certainty should be ensured to the maximum extent possible. Especially with regard to

178. *Cf.* DROBNIG (2004-1), 726–733, who advocates that both generally and in view of a possible future European Civil Code, the traditional regime is to be preferred over the consensual regime of transfer.
179. Arts. 17 and 41 Wge; *see* Ch. 7.4.2.
180. UCC § 8- 501(b). *See* Ch. 8.4.2.
181. Arts. 1583 C. civ. (France) and 1583 BW (Belgium). *See* Ch. 6.4.1 *and* 5.4.1, respectively.
182. Arts. L. 431-2 C. mon. fin. and L. 228-1 ninth paragraph C. com. respectively. *See* Ch. 6.4.2.
183. Art. L. 431-2 fourth paragraph C. mon. fin.
184. *See* Ch. 5.4.2.
185. UNIDROIT draft convention Art. 9 *and see* Legal Certainty Group Advice, 4.
186. *See* Ch. 12.3.7.

such an essential issue as the transfer of securities, factual and legal reality should coincide, and the transfer laws of the jurisdictions that do not in principle adhere to a traditional regime where it concerns book-entry securities transfers should therefore be modernised.

Fortunately, under Dutch law and in most securities transfers under French law, securities transfers take proprietary effect the moment when a transferee's account has been credited. In a minority of securities transfers under French law, however, transfers take proprietary effect at some point in time determined by the settlement system concerned, while this represents the general rule for securities transfers under Belgian law. It is submitted that French and Belgian law should be amended so as to adopt a strict traditional regime for transfers of securities by book-entry.

10.2.9 Security Interests

In recognition of the vital importance of financial collateral in today's financial markets, many studies have stressed the need for the creation of a modern and harmonised regime for security interests in financial assets. More in particular, it has been argued that modern financial collateral arrangements require simple or simplified rules for the creation and enforcement of security interests. Especially the requirement that a collateral taker obtains possession of the collateral, the prohibition of appropriation of the collateralised assets by the collateral taker prior to, or after the debtor's default and some enforcement requirements have been criticised as being unacceptably burdensome for today's markets.[187]

For Europe, these concerns have been addressed in part by the Financial Collateral Directive of 2002 ('FCD'),[188] while national legislatures had already adopted specific rules to accommodate the creation of security interests in clients' assets in favour of their intermediaries. These legislative measures and the FCD's provisions on the creation and enforcement of security interests will be discussed in the following sections.

10.2.9.1 Creation

As the FCD mainly focuses on the harmonisation of rules that concern the enforcement of security interests in financial assets, it contains few provisions on the creation of security rights in book-entry securities. However, it does require Member States to acknowledge the validity of title transfers of securities by way of security, so as to ensure the validity of commonly used financial collateral arrangements based on such title transfers, most notably repurchase agreements; FCD Article 6.[189]

---

187. Guynn *in* Guynn et al. (1996), 41–42.
188. *See* Ch. 9.3.3.
189. *Cf.* FCD Recital 13.

Although it is questionable whether under Dutch law a repurchase agreement would have been classified as a forbidden fiduciary transfer of ownership, or recharacterised as the creation of a pledge, FCD Article 6 has led to an amendment of the *Burgerlijk Wetboek* (Civil Code) so as to exclude financial collateral arrangements from the application of the fiduciary ban.[190] French and Belgian law, on the other hand, already explicitly excluded most securities transfers of title by way of security from their fiduciary prohibition.[191] As a result, no modernisation or harmonisation of the European jurisdictions investigated is needed in this respect.

The FCD determines that all formal requirements for the valid creation of security interests in book-entry securities, such as the registration or filing of such interests, but not including rules that require dispossession, be abolished.[192] Since none of the jurisdictions investigated impose such requirements, no amendments were necessary. Yet it could be argued that a modern and harmonised European book-entry securities regime should introduce a general non-possessory security interest, such as the control agreement of the UCC.[193]

In this view, a non-possessory security interest represents an easy, yet effective way to create a security interest in book-entry securities, resulting in the greater availability of credit and thereby promoting market efficiency. Secondly, it would facilitate the creation of security interests where possessory interests are impossible or more difficult to effectuate, for instance when accountholders wish to vest security interests in their securities in favour of their account provider. Finally, it would facilitate the creation of a security interest in an entire securities account, i.e. in all securities credited in a specific securities account, which is difficult to establish in a system that requires individual securities to be transferred to the collateral taker in order for the security interest to be effective against third parties.

However, most European jurisdictions require, as a traditional principle of property law, some form of dispossession to render a security interest effective against third parties. On the other hand, none of the jurisdictions investigated apply a strict dispossession requirement in the context of book-entry securities, and collateralised securities need not always be transferred to the collateral taker's (pledge) account. Under Belgian law for instance, intermediary liens are effective against third parties, although they are created statutorily,[194] while under Dutch law, these liens are created by a simple pledge agreement.[195] Under French law on the other hand, intermediaries enjoy a statutory right of retention on a client's

190. Art. 7:55 BW. *See* Ch. 7.5.1.
191. Act of 2 January 1991 Arts. 23 and 25bis(1) (Belgium). *See* Chapters 6.5.2. *and* 5.5.2, respectively.
192. Art. 3(1) *and see* FCD Recital 10.
193. UCC § 9-203 (a) in conjunction with UCC § 9-106. *See* Ch. 11.2.4.
194. Act of 2 August 2002 Art. 31(2). *See supra,* Ch. 5.3.8.
195. Art. 21(1) Wge. *See* Ch. 7.5.2.

securities if a client does not fulfil its obligations vis-à-vis the intermediary concerned.[196]

The laws of the European jurisdictions investigated thus facilitate the creation of security interests where possessory interests would be difficult to effectuate, viz. when accountholders wish to vest security interests in their securities in favour of their account provider. Moreover, it is submitted that, at the same time, these laws preserve accountholders' interests, since French law, for instance, permits intermediary liens only when they are related to the client's debts towards the intermediary and Dutch law only facilitates such liens when expressly agreed upon. But also under Belgian law, the intermediary's lien only concerns securities related to the debts an accountholder might have towards his intermediary, while an intermediary remains obliged to obtain the accountholder's explicit consent, should it wish to vest security interests in a client's securities in the context of its own business.[197]

In all other instances, Belgian and Dutch law require that the collateralised securities be transferred to the collateral taker's pledge account for the pledge to be effective against third parties, while under both laws, a pledge of securities that remain registered in the pledgor's name also has that effect, subject to the condition that the pledged securities be blocked or otherwise designated as 'pledged'.[198] Under French law, on the other hand, effective pledges on book-entry securities can only be created through a transfer of the pledged securities to a pledge account registered in the pledgor's name.

It is uncertain in all the European jurisdictions investigated whether a pledge can be created in an entire securities account, so that it extends to all securities registered to that account, even when credited after the conclusion of the pledge agreement. From the requirements for the creation of a security interest as have been discussed, however, it can be inferred that such a pledge would only be possible under Belgian and Dutch law where it concerns an intermediary lien. It is certain, on the other hand, that under French and Belgian law, the pledge vested in book-entry securities also covers the monetary and voting rights that are attached to those securities.[199] Under Dutch law, the creation of security interests in those rights requires different formalities.[200]

In conclusion, no introduction of a general, harmonised non-possessory security interest would be needed in the context of a European modernisation of securities custody and transfer law. Although market efficiency might be promoted by such a security interest, it is submitted that neither investor protection nor market stability warrant its introduction. All European jurisdictions investigated facilitate

196. Art. L. 431-4 C. mon. fin. *See* Ch. 6.3.4.

197. *Cf. supra,* s. 10.2.5 *and see* Ch. 5.3.8 and the Act of 2 August 2002 Art. 31(2).

198. *See* KB no. 62 Art. 7(1) for immobilised securities and the Act of 2 January 1991 Art. 7(1) and Art. 470(1) W. Venn. for dematerialised securities (Belgium), *and* Art. 20(1) Wge (the Netherlands). *See* Ch. 5.3.8 and 7.5.2, respectively.

199. Art. L. 431-4I C. mon. fin. (France). *See* Ch. 6.5.3 and 5.5.3, respectively.

200. In principle, voting rights remain with the pledgor, unless explicitly agreed otherwise; *see* Arts. 3:247 *and* 2:89(3) and 198(3) BW.

the creation of security interests where possessory interests would be difficult to effectuate, but accountholder interests are respected at the same time. Moreover, the dispossession requirement does not seem to be overly onerous, as under all European jurisdictions investigated, security interests can be vested in book-entry securities that remain to be registered in the pledgor's name.

This position is in accordance with that of the Legal Certainty Group. Although it does not address (the creation of) security interests, from its view that no harmonised rules for transfer requirements are needed,[201] it could be inferred that requirements for the creation of security interests should be left to the Member States as well. The UNIDROIT draft convention on the other hand, provides for provisions that specifically describe methods for granting security interests in book-entry securities, but, at the same time, does not preclude participating states from prescribing other methods. Moreover, participating states may opt out of any of the methods the convention prescribes, and can also apply these rules to certain categories of parties.[202]

The UNIDROIT draft convention further determines that security interests may be vested in both an entire securities account and in separate securities credited thereto, but this rule remains subject to the law of the participating states.[203] It is advisable, however, that the European jurisdictions investigated provide more certainty with regard to the possibility of creating a security interest in an entire account. A modernisation of their laws would therefore be needed in this respect.

10.2.9.2 Enforcement, Right of Use

As stated above, it has been argued that modern financial collateral arrangements require the abolition of certain enforcement requirements and the removal of the prohibition of the appropriation of collateralised assets by the collateral taker, which have been criticised as being unacceptably burdensome to today's markets. Moreover, a collateral taker's right to dispose of the collateral, other than due to an event of default, has been considered to be of critical importance in ensuring the liquidity of the market.[204]

These arguments have convinced the European Parliament and Council, as a consequence of which the Financial Collateral Directive was adopted in 2002. Most notably, it requires national laws to allow for the enforcement of security interests by sale or appropriation without court approval or formalities, as well as for collateral agreements to authorise the collateral taker to dispose of the collateralised assets even before the security right is enforced.[205] However, the directive is restricted to certain financial instruments and certain categories of

201. Legal Certainty Group Advice, 4.
202. UNIDROIT draft convention Arts. 8 and 9.
203. Art. 8(3) and 8(4).
204. FCD Recital 19.
205. Art. 4 and 5, respectively. *See supra,* Ch. 9.3.3.

counterparties.[206] The UNIDROIT draft convention on the other hand, copies the FCD's provisions, but extends its scope.[207]

For collateral arrangements concluded by the most important market participants, viz. financial institutions, the recent implementation of the FCD has created a harmonised regime for enforcing security interests in book-entry securities. The Directive's scope is not as broad as it could be, but it is submitted that it meets its principal goal, viz. the facilitation of the economically most important collateral arrangements, and that a modernisation of the issues it addresses is therefore not necessary.[208]

10.2.10 UPPER-TIER ATTACHMENT

Many studies have identified the possibility of upper-tier attachment as a considerable threat to system stability.[209] This threat materialises when creditors of an accountholder attach the assets of their debtor at a higher tier in the custody chain, i.e. at the (omnibus) account registered in the debtor's intermediary's name. As a consequence, the assets of other accountholders are frozen as well, since the attachment affects the entire omnibus or pooled account. Hence, all accountholders at the lower tier are withheld from disposition over their securities, while an intermediary's own securities do not remain available to its accountholders either, should recourse to these assets prove to be needed because of an occurring deficit in the intermediary's insolvency.[210] In sum, this mechanism of freezing assets unjustly harms accountholders and unacceptably hampers the smooth functioning of the market.[211]

The possibility of upper-tier attachment is closely linked to the nature of accountholder interests. If these interests are of a non-traceable nature, upper-tier attachment is logically and categorically impossible. Under US law, for instance, the untraceable nature of a securities entitlement prevents any seizing of assets at other tiers than that of the debtor's immediate intermediary.[212] The same reasoning would apply to French law, under which upper-tier accounts are registered as omnibus accounts in the intermediary's name and accountholders cannot enforce any property law right to fungible assets. However, French law also explicitly forbids upper-tier attachment.[213]

206. Arts. 2(e) and 1(2), respectively. *See* Ch. 9.3.3.
207. UNIDROIT draft convention Arts. 27 through 32.
208. The scope of the FCD has been extensively and heavily debated. *See,* e.g., KEIJSER (2006), 352–364.
209. E.g., CPSS/IOSCO Recommendations 2001,19.
210. *See supra,* s. 10.2.6.
211. *Cf. also* SPINK & PARÉ (2004), 368–369, with regard to the Canadian harmonisation of securities custody and transfer law.
212. Ch. 8.3.2.
213. Arts. 178 and 180 of Decree no. 92-755 of 31 July 1992.

In systems that are based on traceable property rights on the other hand, the threat of upper-tier attachment is substantial, but it could be made impracticable or expressly forbidden. Although under Belgian law, tracing only occurs in intermediary insolvencies, explicit provisions forbid the seizing of the debtor's assets in accounts with upper-tier intermediaries.[214] Under Dutch law, accountholders enjoy a traceable property right and thus a direct link to their securities held at the CSD level, but accountholders' creditors may not attach omnibus accounts maintained by the CSD, as the relevant statute explicitly forbids upper-tier attachment.[215]

Modernisation does not therefore seem to be imperative. Yet, in view of legal certainty, it is to be preferred if a harmonisation instrument would explicitly contain a prohibition of upper-tier attachment.[216] The UNIDROIT draft convention and the Legal Certainty Group Advice propose measures to that effect which are therefore to be welcomed.[217]

10.2.11 CONFLICT OF LAWS

From the perspective of both investor protection and market stability, uniform and clear conflict of laws rules are of paramount importance.[218] But, unlike the private international law of contractual issues of securities transactions, conflict of laws rules on property law aspects of interests in book-entry securities differ widely and are sometimes far from clear. Many studies have therefore suggested that the harmonisation and modernisation of private international law should occur,[219] or, more specifically, that either one version or another of the PRIMA rule should be made uniform,[220] or that accountholder and his immediate intermediary should determine the applicable law.[221] The Convention on the Law Applicable to Certain Rights in Respect of Securities Held With an Intermediary ('Hague Securities Convention', 'HSC'), issued in 2003, chose the last option, but not without making it subject to a PRIMA test.[222] In the following section, the main conflict of laws rule of the HSC, as well as the national private international laws of the jurisdictions investigated will be evaluated.

214. KB no. 62 Art. 11(1) for immobilised securities and the Act of 2 January 1991 Art. 10(2) and Art. 472(2) W. Venn. for dematerialised securities. *See* Ch. 5.5.3.
215. Art. 44 Wge; *see* Ch. 7.5.2.
216. *Cf.* Explanatory Notes to the Preliminary Draft UNIDROIT Securities Convention, 46–48.
217. UNIDROIT draft convention Art. 17 *and* Legal Certainty Group Advice, 6.
218. HAENTJENS (2006), 87–88.
219. Explanatory Notes to the Preliminary Draft UNIDROIT Securities Convention, 46–48, G30 2003 Plan of Action, 10 (Recommendation 15), ISSA Recommendations 2000, 20, GUYNN *in* GUYNN ET AL. (1996), 33–34, Giovannini Group 2001 Report (Recommendation 15).
220. *See* HAENTJENS (2006), 91–94 for a critical examination of PRIMA and other possible conflict rules.
221. GUYNN *in* GUYNN ET AL. (1996), 33-34 and 35-41.
222. *See* Ch. 9.2.4.

10.2.11.1 *Lex Situs*

Lex situs has traditionally been employed as the appropriate conflict of laws rule to determine property law issues regarding bearer securities, but generally shared objections to that rule in its traditional form have already been put forward in the introduction. The main practical objections as discussed there are, briefly: different interpretations of the rule itself; the inaccessibility to information on the exact location of the securities – exacerbated by their fungible nature and their custody within modern holding structures; and the impracticality of a look-through approach in the case of a transfer of a multi-national portfolio, a problem which also arises in the case of arrangements that allow for the substitution of securities.

Although some of these objections do not follow directly from the *situs* rule, but rather from the modern practice of transferring internationally diversified portfolios,[223] the rule has been shown to be impractical in the indirect holding system.[224] In addition, it is not the security itself that is transferred under the laws of the investigated systems, but a right therein; even in the Netherlands – the most 'looking-through' jurisdiction of the ones investigated – the asset transferred is classified as a share in a pool. From this point of view, the location of the securities (to which the asset undoubtedly relates) is an irrelevant factor.

As a consequence, legal thinking in some jurisdictions has developed the *situs* rule from reference to the actual location of certificates to reference to the location of investors' interests.[225] Where and how the accountholder's interests should be located, however, depends on a substantive law classification that is made differently from jurisdiction to jurisdiction. Therefore, the *situs* rule represents a weak theoretical basis for a neutral and predictable conflict of laws rule.

In France and the Netherlands, for instance, it is a highly debated matter where the interests of an investor must be located; regarding the Dutch Wge system, it could be argued that the investors' interests are located at the CSD's securities pool, rather than at the immediate intermediary's securities pool,[226] whereas in France (and Belgium, for that matter), investors' interests are generally considered to be situated at the intermediary's location or at the investor's securities account location. Because the (theoretical) underpinning of this location depends on the highly debated classification of dematerialised securities, no absolute certainty can be obtained as to the French position. Under the US UCC, on the other hand, investors' interests are not located at all.

---

223. Ooi (2003), 103.
224. *Cf.* Austen-Peters (2000), 204: 'Such an obligation [to comply with the formalities of each jurisdiction where the securities are located, MH] would be tedious, time-wasting, expensive and beyond the capabilities of many investors. This process would also permit greater scope for mistakes to be made in the extensive process of due diligence that would have to be undertaken. Such mistakes could be disastrous for the economic value of an investor's rights'.
225. Goode (2003-2), 216 *and* Benjamin & Yates (2002), 80.
226. *See supra,* s. 7.3.5.

To which law this variation of *situs* points thus depends on the *forum,* thereby rendering this rule an uncertain, impractical and unfair one. It does not provide third parties with the clarity which supporters of the *situs* rule proclaim to defend. Moreover, from a more theoretical point of view, it seems highly artificial to allocate a *situs* to an intangible.[227] Not only are the practical problems 'manifest',[228] it is submitted that it would be more coherent to allow the parties who created the asset to designate its law as well.

In many jurisdictions, however, the *lex situs* rule is still predominant, either in its traditional form, or in a form more adapted to the process of immobilisation and dematerialisation. Dutch private international law is an example of the first kind, as it principally refers to the location of the certificates themselves.[229] French private international law, on the other hand, refers to the location of accountholders' interests and can therefore be considered an example of the second type of *lex situs.*[230] Under Belgian law, neither securities nor interests seem to be located, but reference is simply made to the 'register' in which securities are recorded. However, an exception seems to be made where certificates are held abroad in sub-custody for the CSD, and then the *lex rei sitae* applies.

10.2.11.2 PRIMA

PRIMA has been heralded as the conflict of laws rule that is most adapted to the indirect holding system.[231] Admittedly, PRIMA provides a clear rule as it refers to the law of the immediate intermediary, thereby rendering the applicable law readily identifiable; no links in the custody chain have to be taken into account. Moreover, it is considered to be in accordance with existing customary practice in the securities markets whereby security interests are perfected under the law of the jurisdiction where the account is maintained.[232] As seen in the preceding chapters, however, under PRIMA, many variations are understood. On one end of the spectre, an adaptation of the traditional *situs* rule can be discerned, while at the other, PRIMA can mean full party autonomy, such as is provided in the US UCC.

As may be inferred from the preceding paragraph, the PRIMA approach is to be preferred over the traditional look-through approach since it is usually unclear where exactly to look-through to. In many variations however, PRIMA is based on an attempt to locate investors' interests with the intermediary. Such a *situs* approach thus introduces a substantive law classification in a conflict of laws rule.[233] As has been shown, such classification is made in fundamentally different ways in the jurisdictions investigated. Moreover, it is often subject to fierce legal

227. *Cf.*, e.g., LOWENFELD (1978), 122–123, CLARKSON & HILL (2002), 494 *and* Giovannini Group 2001 Report, 58–59.
228. AUSTEN-PETERS (2000), 194.
229. *See* Ch. 7.6.2.
230. *See* Ch. 6.6.
231. E.g., POTOK (2001), 59 *and* POTOK (2004), 220.
232. BENJAMIN (2000), 159.
233. *Cf.* ROGERS (2005), 20.

debate within those jurisdictions, while it is questionable whether intangibles can be located at all. Therefore, such an approach does not represent a theoretically sound basis for a neutral and predictable conflicts rule.[234]

Further, if PRIMA is understood to mean that the law applies to the intermediary that credits the securities on its books (as is the case in the EU Directives, the UCC, Belgian law and the HSC), the following objections can be made. First, it may be objected that such a rule is not neutral. Imagine a situation of 'double dealing', where a second acquirer in good faith claims priority over the first acquirer of the same securities. In this event, the second acquirer claiming an interest may make this claim under his own law, which may be the law of his own choosing (in the case of the UCC and the HSC).[235] At first blush, this is not neutral. The defendant, however, may also defend the claim under his own law, which equalises their positions. This leads to the second possible objection: the priority problem thus created between two different laws is not solved by PRIMA since it does not designate a single law to govern the competing interests.[236] This is true: PRIMA simply shifts liability to the intermediaries concerned.[237]

Finally, attractive as PRIMA may seem, it appears to be difficult to establish the location of the relevant intermediary.[238] In today's world of computer networks, a securities account may be opened in one jurisdiction and may be maintained in another, while the two locations may have nothing to do with either the place of incorporation or the principle place of business of such relevant intermediary. Therefore, and because of the theoretical objections against pinpointing a 'place' of a relevant intermediary, preference must be given, it is submitted, to party autonomy.[239]

---

234. *See* Potok (2004), 211. *Contra* Austen-Peters (2000), 197, Benjamin (2000), 160, n.64, both locating the investors' interests with their immediate intermediaries, holders in trust.
235. Ooi (2003), 255.
236. *Cf. supra,* Ch. 12.3.7.
237. A search for solutions to this dilemma, however, has not led to satisfactory results. Under a so-called Super-PRIMA rule, in which the law of the transferee's intermediary would govern all issues in the chain of custody, such priority conflicts would be governed by a single law. However, such rule would not provide for the desired certainty because the ultimate transferee may be unknown to the transferor; if the law of the ultimate transferee's intermediary would govern all (proprietary) issues, all participants of the custody chain would obtain only retrospective certainty as to their interests. *Cf.* Ooi (2003), 299–300 *and* Rank (2005), 256.
238. *Cf.* Verhagen (2000), 116.
239. Please note that 'party autonomy' refers here and hereinafter to the autonomy of the parties to an account agreement, i.e. between accountholder and account provider, to determine the law applicable to the proprietary issues related to the account agreement. Rogers (2005), 30 has pointed at the possible confusion this use of the term might cause, because 'party autonomy' usually refers to the automy of the parties to a securities transaction. As the present author acknowledges the confusion that the term 'party autonomy' thus might cause in the context of the HSC, it is stressed that the term is used here in the former sense, unless indicated otherwise.

10.2.11.3 Party Autonomy

It has been argued, however, that because accountholders are in a poor position to negotiate with their account providers, party autonomy to choose the applicable law is beneficial solely to the account providers who represent large financial institutions.[240] Such an argument is flawed for two reasons. First, it assumes that accountholders are (invariably) retail consumers. But, as already noted, in many instances, accountholders represent large (financial) institutions, either in a capacity as investor, or as intermediary/account provider for lower-tier accountholders.[241] Second, party autonomy intrinsically entails certainty and predictability as to the applicable law, whereas other connecting factors, such as the *lex rei sitae* have proven to involve arbitrariness and uncertainty, which is in general detrimental to accountholders.[242]

Furthermore, it has been suggested that party autonomy is incompatible with some systems of custody, notably systems whereby a position on a higher tier might change the position of the direct intermediary and the securities in its custody. It has therefore been suggested that the HSC, based on party autonomy, favours the UCC model. However, these incompatibilities appear to be confined to certain specific situations (at least in the jurisdictions investigated).[243] Moreover, such incompatibility results – at least in the case of the Netherlands – from the restrictive nature of the Dutch Wge-system rather than from a prejudiced conflicts rule. Furthermore, the HSC is system-neutral in that it does not localise investors' interests; in contrast to the modern version of the *lex rei sitae,* it is not based on a substantive law classification.

Thus, only party autonomy would ensure a certain and thereby predictable applicable law. Not only would it avoid the arbitrariness of a connecting factor such as the place where the securities are booked in an account, but it would also allow parties to choose the law which is most appropriate to their needs and knowledge.[244] However, neither the national private international laws of the jurisdictions investigated, nor the relevant European directives contain conflict of laws rules that are based on party autonomy. It is submitted therefore, that the EU should either ratify the HSC and amend its directives accordingly, or adopt similar conflict of laws rules in a harmonisation instrument on securities custody and transfer law.

---

240. Johansson (2005), 1114.
241. Rogers (1996), 1529 *and see supra,* s. 10.1.
242. Furthermore, under the PRIMA rules of the EU Directives and France, the Netherlands and the UK, parties may already choose the applicable law by choosing the location of their intermediary; *see* Haentjens (2006), 93.
243. *See* Ch. 7.6.2.
244. *Cf.* Pos (2001), 400. Furthermore, under the PRIMA rules of the EU Directives and France, the Netherlands and Belgium, parties may already choose the applicable law by choosing the location of their intermediary; Potok (2004), 220 *and* ISDA letter of 26 July 2004 to EU Commissioner Frits Bolkestein, 7. *Available at* <www.isda.org>.

However, although the EU Commission had initially expressed its support for the HSC and proposed that the European Council and Parliament should sign the treaty as the representative of all Member States, so that it could prepare legislative action to bring current EU law into congruity with the HSC,[245] no decision to that effect has yet been taken. A cautioning opinion from the European Central Bank has probably contributed to this position.[246] It is submitted, however, that the existing rules should be modified, rather than to hold on to unclear and inconsistent ones.

10.3 CONCLUSION

In this chapter, it has been investigated to what extent the laws of Belgium, France and the Netherlands should be modernised in the context of a possible future European harmonisation instrument for securities custody and transfer law. For that purpose, the laws of these jurisdictions have been evaluated in detail and tested against the standards that can be distilled from the recommendations summarised in the previous chapter. Thus, a new regime of securities custody and transfer law has been proposed, rather than a regime that draws on the solutions of a particular member state or on the *compositum* of all Member States' laws investigated.[247]

Furthermore, it has been shown to what extent this new regime matches the proposed UNIDROIT convention and the advice of the Legal Certainty Group. On the basis of certain policy considerations, viz. the maximisation of investor or account holder protection and the enhancement of market stability by the minimisation of legal risk, normative positions have been taken as to whether or not these proposals should be followed.

(1) More in particular, it has been argued that the costs of harmonising the laws of the jurisdictions investigated would probably outweigh its benefits and would probably *not* serve the realisation of the policy goals just mentioned when a harmonisation instrument would seek to achieve complete dematerialisation or the abolition of all securities certificates, a harmonisation of the characterisation of accountholder interests, the abolition of all tracing mechanisms and the introduction of a general non-possessory security interest.

(2) Furthermore, a modernisation of the laws investigated has been shown to be better left to other (harmonisation) initiatives with regard to the eligibility of intermediaries to maintain and to provide securities accounts, the prohibition on intermediaries from using their clients' assets for their

245. Proposal for a Council decision concerning the signing of the Hague Convention, COM(2003) 783 final. *See also* Communication from the commission to the Council and the European Parliament, COM(2004) 312 final, 24 (28 April 2004) *and* Legal assessment of certain aspects of the Hague Securities Convention, of 3 July 2006, SEC(2006), 910.

246. Opinion of the European Central Bank ('ECB') of 17 March 2005, CON/2005/7, OJ C 81/10.

247. *Cf.* HOMMELHOF (1992), 73.

own businesses (*tirage sur la masse*) and the obligation of intermediaries to segregate their own from those of their clients. Priority rules of claims in intermediary insolvencies, on the other hand, have been shown to be already sufficiently harmonised.

(3) With regard to other specific issues, however, a modernisation of the securities custody and transfer laws of the jurisdictions investigated has been advised. Particularly clarification or an explicit statement in the relevant legislation should be realised where it concerns: an accountholder's right to dispose of his securities by means of instructions to his account provider, an accountholder's right to change the form through which his securities are held, an intermediary's obligation to pass on essential issuer information, an intermediary's obligation to facilitate the accountholders' exercise of the rights attached to their securities, the circumstances under which credit entries in *mala fide* transferees' accounts are subject to challenges, and the impossibility of upper-tier attachment. Moreover, it has been submitted that the jurisdictions investigated should be modified so as to allow for uncovered credit entries, while requiring intermediaries to replace the missing assets and adopting clear rules that protect the accountholders in whose names these credit entries are made.

(4) But perhaps even more importantly, measures of modernisation are needed that protect accountholder interests in intermediary insolvencies against the intermediary('s liquidator) and its creditors, regardless of the number of intermediaries interposed between the issuer and accountholder, while a better rule for allocating shortfalls in such insolvencies should also be implemented. Furthermore, the importance of the finality of securities transfers has been referred to, and it has been submitted that such finality can only be ensured if an abstract and non-consensual securities transfer regime has been realised. Finally, it has been argued that the conflict of laws rules of all jurisdictions investigated should be modernised so as to comply with the rules laid down in the Hague Securities Convention.

These conclusions diverge most strongly from the Legal Certainty Group Advice and the UNIDROIT draft convention where it concerns the possibility of uncovered credit entries, the allocation of shortfalls and the abolition of all causal and consensualist elements in book-entry securities transfer regimes. Yet it must be noted that a modernisation as proposed here will not force market participants to change their practices, but rather follows the market while providing a modern legal foundation to support it.[248] On the other hand, the modernisation proposed will require that the European jurisdictions investigated amend their laws to a certain extent, especially with regard to the issues just listed, but also with regard to the other issues where it was concluded that modernisation would be needed. Whether the systemisation of Belgian, French and Dutch law would permit such a modernisation will be examined in the next chapter.

---

248. *Cf.* SPINK & PARÉ (2004), 344.

Chapter 11

Harmonisation and Coherence of National Laws

11.1 INTRODUCTION

In the preceding chapters, it has been argued that the current legal diversity of securities custody and transfer laws requires harmonisation, and that any harmonisation initiative should be used as an opportunity to effectuate a modernisation of inadequate elements in those laws. Subsequently, measures of modification have been proposed for Belgian, French and Dutch law, while it has been indicated that these measures may deviate from more general principles of law, especially where it concerns the legal regime of securities transfers by book-entry.

However, almost all studies on the subject of securities custody and transfer law stress that the law that governs property, contract and commercial law, traditionally the prerogative of national laws, must be taken into account as 'rooted legal traditions' when drafting a harmonisation instrument.[1] More in particular, they argue that the creation of a harmonisation instrument in this field of securities custody and transfer law will be highly complicated because of its intimate relationship with these other areas of law.[2] Moreover, some have contended that considerations of doctrine or coherence prevent a (comprehensive) harmonisation and modernisation of securities custody and transfer law, at least at the doctrinal

1. *Cf.* Löber (2005), 156 *and* Giovannini Group 2001 Report, 54. *Cf.* letter by G. Morton, Ph. Dupont and A. Maffei to the Legal Certainty Group of 7 February 2005, 2, on the Unidroit project *and* Than *in* Guynn et al. (1996), 75. *And see* De Vauplane & Bornet (2001), no. 1245: *'L'approche factuelle du droit des marchés financiers est simplement le reflet de la complexité des pratiques qu'il est indispensable d'appréhender, de comprendre, et d'encadrer au sein d'un système juridique'.*
2. E.g. Giovannini Group 2001 Report, 54 and 60, EFMLG 2003 Report, 22, BNP Paribas Report, 2 *and* Löber (2006), 62. *Cf. also* CPSS/IOSCO Recommendations 2001, 5.

level,[3] while others claim that the modernisation that has already been effected involves unacceptable exceptions to the more general principles.[4]

Indeed, it has been shown in Chapter 2 that the coherence of national laws is to be taken seriously when drafting a harmonisation instrument, especially because supranational legislation in a specific field may affect the more general areas of national law in which that specific field is embedded. However, it was submitted that these coherence considerations should only prevent (the drafting of) a supranational harmonisation instrument if such legislation would result in a system of strong coherence becoming incoherent or weakly coherent, while the coherence of that system could not be preserved to some extent and coherence would be (felt to be) diminished disproportionately.

Thus, in order to ascertain whether the measures of modernisation as proposed in the preceding chapter interfere unacceptably with the more general areas of the laws investigated, a preliminary, two-pronged investigation must be carried out. First, it must be investigated whether a system has strong coherence in the area of securities custody and transfer law, which has been done extensively in the chapters of Part II and will be summarised and generalised here. Second, it must be examined to what extent the proposed rules of modernisation differ from the current ones, or, to put it differently, to what extent the proposed modernisation will affect present securities custody and transfer law. This has been the main subject of the preceding chapter and will be further elaborated upon in the following sections.

The main focus of the present chapter, however, will be the weighing of (the preservation of) national coherence against the modification or replacement[5] of present securities custody and transfer law. More specifically, it will be separately ascertained for all subjects of securities custody and transfer law whether the laws of Belgium, France and the Netherlands show logical consistency and monism, i.e. whether the relationship of the separate subjects of securities law with the more general areas of law is logically valid and absent of inconsistencies, while sharing common principles. Then, it will be ascertained how the modification of these separate subjects will affect the logical consistency and monism of these jurisdictions.[6] It will be shown that in most instances the present securities laws are either incoherent, i.e. show no logical consistency, or are weakly coherent, i.e. share few common principles, with the more general areas of law in which these national

---

3. *Cf.* Micheler (2006), 53 *and see,* e.g., CPSS/IOSCO Recommendations 2001, 5: 'The various components of the legal framework (eg securities law, contract law, commercial law, bankruptcy law, etc.) should not be inconsistent with or override the rules or procedures of the SSS [Securities Settlement System, MH] or its ability to meet these recommendations'. *See also* Sen (2005), 6, on the Unidroit project. *But cf.* Mooney (1990), 413, arguing that a departure from traditional property law constructs (in the context of the drafting of the US UCC) would be an advantage in view of future harmonisation initiatives.
4. E.g. Johansson (2005).
5. *See* Sono *in* Guynn et al. (1996), 66.
6. As the modernisation proposed in the previous chapter does not concern US law, the following analysis will not involve that system's coherence. For a discussion of some coherence considerations with regard to US law, *see* Ch. 8.7.2.

securities laws are embedded. In other words, the relationship between securities custody and transfer law and more general areas of law is not as intimate as supposed by some, so that most measures that would bring about an urgently needed harmonisation of securities law cannot be convincingly made subject to doctrinal considerations of coherence.

11.2 MODERNISATION AND COHERENCE PERSPECTIVES

11.2.1 Accountholder/Intermediary Relationship

In the chapters of Part II, it has been shown that under the laws of all European jurisdictions investigated, the classification of the contractual relationship between accountholder and his immediate intermediary or account provider is important, as it entails the application of general private or commercial law provisions of a specific contract to the accountholder/intermediary relationship. In all European jurisdictions investigated, however, the classification proved to be problematical.

First, the accountholder/intermediary relationship shows core elements of the mutually exclusive statutory contract of *dépôt régulier* or *bewaargeving* (*depositum*) and the non-statutory contract of *depositum irregulare.*[7] More specifically, under the laws of all jurisdictions investigated, a classification as *depositum* is appropriate since it involves an intermediary's obligation to preserve the assets it holds for its clients. But under French law, for instance, the intermediary's obligation to preserve its clients' securities is also explicitly codified in a separate statute on securities law.[8]

Moreover, under the laws of all European jurisdictions investigated, *depositum* implies a depositor's right to retrieve his assets *in specie,* while under *depositum irregulare,* all the depositor's property rights are transferred to the custodian. Clearly, both characteristics do not correspond with the contractual relationship that a securities accountholder commonly has with his intermediary/account provider. Furthermore, under Dutch law, the classification of the legal act of depositing securities with an intermediary so that these securities are credited to a securities account in the depositor's name is highly controversial, as it shows elements of both the statutorily sanctioned act of deposit and transfer of property, while both clearly do not match the intended result.

Second, under the laws of all European jurisdictions investigated, an additional contract of mandate or *mandat* must be construed to cover the additional duties of an intermediary, such as the processing of corporate information and the facilitating of the exercise of the rights attached to the securities in its custody. The precise scope of this additional contract, however, is unclear under Belgian

7. *See* Chapters 5.3.5 *and* 6.3.4, respectively.
8. Art. L. 533-7 C. mon. fin. *See* Ch. 6.3.4.

law,[9] while under Dutch law, the application of the statutorily sanctioned contract of *lastgeving* (mandate) is contrary to certain aspects of securities custody law.[10] Under French law, on the other hand, most of the intermediary's actions regarding the securities in its custody can be classified so that they are considered to result from a contract of mandate.[11]

In sum, general private law concepts cannot adequately classify the securities accountholder/intermediary relationship. Perhaps more importantly, the most appropriate general private law concepts show characteristics that are contrary to certain aspects of securities custody law. Thus, as the concepts of *depositum, depositum irregulare* and mandate are used differently in general private law and securities custody law, no logically valid connection can be established between those areas of the law, especially because with regard to most aspects of the accountholder/intermediary relationship, the jurisdictions investigated do not explicitly clarify the *sui generis* nature of this relationship.

In other words, the European jurisdictions investigated show incoherence with regard to the contractual aspects of the accountholder/intermediary relationship and a modernisation that would result in clearly stated duties and rights of both accountholders and intermediaries or would explicitly characterise this relationship as *sui generis,* would not diminish the coherence of these jurisdictions. On the contrary, provisions that would explicitly clarify the *sui generis* nature of the securities accountholder/intermediary relationship would render these jurisdictions weakly coherent in lieu of incoherent; although specific and general areas of the law would thus share less common principles, the current inconsistencies resulting from a mismatch between the use of concepts and compartmentalisation are barred by the isolation of the specific area of law.[12]

Moreover, such isolation would allow for explicit provisions that are in accordance with current market practices, but derogate from the norms which traditional concepts prescribe. An accountholder's right to change the form through which his securities are held, other than by physical delivery of the certificates, for example, currently runs contrary to the *depositum* concept, but has been shown to be a principle with which all modern jurisdictions should comply.[13]

---

9. *See supra,* Ch. 5.3.5.
10. *See* Ch. 7.3.4.
11. For instance, if securities are transferred by the intermediary concerned but replaced with securities of the same quantity and quality, this act is considered an *acte de gestion* (and thus an *acte d'administration*) and not an *acte de disposition;* Cass. 1re civ., 2 June 1993, *D.* 1993, p. 613.
12. *See* Thévenoz (2005), 307, in the context of the recent Swiss reform of securities custody and transfer law, which introduced a specific statute for an area of law that was formerly governed by the Swiss civil code.
13. *See* Ch. 10.2.5.

11.2.2 Accountholder Interests

Although the situation under French law is not entirely clear, it can be argued that under the laws of all European jurisdictions investigated, the property law classification of the interests which an accountholder enjoys is fairly certain.[14] Under Belgian and Dutch law, for instance, accountholders enjoy a right of co-ownership in, respectively, a notional and an actual pool of fungible securities. While French securities custody law is not based on a co-ownership construct, the combination of rights which French accountholders enjoy show more similarity to a property right of ownership than to a purely contractual claim.[15]

As can be inferred from the chapters of Part II, however, some general principles that are traditionally associated with property law do not apply to accountholders' property rights. In other words, the European jurisdictions investigated show no monism or unity with regard to this aspect of securities custody and transfer law. Moreover, the characteristics of accountholder interests do not always accord with all traditional elements of ownership, which may therefore lead to inconsistencies.[16] These two issues, as well as the effect of a possible modernisation measure, will be subsequently discussed in the following sections.

11.2.2.1 Principles of Property Law

It is little contested that as a general principle of property law of the (civil law) jurisdictions investigated, an entitlement holder can successfully assert his property rights against all third parties holding the assets to which he is entitled.[17] However, this principle, which is commonly referred to as *droit de suite* or absolutism, is not always applied in securities custody and transfer law.

First, in securities custody law, *droit de suite* involves the tracing of an (ultimate) investor's rights, through the custody chain, up to the securities to which he is entitled and the person holding them.[18] But, although both Belgian and Dutch law represent 'tracing' systems, i.e. they recognise accountholders' direct rights in the securities to which they are entitled, neither system allows accountholders to assert their property interests against persons other than their immediate intermediary. Under Belgian law, it is only in their immediate intermediary's

14. *But see* Ch. 10.2.3.
15. *Cf.* Mouy & De Vauplane (1995), 58 *and* Maffei (2005), 242 *et seq.*
16. It could also be argued that these inconsistencies do not so much result from a discrepancy between securities law and traditional property law principles, but rather demonstrate that in general, modern legal practice can draw little benefit from a (sharp) dogmatic boundary between property law and contract law as Von Savigny had advocated; *cf.*, e.g., Smits (1996), esp. 50 *et seq. and see supra,* s. 10.2.3. The following sections, however, are based on the assumption that the Savignian contrast between property and contract law is still generally accepted.
17. Salomons (2006), 13. *See also* Hansmann & Kraakman (2002), 374 and 378–379, who argue that the *droit de suite* principle represents the distinctive characteristic of property rights, rather than the enforceability of those rights *erga omnes. Contra,* e.g., Schwarcz (2001).
18. *Cf.* Ch. 10.2.4.

insolvency that accountholders can enforce their property rights against upper-tier intermediaries. Under Dutch law, however, accountholders are always barred from enforcing their rights against persons other than their immediate intermediary or its liquidator. French law on the other hand, recognises no direct right in (dematerialised) securities that accountholders can enforce against third parties, but in an intermediary's insolvency, the creditors of that intermediary cannot interfere with the accountholders' right to revendicate the assets to which they are entitled.

Conversely, *droit de suite* would, when applied to securities custody, allow the creditors of an accountholder to trace their debtor's assets and attach those assets at a higher tier. As has been shown in the previous chapter, however, so-called upper-tier attachment is explicitly forbidden under both Belgian and Dutch law.[19] Under French law, (property) rights to securities are normally not traced on other tiers, but upper-tier attachment is not explicitly forbidden by statutory law.

Second, under all jurisdictions investigated, *droit de suite* is usually not applied in securities transfer law. As a general rule, *droit de suite* permits dispossessed entitlement holders to assert their property rights against third party transferees that have acquired the illegally transferred assets. 'Dispossessed' accountholders on the other hand, cannot successfully challenge third party transferees under the securities transfer laws of all jurisdictions investigated, except in extremely rare instances. Both practical and doctrinal considerations prevent such a successful challenge[20] and the *droit de suite* principle is therefore not (fully) upheld in the present securities transfer law of the jurisdictions investigated.[21]

Finally, it has been argued in the preceding chapter that a modernisation of securities custody law should abolish all so-called double bookkeeping requirements, insofar as they withhold credit entries in securities accounts from having proprietary effect when no corresponding credits are made at a higher tier.[22] But under current Belgian and Dutch law, adherence to the *droit de suite* principle requires that accountholders can trace their interest to specific assets and the person holding those assets, as a consequence of which 'uncovered' credit entries are generally withheld from having proprietary effect. A modernisation of securities custody law that would abolish the double bookkeeping requirement and thus extend the proprietary protection of accountholders currently in place, would therefore fit with the general non-adherence to the *droit de suite* principle in the securities custody and transfer laws of the European jurisdictions investigated.[23]

As a corollary to the *droit de suite* principle, under which (property) rights can be asserted against third parties, the traditional property law principle of 'publicity' requires that those third parties should be in a position to assess the rights

19. Ch. 10.2.10.
20. *See* Ch. 10.2.8, where the corollary of the *droit de suite* principle, the *nemo dat quod non habet* rule is discussed.
21. This exception to the *droit de suite* rule is in accordance with the general protection of *bona fide* acquirers of movable tangibles.
22. Ch. 10.2.5.
23. SOMMER (1998), 1202 *et seq.*, links the absence of tracing under US law to the common law principle of privity (of contract).

that can be invoked against them.[24] It is questionable, however, to what extent the publicity requirement is met when capital is expressed through accounts and can only be known from the books of a financial intermediary. More in particular, it is usually only by attachment that creditors and other third parties who rely on the presence of wealth can obtain information as to the content of banking and securities accounts.

Furthermore, under all European jurisdictions investigated, security interests in book-entry securities can be created without strict adherence to the publicity principle, i.e. without the requirement that collateralised assets be transferred to the collateral taker's (pledge) account. First, under the securities laws of Belgium and the Netherlands, a pledge of securities that remain credited to the pledgor's account can be created if the pledged securities are blocked or otherwise designated as 'pledged', while under French law, effective pledges on book-entry securities can only be created through a transfer of the pledged securities to a pledge account registered in the pledgor's name.[25] Second, under the laws of all European jurisdictions investigated, security or similar interests can be created in favour of the intermediary that maintains the account to which collateralised securities are credited, without the performance of any action that would disclose the creation of such an interest.

While the publicity principle is thus not strictly adhered to in the present securities laws of the jurisdictions investigated, the modernisation proposed in the preceding chapter does not introduce a general non-possessory security interest that would further diminish its adherence. On the contrary, the implementation of the modernisation measures advocated would result in better observance of the principle, as it would strengthen the effectiveness of a credit entry in a securities account. First, an argument has been made to implement measures that render effective against third parties both authorised and unauthorised credit entries that are not covered by corresponding credit entries at a higher tier. Moreover, the importance of the finality of securities transfers has been repeatedly stressed, or, more precisely, the undesirability of credit entries being reversed, and modernisation measures have been proposed accordingly.[26] Thus, the measures of modernisation proposed promote the effectiveness of credit entries in securities accounts and reduce the sustainability of interests that are not expressed by entries in securities accounts, such as claims of 'dispossessed' accountholders brought against *bona fide* transferees.

In conclusion, some general principles of property law, such as the *droit de suite* principle and the connected principle of publicity are not (fully) adhered to in the securities custody and transfer laws of the jurisdictions investigated. It has been argued that the implementation of the measures of modernisation proposed in the previous chapter would intensify, but also decrease the current deviation from these principles. The coherence of the jurisdictions investigated would therefore

24. *Cf.* Hansmann & Kraakman (2002), 382 *et seq.*
25. *See* Ch. 10.2.9.
26. Ch. 10.2.5 *and* 10.2.8.

not be fundamentally altered by the modernisation advocated. More precisely, monism would be strengthened with regard to the publicity principle, whereas considerations of market stability and investor protection require measures that may result in an intensification of the existing pluralism with regard to the *droit de suite* principle.

11.2.2.2 Characteristics of Property Interests

It has been stated above that the characteristics of accountholder interests do not always correspond with all traditional elements of ownership and that the characterisation of accountholder interests as (co-)ownership may therefore lead to inconsistencies. More in particular, it will be shown *below* to what extent possession, the right to dispose, the right to vest security interests, the right to receive and exercise the rights attached to the assets owned, as well as the right to revendicate and retrieve the assets owned, match current securities custody and transfer law, or the proposed regime of modernisation.

Under the laws of all European jurisdictions investigated, the concept of ownership is strongly associated with (the possibility of) possession of the asset owned. Under the laws of all jurisdictions analysed, only (co-)ownership of tangible property is therefore dogmatically acknowledged. But although book-entries in securities accounts and accountholder interests therein are by definition intangible and cannot be possessed, Belgian law classifies these interests as co-ownership rights. Recent, yet controversial French case law and legal literature on the other hand, have recognised that proprietary interests such as ownership can relate to intangibles that cannot be possessed, but accountholder interests are generally not considered to be (co-)ownership rights. Dutch law generally only recognises ownership of tangibles, but it also acknowledges that entitlement holders may share equal property rights in intangibles, rights which then classify as 'community rights'. In this regard, Dutch law therefore does not show any inconsistency.[27]

In accordance with the traditional concept of ownership, accountholders in all jurisdictions investigated enjoy a more or less explicit right to dispose of their assets and to vest security interests therein. It is reminded, however, that although accountholders may dispose of their interests, they cannot transfer them. Analysis of the transfer of securities by book-entry shows that when securities are transferred, the transferor's interests in those securities are extinguished by a debit entry in his securities account, while the transferee's interests of the same quantity and quality are created correspondingly by a credit entry.[28] Furthermore, the right of accountholders to dispose of the securities credited to their account is not absolute as it can only be exercised via their account provider. It was therefore

27. Analysis of Dutch securities custody and transfer law, however, shows that accountholder interests do not qualify as 'community rights' in the general private law sense for other reasons; *see* Ch. 7.3.5. The same holds true for current Swiss law; THÉVENOZ (2005), 302–303.
28. *See* Ch. 10.2.8.

submitted that a modernisation of securities custody law should expressly affirm the accountholders' right of disposal.[29]

In further accordance with the traditional characteristics of ownership, accountholders in all jurisdictions investigated enjoy the right to receive and exercise the rights attached to their securities. More in particular, this right usually involves the right to vote and to receive the monetary benefits that flow from interests in securities. But it has been shown that the indirect holding system may hinder the accountholders' (right to) enjoyment of the 'fruits' of their securities and it was therefore argued that a modernisation should result in the introduction of provisions that explicitly state this right.[30]

Finally, accountholders do not enjoy an absolute right to revendicate and retrieve the securities to which they are entitled, although that is a traditional element of ownership and other property rights. The accountholders' right of revendication has already been discussed in the context of the *droit de suite* principle, where it was shown that in instances other that an immediate intermediary's insolvency, accountholders can enforce their right of revendication only in extremely rare circumstances.

Furthermore, securities cannot be (easily) retrieved upon request when they are immobilised in the form of global certificates or dematerialised. Under Belgian and French law, it has therefore been statutorily provided that the retrieval of book-entry securities occurs through the crediting of equivalent securities to a securities account with another intermediary. Moreover, Dutch law allows the issuer to prevent all retrieval of the securities it issued. As a consequence, it was proposed that a modernisation instrument provides that accountholders should have the right to change the form in which their securities are held, either by transfer to another intermediary or, if possible, by delivery.[31]

In conclusion, not all traditional elements of ownership correspond with the characteristics of accountholder interests. It has been shown that a classification of accountholder interests as (co-)ownership rights is contrary to some elements of securities custody and transfer law, in particular where (co-)ownership is considered to involve possession, an absolute right to dispose and to revendicate and retrieve the assets owned. Especially Belgian and Dutch law show inconsistency with regard to these elements, while under French law, accountholder interests are not classified in terms of (co-)ownership, which creates its own problems of coherence as accountholder interests are not explicitly classified *sui generis*.

With regard to an entitlement holder's right to vest security interests in his assets and to receive and exercise the rights attached to those assets on the other hand, none of the securities custody and transfer laws of the European jurisdictions investigated show any logical inconsistency with the traditional concept of ownership. Moreover, the modernisation measures proposed also correspond with these elements of ownership and call for their codification, so as to strengthen the

29. Ch. 10.2.5.
30. Ch. 10.2.7.
31. Ch. 10.2.5.

valid logical connection between securities custody law and general private or commercial law.

Also with regard to the elements where securities laws currently show inconsistency with the (co-)ownership concept of general private law, the proposed modernisation measures would not result in a decrease in coherence. On the contrary, explicit provisions that would carefully state the extent of an accountholder's right of disposal, revendication and retrieval would clarify the relationship of securities custody and transfer law with general private law and thereby eliminate the existing inconsistencies. Thus, the modernisation proposed would result in weak coherence where the jurisdictions investigated currently show incoherence.

To accommodate the introduction of provisions that explicitly refer to differences with traditional private law concepts, it has been argued that accountholder interests should be characterised as a new concept or *sui generis*.[32] However, the laws of all European jurisdictions investigated recognise only a limited number of property rights (*numerus clausus*) and the introduction of a new concept with some property law characteristics might therefore be impossible, or at least more problematical than the introduction of a new concept that would refer to the contractual accountholder/intermediary relationship only.[33] Moreover, it has been seen in the preceding sections that although accountholder interests show some proprietary elements, it is a fundamentally hybrid construct that is of both a contractual and proprietary nature. A new concept that would refer to both elements would therefore be difficult to implement, as under the laws of all jurisdictions investigated, a sharp distinction between contract and property law rights is usually made.[34]

However, it has been argued that this distinction is only of relative value in any modern jurisdiction, while others have shown that the legislature has always been free to introduce new property law concepts, even when it would generally adhere to the property law – contract law divide and the *numerus clausus* principle.[35] Yet it is submitted that the *numerus clausus* principle and the property – contract law distinction is still of such value to the coherence of the European systems investigated that an introduction of pluralism in this regard by the creation of a *sui generis* accountholder interest would result in a disproportionate reduction in coherence. Especially because a functional approach such as that of UNIDROIT could accomplish the harmonisation of accountholder interests by an explicit

32. *See,* e.g., PAECH (2002), 1160: 'If the work [of UNIDROIT, MH] aims at enhancing economic efficiency in cross-border trading and at eliminating legal risk at the same time, it will require the development of a completely new concept which might touch fundamental principles of national legal systems'. *And see* Ch. 10.2.3 and the references provided there.

33. *Cf.,* e.g., HANSMANN & KRAAKMAN (2002), 382 *et seq. and* VAN ERP (2003), III. *But see* SALOMONS (2004), 70, referring to the minor constraints the (Dutch) legislature has when introducing new rights *in rem. Cf.* SNIJDERS (2005), 95.

34. *But see* THÉVENOZ (2005), 307, discussing the recently proposed introduction of such a concept in Switzerland, a civil law jurisdiction.

35. E.g., SMITS (1996), esp. 50 *et seq. and* SALOMONS (2004), 70, respectively.

codification of the characteristics of those interests, but without introducing a new concept, that approach must be supported, for it would to some extent preserve the coherence of the national laws investigated.[36]

11.2.3 Securities Transfer

It has been shown in the previous chapter that investor protection as well as market stability require that accountholders can rely on the credit entries in their securities accounts as evidence of an indisputable interest in securities. Many jurisdictions have therefore endorsed rules that protect accountholders from claims of competing interests and restrict the possibility of reversal. However, in the European jurisdictions investigated, these rules do not always correspond with the general principles of their transfer laws.

More specifically, the special character and economic importance of the finality of credit entries in securities accounts seem opposite to (adherence to): the principles of consensualism, under which property is transferred the moment when an agreement to that effect has been reached (*solo consensu);* causality, under which the validity of a transfer is subject to the validity of the contractual agreement that initiated that transfer; and the already discussed principle of *droit de suite,* under which a (prior) entitlement holder can successfully assert his property rights against all third parties holding the assets to which he is entitled. Moreover, rejection of adherence to either one of those transfer principles would not be inconsistent with current national laws, should one assume a strict dogmatic point of view and accept that a securities transfer by book-entry classifies as novation rather than transfer (as it involves the cancellation of the transferor's interests and the subsequent creation of corresponding interests in the transferee's name).[37] Yet this position is not generally accepted, and in most jurisdictions general principles of transfer law equally apply to the transfer of book-entry securities.

11.2.3.1 Consensualism

Under French and Belgian law, for instance, as a general principle of transfer law, property is legally transferred the moment when parties agree on the price and object of the sale. The principle further requires that the object of the transfer be sufficiently certain, so that in the case of a sale of fungibles, the transfer of ownership usually occurs the moment when the fungibles are delivered.[38] With regard to the transfer of securities by book-entry, however, this principle is abandoned to a certain extent. Particularly under French law, most transfers of book-entry securities are effected by a credit entry in the transferee's securities account. Some transfers of book-entry securities on the other hand, take place the moment

36. *See* Ch. 10.2.3.
37. *See also supra,* s. 10.2.8.
38. *See* Ch. 5.4.2 *and* 6.4.2. *Cf. also* Drobnig (2004-1), 728.

when the transfer has become irrevocable under the rules of the settlement system concerned, while under Belgian law, (interests in) book-entry securities are considered to have been transferred when the transaction is cleared by the CCP/CSD or when the credit entry is made in the transferee's account.[39]

As a matter of general Dutch transfer law, transfers only become effective when both a transfer agreement and delivery of the property have been effectuated. In the case of a transfer of book-entry securities, delivery is considered to have occurred when a credit entry has been made in a securities account. The modernisation proposed in the preceding chapter advocates the implementation of such a rule in all jurisdictions and therefore is in accordance with general Dutch transfer law principles. Thus, it also implies the rejection of adherence to the *solo consensu* principle, the general principle of transfer law in France and Belgium.

However, it is the author's view that the modernisation proposed would not disproportionately diminish the coherence of these jurisdictions' laws, as it would only confirm the existing derogation of book-entry securities laws from general private law with regard to the transfer of securities by book-entry.[40] In other words, it would confirm the existing situation of pluralism and the weak coherence in Belgian and French law, while it would strengthen Dutch monism. Moreover, it would result in stronger monism with regard to (the observance of) the publicity principle discussed *supra,* as the modernisation proposed would strengthen the effectiveness of a credit entry and eliminate the possibility of property interests in securities that are not expressed by credit entries in securities accounts.[41]

11.2.3.2 Causality and *Bona Fide* Acquirer Protection

Apart from the abolition of strict adherence to the *solo consensu* principle, the requirement that accountholders take free of competing claims so that they can rely on the credit entries in their securities accounts has two further ramifications. First, it follows that the transfer of securities by book-entry should not be made subject to the validity of the contractual agreement that initiated the transfer. But under the laws of all European jurisdictions investigated, it is a general principle of transfer law that the underlying contract determines the validity of the transfer and that transfers must therefore be reversed if a party to the contract that initiated the transfer successfully challenges its validity.[42]

Although heavily debated, this principle of causality is currently considered to be applicable to the transfers of securities by book-entry in all the European

39. Ch. 10.2.8.
40. *But see* THAN *in* GUYNN ET AL. (1996), 75: '[I]t would cause considerable problems to a national legislature to set up rules for the transfer of ownership of securities in a totally different way than for the transfer of ownership of other *movables* [emphasis added, MH]'.
41. *Cf.* DROBNIG (2004-1), 733.
42. *Cf.* VAN ERP (2004), 546. *But see* DROBNIG (2004-1), 739: '[T]he basic idea of insulating certain transactions, such as negotiable instruments, from objections derived from an underlying contract, is familiar to all European legal systems'.

jurisdictions investigated.[43] However, it is submitted that the application of the causality principle to book-entry securities transfers leads to inconsistencies; the modern, anonymised stock-market environment does not allow for the necessary identification of a transferee by his transferor and vice versa, except in very rare circumstances. In addition, as has already been argued, the application of the causality principle to transfers of securities by book-entry assumes a transfer in the traditional, private law sense, although no transfer of accountholder interests takes place, but rather a cancellation of the transferor's interests and a creation of corresponding interests in the transferee's name.[44]

The modernisation proposed would explicitly introduce a so-called abstract regime of transfer for book-entry securities and would therefore involve an alteration of the coherence in the jurisdictions investigated, as all European jurisdictions investigated currently consider the causality principle to be applicable to the transfers of securities by book-entry. However, it is submitted that the introduction of pluralism in lieu of monism would be justified here on the grounds of accountholder protection and market stability, while it would eliminate current inconsistencies by responding to current practice and doctrinal considerations. It would therefore render the systems investigated to be weakly coherent where they are currently incoherent.

Second, accountholders that have been credited with securities to their accounts should not suffer from successful challenges by third parties that have allegedly been dispossessed of these securities. However, it has already been ascertained that under the laws of all European jurisdictions investigated, (prior) entitlement holders can successfully assert their property rights against all third parties holding the assets to which they are entitled under the principle of *droit de suite*. On the other hand, it is also a principle in all the jurisdictions investigated that transferees cannot be successfully challenged when they have *bona fide* obtained their interests in the property transferred.[45]

In all European jurisdictions investigated, the principle of *bona fide* acquirer protection also applies to transferees of book-entry securities and to takers of security interests therein, albeit for different reasons.[46] Under Dutch law, for instance, the protection follows from the application of the general principle, whereas Belgian law required a statutory and express extension of that principle to book-entry securities transfers. Under French law, the theoretical basis is unclear, but the protection probably applies. The modernisation proposed, which would explicitly allow for reversal of a credit entry only in the case of a *mala fide* transfer of property interests in book-entry securities, would therefore change little with regard to the coherence of the laws investigated, as it would confirm the monism of Belgian and Dutch law, but also the pluralism of French law in this respect. But it would, at the same time, involve an important improvement, as it would explicitly and

43. *See supra*, Ch. 10.2.8.
44. *See supra*, Ch. 10.2.8.
45. *Cf.* Drobnig (2004-1), 738–739.
46. Ch. 10.2.8.

generally achieve the situation where accountholders can rely on the credit entries in their securities accounts.

11.2.3.3 Conclusion

Implementation of the modernisation measures of securities transfer law as proposed in the previous chapter would thus not result in any system investigated having to change from a system of strong coherence to become incoherent or weakly coherent, while coherence, when diminished, would not be diminished disproportionately. First, the current laws of France and Belgium demonstrate pluralism and thus weak coherence with regard to their adherence to the principle of consensualism where it concerns book-entry securities transfers, a pluralism which will only be strengthened by the modernisation proposed. Moreover, the modernisation proposed will support the monism of Dutch law with regard to its transfer regime based on the *traditio* principle. Second, the laws of all jurisdictions investigated show monism with regard to their adherence to the causality principle, but it has been argued that this monism leads to incoherence. Although the modernisation proposed would therefore cause these laws to be weakly coherent, it would eliminate their current inconsistencies and therewith their incoherence. Finally, the modernisation would not change, but confirm the current (strong) coherence of Belgian, French and Dutch law with regard to their adherence to the *bona fide* acquirer protection principle.

11.2.4 Security Interests

In the preceding chapters, the European harmonisation recently brought about by the Financial Collateral Directive ('FCD') has been discussed. Attention has been paid to the FCD's most prominent provisions, which introduced a general title transfer by way of security for book-entry securities and recently harmonised the enforcement regime for security interests vested in financial instruments. No modernisation was therefore proposed in the previous chapter with regard to these issues. But also with regard to the creation of security interests in book-entry securities, it was submitted that no modernisation was needed. However, the consequences of the implementation of the FCD and of the (not advocated) introduction of a general non-possessory pledge on the coherence of the jurisdictions investigated will be briefly discussed in the following, for the sake of comprehensiveness and as reference.

It has been noted before that although all European jurisdictions investigated prohibit, as a general principle of security law, the title transfer of property by way of security, exceptions to this 'fiduciary ban' were already made for transfers of book-entry securities before the implementation of the SFD.[47] Under French law, for example, title transfer by way of security was already allowed for book-entry

47. Ch. 10.2.9.

securities under specific conditions. Under Belgian law, on the other hand, a statutory provision already excluded the fiduciary ban from securities transfers of title by way of security. Although fiduciary transfers of both securities and other assets were allowed under certain circumstances in the Netherlands, the SFD led to the enactment of an express statutory provision so as to exclude most securities transfers from the fiduciary ban. The FCD can therefore not be argued to have introduced a rule that caused a deterioration of the coherence in the said jurisdictions. Their coherence was already weak as they did not strictly adhere to the fiduciary ban in the case of title transfers of book-entry securities and the SFD only made this pluralism explicit.

While the FCD did not contain harmonisation measures on the creation of security interests in book-entry securities, the previous chapter has discussed the possibility of such a measure and concluded that the introduction of a harmonised, non-possessory pledge in book-entry securities that would not be recorded in any way would not be advisable.[48] However, it is submitted here that the introduction of such a harmonised security interest should not be prevented by coherence considerations.

European jurisdictions traditionally only recognised the possessory pledge (*pignus*), but recent developments in general continental European pledge law increasingly sanction non-possessory pledges in both movables and intangibles.[49] In addition, non-possessory, i.e. not recorded pledges are already possible under Belgian and Dutch law in the case of an intermediary's liens on accountholders' assets. In sum, a modernisation and harmonisation that would introduce a non-possessory pledge in book-entry securities would not have a diminishing effect on the coherence of the jurisdictions investigated as it is in accordance with a similar trend in general private law and also confirms (but, it is agreed, also expands) the weak coherence of those jurisdictions.

As stated previously, the FCD introduced, apart from a general title transfer by way of security for book-entry securities, a harmonised enforcement regime for security interests vested in financial instruments. The main modernisation which the FCD effectuated in that context, concerns a collateral taker's right of appropriation, both before and after an event of the debtor's default. The FCD allows the parties to a financial collateral agreement to authorise the collateral taker to dispose of the securities collateralised prior to an event of the debtor's default, either by transfer of title or by rehypothecation to a third party, while the collateral taker remains under an obligation to return equivalent securities after the payment of the debt.[50] It is generally accepted that such disposal by the collateral taker involves a prior transfer of ownership interests in the collateralised securities

48. It is reminded that the creation of a pledge by the designation of the pledged securities as such in the pledgor's securities account is already possible under the laws of all jurisdictions investigated. *See supra*, Ch. 10.2.9.
49. *See* Drobnig (2004-2), 746, 753 and 754 *and* Salomons (2003).
50. Art. 5.

to the collateral taker.[51] In addition, the FCD introduces the appropriation of the collateralised securities by the collateral taker as a way of enforcement when the debtor defaults.[52] However, this right of appropriation contrasts with a principle of general security law that is common to all continental European jurisdictions and which plainly prohibits appropriation by the creditor.[53] The implementation of the FCD therefore required explicit statutory provisions to derogate from that general rule of private law in all European jurisdictions investigated,[54] although in France a right of appropriation after a debtor's default was already statutorily sanctioned for security interests in exchange-traded securities.[55]

Furthermore, the FCD introduced a liberal regime of enforcement with regard to security interests in financial collateral, so that the Member States had to abolish all provisions which required a collateral taker to give the debtor/collateral giver notice of his intention to realise the security interest. In addition, the requirements that a collateral taker obtains a court approval prior to his enforcement of the security interest, that he realises the enforcement at a public auction and has a certain period of time elapse prior to enforcement, had to be abolished.[56] But since continental European jurisdictions have traditionally strictly regulated the enforcement of security interests by collateral takers,[57] the FCD required the enactment of derogatory provisions to give effect to the abolition of the said requirements in all jurisdictions investigated.[58] Yet in Belgium, more liberal rules already existed for the enforcement of security rights in immobilised securities,[59] while in France the enforcement of a pledge in book-entry securities had also already been made subject to less formalities.[60]

In sum, the FCD involved serious implications for the coherence of the European jurisdictions investigated, especially where the FCD introduced a collateral taker's right of appropriation as an enforcement mechanism. In that regard, the monism of all jurisdictions investigated changed into pluralism, although it must be noted that because the situations to which the derogatory rule applies are well defined,[61] the derogation did not result in incoherence. With regard to the other measures that liberalised the enforcement of security interests in financial collateral, the implementation of the FCD resulted in most of the

51. Although the moment of the transfer of ownership interests might not be unequivocal. *Cf.* Johansson (2005), 1099.
52. Art. 4(1)(a).
53. It has also been argued to contrast with other principles of general pledge law, such as the duty of due care and the right of redemption; Keijser (2006), 347.
54. Act of 15 December 2004 Arts. 10 and 8 (Belgium), Arts. 7:54(1), 7:53(1) and 7:54(5) BW (the Netherlands). *See* Chapters 5.5.3 *and* 7.5.2 respectively.
55. Art. 3 of Decree no. 97-509 of 21 May 1997. *See* Ch. 6.5.3.
56. Art. 4.
57. Drobnig (2004-2), 744.
58. Act of 15 December 2004 Art. 8 (Belgium), Art. L. 431-7-2 C. Mon. Fin. (France) and Art. 7:54(5) BW (the Netherlands).
59. KB no. 62 Art. 7(2).
60. *See* Ch. 6.5.3.
61. *See* Ch. 9.3.3.

jurisdictions investigated in an extension of their weak coherence, rather than a (radical) change in coherence.

However, the collateral taker's right of use can be argued to have led to inconsistencies, as appropriation by the collateral taker involves ambiguities in the classification of the collateral taker's interest, because such interest could then be classified as either outright transfer or as a pledge. In addition, it has been noted that the complete insulation of collateral arrangements from the effects of insolvency proceedings, so that even in the collateral giver's insolvency, he can continue to make payments to the collateral taker under the collateral arrangement, represents an infringement of the principle that creditors should be ranked equally in bankruptcy.[62] As a whole, it can therefore be concluded that the implementation of the FCD changed coherent law in weakly coherent and incoherent law, which constitutes a disproportionate decrease in the coherence of the jurisdictions investigated.

11.2.5 Intermediary Insolvency

Since legal interests are tested *par excellence* in insolvency situations,[63] it is not surprising that in many jurisdictions, strong principles of property law are applied in securities custody law, so as to provide accountholders with (proprietary) protection against their immediate intermediary('s liquidator) and the claims of its creditors. In the following section, it will be further investigated to what extent the current securities custody laws of the European jurisdictions investigated are in accordance with those general principles of property law and what the effect of the modernisation measures as proposed in the previous chapter would be for that relationship. It will be argued that all European jurisdictions investigated show a strong degree of monism, but that this monism sometimes leads to inconsistencies and therewith to incoherence, while the modernisation proposed could contribute to an elimination of that incoherence.

Under the laws of all European jurisdictions investigated, it is a general principle of property law that entitlement holders can assert their property right in insolvency situations as if there were no insolvency.[64] This principle can be seen as an instance of the *droit de suite* principle discussed previously, under which an entitlement holder can successfully assert his property rights against all third parties holding the assets to which he is entitled.[65] Under both Belgian and Dutch law, securities accountholders enjoy a right of co-ownership and, as a general rule, they can assert that right in their intermediary's insolvency accordingly.

---

62. Keijser (2006), 350.
63. An old Dutch publication even referred to insolvency law as the law's gym, where all legal relationships are fully stretched and unfolded most intensively; *ASC Almanak 1911* as cited by Huizink (2005), 22.
64. *Cf.*, e.g., Art. 57 Fw (the Netherlands).
65. *See supra*, s. 11.2.2.

Moreover, under Belgian law, the proprietary character of accountholder interests is only apparent in intermediary insolvencies as it is only then that accountholders can revendicate their assets with higher-tier intermediaries. Under Dutch law, on the other hand, accountholders can only assert their proprietary interests against their immediate intermediary('s liquidator). But, more importantly, the dogmatic consequences of the specific property law construct that was chosen to protect accountholders in the Netherlands, paradoxically makes lower than second-tier accountholders mere unsecured creditors in their intermediary's insolvency.

It is submitted that this distinction presents an example of contradictory valuation or *Wertungswiderspruch,* as the Dutch law here displays contradictory values to situations that do not materially differ.[66] Accountholders usually cannot assess whether an intermediary is a direct CSD participant or not as their securities accounts do not express that difference. Yet, they are treated fundamentally differently when asserting their interests in the account provider's insolvency, which thus shows a telling instance of incoherence. Conversely, under French securities custody law, accountholders do not enjoy a traditional proprietary interest, but are always protected against their intermediary('s liquidator) and its creditors' claims. A special statutory provision grants accountholders a right similar to revendication against their account provider's liquidator so that they can always retrieve their assets.[67]

The modernisation proposed in the previous chapter requires that accountholders take free of the intermediary's general creditors' claims, regardless of the number of intermediaries interposed between accountholder and CSD or issuer. The implementation of that measure would result in the sanctioning of the Belgian adherence to the *droit de suite* principle in securities law and its monism would thus be confirmed. Likewise, French law's pluralism would be underscored and its coherence would remain unaffected. For Dutch law, on the other hand, the modernisation measure would result in a derogation from the general private law construct of co-ownership and its dogmatic consequences. It has been shown, however, that this proposed change of monism into pluralism is justified as it involves the elimination of inconsistent valuation. Weak coherence is thus preferred over incoherence, while the change in coherence would not be disproportionate nor unwarranted.[68]

As another instance of the *droit de suite* principle, the holders of proprietary interests enjoy a direct link with the assets they are entitled to, but must bear the losses that occur with regard to those assets accordingly. Even under French law, where accountholders do not enjoy a traditional proprietary interest, as well as under the laws of all other jurisdictions investigated, this rule is applied when allocating losses that occur in intermediary insolvencies. As a result, a deficit in

66. *Cf.* Ch. 2.3.1 *and* Ch. 10.2.6.
67. *See* Ch. 6.3.6.
68. Moreover, the Dutch application of the co-ownership construct to accountholder interests has led to incoherence in other aspects also. *See* Ch. 7.3.4. *and supra,* s. 11.2.2.

securities maintained by an intermediary for its clients is distributed among the accountholders entitled to the type of securities of which a deficit occurs.

However, as has been argued in the previous chapter, this allocation regime is sub-optimal on both economic and normative grounds and should therefore be modified.[69] Moreover, it is submitted here that the jurisdictions investigated show *Wertungswiderspruch* with respect to this allocation model, on similar grounds as the Dutch law was argued to be inconsistent with respect to its rules on accountholder protection. Accountholders cannot possibly assess the likelihood of a deficit in one pool of securities or another, as that deficit is incurred by the account provider. Yet accountholders who hold entitlements to securities in which the deficit occurs must share, fortuitously, it is submitted, in the loss, while other accountholders, clients of that same account provider, do not suffer. A loss allocation model should therefore be introduced that does not apply contradictory values to situations that do not materially differ and distributes deficits pro rata amongst all accountholders of the same account provider.[70]

For Belgian and Dutch law, the introduction of such an allocation model would involve a change from monism into pluralism as it involves a departure from the *droit de suite* principle. But by removing this inconsistency in valuation or *Wertungswiderspruch,* it would also eliminate the existing incoherence and the change from incoherence to weak coherence would therefore not be unjustified or disproportionate. For French law, on the other hand, no change in coherence would be effected as the new model would merely underscore its current pluralism in this respect.

Finally, the intermediary insolvency rules in none of the jurisdictions investigated apply the general principle of property law that those who have acquired interests in certain assets can assert these interests against others who might have acquired interests in the same assets, but later in time. Under none of the laws investigated does this *prior tempore, potior iure* principle apply to accountholders, as they can always assert their right only pro rata, i.e. as being entitled to fractions of pooled accounts, regardless of the moment when they acquired their interests. Also if a deficit occurs in an account provider's insolvency, accountholders with earlier interests do not trump later accountholders under any of the laws investigated. Yet this inapplicability of the *prior tempore* principle constitutes no pluralism or incoherence of the systems investigated, since it is the result of another general principle of property law that treats co-owners equally when their assets become commingled.[71] Moreover, no modernisation has been proposed to alter this priority rule.

Thus, it has been shown that most European jurisdictions investigated display a strong degree of monism, as they apply the *droit de suite* principle also to intermediary insolvency rules, both with regard to accountholder protection and with regard to the distribution of losses when deficits occur. It has been noted,

69. Ch. 10.2.6.
70. *See* Ch. 10.2.6.
71. *Cf.*, e.g., BURKE (2003), 369 on the common law.

however, that in all jurisdictions, this monism leads to *Wertungswiderspruch* and thus to incoherence where it implies a loss allocation model that unjustly distinguishes between accountholders that are entitled to the type of securities in which the deficit occurs, and other accountholders that maintain securities accounts with the same intermediary. A similar inconsistency in valuation has been established in Dutch law, where it unjustly distinguishes between accountholders that maintain a securities account with the CSD or a direct CSD participant, and other accountholders. The modernisation proposed eliminates those instances of incoherence, and is therefore preferred over maintaining monism. With regard to the current rules of priority between accountholders in their intermediary's insolvency, no incoherence or weak coherence has been found, while no modernisation measure has been proposed in that regard.

11.2.6 Conflict of Laws

In the previous chapter, support has been expressed for the adoption of the Hague Securities Convention ('HSC') or the implementation of similar rules.[72] However, as with modernisation and harmonisation of substantive securities law, one of the strongest objections against the HSC has been that it would fundamentally alter current rules of EU private international law, without being clearly beneficial.[73] More particularly, it has been argued that the HSC departs from the traditional and widely supported *lex rei sitae* in favour of unlimited freedom of contract which would only serve UK and US financial institutions.[74] Coherence considerations have thus been presented as a major argument against ratification of the HSC.

The argument, however, is flawed for several reasons. Firstly, the alteration that the HSC would cause is less fundamental than presented by its objectors.[75] Not only is unlimited freedom of contract with regard to proprietary matters already known in European private international law,[76] but the HSC is also in accordance with (the rationale of) the PRIMA rules as currently codified in the relevant EU directives.[77] It follows from the fallback rules of the HSC that the HSC will in most instances refer to the law of the relevant intermediary's jurisdiction as the applicable law, while an express choice of law in the account agreement will also probably be made to that effect, if only to satisfy the reality check.[78]

Secondly, the current rules of EU private international law clearly do not suffice as conflict of laws rules that make the applicable law readily identifiable. The HSC, on the other hand, would bring about a welcome improvement of European

72. Ch. 10.2.11.
73. Bloch & De Vauplane (2005), 10. *Cf.* Opinion of the ECB of 17 March 2005, 12. For a discussion of other objections, *see*, e.g., Haentjens (2006), 97–98.
74. *Cf.* Johansson (2005) *and see* Haentjens (2006), 97.
75. Potok (2004), 220. *Cf.* Rogers (1996), 1460.
76. *Cf.* Rome Convention Art. 3.
77. *See* Ch. 9.3.3.
78. *Cf.* Rogers (2005), 38-39. *Contra* Rank (2005), 250. *See also supra* s. 9.2.4.

private international law, since it is not based on a concept that has never been intended to serve the cross-border settlement of book-entry securities, viz. the *lex situs*.[79] Moreover, it does not follow a fragmented approach which has been shown to be conceptually and practically unsatisfactory.[80]

In sum, the 'reality check' rules of the HSC correspond with PRIMA which already represents a departure from the traditional *lex rei sitae*. EU conflict of laws rules thus currently display a pluralism that will not be fundamentally changed by the rules of the HSC. In addition, that pluralism is not as dramatic as supposed by some, since the freedom of contract which the HSC introduces corresponds with existing rules of general private international law concerning intangible, as well as tangible movables. Finally, insofar as the HSC constitutes an abandonment of the *rei sitae* rule and thus underscores current pluralism, it is submitted that that change in coherence is clearly neither unjustifiable nor disproportionate.

11.2.7 Clearing and Settlement Systems

Both national and regional legislature increasingly recognise the pivotal role that the providers of clearing and settlement systems, i.e. (I)CSDs and CCPs, play in the settlement process. Specific rules have therefore been enacted to address the systemic risk associated with these key players,[81] but it can be questioned to what extent they should be made subject to specific rules that derogate from rules of a more general nature.[82] In the following section, some of these specific rules and their consequences for coherence will be discussed.

In the previous chapters, it has been seen that the 1998 EU Settlement Finality Directive ('SFD') principally aimed at addressing the systemic risk associated with payment and securities settlement systems, and, more specifically, with the insolvency of a participant in such a system.[83] The SFD therefore provides that the execution of transfer orders is not to be affected by a participant's insolvency when such orders are entered into the settlement system prior to the commencement of insolvency proceedings against the participant that gave the orders, or when the orders are executed by the settlement system while it was legitimately unaware of that participant's insolvency.[84] In addition, the SFD requires that insolvency proceedings against a participant in a settlement system have no retroactive effects with regard to that and other participants' rights and obligations towards

79. *See* Ch. 10.2.11.
80. Benjamin & Yates (2002), 79.
81. *See,* e.g., Moloney (2002), 711. On systemic risk, *see* Ch. 4.4.1.
82. *Cf.* CPSS/IOSCO Recommendations 2001, 5: 'The various components of the legal framework (eg securities law, contract law, commercial law, bankruptcy law, etc.) should not be inconsistent with or override the rules or procedures of the SSS [Securities Settlement System, MH] or its ability to meet these recommendations'.
83. *See* Ch. 9.3.3 *and* 10.2.8.
84. Art. 3.

the system.[85] Thus, the finality or irreversibility of transfer orders and their execution is ensured by insulating the settlement system and its participants from all effects of insolvency proceedings.

These rules derogate from the insolvency laws of all European jurisdictions investigated, under which insolvency proceedings have a retroactive effect as of the beginning of the day on which the proceedings were commenced, so that all actions taken on that day by the insolvent party are void and revocable.[86] Consequently, specific, derogatory rules had to be enacted in all jurisdictions investigated, but especially in France.[87]

The coherence of these jurisdictions has thus been weakened by the introduction of a pluralism in norms. But unlike most other derogatory rules that have been previously discussed, the rules of the SFD do not differentiate between general private or commercial law and securities custody and transfer law, but between general private or commercial law and 'clearing and settlement systems law'. The consequences of an account provider's insolvency therefore differ according to whether or not the account provider is a direct participant of a clearing and settlement system that is covered by the CSD, and whether or not his transfer orders are settled via a settlement system that is covered by the SFD.[88] It is submitted that these distinctions create an unjust dichotomy or *Wertungswiderspruch,* as accountholders who cannot assess whether or not their account provider is a direct clearing and settlement system participant, let alone via which system their transactions are settled, must suffer from the dramatically different consequences which the SFD creates.

In sum, the derogatory rules of the SFD that apply only to transfers and transfer orders involving clearing and settlement systems covered by the SFD, result in incoherence within securities custody and transfer law. Moreover, as these rules can very well apply to all transfers of securities by book-entry and all securities account providers, the incoherence cannot be justified by the special character of clearing and settlement system providers as the highest tier of the custody chain.[89] It is submitted that by the same token, the rule of Belgian law pursuant to which CSDs may obtain a statutory security interest in their participants' omnibus accounts, including these participants' clients' assets, while other intermediaries cannot vest such an extensive lien, also results in an unjustifiable instance of incoherence.[90]

85. Art. 7.
86. *Cf.* Act of 8 August 1997 Arts. 17 *et seq.* (*Loi sur les Faillites/Faillissementswet*) (Belgium), Arts. L. 621-32 and L. 621-24 C. com. (France), Art. 23 Fw (the Netherlands).
87. Act of 28 April 1999 Art. 6 (Belgium), L. 330-1 II C. mon. fin. (France), 212b Fw (the Netherlands). *See* Ch. 5.4.3, 6.4.3 *and* 7.4.4, respectively.
88. It must be noted, however, that the SFD allows Member States to individually designate 'indirect participants' to be covered by the Directive; Art. 2(f) and (g).
89. Unlike, for instance, the rule of the US UCC which provides that creditors of clearing and settlement system providers need not obtain control of securities in order to create an effective security interest in those securities. The derogatory character of this rule is justified, because as settlement providers are the highest tier of the custody chain, their securities simply cannot be transferred; UCC § 8-51 1(c). *See* Ch. 8.3.5.
90. Act of 2 August 2002 Art. 31(5) and Art. 31(1), respectively. *See* Ch. 5.3.8.

Thus, where accountholders cannot evidently ascertain that they are subject to derogatory rules of clearing and settlement systems, and where the derogatory character of those rules cannot be justified by the unique position of settlement system providers, these rules should be reconsidered or extended so as to apply to all of securities custody and transfer law.[91] Not only would such an approach result in the elimination of the found inconsistency in valuation and incoherence within an already specific and functional area of law,[92] it would also prevent any uncertainty that may arise over the scope of the specific rules for clearing and settlement systems.[93] The UNIDROIT draft convention is therefore not supported on normative and coherence considerations, where it provides that specific, non-statutory rules promulgated by the securities settlement systems themselves prevail over the convention's own provisions, should the latter rules be inconsistent with the settlement system's provisions.[94]

11.3 CONCLUSION

In this chapter, it has been separately investigated for a number of subjects of securities custody and transfer law to what extent the current securities laws of Belgium, France and the Netherlands are in coherence with the more general areas of their laws. More accurately, it has been ascertained whether these jurisdictions show strong coherence, weak coherence, or incoherence, i.e. whether they display monism, pluralism or (logical) inconsistencies, an analysis which implied the definition of general principles and characteristics.[95]

In addition, it has been examined how the modernisation measures as proposed in the previous chapter would affect the coherence of the said jurisdictions. It has been shown that the modernisation would result in a change of monism into pluralism, i.e. in less principles shared by both securities law and the more general areas of law, with regard to two subjects of securities custody law only. First, the modernisation proposed would result in a departure from the current adherence of Dutch law to the *droit de suite* principle where it regards an accountholder's proprietary position in his account provider's insolvency. Second, a departure is proposed from the adherence of all jurisdictions investigated to the *droit de suite* principle where that principle leads to the current allocation of deficits that may occur in intermediary insolvencies. In both instances, however, it has been argued

91. *Cf.* LÖBER (2006), 62, who proposes to take the insolvency and finality provisions out of the SFD and to put them into a new EU directive on securities custody and transfer law, to put the SFD provisions that regulate the access of market participants into a new regulatory framework directive, and to put the SFD provisions on the creation and enforcement of security interests in financial collateral into the FCD.
92. *Cf.* PARTSCH-BOBRICHEFF (2005), 45.
93. *Cf.* HAENTJENS (2006), 32 on the problems caused by the unclear scope of the SFD.
94. E.g. Arts. 5(1)(c), 11(2), 12(5), 19(3), 20(1). *Cf.* UCC § 8-111.
95. *Cf.* DE VAUPLANE & BORNET (2001), no. 1245: '*le passage de l'harmonisation à l'unification imposera la définition de ces principes généraux*'.

that the modernisation would also result in the elimination of current inconsistencies due to a *Wertungswiderspruch*. The coherence of the said jurisdictions would therefore be improved by the modernisation as proposed, because it would turn current incoherence into mere weak coherence.

In some instances, the modernisation proposed would merely underscore or make explicit current pluralism, i.e. the current derogation of general principles in securities law. These instances concern the current (and future) derogation from *droit de suite* where it regards the prohibition of upper-tier attachment and the possibility of uncovered credits, the current and future derogation from the principle of consensualism in Belgian and French securities transfer law, the derogation from the ban on fiduciary transfers which has been underscored by the implementation of the FCD in all jurisdictions, and the current derogation from the *lex rei sitae* which will be made explicit if the HSC will be ratified.

However, the modernisation proposed would also eliminate incoherence if it would make explicit the special characteristics of both the contractual relationship between accountholder and his intermediary and the proprietary position of an accountholder. With regard to both subjects, it has been shown that the application of traditional private and commercial law concepts such as *depositum, depositum irregulare,* mandate and ownership to securities custody leads to inconsistencies and that the proposed modernisation would thus improve current coherence. The introduction of a new concept to refer to accountholder interests as a whole, however, has been shown to result in a disproportionate reduction of coherence.

Present incoherence would also arguably be turned into weak coherence by the elimination of the inconsistencies currently caused by adherence to the causality principle in the securities transfer laws of all European jurisdictions investigated. Although the proposed introduction of an abstract transfer regime would change monism into pluralism, it has been shown that that change would be justified on both normative and coherence grounds. As a third instance in which the modernisation proposed would eliminate current inconsistencies, it has been argued that derogatory rules of clearing and settlement systems should be extended so as to apply to all of securities custody and transfer law.

The modernisation proposed would also confirm and strengthen the monism that currently exists where it concerns the publicity principle and the Dutch adherence to its transfer regime by *traditio* in securities transfer law. Moreover, the modernisation proposed would reinforce adherence to the publicity principle in securities law to an important extent as it would intensify the effectiveness of credit entries in a securities account by securing its finality and recognising an accountholder's interests, also when the credit entries are 'uncovered'.

Finally, a harmonisation of the circumstances in which *bona fide* acquirers are protected against competing interests would have no influence on the current coherence of the European jurisdictions investigated, while no modernisation was proposed with regard to the priority of accountholders in intermediary insolvencies.

In sum, none of the modernisation measures diminish current coherence disproportionately and unjustifiably. On the contrary, most measures that have been proposed in the preceding chapter have been shown to improve coherence, which applies especially to the issues that need explicit modernisation most urgently, such as the codification of the different aspects of accountholder interests, accountholder protection in intermediary insolvencies and securities transfers by book-entry. The introduction of a new concept to denote accountholder interests as a whole, however, has been shown to decrease disproportionately the coherence of the jurisdictions investigated and has therefore not been advanced. Consequently, the Giovannini Group was right when it stated: 'there is no need to revolutionise property laws in general, only those dealing with securities'.[96] Except for the introduction of a new accountholder interest concept, it has been shown that no doctrinal objections can indeed be validly made if such a 'revolution' confines itself to the property laws dealing with securities.

96. Giovannini Group 2003 Report, 17. Contrast the statement of the Legal Certainty Group: 'In all cases, book-entry rights are un-classified, un-characterised and doctrinally neutral at the harmonising EU level. They neither replace nor alter national property rules concerning securities.' Legal Certainty Group Advice, 8.

Chapter 12

Towards the European Harmonisation of Securities Law

12.1 INTRODUCTION

As has been noted previously, UNIDROIT aims at a global harmonisation of securities custody and transfer law that reduces legal or systemic risk and improves market efficiency.[1] Consequently, the UNIDROIT Secretariat has stated that it would only consider the drafting of a harmonisation instrument if that would be evidently needed to ensure the internal soundness of national systems and their interoperability or compatibility.[2] With regard to the European harmonisation, a similar argument can be made, especially in the light of the constraints imposed by European, i.e. Community law.

Chapter 10 scrutinised the 'internal soundness' of selected European systems and advanced proposals for modernisation accordingly. These proposals have subsequently been tested against coherence considerations in the chapter that followed, but the 'interoperability' or 'compatibility' of the European jurisdictions investigated has not been examined in detail and will therefore be further elaborated upon in this chapter. Moreover, although this book is not primarily concerned with European law *stricto sensu* and its institutional matters, some remarks will be made here on the question of whether the harmonisation measures that would satisfy the requirements of internal soundness and interoperability could withstand the constraints of EU law.

Thus, the possible scope of future EU legislative action in the field of securities custody and transfer law will be the main focus of this chapter, and the most important issue to be discussed in that context will be to what extent a

1. Ch. 9.2.3 *and* 10.1.
2. *See,* e.g., PAECH (2002), 1158 *and* UNIDROIT 2003 Position Paper, 6 and 14.

harmonisation instrument should be comprehensive. It could be questioned, for instance, whether such an instrument should take a functional approach, or be more systematic and prescribe classifications. In other words, it could be questioned whether it should achieve minimum or maximum harmonisation, and to what extent it should touch on different, other relevant areas of the law. Closely connected with this issue is what form the EU harmonisation instrument should take, which could be determined, in part, by ascertaining the extent to which national legislation must be changed and the range of subjects that should be covered. In that vein, it will be discussed whether a soft law instrument, a directive or a regulation should be chosen.

In the following sections, the legal basis for any EU harmonisation instrument in the field of securities custody and transfer law will be discussed first, after which views will be advanced on the preferred scope of such instrument. Finally, the argument will be made that a directive would be the most appropriate form for the measure of harmonisation and modernisation proposed above.

12.2 LEGAL BASIS

As a general principle, a restrictive approach enhances any harmonisation initiative's chances of success, while such an approach might also be warranted to preserve competition between legal systems.[3] For the EU, the limits to harmonisation are set by the Treaty Establishing the European Community ('EC Treaty') Article 5. First, it states that the European legislature should restrict itself to matters for which the Treaty has explicitly granted legislative authority. Second, it provides that EU legislation should comply with the principles of subsidiarity and proportionality, meaning that the Community should only consider the regulation of matters that cannot be better left to the national sphere, and that it should not go beyond what is necessary to achieve the objectives of the Treaty. In the following, it will therefore be examined first, whether the EC Treaty empowers the European legislature to adopt a harmonisation instrument in the field of securities custody and transfer law, and second, for what matters of securities custody and transfer law a need for harmonisation exists.

It is submitted that EC Treaty Article 95 provides the most appropriate legal basis for Community legislation on securities custody and transfer law, as the article empowers the European legislature to adopt harmonisation measures that 'have as their object' the enhancement of the internal market.[4] But in the Tobacco case of 2000, the European Court of Justice ('ECJ') ruled that EC Treaty Article 95 does not provide a legal basis for harmonisation measures in all areas where legal disparities between national rules exist. According to the Court, EC Treaty Article

3. *Cf.* Ch. 9.1.1.
4. EC Treaty Art. 14(2) further defines 'internal market' as being an area of free movement of goods, persons, services and capital.

95 provides a legal ground for harmonisation, only where it 'genuinely has the improvement of the functioning of the internal market as its object'.[5]

Without reiterating all the arguments that have been brought forward previously, a harmonisation of securities custody and transfer law will be 'genuinely' beneficial to the functioning of the internal market, as the research referred to *above* clearly shows the significant economic benefits of harmonisation in that field.[6] More specifically, a harmonisation that would eliminate current legal diversity would contribute to the reduction of post-trading costs, resulting in a higher GDP of 0.2 per cent or more in the subsequent years.[7] Moreover, it would control the existing legal uncertainty which involves unacceptable (systemic) risks in view of the economic importance of today's securities markets and their smooth functioning.

Taking into account the measures of modernisation as proposed above, Community harmonisation of securities custody and transfer law would also improve accountholder protection and market stability, and thus support the freedom to provide services and the free movement of capital.[8] In addition, it would serve consumer protection and enhance the competitiveness of the European market by making it globally compatible, which are all explicit policy goals of the European Union.[9]

In sum, EC Treaty Article 95 empowers the European legislature to draft a harmonisation instrument in the field of securities custody and transfer law, if it would bring about a harmonisation and modernisation as proposed. Such a harmonisation instrument would therefore most probably comply with the constraints as codified in EC Treaty Article 5 and as interpreted by the ECJ.

12.3 SCOPE AND INTEROPERABILITY

12.3.1 INTRODUCTION

As just stated, EU law dictates that legislative action may only be undertaken on the Community level if it would not be better left to the national legislatures.[10] In the case of securities custody and transfer law, this requirement comes particularly into play when considering the 'interoperability' of national systems,

5. Case C-376/98, Germany v. Parliament and Council, 2000 ECR I-8419 (*Tobacco Advertising*). *See,* e.g., MOLONEY (2002), 722, ROTH (2002), 764, VAN ERP (2004), 538 *and* VAN GERVEN (2004), 505–506. *See also* HESSELINK (2005), especially 76–77, on the legal basis for a European harmonisation of non-mandatory rules in contract law, *and* WEATHERILL (2006), 105 *et seq.*, on the case law subsequent (but not contrary) to the Tobacco case, in particular Case 210/03, 2004 ECRI–11893 (*Swedish Match*).
6. E.g., G30 2003 Plan of Action, 4–5 *and* Giovannini Group 2001 Report, ii. *See* Ch. 9.1.1.
7. EC Economic Impact Study (2006), 18.
8. *See also* EFMLG 2003 Report, 27. *Cf.* SFD Recital 3.
9. EC Treaty Art. 3(1)(c), (h), (m) and (t).
10. EC Treaty Art. 5.

as a supranational legislature is evidently in a better position to establish such interoperability when that is absent than the national legislatures themselves. The scope of a harmonisation instrument, or whether that instrument matches the EU requirement of subsidiarity, should therefore be determined by an assessment of whether interoperability is currently absent and, subsequently, whether particular measures of harmonisation would significantly contribute to the interoperability of the national systems concerned.

In the context of the national Canadian harmonisation of securities custody and transfer law, it has been considered that the interoperability of national systems is established when those systems display either 'technical uniformity' or 'functional consistency'. It was noted that a limited number of matters, such as conflict of laws and the description of accountholder interests, requires technical uniformity, but that for other issues, functional consistency suffices to achieve 'the desired level of safety and efficiency'.[11] In the following sections, it will be examined for a number of issues that have been investigated in the previous chapters whether harmonisation is needed to establish true interoperability in the form of either 'technical uniformity' or 'functional consistency'.

12.3.2 Definitions

For the interoperability of national systems, as well as for the certainty of scope, it is of critical importance that a harmonisation instrument in the field of securities custody and transfer law provides clear definitions of the categories of financial instruments, the account providers and CSDs it covers. On the one hand, exhaustive definitions that specifically describe the categories of financial instruments covered by the harmonisation instrument envisaged would facilitate the smooth cross-border settlement of securities transactions. A clear set of criteria for the eligibility of financial instruments would prevent disputes over instruments that are eligible to be credited to a securities account in one jurisdiction, but are excluded in another.[12]

Precisely defined categories of securities would thus enhance legal certainty, but would also necessarily leave out certain categories, which might be particularly undesirable in view of the ever evolving (securities) markets and the emergence of new financial instruments.[13] Moreover, because of such developments, a theoretically satisfactory and broadly acceptable definition of financial instruments has

11. Spink & Paré (2004), 355.
12. In some jurisdictions, for instance, derivatives are subject to securities custody and transfer laws, while these instruments are excluded from those laws in others. The US UCC for example, can apply to derivatives, while statutory provisions of, for example, French and Dutch law expressly do not cover derivatives. *See* Ch. 8.3.2 (US), Ch. 6.3.1 (France), *and* 7.2 (the Netherlands), respectively.
13. Bernasconi (2000), 43–45.

proven to be extremely difficult.[14] In addition, normative reasons require that the financial instruments covered by a future harmonisation be defined as broadly as possible, since the legal regime determining accountholders' rights and duties should not differ, depending on whether the accountholders are entitled to securities which may or may not fall within certain contestable definitions.

The better view would therefore be that a future EU harmonisation instrument should cover all (entitlements to) securities and financial instruments that are credited to a securities account, but that it should be left to supranational regulatory authorities to further define the categories of those securities and other financial instruments that are eligible for being credited to a securities account. This also seems to be the view of the Legal Certainty Group and corresponds with existing Community legislation, but also with the approach taken in the US UCC, the UNIDROIT draft convention, and the HSC.[15]

A similar line of argumentation can be made with regard to securities account providers. As in the case of financial instruments, it is submitted that a possible future instrument of EU harmonisation should define 'intermediary' or 'account provider' as broadly as possible, so that all accountholders are protected by that instrument.[16] To ensure the necessary degree of interoperability, it is submitted that the requirements for eligibility should be determined by (prudential) regulatory law at the Community level, and that it should include at least credit institutions, investment firms and all (I)CSDs.[17] That view has also been taken by the Legal Certainty Group, and corresponds with existing Community legislation, such as the Directive on Markets in Financial Instruments ('MiFID').[18]

Further, it is the Legal Certainty Group's view that a future harmonisation instrument should cover not only settlements within certain securities settlement systems, but all settlements of securities by book-entry. It follows that both purely

---

14. In France, for instance, no consensus exists on the precise scope of the term *valeurs mobilières* (securities) and its relation to the term *instruments financiers* (financial instruments). In short, the only common characteristic which seems to be uncontested to some extent is tradability on a stock exchange, a characteristic which has been codified in Art. L. 228-1 C. com. Under US law, on the other hand, UCC § 8-102(a)(15)(ii) required 'securities' to be also tradable on a securities market. Furthermore, when an instrument is not tradable, issuers can opt for application of Art. 8, provided the instrument is a medium for investment. Provided they can be registered by means of a securities account, the UCC can also apply to other financial instruments such as derivatives; UCC § 8-103(e). *See* Ch. II.3.2.1. *Cf. also* Rank *in* EISMA ET AL. (2002), 19–49.
15. *See* Legal Certainty Group Advice, 8, MiFID Annex I, Section C, Ch. 8.3.2 (US) *and* UNIDROIT draft convention Art. 1(a) and (b), and Explanatory Report (2005), 31, respectively. The EFMLG on the other hand, did not favour extension to derivatives, but also advised against an exhaustive definition of securities; EFMLG 2003 Report, 20, 22 and 28.
16. The Legal Certainty Group decided to use 'account provider', as the most appropriate term to denote a person who maintains positions regarding securities by way of book-entry. *See* MARKT/G2/MNCT D(2005), memo on 'account provider', Brussels, 6 April 2005, *available at* <http://ec.europa.eu/internal_market/financial-markets/clearing/certainty_en.htm>.
17. *Cf.* the EFMLG 2003 Report, which proposed to further include corporate issuers and supervised insurance undertakers.
18. Legal Certainty Group Advice, 9 *and see* MiFID Art. 5(1).

domestic settlements and cross-border settlements should be made subject to the instrument. As has been shown in the context of the Settlement Finality Directive ('SFD'), rules of securities custody and transfer law that apply only to certain, specific clearing and settlement systems can easily result in unjust dichotomies and incoherence within an already specific and functional area of law.[19] The view of the Legal Certainty Group must therefore be supported from a coherence and normative perspective, as derogatory rules on certain securities settlements are only justified when they result from the unique position of securities settlement providers as the highest tier of the custody chain.

In sum, normative and coherence considerations require that a possible future harmonisation instrument of securities custody and transfer law should cover all categories of financial instruments that can be credited to a securities account, account providers, CSDs and securities settlements, so that virtually all accountholders are equally protected by the harmonisation instrument's provisions. While the definitions of that instrument should thus be as broad as possible, legal certainty and interoperability require that regulatory law at the Community level should determine the eligibility of financial instruments to be credited in securities accounts, as well as account providers and CSDs.

12.3.3 Characterisation

In the preceding chapter, it has been argued that the introduction of a new concept that would refer to accountholder interests as a bundle of rights would be unwarranted from a coherence perspective. Unidroit, the Hague Conference and the Legal Certainty Group also considered a functional approach that would refrain from the introduction of legal classifications as the best course to take and drafted or advised accordingly.[20] It can be questioned, however, whether such a functional approach can guarantee the required degree of interoperability.[21]

More specifically, it might be objected that re-characterisation remains problematical without harmonisation on the conceptual level.[22] Recharacterisation occurs when the applicable (substantive) law classifies a certain interest differently than parties originally intended, which thus involves considerable (legal) risk for the parties concerned. Assume, for instance, that a Dutch judge classifies a securities entitlement that has been established under US law as a contractual claim and consequently does not give the accountholder the protection normally awarded to accountholders under Dutch law. But from this example, it can only be concluded that the issue of re-characterisation must be addressed by a unification of private international law, so that the applicable law is easily ascertainable

19. Ch. 11.2.7.
20. *See* Ch. 10.2.3.
21. *Cf.* Unidroit Implementation Report, February 2006, Doc. 26 of Study LXXVIII, 9.
22. *Cf.* Explanatory Notes to the Preliminary Draft Unidroit Securities Convention, 46–48 *and* Spink & Paré (2004), 343.

and indeed identically determined by all forums. In addition, it showed that such unification of conflict of laws rules should give effect to the parties' intent, which arguably is the most appropriate way to make the applicable law, and thus the consequent characterisations predictable.[23]

Moreover, harmonisation or unification of the separate elements of accountholder interests, i.e. of the effects of a credit entry in a securities account, also minimises the risk of differing characterisations by the courts and their unwanted consequences. Thus, when no harmonisation is established on the conceptual level, the interoperability of national systems must be ensured by specific and precise harmonisation of the effects of a credit in a securities account, because these effects normally follow from the classification of either the accountholder/intermediary relationship, or the accountholder interest.

An accountholder's right of disposal, retrieval, to vest security interests, and to receive and exercise the rights attached to his securities typically follow from the classification of his interests,[24] and the harmonisation of these rights by explicit provisions is therefore advisable for considerations of interoperability. Furthermore, it has been noted that the (im)possibility of upper-tier attachment and uncovered credit entries in a securities account also follows from the classification of accountholder interests as a direct property right.[25] The prohibition of upper-tier attachment and the proprietary effect of uncovered credits should therefore be also explicitly provided for in a harmonisation instrument on interoperability considerations, even when all jurisdictions investigated currently prohibit upper-tier attachment in a similar way.

12.3.4 Accountholder Protection in Intermediary Insolvency

It has been shown *above* that as a result of its classification of accountholder interests, Dutch law does not give accountholders (proprietary) protection in their account provider's insolvency under certain circumstances and it has been argued that such law should be modernised on normative and coherence grounds.[26] As a third ground, it is added here that such law renders the system concerned not fully interoperable with other systems of custody law.

For instance, if an investor holds a securities account with a Dutch intermediary, which in turn holds a cross-border securities account with a foreign participant of a foreign settlement system, Dutch law applies to the said investor's interests pursuant to PRIMA. However, Dutch law does not grant this investor the proprietary protection that is enjoyed by other Dutch accountholders, or more accurately, by the holders of (Dutch) securities that have been admitted by the Dutch CSD and are thus covered by the relevant Dutch statute. In the Dutch intermediary's

23. *See* Ch. 10.2.11.
24. *See* Ch. 11.2.2.
25. Ch. 10.2.10 *and* 10.2.5.
26. Ch. 10.2.6 *and* 11.2.5.

insolvency, the said investor would therefore be left with a mere contractual claim, which is probably contrary to his expectations, as he might have assumed to be protected by the Dutch statute. Systems such as the Dutch thus do not allow for cross-border links without serious consequences for accountholder protection and therefore distort the interoperability between systems of securities law.

Conversely, when an accountholder holds a securities account with an intermediary of a jurisdiction that grants proprietary protection or otherwise confers top priority to accountholders in intermediary insolvency (such as France and Belgium), while this intermediary holds the corresponding securities with an intermediary from a jurisdiction where the accountholders are not so protected under all circumstances (such as the Netherlands), the upper-tier intermediary's insolvency would prove to be problematical for the lower one, since it cannot pass on its loss of securities under the law that governs its relationship with its clients. This poses a serious risk which would most likely be passed on to the clients of the lower intermediary in the form of higher custody costs, but also indicates the defective interoperability of the system that does not grant accountholders a top priority in intermediary insolvencies under all circumstances.

It is submitted therefore, that 'functional consistency' is currently not achieved with regard to the consequences of intermediary insolvencies to accountholder interests and that systems like the Dutch should be harmonised with systems that better protect accountholder interests. Thus, the Legal Certainty Group's advice that such harmonisation (and modernisation) of accountholders' priority in intermediary insolvencies be established on the EU level has been shown to comply with the principle of subsidiarity as a necessary measure to achieve full EU interoperability.

12.3.5 Corporate and Other Areas of Law

Of several matters that play an important role in the custody of book-entry securities, it can be questioned whether they are better harmonised at other places than in a future instrument on securities custody and transfer law. This applies particularly to matters of corporate law, regulatory, insolvency, and agency law, as well as private international law, which will be successively discussed in the following section.

First, it has been argued above that an accountholder's right to receive and exercise the rights attached to his securities typically follows from the classification of his interests, and that a harmonisation instrument that refrains from classifications should therefore make this right explicit in view of the interoperability of the jurisdictions concerned. The Unidroit draft convention, as well as the Legal Certainty Group Advice, propose such provisions,[27] but it can be questioned whether the harmonisation of corporate action processing by intermediaries should take place in an instrument that focuses on securities custody and transfer law.

27. *See* Ch. 10.2.7.

Indeed, some jurisdictions consider these issues to lie more within the scope of company law than of securities custody and transfer law, while the proposal for the Shareholders' Rights Directive also addresses the exercise of clients' voting rights by intermediaries.[28] It could therefore be argued that a harmonisation of securities custody and transfer law should not be concerned with 'corporate action processing'.

However, the enjoyment of the rights attached to an accountholder's securities concern both corporate securities and non-corporate financial instruments, while the indirect holding system has the potential to hamper that enjoyment for both types of instruments.[29] Consequently, it is submitted that a securities custody law harmonisation should contain general provisions that ensure accountholders' enjoyment of their rights as a traditional element of ownership of securities, but that specific rules on the corporate consequences of voting should be codified elsewhere. Thus, the exercise by intermediaries of the rights attached to accountholders' securities, as well as the intermediaries' obligations to pass on corporate and monetary rights to their clients should be addressed by the same harmonisation instrument. Such an approach would avoid difficult issues of scope, and, at the same time, respond to the need for an internally coherent and comprehensive harmonised securities custody and transfer law within the EU.

Second, it is reiterated that the eligibility of financial instruments for being credited in securities accounts, as well as the eligibility of account providers and CSDs for providing custody services, should be determined by (prudential) regulation at the Community level. Furthermore, it has been argued *above* that the separation of an intermediary's own assets from those of its clients, as well as the enforcement of the *tirage sur la masse* prohibition and supervision concerning the intermediaries' obligation to replace missing securities should also be left to regulatory law.[30]

More generally, it is submitted that regulatory authorities are in the best position to effectively monitor and enforce these matters of bookkeeping by intermediaries, to which compliance with the delivery versus payment rule[31] and other rules that regulate the technical operation of securities custody and settlement can be added. In sum, regulation is of critical importance in contributing to the safekeeping of investors' assets and thereby to the stability of the market, and should therefore complement any harmonisation instrument of securities custody and transfer law, but should not find a place in such instrument.[32]

Third, it seems generally accepted that true certainty in international securities settlements can only be obtained if securities custody law is jointly harmonised

---

28. It further facilitates proxy voting and provides that an intermediary does not necessarily have to vote identically on all securities in its custody. *See* Ch. 9.3.3.
29. *See also supra,* Ch. 9.3.3 and 10.2.7. A similar argument could be made with regard to all issues of securities custody and transfer law; *cf.* SPINK & PARÉ (2004), 347.
30. Ch. 10.2.5.
31. *Cf.* CPSS/IOSCO recommendations 2001, 19.
32. *Cf.* Legal Certainty Group Advice, 10.

with substantive insolvency law.[33] But it is submitted that a harmonisation of securities custody law should not extend to rules on fraudulent preferences or other, specific rules of insolvency law.[34] The rules of loss allocation in intermediary insolvencies on the other hand, are only characteristic of the custody of book-entry securities and should therefore be harmonised in that context. Moreover, technical uniformity is arguably needed with regard to those rules, as an element of vital importance in view of legal certainty in critical situations.[35]

Fourth, it has been claimed above that since an accountholder's right of disposal typically follows from the classification of his interests, a harmonisation instrument that avoids all classifications should explicitly codify this right for considerations of interoperability. More specifically, it has also been argued that such an instrument should state that this right of disposal must be effected against the account provider by means of an instruction.[36] Yet it is submitted that a EU harmonisation instrument of securities custody law should not be extended so as to determine under what circumstances such an instruction is validly given, which should be left to (national) rules of agency law. Consequently, the liability of intermediaries for not or unjustifiably having given effect to accountholder instructions and, generally, an intermediary's liability for deficits in the securities pools it administers, should also be left to other rules of law and is not a necessary element of a securities law harmonisation.[37]

Finally, it has been argued that the EU should ratify the Hague Securities Convention ('HSC') or implement similar provisions.[38] If the European Council will soon follow the European Commission's proposal and recommendation,[39] the HSC will become law for all Member States of the EU and separate conflict of laws provisions would not be needed in a future instrument on securities custody law. But if the EU persists in its reluctance to ratify the convention, it might be advisable (perhaps as a preliminarily measure) to introduce similar conflict of laws rules via a harmonisation instrument of custody law, as it is generally believed that the harmonisation of private international law requires simultaneous harmonisation of related rules of substantive law and vice versa.[40] Yet in view of global consistency in a matter of critical importance for legal certainty, it is submitted that the former would be the better course to take.

33. *See* HAENTJENS (2006), 97 and the references provided there.
34. *Cf.* UNIDROIT 2003 Position Paper, 28 *and* UNIDROIT draft convention Art. 16.
35. *See* Giovannini Group 2001 Report, 56. *But cf.* the position taken by the UNIDROIT draft convention and the Legal Certainty Group; *see* Ch. 10.2.6.
36. Ch. 10.2.5.
37. As has already been shown, these positions are in accordance with the current systemisation of law in all European jurisdictions investigated. *But cf.* the US UCC and the UNIDROIT draft convention; Ch. 10.2.5.
38. Ch. 10.2.11.
39. Proposal for a Council decision concerning the signing of the Hague Securities Convention, COM(2003) 783 final *and* Legal assessment of certain aspects of the Hague Securities Convention, of 3 July 2006, SEC(2006), 910.
40. *Cf.* HAENTJENS (2006), 97 and the references provided there.

12.3.6 Uncovered Credits

In the previous chapters, it has been argued that a harmonisation instrument should give proprietary effect or render effective against third parties uncovered credit entries in a securities account, i.e. credit entries that do not correspond with identical credits at the higher tier. But under the UNIDROIT draft convention and the Legal Certainty Group's advice, states may opt for imposing the requirement of double bookkeeping.[41] It has been shown above that a harmonisation in this respect is warranted as well as justified on normative and coherence grounds, but it is added here that it would also be a necessary measure so as to establish true interoperability within the EU.

For instance, an intermediary runs a serious risk when it holds an omnibus account for its clients with a foreign account provider under a law that does not give proprietary effect to uncovered credits, while its domestic law, which applies to its clients' accounts, does give proprietary effect to uncovered credits. The risk materialises when the intermediary's account provider proves to maintain insufficient securities, and the intermediary is under the obligation of its own law to satisfy its clients' claims. It is submitted, therefore, that uncovered credits should be given proprietary effect in a harmonisation instrument, not only because this allocates the risk where it belongs, viz. with the intermediary that makes the credit entry without having obtained a prior corresponding credit at the higher tier, but also because it considerably enhances the interoperability between systems. Thus, the harmonisation of the legal effect of uncovered credits prevents mismatches between systems that give proprietary effect to uncovered credit entries and those that do not. In addition, because the effect of uncovered credits usually follows from a classification of investor interests, it should be explicitly determined in a harmonisation instrument that refrains from classifications.

12.3.7 Securities Transfers

Although the importance of the finality of securities transfers is generally acknowledged and the current situation has been shown not to establish that, neither the Legal Certainty Group nor UNIDROIT have proposed dramatic harmonisation measures that would contribute to achieving legal certainty in that regard.[42] It has been shown that of the issues that determine the finality of (securities) transfers, viz. negotiability, the moment of transfer and the effect of contractual validity on the validity of the transferee's interests, harmonisation is the least needed for negotiability, and, related thereto, the possibility of a reversal of entries in *mala fide* transferees' accounts.

Yet the Legal Certainty Group concluded that the circumstances under which credit entries in *mala fide* transferees' securities accounts may be successfully

41. Ch. 10.2.5 *and* 11.2.2.
42. *See* Ch. 10.2.8.

challenged should be codified in a future harmonisation instrument, while no harmonised rules for the moment of transfer, or for transfer requirements would be needed. Explicit harmonisation of the circumstances under which credit entries in *mala fide* transferees' securities accounts may be successfully challenged, and its corollary, the protection of *bona fide* transferees, is indeed advisable in view or existing legal uncertainty and the systemisation of law in the jurisdictions investigated.[43] Moreover, such a harmonisation measure would comply, not only with the restraints dictated by coherence considerations, but also with the principle of subsidiarity, since a harmonisation measure in this regard would arguably establish interoperability where it is presently absent.

More specifically, a harmonisation of the *bona fide* acquirer protection principle would solve the priority problems occurring in so-called 'double-dealing' situations. In these situations, the same securities are transferred twice, both to *bona fide* transferees, and the second acquirer in good faith claims priority over the first. Assuming the application of PRIMA, both acquirers make their claims under their respective laws, while PRIMA does not determine the priority of one claim or law over the other. Should both claims be sustained, one of the two intermediaries thus has to honour his client's interests without having obtained the corresponding assets. An explicit harmonisation of the law that governs the protection of *bona fide* transferees and the priorities between those transferees would therefore eliminate a serious risk that materialises because the 'uncovered intermediary' is not able to pass on the loss.[44]

With regard to the moment of transfer and the effect of contractual validity on the validity of the transferee's interests, the Legal Certainty Group first took the position that securities transfer requirements should be harmonised, but that the moment of transfer should be left to the discretion of the Member States.[45] In its final advice, however, the Group concluded that neither harmonised rules for the moment of transfer, nor for transfer requirements would be needed.[46] This position is puzzling for several reasons.

First, the Group thus seems to take the view that it should be left to the Member States to determine the moment that credit entries in securities accounts take proprietary effect. It follows that consensual regimes of transfer will not be harmonised with traditional regimes, so that ownership of book-entry securities might still be transferred by party agreement alone in some jurisdictions.[47] However, the Group states elsewhere that '[t]he account holder becomes entitled to the rights as of the moment on which the credit entry is made by the account provider on the account holder's account and ceases to be entitled to them upon a debit entry being

43. *See* Ch. 10.2.8 *and* 11.2.3.
44. The priority problem occurring in 'double-dealing' situations cannot to be solved by a better conflict of laws rule. *See* Ch. 10.2.11.
45. *See* MARKT/G2/MNCT D(2006), minutes of meeting 25 and 26 April 2006, available at <http://ec.europa.eu/internal_market/financial-markets/clearing/certainty_en.htm>.
46. Legal Certainty Group Advice, 4.
47. *Cf.* Ch. 10.2.8.

made'.[48] It is submitted that these two positions are mutually exclusive, since under the consensual regime of transfer, a transferee becomes entitled to the rights of an accountholder without a credit entry having been made on his account.

Second, the previous chapters have shown that the finality of securities transfers can only be ensured by the realisation of a harmonised abstract and non-consensual transfer regime, while such modernisation would not result in any system investigated having to change from a system of strong coherence to become incoherent or even weakly coherent.[49] The Legal Certainty Group, however, does not justify its view that harmonisation of the requirements and the moment of securities transfer would not be needed, although these issues have explicitly been identified by the European Commission as core issues for harmonisation in view of the current legal uncertainty.[50]

Third, the absence of a harmonised regime of securities transfer law leads to unacceptable complications in cross-border securities settlements. Consider, for instance, the following situations, where the application of PRIMA is assumed. Dutch transfer law is characterised as a causal transfer regime and, thus, a transfer requires a valid agreement so as to be proprietarily effective. Although debatable,[51] the causal regime is probably applied to the transfer of securities by book-entry also and if a transfer agreement is defective, the transferor who holds a securities account with a Dutch intermediary thus remains the owner, even though his securities account has already been debited. The transferee, however, might hold a securities account with an intermediary of a so-called abstract jurisdiction (such as the US), where an invalid agreement does not affect the proprietary effects of a transfer. As a consequence, the transferee has become the owner notwithstanding a defective agreement, while the transferor has remained the owner under his law.[52] Because a court applying PRIMA would have to respect both claims, two different accountholders must be considered to be the owners of the same securities at the same time in such a situation.

The reverse would happen if a transferor holding his securities with an intermediary of a consensual jurisdiction (such as France and Belgium) would transfer his securities to a transferee that holds an account with an intermediary of a so-called traditional regime (such as the Netherlands). It has been shown that under Belgian law, the consensual transfer regime applies to transfers of securities by book-entry, or, more accurately, that under Belgian law, rights in securities are transferred when cleared by the CCP or CSD. From that moment on, the transferor ceases to be the entitlement holder and the transferee is considered to be the owner. But if securities are transferred to an accountholder holding an account with a Dutch intermediary, that transferee only becomes the entitlement holder

48. Legal Certainty Group Advice, 8.
49. Ch. 10.2.8 *and* 11.2.3.
50. Communication from the Commission to the Council and the European Parliament, *Clearing and Settlement in the European Union, Main policy issues and future challenges,* COM(2002) 275, 25. *Cf. also* Giovannini Group 2001 Report, 56. *See* Ch. 9.3.4.
51. *See* Ch. 9.3.4.
52. VAN BEEK & VAN BRUGGEN (2002), 81.

the moment when his securities account is credited. Thus, after a CSD has cleared the transfer, but before the transferee's account has been credited, the transferred securities do not (yet) belong to the transferee, but neither do they belong to the transferor. Should the Dutch transferee then become insolvent, the transferred securities could therefore – *horribile dictu* – be considered to belong to one of the intermediaries interposed and thus not be available to the transferor's creditors.

It is submitted that these examples show that not even functional consistency is currently achieved between the European jurisdictions investigated and that this lack of interoperability represents a grave legal risk. An explicit harmonisation of the law that governs the protection of *bona fide* transferees and the priorities between those transferees, the requirements for and the moment of the transfer of securities by book-entry is therefore not only urgently needed, but also complies with the requirements of subsidiarity.

12.4 FORM

12.4.1 Introduction

In the above, some remarks have been made on the scope, as well as on the legal basis for a future Community instrument in the field of securities custody and transfer law. The last remaining issue therefore, would be what form such an instrument should take. As it should seek to achieve the goals common to all legislative initiatives, it should aim at achieving comprehensiveness and coherence, the reduction of uncertainty and the enhancement of predictability, as well as the adaptability to change.[53] But a European instrument would also be constrained by the principles of subsidiarity and proportionality, and it is against the background of the combination of these principles that the best possible form of a Community instrument on securities custody and transfer law will be sought in the following sections.

12.4.2 European Uniform Securities Code

It has been argued in various contexts that existing European legislation fails to meet the first two of the objectives just mentioned, i.e. comprehensiveness and coherence. More specifically, the piece-meal approach of the Community legislature and the lack of systematic relationships between directives has often been criticised,[54] and the EU Commission has therefore proposed that future EU legislation on securities custody and transfer law should be as broad as possible. The

53. These ideals of harmonisation, which further include uniformity, have been formulated in the context of the drafting of the US UCC; White & Summers (2001), 181–182.
54. *See,* e.g., Roth (2002), 766 *and* Smits (2006), 65–76. Van Gerven (2004), 525, even called it the 'dark side' of harmonisation.

Commission suggested that it should become part of a larger 'European Uniform Securities Code', which would contain securities custody and transfer law, but also include private international law rules and rules of company and insolvency law.[55]

However, the Commission's proposal did not find support, for, it is submitted, convincing reasons.[56] First, it is questionable whether a European Securities Code could comply with the subsidiarity and proportionality principles, as any Securities Code claiming comprehensiveness would have to include matters of, for instance, regulatory, corporate and insolvency law that have been firmly established as belonging to the Member States' discretion. Thus, it would be likely to include issues for which no harmonisation would be (immediately) needed and no explicit legal basis would exist.[57]

Moreover, a European Securities Code would be likely to infringe unacceptably on the national systemisation of law, or be otherwise unwarranted from a coherence perspective. First, such a Code would probably not be able to take a functional approach and categorise differently than some of the Member States currently do, which would disproportionately and unjustifiably diminish current coherence.[58] Second, it would include rules that necessarily derogate from other, more general rules of law in some jurisdictions. But, as it has been noted that derogatory rules might be justified by the specific nature of book-entry securities and subject to the condition that they do not diminish current coherence disproportionately, it is unlikely that the weakening of coherence in other areas that do not require modernisation or harmonisation would be similarly justifiable.

It is submitted, therefore, that a harmonisation instrument in the area of securities custody and transfer law should refrain from infringements on other areas of law and, more generally, from distortions of national coherence where possible, but that a European Securities Code would not be able to achieve that. Likewise, the Giovannini Group did not endorse the Commission's proposal for a Code, but argued instead that legislative action on the Community level should be confined to the reform and harmonisation of, mainly, the ownership of book-entry securities. The EU Commission, in its second Communication, acknowledged this position and it is now generally felt that limited harmonisation should be the objective of a future EU harmonisation instrument.[59]

55. Communication from the Commission to the Council and the European Parliament, *Clearing and settlement in the European Union* of 28 May 2002, COM(2002)257, 12.
56. E.g., EFMLG 2003 Report, 5–6 and 22 *and* Löber (2005), 178. From the European Parliament's position that no framework directive on the regulation of clearing and settlement was needed, it may be inferred that it would even more strongly oppose a codification of the whole of securities law; *see* Motion of the European Parliament of 6 June 2005, A6-0180/2005 final, 14.
57. *Cf. supra,* s. 12.2 *and see* Giovannini Group 2003 Report, 17.
58. *Cf.* Ch. 11.2.2.
59. *Cf.* Löber (2005), 178 *and* Löber (2006), 9. *Cf. also* Giovannini Group 2003 Report, 17.

12.4.3 Directive, Regulation and Other Forms

Of the various forms that the European harmonisation of securities custody and transfer law may theoretically take, it follows from the preceding section that it will not and should not take the form of a European Uniform Securities Code. Other possible forms, such as a model act or recommendation, a directive, a regulation or a treaty, have not yet been discussed, but will be examined in the next section.[60]

The Legal Certainty Group has not explicitly stated what it considers to be the most appropriate form for a European harmonisation of securities custody and transfer law, but has indicated, however, that the ratification of a future Unidroit convention might be preferable to a separate EU instrument.[61] On the other hand, it has been argued that a European harmonisation of securities custody and transfer law should aim at a higher degree of uniformity than a convention or similar instrument could achieve.[62] This seems to be the better view, for several reasons.

First, European systems already show a degree of integration that is absent at the global level, so that the European legislature could, and, in fact, should, aim at a higher degree of harmonisation than would be possible globally.[63] Second, a European directive or regulation by definition binds all EU countries, whereas a convention or similar instrument, including model acts and recommendations, has less binding force. Therefore, the latter might not be the most appropriate tool to establish difficult changes in existing statutory laws. As the development of the Unidroit project shows, non-directly binding instruments that are created on an inter-governmental basis have a poor possibility to realise sometimes radical changes that are nonetheless urgently needed for the reduction of current uncertainty.[64] Moreover, treaties have but a limited adaptability to change, which might be problematical in the context of a convention on securities law, a rapidly moving area of law that is subject to constant developments. A not directly binding instrument such as a treaty therefore does not seem to be the most appropriate instrument to harmonise European securities custody and transfer law, particularly

60. *See* EC Treaty Art. 249. The Art. also lists 'Decisions' as a possible EC instrument, but that instrument is only applicable to specified situations and parties, and is thus not appropriate for a general harmonisation of securities custody and transfer law.
61. Legal Certainty Group Advice, 10.
62. *Cf.* Löber (2005), 188.
63. *Cf.* Löber (2005), 188.
64. At an earlier stage in the project, Paech (2002), 1160, chief research officer at the Unidroit Secretariat for the securities custody and transfer law project, stated: 'If the work [of Unidroit, MH] aims at enhancing economic efficiency in cross-border trading and at eliminating legal risk at the same time, it will require the development of a completely new concept which might touch fundamental principles of national legal systems'. *But compare* this statement with the current draft convention as summarised *supra,* Ch. 9.2.3, where it was concluded that the draft Unidroit convention will probably enhance the interoperability and internal soundness of these jurisdictions investigated to a limited extent only.

because of the critical and urgent need for modernisation and the availability of quicker and more efficient forms of legislation.[65]

A regulation, for instance, is 'binding in its entirety and directly applicable in all Member States'[66] and would thus achieve a high level of uniformity. Consequently, it would minimise legal uncertainty, while changes to that instrument can be made relatively easily. Furthermore, a regulation effectuating the modernisation of securities custody and transfer law proposed in the previous chapters would be relatively easily adopted, since, as an instrument of harmonisation that purports to further the internal market, it would require only a qualified majority in the European Council rather than unanimity to be adopted.[67]

However, because of its binding character, a regulation does not allow for diverging ways of implementation, so that in the case of a securities custody and transfer law regulation, Member States would not be able to provide accountholders with more protection than the regulation would establish.[68] Yet it is submitted that the measures proposed in the previous chapters would ensure the highest level of accountholder protection possible from a commercial law perspective, and that it should be left to national regulatory law to guarantee the enforcement of additional protective rules.[69] More generally, a regulation would prevent the possibility of experimentation in Member States, which, as has been noted *above*, would not be advisable in view of the furthering of (legal) innovation and the satisfaction of different preferences of the subjects of these states.[70]

In addition, a regulation would not be the most appropriate instrument of harmonisation from a coherence perspective, since it would involve the introduction of a separate, alien body of legislation, without respecting the specifics of Member States' legal systemisation, which has been noted as a serious objection also with regard to the European Securities Code.[71] While it has been shown that most of the harmonisation measures discussed *above* would not encroach detrimentally or disproportionately on the coherence of the jurisdictions investigated, that discussion presupposed that the least intrusive approach would be taken. As a consequence, it concluded, for instance, that a functional approach should be taken and that no new concept to denote accountholder interests should be introduced. Thus, a less intrusive instrument than a regulation would be more appropriate, which would also be in accordance with the constraints imposed by the subsidiarity principle.

A directive is such an instrument, as it is binding only with regard to the substantive result and allows the Member States to choose the form and method of implementation. It is submitted that a directive would therefore not encroach disproportionately on Member States' systemisation of law, and would, at the same time, bring about the harmonisation and modernisation currently needed.

65. *Cf.* Partsch-Bobricheff (2005), 31–38.
66. EC Treaty Art. 249.
67. EC Treaty Art.s 95 and 251.
68. *Cf.* Smits (2006), 85–87, in the context of consumer law harmonisation.
69. *Cf. supra,* s. 12.3.5.
70. Ch. 9.1.1.
71. EFMLG 2003 Report, 28.

Moreover, the risk of supererogatory implementation would probably not materialise, because the harmonisation of securities custody and transfer law are not likely to be implemented in a civil code.[72] Furthermore, the instrument would be as comprehensive as possible and therefore meet the objection of fragmentation commonly brought forward against Community legislation, provided it would contain all the measures of modernisation proposed above.[73]

On the other hand, the uniformity which a directive can achieve is necessarily less than a regulation usually accomplishes, *inter alia* because a directive might be implemented and amended differently by the national legislatures, notably with respect to the terminology used, while national courts might also interpret the implemented provisions differently.[74] It is submitted, however, that in the instance of securities custody and transfer law, a directive would ensure the harmonisation needed by adopting a functional approach where less uniformity is needed, while containing provisions of a more detailed nature where technical uniformity is necessary. Alternatively, a framework directive could be drafted which would set out the overarching policy goals, while a more detailed directive or regulation could prescribe specific implementing measures that require (near) uniformity.[75] The classification of accountholder interests for instance, could be left to national law, while provisions ensuring accountholder protection in intermediary insolvencies should be drafted so as to achieve technical uniformity.

In sum, a directive would be the most appropriate legislative form to achieve the harmonisation and modernisation so urgently needed for the European Union. It has been shown that a directive would represent the best possible medium between respecting the current systemisation of the national laws investigated and having enough binding force to accomplish the necessary reduction of uncertainty. If a directive would contain all the measures proposed in the preceding chapters, it could also claim to be as comprehensive as possible, while observing the constraints imposed by the principles of subsidiarity and proportionality at the same time.

12.5 CONCLUSION

The scope of a future EU legislative action in the field of securities custody and transfer law has been the main focus of this chapter, where it has been shown that a restrictive approach should be chosen, both to preserve some competition between legal systems and to comply with the principles of subsidiarity and proportionality codified in the EC Treaty. More generally, a restrictive and functional approach

---

72. Currently, none of the jurisdictions investigated have codified securities custody and transfer law in their civil codes.
73. Ch. 10.3.
74. *Cf.* Taylor (1978), 101–102 in the context of the US UCC.
75. Such an approach is called the 'Lamfalussy approach'; *cf.* <http://ec.europa.eu/internal_market/securities/transposition/index_en.htm>, for examples of directives that have already been adopted on that basis.

that would result in minimum harmonisation has been concluded to provide for the greatest opportunity of success.

EC Treaty Article 95, as interpreted by the ECJ in the Tobacco case, proved to provide a legal basis for a Community instrument on securities custody and transfer law. In addition, the principle of subsidiarity would be complied with, as it has been shown that interoperability is currently most notably absent with regard to the protection of accountholder interests in intermediary insolvencies, the possibility of uncovered credits and the regimes for securities transfers by book-entry. Consequently, it has been submitted that the protection of *bona fide* transferees and the priorities between those transferees, as well as the requirements for and the moment of the transfer of securities by book-entry should be included in the harmonisation.

Furthermore, it was concluded that functional consistency should be sufficient where it regards the classification of the accountholder/intermediary relationship, and, more generally, of accountholder interests. But, as a consequence, technical uniformity should be established with regard to the elements of accountholder interests, such as an accountholder's right of disposal, retrieval, to vest security interests and to receive and exercise the rights attached to his securities. In the same vein, the prohibition of upper-tier attachment and the possibility of uncovered credit entries in a securities account should be codified, so as to establish the required degree of interoperability.

Thus, a EU harmonisation instrument on securities custody and transfer law that would contain derogatory rules should be confined to the rules traditionally classified as property law rules, and it has accordingly been submitted that it should include neither specific issues of corporate, regulatory or insolvency law, nor general issues of contract law. Moreover, it was concluded that separate conflict of laws provisions would not be needed in a future instrument on securities custody law, provided the EU would ratify the HSC, which was strongly advised.

Normative and coherence considerations on the other hand, have been shown to require that a harmonisation instrument cover all categories of financial instruments that can be credited to a securities account, account providers, CSDs and securities settlements, so that virtually all accountholders are equally protected by the harmonisation instrument's provisions. Except for the author's position on the harmonisation of the transfer regime for book-entry securities, these positions are in accordance with those of the Legal Certainty Group and existing Community legislation.[76]

76. *See* Löber (2006), 51–52 *and* MARKT/G2/MNCT D(2006), minutes of meeting 25 and 26 April 2006, available at <http://ec.europa.eu/internal_market/financial-markets/clearing/certainty_en.htm>, a position which was supported by the clearing and settlement industry, witness their responses to earlier consultation documents, available at the same website. The EFMLG on the other hand, suggested that a European harmonisation should bring about full statutory dematerialisation at a Community level and provide the exact nature and extent of an investor's rights, for the protection of investor's rights in intermediary insolvencies, for the full tradability of book-entry securities including the protection of good faith acquirers, for the safeguarding of the safety of settlement system by double-entry bookkeeping (implying the direct correspondence of credits and debits with the crediting and debiting of beneficiaries

Finally, it was determined that a directive would be the most appropriate form for the measure of harmonisation and modernisation proposed above, as a treaty or similar, less directly binding instrument would not be able to achieve the level of harmonisation and modernisation which is currently lacking, but is so urgently needed, while a regulation or a Uniform Securities Code proved to involve a disproportionate encroachment on the coherence of national systems.

In the context of the US UCC, it had been concluded that the harmonisation of commercial law at the federal level would be 'politically unattainable, philosophically unwise and practically unfeasible' as it would sacrifice state interests and the possibility of experimentation, but that it would also be a remedy against 'territorial instincts, self-identity need, provincial chauvinism and the fear of a federal tyrant'.[77] It is shown here that the harmonisation of commercial law at the EU Community level should equally steer between these Skylla and Charybdis, but that, generally, 'federalisation' should be preferred over 'provincial chauvinism'.

accounts) and separation of an intermediary's own assets from its clients' and rules on securities transfers. *See* EFMLG 2003 Report, 19 *et seq. See also supra,* Ch. 9.3.4. The EU Commission, in its turn, thought that apart from a reform of investors' ownership rights, investor protection from intermediary insolvency, the tradability of book-entry securities, priority issues and shortfalls, the processing of corporate actions and the issuer's ability to choose the location of its securities should be included in a harmonisation instrument; Communication from the Commission to the Council and the European Parliament, Clearing and settlement in the European Union of 28 May 2002, COM(2002)257.

77. Taylor (1978), 101–102.

Summary and Recommendations

omnia mutantur, nihil interit
everything changes, nothing perishes

OVID[1]

As practices change, so too must language and concepts. That, in a nutshell, is the lesson to be drawn from the past few decades' work on the commercial law of investment securities.

ROGERS[2]

INTRODUCTION

The present book started from the premise, stated in Chapter 1.1, that whereas practices may converge on the functional level, doctrinal path dependence prevents, or at least shapes, a corresponding convergence at the formal, i.e. legal level.[3] It is submitted that this premise has not been falsified by the chapters that followed. Rather, it has been shown that current practices of book-entry securities custody and transfer have been principally shaped by market forces, and that those practices show a remarkable

1. P. OVIDIUS NASO, METAMORPHOSES 15.165.
2. ROGERS (1995), 689–690.
3. MICHELER (2006). *Cf. also* CANIVET (2003), 50-51: *'(...) la convergence ne peut se faire qu'au prix de concessions parfois difficiles à accepter lorsqu'elles atteignent des pratiques fortement enracinées'.*

convergence, both globally and regionally. But the underlying legal infrastructure has not uniformly followed that convergence, and, where modifications to the law have been made, those modifications have been largely shaped so as to be in accordance with existing rules and general principles of private and commercial law.

Such 'doctrinal path dependence' proves to be particularly problematical when the accountholder – intermediary relationship is defined in traditional, private law concepts, when the rules on tangible movables are applied to credit-entries in securities accounts, and when traditional transfer regimes are applied to securities transfers. For instance, it has been shown that the conflict of laws rules in many jurisdictions are still based on the *lex situs* rule, which applies the law of the place where the securities are located. From the perspective of accountholder protection and market stability, these discrepancies between, on the one hand, the reality of securities custody and transfer, and its inflexible legal underpinnings on the other, contribute to an undesirable situation of legal uncertainty. More in particular, the application of ill-fitting concepts of general private law has proven to create uncertainty for securities accountholders and account providers alike, about which rights they can enforce, and against whom. As the most unwarranted consequence of such discrepancy, a strict application of a 'property law construct' or a consensualist transfer regime leaves accountholders with a mere contractual claim in their account provider's insolvency.

However, these discrepancies also show to what extent legal systems are 'path dependent', i.e. what value is attributed to the preservation of their internal coherence. On a more theoretical level, Chapter 2 summarised how legal theorists currently assess the relevance of coherence, and coherence proved to further equality, legal certainty and rationality in a given legal system. Current coherence of national systems of law must therefore be taken into account when proposing alterations to parts of those systems, or as De Vauplane & Bornet stated:

> *Seuls les principes généraux du droit structurent ce système juridique qui sans eux deviendrait fragile et évanescent car sans réelle charpente. [. . . .] L'approche factuelle du droit des marchés financiers est simplement le reflet de la complexité des pratiques qu'il est indispensable d'appréhender, de comprendre, et d'encadrer au sein d'un système juridique.*[4]

PART I

Chapter 2 therefore developed a coherence model as a tool to assess the consequences of a harmonisation of securities custody and transfer law. It concluded that in the context of the present study, harmonisation proposals should be tested against a non-foundationalist coherence concept that allows for value-pluralism. In other words, it was neither assumed that only coherence considerations

4. De Vauplane & Bornet (2001), no. 1245. *Cf. also* Micheler (2006), 16–17, Van Erp (2004), 540 and 546, *and* Wilhelmsson (2002), 92.

determine what the law is, nor that only coherence considerations determine what the law should be.

It was also shown, however, that as an important principle of systemisation, coherence should always be realised to the maximum extent possible, as it furthers equality, legal certainty and rationality in a given legal system. More in particular, it has been shown that a system of law is considered coherent when its elements, i.e. its norms, values and principles, are logically consistent and show some monism, i.e. unity of principle. Logical consistency is established when a given system of law shows a sound internal architecture, i.e. if all norms of a specific area of law fit logically into the more general parts of the law, and when it is both absent of intrinsic contradictions and of instances of inconsistent valuation (*Wertungswiderspruch*).

If these conditions are not met, the legal system under scrutiny must be considered not to be coherent or in-coherent. But if no inconsistencies can be found, whilst the rules and norms of the given system are supported by many different principles, that system is weakly coherent. With regard to harmonisation legislation on a supra-national level, it was therefore concluded that coherence considerations should only prevent a harmonisation proposal if it would cause a system of strong coherence to become incoherent or weakly coherent, while coherence could not be preserved to some extent and coherence would be (felt to be) diminished unjustifiably and disproportionately.

In Chapter 3, a brief historical overview was given of securities custody and transfer law. It discussed major developments in the practice of the custody and transfer of securities, and showed that during the last few centuries, the law had constantly been adapted to those changes, in some instances after crises had painfully demonstrated the inadequacy of the contemporary framework. It was also shown that while the immobilisation and dematerialisation of securities has dramatically changed the practice of securities custody in the second half of the 20th century, neither substantive, nor private international law has kept pace with that development. It was argued that the main underlying problem is posed by the fact that most European jurisdictions still base their securities custody and transfer laws on traditional property law concepts, while they still characterise securities as tangible movables.

In Chapter 4, operational aspects of the current practice of global securities transfers were explained, and it was shown how, in an overwhelming variety of possibilities, securities may be transferred. Some characteristics of the pre-transfer stage (clearing) were discussed, as well as typical fact patterns in the actual transfer of securities by book-entry (settlement) and the creation of security interests in such securities. As a consequence of the current so-called 'multiple access model', settlement appeared to be extremely complicated in a cross-border context, although key market participants continue to consolidate and integrate.

It was argued that most of the risks inherent in the current financial markets and, more specifically, to securities settlement systems, can be mitigated by operational measures, which have indeed been implemented in many systems. These measures have also been recommended in reports and recommendations drafted mainly by international organisations. Legal risk, however, caused by a mismatch between law and practice, is still substantial and thus presents a threat to the financial markets as a whole (systemic risk). It was therefore concluded that risk has not yet been properly addressed.

PART II

In the chapters of Part II (Chapters 5 through 8), an analysis has been made of current Belgian, French, Dutch and US securities custody and transfer law. These jurisdictions have been chosen because they represent typical and economically important systems of securities law. Each of these jurisdictions is examined on two levels: first, a comparative analysis has been made on the basis of specific legal questions which will be listed immediately below, and second, the interaction is examined between the securities laws of the said jurisdictions and the more general areas of law in which these securities laws are embedded, on the basis of the coherence concepts discussed in Chapter 2.

Thus, for each of the said jurisdictions, answers to specific questions have been sought that mainly concern either the rights and duties of a securities accountholder, or the integrity of the custody system. More in particular, it was asked, as a preliminary issue, which categories of securities are eligible to be credited in a securities account. Second, it was asked what the nature of the interests is that an accountholder enjoys with regard to the securities to which he is entitled. That issue encompassed the following questions: how are an accountholder's interests characterised? How are they evidenced? For example, is a credit entry in a securities account a proof of ownership or is it a constitutive element for the existence of securities? Are informal dispositions over securities, i.e. dispositions that are not registered by a book-entry in a securities account possible? Are provisional credit entries in securities accounts possible?

Third, as another important question related to the nature of accountholder interests, it was questioned how an accountholder's interests in his securities are protected against the account provider and third parties. This question becomes particularly acute when the account provider becomes insolvent, and the most pertinent questions then become: how are shortfalls availed that occur as to the securities held by the account provider? How are an accountholder's interests in securities separated from the account provider's property, and, more generally, how are accountholder interests protected against the claims of the account provider's general creditors?

Fourth, it was investigated what the requirements for a transfer of securities by book-entry are. Other questions in that respect included: When is a transfer of securities by book-entry effective, i.e. when can the transferee assert his interests in the transferred securities against third parties? Under what circumstances can *bona fide* transferees rely on the crediting of their securities account, especially when having acquired *a non domino,* and, more generally, under what circumstances may credit entries in a securities account be reversed?

Fifth, the creation, perfection and enforcement of security rights that can be vested in securities were examined. More specifically, it was questioned what the requirements are for the creation of a security right in book-entry securities and how such a security interest may be enforced. Moreover, it was asked whether upper-tier attachment is possible, i.e. whether it is possible for an accountholder's creditor to exercise his rights against higher-tier account providers. Finally, the conflict of laws rules of the selected jurisdictions were analysed and compared, insofar as they concerned the custody and transfer of securities, both as title transfer and by way of security.

As stated, the coherence of the jurisdictions thus investigated has also been studied. More accurately, the relationship between national securities laws and the more general areas of law in which those securities laws are embedded has been analysed. It was concluded that Belgian law has created a very modern and clearly successful legal infrastructure for the custody and transfer of book-entry securities, and that under Belgian law, accountholders are, overall, well protected, while (legal) certainty of the settlement system seems ensured. But the relationship of the book-entry securities custody and transfer law with the more general areas of Belgian law was often concluded to be weakly coherent and sometimes incoherent, in spite of recent legislative amendments (Chapter 5.7.2).

French securities law was shown to be characterised mainly by its statutory and comprehensive dematerialisation. As a result of that dematerialisation, realised in the 1980s, almost no French securities can today be found in a physical form. The dematerialisation sparked intense scholarly debate about almost every aspect of French securities custody and transfer law, and that debate showed that only a few rules of general private and commercial law match the current practice of securities custody and transfer. As a reaction, the French legislature and judiciary introduced for some specific issues rules of securities law that clearly derogate from general private law principles, and it was concluded that these rules established a weakly coherent relationship between French securities law and general private law. But in other instances, where such clear rules are absent, it was argued that this relationship is unclear and sometimes even incoherent (Chapter 6.7.2).

Unlike French securities law, Dutch law is (still) primarily framed so as to accommodate the circulation of bearer securities. Yet it has been shown that virtually none of the cornerstones of Dutch securities custody and transfer law are fully consistent with general private law principles. Because of the strict dogmatic structure of Dutch private law, and the application of general private law principles to specific and functional areas of law, the inconsistencies and derogations are clearly apparent, perhaps even more so than in less dogmatic systems. It was concluded, therefore, that the relationship between Dutch securities law and the more general areas of law in which it is embedded, is characterised by incoherence and weak coherence. Where the inconsistencies result in unwarranted consequences, notably the corrosion of accountholder protection, it was argued that they should be solved (Chapter 7.7.2).

In the US, the UCC harmonised state securities custody and transfer law through its Article 8, which underwent a major modification in 1994. That revision introduced new concepts for *sui generis* phenomena of securities custody law, and (functionally) maintained coherence with other parts of the law. Thus, the 1994 revision of UCC Article 8 has turned previously existing incoherence into weak coherence, and also retained its strong coherence with general principles of US private and commercial law. In sum, it was concluded that the UCC should be regarded as an example for a future European harmonisation of securities custody and transfer law, both from a substantive law and a coherence point of view (Chapter 8.7.2).

PART III

Chapter 9 starts with a summary of the arguments that have been made for, as well as against, harmonisation and concludes mainly on economic grounds, that the harmonisation of securities custody and transfer law is strongly advisable. Subsequently, the global and European initiatives that have been undertaken so far to achieve such harmonisation were discussed. On the global level, attention was paid to the recommendations drafted by various international organisations such as the G30, BIS and IOSCO, and the draft convention of UNIDROIT on substantive securities law and the Hague Conference on conflict of laws were also separately discussed. On the EU level, several Directives and the work of the Legal Certainty Group were explained.

It was concluded, however, that the global recommendations could not result in the dramatic legal modernisation and harmonisation that is currently needed, while the EU instruments currently in place were proven to be too limited in scope. In addition, it was demonstrated that the EU lacks harmonisation of, notably, the national differences that still exist with regard to investors' ownership rights, investor protection from intermediary insolvency, the tradability of book-entry securities, priority issues and shortfalls. Moreover, it was argued that harmonisation of the conflict of laws rules is urgently needed, as current EU legislation in that field is neither consistent, nor globally compatible.

In Chapter 10, it was discussed in detail to what extent the European jurisdictions analysed in Part II should be modified, in order to meet the policy goals of investor protection and market integrity. Thus, the findings of the analyses made in Chapters 5 through 8 were compared and evaluated against the standards of modern securities custody and transfer practice, with the harmonisation brought about in the US, with the UNIDROIT draft convention and with the advice of the Legal Certainty Group. It was concluded that the costs of harmonising the laws of the jurisdictions investigated would probably outweigh its benefits and would probably *not* serve the realisation of the policy goals just mentioned when a harmonisation instrument would seek to achieve complete dematerialisation or the abolition of all securities certificates, a harmonisation of the characterisation of accountholder interests, the abolition of all tracing mechanisms and the introduction of a general non-possessory security interest.

In addition, it was argued that a modernisation of the European jurisdictions investigated should to be better left to other (harmonisation) initiatives with regard to the eligibility of intermediaries to maintain and to provide securities accounts, with regard to the prohibition on intermediaries from using their clients' assets for their own businesses (*tirage sur la masse*), and with regard to the obligation of intermediaries to segregate their own assets from those of their clients. Priority rules of claims in intermediary insolvencies, on the other hand, were shown to be already sufficiently harmonised.

With regard to other issues, however, it was concluded that a modernisation of the securities custody and transfer laws of the jurisdictions investigated were advisable. Particularly clarification or an explicit statement in the relevant legislation should be realised where it concerns: an accountholder's right to dispose of his securities by means of instructions to his account provider, an accountholder's right to change the form through which his securities are held, an intermediary's obligation to pass on essential issuer information, an intermediary's obligation to facilitate the accountholders' exercise of the rights attached to their securities, the circumstances under which credit entries in *mala fide* transferees' accounts are subject to challenges, and the impossibility of upper-tier attachment. Moreover, it was submitted that the jurisdictions investigated should be modified so as to allow for uncovered credit entries, while requiring intermediaries to replace missing assets and adopting clear rules that protect the accountholders in whose names these credit entries are made.

Most importantly, however, it was concluded that measures of modernisation are needed that protect accountholder interests in intermediary insolvencies against the intermediary('s liquidator) and its creditors, regardless of the number of intermediaries interposed between issuer and accountholder, while a better rule for allocating shortfalls in such insolvencies should also be implemented. Furthermore, the importance of the finality of securities transfers was stressed, and it was shown that such finality can only be ensured if an abstract and non-consensual securities transfer regime has been realised. Finally, it was argued that the conflict of laws rules of all jurisdictions investigated should be modernised so as to comply with the rules set forth in the Hague Securities Convention.

In Chapter 11, the advocated modernisation measures were tested against the coherence analyses made in Chapters 5 to 8. It was concluded that none of the modernisation measures proposed in the preceding chapter would unacceptably infringe on the current systemisation of the European jurisdictions investigated, i.e. none of the modernisation measures advocated would disproportionately and unjustifiably diminish the current coherence of the said jurisdictions. Rather, most measures were shown to improve present coherence, except for the introduction of a new concept to define accountholder interests. It was therefore advised that the different aspects of accountholder interests should be expressly codified, that accountholder protection in intermediary insolvencies should be (further) ensured, that securities transfers should be made effective only upon a credit-entry in the transferee's securities account, and that the applicable law should be chosen by accountholder and account provider, within the limits set by the Hague Securities Convention.

In the last Chapter, it was shown that the present institutional form of the European Union provides a legal basis for a harmonisation instrument that could achieve the securities law harmonisation needed. In addition, it was argued that such harmonisation would comply with the subsidiarity principle, as interoperability is currently most notably absent with regard to the protection of accountholder interest in intermediary insolvencies, the possibility of uncovered credits and the regimes for securities transfers by book-entry. Consequently, it was concluded that the protection of *bona fide* transferees and the priorities between those transferees, as well as the requirements for and the moment of the transfer of securities by book-entry should be included in the harmonisation.

Furthermore, it was concluded that functional consistency should be sufficient where it regards the classification of the accountholder – intermediary relationship, and, more generally, of accountholder interests. But, as a consequence, technical uniformity should be established with regard to the elements of accountholder interests, such as an accountholder's right of disposal, retrieval, to vest security interests and to receive and exercise the rights attached to his securities. In the same vein, the prohibition of upper-tier attachment and the possibility of uncovered credit entries in a securities account should be codified, so as to establish the required degree of interoperability.

Finally, it was determined that a directive would be the most appropriate form for the measure of harmonisation and modernisation proposed *above*, as a treaty or similar, less directly binding instrument would not be able to achieve the level of harmonisation and modernisation which is currently lacking, but is so urgently needed, while a regulation or a Uniform Securities Code proved to involve a disproportionate encroachment on the coherence of national systems.

FINAL REMARK

The harmonisation and modernisation measures proposed would eliminate current legal uncertainty and the existing discrepancies between practice and legal infrastructure, but they would also necessarily require alterations in current national laws. Especially with regard to the enforceability of credit entries in securities accounts, these proposals go further than the less ambitious proposals of UNIDROIT and the Legal Certainty Group. A different coherence analysis might be the main reason for that,[5] but the said institutions may not have recognised that coherence is enhanced, rather than reduced when new and different rules are applied to new

5. Unfortunately, the coherence concept employed is not expressly formulated by either of the said institutions. *Cf.* BERTEA (2005), 171–172, pointing at the unclear coherence concept of the European Court of Justice, and its inconsistent consequences. But coherence considerations do not, of course, solely determine the position of any supranational body. Xenophobia, lobbying by interested parties and simple unfamiliarity with other solutions have also been noted as factors that might prevent harmonisation instruments from eliminating legal diversity and uncertainty; HARTKAMP (1989), 104.

and different phenomena.[6] Thus, modern developments regarding the custody and transfer of securities require new rules, especially when the application of old rules results in incoherence and legal uncertainty, so unacceptable in a vital element of our present economies.[7]

6. *Cf.* THEVENOZ (2005), 308.
7. *Cf.* ROGERS (1995), 689–690, *and* SALOMONS (2000), 907, with regard to the legal changes in private law that the 'internet revolution' requires.

Résumé et Recommandations

omnia mutantur, nihil interit
tout change, rien ne périt

OVIDE[1]

Lorsque les pratiques changent, le langage et les concepts doivent changer de même. C'est, en quelques mots, la leçon à tirer du travail de ces dernières décennies sur le droit commercial concernant les titres d'investissement.

ROGERS[2]

INTRODUCTION

Le présent livre partit de la prémisse formulée dans le Chapitre 1.1 ainsi: tandis que les pratiques convergent au niveau fonctionnel, la dépendance doctrinale de la précédente législation ('path dependence') prévient, ou, au moins, forme une convergence correspondante au niveau formel, c.-à-d. juridique.[3] Il a été soutenu que cette prémisse n'a pas été contredite par les chapitres qui suivaient. Il a été

1. P. OVIDIUS NASO, METAMORPHOSES 15.165.
2. ROGERS (1995), 689–690.
3. MICHELER (2006). *Cf. aussi* CANIVET (2003), 50–51: 'la convergence ne peut se faire qu'au prix de concessions parfois difficiles à accepter lorsqu'elles atteignent des pratiques fortement enracinées'.

montré plutôt que les pratiques courantes de conservation et de virement de titres dématérialisés ont été formées principalement par les forces du marché, et que ces pratiques montrent une convergence remarquable, au niveau mondial ainsi qu'au niveau régional. Mais l'infrastructure juridique sous-jacente n'a pas suivi uniformément cette convergence et, là où la loi a été modifiée, ces modifications ont été largement façonnées de manière à être conformes à la réglementation existante et aux principes généraux de droit privé et commercial.

Une telle 'dépendance du chemin parcouru' se révèle surtout problématique quand la relation titulaire de compte – intermédiaire est définie en concepts traditionnels de droit privé, quand la réglementation sur les biens corporels est appliquée aux inscriptions en comptes de titres, et quand les règles traditionnelles de transfert de propriété sont appliquées au virement de titres. Il a été montré, par exemple, que, dans beaucoup de juridictions, les règles de droit international privé se basent toujours sur la règle de *lex situs,* qui applique la loi du lieu où se trouvent les titres. Dans la perspective de la protection du titulaire de compte et de la stabilité du marché, ces divergences entre, d'un côté, la réalité de conservation et virement de titres et, de l'autre côté, ses étayages juridiques inflexibles contribuent à créer une situation indésirable de flou juridique. Plus précisément, l'application de concepts inappropriés de droit privé général s'est révélée créatrice d'incertitude pour les titulaires de comptes de titres ainsi que pour les prestataires de comptes concernant les droits qu'ils peuvent faire valoir et envers qui. Conséquence la plus injustifiée d'une telle divergence, une application stricte d'un système juridique du droit des biens ou du principe du consensualisme ne laisse aux titulaires de compte rien d'autre qu'une créance contractuelle en cas d'insolvabilité de leur prestataire de compte.

Toutefois, ces divergences montrent dans quelle mesure les systèmes juridiques sont 'path dependent', c.-à-d. quelle valeur on attribue à la conservation de leur cohérence interne. A un niveau plus théorique, le Chapitre 2 résumait comment les théoriciens juridiques évaluent couramment la pertinence de cohérence, et comment la cohérence s'est révélée favorable à l'égalité, la sécurité juridique et la rationalité dans un système juridique donné. Par conséquent, il faut prendre en compte la cohérence actuelle de systèmes juridiques nationaux en proposant des altérations de certaines parties de ces systèmes, ou, comme l'ont affirmé De Vauplane & Bornet:

> Seuls les principes généraux du droit structurent ce système juridique qui sans eux deviendrait fragile et évanescent car sans réelle charpente. [. . . .] L'approche factuelle du droit des marchés financiers est simplement le reflet de la complexité des pratiques qu'il est indispensable d'appréhender, de comprendre, et d'encadrer au sein d'un système juridique.[4] (En français dans le texte.)

---

4. De Vauplane & Bornet (2001), no. 1245. *Cf. aussi* Micheler (2006), 16–17, Van Erp (2004), 540 et 546, *et* Wilhelmsson (2002), 92.

PREMIÈRE PARTIE

Par conséquent, le Chapitre 2 a développé un modèle de cohérence en tant qu'outil à l'évaluation des conséquences d'une harmonisation des lois sur la conservation et le transfert de propriété des titres. Il a conclu que, dans le contexte de la présente étude, les propositions d'harmonisation devraient être mises à l'épreuve envers un concept 'non foundationalist' de la cohérence qui permet un pluralisme des valeurs. Autrement dit, il n'a pas été présumé que seulement des considérations de cohérence déterminent quelle est la loi, ni que ces considérations déterminent quelle devrait être la loi.

Il a également été montré, toutefois, que, étant un principe important de systématisation, la cohérence devrait toujours être réalisée à un degré maximal, car elle sert l'égalité, la sécurité juridique et la rationalité dans un système juridique donné. Plus précisément, il a été montré qu'un système juridique est censé être cohérent quand ses éléments, soit ses normes, valeurs et principes, sont logiquement consistants et montrent un certain monisme, c.-à-d. une unité de principe. Une consistance logique est réalisée lorsque un système juridique donné présente une architecture interne solide, c.-à-d. si toutes les normes dans un domaine spécifique du droit s'intègrent logiquement dans les parties plus générales de la loi et lorsqu'il est dépourvu de contradictions intrinsèques ainsi que de cas d'évaluation inconsistante ('Wertungswiderspruch').

Si ces conditions ne sont pas remplies, le système juridique en question doit être considéré comme n'étant pas cohérent ou alors incohérent. Mais s'il n'est pas question d'inconsistances, tandis que la réglementation et les normes du système donné sont soutenues par de nombreux principes différents, ce système-là est faiblement cohérent. Concernant la législation sur l'harmonisation au niveau supranational, il a donc été conclu que des considérations de cohérence ne devraient prévenir une proposition d'harmonisation que si celle-ci devait amener un système fortement cohérent a devenir incohérent ou faiblement cohérent, alors que un certain degré de cohérence ne pouvait pas être conservé et la cohérence aurait (ou serait considérée comme) diminuée d'une manière injustifiable et disproportionnelle.

Dans le Chapitre 3 est présenté un aperçu historique du droit concernant la conservation et le transfert de propriété des titres. Il traite des développements majeurs de la pratique de la conservation et du transfert de titres, et montre que, pendant ces derniers siècles, le droit a été constamment adapté à ces changements, dans certains cas après que des crises avaient démontré douloureusement l'inadéquation du cadre contemporain. Il a été également montré que, tandis que l'immobilisation et la dématérialisation de titres ont radicalement changé la pratique de conservation de titres dans la seconde moitié du 20me siècle, ni le droit matériel, ni le droit international privé n'ont emboîté le pas à ce développement. Il a été argumenté que le plus important problème sous-jacent repose sur le fait que la plupart des juridictions européennes fondent toujours leur droit concernant la conservation et le transfert de propriété des titres sur des concepts traditionnels du droit des biens, puisque elles caractérisent toujours les titres comme des biens corporels.

Dans le Chapitre 4 ont été expliqués des aspects opérationnels de la pratique actuelle du virement de titres au niveau mondial, et il a été montré comment, parmi une immense variété de possibilités, des titres peuvent être transférés. Quelques particularités de la phase pré-transfert (compensation) ont été traitées, ainsi que des configurations typiques de faits dans le transfert actuel de titres par écriture (règlement-livraison) et la création de garanties sur de tels titres. Conséquence du modèle courant, dit 'modèle d'accès multiple', le règlement-livraison s'est révélé extrêmement compliqué dans un contexte transfrontalier, bien que les participants essentiels du marché continuent de consolider et d'intégrer.

Il a été argumenté que la plupart des risques inhérents aux marchés financiers actuels et, pour être plus précis, aux systèmes de règlement-livraison, peuvent être mitigés par des mesures opérationnelles, qui, en effet, ont été implémentées dans beaucoup de systèmes. Ces mesures ont été également recommandées dans des rapports et recommandations établis notamment par des organisations internationales. Toutefois, le risque juridique, causé par une disparité entre le droit et la pratique, est toujours considérable et forme ainsi une menace pour les marchés financiers dans leur ensemble (risque systémique). Par conséquent, il a été conclu que le risque n'a pas encore été correctement abordé.

DEUXIÈME PARTIE

Dans les chapitres de la deuxième partie (Chapitres 5 à 8), une analyse a été faite du droit positif sur la conservation et le transfert de propriété des titres en Belgique, en France, aux Pays-Bas et aux EU. Ces juridictions ont été choisies parce qu'elles représentent des systèmes typiques et importants du point de vue économique et juridique dans le domaine des titres. Chacune de ces juridictions a été étudiée à deux niveaux: premièrement, une analyse comparative a été effectuée sur la base de questions juridiques spécifiques citées immédiatement ci-dessous, et deuxièmement, l'interaction entre les lois sur les titres dans les dites juridictions et les domaines plus généraux du droit dans lesquels ces lois sont incorporées a été examinée, sur la base des concepts de cohérence traités dans le Chapitre 2.

Ainsi, pour chacune des dites juridictions, des réponses ont été cherchées à des questions spécifiques concernant notamment soit les droits et les obligations d'un titulaire de compte de titres, soit l'intégrité du système de conservation. Plus précisément, il a été demandé, en tant que question préalable, quelles catégories de titres sont susceptibles d'être inscrites en compte. Deuxièmement, il a été demandé quelle est la nature des droits dont bénéficie un titulaire de compte concernant les titres qu'il détient. Cette matière comprenait les questions suivantes: quelle est la nature juridique d'un inscription en compte? Comment sont attestés les droits d'un titulaire de compte? Par exemple, une inscription en compte de titres est-elle une preuve de propriété ou alors est-elle un élément constituant de l'existence des titres? Des dispositions informelles concernant des titres, c.-à-d. des dispositions non registrées par une écriture dans un compte de titres, sont-elles possibles? Des inscriptions en compte provisoires sont-elles possibles?

En troisième lieu, en tant qu'autre question importante quant à la nature des droits du titulaire de compte, il a été demandé comment les droits de celui-ci sur ses titres sont protégés contre le prestataire de compte et des tiers. Cette question s'impose notamment quand le prestataire de compte devient insolvable, et alors les questions les plus pertinentes seront: comment sont utilisés les déficits qui se présentent concernant les titres détenus par le prestataire de compte? Comment les droits en titres d'un titulaire de compte sont-ils séparés de la propriété du prestataire de compte, et, plus en général, comment sont protégés les intérêts du titulaire de compte contre les réclamations des créanciers généraux du prestataire de compte?

En quatrième lieu, il a été examiné quelles sont les formalités à accomplir pour un transfert de propriété des titres par écriture. D'autres questions à cet égard comprenaient: Quand prend effet un transfert de titres par écriture, c.-à-d. quand est-ce que les droits de l'acquéreur seront opposable aux tiers? Dans quelles circonstances sont les inscriptions en compte opposables aux tiers, surtout quand il s'agit d'une inscription en compte d'un sous-acquéreur de bonne foi, et plus en général, dans quelles circonstances lesdites inscriptions peuvent-elles être annulées?

En cinquième lieu, la constitution et la réalisation d'un gage sur compte de titres, ont été étudiées. Pour être plus précis, il a été demandé quelles sont les formalités pour la constitution d'un gage sur des titres dématérialisés et comment on pourrait réaliser une telle garantie. En plus, il a été demandé si une saisie à l'échelon supérieur est possible, c.-à-d. s'il est possible pour le créancier d'un titulaire de compte de faire valoir ses droits à l'encontre de prestataires de compte d'ordre plus élevé. Finalement, les règles de droit international privé dans les juridictions choisies ont été analysées et comparées, pour autant qu'elles concernent la conservation et le virement de titres, aussi bien en tant que transfert de propriété strict qu'à titre de garantie.

Comme mentionné plus haut, la cohérence des juridictions ainsi examinées a également été étudiée. Plus précisément, la relation entre les lois nationales sur les titres et les domaines plus généraux du droit dans lesquels ces lois sont incorporées, a été analysée. Il a été conclu que le droit belge a créé une infrastructure juridique très moderne et bien réussie pour la conservation et le virement des titres dématérialisés, et que, selon la législation belge, les titulaires de compte sont globalement bien protégés, alors que la sécurité (juridique) du système de règlement-livraison semble assurée. Toutefois, il a souvent été conclu que la relation entre la législation concernant la conservation et le transfert de propriété des titres dématérialisés et les domaines plus généraux du droit belge est faiblement cohérente et parfois incohérente, malgré des amendements législatifs récents (Chapitre 5.7.2).

Le droit français sur les titres s'est révélé être caractérisé notamment par sa dématérialisation globale et codifiée. Résultant de cette dématérialisation, réalisée dans les années 1980, on ne trouve, à présent, guère plus de titres français en forme physique. La dématérialisation a suscité un vif débat doctrinal sur à peu près tout aspect de la législation française sur la conservation et le transfert de propriété des titres, et ce débat a montré que seulement quelques règles du droit général privé et commercial correspondent à la pratique actuelle de conservation et virement de titres. En réaction, la législature et la magistrature françaises ont introduit pour certains cas spécifiques des règles de droit sur les titres qui dérogent nettement aux principes généraux de droit privé, et il a été conclu que ces règles ont établi une relation faiblement cohérente entre le droit français sur les titres et le droit privé général. Toutefois, dans d'autres cas, en l'absence de telles règles claires, il a été argumenté que cette relation est floue, voire parfois incohérente (Chapitre 6.7.2).

Contrairement au droit français sur les titres, le droit néerlandais est (toujours) cadré en premier lieu de manière à faciliter la circulation de titres au porteur physiques. Pourtant, il a été montré que presque aucune des pierres angulaires du droit néerlandais sur la conservation et le transfert de propriété des titres n'est complètement compatible avec les principes généraux de droit privé. En raison de la structure rigoureusement dogmatique du droit privé néerlandais, et de l'application de principes généraux de droit privé dans des domaines spécifiques et fonctionnels du droit, les incohérences et dérogations sont nettement visibles, peut être encore davantage que dans des systèmes moins dogmatiques. Par conséquent, il a été conclu que la relation entre la législation néerlandaise sur les titres et les domaines plus généraux du droit dans lesquels elle est incorporée se caractérise par l'incohérence et une faible cohérence. Là où les disparités mènent à des conséquences injustifiées, notamment l'érosion de la protection du titulaire de compte, il a été argumenté qu'elles devraient être résolues (Chapitre 7.7.2).

Aux Etats-Unis, le 'UCC' (Code Commercial Uniforme) a harmonisé la législation des états sur la conservation et le transfert de propriété des titres par son Article 8, qui a été réformée en 1994. Cette révision a introduit de nouveaux concepts pour des phénomènes *sui generis* de droit sur la conservation de titres, et a maintenu (de manière fonctionnelle) une cohérence avec d'autres éléments du droit. Ainsi, la révision de 1994 de l'Article 8 de l'UCC a changé l'incohérence préexistante en faible cohérence, et a également retenu sa forte cohérence avec les principes généraux du droit américain privé et commercial. En somme, il a été conclu que l'UCC devrait être considéré comme un exemple en vue d'une future harmonisation européenne de la législation sur la conservation et le virement de titres, d'un point de vue du droit matériel ainsi que de la cohérence (Chapitre 8.7.2).

TROISIÈME PARTIE

Le Chapitre 9 commence par un résumé des arguments pour et contre une harmonisation et conclut, surtout pour des raisons économiques, que l'harmonisation de la législation sur la conservation et le virement de titres est fortement conseillée. Ensuite, les initiatives mondiales et européennes entreprises jusqu'ici en vue d'une telle harmonisation ont été traitées. Au niveau mondial, il a été question des recommandations formulées par des organisations internationales telles que le G30 (Groupe des Trente), La BIS (Banque des Règlements Internationaux, BRI) et la IOSCO (Organisation Internationale des Commissions de Valeurs, OICV), puis le projet de convention de UNIDROIT sur le droit matériel sur les titres et la Conférence de La Haye sur le droit international privé ont été traités séparément. Au niveau de l'Union Européenne, plusieurs Directives et le travail du 'Legal Certainty Group' (Groupe 'Sécurité Juridique') ont été expliqués.

Toutefois, il a été conclu que les recommandations mondiales ne pouvaient conduire aux modernisation et harmonisation juridiques radicales actuellement exigées, tandis que les instruments à présent en vigueur dans l'UE se sont révélés être d'une portée trop limitée. En plus, il a été démontré que l'UE manque d'harmonisation, notamment des différences nationales toujours existantes concernant les droits de propriété de l'investisseur, la protection de l'investisseur contre l'insolvabilité de l'intermédiaire, la négociabilité de titres dématérialisés, les questions de rang et les déficits. En outre, il a été argumenté que l'harmonisation des règles de droit international privé est absolument nécessaire, puisque la législation européenne dans ce domaine n'est ni cohérente, ni compatible au niveau mondial.

Dans le Chapitre 10, il a été question, en détail, du degré jusqu'où les juridictions européennes analysées dans la Deuxième Partie devraient être modifiées pour atteindre les buts politiques de protection de l'investisseur et d'intégrité du marché. Ainsi, les résultats des analyses effectuées dans les Chapitres 5 à 8 ont été comparés et évalués envers les standards de la pratique moderne de conservation et virement de titres, l'harmonisation réalisée aux EU, le projet de convention UNIDROIT et la recommandation du Groupe Sécurité Juridique. Il a été conclu que les coûts de l'harmonisation des lois des juridictions étudiées dépasseraient ses bénéfices et *ne* serviraient probablement *pas* à la réalisation des buts politiques cités, quand un instrument d'harmonisation chercherait à atteindre une dématérialisation complète ou l'abolition de tous les certificats de titres, une harmonisation de la nature juridique des droits du titulaire de compte, l'abolition de tous les mécanismes d'individualisation ('tracing') et l'introduction d'une garantie générale non-possessoire.

En outre, il a été argumenté qu'une modernisation des juridictions européennes étudiées devrait être laissée plutôt à d'autres initiatives (d'harmonisation) concernant l'habilitation des intermédiaires teneurs de compte, l'interdiction aux intermédiaires d'utiliser les actifs de leurs clients pour leurs propres affaires (*tirage sur la masse*) et l'obligation des intermédiaires de séparer leurs propres actifs de ceux de leurs clients. Par contre, les règles de rang des créances en cas d'insolvabilité d'intermédiaires se sont trouvées déjà suffisamment harmonisées.

Toutefois, quant à d'autres aspects, il a été conclu qu'une modernisation de la législation sur la conservation et le transfert de propriété des titres dans les juridictions étudiées était opportune. En particulier devrait être réalisée une clarification ou une déclaration explicite dans la législation pertinente concernant: le droit d'un titulaire de compte de disposer de ses titres en donnant des instructions à son prestataire de compte, le droit d'un titulaire de compte de changer la forme sous laquelle sont tenus ses titres, l'obligation d'un intermédiaire de transmettre de l'information essentielle de l'émetteur, l'obligation d'un intermédiaire de faciliter pour les titulaires de compte l'exercice des droits liés à leurs titres, les circonstances dans lesquelles les inscriptions en compte d'un sous-acquéreur de mauvaise foi ne sont pas opposable aux tiers, et l'impossibilité d'une saisie à l'échelon supérieur. En outre, il a été exposé que les juridictions examinées devraient être modifiées de manière à permettre des crédits non couverts, en exigeant des intermédiaires de remplacer les actifs manquants et en appliquant des règles claires pour protéger les titulaires de compte au nom desquels ces crédits ont été effectués.

Le plus important, pourtant, c'est qu'il a été conclu que des mesures de modernisation sont nécessaires qui protègent les droits du titulaire de compte en cas d'insolvabilité de l'intermédiaire contre (le liquidateur de) l'intermédiaire et ses créanciers, indépendamment du nombre d'intermédiaires posés entre l'émetteur et le titulaire de compte, alors qu'il faudrait aussi mettre en oeuvre une meilleure règle pour répartir les déficits dans ces cas d'insolvabilité. En plus, l'importance de l'irrévocabilité de virements de titres a été soulignée, et il a été montré qu'une telle irrévocabilité ne peut être garantie que si l'inscription en compte est faite translative de propriété des titres. Finalement, il a été argumenté que les règles de droit international privé dans toutes les juridictions étudiées devraient être modernisées, de manière à se conformer aux règles établies par la Convention de La Haye sur les Titres.

Dans le Chapitre 11, les mesures de modernisation préconisées ont été confrontées aux analyses de cohérence effectuées dans les Chapitres 5 à 8. Il a été conclu qu'aucune des mesures de modernisation proposées dans le chapitre précédent n'enfreindrait, de manière inacceptable, la systématisation actuelle des juridictions européennes examinées, c.-à-d. aucune des mesures de modernisation préconisées ne diminuerait, de façon disproportionnée et injustifiable, la cohérence actuelle des dites juridictions. De la plupart des mesures il a été montré qu'elles ont plutôt amélioré la présente cohérence, excepté l'introduction d'un nouveau concept pour qualifier la nature juridique du droit de titulaires de compte. Par conséquent, il a été recommandé de codifier explicitement les divers aspects des droits de titulaires de compte, de (mieux) garantir la protection de titulaires de compte en cas d'insolvabilité d'intermédiaire, de ne faire prendre effet les transferts de propriété des titres qu'après le crédit sur le compte de titres de l'acquéreur et de laisser le choix de la loi à appliquer au titulaire de compte et au prestataire de compte, dans les limites fixées par la Convention de La Haye sur les Titres.

Dans le dernier Chapitre, il a été montré que la présente forme institutionnelle de l'Union Européenne fournit une base constitutionnelle à un instrument d'harmonisation capable de réaliser l'harmonisation nécessaire de la législation sur les titres. En plus, il a été argumenté qu'une telle harmonisation respecterait le principe de subsidiarité, puisque, actuellement, l'interopérabilité manque surtout regardant la protection des droits du titulaire de compte en cas d'insolvabilité d'intermédiaire, la possibilité de crédits à découvert et les régimes de transfert de propriété des titres par écriture. Par conséquent, il a été conclu que l'opposabilité aux tiers des droits de l'acquéreur de bonne foi et les questions de rang entre ces acquéreurs, ainsi que les formalités à accomplir pour et le moment du transfert de propriété des titres par écriture devraient être inclus dans l'harmonisation.

En outre, il a été conclu qu'une cohérence fonctionnelle devrait suffire en ce qui concerne la qualification de la relation: titulaire de compte – intermédiaire, et, plus généralement, des droits du titulaire de compte. Mais, en conséquence, une uniformité technique devrait être réalisée concernant les éléments de droits du titulaire de compte, tels que les droits d'un titulaire de compte de disposition, de revendication, de faire constituer un gage et de recevoir et d'exercer les droits liés à ses titres. Parallèlement, l'interdiction de saisie à l'échelon supérieur et la possibilité de crédits à découvert dans un compte de titres devraient être codifiées, de manière à réaliser le degré nécessaire d'interopérabilité.

Finalement, il a été affirmé qu'une directive serait la forme la plus adéquate pour les mesures d'harmonisation et de modernisation proposées plus haut, car un traité ou un instrument similaire moins contraignant serait incapable de réaliser le niveau d'harmonisation et de modernisation qui fait défaut actuellement tout en étant absolument nécessaire, tandis qu'une réglementation ou un Code Uniforme des Titres ont prouvé d'entraîner un empiètement disproportionné sur la cohérence des systèmes nationaux.

REMARQUE FINALE

Les mesures d'harmonisation et de modernisation proposées pourraient éliminer l'insécurité juridique actuelle et les divergences existant entre la pratique et l'infrastructure juridique, mais elles nécessiteraient également des modifications de lois nationales actuelles. Surtout en ce qui concerne le droit absolue que constitue l'inscription en compte de titres, ces propositions sont plus avancées que celles, moins ambitieuses, de UNIDROIT et du Groupe Sécurité Juridique. Une analyse différente de cohérence en pourrait être la raison la plus importante,[5] mais les institutions en question n'ont peut-être pas reconnu que la cohérence est améliorée, plutôt que réduite quand des règles nouvelles et différentes sont appliquées à des phénomènes nouveaux et différents.[6] Ainsi, des développements modernes concernant la conservation et le transfert de propriété des titres nécessitent des règles nouvelles, surtout quand l'application de règles anciennes mène à de l'incohérence et de l'insécurité juridique, tellement inacceptables dans un élément vital de nos économies actuelles.[7]

---

5. Malheureusement, le concept de cohérence utilisé n'est formulé explicitement par aucune des dites institutions. *Cf.* BERTEA (2005), 171–172, indiquant le vague concept de cohérence de la Cour Européenne de Justice, et ses conséquences inconsistantes. Mais il est évident que ce ne sont pas uniquement des considérations de cohérence qui déterminent la position de tout organisme supranational. Xénophobie, lobbying par des parties intéressées et tout simplement la méconnaissance d'autres solutions sont également cités en tant que facteurs susceptibles de prévenir que des instruments d'harmonisation éliminent la diversité et l'insécurité juridiques; HARTKAMP (1989), 104.
6. *Cf.* THEVENOZ (2005), 308.
7. *Cf.* ROGERS (1995), 689–690, *et* SALOMONS (2000), 907, à propos des modifications juridiques de droit privé imposées par 'la révolution internet'.

Samenvatting en Aanbevelingen

omnia mutantur, nihil interit
alles verandert, niets gaat teniet

OVIDIUS[1]

Wanneer de praktijk verandert, dienen taal en terminologie mee te veranderen. Dat is in een notendop de belangrijkste les die het werk van de laatste tientallen jaren op het gebied van privaatrecht en effectenrecht ons geleerd heeft.

ROGERS[2]

INLEIDING

Deze dissertatie gaat uit van de stelling, dat waar op praktisch niveau vèrgaande harmonisering bereikt kan worden, harmonisering op het formele of juridische niveau verhinderd of althans gevormd wordt door oude en reeds bestaande kaders (*path dependence*).[3] Deze stelling, geformuleerd in hoofdstuk 1.1, wordt aan de hand van een onderzoek naar het giraal effectenverkeersrecht uitgewerkt in de rest

1. P. OVIDIUS NASO, METAMORPHOSES 15.165.
2. ROGERS (1995), 689–690.
3. *Zie* MICHELER (2006). *Vgl. ook* CANIVET (2003), 50–51: *'(...) la convergence ne peut se faire qu'au prix de concessions parfois difficiles à accepter lorsqu'elles atteignent des pratiques fortement enracinées'.*

van dit proefschrift. In het bijzonder worden de juridische aspecten van bewaring en overboeking van effecten belicht, waarbij de spanning tussen recht en (internationale) praktijk centraal staat. Op het praktische niveau van effectenadministratie heeft zich namelijk in de afgelopen decennia een ingrijpende en wereldwijd vrijwel uniforme evolutie voltrokken, terwijl de nationale rechtsordes zich noch aan die praktische veranderingen, noch aan elkaar hebben aangepast.

Effecten worden tegenwoordig voornamelijk bij een bank of andere financiële instelling aangehouden. De gerechtigdheid van een belegger tot deze effecten wordt uitgedrukt door een tegoed op een effectenrekening en effecten kunnen dan ook over het algemeen slechts door het geven van een overboekingsopdracht overgedragen worden. In vele rechtstelsels is het juridisch kader van de effectenbewaring echter nog steeds gebaseerd op de oude situatie, waarin beleggers zelf de (fysieke) stukken onder zich hielden. Bovendien verschillen de rechtstelsels aanzienlijk van elkaar, hetgeen problemen en onzekerheden oplevert wanneer effecten het voorwerp zijn van grensoverschrijdende transacties.

Aangezien deze rechtsonzekerheid de soepele werking van een zo elementair onderdeel van onze hedendaagse economieën belemmert, zijn zowel op wereldwijd als op regionaal niveau harmoniseringsinitiatieven ontplooid om door middel van juridische modernisering en integratie de rechtsonzekerheid het hoofd te bieden. Dergelijke initiatieven ondervinden echter vaak bezwaren van dogmatische aard. Men stelt zich op het standpunt dat een vèrgaande aanpassing van bijvoorbeeld de bepalingen omtrent eigendom en overdracht van effecten verhinderd wordt door de strakke structuur van het (privaat)recht, die vereist dat bijzondere bepalingen synchroon lopen met bepalingen van meer algemene aard, terwijl deze algemene bepalingen over het algemeen niet (kunnen) worden aangepast.

Deze *path dependence* is illustratief voor de waarde die in een zeker rechtstelsel toegekend wordt aan het behoud van de interne coherentie. In het tweede hoofdstuk van dit proefschrift vat ik dan ook samen hoe rechtstheoretici thans de interne coherentie van een rechtssysteem analyseren en waarderen, en stel vast dat coherentie bijdraagt aan de gelijkheid, rechtszekerheid en de rationaliteit binnen een gegeven stelsel. Mijns inziens dient bij aanpassing van enig rechtstelsel de interne coherentie ervan dan ook in ogenschouw genomen te worden. Of, zoals De Vauplane & Bornet het formuleren:

> *Seuls les principes généraux du droit structurent ce système juridique qui sans eux deviendrait fragile et évanescent car sans réelle charpente. [. . . .] L'approche factuelle du droit des marchés financiers est simplement le reflet de la complexité des pratiques qu'il est indispensable d'appréhender, de comprendre, et d'encadrer au sein d'un système juridique.*[4]

Dit proefschrift gaat met name in op de Europese dimensie van de harmonisering van het effectenrecht. Onderzocht wordt in hoeverre een eventuele Europese harmonisering en modernisering van het huidige recht van invloed zou zijn op het gebouw van (privaat)recht, zoals dat thans in België, Frankrijk en Nederland

4. De Vauplane & Bornet (2001), no. 1245. *Vgl. ook* Micheler (2006), 16–17, Van Erp (2004), 540 en 546, *en* Wilhelmsson (2002), 92.

bestaat. Dat onderzoek wordt afgezet tegen de ontwikkelingen zoals deze zich in de Verenigde Staten hebben voorgedaan, waar het statelijk recht sinds 1994 vrijwel volledig is geüniformeerd. Daarnaast wordt aandacht besteed aan ontwikkelingen op wereldwijd niveau, zoals de recente harmoniseringsinitiatieven van UNIDROIT en de Haagse Conferentie.

DEEL I

Het dissertatieonderzoek is als volgt opgezet. Na een (korte) inleiding in hoofdstuk 1, wordt in hoofdstuk 2 tegen de achtergrond van de op dat punt reeds bestaande rechtstheorie een coherentiebegrip ontwikkeld dat de kern zal vormen van de analyse van de huidige structuur van privaatrecht in de genoemde landen. Bovendien zal aan de hand van dat begrip onderzocht worden, in hoeverre een harmonisering van het effectenrecht die huidige structuur zou aantasten.

Het door mij gehanteerde coherentiebegrip is *non-foundationalist* en bovendien (norm)pluralistisch. Een en ander betekent dat in deze studie niet wordt aangenomen, dat slechts coherent recht 'recht' in strikte zin is, en bovendien dat behalve coherentieoverwegingen, ook normatieve overwegingen dienen te bepalen wat het recht zou moeten zijn. Hoewel deze opvatting van coherentie als normatief weinig dwingend zou kunnen worden beschouwd, toon ik aan dat coherentie een belangrijk beginsel is van systematisering van het recht en dat het om die reden gemaximaliseerd dient te worden. Ik betoog namelijk, dat coherentie een niet onaanzienlijk bijdrage levert aan de gelijkheid, rechtszekerheid en rationaliteit in een gegeven rechtstelsel.

Het ontwikkelde coherentiebegrip gaat verder uit van het volgende. Een rechtstelsel wordt als 'coherent' beschouwd indien de afzonderlijke elementen van dat stelsel, dat wil zeggen de normen, waarden en beginselen ervan, logisch consistent zijn en dat stelsel bovendien een zekere mate van monisme vertoont. Monisme betekent in dit verband dat alle normen in het rechtstelsel geschraagd worden door één of slechts een beperkt aantal beginselen. Men spreekt van een logisch consistent rechtstelsel indien alle onderdelen of rechtsgebieden van dat rechtstelsel logisch in elkaar passen en op elkaar aansluiten. Daarnaast dient het geen innerlijke tegenstrijdigheden of tegenstrijdige waarderingen (*Wertungswiderspruch*) te bevatten. Wanneer een rechtssysteem logisch inconsistent is, noemt men dat systeem incoherent. Wanneer het rechtssysteem logisch consistent is, maar de normen en waarden ervan worden gesteund door een groot aantal verschillende beginselen, dan is dat systeem 'zwak coherent'.

Ik concludeer in hoofdstuk 2 dat een harmonisatie-initiatief aldus zou moeten worden ingericht, dat het de coherentie van de rechtsstelsels waarop het betrekking heeft, niet op disproportionele en ongerechtvaardigde wijze aantast. Preciezer gezegd, wanneer een supranationale instantie harmoniserende regelgeving voorbereidt, dient zij te voorkomen dat die regelgeving coherente rechtssystemen zou doen verworden tot zwak coherent of incoherente systemen. Bovendien dient de coherentie van deze systemen zoveel mogelijk te worden behouden en mag zij niet disproportioneel en ongerechtvaardigd verminderd zou worden. Ook indien zwak coherente stelsels incoherent zouden worden ten gevolge van de implementatie van het harmonisatie-initiatief, zou het initiatief herzien dienen te worden.

Hoofdstuk 3 bevat een korte, historische inleiding tot de materieel en internationaal privaatrechtelijke aspecten van het effectenverkeer. De belangrijkste ontwikkelingen in de afgelopen eeuwen met betrekking tot de praktijk van effectenbewaring en effectenverkeer worden onder de loep genomen. Er wordt aangetoond dat het recht steeds werd aangepast aan genoemde ontwikkelingen, niet zelden nadat (economische) crises de onvolkomenheden van het juridisch kader bloot hadden gelegd. Daarnaast wordt bezien hoe noch het materiële recht, noch het internationaal privaatrecht de ingrijpende ontwikkeling van immobilisatie en dematerialisatie van effecten heeft gevolgd. Als voornaamste reden daarvoor wordt aangevoerd dat het giraal effectenverkeersrecht van de meeste (Europese) rechtstelsels nog immer op traditioneel goederenrechtelijke begrippen gestoeld is, en dat zij effecten nog immer als roerende goederen kwalificeren.

In hoofdstuk 4 worden enkele operationele aspecten van de huidige praktijk van mondiale effectentransacties uiteen gezet. Ik leg in dit hoofdstuk onder andere uit, hoe effecten in duizelingwekkende variaties internationaal kunnen worden overgeboekt. Enkele aspecten van de fase vóór de daadwerkelijke overboeking, *clearing* genaamd, worden besproken. Ook worden enkele typische casusposities besproken waarbij effecten daadwerkelijk worden overgeboekt (*settlement*) of zekerheden op girale effecten worden gevestigd. Met name de afwikkeling van internationale transacties blijkt extreem gecompliceerd, hoewel de belangrijkste partijen op de clearing en settlement markt blijven fuseren en integreren.

Gesteld wordt dat de meeste risico's zoals die zich thans voordoen in de financiële markten en afwikkelingssystemen opgevangen kunnen worden door maatregelen op operationeel niveau. Dergelijke maatregelen, die meestal zijn aanbevolen in rapporten en aanbevelingen van internationale organisaties, blijken dan ook vaak reeds genomen te zijn. Rechtsonzekerheid (in effectenrechtelijke context veelal aangeduid als *legal risk*) blijkt echter nog immer een aanzienlijke bedreiging te vormen voor de financiële markten als geheel. Dergelijk risico vindt zijn oorzaak in een discrepantie tussen recht en praktijk, waarvoor mijns inziens dan ook een oplossing gezocht dient tc worden.

DEEL II

In de hoofdstukken die deel II uitmaken (hoofdstukken 5 tot en met 8), worden het huidige Belgische, Franse, Nederlandse en Amerikaanse effectenverkeersrecht aan een nadere analyse onderworpen. In hoofdstuk 1 was reeds uiteengezet dat juist voor deze rechtstelsels is gekozen omdat zij typische regels van effectenrecht bevatten en bovendien een belangrijke economische rol spelen. Het onderzoek naar elk stelsel vindt op twee niveaus plaats: op het eerste niveau wordt een rechtsvergelijkende analyse verricht op basis van nader te bespreken, welomschreven vragen, terwijl op het tweede niveau de wisselwerking wordt onderzocht tussen het Belgisch, Frans en Nederlands effectenrecht enerzijds en de meer algemene rechtsgebieden waarin dat effectenrecht is ingebed anderzijds, dit laatste op basis van het in de vorige paragraaf uiteengezette coherentiebegrip.

Antwoord is derhalve gezocht op enkele specifieke vragen, die hoofdzakelijk ofwel de rechten en verplichtingen van de effectenrekeninghouder, ofwel de integriteit van het effectenverkeer betreffen. Meer in het bijzonder doet zich als preliminaire vraag voor, welke categorieën effecten gecrediteerd kunnen worden op een effectenrekening, of opgenomen kunnen worden in het giraal effectenverkeer. Bovendien heb ik mij afgevraagd wat de rechten van een effectenrekeninghouder behelzen. Deze vraag valt uiteen in de volgende subvragen: Hoe worden de rechten van een effectenrekeninghouder gekwalificeerd? Hoe worden zij bewezen? Is een tegoed op een effectenrekening bijvoorbeeld een constitutief vereiste voor (het bewijs van) eigendom van de aldus gecrediteerde effecten? Of van het bestaan van de effecten zelf? Zijn niet-geregistreerde beschikkingshandelingen met betrekking tot girale effecten mogelijk? Zijn voorwaardelijke boekingen mogelijk?

Ten derde heb ik onderzocht hoe de rechten van een effectenrekeninghouder beschermd worden tegen de financiële instelling die de rekening bijhoudt en tegen derden. Deze vraag wordt vooral relevant in het faillissement van genoemde financiële instelling, en de belangrijkste vragen die zich dan voordoen zijn: Hoe worden de tekorten gedolven die wellicht optreden in het door de instelling beheerde vermogen? Hoe worden de goederen waartoe de rekeninghouders gerechtigd zijn, gescheiden van de goederen die toebehoren aan de beherende instelling zelf? En, meer in het algemeen: hoe worden de rechten van de effectenrekeninghouders beschermd tegen aanspraken van de crediteuren van de beherende instelling?

Ten vierde heb beschreven wat de vereisten zijn voor de overboeking van girale effecten. Ten behoeve van die beschrijving heb ik voor elk van de genoemde rechtstelsels onderzocht op welk moment een overboeking van effecten aan derden tegenstelbaar wordt, dat wil zeggen: wanneer zij goederenrechtelijk effect verkrijgt. Andere vragen die ik getracht heb te beantwoorden in dit verband zijn: onder welke omstandigheden kunnen verkrijgers te goeder trouw vertrouwen op de creditering van hun effectenrekening, met name wanneer zij van een beschikkingsonbevoegde verkregen hebben? En meer in het algemeen: wanneer mag een creditering teruggedraaid worden?

Ten vijfde heb ik het vestigen en uitwinnen van een zekerheidsrecht op girale effecten nader onderzocht. De belangrijkste vragen hier zijn: aan welke voorwaarden dient te zijn voldaan om een geldig zekerheidsrecht op girale effecten te doen ontstaan? En: hoe dient een dergelijk zekerheidsrecht te worden uitgeoefend? Tevens stelt zich de vraag of *upper-tier attachment* toegestaan is, dat wil zeggen: mag men beslag leggen op de effecten van zijn schuldenaar, wanneer deze effecten beheerd worden door een ander dan de instelling die de effectenrekening bijhoudt? Ten slotte wordt het internationaal privaatrecht van de onderzochte rechtstelsels geanalyseerd, voorzover het het giraal effectenverkeer betreft.

Als gezegd heb ik de onderzochte rechtstelsels niet alleen geanalyseerd op het niveau van de zojuist besproken vragen, maar ook op basis van het in hoofdstuk 2 uiteengezette coherentiebegrip. Zo heb ik de wisselwerking onderzocht tussen het Belgisch, Frans, Nederlands en Amerikaans effectenrecht enerzijds en de meer algemene rechtsgebieden waarin dat effectenrecht is ingebed anderzijds. Voor het Belgisch recht heb ik kunnen vaststellen dat het een uiterst modern en effectief juridisch kader heeft geschapen voor het giraal effectenverkeer. Meer in het bijzonder blijkt het Belgisch recht effectenrekeninghouders over het algemeen goed te beschermen en blijkt de rechtszekerheid in het effectenverkeer gegarandeerd te zijn. De relatie tussen het effectenverkeersrecht en meer algemene rechtsgebieden blijkt echter vaak zwak coherent en soms zelfs incoherent, hoewel recente wetswijzigingen het tegendeel zouden kunnen doen vermoeden (Hoofdstuk 5.7.2).

Het Frans effectenrecht wordt gekenmerkt door een volledige, wettelijke dematerialisatie van de effectenbewaring. Ten gevolge van deze dematerialisatie, die in de jaren 1980 werd voltrokken, worden Franse effecten sindsdien niet meer in fysieke vorm uitgegeven en/of bewaard, maar slechts via effectenrekeningen geadministreerd en overgedragen. De dematerialisatie gaf echter ook aanleiding tot een herwaardering van alle centrale begrippen van het effectenverkeersrecht. Uit dat juridisch discours kwam naar voren dat slechts weinig begrippen van algemeen privaatrecht zonder meer toepasselijk zijn op de moderne praktijk van giraal effectenverkeer. Daarom heeft wetgeving en rechtspraak voor enkele specifieke aspecten van het effectenrecht expliciet derogerende bepalingen geïntroduceerd, en op deze punten blijkt Frans recht derhalve zwak coherent. Waar dergelijke expliciete bepalingen echter ontbreken, blijkt de verhouding effectenrecht – algemeen privaatrecht onduidelijk en soms zelfs incoherent te zijn (Hoofdstuk 6.7.2).

Anders dan het Franse effectenrecht, is het Nederlandse effectenrecht nog hoofdzakelijk op de bewaring en overdracht van toonderstukken gebaseerd. Het blijkt echter, dat geen van de kernelementen van het Nederlands giraal effectenverkeersrecht consistent is met de algemene beginselen van privaatrecht. Door de dogmatische structuur van het Nederlands privaatrecht vinden de algemeen privaatrechtelijke bepalingen toepassing waar bijzondere bepalingen ontbreken, hetgeen wellicht (nog) meer dan elders de bestaande inconsistenties aan het licht doet komen. Ik heb daarom moeten concluderen dat de relatie tussen het Nederlands effectenverkeersrecht en algemeen privaatrecht zwak coherent en (vaak) incoherent is. Deze inconsistenties leiden in sommige gevallen tot buitengewoon onwenselijke resultaten, zoals de vermindering van bescherming van de effectenrekeninghouder. Ik acht het daarom wenselijk dat deze inconsistenties opgelost worden (Hoofdstuk 7.7.2).

In de Verenigde Staten heeft de *Uniform Commercial Code* ('UCC') een harmonisatie van het statelijk effectenverkeersrecht bewerkstelligd. De relevante bepalingen van deze 'Code' (voornamelijk te vinden in *Article* 8), werden ingrijpend gewijzigd in 1994. De wijzigingen betroffen de invoering van nieuwe begrippen voor *sui generis* aspecten van de effectenbewaring en brachten aldus een functionele coherentie met de meer algemene rechtsgebieden tot stand. Deze functionele coherentie wijzigde de bestaande incoherentie in zwakke coherentie, maar behield de sterke coherentie met enkele algemene beginselen van Amerikaans vermogensrecht. Naar mijn mening zou de UCC daarom beschouwd moeten worden als voorbeeld voor een eventueel toekomstig Europese harmonisering van het effectenverkeersrecht, zowel vanuit een materieel rechtelijk als rechtstheoretisch oogpunt (Hoofdstuk 8.7.2).

DEEL III

In het negende hoofdstuk passeren eerst de argumenten de revue, zoals die in het wetenschappelijk debat voor en tegen harmonisatie van privaatrecht naar voren zijn gebracht. Naar aanleiding van deze bespreking concludeer ik dat het effectenverkeersrecht geharmoniseerd dient te worden, hoofdzakelijk om economische redenen. Vervolgens behandel ik de harmoniseringsinitiatieven die ontplooid zijn op zowel Europees, als wereldwijd niveau. De mondiale initiatieven betreffen enerzijds de aanbevelingen zoals deze gepubliceerd zijn door verschillende internationale organisaties als de G30, BIS en IOSCO, en anderzijds het ontwerpverdrag materieel giraal effectenverkeer als opgesteld onder auspiciën van UNIDROIT, en het internationaal privaatrechtelijke verdrag opgesteld door de Haagse Conferentie. Ten aanzien van de harmonisering op Europees niveau wordt aandacht geschonken aan verschillende, reeds ingevoerde richtlijnen alsmede aan het werk van de zogeheten *Legal Certainty Group,* dat de mogelijkheden onderzoekt om tot een Europese harmonisatie te komen.

Ik heb echter moeten concluderen dat de mondiale aanbevelingen niet hebben kunnen resulteren in de vereiste, ingrijpende hervormingen van giraal effectenverkeersrecht, en dat de Europese regelgeving op dit punt te beperkt is geweest. Tevens toon ik aan dat harmonisering thans ontbreekt, met name waar het nationale verschillen betreft ten aanzien van de rechten van effectenrekeninghouders, de bescherming van effectenrekeninghouders in het faillissement van de beheerder van hun effecten, de overdraagbaarheid van effecten, de regels van voorrang en de mogelijke tekorten die in faillissement optreden. Bovendien blijkt dat harmonisering van het internationaal privaatrecht dringend vereist is, nu de huidige Europese regelgeving op dit punt inconsistent en (wereldwijd) incompatibel is.

In Hoofdstuk 10 bespreek ik in detail in hoeverre de Europese rechtstelsels als geanalyseerd in Deel II dienen te worden aangepast, willen zij voldoen aan de algemene beginselen van beleggersbescherming en marktintegriteit. Daartoe worden de bevindingen van Deel II vergeleken en geëvalueerd. De onderzochte stelsels vergelijk ik met elkaar, met het UNIDROIT ontwerpverdrag en met het advies van de *Legal Certainty Group,* terwijl de evaluatie plaats vindt op basis van een vergelijking met de algemeen aanvaarde beginselen van giraal effectenverkeer zoals deze naar voren zijn gebracht in de reeds genoemde internationale aanbevelingen. Uit deze vergelijking en evaluatie trek ik een aantal conclusies.

Ten eerste moet geconcludeerd moet worden dat de kosten van een eventuele harmonisering van de onderzochte stelsels niet op zouden wegen tegen de baten, en dat bovendien beleggersbescherming en marktintegriteit *niet* per definitie gerealiseerd zouden worden indien een Europees harmoniseringsinstrument zou strekken tot: volledige dematerialisatie, dat wil zeggen de afschaffing van elk toondereffect, tot harmonisering van de kwalificatie van de rechten van een effectenrekeninghouder, tot harmonisering van elk *tracing* mechanisme en tot invoering van een algemeen bezitloos zekerheidsrecht op girale effecten.

Ten tweede stel ik vast dat harmonisering van de onderzochte Europese rechtstelsels dient te worden overgelaten aan andere harmoniseringsinitiatieven waar het betreft de toelatingscriteria voor effecten om in het giraal verkeer te worden opgenomen, de toelatingscriteria voor instellingen om als beheerder van effecten op te treden en als zodanig effectenrekeningen bij te houden, het verbod voor beheerders om de effecten van hun cliënten aan te wenden voor eigen rekening, en de verplichting voor beheerders om de effecten van hun cliënten te scheiden van de eigen effecten. Regels van voorrang bleken daarentegen reeds voldoende geharmoniseerd.

Ten derde blijkt dat andere aspecten van het effectenverkeersrecht wel degelijk harmonisering en modernisering behoeven. Met name verduidelijking of expliciete vermelding blijkt aangewezen waar het betreft het recht van de effectenrekeninghouder om beschikkingshandelingen te verrichten met betrekking tot 'zijn' effecten, het recht van een effectenrekeninghouder om de wijze waarop zijn effecten gehouden worden te wijzigen, de verplichting van een beheerder van effecten om relevante informatie van uitgevende instellingen aan zijn cliënten door te geven, de verplichting van een beherende instelling om de uitoefening door haar cliënten van de aan effecten verbonden rechten te faciliteren, de omstandigheden waaronder te kwader trouw verkregen effecten kunnen worden gerevindiceerd door de rechtmatig eigenaar, en de onmogelijkheid van *upper-tier attachment*. Daarnaast ben ik van mening dat de onderzochte rechtstelsels dienen te voorzien in de mogelijkheid van 'niet gedekte', maar wel (goederenrechtelijk) beschermde creditering van effecten. Tegelijk zou echter een helder geformuleerde verplichting voor beherende instellingen om ontstane tekorten aan te vullen dienen te worden geïntroduceerd, alsmede duidelijke regels die de effectenrekeninghouders beschermen.

Wellicht belangrijker nog, vastgesteld moet worden dat modernisering dringend noodzakelijk is om de rechten van effectenrekeninghouders te beschermen. In het faillissement van een effectenbeheerder blijken effectenrekeninghouders namelijk niet altijd een vordering te hebben die boven die van de curator en de concurrent crediteuren van de beheerder gaat. Naar Nederlands recht bijvoorbeeld, hangt de positie van de effectenrekeninghouder af van het aantal 'schakels', dat wil zeggen het aantal financiële (bewaar)instellingen tussen belegger en centrale bewaarinstelling. Ik betoog derhalve dat de positie van de effectenrekeninghouder gewaarborgd dient te worden, onafhankelijk van het aantal schakels. Bovendien stel ik voor een ander verdelingsmechanisme in te voeren wanneer een eventueel tekort optreedt, en de onaantastbaarheid van de creditering van een effectenrekening te verzekeren door een abstract en niet-consensueel overdrachtregime voor de overboeking van effecten. Tenslotte bepleit ik aanpassing van het internationaal privaatrecht van de onderzochte Europese stelsels in die zin, dat het overeenkomt met de regels als opgenomen in het Haags Effectenverdrag.

In Hoofdstuk 11 worden de voorgestelde moderniseringsmaatregelen tegen de achtergrond van het coherentiemodel zoals ontwikkeld in Hoofdstuk 2 getoetst aan, en vergeleken met de coherentieanalyses van de Hoofdstukken 5 tot en met 8. Met andere woorden, bepaald wordt of de voorgestelde maatregelen op onacceptabele wijze, dat wil zeggen: disproportioneel en ongerechtvaardigd, zouden ingrijpen in de onderzochte rechtsordes. Ik concludeer dat dit niet het geval is, met uitzondering van het voorstel om een nieuw (verzamel)begrip in te voeren dat de rechten van een effectenrekeninghouder zou kwalificeren. Sterker nog, het merendeel van de voorstellen blijkt de huidige coherentie eerder te bevorderen dan daaraan afbreuk te doen. Ik adviseer derhalve om de onderscheiden aspecten van de (juridische) positie van een effectenrekeninghouder expliciet te codificeren, om die positie in het faillissement van de effectenbeheerder te waarborgen, om de tegenstelbaarheid van de creditering van een effectenrekening te verzekeren en om – zij het binnen de grenzen van het Haags Effectenverdrag – een keuzevrijheid toe te staan met betrekking tot het toepasselijk recht.

In het laatste hoofdstuk wordt aangetoond dat de huidige institutionele structuur van de EU de invoering van een richtlijn zou toelaten die de noodzakelijke harmonisering van het giraal effectenverkeersrecht zou kunnen bewerkstelligen. Ik stel daar namelijk vast dat nationale verschillen met betrekking tot de bescherming van effectenrekeninghouders in het faillissement van hun bewaarders, met betrekking tot de (on)mogelijkheid van 'ongedekte' creditering en met betrekking tot de regimes voor de overdracht van effecten, substantiële belemmeringen vormen voor het optimaal functioneren van de interne Europese markt. Ik concludeer vervolgens dat een toekomstig harmoniseringsinstrument dat deze belemmeringen opheft zou voldoen aan het subsidiariteits- en proportionaliteitsvereiste. Zodoende zou het ook regelingen kunnen (en dienen te) bevatten die verkrijgers van effecten te goeder trouw ruimhartig beschermen, die de vereisten voor een geldige overboeking regelen en die het moment van overboeking bepalen.

Tevens betoog ik dat functionele overeenstemming tussen de onderzochte rechtstelsels zou volstaan waar het de kwalificatie van de relatie effectenrekeninghouder – effectenbewaarder betreft, en, meer in het algemeen, waar het de kwalificatie van de rechten van de effectenrekeninghouder betreft. Een dergelijke functionele benadering zou derhalve geen harmonisering van kwalificering(en) vereisen, maar wel van de onderscheiden rechten van de effectenrekeninghouder, zoals zijn recht om beschikkingshandelingen te verrichten met betrekking tot zijn effecten, om uitlevering van zijn effecten te verkrijgen, en om de rechten uit te oefenen die aan zijn effecten verbonden zijn. Eveneens zou het verbod op *upper-tier attachment* en de mogelijkheid van 'ongedekte' crediteringen in een harmoniseringsinstrument gecodificeerd dienen te worden, om aldus de vereiste mate van internationale compatibiliteit te garanderen.

Tenslotte bepleit ik dat een richtlijn de meest aangewezen vorm zou zijn om de voorgestelde harmonisering en modernisering van het effectenverkeersrecht te verwezenlijken. Een verdrag of ander, minder direct bindend instrument zou immers niet de benodigde harmonisering kunnen bewerkstelligen, terwijl een verordening of *Uniform Securities Code* een disproportionele aantasting van de nationale rechtsordes zou betekenen.

CONCLUSIE

De voorgestelde harmoniseringsmaatregelen zouden de huidige rechtsonzekerheid en bestaande discrepantie tussen recht en praktijk effectief verhelpen, maar zouden ook aanpassingen van de nationale rechtsordes eisen. Met name ten aanzien van de afdwingbaarheid van elke creditering van een effectenrekening gaan de hier voorgestelde maatregelen verder dan de minder ambitieuze maatregelen zoals UNIDROIT en de *Legal Certainty Group* naar voren hebben gebracht. Dit verschil zou gelegen kunnen zijn in een andere coherentieanalyse,[5] maar genoemde instanties zouden ook hebben kunnen miskend dat de coherentie van een (nationale) rechtsorde eerder gebaat is bij, dan lijdt onder de introductie van nieuwe en aparte regels voor nieuwe en aparte fenomenen.[6] Het moge duidelijk zijn dat het giraal effectenverkeer nieuwe regels vereist, met name omdat toepassing van de oude regels resulteert in onacceptabele gevolgen voor een zo essentieel onderdeel van onze huidige economie: incoherentie en rechtsonzekerheid.[7]

5. Helaas heeft geen van genoemde instellingen het door hen gehanteerde coherentiebegrip geëxpliciteerd. *Vgl.* BERTEA (2005), 171–172, waar hij wijst op het vage coherentiebegrip dat het Europees Hof van Justitie hanteert en de inconsistente gevolgen daarvan. Wat daar ook van zij, het succes van harmonisatie-initiatieven wordt uiteraard niet alleen bepaald door coherentie overwegingen. Zoals HARTKAMP (1989), 104, opmerkte: 'Mijn ervaring in vele internationale vergaderingen, onder meer in het kader van Unidroit en van Uncitral, heeft mij geleerd dat de vraag of staten aan hun eigen recht willen vasthouden, door geheel andere factoren wordt beslist, zoals gehechtheid aan nationale tradities, xenofobie, lobbies van belanghebbenden, of gewoon onbekendheid met andere oplossingen'.
6. *Vgl.* THEVENOZ (2005), 308.
7. *Vgl.* ROGERS (1995), 689–690, *en* SALOMONS (2000), 907, de laatste met betrekking tot de veranderingen die de 'internet revolutie' vereist ten aanzien van het privaatrecht.

Bibliography

ALEXY & PECZENIK (1990)
R. Alexy & A. Peczenik, *The Concept of Coherence and Its Significance for Discursive Rationality,* 3 RATIO JURIS 130-47 (1990)

VAN ARDENNE-STACHIW (1991)
E.M. van Ardenne-Stachiw, *Medium Term Notes,* 5 TIJDSCHRIFT VOOR VENNOOTSCHAPPEN, VERENIGINGEN EN STICHTINGEN 118–123 (1991)

VAN ARDENNE-STACHIW (1998)
E.M. van Ardenne-Stachiw, *De voorwaardelijke overdracht van effecten in de zin van de Wet giraal effectenverkeer, in* ONDERNEMING EN EFFECTEN 169–182 (S.C.J.J. Kortmann et al. eds, 1998)

ASSER-MIJNSSEN-DE HAAN 3-I (2001)
3 F.H.J. MIJNSSEN & P. DE HAAN, MR. C. ASSER'S HANDLEIDING TOT BEOEFENING VAN HET NEDERLANDS BURGERLIJK RECHT, 1 GOEDERENRECHT (14th ed. 2001)

ASSER-VAN DAM-MIJNSSEN-VAN VELTEN 3-II (2002)
3 C.C. VAN DAM, F.H.J. MIJNSSEN & A.A. VAN VELTEN, MR. C. ASSER'S HANDLEIDING TOT BEOEFENING VAN HET NEDERLANDS BURGERLIJK RECHT, 2 GOEDERENRECHT (14th ed. 2002)

ASSER-HARTKAMP 4-I (2004)
4 A.S. HARTKAMP, MR. C. ASSER'S HANDLEIDING TOT BEOEFENING VAN HET NEDERLANDS BURGERLIJK RECHT, 1 VERBINTENISSENRECHT (12th ed. 2000)

ASSER-KORTMANN-DE LEEDE-THUNNISSEN 5-III (1994)
5 S.C.J.J. KORTMANN, L.J.M. DE LEEDE & H.O. THUNNISSEN, MR. C. ASSER'S HANDLEIDING TOT BEOEFENING VAN HET NEDERLANDS BURGERLIJK RECHT, 3 BIJZONDERE OVEREENKOMSTEN (7th ed. 1994)

AUCKENTHALER (2004)
F. AUCKENTHALER, DROIT DES MARCHES DE CAPITAUX (2004)

AUDIT (2000)
B. AUDIT, DROIT INTERNATIONAL PRIVE (3rd ed. 2000)
AUSTEN-PETERS (2000)
A.O. AUSTEN-PETERS, CUSTODY OF INVESTMENTS: LAW AND PRACTICE (2000)
AVEZAAT (2002)
R.M. AVEZAAT, DE KWALITEITSREKENING (2002)
BANE (1983)
C. Bane, *The Progressive Development of Commercial Law,* 37 U. MIAMI L. REV. 351 (1983), *reprinted in* PERSPECTIVES ON THE UNIFORM COMMERCIAL CODE, 4–13 (D. Litowitz ed. 2001)
BARTOS (2002)
J.M. BARTOS, UNITED STATES SECURITIES LAW: A PRACTICAL GUIDE (2002)
VAN BEEK (2002)
B.M. van Beek, *Clearing van transacties op Euronext Amsterdam, in* LUSTRUMBUNDEL 2002 VERENIGING VOOR EFFECTENRECHT, EEN BEWEZEN BESTAANSRECHT 1–10 (2002)
VAN BEEK & VAN BRUGGEN (2002)
B.M. VAN BEEK & D. VAN BRUGGEN, DE AFWIKKELING VAN GRENSOVERSCHRIJDENDE EFFECTENTRANSACTIES (2002)
VAN DER BEEK (2003)
J. van der Beek, *Aspecten van levering en verpanding van Wge-aandelen,* 7 ONDERNEMINGSRECHT 244–247 (2003)
BENABENT (2004)
BENABENT, DROIT CIVIL, LES CONTRATS SPECIAUX, CIVILS ET COMMERCIAUX, (6th ed. 2004)
BENJAMIN (2000)
J. BENJAMIN, INTERESTS IN SECURITIES, A PROPRIETARY LAW ANALYSIS OF THE INTERNATIONAL SECURITIES MARKETS (2000)
BENJAMIN (2003)
J. Benjamin, *Overview of Post-trade Infrastructure,* 3, 4 & 5 BUTTERWORTHS JOURNAL OF INTERNATIONAL BANKING AND FINANCIAL LAW 127–131, 171–177 & 223–228 (2003)
BENJAMIN & YATES (2002)
J. BENJAMIN, M. YATES & R. MONTAGU, THE LAW OF GLOBAL CUSTODY (2nd ed. 2002)
BERGEL, BRUSCHI & CIMAMONTI (1999)
J.-L. BERGEL, M. BRUSCHI & S. CIMAMONTI, TRAITE DE DROIT CIVIL, LES BIENS (1999)
BERNASCONI (2000)
Christophe Bernasconi, *The law applicable to dispositions of securities held through indirect holding systems* (November 2000) (Preliminary Document no. 1 to the Hague Conference on Private International Law), *available at* <www.hcch.net>

BERNASCONI & POTOK (2002)
C. Bernasconi & R. Potok, *The future Hague Convention on indirectly held securities, in* CROSS BORDER COLLATERAL: LEGAL RISK AND THE CONFLICT OF LAWS 615-623 (R. Potok ed., 2002)

BERTEA (2005)
S. Bertea, *Looking for Coherence within the European Community,* 2 EUROPEAN LAW JOURNAL 154–172 (2005)

BESSON (2004)
S. Besson, *From European Integration to European Integrity: Should European Law Speak with Just One Voice?,* 3 EUROPEAN LAW JOURNAL 257–281 (2004)

BIS Glossary 2003
BIS Committee on Payment and Settlement Systems, *A glossary of terms used in payments and settlement systems* (March 2003), *available at* <www.bis.org>

BLOCH (1999)
P. Bloch, *La directive 98/26/CEE concernant le caractère définitif du règlement dans les systèmes de paiement et de règlement des opérations sur titres, in* DROIT BANCAIRE ET FINANCIER, MELANGES AEDBF-FRANCE II 49–81 (J.-P. Mattout & H. de Vauplane eds, 1999)

BLOCH & DE VAUPLANE (2005)
P. Bloch & H. de Vauplane, *Loi applicable et critères de localisation des titres multi-intermédiés dans la Convention de La Haye du 13 décembre 2002,* REVUE TRIMESTRIELLE LEXISNEXIS IURISCLASSEUR-J.D.I. 3–40 (2005)

BLOEMBERGEN (1992-1)
A.R. BLOEMBERGEN, *De eenheid van het recht, in* BLOEMBERGENS WERK, 557–569 (1992)

BLOEMBERGEN (1992-2)
A.R. BLOEMBERGEN, *De eenheid van privaatrecht en administratief recht, in* BLOEMBERGENS WERK, 305–351 (1992)

BLOEMBERGEN ET AL. (2001)
A.R. BLOEMBERGEN ET AL., RECHTSHANDELING EN OVEREENKOMST (3d ed. 2001)

BLOM (1998)
M.A. Blom, *Dematerialisatie van effecten en ontwikkelingen rond de Wge, in* ONDERNEMING EN EFFECTEN 183–206 (S.C.J.J. Kortmann et al. eds, 1998)

BLOM (1999)
M.A. Blom, *Effecten en the law of the intermediary,* 14 ONDERNEMINGSRECHT 376–384 (1999)

BNP Paribas Report
BNP Parisbas, *EU Legal Certainty Project, Priorities for the legal expert group, available at* ec.europa.eu/internal_market/financial-markets/clearing/certainty_en.htm

BODDAERT (2004)
C. Boddaert, FINANCIEEL RECHT, Looseleaf Commentary on KB. no. 62, 81–246 (supp. 21, 2004)
BOELE (1997)
S.A. Boele, *Enkele civielrechtelijke aspecten van de global note, in* LUSTRUMBUNDEL 1997 VERENIGING VOOR EFFECTENRECHT, DE OPKOMST VAN EEN RECHTSGEBIED 15–24 (1997)
BOGERT (1987)
G.T. BOGERT, TRUSTS (6th ed. 1987)
BONNEAU (2003)
TH. BONNEAU, DROIT BANCAIRE (5th ed. 2003)
BONNEAU & DRUMMOND (2005)
TH. BONNEAU & F. DRUMMOND, DROIT DES MARCHES FINANCIERS (2nd ed. 2005)
VAN DEN BOSCH (2000)
A.F.M. van den Bosch, *Voorstel tot beperkte wijziging van de Wet giraal effectenverkeer,* 9 VENNOOTSCHAP & ONDERNEMING 136–139 (2000)
BROUWER (1992)
P.W. Brouwer, *Over coherentie in recht,* 3 NEDERLANDS TIJDSCHRIFT VOOR RECHTSFILOSOFIE EN RECHTSTHEORIE 178–192 (1992)
BROUWER (1999)
P.W. Brouwer, *Systematisering van recht, in* DRIE DIMENSIES VAN RECHT: RECHTSTHEORIE, RECHTSGELEERDHEID, RECHTSPRAKTIJK 219–237 (P.W. Brouwer et al. eds, 1999)
BROWN (1975)
R.A. BROWN, THE LAW OF PERSONAL PROPERTY (W.B. Raushenbush ed., 3d ed. 1975)
BURG (2000)
H.J.M. BURG, THE MODEL OF PRINCIPLES, THE QUEST FOR RATIONALITY IN THE IMPLEMENTATION OF CONFLICTING PRINCIPLES (2000)
BURKE (2003)
B. BURKE, PERSONAL PROPERTY IN A NUTSHELL (3d ed. 2003)
CABRILLAC & MOULY (1992)
M. CABRILLAC & C. MOULY, DROIT DES SÛRETÉS (6th ed. 2002)
CANARIS (1969)
C.-W. CANARIS, SYSTEMDENKEN UND SYSTEMBEGRIFF IN DER JURISPRUDENZ (2nd ed. 1983)
CANIVET (2003)
G. Canivet, *La Convergence des Systèmes Juridiques du Point de Vue du Droit privé Français,* 1 EUROPEAN REVIEW OF PRIVATE LAW 50–65 (2003)
CERFONTAINE (2004)
J. Cerfontaine, *Effectenbewaarneming door financiële instellingen, in* BANK-CONTRACTEN 475–519 (B. Tilleman & B. Du Laing eds, 2004)
CLARKSON & HILL (2002)
C.M.V. CLARKSON & J. HILL, JAFFEY ON THE CONFLICT OF LAWS (2nd ed. 2002)

CNCT 1997 Report

Conseil National du Crédit et du Titre, *Problèmes Juridiques liés à la Dématérialisation des Moyens de Paiement et des Titres* (May 1997)

COHEN (2005)

E.E. Cohen, *Commercial Law, in* ANCIENT GREEK LAW 290–302 (M. Gagarin & D. Cohen eds, 2005)

COOPER (2000)

C. COOPER, THE NEW ARTICLE 9 UNIFORM COMMERCIAL CODE (2nd ed. 2000)

CORNU (2004)

G. CORNU, VOCABULAIRE JURIDIQUE (6th ed. 2004)

COURET & LE NABASQUE (2004)

A. COURET & LE NABASQUE, VALEURS MOBILIERES AUGMENTATIONS DE CAPITAL, NOUVEAU REGIME (2004)

CPSS 1995 Report

Committee on Payment and Settlement Systems, *Cross-border Securities Settlements* (March 1995), *available at* <www.bis.org>

CPSS Red Book

Committee on Payment and Settlement Systems, *Red Book statistical update* (April 2003), *available at* <www.bis.org>

CPSS/IOSCO Recommendations 2001

Committee on Payment and Settlement Systems & Technical Committee of the International Organization of Securities Commissions, *Recommendations for securities settlement systems* (November 2001), *available at* <www.bis.org>

CURTIN & DEKKER (1999)

D.M. Curtin & I.F. Dekker, *The EU as a 'Layered' International Organization: Institutional Unity in Disguise, in* THE EVOLUTION OF EU LAW 83–136 (P. Craig & G. de Búrca eds, 1999)

DALHUISEN & VAN SETTEN (2003)

J.H. DALHUISEN & L.D. VAN SETTEN, ZEKERHEID IN ROERENDE ZAKEN EN RECHTEN (2003)

VAN DELDEN (1988)

R. van Delden, *Giraal verkeer en registratie, in* TOT VERMAAK VAN SLAGTER, FEESTBUNDEL AANGEBODEN AAN PROF. MR. W.J. SLAGTER 51–64 (1988)

DESMET (1987)

J. Desmet, *The Structure of Law from a Legislative Point of View, in* THE STRUCTURE OF LAW 115–139 (Å. Frändberg & M. van Hoecke eds, 1987)

DEVOS (2000)

D. Devos, *Aspects juridiques intéressants les systèmes de règlement-titres, in* NIEUW VENNOOTSCHAPS- EN FINANCIEEL RECHT 1999 527–552 (2000)

DICKSON (2001)

J. Dickson, *Interpretation and Coherence in Legal Reasoning,* The Stanford Encyclopaedia of Philosophy (Summer 2001 Edition), *at* <http://plato.stanford.edu/archives/sum2001/entries/legal-reas-interpret/>

VAN DIJK (2001-1)
J.M. van Dijk, *Wijziging van de Wet giraal effectenverkeer,* 6 ONDERNEMINGSRECHT 146–153 (2001)
VAN DIJK (2001-2)
J.M. van Dijk, *Giraliseren bij uitgifte van effecten op naam,* 11 ONDERNEMINGSRECHT 336–338 (2001)
DIRIX (1998)
E. Dirix, *Kwaliteitsrekeningen; algemene inleiding en toepassingsgevallen, in* INZAKE KWALITEIT, DE KWALITEITS- OF DERDENREKENING NAAR BELGISCH EN NEDERLANDS RECHT 3–16 (E. Dirix & R.D. Vriesendorp eds, 1998)
DROBNIG (1988)
U. Drobnig, *Dokumenteloser Effektenverkehr, in* ABSCHIED VOM WERTPAPIER? DOKUMENTELOSER WERTBEWEGUNGEN IM EFFEKTEN-, GÜTERTRANSPORT- UND ZAHLUNGSVERKEHR 11–41 (K. Kreuzered., 1988)
DROBNIG (2004-1)
U. Drobnig, *Transfer of Property, in* TOWARDS A EUROPEAN CIVIL CODE 725-740 (A. Hartkamp et al. eds, 3d ed. 2004)
DROBNIG (2004-2)
U. Drobnig, *Security Rights in Movables, in* TOWARDS A EUROPEAN CIVIL CODE 741–755 (A. Hartkamp et al. eds, 3d ed. 2004)
DTCC 2001 White Paper
The Depository Trust & Clearing Corporation, *A White Paper to the Industry on T+1* (July 2000), *available at* <www.dtcc.com>
DWORKIN (1986)
R. DWORKIN, LAW'S EMPIRE (1986)
EBELING (1978)
C.B.J. Ebeling, *Giraal effectenverkeer, enige notities bij de Wet giraal effectenverkeer,* 5 TVVS/ONDERNEMINGSRECHT 137–143 (1978)
EC Economic Impact Study (2006)
N. Schulze & D. Baur, Economic Impact Study on Clearing & Settlement – Annex II (May 2006), *available at* ec.europa.eu/internal_market
EFMLG 2000 Proposal
EFMLG, *Proposal for EU Directive on Collateralisation* (2000), *available at* <www.efmlg.org>
EFMLG 2003 Report
EFMLG, *Harmonisation of the legal framework for rights evidenced by book-entries in respect of certain financial instruments in the European Union* (June 2003), *available at* <www.efmlg.org>
EINSELE (1997)
D. Einsele, *Das neue US-amerikanische Wertpapierrecht als Modell für einen funktionsfähigen Effektengiroverkehr,* 43 RECHT DER INTERNATIONALEN WIRTSCHAFT 269–274 (1997)
EINSELE (2005)
D. Einsele, *Modernising German Law : Can the UNIDROIT Project on Intermediated Securities Provide Guidance?,* 1/2 UNIFORM LAW REVIEW 251–261 (2005)

EISMA ET AL. (2002)
S.E. EISMA (ED.), J.M. VAN DIJK, W.A.K. RANK ET. AL., LEERBOEK EFFECTENRECHT (2nd ed. 2002)
VAN ERP (2003)
J.H.M. van Erp, *A* Numerus Quasi-Clausus *of Property Rights as a Constitutive Element of a Future European Property Law?,* 7.2 ELECTRONIC JOURNAL OF COMPARATIVE LAW (2003)
VAN ERP (2004)
J.H.M. van Erp, *De osmose van Nederlands en Europees goederenrecht,* 10 NEDERLANDS TIJDSCHRIFT VOOR BURGERLIJK RECHT 533–546 (2004)
ESCB-CESR 2004 Report
Committee of European Securities Regulators and the European Central Bank, *Standards for Securities Clearing and Settlement in the European Union* (September 2004), *available at* <www.cesr.eu>
Euroclear Annual Report 2002
Euroclear plc, Euroclear Bank S.A./N.V. and subsidiaries, *Annual Report 2002, available at* <www.euroclear.com>
Euroclear France 2003 Disclosure Framework
Euroclear France, *Disclosure Framework Euroclear Netherlands* (27 March 2003), *available at* <www.euroclear.com>
Euroclear Netherlands 2003 Disclosure Framework
Euroclear Netherlands, *Disclosure Framework Euroclear Netherlands* (22 January 2003), *available at* <www.euroclear.com>
Explanatory Notes to the Preliminary Draft UNIDROIT Securities Convention
UNIDROIT Secretariat, *Explanatory Notes to the Preliminary Draft UNIDROIT Convention on Harmonised Substantive Rules regarding Securities Held with an Intermediary,* 1/2 UNIFORM LAW REVIEW 36–115 (2005)
Explanatory Report (2005)
R. Goode, H. Kanda & K. Kreuzer, *Explanatory Report on the Hague Convention on the Law Applicable to Certain Rights in Respect of Securities held with an Intermediary* (2005), *available at* <www.hcch.net>
FIALHO DE OLIVEIRA (2005)
R. Fialho de Oliveira, *The São Paulo UNIDROIT Seminar,* 4 UNIFORM LAW REVIEW 827–831 (2005)
FILOTT (2000)
W.H.G.A. FILOTT, ALGEMENE BANKVOORWAARDEN (4th ed. 2000)
FREDERICQ (1952)
L. FREDERICQ, TRAITE DE DROIT COMMERCIAL BELGE, TOME IX (1952)
FRIELINK (1990)
K. Frielink, *Open bewaargeving van effecten en giraal effectenverkeer,* 5944 & 5945 WEEKBLAD VOOR PRIVAATRECHT, NOTARIAAT EN REGISTRATIE 19–24 & 35–38 (1990)
G30 1989 Report
Group of 30, *Clearance and Settlement in the World's Securities Markets* (1989)

G30 2003 Plan of Action
Group of 30, *Global Clearing and Settlement, A plan of Action* (executive summary) (January 2003), *available at* <www.group30.org>
GAO (1997)
US Government Accounting Office, *Financial Crisis Management, Four financial crises in the 1980s* (1997), *available at* <www.gao.gov>
GAVALDA & STOUFFLET (2002)
C. GAVALDA & J. STOUFFLET, DROIT BANCAIRE, INTITUTIONS, COMPTES, OPERATIONS, SERVICES (5th ed. 2002)
GELDERBLOM & JONKER (2005)
O. Gelderblom & J. Jonker, *Amsterdam as the Cradle of Modern Futures and Options Trading, 1550–1650, in* THE ORIGINS OF VALUE 189–205 (W.N. Goetzmann & K.G. Rouwenhorst eds, 2005)
VAN GERVEN (1996)
W. van Gerven, *Toward a Coherent Constitutional System within the European Union,* 1 EUROPEAN PUBLIC LAW 81–101(1996)
VAN GERVEN (1997)
W. van Gerven, *Coherence of Community and national laws. Is there a legal basis for a European Civil Code,* 5 EUROPEAN PUBLIC LAW 465–470 (1997)
VAN GERVEN (2004)
W. van Gerven, *Harmonization of Private Law: Do We Need It?,* 41 COMMON MARKET LAW REVIEW 505–532 (2004)
GILSON (2001)
R.J. Gilson, *Globalizing Corporate Governance: Convergence of Form or Function,* 49 AMERICAN JOURNAL OF COMPARATIVE LAW 329–357 (2001)
GIORDIANO (2002)
F. Giordiano, *Cross-border Trading in Financial Securities in Europe: The Role of the Central Counterparty* (December 2002)(ECMI Short Paper no. 3), *available at* <www.ecmi.es>
Giovannini Group 2001 Report
Giovannini Group, *Cross-border clearing and settlement arrangements in the European Union* (November 2001), *available at* ec.europa.eu/internal_market/financial-markets/
Giovannini Group 2003 Report
Giovannini Group, *Second report on EU clearing and settlement arrangements* (April 2003), *available at* ec.europa.eu/internal_market/financial-markets/
GOODE (1996)
R. Goode, *The nature and transfer of rights in dematerialised and immobilised securities,* 4 JOURNAL OF INTERNATIONAL BANKING AND FINANCIAL LAW 167–176 (1996)
GOODE (2003-1)
R. Goode, *Contract and Commercial Law: the Logic and Limits of Harmonisation,* IUS COMMUNE LECTURES ON EUROPEAN PRIVATE LAW, 2003

GOODE (2003-2)
R. GOODE, LEGAL PROBLEMS OF CREDIT AND SECURITY (3d ed. 2003)
GRAAF (1991)
F.G.B. GRAAF, EUROMARKET FINANCE: ISSUES OF EUROMARKET SECURITIES AND SYNDICATED EUROCURRENCY LOANS (1991)
GROENHUJSEN & KRISTEN (1999)
M.S. Groenhuijsen & F.G.H. Kristen, *Verduistering van girale effecten,* ONDERNEMINGSRECHT 214–219 (1999)
GRUNDMANN-VAN DE KROL (2002)
C.M. GRUNDMANN-VAN DE KROL, KOERSEN DOOR HET EFFECTENRECHT, BESCHOUWINGEN OMTRENT HET NEDERLANDSE EFFECTENRECHT (4th ed. 2002)
GUTTMAN (1990)
E. Guttman, *Transfer of Securities: State and Federal Interaction,* 12 CARDOZO L. REV. 437–469 (1990)
GUTTMAN (2005)
E. GUTTMAN, MODERN SECURITIES TRANSFERS, Vols. 28 and 28A (2005)
GUYNN ET AL. (1996)
R.D. GUYNN ET AL., MODERNIZING SECURITIES OWNERSHIP, TRANSFER AND PLEDGING LAWS (1996)
GUYNN & ROGERS (2002)
R.D. Guynn & J.S. Rogers, *United States (New York) in* CROSS BORDER COLLATERAL: LEGAL RISK AND THE CONFLICT OF LAWS 603–614 (R. Potok ed., 2002)
HAENTJENS (2004-1)
M. Haentjens, *Privaatrechtelijke aspecten van giraal effectenverkeer,* 6582 WEEKBLAD VOOR PRIVAATRECHT, NOTARIAAT EN REGISTRATIE, 472–481 (2004)
HAENTJENS (2004-2)
M. Haentjens, *Naschrift: Zicht op onduidelijkheid; over aanspraak, overdracht en vertegenwoordiging in de Wge,* 6602 WEEKBLAD VOOR PRIVAATRECHT, NOTARIAAT EN REGISTRATIE 988–990 (2004)
HAENTJENS (2006)
M. HAENTJENS, THE LAW APPLICABLE TO INDIRECTLY HELD SECURITIES (2006)
HAENTJENS (forthcoming, 2007)
M. Haentjens, SDU COMMENTAAR FINANCIEEL RECHT, Commentary on the Wge (forthcoming, 2007)
HANSMANN & KRAAKMAN (2002)
H. Hansmann & R. Kraakman, *Property, Contract, and Verification: The Numerus Clausus Problem and the Divisibility of Rights,* 31 JOURNAL OF LEGAL STUDIES 373–420 (2002)
HARTKAMP (1989)
A.S. Hartkamp, *Opmerkingen over de verhouding tussen internationale unificatie en nationale (her)codificatie,* 4 KWARTAALBERICHT NIEUW BW 101–104 (1989)
HARTKAMP (2002)
A.S. HARTKAMP, MONOGRAFIEËN NIEUW BW, A1 AARD EN OPZET VAN HET NIEUWE VERMOGENSRECHT (3d ed. 2002)

HARTKAMP (2003)

A.S. Hartkamp, *Eenmaking en harmonisering van het contractenrecht: doeleinden en methoden, in* PRIVAATRECHT TUSSEN AUTONOMIE EN SOLIDARITEIT 97–105 (M.W. Hesselink, C.E. du Perron & A.F. Salomons eds, 2003)

HARTKAMP ET AL. (2004)

A.S. HARTKAMP ET AL. EDS, TOWARDS A EUROPEAN CIVIL CODE (3d. ed. 2004)

HELLNER (1987)

J. Hellner, *The Structure of Law in a Legislative Perspective, in* THE STRUCTURE OF LAW 101–114 (Å. Frändberg & M. van Hoecke eds, 1987)

HESSELINK (2001)

M.W. HESSELINK, THE NEW EUROPEAN LEGAL CULTURE (2001)

HESSELINK (2005)

M.W. Hesselink, *Non-Mandatory Rules in European Contract Law,* 1 EUROPEAN REVIEW OF CONTRACT LAW 44–86 (2005)

HESSELINK (2006)

M.W. Hesselink, *The Ideal of Codification and the Dynamics of Europeanisation: The Dutch Experience,* 3 EUROPEAN LAW JOURNAL 279–305 (2006)

VAN DEN HOEK (2003)

M.P. van den Hoek, *Wge moet af van 'mede-eigendom',* 6536 WEEKBLAD VOOR PRIVAATRECHT, NOTARIAAT EN REGISTRATIE 432–438 (2003)

VAN DEN HOEK (2004)

M.P. van den Hoek, *Waar zijn gedematerialiseerde aandelen?,* 6567 WEEKBLAD VOOR PRIVAATRECHT, NOTARIAAT EN REGISTRATIE 147–156 (2004)

HOMMELHOF (1992)

P. Hommelhof, *Zivilrecht unter dem Einfluß europäischen Rechtsangleichung,* 192 ARCHIV FÜR DIE CIVILISTISCHE PRAXIS 71–107 (1992)

HUET (2001)

J. HUET, TRAITE DE DROIT CIVIL, LES PRINCIPAUX CONTRATS SPECIAUX (2nd ed. 2001)

HUIZINK (2005)

J.B. HUIZINK, INSOLVENTIE (5th ed. 2005)

HYNES & LOEWENSTEIN (2005)

J.D. HYNES & M.J. LOEWENSTEIN, AGENCY, PARTNERSHIP, AND THE LLC IN A NUTSHELL (3d ed. 2005)

DE IONGH (1926)

A.W. IONGH, GEDENKBOEK 1876–1926, VEREENIGING VOOR DEN EFFECTENHANDEL (1926)

ISSA Recommendations 2000

International Securities Services Association, *Recommendations 2000* (June 2000), *available at* <www.issa.org>

JOERGES (1997)

C. Joerges, *The Impact of European Integration on Private Law: Reductionist Perceptions, True Conflicts and a New Constitutional Perspective,* 4 EUROPEAN LAW JOURNAL 378–406 (1997)

JOHANSSON (2005)
E. Johansson, *Transfer and Settlement of Securities: The New Order,* EUROPEAN BUSINESS LAW REVIEW 1093–1115 (2005)

DE JONG (1998)
W. de Jong, *Beleggersgiro: een effectenrechtelijk kameleon?, in* ONDERNEMING EN EFFECTEN 53–71 (S.C.J.J. Kortmann et al. eds, 1998)

KEIJSER (2002)
T.R.M.P. Keijser, *De collateral richtlijn, in* ONDERNEMING EN 10 JAAR NIEUW BURGERLIJK RECHT 165–192 (S.C.J.J. Kortmann et al. eds, 2002)

KEIJSER (2003)
T.R.M.P. Keijser, *De rechtspositie van de pandgever op de schopstoel, Het 'gebruiksrecht' van de Collateral Richtlijn beschouwd naar Nederlands en Duits recht,* 8 NEDERLANDS TIJDSCHRIFT VOOR BURGERLIJK RECHT 432–442 (2003)

KEIJSER (2006)
T.R.M.P. KEIJSER, FINANCIAL COLLATERAL ARRANGEMENTS (2006)

KENNEDY (2006)
D. Kennedy, *Thoughts on Coherence, Social Values and National Tradition in Private Law, in* THE POLITICS OF A EUROPEAN CIVIL CODE 9–31 (M.W. Hesselink ed., 2006)

KLIEBISCH (1997)
Th.A.L. Kliebisch, *Vijf jaar fiducia-verbod, in* ONDERNEMING EN 5 JAAR NIEUW BURGERLIJK RECHT 75–86 (S.C.J.J. Kortmann et al. eds, 1997)

KLIK & KUIPERS (1992)
P. KLIK & P. KUIPERS, CONTRACTSDWANG DE GLOBAL NOTE EN DE NEMO PLUS-REGEL (1992)

KRESS (1996)
K. Kress, *Coherence, in* A COMPANION TO PHILOSOPHY OF LAW AND LEGAL THEORY 533–552 (1996)

KROPHOLLER (2004)
J. KROPHOLLER, INTERNATIONALES PRIVATRECHT (5th ed. 2004)

LAGA & LIETAER (2001)
H. Laga & V. Lietaer, *Eigendomsbetwistingen bij aandelen, in* ONDERNEMING EN EFFECTEN 465-491 (B. Tilleman & B. Du Laing eds, 2001)

DU LAING (2001)
B. du Laing, *Aspecten van Aandelenbewa(a)r(gev)ing, in* ONDERNEMING EN EFFECTEN 335–382 (B. Tilleman & B. Du Laing eds, 2001)

LAMBRECHT & HALJAN (1999)
P. Lambrecht & D. Haljan, *Investor Protection and the European Directives Concerning Securities, in* THE LAW OF CROSS-BORDER SECURITIES TRANSACTIONS 257–276 (H. van Houtte ed., 1999)

Lamfalussy 1990 Report
Bank for International Settlements, *Report of the Committee on Interbank Netting Schemes of the Central Banks of the Group of Ten Countries* (November 1990)

LAWRENCE (2005)
L. LAWRENCE, LAWRENCE'S ANDERSON ON THE UNIFORM COMMERCIAL CODE (3d. ed. supp. 2005)
LCG Draft Advice
EU Clearing and Settlement Legal Certainty Group, *Draft advice of 11 August 2006, available at* <http://ec.europa.eu/internal_market/>.
Legal Certainty Group Advice
EU Clearing and Settlement Legal Certainty Group, *Advice of 11 August 2006, available at* <http://ec.europa.eu/internal_market/>.
LEGRAND (1997)
P. Legrand, *Against a European Civil Code,* THE MODERN LAW REVIEW 44–63 (1997)
LEVENBOOK (1984)
B.B. Levenbook, *The Role of Coherence in Legal Reasoning,* 3 LAW AND PHILOSOPHY, 355–74 (1984)
LITOWITZ (2001)
D. LITOWITZ, PERSPECTIVES ON THE UNIFORM COMMERCIAL CODE (2001)
LÖBER (2005)
K.M. Löber, *The Changing Legal Landscape for Clearing and Settlement in the European Union,* 1/2 UNIFORM LAW REVIEW, 155–188 (2005)
LÖBER (2006)
K.M. Löber, *The Developing EU Legal Framework for Clearing and Settlement of Financial Instruments,* ECB LEGAL WORKING PAPER SERIES NO. 1 (February 2006)
LOOS (2006)
M.B.M. LOOS, SPONTANE HARMONISATIE IN HET CONTRACTEN- EN CONSUMENTENRECHT (2006)
LOWENFELD (1978)
A. Lowenfeld, *In Search of the Intangible: A Comment on* Shaffer v. Heitner, 53 NEW YORK UNIVERSITY L. REV., 102–124 (1978)
MACCORMICK (1984a)
N. MacCormick, *Coherence in Legal Justification, in* THEORY OF LEGAL SCIENCE 235–251 (A. Peczenik et al. eds, 1984)
MACCORMICK (1984b)
N. MacCormick, *Coherence in Legal Justification, in* THEORIE DER NORMEN: FESTGABE FÜR OTA WEINBERGER 37–53 (W. Krawietz ed., 1984)
MAFFEI (2005)
A. Maffei, *De la nature juridique des titres dématérialisés intermédiés en droit français,* 1/2 UNIFORM LAW REVIEW 237–249 (2005)
MALAURIE, AYNES & GAUTIER (2001)
P. MALAURIE, L. AYNES & P.-Y. GAUTIER, COURS DE DROIT CIVIL TOME VIII, LES CONTRATS SPECIAUX (14th ed. 2001)
MALMENDIER (2005)
U. Malmendier, *Roman Shares, in* THE ORIGINS OF VALUE 31–42 (W.N. Goetzmann & K.G. Rouwenhorst eds, 2005)

DE MAREZ OYENS & FRAENKEL (1990)
G.H. de Marez Oyens & D.G. Fraenkel, *Internationale Clearing en Settlement,* 16 BEDRIJFSJURIDISCHE BERICHTEN, 166–168 (1990)
MARTIN (1996)
D.R. Martin, *De la nature corporelle des valeurs mobilières (et autres droits scripturaux),* Dalloz Chronique, 47–52 (1996)
MAYER & HEUZÉ (2004)
P. MAYER & V. HEUZÉ, DROIT INTERNATIONAL PRIVÉ (8th ed. 2004)
MEIJER (1974)
W.R. MEIJER, EFFECTENBEWARING (1974)
MEIJER (1999)
S.Y.TH. MEIJER, MIDDELLIJKE VERTEGENWOORDIGING (1999)
MICHELER (2006)
E. MICHELER, DOCTRINAL PATH DEPENDENCE AND FUNCTIONAL CONVERGENCE: THE CASE OF INVESTMENT SECURITIES (2006), *available at* <www.ssrn.com>
MIJNSSEN (1975)
F.H.J. Mijnssen, *Het voorstel tot regeling van giraal effectenverkeer,* DE NAAMLOZE VENNOOTSCHAP 199–211 (1975)
MOLONEY (2002)
N. MOLONEY, EC SECURITIES REGULATION (2002)
MOONEY (1990)
C.W. Mooney Jr., *Beyond Negotiability: A New Model for Transfer and Pledge of Interests in Securities Controlled by Intermediaries,* 12 CARDOZO L. REV. 305–427 (1990)
MOONEY (1998)
C.W. Mooney Jr., *Practising Safer Lex: The Proper Domein of Property, Secured Transactions and Insolvency Laws in the Regulation of Securities Intermediaries, in* EUROPEAN SECURITIES MARKETS 85–94 (G. Ferrarini ed., 1998)
MORTON, POTOK & BENJAMIN (2002)
G. Morton, R. Potok & J. Benjamin, *England, in* CROSS BORDER COLLATERAL: LEGAL RISK AND THE CONFLICT OF LAWS 217–247 (R. Potok ed., 2002)
MOUY & DE VAUPLANE (1995)
S. Mouy & H. de Vauplane, *Dématérialisation et titres internationaux,* 565 BANQUE, 56–59 (1995)
MÜLLER-GRAFF (2004)
P.-C. Müller-Graff, *Private Law Unification by Means other than of Codification, in* TOWARDS A EUROPEAN CIVIL CODE 77–89 (A.S. Hartkamp et al. eds, 3d. ed. 2004)
VAN NESTE (1990)
F. VAN NESTE, BEGINSELEN VAN BELGISCH PRIVAATRECHT; V ZAKENRECHT, BOEK I (2nd ed. 1990)
ODERKERK (1999)
M.E. ODERKERK, DE PRELIMINAIRE FASE VAN HET RECHTSVERGELIJKEND ONDERZOEK (1999)

Ooi (2003)
M. Ooi, Shares and Other Securities in the Conflict of Laws (2003)
Paech (2002)
P. Paech, *Harmonising Substantive Rules for the Use of Securities held with Intermediaries as Collateral: the Unidroit Project,* 4 Uniform Law Review 1140–1160 (2002)
Van Pappelendam-Hemmen (2000)
E.M. van Pappelendam-Hemmen, *Wetsvoorstel 27 164 tot wijziging van de Wge,* 13 Ondernemingsrecht 376–381 (2000)
Pardoel (1997)
D. Pardoel, Les Conflits de Lois en Matiere de Cession de Creance (1997)
Partsch-Bobricheff (2005)
O. Partsch-Bobricheff, *Analysis of the Current Legal Framework for Clearing and Settlement Services in the European Union, together with Some Tentative Considerations Concerning the Future,* 1 Euredia 15–72 (2005)
Peeters & Van der Vorst (2001)
I. Peeters & C. Van der Vorst, *Pand en andere zekerheden op aandelen in diverse verschijningsvormen. Een goederenrechtelijke analyse, in* Onderneming en Effecten 427–461 (B. Tilleman & B. Du Laing eds, 2001)
Du Perron (1993)
C.E. Du Perron, *De overeenkomst van opdracht,* 29 Nederlands Juristenblad 1044–1048 (1993)
Du Perron (1999)
C.E. Du Perron, Overeenkomst en derden (1999)
Peters (2003)
M.J. Peters, Clearing, settlement and taxation in Securities Markets (2003)
Pezzolo (2005)
L. Pezzolo, *Bonds and Government Debt in Italian City-States, 1250–1650, in* The Origins of Value 145–164 (W.N. Goetzmann & K.G. Rouwenhorst eds, 2005)
Pos (2001)
D.M. Pos, *Rechtskeuze in het internationaal zakenrecht,* 4 Nederlands Internationaal Privaatrecht 398–405 (2001)
Potok (2001)
R. Potok, *Cross-border collateralisation – legal risk, in* Internationaal Privaatrecht en Financiële Transacties 55–63 (F.G.B. Graaf & W.A.K. Rank eds, 2001)
Potok (2002)
R. Potok, *General introduction: legal nature of interests in indirectly held securities and resulting conflict of laws analysis, in* Cross Border Collateral: Legal Risk and the Conflict of Laws 7–47 (R. Potok ed., 2002)
Potok (2004)
R. Potok, *The Hague Securities Convention – closer and closer to reality,* 15 Journal of Banking and Finance Law and Practice 204–220 (2004)

QUINN (2001)
TH.M. QUINN, QUINN'S UNIFORM COMMERCIAL CODE COMMENTARY AND LAW DIGEST (2nd ed., revised volume 2,2001)

QUINN (2005)
TH.M. QUINN, QUINN'S UNIFORM COMMERCIAL CODE COMMENTARY AND LAW DIGEST (2nd ed., 2005 Cumulative Supplement No. 2, 2005)

RAIJMAKERS & VAN BEEK (2003)
J.A.A.J. Raijmakers & B.M. van Beek, *Financiëlezekerheidsovereenkomsten,* 10 TIJDSCHRIFT VOOR EFFECTENRECHT 183–192 (2003)

RANK (1996)
W.A.K. Rank, *Custody of Securities in The Netherlands, in* VERTROUWD MET DE TRUST, TRUST AND TRUST-LIKE ARRANGEMENTS 319–338 (D. Hayton et al. eds, 1996)

RANK (1998)
W.A.K. Rank, *Repo's en repowet: van de regen in de drup?, in* ONDERNEMING EN EFFECTEN 371–418 (S.C.J.J. Kortmann et al. eds, 1998)

RANK (1999)
W.A.K. Rank, *Aangaan en afwikkeling van transacties op de AEX-Effectenbeurs, in* GELDIGE EFFECTEN 71–88 (1999)

RANK (2001)
W.A.K. Rank, *Cross-border collateralisation under Dutch law, in* INTERNATIONAAL PRIVAATRECHT EN FINANCIËLE TRANSACTIES 65–71 (F.G.B. Graaf & W.A.K. Rank eds, 2001)

RANK (2002)
W.A.K. Rank, *EU Collateral Directive vastgesteld: zekerheid voor financiële zekerheidsovereenkomsten?, in* LUSTRUMBUNDEL 2002 VERENIGING VOOR EFFECTENRECHT, EEN BEWEZEN BESTAANSRECHT 319–328 (2002)

RANK (2005)
W.A.K Rank, *Vaststelling* Hague Securities Convention: *meer rechtszekerheid in het internationale effectenverkeer?,* 3 NEDERLANDS INTERNATIONAAL PRIVAATRECHT 249–265 (2005)

RANK ET AL. (1997)
W.A.K. RANK, E.M. VAN ARDENNE-STACHIW & CH.W. LE RÛTTE, BEWARING EN EIGENDOM VAN EFFECTEN (1997)

RANK & BIERMAN (2006)
W.A.K Rank & B. Bierman, *Europese Commissie evlueert* Hague Securities Convention: *met grote stappen snel thuis?,* 10 TIJDSCHRIFT VOOR FINANCIEEL RECHT 255–261 (2006)

RANK & VAN DER LELY (2002)
W.A.K. Rank & A.-J. van der Lely, *The Netherlands,* in CROSS BORDER COLLATERAL: LEGAL RISK AND THE CONFLICT OF LAWS 397–416 (R. Potok ed., 2002)

RANK-BERENSCHOT (1998)
E.B. Rank-Berenschot, *Het Wge-aandeel: een recht op naam van eigen aard, in* ONDERNEMING EN EFFECTEN 149–167 (S.C.J.J. Kortmann et al. eds, 1998)

VAN RAVENHORST (1995)
C. VAN RAVENHORST, BANKREKENINGEN/BANKVERRICHTINGEN (PASSIEF BEDRIJF) (1995)

RAZ (1992)
J. Raz, *The Relevance of Coherence,* 72 BOSTON UNIVERSITY LAW REVIEW 273–321 (1992)

RAZ (1994)
J. RAZ, *The Relevance of Coherence, in* ETHICS IN THE PUBLIC DOMAIN 260–309 (1994)

REIGNE & DELORME (2001)
Ph. Reigné & Th. Delorme, *Le code monétaire et financier et les valeurs mobilières,* 5 JCP – LA SEMAINE JURIDIQUE ENTREPRISE ET AFFAIRES, 214–218 (2001)

REITZ (2005)
C.R. Reitz, *Reflections on the Drafting of the 1994 Revision of Article 8 of the US Uniform Commercial Code,* 1/2 UNIFORM LAW REVIEW 357–367 (2005)

REYGROBELLET (1999)
A. Reygrobellet, *Le droit de propriété du titulaire d'instruments financiers dématérialisés,* 52 REVUE TRIMESTRIELLE DE DROIT COMMERCIAL, 305–316 (1999)

RIPERT & ROBLOT I-2 (2002)
G. RIPERT & R. ROBLOT, TRAITE DE DROIT COMMERCIAL, TOME 1- VOLUME 2 (M. Germain ed., 18th ed. 2002)

RIPERT & ROBLOT II (1976)
G. RIPERT & R. ROBLOT, TRAITE DE DROIT COMMERCIAL, TOME 2 (8th ed. 1976)

RIPERT & ROBLOT II (1996)
G. RIPERT & R. ROBLOT, TRAITE DE DROIT COMMERCIAL, TOME 2 (P. Delebecque & M. Germain eds, 15th ed. 1996)

ROCKS (2003)
S.M. Rocks, *The Hague Convention on the Law Applicable to Certain Rights in Respect of Securities Held with an Intermediary,* 36 UNIFORM COMMERCIAL CODE LAW JOURNAL 1–14 (2003)

ROCKS & BJERRE (2004)
S.M. ROCKS & C.S. BJERRE, THE ABCs OF THE UCC, ARTICLE 8: INVESTMENT SECURITIES (2nd ed. 2004)

ROGERS (1995)
J.S. Rogers, *An Essay on Horseless Carriages and Paperless Negotiable Instruments: Some Lesons From the Article 8 Revision,* 31 IDAHO L. REV. 689–698 (1995)

ROGERS (1996)
J.S. Rogers, *Policy Perspectives on Revised U.C.C. Article 8,* 43 UCLA L. REV. 1431–1545 (1996)

ROGERS (2004)
J.S. ROGERS, THE EARLY HISTORY OF THE LAW OF BILLS AND NOTES (2nd reprint 2004)

ROGERS (2005)

J.S. ROGERS, CONFLICT OF LAWS FOR TRANSACTIONS IN SECURITIES HELD THROUGH INTERMEDIARIES, BOSTON COLLEGE LAW SCHOOL RESEARCH PAPER 80 (2005), *available at* <www.ssrn.com/abstract=815005>, *also published in* 39 CORNELL INTERNATIONAL LAW JOURNAL 285 (2006)

RONGEN (1996)

M.H.E., Rongen, *De strekking van het fiduciaverbod, in het bijzonder in verband met financiering op basis van vorderingen, in* VERTROUWD MET DE TRUST, TRUST EN TRUST-LIKE ARRANGEMENTS 263-301 (D.J. Hayton et al. eds, 1996)

DE ROOVER (1974)

R. DE ROOVER, *New Interpretations of the History of Banking, in* BUSINESS, BANKING, AND ECONOMIC THOUGHT IN LATE MEDIEVAL AND EARLY MODERN EUROPE 200–238 (J. Kirshner ed. 1974)

ROTH (2002)

W.-H. Roth, *Transposing "Pointillist" EC Guidelines into Systematic National Codes – Problems and Consequences,* 6 EUROPEAN REVIEW OF PRIVATE LAW 761–776 (2002)

RUTGERS (1998)

G.R. RUTGERS, MONOGRAFIEËN NIEUW BW, B73 BEWAARNEMING (1998)

LE RÛTTE (1992)

Ch.W. Le Rûtte, *Stukkenloze effecten,* 3 TIJDSCHRIFT VOOR VENNOOTSCHAPPEN, VERENIGINGEN EN STICHTINGEN 63–65 (1992)

VAN RYN & HEENEN (1981)

J. VAN RYN & J. HEENEN, PRINCIPES DE DROIT COMMERCIAL, TOME III (2nd ed. 1981)

VAN RYN & HEENEN (1988)

J. VAN RYN & J. HEENEN, PRINCIPES DE DROIT COMMERCIAL, TOME IV (2nd ed. 1988)

SAGAERT (2003)

V. SAGAERT, ZAKELIJKE SUBROGATIE (2003)

SALOMONS (1994)

A.F. Salomons, *Op de bres voor het fiducia-verbod. Ofwel: Meijers als kampioen der concurrent crediteuren,* 37 NEDERLANDS JURISTENBLAD 1261–1266 (1994)

SALOMONS (2000),

A.F. Salomons, *Inpassen of aanpassen? Vermogensrecht voor het digitale tijdperk,* 6427 WEEKBLAD VOOR PRIVAATRECHT, NOTARIAAT EN REGISTRATIE 901–907 (2000)

SALOMONS (2003)

A.F. Salomons, *Het wetsvoorstel tot aanpassing van Article 3:94: Nederland introduceert de 'stille cessie,'* 6546 WEEKBLAD VOOR PRIVAATRECHT, NOTARIAAT EN REGISTRATIE 670–675 (2003)

SALOMONS (2004)

A.F. Salomons, *Should we Ratify the* Convention on International Interest in Mobile Equipment *and the* Air Equipment Protocol? *Some Remarks from a Dutch Point of View,* 1 EUROPEAN REVIEW OF PRIVATE LAW 67–74 (2004)

SALOMONS (2006)
A.F. SALOMONS, TRANSFER OF TITLE CONCERNING MOVABLES PART IV (2006)
SCHIM (2002)
B.F.L.M. Schim, *Girale levering als girale betaling; over artikelen 17 en 41 Wge en artikel 3:84 BW, in* ONDERNEMING EN 10 JAAR NIEUW BURGERLIJK RECHT 193–209 (S.C.J.J. Kortmann et al. eds, 2002)
SCHIM (2004)
B.F.L.M. Schim, *Verpanding van girale effecten,* ONDERNEMINGSRECHT 418–424 (2004)
SCHIM (2006)
B.F.L.M. SCHIM, GIRAAL EFFECTENVERKEER EN GOEDERENRECHT (2006)
SCHOORDIJK (1975)
H.C.F. Schoordijk, *Enige aantekeningen n.a.v. het voorontwerp van wet betreffende het giraal effectenverkeer,* 5316 & 5317 WEEKBLAD VOOR PRIVAATRECHT, NOTARIAAT EN REGISTRATIE 629–638 & 649–655 (1975)
SCHRANS & STEENNOT (2003)
G. SCHRANS & R. STEENNOT, ALGEMEEN DEEL VAN HET FINANCIEEL RECHT (2003)
SCHWARCZ (2001)
S.L. Schwarcz, *Indirectly Held Securities and Intermediary Risk, 2* UNIFORM LAW REVIEW 283–299 (2001)
SCOLES ET AL. (2000)
E.F. SCOLES, P. HAY, P.J. BORCHERS & S.C. SYMEONIDES, CONFLICT OF LAWS (3rd ed. 2000)
SCOTT & FRATCHER (1987)
A.W. SCOTT & W.F. FRATCHER, THE LAW OF TRUSTS (4th ed. 1987)
SCOTT (2006)
H.S. SCOTT, INTERNATIONAL FINANCE: TRANSACTIONS, POLICY AND REGULATION (13th ed. 2006)
SEN (2005)
B. Sen, *Preface,* 1/2 UNIFORM LAW REVIEW 4–8 (2005)
SERVAES (2000)
B. Servaes, *Het immobiliseren van effecten: het Belgisch juridisch kader, in* NIEUW VENNOOTSCHAPS- EN FINANCIEEL RECHT 1999 513–526 (2000)
VAN SETTEN (1998)
L.D. VAN SETTEN, DE COMMISSIONAIR IN EFFECTEN (1998)
VAN SETTEN (2003)
L. van Setten, *Implementation in The Netherlands, in* SETTLEMENT FINALITY IN THE EUROPEAN UNION, THE EU DIRECTIVE AND ITS IMPLEMENTATION IN SELECTED JURISDICTIONS (M. Vereecken & A. Nijenhuis eds, 2003)
SIEGEL (1994)
D.D. SIEGEL, CONFLICTS IN A NUTSHELL (2nd ed. 1994)
SMITS (1996)
J. Smits, *Van partijen en derden: over de interpretatie van numerus clausus van zakelijke rechten,* 13 GRONINGER OPMERKINGEN EN MEDEDELINGEN 41–64 (1996)

SMITS (2006)
J. Smits, *Europese integratie in het vermogensrecht: een pleidooi voor keuzevrijheid, in* EUROPESE INTEGRATIE 57–104 (2006)
SNIJDERS (1972)
W. Snijders, *Betaling per giro, in* VAN OPSTALL-BUNDEL, OPSTELLEN AANGEBODEN AAN PROF. MR. S.N. VAN OPSTALL 173–178 (1972)
SNIJDERS (2005)
W. Snijders, *Ongeregeldheden in het vermogensrecht,* 6607 and 6608 WEEKBLAD VOOR PRIVAATRECHT, NOTARIAAT EN REGISTRATIE, 79–85 and 94–102 (2005)
SNIJDERS & RANK-BERENSCHOT (1996)
H.J. SNIJDERS & E.B. RANK-BERENSCHOT, GOEDERENRECHT (2d ed.1996)
SOMMER (1998)
J.H. Sommer, *A Law of Financial Accounts: Modern Payment and Securities Transfer Law,* 53 THE BUSINESS LAWYER 1181–1215 (1998)
SORIANO (2003)
L.M. Soriano, *A Modest Notion of Coherence in Legal Reasoning. A Model for the European Court of Justice,* 3 RATIO JURIS 296–323 (2003)
SPINK & PARÉ (2004)
E.T. Spink & M.A. Paré, *The* Uniform Securities Transfer Act: *Globalized Commercial Law For Canada,* 19 BANKING & FINANCE L. REV. 321–391 (2004)
STEFFENS (1997)
L.F.A. Steffens, *Goederenrechtelijke aspecten van cessie in het IPR,* 7 NEDERLANDS TIJDSCHRIFT VOOR BURGERLIJK RECHT 212–219 (1997)
STEFFENS (2005)
L.F.A. Steffens, *De Europese Richtlijn Financiëlezekerheidsovereenkomsten en de implementatie in de Nederlandse wetgeving,* NEDERLANDS TIJDSCHRIFT VOOR HANDELSRECHT 56–66 (2005)
STRIKWERDA (2002)
L. STRIKWERDA, INLEIDING TOT HET NEDERLANDSE INTERNATIONAAL PRIVAATRECHT (7th ed. 2002)
STRUYCKEN (1998)
T.H.D. Struycken, *The proprietary aspects of international assignment of debts and the Rome Convention, Article 12,* LLOYD'S MARITIME AND COMMERCIAL LAW QUARTERLY 345–360 (1998)
SUNT (1996)
Ch. Sunt, *Dematerialisatie van vennootschapseffecten, in* DE GEWIJZIGDE VENNOOTSCHAPSWET 1995 495–467 (K. Byttebier, R.R. Feltkamp & A. François eds, 1996)
TAYLOR (1978)
H. Taylor, *Uniformity of Commercial Law and State-by-State Enactment: A confluence of Contradictions,* 39 HASTINGS L.J. 337 (1978), *reprinted in* PERSPECTIVES ON THE UNIFORM COMMERCIAL CODE, at 104 (D. Litowitz ed. 2001)

TENENBAUM (2004)
A. Tenenbaum, *Réflexions sur la Convention de La Haye du 13 décembre 2002 sur la loi applicable à certains droits sur des titres détenus auprès d'un intermédiaire,* 4 REVUE DES SOCIETES 835–854 (2004)

TEUBNER (1998)
G. Teubner, *Legal Irritants: Good Faith in British Law or How Unifying Law Ends Up in New Divergences,* 61 THE MODERN LAW REVIEW 11–32 (1998)

THÉVENOZ (2005)
L. Thévenoz, *New Legal Concepts regarding the Holding of Investment Securities for a Civil Law Jurisdiction – The Swiss Draft Act,* 1/2 UNIFORM LAW REVIEW 301–311 (2005)

THOMAS (2005)
R. Thomas, *Writing, Law and Written Law, in* ANCIENT GREEK LAW 41–60 (M. Gagarin & D. Cohen eds, 2005)

TIMMERMAN & DOORMAN (2005)
L. Timmerman & A. Doorman, *Rights of Minority Shareholders in the Netherlands, a report written for the XVIth World Congress of the International Academy of Comparative Law* (2005), *available at* rechten.eldoc.ub.rug.nl

TISON (1996)
M. Tison, *De uitgifte van gedematerialiseerde vennootschapseffecten; bemerkingen bij de wet van 7 april 1995, in* HET GEWIJZIGDE VENNOOTSCHAPSRECHT 1995 229–261 (H. Braeckmans & E. Wymeersch eds, 1996)

UMBGROVE (1991)
J.H.F. Umbgrove, *NIEC start effectengiro,* 3 BEDRIJFSJURIDISCHE BERICHTEN 18–20 (1991)

UNIKEN VENEMA (2003)
C.&Æ UNIKEN VENEMA, EFFECTENGIRO-RECHT IN BEWEGING (2003)

UNIDROIT 2003 Position Paper
UNIDROIT Study Group on Harmonised Substantive Rules Regarding Indirectly Held Securities, *Position Paper* (August 2003), *available at* <www.unidroit.org>

DE VAUPLANE & BORNET (2001)
H. DE VAUPLANE & J.-P. BORNET, DROIT DES MARCHES FINANCIERS (3d ed. 2001)

DE VAUPLANE & DAIGRE (2003)
H. de Vauplane & J.-J. Daigre, *Chronique financière et boursière,* 89 BANQUE ET DROIT 30–40 (2003)

DE VAUPLANE & NIZARD (2001)
H. de Vauplane & F. Nizard, *Les titres inscrits en compte en droit international privé,* in DROIT BANCAIRE ET FINANCIER, MELANGES AEDBF-FRANCE III 401–423 (H. de Vauplane & J.-J. Daigre eds, 2001)

VEREECKEN & NIJENHUIS ET AL. (2003)
M. VEREECKEN & A. NIJENHUIS (EDS), SETTLEMENT FINALITY IN THE EUROPEAN UNION, THE EU DIRECTIVE AND ITS IMPLEMENTATION IN SELECTED JURISDICTIONS (2003)

VERHAGEN (1997)
H.L.E. Verhagen, *Vijf jaar NBW: artikel 3:84 lid 3 en de financieringspraktijk,* 2 TREMA 54–59 (1997)
VERHAGEN (1998)
H.L.E. Verhagen, *De girale levering in het international privaatrecht, in* ONDERNEMING EN EFFECTEN 333–271 (S.C.J.J. Kortmann et al. eds, 1998)
VERHAGEN (2000)
R. Verhagen, *Book-entry Securities and the Conflict of Laws,* EUROPEAN BUSINESS LAW REVIEW 112–127 (2000)
VERJANS (2002)
R.L.S. Verjans, *Dematerialisatie van toondereffecten,* 6495 WPNR 465–471 (2002) (and the reaction thereupon by M.P. van den Hoek, 6504 WEEKBLAD VOOR PRIVAATRECHT, NOTARIAAT EN REGISTRATIE 675–677 (2002)
VINCENT (1997)
L.J.K. Vincent, *Eigendom van effecten in het effectengiro-systeem,* NAAMLOZE VENNOOTSCHAP 42–49 (1975)
VINK (1998)
J-W.G. Vink, *De clearingmemberstructuur van de AEX-effectenclearing, in* ONDERNEMING EN EFFECTEN 273–292 (S.C.J.J. Kortmann et al. eds, 1998)
VISSER (1938)
L.E. Visser, *Het B.W. en het Handelsrecht, in* GEDENKBOEK BURGERLIJK WETBOEK 1838–1938, 559–578 (P. Scholten & E.M. Meijers eds, 1938)
VAN VLIET (2005)
L.P.W. van Vliet, *De financiëlezekerheidsovereenkomst, een tussenbalans,* NEDERLANDS TIJDSCHRIFT VOOR BURGERLIJK RECHT 190–203 (2005)
DE VRIES (2003)
G. de Vries, *Kroniek titel 3.3 (volmacht),* 9 NEDERLANDS TIJDSCHRIFT VOOR BURGERLIJK RECHT 524–530 (2003)
G. WAGNER (2002)
G. Wagner, *The Economics of Harmonization: The Case of Contract Law,* 39 COMMON MARKET LAW REVIEW 995–1023 (2002)
H. WAGNER (2005)
H. Wagner, *Economic Analysis of Cross-Border Legal Uncertainty; The Example of the European Union, in* THE NEED FOR A EUROPEAN CONTRACT LAW 27–54 (J. Smits ed., 2005)
WATSON (2000)
A. Watson, *Legal Transplants in European Private Law,* IUS COMMUNE LECTURES ON EUROPEAN PRIVATE LAW (2000)
WEATHERILL (2006)
S. Weatherill, *Recent developments in the law governing the free movement of goods in the EC's internal market,* 1 EUROPEAN REVIEW OF CONTRACT LAW 90–111 (2006)
WHITE & SUMMERS (2000)
J. WHITE & S. SUMMERS, UNIFORM COMMERCIAL CODE, REVISED (1999) ARTICLE 9 SUPPLEMENTARY PAMPHLET (4th ed. 2000)

WHITE & SUMMERS (2001)
J. White & S. Summers, *Uniform Commercial Code: Secured Transactions, in* PERSPECTIVES ON THE UNIFORM COMMERCIAL CODE, 181 *et seq.* (D. Litowitz ed. 2001)

WICHERS (2002)
J.E. WICHERS, NATREKKING, VERMENGING EN ZAAKSVORMING (2002)

WILHELMSSON (2002)
Th. Wilhelmsson, *Private Law in the EU: Harmonised or Fragmented Europeanisation?,* 1 EUROPEAN REVIEW OF PRIVATE LAW 77–94 (2002)

WINTER (1998)
J.W. Winter, *Voetbalaandelen, Ajax naar de beurs,* 7 TIJDSCHRIFT VOOR VENNOOTSCHAP EN STICHTING 189–193 (1998)

WOUTERS (1998)
J. Wouters, *De Finaliteitsrichtlijn, in* ONDERNEMING EN EFFECTEN 103–115 (S.C.J.J. Kortmann et al. eds, 1998)

ZEBREGS (2005)
B.J.A. Zebregs, *De toelating van effecten tot het Wge-systeem door Euroclear Nederland,* 7 TIJDSCHRIFT VOOR FINANCIEEL RECHT 196–205 (2005)

ZWEIGERT & KÖTZ (1998)
K. ZWEIGERT & H. KÖTZ, INTRODUCTION TO COMPARATIVE LAW (3d ed. 1998)

Table of Cases

BELGIUM

Cas. 1re civ., 26 September 1940, *Pas.* 1940, III, 228	5.3.5
Cass. 1re civ., 17 October 1996,2 *Revue de la Banque/Bank en Financiewezen* 1997, 114	**5.5.2**
Hof van Beroep te Antwerpen (Antwerp Court of Appeal), 17 May 1984, *R.W.* 1984–1985, 264	5.4.2
Hof van Beroep te Antwerpen 20 August 1990, *T.R.V.* 1990, 540	5.3.1, **5.3.3**, 5.3.5
Hof van Beroep te Antwerpen 21 November 2002, *Forum Financier/Droit Bancaire et Financier* 2003, 313	**5.3.2**

EU

Case 26/62, Van Gend en Loos v. Nederlandse Administratie der Belastingen, 1962 ECR 3	2.4.1
Case C-376/98, Germany v. Parliament and Council, 2000 ECR I-8419 (*Tobacco Advertising*)	**12.2,** 12.5
Case 210/03,2004 ECR I-11893 (*Swedish Match*)	12.2

FRANCE

Cass. 1re civ., 25 January 1966, *Dalloz Sirey* 1966, 390	6.6
Cass. 1re civ., 8 July 1969, *Revue critique de Droit International Privé* 1971, 75	**6.6**
Cass. 1re civ., 17 October 1972, *Revue critique de Droit International Privé* 1973, 520	6.6

THE NETHERLANDS

THE UNITED STATES OF AMERICA

Table of Legislation

BELGIUM

EU

FRANCE

PEOPLE'S REPUBLIC OF CHINA

ROMAN LAW

THE NETHERLANDS

THE UNITED STATES OF AMERICA

CONVENTIONS

Index

Private Law in European Context Series

1. M. Bussani and U. Mattei (eds): *The Common Core of European Private Law.* Essays on the Project. 2002 ISBN 90-411-2004-1
2. S. Grundman and J. Stuyck (eds): *An Academic Green Paper to European Contract Law.* 2002 ISBN 90-411-1853-5
3. M.W. Hesselink: *The New European Private Law,* Essays on the Future of Private Law in Europe. 2002 ISBN 90-411-1962-0
4. M. Bussani: *The Common Core of European Private Law.* 2003 ISBN 90-411-1852-7
5. H. Collins (ed.): *The Forthcoming EC Directive on Unfair Commercial Practices.* 2004 ISBN 90-411-2224-9
6. S. Grundmann and D. Mazeaud (eds): *General Clauses and Standards in European Contract Law.* 2005 ISBN 90-411-2432-2
7. M.W. Hesselink (ed.): *The Politics of a European Civil Code.* 2006 ISBN 90-411-2410-1
8. S. Grundmann and M. Schaner (eds): *The Architecture of European Codes and Contract Law.* 2006 ISBN 90-411-2530-2
9. F. Cafaggi (ed.): *Reframing Self-Regulation in European Private Law.* 2006 ISBN 90-411-2531-0
10. T. Wilhelmsson (ed.): *Private Law and the Cultures of Europe*. 2007 ISBN 978-90-411-2593-4
11. M. Haentjens: *Harmonisation of Securities Law: Custody and Transfer of Securities in European Private Law*. 2007 ISBN 978-90-411-2639-9

www.ingramcontent.com/pod-product-compliance
Lightning Source LLC
Chambersburg PA
CBHW071236230926
51849CB00001B/127